Europe's Long Century

Society, Politics, and Culture
1900–1945

Volume One

SPENCER M. DI SCALA
University of Massachusetts Boston

New York   Oxford

OXFORD UNIVERSITY PRESS

Oxford University Press is a department of the University of Oxford.
It furthers the University's objective of excellence in research, scholarship,
and education by publishing worldwide.

Oxford New York
Auckland Cape Town Dar es Salaam Hong Kong Karachi
Kuala Lumpur Madrid Melbourne Mexico City Nairobi
New Delhi Shanghai Taipei Toronto

With offices in
Argentina Austria Brazil Chile Czech Republic France Greece
Guatemala Hungary Italy JapansPoland Portugal Singapore
South Korea Switzerland Thailand Turkey Ukraine Vietnam

For titles covered by Section 112 of the US Higher Education
Opportunity Act, please visit www.oup.com/us/he for the latest
information about pricing and alternate formats.

Published by Oxford University Press
198 Madison Avenue, New York, New York 10016
http://www.oup.com

Library of Congress Cataloging-in-Publication Data
Di Scala, Spencer.
Europe's long century: politics, society, culture, 1900-present / Spencer Di Scala.
p. cm.
Includes bibliographical references and index.
ISBN 978-0-19-977850-8 (acid-free paper)—ISBN 978-0-19-977851-5—ISBN 978-0-19-977852-2
1. Europe—History—20th century.   2. Europe—Politics and government—20th century.
3. Europe—Biography.   I. Title.
D424.D497 2012
940.5—dc23   2012015473

CONTENTS

✍

PREFACE

The twentieth century has been interpreted as a short century marked by extremes. According to this view, the century lasted only from 1914 to 1989 or 1991. These dates coincide with the rise and fall of communism, which came to power in Russia in 1917 and ended with the fall of the Berlin wall (1989) or that of the Soviet Union (1991). Thus, the concept of a short century seems to be influenced by a cold war perspective that considers the struggle between communism and capitalism the overriding aspect of the past century.

What I have learned as a result of my research for this book is that, in contradistinction to the idea of the "short" twentieth century, we are talking about a "long" century that lasted approximately from 1900 to 2000, characterized by three overriding movements, with antecedents before the century began, that continued to be elaborated after it ended. In international politics, a struggle for hegemony that pitted the German Empire against its British and French rivals intensified. The Germans challenged the British and French for control of Europe and, indeed, the world. After World War I, the struggle continued with the rise of Nazism, which, albeit with a radically different and odious ideology, reinvigorated the German challenge. The German defeat of 1945 brought the fear that S Russia would rule the entire continent and, more clearly than had been the Germany, perhaps the world. Complicating these fights were exasperated alism, religious differences, and the desire to right what one side or and sidered historical wrongs. International communism submerged these an all-embracing ideology, but they resurfaced after it collapsed.

In fact, it will be increasingly necessary to view the hundred yea tieth century in a post–cold war perspective. In my opinion, the date or were independent of the cold war, even if they were will forcefully emerge as more important than they were seen itself or in the years that immediately followed its end. Despi duration of the Communist movement, it was, in the conte and world history, a transitory phase that is unlikely to age of extremes is also less helpful than appears at first s

always characterized European history. The twe'
alleled atrocities, also because new technolog
It is important not only to learn from the lesso.
developments during the period that had earlier .
manent effects.

In this book, I have emphasized another factor .
neglected in the past: modern science. The past hundred
characterized by great innovations in science and technology,
affect the common person with unparalleled speed, a trend th
throughout the past century. However, the changes in mentality th.
century science brought about were not confined to scientists, but eve.
tered down to ordinary people and influenced them even if they were u.
of it. This is clear not only in the concrete case of nuclear physics, for exan.
which developed nuclear weapons under whose shadow the world has lived unde.
since 1945, but in the modern mentality. The "uncertainty" (or "indeterminacy")
principle that came out of quantum mechanics affected the culture of most of the
twentieth century, and who can argue that the discovery of DNA and the genetic
engineering that it made possible during the latter part of the century has not
affected people's thinking and society itself?

I have tried to bring these questions to the fore in this book while covering
a large amount of information. In my many years of teaching, I have been struck
by the intellectual curiosity of students who constantly challenged the opinions
of even the most celebrated historians. In my discussions with them, the students
always resisted quick explanations. In a twist that might be considered ironic,
given the present-mindedness of the current age, when I presented relevant material to them, they were always interested in going back further to understand the
origins of a particular dispute, war, social condition, or cultural phenomenon. It
slowly dawned on me that full explanations of events must be given in their *historical* contexts, so that, for example, twentieth-century events may have been influenced by facts dating from the nineteenth or previous centuries. If such facts are
relevant for a complete understanding of certain developments, I have considered
them in this book, so that the reader should not be surprised to find information
on the Turkish occupation in the discussion of the states of southeastern Europe,
or a reference to the seventeenth century when considering social conditions in
modern Spain.

Perhaps fuller explanations will make history, even modern history, less
remote. I have always wondered why history seems so boring to many people and
have come to at least a tentative conclusion. Professional historians are frequently
carried away by generalizations, trying to make everything fit into a scheme. To
a certain extent, this is necessary, but historians risk being too abstract, making
istory "dry" and of seemingly doubtful relevance to the present. I have attempted
strike a balance among political, social, and cultural history. Because history
als primarily with people, I have tried to bring the real lives of people into the
ture, not only at strategic points in the book, but in another significant way.
ve included "Biographical Sketches" within each chapter. These sketches tell
t the lives of prominent—but not necessarily the most important—persons

during the period discussed. They emphasize the *life* of a person as a whole, not just the factor that made him or her significant. Real people do not live by their accomplishments alone, but by their hopes and disappointments, achievements and sorrows. The great German scientist Max Planck, for example, will live in history for his formulation of the quantum theory, but that achievement makes Planck remote from most of humanity. His suffering when the Nazis executed his son brings him closer to us on a human level. Another important aspect of this book is the extensive bibliographical essay that I have included for each chapter. This essay, wide-ranging in scope, attempts to give an idea of the arguments confronted by the books that are cited in it. The "Note on the Bibliographical Essay" provides a more detailed explanation of the purposes of the essay.

After World War II Europe underwent a profound transformation. It responded to the two world wars by earnestly seeking economic and political unity. The ideal of European unity as an antidote to war has a long and respectable history, even though it had few practical results before the mid-twentieth century. Because of national cultural differences, creating a European political unity had, by the end of the century, produced an imperfect but viable union with a world role. In domestic politics and society, the contrast between the beginning of the century and its end could hardly be greater. In 1900, elite governments, staffed primarily by aristocrats and very wealthy men, ruled throughout Europe. In most countries, ordinary people and workers had little voice in governing themselves. The ruling classes frowned on governmental intervention in the economy to help the weaker sectors of society. Many men and all women could not vote. Women chafed under the tutelage of their fathers and husbands; lacked social, economic, and sexual equality; and did not have control of their own resources. Socialist parties struggled to alter the political and social system, encountering stiff and sometimes violent resistance.

At the end of the century, wealth and social standing, while still important, were not considered criteria that automatically qualified people for governing—frequently the opposite. Governments claimed the right to rule on grounds of competence and because they had the sanction of the majority in elections in which all persons over a minimum age could vote. Members of the middle and lower classes regularly rose in politics to the highest offices, despite real practical difficulties. Governments paid great attention to the principle of political and social equality of the sexes, even if this ideal remained a work in progress. The European welfare state helped redress the social inequality between the rich and the poor, and governmental officials openly guided the economy. Indeed, the scope and cost of the welfare state provoked a backlash in the latter years of the century.

The increasingly important role of science and technology also characterized European life. The century began with a revolution in physics and ended with one in biology. Work done by European scientists during the early years of the century allowed them to discover nuclear fission, an event that led to both new energy sources and weapons of mass destruction. The last years of the century found Europeans in the forefront with Americans engaged in genetic engineering, on the brink of cloning humans, and confronting new ethical questions raised by the biological revolution.

This book is unusual in considering the smaller countries in detail because the inhabitants of all the countries of Europe, not just the large ones, contributed to the progress of politics, society, and science in the twentieth century. In keeping with the emphasis on science, the book points out that smaller countries were important in the development of atomic physics, as exemplified by Copenhagen as a prime center in the revolution in physics and the prominence of Hungarian scientists as pioneers in the same field. The Scandinavian countries pioneered the social democracy and the emancipation of women that spread all over Europe. Belgium, the Netherlands, and Luxembourg provided a model for the European economic cooperation that knit the continent together. The practical influence of the smaller states in economics and politics increased as the century progressed, and the EU's structure ensured that the trend would intensify.

The high level of violence in Europe and the crucial political events that marked the past century are properly the focus of this book, but so are the end of the struggle for hegemony, the establishment of common economic and political institutions, the affirmation of social democracy, and the stunning advance of science.

A NOTE ON THE BIBLIOGRAPHICAL ESSAY

The aim of the Bibliographical Essay is to give the reader the possibility to expand on the issues discussed in the text. I have attempted to achieve this goal in three ways. First, I have included general works that allow readers to broaden their knowledge of an entire period. Second, specialized books on important themes facilitate the investigation of relevant topics in depth. Third, while these two categories necessarily include points of view, I have also cited books that are notable primarily for their interpretations, even when controversial.

I hope that in this manner readers will not only become familiar with major topics that are relevant to the history of twentieth-century Europe, but will be better able to investigate those of their choice in greater depth and from various points of view. Readers who are interested in further investigation should also remember to take advantage of the Internet sources, of reference bibliographies, and of bibliographies in individual books that could not be mentioned here, in addition to other research tools that are available in libraries. Internet resources should be integrated with books to get a fuller and more accurate discussion of important issues. In order not to weigh down the text, I have not included footnotes. I have cited the sources for the quotations used in the text in the Bibliographical Essay.

Spencer M. Di Scala
Boston, Massachusetts
May 2012

ACKNOWLEDGMENTS

No one writes a book without incurring debts of all kinds with persons who have given their time willingly and generously. I am grateful to the staff of Oxford University Press who were connected with the development and production of this work not only for their skills, but for their kindness; they gave me their much-needed encouragement and suggestions as the book went through its different phases from planning to writing to production. I am particularly grateful to my editor Charles Cavaliere, who shepherded this book though its planning stages and its production, for his encouragement, wise counsel, and excellent suggestions. I also thank Assistant Editor Lauren Aylward, who did the difficult and sometimes maddening technical work of getting this book into production, Marianne Paul, the Production Editor who took it through the production process, and Wendy Ameleh, the Copyeditor.

I want to thank the persons who read the manuscript and gave me their suggestions for improvement, from which I greatly profited: Eugene Boia, Cleveland State University; John Cox, Florida Gulf Coast University; Axel Fair-Schulz, SUNY Potsdam; Martin Menke, Rivier College; David A. Messenger, University of Wyoming; Thomas J. Schaeper, St. Bonaventure University; Robin Underhill, University of Delaware.

I would also like to thank my students at the University of Massachusetts, Boston, for their probing questions, their interest and curiosity, and even their skepticism, all of which spurred me to think about issues that are discussed in this book in ways I would not otherwise have done.

Finally, I would like to acknowledge my two most important personal debts. Although she does not suspect it, my daughter Ashley (not a history buff) gave me valuable insight into the thinking of young people and to what may be most important to them in learning about the past as they mature. To my wife Laura, to whom this book is dedicated, my thanks once again for putting up with too many bouts of introspection alternating with too much boring talk of the past, for reading portions of the manuscript at crucial intervals, for making essential suggestions—and for making the book possible.

ABOUT THE AUTHOR

Spencer M. Di Scala is full professor, Research Professor, and past Graduate Program Director in the history department at the University of Massachusetts Boston. He has been awarded Fulbright scholarships and has published numerous books and articles in modern Italian and European history. His books are: *Dilemmas of Italian Socialism: The Politics of Filippo Turati*; *Renewing Italian Socialism: Nenni to Craxi*; *Italian Socialism Between Politics and History*; *Italy: From Revolution to Republic* (1st ed., 1995; 2nd ed., 1999; 3rd ed., 2004; 4th ed., 2009); *European Political Thought, 1815–1989* (with Salvo Mastellone); *Twentieth Century Europe*; *Makers of the Modern World. Vittorio Orlando: Italy. Italy: From Revolution to Republic* was chosen as an alternate selection of the History Book Club and three of his other books have been translated. He has published over 250 articles in scholarly journals, encyclopedias, historical dictionaries, and newspapers in the United States and Europe. Di Scala has also edited a book series on Italian and Italian-American history. In 2011 he held visiting professorships at the University of Rome "Tor Vergata" and at the Free Italian University of the Social Sciences "Guido Carli" (LUISS). Di Scala is President of the Dante Alighieri Society of Massachusetts, the largest Italian-American cultural association in New England. He travels and lectures widely in Europe, consults regularly with European statesmen, and serves on the editorial boards of scholarly journals.

In 1995 Spencer Di Scala was named "Commander" in the Order of Merit of the Italian Republic for the excellence of his research. He received the 2006 award from the New England Chapter of the University Continuing Education Association (UCEA) "in recognition of outstanding teaching, programming, and service." In 2007 UCEA presented him with its national "Excellence in Teaching" award. He teaches face-to-face and online courses.

More information can be found at www.spencerdiscala.com.

Introduction: What Is Europe?

✒

Whathat characterizes Europe, and how do Europeans characterize themselves? Europe does not encompass a large landmass, but its topography and climate are extraordinarily varied. Europe diverges from the lowlands of the Netherlands to the heights of Mont Blanc; from the moderate, wet climate of the British Isles to the extreme cold of Russia; and from Scandinavia to the torrid summers of Greece, Spain, and southern Italy.

EUROPE AS A CULTURAL CONCEPTION

Definitions of people are more difficult to summarize. People compare themselves to others in defining themselves but frequently discover who they are not. The ancient Greeks first fixed the limits of Europe but rejected a geographic for a cultural definition. For the Greek orator Isocrates, Europe meant Greece, that is, Greek culture. With the spread of Greek civilization, the "father of history," Herodotus, extended the idea of Europe to include areas that were influenced by Greek culture. Even persons living within the geographic confines of Europe were not European, Herodotus wrote, if they did not live in cities and were not politically free. In his account of the Persian Wars (6th century BC), in which the Greek city-states defeated the Persian Empire's attempt to conquer them, Herodotus interpreted the conflict as one between liberty (Europe) and despotism (Asia). Both the Greeks and their cultural heirs, the Romans, viewed struggles between themselves and their enemies as civilization versus barbarism.

These ideas remained in the consciousness of Europeans into the twentieth century and still do. In his massive *Decline and Fall of the Roman Empire*, the eighteenth-century British historian Edward Gibbon emphasized how Roman acceptance of despotic Asiatic forms of government signaled the empire's degradation.

THE IDEA OF EUROPE AND CHRISTIANITY

Far from ending the identification of Europe as a cultural unit counterposed against common enemies, the political dismemberment of the Roman Empire marked continuation of the idea, thanks to the empire's conversion to Christianity in the fourth century and to Rome's survival as a unifying ideal. Paradoxically, powerful German tribes that settled in the former Roman Empire converted to Christianity, defended the empire's religion, and championed its political revival. In the ninth century, the Frankish king, Charlemagne, unified large parts of what had been the Roman Empire in the West, and, in a conscious attempt to reclaim Rome's heritage, had himself crowned emperor by the pope. By then, the term *Frank* included both descendants of Teutons and Latins, and western Europeans considered themselves the same people, primarily because of their common religion. A new religious consciousness—East versus West—replaced German against Roman. The bishop of Cremona labeled the East as the land of heresies, while "we westerners" extirpated them. In 960, proclamation of the Holy Roman Empire, based in Germany, demonstrated that Europe remained identified with Rome and Christianity and that these concepts had triumphed in the former homeland of barbarism.

Both popes and secular leaders equated Europe with Christendom when the Muslims invaded Europe in the seventh and eighth centuries. Later, the growing power of the church provoked a reaction by the European monarchs of the twelfth and thirteenth centuries and the decline of papal power in the fourteenth. Even with the weakening of church power, however, the cry went out for Europe to unite against the Turks during the next century when the Muslim threat increased with the rise of the Ottoman Turks, demonstrating the identification of Europe with Christianity.

Within this context of intertwined religious and political conflict, the idea of Europe took hold. The contemporaneous decline of the papacy and the Holy Roman Empire in the fourteenth and fifteenth centuries favored the emergence of individual states with their own interests. This situation made it difficult to unite and oppose the Turkish threat. In 1458, the Italian humanist Aeneas Sylvius Piccolomini, elected Pope Pius II, specifically identified Europe and Christendom. In trying to rally Europe, Pius cataloged the power of the individual "Christian" nations—all European—and warned the Turks that the closer they came to the center of Christendom, the more Europeans would unify. In the course of his discussion, Pius turned the word *Europe* into the adjective—*European*—a linguistic change that enjoyed little support in classical Latin.

THE EUROPEAN IDEA BECOMES SECULARIZED

Pius's yearning for a unified Europe to fight the Muslims remained unfulfilled as the Europeans continued their wars. The idea of Europe as a *cultural* unit, however, survived and became secularized, thanks to the Italian political philosopher Niccolò Machiavelli. Machiavelli defined Europe according to the government and political styles of the individual states, not their religion. States are governed either by one person, with everyone being a servant of the ruler, or by a prince and other groups who have independent power bases, Machiavelli wrote in his famous treatise *The Prince*. In the first case, the ruler may do anything he wishes, while in the second, law, custom, and habit limit monarchs. Machiavelli argued that the second case characterized European states, whether republics or monarchies, but led to conflicts. However, this competition produced diversity and differentiation that favored creative energy and stimulated individual virtue.

This idea led Machiavelli to define Europe by what it is not. Asia, characterized by despotism, permanently repressed the individual. In Europe, political diversity had encouraged the concept of individual liberty. During the seventeenth and eighteenth centuries, European writers strengthened this political interpretation because it fitted well with the existence in Europe of a multiplicity of states.

Unfortunately, constant warfare turned out to be the pernicious other side of the coin of the emergence of powerful states. Many European thinkers considered conflict a necessary evil for the maintenance of freedom. In order to preserve the independence of the individual states and to prevent any one from dominating

Since antiquity, Europe has traditionally been represented as a woman. The painting shown here, by the sixteenth-century Italian artist Titian, depicts a famous Greek myth—"The Rape of Europa." The god Zeus, in the form of a bull, ravishes Europa.

the entire continent, the balance of power concept emerged. First developed in fourteenth-century Italy, this concept spread throughout the continent. Maintaining a political equilibrium required continual diplomatic vigilance and military preparedness that heightened tensions and increased the risk of warfare. Opposing this concept, however, some utopian thinkers elaborated projects for European international organizations that would be capable of keeping the peace and replacing the balance of power while ensuring liberty. As European conflicts became bloodier over the centuries, the desire for some kind of supranational organization strengthened and reached its culmination after World War II.

During the eighteenth-century Enlightenment, the most influential philosophe (a French term signifying Enlightenment intellectuals) of the period, Voltaire, compared Europe to a republic consisting of many states, with diverse forms of government, but fundamentally linked by Christianity and common legal and political principles found nowhere else. Voltaire believed that the principle of freedom for women set the tone for European society, even if women, as most men, did not enjoy political rights. By the eighteenth century, the habit of defining Europe by "who we are not" had become widespread because the discovery of America and subsequent explorations had revealed the existence of peoples living in radically different societies. Paradoxically, the philosophes exploited these exotic societies as a means of criticizing the West by citing their unspoiled character but contrasted European sophistication to the primitivism of other cultures. As more of these different cultures became known, Europeans realized how similar they were despite their own diversity.

The growth of science strengthened this common bond. The scientific revolution of the seventeenth century convinced European thinkers that the scientific method of investigation had ramifications beyond science: Intellectuals considered it an ideal for the secular organization of society and the guiding principle of human development. Ever since then, science, pure, applied, and social, has retained an authority in Europe that has only recently been emulated in other parts of the world. Thus, their scientific culture helped convince Europeans that they were different from, and superior to, other peoples.

In his definition of Europe, Voltaire excluded Russia. If Europe meant a way of life, Russia did not qualify as European. European writers continued to disagree about Russia's character as an Asiatic or a European entity. Even if some observers conceded that, geographically, Russia was in Europe, most agreed that it had the characteristics of an Asian not a European state. Depending on the author, Russia might be included or excluded from the schemes for closer cooperation that emerged from the pens of European writers. In the seventeenth century, Tsar Peter the Great attempted to westernize his country by introducing Western economic methods, but his campaign did not resolve the important issue. If Europe stood for liberty, and Asia for despotism, Russia clearly fit into the latter camp.

During the nineteenth century, however, Russia played a significant role in defeating Napoleon, whose enemies considered him a despot, but it was still generally considered "Asiatic." Only during the late nineteenth and twentieth centuries did Russia become more acceptable as a European country, largely because of an extraordinary series of great writers who reflected important European values, but the debate about whether it was truly European continued not only among West

Europeans. but among Russians themselves. The discussion over Russia's position illustrates how the definition of *Europe* continued to revolve around culture rather than geography.

The increasingly brutal wars, however, encouraged European thinkers and statesmen to focus on unity as a means of ending them and maximizing the continent's potential. The methods for accomplishing this aim can be broadly viewed as either hegemonic or ideological.

HEGEMONY VERSUS CONSENSUS

In substance, the "hegemonic" method meant conquering diverse areas and integrating their inhabitants socially, culturally, and economically into a cohesive, centralized political unit. Proponents of the "ideological" technique, based on consensus instead of force, considered Europe a unit and Europeans as sharing basic beliefs, institutions, and values. In short, despite their differences, Europeans had a common outlook. If they emphasized their common traits, they could form a single economic and political unit on a voluntary basis in order to improve their lot. Concretely, advocates of this ideal believed that a federation would respect the diversity among Europeans while uniting them politically.

The hegemonic ideal can be traced to the Roman Empire. Rome conquered all of known Europe in ancient times and imposed its culture and the Pax Romana, a long-term peace that Europeans considered a golden age. In the Middle Ages, the Roman example inspired imitators, such as Charlemagne, the Holy Roman emperors, and the popes. During the eighteenth century, France seemed destined to conquer all of Europe, first under its powerful monarchs and then under the ideological and political impact of the French Revolution and Napoleon. This last development created a new paradox. Napoleon asserted that he favored a European confederation, with common political and judicial institutions, laws, monetary system, and weights and measures. He would have created a community of European peoples, he professed, ending war among Europeans. Napoleon set up states run by natives that introduced French-style reforms into different areas of Europe; he established a multinational army to invade Russia in 1812 that might be seen as the forerunner of a European army.

Despite Napoleon's claims, he and his French revolutionary predecessors retained real control of the areas they "liberated." At the same time, French revolutionary ideology stimulated the growth of nationalism: the idea that all nationalities should have control of the areas in which they lived and should be free to follow their own interests. Paradoxically, this belief provoked powerful revolts against the French themselves and, later, competition among the various European nationalities. The French Revolution thus created a new tension between the idea of a common European identity and a fight for supremacy among nation-states, each convinced of its superiority. This heightened nationalism culminated in the ruinous wars of the twentieth century, but the theme of a common cultural heritage led Europeans to search for a balance between individuality and commonality when those wars ended.

When the fear of French hegemony faded, the German threat followed. After German unification in 1871, Germany's industrial development eclipsed Britain's and France's. Had Germany won in World War I, its war aims envisioned economic and military domination of the continent through the creation of Middle Europe, a combination of strategic annexations and a customs union, and of Middle Africa to ensure raw materials. Germany also desired the breakup of Russia. German culture, already extremely influential, would have become paramount.

Following Germany's defeat in 1918 and its treatment after the war, the rise of Nazism signaled the approach of a new conflict of the kind that Europeans increasingly considered "a civil war between the forces of oligarchy, aristocracy, authoritarianism, Fascism and those of popular democracy, socialism, revolution." Italian Fascism found support in such traditionally democratic countries as France, England, and Belgium. In France, the triumph of a leftist electoral alliance, including the Communists, and a Jewish Socialist prime minister, forced industrialists to accept the Matignon Agreements that extended benefits for French workers and enraged the industrialists. The far right popularized the slogan, "Better Hitler than Blum." When the Nazis overran Europe in the early days of World War II, they found willing collaborators in the different parts of the continent, and later the Resistance movements took on a clearer civil war aspect. For a continent that considered itself family, wars among its member nations had been civil conflicts for some time, and World War II intensified this feeling.

In their attempt to control the continent, even the Nazis exploited the idea of a common heritage and feeling for European unity and claimed that they defended European interests from "Asian" Bolshevism. In this context, the defeat of Russia was an important step in the process of uniting Europe, which would exclude Russia. According to a German-drafted European Charter, no European country could maintain its freedom and economic viability acting alone.

The grotesque Nazi attempt to exploit Europeanist ideas marked the last gasp of the hegemonic model. The emphasis now shifted to doing so by consensus. Although various ideas to unite the continent had circulated for centuries, only the conditions following World War II's devastation allowed European intellectuals and statesmen to take concrete steps toward some form of unity.

The modern beginnings of an ideological concept of Europe can be found in the eighteenth-century Enlightenment and the French Revolution, during which ideas for all-European institutions combining common principles, the desire for peace, and the basic political restructuring of the continent were discussed. The trend accelerated in the nineteenth century with the growth of democratic and revolutionary movements. French revolutionary thinkers built on philosopher Jean-Jacques Rousseau's concept of the general will. Although subject to different interpretations, the general will opposed rule by divine-right monarchs and was perceived as the people governing by a majority vote. French revolutionaries believed that their reforms, along with "Liberty, Equality, and Fraternity," were the birthright of all nations.

French armies carried these ideals to other European countries despite their ruthlessness. After the Revolution's defeat, the conservative powers banded together to prevent the diffusion of Liberal and Nationalist sentiments that had been unleashed by revolutionary ideology that shook the continent in 1820 and 1821, 1830 and 1831, and especially in the "year of revolutions," 1848. Democratic leftist leaders called for revolutionary Europe to band together against the conservative powers. Italian patriot Giuseppe Mazzini established a secret society to fight for Italian freedom and favored the establishment of similar societies to struggle against the monarchs in favor of Europe's common Liberal heritage. In addition to "Young Italy," Mazzini inspired the foundation of similar organizations in other countries, capped off by Young Europe, which he defined as "a federation of peoples, based on the principles of national independence and the freedom of each in internal affairs." The French utopian Socialist Claude-Henri de Saint Simon called for common European political institutions in which national parliaments would select a European Parliament to elect a king of Europe. This European federation would end war and stimulate industry. Similarly, the nineteenth-century pacifist movement advocated a European federation as a means of eliminating war. It looked to the American model and coined the term "United States of Europe," a popular concept during the nineteenth century. European Socialists preached peace and cooperation on a worldwide scale and coordinated their actions through the Second International.

The outbreak of World War I destroyed the International and seemed to make a mockery of peace based on collaboration among nations, but the idea of European unity survived that conflict. Discussing the shape of a postwar Europe in 1916, former French foreign minister Gabriel Hanotaux advocated a "Constituent Assembly of united European states," a European government with legislative, judicial, and executive powers commanding an armed force capable of enforcing its decisions. Similarly, during the war's early months, the British press emphasized that only a United States of Europe could bring permanent peace to the continent. In Italy in 1917, Fiat owner Giovanni Agnelli and University of Genoa professor Attilio Cabiati argued for the establishment of a European federal structure complete with a parliament and an army as the only means of reconciling European nationality with the political, strategic, and economic goals of different states, and German writers expressed like ideas.

THE IDEAL OF UNITY BETWEEN THE TWO WORLD WARS

In the 1920s and 1930s, books, the press, conferences, and high governmental officials advocated European unification. The debut of the United States on the world scene stimulated the discussion because World War I had left the European powers exhausted and bankrupt; with the United States eclipsing Europe, many Europeans believed that only a unified continent would be capable of confronting American economic and political power. In the 1920s, the hopes for a practical outcome to projects for European unity seemed bright because the French and Germans resolved some of the important diplomatic problems left over from the war, and a new spirit of cooperation between them emerged. While no concrete results appeared, the discussion on unity between the wars set the tone for practical action after World War II. The editor of the French newspaper Le Figaro answered the old question "What is Europe?" He wrote: "Geographically, racially, and linguistically, Europe is characterized by diversity, but in its intellectual and spiritual tradition, it is a unity. The essence of this unity is a fusion of Hebrew religion, Greek intelligence, and Roman law."

The increasing interest that influential statesmen took in the question of unity was demonstrated in talks on the subject among French foreign minister Aristide Briand, German chancellor Gustav Stresemann, and other European statesmen. These talks ultimately failed because the Germans linked unity to a revision of the Versailles settlement, the British believed that their destiny lay with their colonies and dominions, and, predictably, the nationalistic Italian Fascist regime was unsympathetic. But Briand insisted, stating in a July 16, 1929, speech to the Chamber of Deputies that he advocated a European federation as a means of preventing future European wars. On May 17, 1930, the French Foreign Office followed up the speech by releasing a long memorandum on a federal union for Europe. This document linked a European union to the new League of Nations by replicating that body's organization by establishing a European Conference—a general assembly representing all member states—a permanent Political Committee composed only of certain nations, and a Secretariat working closely with the League Secretariat. The union would retain enough flexibility to consider the sovereign needs of nations but would be firm enough to guarantee the benefits of collective security. In the economic sphere, the union would create a common market to achieve the highest standard of living possible for Europeans.

In September 1930, the French attempted to secure the adoption of Briand's proposal by the Europeans, but by then the rise of the Nazis in Germany had already begun. While the political and economic crises of the 1930s scuttled Briand's initiative, it was an important anticipation of the efforts to create the European Union following World War II.

THE EUROPEAN CONCEPT DURING THE LATE TWENTIETH CENTURY

The brutality of World War II, the concentration camps, the persecutions, and the division between resisters and collaborators in Nazi-occupied Europe produced a definitive turn toward the idea of a united Europe as the only way to end the wars that systematically destroyed the European continent. The armed European Resistance itself took on the aspect of a pan-European movement, with fighters of diverse nationalities taking part in different national resistance movements. Even though the Communists were major elements in the resistance, its domination by Moscow prevented it from taking a major role in the new drive for European unity, which came most prominently through the writings of moderate Liberals and Catholics. In Italy, the earliest postwar center of major ideas and leadership for the Europeanist ideal, the Communist-dominated Resistance did not have a major role in the 1943 elaboration of the "Ventotene Manifesto" (from the name of a Mediterranean island used as a prison). Inspired by Mazzini's ideas of a United States of Europe, this declaration linked the postwar European structure to the development of European unity. Altiero Spinelli, one of postwar Europe's most influential advocates for unity, found the cause of wars in the nature of the nation-state itself, regardless of its social or political organization. Patriotism produced degenerate nationalism, Spinelli argued, and federalism was the antidote. In 1944, a conference held in Geneva adopted a "Manifesto of European Resistance" advocating a European Federal Alliance. In addition, the postwar Catholic movement would produce great parties in Germany, Italy, and France that strongly supported European unity.

For Europeans, World War II forcefully posed the question of how to create common European institutions, not whether to do so. Given American predominance and the danger that the continent would rapidly be transformed into an American economic colony, French statesmen Jean Monnet and Robert Schuman prodded the Europeans to cooperate on the economic plane, calculating that economic collaboration would favor political agreements. In fact, Western European economic collaboration culminated in the European Economic Community and, with the demise of its British-led rival, the European Free Trade Association, its enlargement and transformation first into the European Community and then into the EU. East Europe's attempt at cooperation among Communist countries beginning in 1949 (the Council for Mutual Economic Assistance) failed not only because of its domination by the USSR but also because of the inequality among the different member states. Following the fall of communism between 1989 and 1991, the Eastern European countries applied for admission to the EU, which, in the meantime, had eliminated tariff barriers and had established a common currency.

Despite difficulties and crises, the EU proceeded apace in its development of common political institutions and in its efforts to refine its decision-making powers. These institutions included a European Parliament regularly elected by EU citizens and an executive body, the European Commission, consisting of commissioners from the different nations that made policy and uniformly enforced legislation. The Europeans also attempted with less success to work out a common foreign policy and to set up a common armed force. Given Europe's divisive history despite its common heritage, however, these successes did not come easily and were threatened by the crisis following the attack on the United States on September 11, 2001. The process of European unity periodically went through grave political and economic crises, alternating between periods of optimism and pessimism. However, there is no doubt about the substantial success of the experiment, with Europe emerging as a major trading bloc and as a major influence in the world through its influence ("soft power"), rather than through its military strength. Europeans understand that without the EU, they would scarcely count for much in the world. They have evolved their own perspectives on modern economic and social problems that contrast with those of the United States, once more defining themselves as what they "are not."

A POST–COLD WAR PERSPECTIVE

This rapid survey illustrates how the history of Europe transcends short-term events. After World War II, European influence fell to its lowest point in modern times, and the continent became a battleground for the struggle between the United States and the Soviet Union for world domination. Because the cold war lasted almost fifty years, observers assumed that it would be a permanent feature in European history. This turned out to be a false perspective. Long-term

European trends that seemed to have disappeared, especially in the Soviet bloc, rapidly reasserted themselves following the fall of the Soviet Union. Crucial and important as it was, the cold war turned out to be an episode in time that is unlikely to be repeated. In considering the history of Europe, therefore, this book emphasizes long-term trends and tendencies that have determined the continent's course, have marked Europe in the past, and seem likely to do so in the future—along with new developments, such as the great increase in immigration, that are likely to change it. It seems judicious to keep in mind that tendencies that seem minor or that were overwhelmed by more spectacular events, such as the cold war, can later come to the fore, sometimes as the result of those events.

This is the case with the desire for unity, muted but always present in the European background; with nationalism, suppressed by the USSR in the East and overwhelmed by guilt in the West; and with religion, given new life by the challenge of Muslim immigration. The twentieth century opened with the European nations dominating the world but poised for a disastrous civil war. It ended with great progress toward the establishment of what the Soviet Union's last leader, Mikhail Gorbachev, dubbed a "Common Home" because, despite the conflicts, Europeans did have much in common and needed to stop the wars. Thus, their future during the twenty-first century will depend on whether they can truly cooperate to make Europe a working economic and political unit while preserving their individuality. The answer to this question promises to affect Europe and the world.

Bibliographical Essay

There is an ample literature on the topics treated in this section. A good, brief, introduction is Denys Hay, *Europe: The Emergence of an Idea* (New York, 1966). Denis de Rougemont, *The Idea of Europe* (New York, 1966), is a fuller treatment of the themes. Anthony Pogden, *The Idea of Europe: From Antiquity to the European* Union (Washington, D.C., 2002), includes a broad range of essays analyzing the European idea from the distant past up to the most important contemporary issues. Alexander Tchoubarian, *The European Idea in History in the Nineteenth and Twentieth Centuries: A View from Moscow* (Essex, UK, 1994), is full of interesting information that is difficult to get in one source, despite a sometimes naive tone and some printing errors. Carl H. Pegg's *Evolution of the European Idea, 1914–1932* (Chapel Hill, N.C., 1983) is a well-researched work on the period, from which the quote by Lucien Romier was taken (p. 57). The quotation on the period between the First and Second World Wars as the approach of civil strife may be found on p. 13 of Donald Cameron Watt, *Too Serious a Business: European Armed Forces and the Approach to the Second World War* (New York, 1975). The book edited by Peter M. R. Stirk, *European Unity in Context: The Interwar Period* (London, 1989), examines the period from 1918 to 1940. Stirk and David Willis also edited a collection of essays on important themes discussed after World War II, *Shaping Postwar Europe: European Unity and Disunity, 1945–1957* (New York, 1991). Martin Dedman published a good introduction to the subject of the EU: *The Origins and Development of the European Union 1945–2008* (London and New York, 2010). A critical work that brings the question past the cold war's end and takes a skeptical view of European unity, Gerald Delanty's *Inventing Europe: Idea, Identity, Reality* (New York, 1995) argues that the idea of Europe is based more on adversity than on unity and that there is little within the national traditions fostering unity; the work emphasizes a political science rather than a historical approach. As Europe became increasingly more important because of its economy and social policies, the debate about whether the American or European ways of life were better heated up. Jeremy Rifkin, *The European Dream: How Europe's Vision of the Future Is Quietly Eclipsing the American Dream* (New York, 2004), argues for the superiority of the European approach to life and believes that it is eclipsing America's style by emphasizing cooperation and social networks instead of competition and individualism. Mark Leonard's *Why Europe Will Run the 21st Century* (New York, 2005) reasons that Europe will become supreme not through military means ("hard power") but by making use of its enormous and rising cultural and economic influence in the world ("soft power"). Another book favoring the European lifestyle is Steven Hill's *Europe's Promise: Why the European Way Is the Best Hope in an Insecure Age* (Berkeley, Calif., 2010). Alberto Alesina and Francesco Giavazzi take the opposite—and more pessimistic view—arguing in *The Future of Europe: Reform or Decline* (Cambridge, Mass., 2006) that the American economic system is more efficient that that of Europe and assures greater prosperity for its people. Although not specifically concerned with unification, Sam Huntington in *The Clash of Civilizations* (New York, 1996) argues that Europe's borders are those of Western Christianity and have became increasingly relevant after the terroristic attacks on the West after September 11, 2001.

ABBREVIATIONS

ARP	Protestant Anti-Revolutionary Party
BANU	Bulgarian Agrarian Party
BBC	British Broadcasting Corporation
BEF	British Expeditionary Force
BVP	Bavarian People's Party
CEDA	Confederation of Autonomous Rightist Groups
CGL	General Confederation of Labor (Italy)
CGT	General Confederation of Labor (France)
COMINTERN	Communist International
CNT	Anarchist Labor Union
CPC	Communist Party of Czechoslovakia
CPSU	Communist Party of the Soviet Union
DAF	German Labor Front
DAP	German Workers' Party
DGB	German Federation of Trade Unions
DNVP	German Nationalist Party
EDES	Greek Monarchist Resistance Movement
ELAS	Greek Communist Resistance Movement
ETA	Basque Separatist Organization
FFI	French Forces of the Interior
Gestapo	Nazi Secret Police
GNP	Gross National Product
GUF	Fascist University Youth
ILP	Independent Labour Party
IMRO	Macedonian Revolutionary Organization
IRA	Irish Republican Army
IRI	Institute for Industrial Reconstruction
KGB	Soviet Secret Police
KKE	Greek Communist Party
KPD	German Communist Party

MRP	Popular Republican Movement
NEP	New Economic Policy
NKVD	Soviet Secret Police
NSDAP	National Socialist German Workers' Party (Nazi)
NSF	Nazi Women's Group
ONB	Italian Fascist Youth Movement (Balilla)
OND	Italian Fascist Leisure Movement (Dopolavoro)
OSS	Office of Strategic Services
OVRA	Italian Fascist Secret Police
OZN	Camp of National Unity
PCF	French Communist Party
PCI	Italian Communist Party
PNF	National Fascist Party
PPF	French Popular Party
PPI	Italian Popular Party
PPS	Polish Socialist Party
PSOE	Spanish Socialist Workers' Party
RSFSR	Russian Soviet Federated Socialist Republic
SD	Security Service (Nazi)
SFIO	French Socialist Party
SPD	German Socialist Party
SS	Security Guards
UGT	Spanish Trade Workers' Union
USPD	Independent Social Democratic Party
USSR	Union of Soviet Socialist Republics

The European Age

✍

December 14, 1900

Chronology aside, some centuries seem to arrive early; others, late. It can be argued that the eighteenth century began in 1715 with the death of France's Sun King, Louis XIV, which removed the political obstacles to the full application of Enlightenment ideas. The nineteenth century may have begun late, in 1815, with the end of the Napoleonic wars, or early, in 1789, with the French Revolution. In considering when historical periods begin or end, historians look at the defining characteristics of an age, then attempt to determine when those attributes became dominant and when they ceased to be so.

THE TWENTIETH CENTURY: SCIENCE AND IDEOLOGY

In this sense, the twentieth century appears unusual, generally being considered an age of conflict, or extremes, beginning in 1914 with the First World War. Certainly the peaceful age preceding World War I lends credence to this interpretation, but it also may mislead observers because wars do not come out of nowhere. A detailed examination of the pre-1914 period is essential to understand the causes of World War I, but this leads also to the conclusion that the attributes of a new age that had already emerged before it.

In volume 5 of his collected papers, philosopher Isaiah Berlin identified the factors characterizing the twentieth century as the dramatic development of the natural sciences and technology and the ideological cyclones that affected everyone's life: totalitarianism of different political hues, nationalism, and racism.

If Berlin is correct in his assessment, the twentieth century entered the scene right on time. On December 14, 1900, German physicist Max Planck elaborated the quantum theory. This hypothesis was the foundation of new theories of the atom, motion, and the universe eventually worked out by Albert Einstein and others over the next thirty years. The early years of the century were also the seedtime for new political movements—populist nationalism, fascism, and communism. Both trends shook the comfortable assumptions that had been painfully constructed in Europe over the previous two centuries, even if economic and social changes increased self-confidence. Most Europeans were unaware that they were living an all-too-brief optimistic moment and that their lives were in the process of being pulled apart.

EUROPEAN SOCIETY

In 1900, French philosopher Charles Peguy noted that society had changed more in the past thirty years than it had since the birth of Christ. Indeed, the period from 1890 to 1914 witnessed the second industrial revolution—the spread of heavy industry, electrification, construction of a telephone network, improved transportation, rapid urbanization, increased purchasing power, and a general improvement of living conditions. Europeans were the first to adjust to this rapid modernization of society. However, because large sectors of the population remained desperately poor and resentful, they mobilized politically to oppose existing governments, and socialist parties grew rapidly during the "belle époque."

Private Lives in a Modernizing Society

Interestingly enough, much of the discontent at the twentieth century's dawn appears to have been owing to rising expectations. People expected that life would improve even more rapidly and continuously. Those classes whose lot improved slowly resented being left behind. Yet, despite the high levels of poverty that existed in Europe when compared to the late twentieth century, the continent (and the United States) led the world in the extent and depth of its economic development. After the 1890s, a greater proportion of the European populace enjoyed more goods and services at a lower price than ever before in history. In Britain, a worker's purchasing power increased by 40 percent in only two decades, and real wages also rose dramatically for other Western European workers. An agricultural depression that lasted from the 1870s to the early 1890s lowered the price of food. Coupled with a great increase in industrial production, this drop allowed Europeans to spend a smaller percentage than before of their income on food, clothes, health, entertainment, and education. Moreover, the crisis on the land forced many peasants to move to the cities, which grew enormously. Greater London's population exploded from 1,405,000 in 1891 to 2,045,000 at Queen Victoria's death in 1901, and other European cities had a similar growth pattern. Conditions in the cities were miserable for these new residents, but eventually their children were better off than if they had remained in rural areas.

While heavy industry accounted for much of the increase in Western Europe's prosperity, light industry, stimulated by technological advances, contributed to the greater comfort of its inhabitants. The increased manufacture of such amenities as soap, processed foods, and newspapers raised the standard of living for ordinary people. With the proliferation of trams (initially horse-drawn, then electric), subways, bicycles, and the creation of dense railway networks, a revolution in transportation occurred. Growing numbers of department stores, telephone networks, and other service-sector industries such as teaching, and the typewriter, enabled women to find employment outside the home in greater numbers. Women still suffered discrimination and were obliged to resign from their jobs when they married, but the process of emancipation had begun.

The increased efficiency and lower prices brought about improvements in transportation, and banking increased the pace of economic activity. Improved sanitary conditions reduced the death rate, and Europe's population grew at the extraordinary rate of about 1 percent a year between 1890 and 1914. The increase in production, however, counterbalanced the population expansion and created greater wealth, while the bigger population and improved technology stimulated demand. For example, in the home, heaters capable of warming several rooms efficiently became more common; matches—once very expensive—became cheap; economical and efficient coal- or gas-burning stoves appeared; electric irons replaced their coal-burning predecessors; and iceboxes kept foods fresh. Frozen meats and exotic fruits, such as bananas and coconuts, arrived from faraway places.

Men's lives changed dramatically in the last years of the nineteenth and the first decade of the twentieth century. Paternal authoritarianism in the extended family had afflicted young men in different ways than it had women, but was equally stifling. Fathers kept a tight financial rein on their children's lives and controlled them even if they were away at school, but now real salaries rose and men could live in their own homes with their wives after marriage. National governments sponsored reduced railway fares, encouraging tourism and attendance at sports events in different cities, and the ubiquitous tourist with a Kodak camera slung around his neck appeared. Participation in individual sports, such as swimming, canoeing, and mountain climbing, became common middle-class activities. Politics also aroused their enthusiasm, since by 1900 most men could vote, and more of them participated in discussions in the many cafés. Life for men became less provincial.

The City
Life in the expanding city changed significantly. In places long characterized by pollution, areas of extreme poverty, and unhealthful conditions, better illumination and improved sanitation reduced crime and disease. Electric street lighting gradually replaced gaslights and encouraged people to stay out late at night in greater safety in cafés and theaters or to attend movies—a new art form. Their evening over, electrified streetcars whisked the revelers home. The rapid transportation systems had an important impact on city government by stimulating the incorporation of once outlying regions into major metropolitan areas. In personal transportation, the bicycle, formerly made of wood, acquired rubber tires and gears and revolutionized personal mobility. The first automobiles, expensive

and unreliable, did not clog city streets on December 14, 1900, when Max Planck elaborated his quantum theory.

Despite the great improvements in health care and city services, social and economic conditions remained backward by present standards. Only an estimated 20 percent to 30 percent of people belonged to the middle class in England, Europe's most advanced industrial and urban region. Almost 31 percent lived in dire poverty in London in 1900, the world's most advanced city, according to a study in that year. This extreme poverty meant constant hunger and cold, frequent death on the street, and burial in a pauper's grave. Nevertheless, these statistics demonstrate that poverty afflicted a smaller percentage of Europeans than the rest of the world population, and municipalities began keeping records on the changes in daily life—births, marriages, deaths—that are fundamental in implementing governmental support for ordinary people.

The Countryside

In addition to changes in the cities, the agricultural depression's end in the late 1890s produced major alterations in the countryside. The depression forced many rural wage earners and marginal farmers off the land, but the decrease in the labor supply gradually resulted in an improved income for those who remained. Taking advantage of new machinery, such as threshers and reapers, and stimulated by knowledge of improving city life brought to them by newspapers, peasants aspired to higher living standards and organized politically to achieve them. Denmark stands out as a country that transformed its agriculture. It decided to specialize in the production of dairy products for export, resulting in increased agricultural wages at a time when politics dictated high tariff policies for the big European powers. In France and other Western European countries, incomes also increased significantly during the century's first decade, but there political action instead of crop changes played a major role. When phylloxera devastated vineyards in southern France, for example, peasant demonstrations forced the government to intervene in their favor, and similar developments occurred in other countries.

Land tenure varied in different parts of Europe and influenced the economic well-being of rural areas. In France, small independent proprietors and tenant farmers accounted for a large proportion of males who were engaged in agriculture (70 percent), while both categories declined significantly in England. In central and southern Europe, conditions differed considerably. In southern Italy, large latifundia owned by the rich and worked by day laborers contrasted with scattered landholdings that were too small to support a family, a large number of very poor day laborers, and peasant villages located at long distances from farms; these conditions and the lack of industry favored large-scale emigration from the South to other parts of Europe, the United States, and Latin America. In southern Spain and Prussia east of the Elbe river, most peasants did not own land and worked for large landowners, while many German, Czech, Austrian, Hungarian, and Polish peasant families worked their own land. In Russia the peasants were the worst off. The serfs had been emancipated in 1861 and in 1900 could not own land as individuals. Peasants lived in village communities that owned the land and regulated how they paid their taxes and the fees owed to local landowners for land purchased from them. Peasants also required permission from the head of the household and the commune to leave their village for any length of time.

Peasant psychology differed dramatically from that of city folk. Peasants incorporated technological advances into their farming readily enough, but they stubbornly adhered to their traditional cultures and abhorred the changing social attitudes of the cities. Eastern European peasants considered themselves "the people," thought city dwellers strange, and rejected outsiders, especially intellectuals. Russian peasants attacked radical university students who came to the countryside to help them. As a rule, peasants proved impervious to outside movements that hoped to win them over to revolutionary ideals, but they frequently rose spontaneously when circumstances provoked them.

Women

Despite these anomalies, alterations in social conditions affected the lives of social groups everywhere in Europe to a much greater extent than had been true in the past. The breakup of the large extended family and better economic conditions improved women's lives. Living in their own homes instead of with their extended families had become socially acceptable and economically feasible by 1900. Economic progress and better transportation allowed middle-class families to take vacations, and, in general, leisure time increased. In 1900 women still had more children than they did in 1914, but, because peasant girls preferred to come to the city to work as maids, rather than toil in the fields, plentiful domestic help made it easier for middle-class women to go out by themselves, especially in northern Europe, but in some areas women still could not to go out on their own or stay in hotels even if accompanied by their husbands. Where they went out by themselves, shopping was a favorite activity for women, and they changed the whole experience. With more female customers, the shops that had been primarily warehouses acquired a modern aspect with windows that attractively displayed merchandise. In the past women had sewn the family's clothes, but the new century brought more ready-made clothing. Fashion reflected women's new mobility and freedom as skirts shortened and women's suits became more common. More of their offspring survived because of better hygienic practices, so women married later and had fewer children as the century advanced. Fewer children meant more independence for women and allowed more of the middle class's resources to be spent on education and other amenities.

As women became freer, they attended school in greater numbers and in Western Europe studied the same subjects as their male counterparts and made important contributions in diverse fields. In 1894 Maria Montessori became the first woman in Italy to win a medical degree. Specializing in education, she lectured on pedagogy at the University of Rome from 1901 to 1907 and developed educational methods that worked effectively that she applied in a special school she founded in 1906; her educational techniques spread throughout the world. Several women won Nobel Prizes in literature, and in science Madame Marie Curie shared a Nobel Prize and was awarded one for chemistry in 1911.

The real improvements in conditions for women did not bring full equality to women, however,. The doors of Russian institutions of higher learning were still closed to women, and in Maria Montessori's Italy lawyers argued against women's entrance to the bar. Women had only restricted control over their own property and faced discrimination in many professions. As late as the 1920s and 1930s, women were expected to resign from their jobs when they married, and governments placed quotas on the number of women who could be employed in state service. Women could not vote except in some Scandinavian countries, and the major West European countries gave them the vote in general elections only after World War I or II. Women rebelled by establishing feminist organizations, participating in political life, founding newspapers and other publications to advance their cause, and demonstrating. Socialist parties welcomed them into their organizations, but their leaders gave priority to the struggle for men's rights. European Socialism nevertheless numbered among its most innovative thinkers and key political leaders Rosa Luxemburg, Anna Kuliscioff, Angelica Balabanoff, and Clara Zetkin.

Social Classes

Despite the accelerating modernization of European society, the social classes remained separate and distinct in 1900. Part of the aristocracy still boasted

Feminist associations and publications were widespread by the beginning of the twentieth century. This photo dates from the early 1900s and shows suffragists holding a copy of the newspaper *The Vote*.

fabulous wealth and had political power out of proportion to its numbers. In Britain, unlike the continent, the aristocracy had its own house in Parliament, the House of Lords, which wielded real power and comprised a significant bloc in the House of Commons. Nobles dominated the established churches; the higher ranks of the military; the bureaucracies, especially in the East; and society. Suave cosmopolitanism distinguished the European aristocracy, and nobles in different countries had more in common with each other than with the lower or middle classes of their own nations. A common mentality distinguished European nobles: "He [an aristocrat] behaved as if his birth and leisure made him superior but never argued the point."

BIOGRAPHICAL SKETCHES

Anna Kuliscioff
Cofounder of Italian Socialism

Born in Russia on January 9, 1854, the flame-haired Anna Kuliscioff attended the University of Zurich in 1871 to study engineering because Russian institutions of higher learning excluded women. At Zurich, a center of Russian exile activity, she became a revolutionary. Upon returning to her homeland in 1874, she participated in the return-to-the-people movement, an ill-fated attempt to convert Russian peasants to revolutionary activity. Forced to flee the country for Switzerland, she began a liaison with Andrea Costa, a prominent Italian Anarchist, and had a leading role in the European anarchism of the period. In the late 1870s she converted to Marxism and influenced Costa to make a similar change.

When her relationship with Costa ended, Kuliscioff moved to Naples with their daughter Andreina and fell in love with Milanese democrat Filippo Turati. She exercised a decisive influence on Turati, who converted to Marxism. In the meantime, she received a medical degree and practiced medicine among the poor in Milan (this did not stop her from resisting Turati's pleas to stop smoking). The partners founded the country's most important Socialist journal, *Critica Sociale*, and the Milanese Socialist League became a cell for the county's first modern political organization in 1892, the Italian Socialist Party. The articles in *Critica Sociale* and Kuliscioff's salon located in Milan's famous Galleria converted Italy's most famous intellectuals to Marxist socialism. Kuliscioff advised Turati during his many years in Parliament, and the two are still revered as icons of Italian democracy. In 1898, the Italian government cracked down on Socialists, imprisoning the couple. Released after some months, they later guided the Socialist Party in its drive for social and political reforms.

Within the party, the couple fought the revolutionary wing, led after 1912 by Benito Mussolini. The two had political differences, with Kuliscioff pushing for an immediate campaign in favor of women's suffrage and Turati advocating for more gradual action. Kuliscioff headed the feminist movement and in 1911–12 edited its newspaper *La Difesa delle Lavoratrici* [Defense of Women Workers]. Following World War I, the pair led the Socialist revisionists in an unsuccessful fight to block the rise of fascism. Kuliscioff was so closely identified with the antifascist

continued

continued

resistance that when she died on December 29, 1925, her funeral procession to Milan's Monumental Cemetery provided the occasion for the last epic street battle between Socialists and Fascists. Her companion died in exile fighting fascism on March 29, 1932, and joined her in the same cemetery after World War II.

Kuliscioff's daughter married a rich Catholic Milanese businessman, which prompted Kuliscioff to write dejectedly that there must be a balancing force in the world: She rebelled against everyone and everything, while her daughter, raised by two revolutionaries, conformed to bourgeois life. She would have appreciated the irony when her grandson became a monk.

Below the aristocracy, the upper middle class enjoyed life at the beginning of the new century. Composed of administrators, successful entrepreneurs, and professionals, this group made up between 10 percent and 15 percent of the population in the most developed Western European societies, but much less in Eastern and Southern Europe. Seeking to imitate aristocratic values, the group honored intellectual pursuits, such as reading and listening to good music. They valued a good general culture but disdained the specialized knowledge that doctors or skilled craftsmen might possess to earn their living.

The lower middle class, estimated at 20 percent to 30 percent of Western Europe's working population, in turn, emulated the upper bourgeoisie. Consisting of persons, such as craftsmen, elementary schoolteachers, office clerks, bank employees, shop assistants, and white-collar employees, this class dreaded being thrown into the lower class that they resented. Members of the lower-middle class earned about the same as skilled industrial workers, but prided themselves on earning salaries instead of wages and not getting their hands dirty to make a living and flaunted social and cultural mannerisms copied from the upper classes.

All social groups looked down on the working classes, among whom important differences existed. In Northern Europe they were more stable than in the South. Because industrialization had begun earlier, by 1900 they were two or three generations removed from the farm, had organized politically, and were less violent; in southern Europe the industrial revolution had begun later, and workers frequently took to the streets seeking to overthrow the established political system. Even in the North, however, the workers' past unruly behavior fixed their image among the middle classes, who considered them riotous, lawless, and inferior. In the new century, workers still frequently led segregated, miserable lives in isolated city neighborhoods or, as in the case of miners, subdivisions outside the cities. They drank hard and kept to themselves.

At the beginning of the twentieth century, a "second" industrial revolution brought important technical changes, such as electrification, greater mechanization, an increased work pace, larger industrial organizations, and more impersonal relationships with employers that rapidly transformed the workplace by demanding greater skills from workers than in the past. As a consequence, a larger proportion of the workers in the new century had more education, were better paid, and were family oriented. Children, earlier seen solely as sources of income and sent into the factories at a tender age, tended to be withdrawn from the labor force to receive more education, while the average age of male workers increased and more women entered the labor force.

Along with opportunities, however, shifting economic conditions brought new insecurity. Workers adapted to the new conditions with increasing difficulty, men felt threatened by women workers, and the wages that had risen earlier leveled off in the early years of the twentieth century. Work became more routine and monotonous, and workers objected to the legal discrimination against them in such matters as debt and divorce and to the increasingly harsh police methods. Workers became convinced that they and their children had very little chance for advancement and flocked to join Socialist parties and other opposition groups.

Emigration

These factors heavily influenced another characteristic of Europe during the early twentieth century: migration. Emigration and immigration had been common throughout the nineteenth century, but from the 1890s on, movements of populations between and within countries accelerated because several important elements came together. Europe's population jumped from 266 million in 1850 to

The massive emigration of people from Europe to other parts of the world in the late nineteenth and early twentieth centuries had an enormous effect on the continent and on the lands in which the immigrants settled. Here is a picture of immigrants arriving at Ellis Island in New York Harbor in 1904.

429 million in 1900. Old barriers to emigration within countries, such as serfdom, broke down at the same time that the transportation infrastructure was being extended and economies were modernizing. Accelerating industrialization in countries, such as Italy and Russia, brought new employment opportunities abroad or in different areas of the same country. More opportunities to work stimulated travel, widened horizons, intensified communications, broke down traditional communities, increased social mobility, and inspired a desire to move. Even where industrialization did not spread, such as southern Italy, or among populations left behind, such as Russian Jews, industrializing countries needing cheap labor beckoned to people in search of a better life.

The geographic target areas and qualitative nature of the great European migration deserve special emphasis. The emigrant trek across the Atlantic Ocean to the United States, Argentina, Brazil, and Canada is only part of the story. Europeans first migrated within the continent, especially to France. By 1911, the Italian-born population of France was one-third that of the United States, and the country counted large numbers of Poles, Spaniards, and Belgians. Italy, the largest source of immigrants during this period, also sent people to Germany during Germany's intense industrialization after 1890, as did Austria-Hungary. Skilled craftsmen regularly left their native regions to work in other European countries; British technicians transferred advanced technology to the entire European continent as far as Russia; Scottish engineers designed railways the world over; Welsh foundry men developed iron making in France, Russia, and Pennsylvania; Greeks labored in Romania and Bulgaria and traded in Turkey before going to Africa, North America, and South America; Sicilian and Greek peasants tilled the soil in Tunis and the Argentine wheat fields or worked in the American construction industry. Many emigrants started their own businesses, and a sizable number returned home with a nest egg large enough to buy property in their native regions. The money they brought or sent back buoyed the old country's economy, and their foreign experience influenced their country's politics.

The Jewish exodus from Eastern Europe was an important feature of the European migration of the early twentieth century and illustrates the wide-ranging effects of the population movement. Although religious persecution and pogroms played an important role in this vast migration, the decline of the non-Jewish market in proportion to the high percentage of small tradesmen among Jews and workers in consumer-goods industries seems to have had a greater role. An estimated 1.5 million Jews migrated to the United States between 1899 and 1914, many of whom contributed to the growth of the garment trade in New York City.

The great population movements of the late nineteenth and early twentieth centuries brought Europeans into contact with different peoples and customs, preparing them for the late twentieth-century immigration into Europe.

CHANGING CULTURAL AND POLITICAL OUTLOOKS

Unbeknownst to most people at the time, ferment and change also characterized European culture. In 1900 the majority of Europeans led their lives according to comfortable assumptions that had originated during the Enlightenment two hundred years earlier. However, while ordinary Europeans would easily have recognized and subscribed to a common set of ideas and assumptions, new ideas circulating among the cultural elite drastically changed the cultural outlook of ordinary people over the next quarter century.

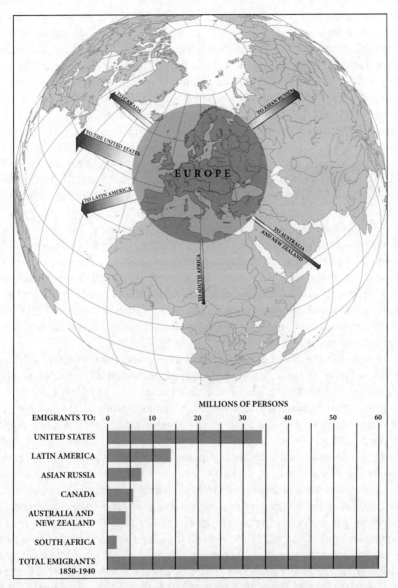

European Exodus. This map and graph give a good idea of where the approximately 60 million emigrants from Europe went between 1850 and 1940. People leaving the different European countries brought a new social and cultural diversity, stimulated the export of manufactured goods and capital from the old continent, and increased European economic influence throughout the world.

The Nation as a Community

Europeans believed in the nation as the ideal form of organization for a community. Before the eighteenth century, generals frequently led armies of a different nationality against their own countries of origin, and foreigners could lead countries. With the French Revolution in 1789, this attitude changed as the French fought savagely to defend their fatherland because of the benefits the Revolution had bestowed on them. During the revolutionary era, French armies fought to extend those advantages to other areas and encouraged the development of nationalism in the hope of utilizing it against the former rulers. However, nationalism worked not only against the old regimes but backfired against the French as different national groups preferred independence under their own leaders who they hoped would implement French-style reforms. Conflicts between the champions of oppressed nationalities and of the status quo marked the early and mid-nineteenth century. In the West, the major enemy of nationalism was Austria, whose existence nationalism threatened because it was composed of many nationalities but ruled by German-speaking Austrians. The struggle produced waves of revolutionary disorder in 1820 to 1821, 1830 to 1831, and 1848 and several wars between 1859 and 1870 and was an important cause of World War I.

Nationalism resulted in a united Italy and Germany, the high point of nineteenth-century nationalism, and, despite the continuing struggle of East European nationalities to free themselves from Austrian, Russian, or German domination, in the West the nation-state seemed to provide the essential framework necessary to confront the demands of the second industrial revolution. Modern industrial economies demanded more educated workers, for example, and modern nation-states created popular school systems with compulsory attendance to provide these workers.

Accelerating industrialization, secular schools and the population shift from the countryside to the cities weakened traditional habits and religious beliefs. Intellectuals confidently predicted the disappearance of traditional churches as the nation-state increasingly inherited the mystique, loyalties, and emotions that religions once possessed and took over the role of the medieval church—regulating public and private business and behavior, controlling education, and replacing charity with social assistance, such as pensions, unemployment insurance, poor relief, and medical help.

The nation-state gave people an identity and appeared as the concrete emanation of a nationality's collective personality and pride. It implemented economic and social principles for the benefit of all, created a legal structure to mediate disputes, set policy to protect the community's interests, and built armed forces to defend them. Because of the benefits it provided, the nation-state legitimately demanded sacrifices and cooperation from different classes and replaced the political struggles of the early and mid-nineteenth century with internal peace. Unfortunately, Europeans considered colonies essential for economic development and big-power status, and the resulting competition intensified tensions among them, stimulated racist ideas, and made war more likely.

Liberalism

Liberalism, the ideology that pervaded the West, originated in eighteenth-century Britain at the dawn of the industrial revolution, when manufacturers demanded that governments cease interfering in economic processes because they believed that the free operation of the market stabilized society. From economics they extended this theory into a political one, according to which the state should intervene only minimally in the lives of free individuals and concern itself only with defense and maintaining internal order.

Throughout the nineteenth century, liberalism was the antithesis of French revolutionary Jacobinism, which called for greater state regulation on behalf of the poor. By the beginning of the twentieth century, the bourgeoisie had become supreme in Western Europe, and liberalism had changed. In the late nineteenth century, Liberal thinkers, such as John Stuart Mill, adapted bourgeois liberalism to changing social, economic, and political conditions by acknowledging an expanded role for the state, although not a dominant one. In 1911 liberal theory reached its culmination with L. T. Hobhouse's famous essay *Liberalism*. Hobhouse argued that the state must interfere in society as little as possible but that it must help create conditions to enable all citizens to obtain everything necessary to their own well-being through their own efforts.

While in theory Liberals continued to believe that the law of supply and demand must be allowed the freest possible reign and that the government must keep out of individuals' lives, in practice the bourgeoisie sought to blunt the social struggles that threatened the economic order and its own political supremacy. Thus, bourgeois-dominated governments favored social legislation to soften the harshest effects that the economic system had on workers and peasants. Moreover, in the early 1900s, many Liberals believed that individuals could achieve their fullest expression within the nation-state's framework. Liberal theory favored free trade, but when confronted with fierce foreign competition that threatened to drive them out of business, Liberals turned to their governments for protection. They argued that jobs would disappear and that the nation would become vulnerable to hostile powers if industrial capacity diminished. In brief, they identified their own interests with the national interest and argued that governmental support of business would stimulate the economy, create jobs, and boost national prestige. For the same reasons, Liberals believed that the nation should help industrialists gain cheap raw materials and world markets and consequently supported the imperialism that had an important role in the foreign policy of the major powers.

Ironically, because the best-paid workers benefitted from these policies, an important segment of the working class supported them, while the bourgeoisie supported labor reforms because they brought economic and social peace. These measures included extension of the right to vote (by 1912 all Western countries had granted universal male suffrage), functioning parliamentary systems, strengthened civil rights, compulsory elementary education, unemployment compensation, old-age pensions, industrial accident insurance, and legislation protecting woman and child labor. In addition, skilled, organized workers in the most advanced industries directly benefited from the protectionist and imperialist policies of the bourgeoisie because they favored good jobs and high salaries. This situation created divisions among sectors of the working class.

Socialism

Despite concessions, the bourgeois refusal to accept the working class as a major partner in government stimulated the growth of Socialist parties, which, however, split on conflicting interpretations of how socialism would come to power.

This is the philosophical crux of Karl Marx's argument predicting the triumph of socialism: Economic relationships (the substructure) determine social relationships (the superstructure). Economic changes demand corresponding alterations in the governmental and the legal structure of society. As the productive system develops, however, the governing class, which was put into power by previous economic conditions (the bourgeoisie), refuses to abdicate. The new means of production and the class it has produced (the workers) come into conflict with the dominant political class; continued development of the new economic system, combined with resistance by the old government, culminates in revolution and the victory of the workers and socialism.

In elaborating his theory, Marx described certain concrete developments that would signal the decline of capitalism—deeper and more frequent economic crises would produce a revolution. When Marx's predictions did not materialize, Socialist theoreticians closely examined his analysis. In *Evolutionary Socialism* (1899), the German Socialist Eduard Bernstein argued that the signs of capitalism's impending collapse not only had failed to appear, but that the opposite seemed to be happening. Economic crises were less frequent and milder, and the middle class was increasing instead of disappearing. Bernstein concluded that Marx was wrong and advocated achieving socialism not by revolution but gradually through parliamentary reforms.

Before World War I, the Bernstein Debate wracked all European Socialist movements as social democratic revisionists or reformists fought with orthodox Marxist revolutionaries for control of the Socialist parties. In general, the revisionists gained control of the organizations against stiff opposition and followed a reformist policy, but stopped short of revising official party theory that called for the violent overthrow of capitalism. In all European countries, Socialist parties split into warring social-democratic and revolutionary factions.

The Belief in Science

The importance of Marx and Liberal economic theories illustrated the European penchant for applying scientific precepts to the analysis of society. This tendency, unique to Europe, originated during the eighteenth-century Enlightenment, when Isaac Newton's scientific method had been applied to the examination of social problems (social Newtonianism). In the nineteenth century, sociologists applied biological precepts to society. Ideas coming both from physics and biology were still important for the ordinary European during the first decade of the twentieth century.

In 1859, Charles Darwin's *The Origin of Species* enunciated the principles of evolution, including natural selection, which Social Darwinists transformed

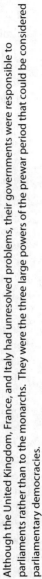

Although the United Kingdom, France, and Italy had unresolved problems, their governments were responsible to parliaments rather than to the monarchs. They were the three large powers of the prewar period that could be considered parliamentary democracies.

into the survival of the fittest. They argued that, through a process of struggle, nature selected certain families, classes, nations, or races to rule over others while reserving on inferior status for other groups. This tendency contributed to racist theories that justified imperialism. Philosopher Hannah Arendt wrote that European race-thinking was based primarily on an interpretation of Darwin's survival of the fittest and that it would have disappeared had it not served as an excuse for imperialism. Racism persisted in the European psyche until its culmination as a fundamental Nazi tenet.

The application of scientific principles to different fields of human endeavor abetted materialism, another concept in which many Europeans believed. As science explained more material phenomena, the trend toward a diminished religiosity intensified, and the ability of religion to impose limits on human behavior diminished. Protestant Liberals responded by seeking to demonstrate that the religious and scientific spheres were separate, although most Protestants seemed to believe that science and the Bible should be harmonious because God had revealed both. The Catholic Church, led by Pius X, frowned on new scientific doctrines. As the new century opened, a struggle raged over modernism, an attempt to apply new scientific and social theories to religious dogma that gained some success among Protestants but brought excommunication to its Catholic adherents. Both the more flexible Protestant approach and the rigid Catholic method failed to halt the declining appeal of the churches for the urban masses.

However, the twentieth century overthrew not only traditional religion but the comforting worldview based upon the scientific precepts and cultural assumptions of the Enlightenment.

Scientific Revolution

For Europeans, science had been important for the technological improvements it engendered and for how it defined the world. The diffusion of Newton's physics among eighteenth-century intellectuals had fundamental effects on politics and society. In the fourth century, St. Augustine's view of history as the unfolding of God's will justified the church's prominent role in politics because God directly intervened in the affairs of the world through His church. A universe composed of spheres pushed by angels completed this picture of God's direct intervention in human affairs. Newton, however, argued that the universe operated automatically, according to a series of laws that he described: God had created the universe and left it to run by itself like a clock. Because God did not intervene directly in the running of the universe, He did not directly intervene in the operation of society through the clergy. This rationale bolstered the claim that secular governments should rule and reduced the church's role in politics. Enlightenment intellectuals extended Newton's concept to all society and attempted to discover its fundamental laws of operation. They described the universe, and society, as a smooth-running machine with easily understandable laws, a view to which most people still subscribed in 1900.

During the early years of the twentieth century, however, a new scientific revolution that had its roots in the last years of the previous decade overthrew Newtonianism's comfortable worldview. This new science gradually shattered previous assumptions and fundamentally changed European culture and society.

The old conception of matter went first. The way in which most people understood matter in 1900 had its roots in the Greek philosophy of the fifth century B.C. The ancient Greeks had reasoned that by continually cutting a material, eventually the smallest indivisible piece of matter would be achieved—the atom—but in the last years of the nineteenth century, this commonsense argument broke down, and in the early years of the new one, it was proved false. In 1895, the German physicist Wilhelm Roentgen accidentally discovered X-rays and learned that when he passed them through a gas, they dislodged minute, electrically charged particles. In 1897, the Englishman J. J. Thompson, working at the famous Cavendish laboratory in Cambridge, England, reasoned that bodies made up of *parts* of atoms accounted for electricity, a conclusion independently reached by the Dutch physicist Hendrik Lorentz, who named the particles "electrons." Scientists had demonstrated that atoms consisted of smaller parts and therefore were not irreducible, as had been believed for over two thousand years. Further investigation into the atom made use of quantum and relativity theories elaborated by German physicists Max Planck and Albert Einstein in 1900 and 1905. Additional research by two of Thompson's collaborators at the Cavendish laboratory—the New Zealand-born and educated Ernest Rutherford (1911) and the Dane Niels Bohr (1913)—produced a model of the atom resembling a miniature solar system.

The roster of names involved in crucial discoveries confirms that early twentieth-century science was a common European endeavor. Roentgen sent a reprint of his work to the famous French mathematician Henri Poincaré, who passed it on to physicist Henri Becquerel, discoverer of uranium's radioactive properties in 1896. Inspired by Becquerel, a young Polish-born graduate student at the Sorbonne, Maria Sklodowska, began work in the new field, and, in collaboration with her French husband Pierre Curie, she discovered two new elements that won the couple and Becquerel a Nobel Prize in 1903. The implications of the Curies' research into radioactivity was proof positive that different particles made up the atom and that elements could be changed or transmuted by changing particles within an atom. In April 1902, Rutherford and his colleague Frederick Soddy demonstrated that radioactivity is not only a "manifestation of subatomic chemical change," but produces "new kinds of matter." Their work blazed the way for an understanding of the forces encapsulated within the atom's nucleus over the next forty years. This research influenced society by spurring intellectuals to delve into the characteristics of reality that were not visible.

Indeed, even more revolutionary developments in theoretical physics gave impetus to this search. While examining questions related to the intensity of colors in the radiation emerging from a small hole in an electric oven (cavity radiation), Max Planck, a professor of theoretical physics at the University of Berlin, concluded that energy was emitted not in different amounts but *only* in standard packets he called the "quantum of action." The science historian J. L. Heilbron explained the concept in the following words: "In ordinary or classical physics, energy is a continuous quantity and can be . . . [dispensed] as ordinary people drink beer, in any quantity they wish; in Planck's theory as reinterpreted by

Einstein, the . . . energy [can be dispensed] only in certain amounts, as a guzzler who insists on consuming only by the pint. Why nature guzzles rather than sips became a fundamental problem for physicists."

Max Planck's presentation of his quantum theory at a scientific meeting on December 14, 1900, proved fundamental in touching off the twentieth-century scientific revolution. Applied initially by Planck only to the field of thermodynamics, the quantum concept of the discontinuity of energy contradicted Newton's system, which assumed continuity in all of nature's causal relationships. It soon became clear to scientists that quantum theory was relevant not only to thermodynamics but to many other fields, and the quantum became recognized as a constant of nature fundamental to the study of X-rays, gases, the photochemical effects of light, and atomic structures. During the rest of the century, quantum theory (and its offshoot, quantum mechanics) had increasingly greater revolutionary implications about the nature of matter and its behavior so as to make reality at the subatomic level seem downright bizarre.

Albert Einstein utilized Planck's quantum theory in his famous 1905 paper describing his special theory of relativity (one of three brilliant papers published that year) by demonstrating that light also emits energy in packets or quanta. Relativity proved to be an equally revolutionary formulation that Planck forcefully defended, along with its author, so that, an observer commented: "Einstein may be considered Planck's second great discovery in physics."

BIOGRAPHICAL SKETCHES

Max Planck
An Upright German

A mild man with a conventional demeanor, the scientist who revolutionized twentieth-century physics led an upright public life and a tragic personal one. Born in 1858, descended from a long line of pastors and scholars, Max Planck appeared to his teachers as a steady but not a brilliant student with no special aptitude for physics. His first wife died in 1909 after twenty-three years of marriage. He remarried at age fifty and led a pleasant life with his second wife and four children for an all-too-brief while. An accomplished pianist, Planck composed songs and an operetta as a boy. As a university professor, he kept up with his music at his villa in a Berlin suburb by acting as a choirmaster, by playing the organ at services, and by inviting guests to regular musical evenings. The most famous participants included Albert Einstein, who played along on his violin, and Lise Meitner and Otto Hahn, both renowned for their research into nuclear fission.

After he achieved fame by enunciating the quantum theory, Planck spared no effort to help his fellow scientists and his students. Einstein found in him his first and greatest supporter. Planck's students praised his clear and brilliantly organized lectures and flocked to them. He sat through 650 doctoral examinations. Many of his students became famous, two of them winning Nobel Prizes. Although he believed that nature had determined that women should be mothers and homemakers, he sympathized with their causes and gave them permission to attend his lectures. When he was rector in 1913 to 1914, 770 women attended courses at the University of Berlin. He also appointed as his assistant Austrian physicist Lise Meitner, the first scientist to explain nuclear fission.

On October 4, 1914, Planck signed the "Appeal to the Cultural Peoples of the World," a declaration by ninety-three German intellectuals denying that German troops had committed atrocities and identifying themselves with the army. He later regretted this action and championed the cause of international cooperation among scientists when nationalist sentiments threatened to destroy it. After the war, he helped save German science during the difficult times of hyperinflation by securing grants from the Rockefeller Foundation, the General Electric Corporation, and a Japanese industrialist.

Planck's world changed in January 1933, when Adolf Hitler came to power. In May he attempted to convince Hitler that his anti-Semitic policies would ruin German science, causing the Fuehrer to fly into a rage. Planck attempted to find posts for dismissed Jewish scientists and, if necessary, help them emigrate. He fought Nazi scientists who attacked "Jewish" physics, not openly but indirectly, an attitude that later earned him criticism from some quarters. He continued the battle even after his forced retirement at age eighty, despite the heartache that weighed him down. His oldest son Karl died of his wounds in World War I. His twin daughters both died within two years of each other following childbirth. Bombing during World War II completely destroyed his home and possessions, with all their memories, but that loss paled in comparison to a blow that almost killed him. In February 1945 the Nazis executed his son Erwin, an opponent of the regime, just when the father had high hopes for a pardon.

War and declining health brought more suffering. As he fled from the last bombings of the conflict, his vertebra fused, causing him immense pain. Before his death from a stroke on October 4, 1947, at age 89, he at least had the satisfaction of seeing Germany's premier research institution, the Kaiser Wilhelm Institute, renamed after him and staffed by his friends.

Einstein's relativity theory revolutionized scientific thinking and its implications were still important at the end of the twentieth century. The theory's departure is the constancy of the speed of light for all observers everywhere, conclusively demonstrated in a famous 1887 experiment by two Americans, Albert Michelson and Edward Morley. The only way the speed of light can remain constant is for space and time to change according to one's framework. Einstein's theory produced consequences that ordinary persons would consider weird. Relativity required people to give up their conventional and commonsense ideas of space and time as universal constants that remained the same everywhere for all people. Einstein's theory also postulated that mass and energy were convertible one into the other, as represented by the famous equation $E = MC^2$ (where E is energy, M is mass, and C is the speed of light). Because the speed of light is such a large number, the destruction of even a small amount of mass would produce amounts of energy so great that they were inconceivable at the time. This equation eventually made the atomic bomb possible.

Quantum theory and relativity created conceptions of space, time, motion, and matter that struck observers as fantastic and bounded only by the imagination of individual scientists. By the 1920s, this idea proceeded even further as the "uncertainty (or indeterminacy) principle" elaborated by German physicist Werner Heisenberg disrupted the ordinary person's view of the universe. The uncertainty principle stated that it was possible, at a given moment, to know either the speed or the position of a particle, but not both. Uncertainty evolved into a dominant principle of the cosmos, which had to be interpreted according to statistics. Intellectuals would learn from science not only that reality lay hidden from view and was mysterious, but was, like time and space, flexible.

Taken together, the theories of Planck and Einstein shattered the Newtonian worldview, substituting a cosmos that was difficult to comprehend, apparently unstable, contrary to common sense, irrational, and variable according to a person's frame of reference. The comforting assumption that ordinary people had of the universe as a smooth-operating machine disappeared.

Cultural Rebellion

In 1919 British scientists confirmed relativity by observing the bending of light during a solar eclipse as Einstein's theory predicted, but the new ideas had had an impact on European intellectuals. Max Planck himself acknowledged the close relationship between the natural and intellectual sciences and their mutual influences. Unfortunately, for many nonscientists, "Mistakenly but perhaps inevitably, relativity became confused with relativism [the idea that truth depends on the individuals or groups holding them]." This notion circulated at a popular level primarily after World War I, but long before then, intellectuals demolished the Enlightenment values underpinning European culture and society that were linked to the Newtonian worldview, igniting the cultural and political revolutions that marked the twentieth century.

Like the physicist Einstein, French philosopher Henri Bergson contemplated the nature of time. He declared it a subjective experience, a duration that is lived differently by each individual. In that sense, reality was relative for Bergson. A mystical life force flowed somewhere, Bergson believed, and individuals must be in touch with it through "intuition," rather than rational analysis. Reality was not universal but differed for each individual, and artists or thinkers who understood that were superior to those who did not. In his 1907 book, *Creative Evolution,* Bergson enunciated the concept of the élan vital, the quality that enables people to keep in touch with the mysterious wellspring of life. Bergson's philosophy paralleled physics by stressing the sources of life that were not susceptible to simple rational analysis and varied for different people. Intuition had as great a role in life as it did in science.

In the course of his work, Bergson emphasized psychology, arguing for the importance of dreams, referring to the false realities that people construct as masks. He also considered unconscious influences, a field in which the Austrian physician Sigmund Freud opened up an entirely new dimension for humanity. Successfully working with a patient whose disorder had proved intractable by getting her to remember long-forgotten incidents that had affected her—through free association—Freud became convinced that many mental disorders could be traced back to traumatic, repressed childhood sexual events. He discovered that individuals lived an intense unconscious life. In short, reason alone did not determine people's behavior, but the unconscious—hidden and mysterious. Freud's work cast further doubt on the dominant role of rationality as developed during the Enlightenment in the eighteenth century.

In the cases of Bergson and Freud, as in science, the clear-cut, commonsense approach to life that characterized the beliefs of ordinary people broke down, and the same development occurred in art. In Germany, the Russian-born painter Wassily Kandinsky condemned the materialism that determined the outlook of traditional artists, scientists, leftist politicians, and ordinary people. These materialists, he wrote in 1910, "know nothing of the vital impulse of life." For Kandinsky, the scientific revolution of those years had "cast doubt on that very matter which was yesterday the foundation of everything, so the whole universe is shaken." Kandinsky is an outstanding example of how, stimulated by new scientific developments and philosophical currents uncovering mysterious impelling forces, artists turned to the intuitive study of underlying reality, producing Expressionism—an artistic style affecting all spheres of thought between 1910 and 1924. Thus, Kandinsky, the movement's theoretician, stated that art must appeal to the emotions. In painting, for example, this meant examining the nature and impact of color. Kandinsky explained that colors produce a spiritual vibration in the observer

This painting illustrates some of the central themes of Futurism. "Brawl in the Galleria," by Umberto Boccioni (1882-1916), pictures a riot in Milan's famous Galleria Vittorio Emanuele II. The painting illustrates the sights and sounds of violence among the elegant shops and restaurants of the northern Italian industrial city's famous landmark.

and should, therefore, be chosen *for their psychic effect*. He favored abstract painting for that reason, bolstering his argument by citing the emotional force of music, the least representational of the arts. In line with these ideas, German Expressionist painters of the Blue Rider school founded by Kandinsky produced abstract pictures that attempted to transmit extreme feeling primarily through intense color.

Kandinsky had been greatly influenced by artistic developments in Paris during a 1906–07 stay. In Paris, the Fauves (Wild Beasts) employed violent color and distorted, flat forms in their paintings, even though their best-known representative, Henri Matisse, did not paint in a completely abstract manner. Another artistic school centered in Paris, Cubism, attempted to get at inner reality through the structure of paintings and distorted forms. Cubism counted Pablo Picasso and Georges Braque as its major representatives. Like Kandinsky, Picasso emphasized emotion and considered painting visual music. Although the different schools debated about which one best conveyed emotions on canvas, avant-garde artists of this period broke with earlier naturalistic traditions representing external reality in an attempt to get at the real nature of things, as science had done. Their work included "references to the artist's thoughts, feelings, and unconscious impulses, to the perceptions of his or her nonvisual senses, or to the physical laws governing the universe." The denial of external aspects of life in favor of its intangible and mysterious qualities accelerated the decline of the rationalism that the twentieth century had inherited from the Enlightenment, confirming artists' views of themselves as revolutionaries against the bourgeois world of their elders.

Most avant-garde artists seemed to be interested in social and political issues only tangentially. The great exception was the most iconoclastic of the prewar movements, Italian Futurism. Futurism's political and social outlook formed a whole with its artistic philosophy and had wide-ranging implications. Primarily concerned with reviving Italy from bottom to top, the Futurists issued a manifesto in the Parisian *Le Figaro* on February 20, 1909. Inspired by Egyptian-born, 33-year-old, well-off, well-dressed poet Filippo Tommaso Marinetti, the manifesto took the European art world by storm.

The Futurists felt compelled to speak because "Time and Space died yesterday." They aimed to "break down the doors of the mysterious Impossible" and never look back. This task required an all-out war on the past, against the bourgeoisie, existing society in all its manifestations, and all their supporters (Pastists). Among the instruments and values of the past that were slated for destruction were museums and libraries, schools, and academies, "moralism, feminism, vile and utilitarian opportunism."

The Futurists glorified modern civilization—a culture dominated by speed, the machine, and technology. They aimed to bring this new civilization to Italy in anticipation of a modern Italian art. The great Renaissance tradition weighed heavily on Italian artists and writers, which explains why so many Futurist artists rebelled, why they congregated in Paris, and why they published their founding manifesto in the French capital. They dedicated themselves to the theme of speed and industrialization—symbolized by the airplane, the automobile, and the machine—attempting to reproduce the sounds, noises, and smells of modern life.

Futurist painter Umberto Boccioni portrayed rising cities and speed on his canvases; architects, such as Antonio Sant'Elia, designed ultramodern cities; and poets composed sacred hymns to coal and electricity. Futurists shocked audiences with their weird and violent behavior that was designed to ridicule the placid bourgeoisie during infamous Futurist evenings that ended in riots as the artists jumped from the stage and "dynamically altered" the faces of people in the audience by beating them. Italian Futurism influenced subsequent artistic movements, such as Dadaism.

From Cultural to Political Revolt

The Futurist lifestyle, dominated by danger and rebellion, culminated in a love for war, which the Futurists glorified as the "hygiene of the world." Marinetti saw action in the Libyan War (1911–12) and covered the Balkan Wars (1912–13), and Marinetti and the Futurists pushed for Italian entrance into World War I and volunteered for action in World War I and World War II. He linked up with former revolutionary Socialist and founder of fascism Benito Mussolini. Like Futurism, Italian Fascism adored violence, loved action, and aimed to destroy bourgeois society. (From now on in the book, Fascism with a capital means the Italian movement and the lower case, fascism, refers to the generic movement.) Both movements hated pacifist socialism and its goal of a comfortable materialistic life. In 1919, Futurists and Fascists collaborated in violent physical attacks on their enemies that was the hallmark of early fascism.

The path to fascism, however, was complex. During the century's first decade, political thinkers attempted to connect with the mystical life sources not only of individuals, but of nations. In Italy, intellectuals were obsessed with Italian weakness and the parliamentary rule of pragmatist Prime Minister Giovanni Giolitti, whom they blamed for the country's flaws. The nineteenth-century movement for national unification, the Risorgimento, they believed, had been betrayed, and they dreamed of moral regeneration, grandeur, and a new political system. The primary political exponents of these ideas were the Nationalists, whose theoretician Enrico Corradini founded an influential journal in 1903. Corradini believed that the nation was the highest expression of fellowship and embodied the instincts of association and struggle. Because civilization without war was impossible, imperialism was the natural consequence of nationalism. Corradini stated that since Italy was a poor, "proletarian" nation, it must lead a revolutionary struggle against the rich countries that held it down. Using the Socialist analogy, he argued that this struggle required internal unity that parliaments destroyed and, internationally, a war of the proletarian nations led by Italy against the rich countries. This emphasis on war, antiparliamentarianism, and internal revolution linked the Nationalists and Futurists and, after World War I, the Fascists.

Similar developments occurred in France, exacerbated by the case of Alfred Dreyfus, a Jew accused of treason. This famous case split French society between his accusers and supporters, stimulating French nationalism and anti-Semitism (the strongest in Europe at the time), and bringing together groups that hoped for a national regeneration through authority and force, action and strong leaders, and antiparliamentarianism. Two prominent thinkers provided ideological consistency, clarity, and force to this movement, Maurice Barrès and Charles Maurras. Barrès argued in 1902 that a French essence defined the French people and emphasized the importance of the nation as a tight-knit community working together—organic nationalism. Barrès saw the fatherland as resembling the individual in that it is the sum of a long history of effort, sacrifice, loyalty, and a long struggle against internal and external enemies for survival. Similarly, Charles Maurras developed integral nationalism between 1900 and 1909. Maurras viewed the monarchy as the culminating institution of the French nation, the only one capable of representing it and of imposing a truly national policy. Maurras denounced parliaments as the embodiment of egotistical minorities that a prince who based his dictatorial authority on the French people would eliminate. In the case of both Barrès and Maurras, the French nation embodied the mystical qualities that excluded not only foreigners but French opponents of their ideas.

In Germany as well, to intellectuals, the central theme was the harm that liberalism and parliamentary government had done to the Germans. The intellectuals railed against parliamentary corruption and demanded the ethical revamping of bourgeois society and a culture that would put politics on a new course. The brilliant philosopher and theoretician of the "superman," Friedrich Nietzsche, was repeatedly cited as the enemy of democratic mediocrity. German nationalist exponents demanded a leader who would unite German society, rid it of its impure elements, and lead the country to glory. As in France, the anti-Semitic component of this current of thought was powerful, and the Jew was considered the primary scoundrel. The cultural discontent expressed by these intellectuals had a great influence on German politics and pointed the way toward ideas expressed by Adolf Hitler in the 1930s.

Reinforcing these feelings were the critics of the prevailing European political systems who examined the rules of political behavior. Gaetano Mosca had criticized the corruption and mediocrity of elected parliaments that, he believed, made democracy a sham. Best known for his 1896 work, *The Ruling Class,* Mosca argued that the only real classes in any form of government are the governing (always a minority) and the governed (the majority). Vilfredo Pareto, an Italian political thinker teaching in Switzerland, reaffirmed this view by arguing that in every society, the upper classes constitute an aristocracy or an elite. When the social equilibrium is stable, the power elite appears competent and is accepted; when crises cause political systems to fail, a new elite replaces the old. This cycle always repeats itself, Pareto wrote, no matter what the form of government. The German political theoretician Robert Michels expanded these ideas to party organizations, including democratic ones, in *Political Parties: A Sociological Study of the Oligarchic Tendencies of Modern Democracies* (1911). This work stated his "iron law of oligarchy": in every organization, including democratic parties and parliaments, political groups that cannot be removed have real control.

The ideas seemed to confirm "scientifically" the feelings of avant-garde artists, nationalists, and intellectuals that an underlying reality determined the visible one in politics, a view that permeated Marxism as well. By the end of the nineteenth century, the European Socialist parties, dominated by revisionism, had lost their revolutionary edge. In France and Italy, a new political philosophy, revolutionary syndicalism, incited workers to organize in unions, overthrow the bourgeois political and economic system, and create a new society based on their organizations. The French philosopher Georges Sorel and his Italian disciples put into effect what historian Zeev Sternhell called the revolutionary revision of Marxism. In his *Reflections on Violence* (1906), Sorel lauded violence as the necessary element of change. Because the economic forces that Marx believed would produce a revolution had failed to do so, Sorel emphasized the power of myths, which could mobilize the proletarian to overthrow the bourgeoisie by violence. Sorel thus shifted the main emphasis of Marxist doctrine from economics to psychology by injecting irrationalism into Marxism. Given their limited ability to influence the established French and Italian Socialist parties, revolutionary syndicalist theoreticians turned to the nationalism existing in both France and Italy and, with the objective of "the destruction of the liberal democratic regime and its intellectual norms and moral values," contributed to the birth of Fascist ideology.

A Society in Movement

At the beginning of the twentieth century, European society presented a curious picture of a civilization balanced between stability and transformation. Europeans were better off economically than they had ever been, despite the existence of deep pockets of poverty. However, instead of bringing peace, the new prosperity generated resentment among the categories that were left out or could not keep up with the speed of economic and technical change. These groups linked up with influential intellectuals who aimed to destroy existing society just as quantum and relativity demonstrated that reality could no longer be understood by relying upon appearances and was destroying Newtonianism. Artists and intellectuals went on a search for the hidden and mystical aspects of life, resulting in a cultural and political rebellion that shattered the intellectual basis of the European world even before World War I destroyed its political, economic, and social foundations and brought to power irrational movements that formed in the crucible of early twentieth-century thought.

Bibliographical Essay

A good survey of social conditions at the beginning of the twentieth century is Edward R. Tannenbaum, *1900: The Generation before the Great War* (Garden City, N.Y., 1976). Wider ranging, more complete, and possessing a wealth of historical statistics is Peter N. Stearns, *European Society in Upheaval: Social History Since 1800* (New York, 1967). An older work that gives a good idea of the social life of this period is B. Seebohm Rowntree, *Poverty: A Study of Town Life* (New York, 1971); originally published in 1901, this is the classic study of British social conditions that modern scholars rely on. Peter Laslett, *The World We Have Lost* (New York, 1965), discusses Britain before the industrial revolution but has an excellent chapter on the beginning of the twentieth century; the work includes a wealth of interesting information. Asa Briggs, *Victorian Cities* (New York, 1963), presents a good picture of urban living in approximately the same period as discussed in this chapter. An indispensable starting point in understanding the nature of European population movements during this period is Frank Thistlethwaite's chapter "Migration from Europe Overseas in the Nineteenth and Twentieth Centuries," in Herbert Möller, ed., *Population Movement in Modern European History* (New York, 1964), pp. 73–92.

D. V. Glass and Roger Revelle, eds., *Population and Social Change* (London, 1972), collects a number of papers mostly dealing with Europe. Sandra Halperin, *War and Social Change in Europe: the Great Transformation Revisited* (Cambridge, UK, 2004) describes the continuation of the traditional classes. J. M. Houston's *A Social Geography of Europe*, rev..ed.. (New York, 1963), looks at the development of European cities in historical perspective. Gerold Ambrosius and William H. Hubbard published *A Social and Economic History of Twentieth-Century Europe* (Cambridge, MA, 1989). Books that include material on twentieth-century social conditions in Europe include Robert Clifford Ostergren and John G. Rice, *The Europeans: A Geography of People, Culture and Environment* (New York, 2004), and Richard Vinen, *A History in Fragments: Europe in the Twentieth Century* (Cambridge, Mass., 2001).

On the issue of women, the memoirs of Angelica Balabanoff, *My Life as a Rebel* (New York, 1968), originally published in 1938, not only provides excellent portraits of the important characters she knew well, such as Mussolini and Lenin, but is a mine of information on the period. The British feminist Emmeline Pankhurst wrote her auto-biography, first published in 1914, *My Own Story* (London, 1979); see also the biography by her daughter, E. Sylvia Pankhurst, *The Life of Emmeline Pankhurst* (London, 1969). Sandra Stanley Holton, *Feminism and Democracy: Women's Suffrage and Reform Politics in Britain, 1900–1918* (Cambridge, 1986), is a clear, brief overview of the women's movement for reform and the vote in Britain between 1900 and 1918. For France, there is Steven C. Hause and Anne R. Kenney, *Women's Suffrage and Social Politics in the French Third Republic* (Princeton, N.J., 1984), a work seeking to combine the political and social history of the issue, especially between the 1890s and 1920s. Two general histories that consider this period are Deborah Simonton, *The Routledge History of Women in Europe Since 1700* (London, 2006), and Olwen H. Hufton, *The Prospect Before Her: A History of Women in Western Europe* (New York, 1996). Lynn Abrams wrote *The Making of Modern Woman: Europe 1789–1918* (Harlow, 2002), which includes material on the 20th century. Tito Boeri et al. present problems faced by working women in *Women at Work: An Economic Perspective* (Oxford 2005).

Immigration from Europe has been well covered, but it is more difficult to find sources on the material presented in this volume. The following books are helpful: Andrew Geddes, *The Politics of Migration and Immigration in Europe* (London, 2003), an overview of problems linked to immigration; Walter T. K. Nugent, *Crossings: The Great Transatlantic Migrations, 1870–1914* (Bloomington, 1992), an account of migration to the New World that includes some of the countries discussed here; and Eli Lederhendler, *Jewish Immigrants and American Capitalism, 1880–1920: From Caste to Class* (Cambridge, UK, 2009), an account of European Jews and immigration.

Good general surveys of the entire period, which also deal with social and cultural issues in addition to the political and diplomatic, include Carlton J. H. Hayes, *A Generation of Materialism, 1871–1900* (New York, 1941), from which the quotation regarding Darwinism was taken (p. 12), and Oron J. Hale, *The Great Illusion, 1900–1914* (New York, 1971). Hannah Arendt's opinion, cited on the connection between imperialism and racism and its results, is found in her *The Origins of Totalitarianism*, rev..ed...(New York, 1966), pp. 183–84.

Unfortunately, the history of socialism in the twentieth century has been neglected in recent scholarship, and many of the good books are also old. George Lichtheim, *Marxism: An Historical and Critical Study* (New York, 1961), provides a one-volume introduction to the subject. G. D. H. Cole, *A History of Socialist Thought* (New York, 1953), is a thorough examination in five volumes. Peter Gay, *The Dilemma of Democratic Socialism: Edward Bernstein's Challenge to Marx* (New York, 1962), is a classic analysis of Eduard Bernstein's revisionism and its problems and implications. Albert S. Lindemann, *A History of European Socialism* (New Haven, Conn., 1983), examines the European movements. Good studies of socialism, too numerous to cite here, exist for most of the individual European countries during this period. Daryl Glaser et al., *Twentieth Century Marxism: A Global Introduction* (London, 2007) is a recent book. Sheri Berman's *The Primacy of Politics: Social Democracy and the Making of Europe's Twentieth Century* (New York, 2006) emphasizes revisionism and social democracy.

Although the scientific revolution of the early twentieth century has received attention, books that make the issues understandable to nonscientists are unfortunately not plentiful. Thomas H. Kuhn's *The Structure of Scientific Revolutions* (Chicago, 1972), first published in 1962, emphasized the role of paradigms in the history or science; this work achieved a wide following, but his concept of scientific revolutions has been challenged. Alfred North Whitehead's *Science and the Modern World* (Cambridge, U.K., 1929) is a readable classic with a good discussion of relativity and the quantum theory and their impact on modern science. James B. Conant, *On Understanding Science* (New Haven, Conn., 1947), remains useful.

Max Planck attempted to explain the principles of modern physics and their relationship to a philosophy of life in a brief work, *The Philosophy of Physics* (New York, 1936). J. L. Heilbroner, *The Dilemmas of an Upright Man: Max Planck as a Spokesman for German Science* (London, 1986), discusses Planck's discoveries and his role in German physics up to his death; the citation describing the nature of the "quantum" is taken from this work, p. 21, and the quote regarding his relationship to Einstein is from p. 28. Jane Weir has written a more recent biography, *Max Planck: Revolutionary Physicist* (Minneapolis, 2009). Lise Meitner received a well-deserved biography by Patricia Rife, *Lise Meitner and the Dawn of the Nuclear Age* (Boston, 1999). The reader will find biographies of Einstein readily available but no easy description of his relativity theory, even though the effort has been made. The best biography for the nonspecialist is Michael White and John Gribbin, *Einstein: A Life in Science* (New York, 1994); a more detailed work is Ronald W. Clark, *Einstein: The Life and Times* (New York, 1971). Both Denis Brian, *Einstein: A Life* (New York, 1996), and Walter Isaacson's *Einstein: His Life and Universe* (New York, 2007), are excellent. Stanley Goldberg's *Understanding Relativity: Origin and Impact of a Scientific Revolution* (Boston, 1984), is more technical than one would wish, although an indication of its impact is provided. A clearer work about the implications of relativity on the concept of time and some of its strange derivations is Paul Davies, *About Time: Einstein's Unfinished Revolution* (New York, 1995); Davies uses the term *unfinished revolution* to describe the continuing effects of Einstein's theories. An interesting work comparing the influence of science at the beginning of the twentieth century and at its end is Gerald Holton, *Einstein, History, and Other Passions* (Reading, Mass., 1996); this book also provides interesting insights into Einstein's personal life. Susan Quinn's biography, *Marie Curie: A Life* (New York, 1995), is an insightful work dealing with the personal and research aspects of the science of the period. The segments of letters reproduced in Ilse Rosenthal-Schneider, *Reality and Scientific Truth: Discussions with Einstein, von Laue, and Planck* (Detroit, 1980), edited by Thomas Braun, gives a fascinating glimpse of the views that the era's most famous scientists had of their own findings.

A clear analysis of Bergson's thought, especially his concept of time, is Leszek Kolakowski, *Bergson* (Oxford, 1985), to which must be added the more recent *Thinking in Time: An Introduction to Henri Bergson* (Ithaca, N.Y., 2006) by Suzanne Guerlac. Thomas Hama, ed., *The Bergsonian Heritage* (New York, 1962), includes essays on those aspects of Bergson's thought that survive. The collection of essays edited by

P. A. Y. Gunter, *Bergson and the Evolution of Physics* (Knoxville, Tenn., 1969), turns the tables and discusses Bergson's insights on the physical sciences and on the philosophy of science. The reader will find many treatments of the different aspects of Freud's work and thought. The classic biography is the massive three-volume work by a close friend of the early period, but see especially the first volume, Ernest Jones, *The Life and Work of Sigmund Freud. Volume I: The Formative Years and the Great Discoveries, 1856–1900* (New York, 1953). The best one-volume biography is Peter Gay, *Freud: A Life for Our Time* (New York, 1988).

Paul Johnson makes the application of relativity to politics and society the main theme of his *Modern Times: The World from the Twenties to the Eighties* (New York, 1983), in which the reader may find the remark on relativity and relativism (p. 4). Wassily Kandansky's brief, influential work, originally published in 1910, is *Concerning the Spiritual in Art,* translated by M. D. H. Sadler (New York, 1977); the relevant citations are found on pp. 12 and 24. An excellent brief general introduction to Expressionism in its different aspects is R. S. Furness, *Expressionism* (London, 1973); a fuller treatment is Richard Samuel and R. Hinton Thomas, *Expressionism in German Life, Literature and the Theatre (1910–1924)* (Philadelphia, 1971); for a more recent book, see Ashley Bassie's *Expressionism* (New York, 2008). The best work on Picasso during the crucial decade mentioned in the text is John A. Richardson, *A Life of Picasso. Volume 2: 1907–1917*. Matisse is covered in Alfred H. Barr, *Matisse: His Art and His Public* (New York, 1966).

Probably the best work on the active political lives of painters and a smattering of other intellectuals during this period is Theda Shapiro, *Painters and Politics: The European Avant-Garde and Society, 1900–1925* (New York, 1976), on p. 91 of which may be found the citation about artists bringing into their work the invisible elements and the physical laws of the universe. There is an excellent portrait of Marinetti, his action, influence, and link to fascism in James Joll, *Three Intellectuals in Politics* (New York, 1965); the citation regarding Futurism is on p. 144. The quotations in the text regarding Futurist theory are taken from the 1909 Manifesto that founded the movement. Walter L. Adamson examines the crucial role of the Florentine milieu and Futurism in *Avant-Garde Florence: From Modernism to Fascism* (Cambridge, Mass., 1993). The impact of Futurism and its aesthetics on avant-garde European writers and artists is thoroughly discussed by Marjorie Perloff, *The Futurist Moment: Avant-garde, Avant guerre, and the Language of Rupture* (Chicago, 1986). For the technological themes in the movement, see the essays in Gunter Berghaus, *Futurism and the Technological Imagination* (Amsterdam, 2009). Robert C. Williams, *Artists in Revolution: Portraits of the Russian Avantgarde, 1905–1925* (Bloomington, Ind., 1977), discusses the Russian avant-garde at the beginning of the century.

Michael Curtis examines the attacks of three intellectuals discussed in the text against the political and social structure of France during this period: *Three Against the Third Republic: Sorel, Barrès, and Maurras* (Westport, Conn., 1976). The standard work on Germany is Fritz Stern's *The Politics of Cultural Despair: A Study in the Rise of the Germanic Ideology* (Berkeley, Calif., 1963). Armand Patrucco's *The Critics of the Italian Parliamentary System, 1860–1915* (New York, 1992) is an excellent discussion of the ideas of Mosca, Pareto, and Michels in action.

Richard D. Humphrey, *Georges Sorel: Prophet Without Honor* (Cambridge, Mass., 1951), is a general study of Sorel's contribution to the analysis of modern social forces while Larry Portis, *Georges Sorel* (London, 1980) is a biography. John Stanley, *The Sociology of Virtue* (Berkeley, Calif., 1981), concentrates on Sorel's early work and on his revolutionary syndicalism. J. R. Jennings, *Georges Sorel: The Character and Development of His Thought* (New York, 1985), is a good discussion of Sorel's complexity and contradictions.

Mark Antiff's *Avant-garde Fascism: The Mobilization of Myth, Art, and Culture in France, 1909–1939* (Durham, N.C., 2007) discusses some of the themes elaborated on these pages. Jack J. Roth, *The Cult of Violence: Sorel and the Sorelians* (Berkeley, Calif., 1980) remains a good study of the general impact of Sorel and the Sorelians.

The major work on the link between revolutionary syndicalism, Sorel, and Fascist ideology is Zeev Sternhell, *Birth of Fascist Ideology: From Cultural Rebellion to Political Revolution* (Princeton, N.J., 1994); the quotation is on p. 22.

CHAPTER 2

◢

The Democracies and
Their Dilemmas

CHAPTER OUTLINE

Britain: Accommodation and Militancy • France Muddles Through •
Italian Democracy in the Making

BIOGRAPHICAL SKETCHES

Emmeline Pankhurst, "Votes for Women!" • Jean-Joseph-Marie-Auguste
Jaurès, Martyr

At the beginning of the twentieth century, the major European states could be divided into two categories according to their political structure. Three had functioning parliamentary systems that included ministerial responsibility, the principle
that no government could be installed or continue to rule without the majority approval of a popularly elected Parliament. Furthermore, members of Parliament could
call a vote of confidence that might provoke the fall of a cabinet at any moment. If the
government lost such a vote, it had to resign, whether or not the king or president (the
executive) agreed. This procedure gave the legislative branch real power in these countries, the outcome of a centuries-long dispute between kings and elected assemblies.

Despite a variety of political, social, and still-unresolved governmental problems, Great Britain, France, and Italy fit the category of parliamentary democracies. In three other major European states—Germany, Austria-Hungary, and
Russia—the governments were responsible not to parliaments, but to the monarchs. According to the constitutional structures of these states, the emperors
named governmental ministers who served at their pleasure, not the Parliament's.
As the new century opened, a number of serious domestic issues faced both the
parliamentary democracies and the authoritarian states.

BRITAIN: ACCOMMODATION AND MILITANCY

Following a reign of sixty-three years, Queen Victoria died on January 22,
1901, and because of her longevity at the height of the country's power, her

name symbolized the age. Considered rather dull, she at least took her duties seriously.

The opposite is true of her son, who succeeded her as Edward VII at age sixty. Edward loved hobnobbing with the rich and representing his country during a showy age, but, unsuited for governmental affairs, "his reign marks the real transition of the English monarchy from a significant political institution to its present primarily social function." In 1910, his son succeeded him as George V. Solemn and serious, this king resembled his grandmother but ably carried on the reduced role that his father had conferred on the monarchy.

Parliament and Reform

In contrast to the monarchy's decline, the English Parliament still represented the classic parliamentary model, with a long tradition of opposing groups alternating in power, cabinet stability, and parliamentary responsibility but faced a major institutional problem that threatened its ability to meet the growing social demands of modern society: the House of Lords was better able and ready to veto legislation than were the French and Italian senates. As Britain faced the growing lower-class demands, the anomaly of a hereditary branch of Parliament capable of blocking pressing reforms appeared intolerable.

The struggle to reduce the power of the Lords had been ongoing, but the Tories had blocked major changes. In July 1895 they had beaten back a challenge from radicals working with the Liberal Party and won a crushing victory in the general election. Conservative domination of British politics remained secure, despite the poor British performance in the South African Boer War (1899–1902), and continued with the elections of 1900 and 1902, when the new Conservative leader Arthur Balfour controlled the office of prime minister for the next three years.

Nevertheless, Conservative strength slowly eroded. In 1902, the Conservatives passed the Education Act, which alienated Dissenters because they perceived it as strengthening schools run by the Church of England. The temperance movement had brought general recognition that the great number of pubs constituted a grave social problem, but the method of reducing the number of pubs under the Licensing Act of 1904 created dissension, as did the question of whether owners whose licenses to sell alcoholic beverages had not been renewed should be compensated.

In 1903 and 1904, an economic downturn and long-term industrial changes increased labor agitation and spurred inflation. Labor power had ironically grown because of a 1901 House of Lords ruling stating that labor unions did not have immunity from suits and could be sued for the actions of their agents. Anger ignited resistance among the unions, whose political action committee successfully elected two candidates to Parliament, including labor's most notable leader Keir Hardie. Labor's growing clout and the increased industrial unrest came at a bad time for the Conservatives, who were split between the free-trade majority and advocates of protectionism and closer economic links with the British colonies led by Joseph Chamberlain. An attempted compromise and a cabinet reshuffle by

Balfour did not resolve the issue; Chamberlain challenged the prime minister for control of the party, and Balfour resigned in December 1905.

The Conservative decline altered Britain's political complexion. A wealthy, good-looking Scot, Liberal leader Sir Henry Campbell-Bannerman—known as CB—installed a cabinet and prepared for new elections with a successful appeal to Britons who were tired of the high cost of living and sick of the conservative inefficiency. Most important, the Liberals had powerful union support that established the well-organized Labour party. The January 1906 elections resulted in a Liberal majority of eighty-four seats, with twenty-nine seats going to its Labour allies.

CB's new cabinet was committed to reform and included Herbert Henry Asquith, future prime minister, as chancellor of the exchequer (treasury secretary) and Edward Grey, who directed British foreign policy until World War I. The Liberals embraced a serious social reform program based on the ideas of the Fabians, Socialist intellectuals led by Beatrice and Sidney Webb who pressed for reforms that would allow the country to catch up with social legislation that had already been implemented on the continent. The Liberal social-reform program included improvements in education, regulation of the liquor business, and health and accident insurance for working people.

The Liberals addressed the problems of children with legislation in 1906 and 1907 that provided free meals and medical attention for poor children in the schools. Furthermore, in a move aimed at breaking down class barriers in British society, the Liberals obliged every secondary school that received state aid, including private ones, to reserve a quarter of their places for graduates of state elementary schools. In 1908, the Children's Act banned imprisonment of children under age 14 and improved the reformatory system. In a related area, a royal commission recommended modifications in Britain's stringent Poor Laws, but divisions and World War I delayed changes until 1929.

The Liberals also favored the workers who had helped them come to power. In 1908, miners received the eight-hour day. In the same year, the government established old-age pensions and provided for retirement at age seventy, marking acceptance of an important principle by the British. Two other important pieces of labor legislation, backed by Winston Churchill, passed in 1909: creating labor exchanges that matched up workers and employers with available jobs and instituting mixed bodies of workers, employers, and state representatives with the power to set wages (subject to approval of a higher body, the Board of Trade) in industries that were noted for sweatshop conditions. In 1911 legislation patterned on the pioneering German social insurance law of 1889 was passed, the British National Insurance Act. This law established unemployment-limited insurance, national health insurance, maternity assistance, and sick pay, all funded by a modern contributory system.

Struggle with the House of Lords

In the course of implementing this ambitious reform platform, the Liberals ran into stiff opposition from the House of Lords, which it lost.

The Lords hoped to wear down the government by defeating land reform bills in 1907 and an important temperance measure in 1908. Liberal losses in by-elections signaled that the strategy was working, and the Liberals were further weakened by CB's death in 1908 and by the need for his successor Asquith to raise new funds to pay for the expensive social legislation and for new warships to meet the German naval challenge.

Fiery Chancellor of the Exchequer David Lloyd George decided to resolve both the monetary and the political problem in one bold stroke. In 1909 he presented a budget proposal that sharply increased existing estate and luxury taxes and introduced new duties aimed at the rich. His proposal included a supertax on incomes over 5,000 pounds, a 20 percent capital gains tax on land, and a levy on the value of undeveloped land. The high amounts involved, the principle of taxing high income, and the land duties shocked the Lords, who summarily rejected the proposed budget following its passage by the House of Commons. This development raised an important constitutional issue: constitutional experts agreed that the elected House of Commons had complete control of finance measures that should not be subject to reversal by the hereditary House of Lords. Lloyd George took his case to the people in an effective campaign in which he stated ironically: "a fully equipped duke costs as much to keep up as two Dreadnoughts; and dukes are just as great a terror and they last longer."

The Liberals won the January 1910 elections, fought over these issues, keeping their majority in the Commons with 377 seats to 275 with the help of its Labour and Irish Nationalist allies who won forty and eighty-two seats, respectively. This result induced the Lords to accept Lloyd George's budget, but the principle of whether they should have power at all had been raised. The problem the Liberals faced would be that the Lords would veto the legislation when the bill reached their chamber. The only way to get around the obstacle was to have the monarch appoint enough new peers to reverse the majority in the House of Lords, a procedure that had been used in the past. King Edward, therefore, had to agree, but he insisted on a second election, which took place in December 1910 and yielded similar results as the previous election. In the meantime, Edward died, and his successor George V, favored negotiations, but the Lords still rejected the bill and set the stage for its reintroduction under George V's threat to create new peers in case of a new rejection.

In August 1911 the bill became law. It deprived the Lords of their veto power by providing that the budget (or any bill certified as a money bill by the Speaker of the House of Commons) would become law without the consent of the House of Lords after a month. The Lords could hold up legislation other than money bills only for two years if the legislation passed in the Commons three times during that period. Finally, the duration of a parliament was reduced from seven years to five. In this way, the House of Commons gained control of the country's political affairs with the possibility of interference by the Lords reduced to a minimum.

The disputes over constitutional issues and social legislation weakened the British political system's ability to confront other questions threatening the country's stability. Despite British labor's success in attaining social reforms, salaries failed to catch up with the rising cost of living. In 1909, acting in its judicial capacity, the House of Lords dealt a blow to unions by ruling that they could not use members' dues to finance political action (the Osborne case).

Liberal Chancellor of the Exchequer David Lloyd George took on the House of Lords in 1909 with a famous program taxing the rich in a successful attempt to extend social programs and bolster the country's defenses by appealing to the British people. Lloyd George had a long career and led Britain to victory during World War I. Here is a picture of the "People's Champion" at ease with his dog, "Peggy."

The Liberals attempted to nullify the ruling in 1911 and 1913 by instituting salaries for members of Parliament and establishing criteria regulating the utilization of union funds for politics. The Labour Party saw these measures as a compromise, but the workers interpreted them as a sign that the party had been seduced by the parliamentary system. The increased aggressiveness of British workers coincided with agitation in Australia and the rise of revolutionary syndicalism in France and Italy. This ideology criticized parliamentary blandishments and advocated the supremacy of workers in politics and direct action through strikes. The British had won the right to strike in 1906, and labor leaders who had recently returned from Australia urged them to exercise it frequently.

Increasing Militancy

Labor militancy increased dramatically between 1906 and World War I. Union membership doubled, and in 1908 strikes caused the loss of more hours in one year than in the previous ten. Strikes particularly affected the mining, shipping, and railway industries. In 1911 striking seamen and firemen won important concessions. The first national railway strike took place during the same year and paralyzed the nation for two days. In 1912 the dockers' strike brought violence. The government's response ranged from conciliation to force, and the strike met defeat, as did similar actions by the miners. Frustrated by the spotty success of their strike tactics and dissatisfied with governmental concessions, the militant miners', transport, and railway unions signed an agreement to coordinate their action, the triple alliance, in June 1914. Before the agreement could be formally implemented, however, World War I broke out, and the government had little trouble persuading the unions to end their agitation on patriotic grounds—but the labor agitation brought a foretaste of future developments.

Militancy also increased among other groups, especially women. Before 1907, women had attained the vote in local elections, but the "suffragettes" demanded the ballot in national elections. Prime Minister Asquith remained cool to the request. In 1908 and 1909, Emmeline Pankhurst, founder of the Women's Social and Political Union (WSPU), led her organization to adopt militant tactics—demonstrations, violence, and destruction of property. In 1910 the government seemed willing to consider concessions, but the fight with the Lords and parliamentary maneuvering subsequently delayed legislation that was designed to grant them. In the meantime, the WSPU split because of the authoritarian manner in which the Pankhurst family administered the organization. Emmeline then quarreled with her daughters over ideology—were women repressed as a sex or a class? The women, however, like the workers, put the struggle for their rights on hold after the outbreak of war.

BIOGRAPHICAL SKETCHES

Emmeline Pankhurst
"Votes for Women!"

When Emmeline Pankhurst was born on July 14, 1858, her father Robert Goulden exclaimed: "She should have been a lad!" She very quickly learned to play the piano at sight, and her ability to spell earned her the nickname "the dictionary." Growing up in Manchester, then the center of the movement for the right of women to vote, fourteen-year-old Emmeline asked to be taken along when her mother attended a lecture by an advocate for the franchise. The event inspired her life's work.

In 1878, Emmeline and her parents attended a lecture by Dr. Richard Marsden Pankhurst, a strong advocate of equal suffrage for both sexes. The cab pulled up close to the family, and Pankhurst's delicate hand reached out to open the door. Her daughter Sylvia wrote: "Thenceforward all happened as if by magic." They married in the winter of 1879, and within a short time had four children. Emmeline had entered the political world and, spurred by the death of a son who she believed would have survived had the family been better off, became a Socialist and a champion of the poor.

Mrs. Pankhurst campaigned for the rights of married women during debates on a law that would allow women to vote on the local level. Politicians argued that married women should not have the vote because of the protection their husbands afforded them. In fact, once married, a woman did not exist legally. Her property became her husband's, and she could neither sue nor be sued in court.

continued

continued

Mrs. Pankhurst won her battle, and in 1894 all women gained local voting rights without regard to marriage.

During the early years of the new century, she took the lead in the women's movement and instituted militant means to obtain voting rights for women in national elections. Mrs. Pankhurst was intimately involved with the nascent Labour Party, but this organization disappointed her. She founded the WSPU as the instrument of fighting for women's rights. Its slogan was "Votes for Women!" Its members employed disruptive techniques, with many going to jail. During her career, courts sentenced Emmeline to a total of four years in prison, and she served several months. Her jail time compromised her delicate health, as it did that of other militant women who undertook hunger strikes and whom the authorities force-fed. When World War I broke out, Mrs. Pankhurst ended her militant campaign, giving top priority to supporting the war. In 1917, she led a WSPU delegation to Russia to convince that country to remain in the war against Germany. During the trip, she developed an abiding hatred for Bolshevism, an attitude that alienated her from her daughter Sylvia. In 1918 the climax of her campaign came, when women aged thirty and older received the right to vote and ironically the right to be elected to Parliament at age twenty-one.

Mrs. Pankhurst had a difficult relationship with her daughters, but suffered from her daughter Christabel's loss in her attempt to be the first woman elected to Parliament and from the subsequent collapse of her Women's Party. She remained active, however, in helping war orphans and in a number of other worthy causes. In 1928 she surprised the country when she agreed to present herself as a Conservative candidate for Parliament. During the campaign, she fell ill with the jaundice that had plagued her since her prison days. In May her daughters moved her into a nursing home, but she died on June 14, 1928, leaving her worldly possessions of eighty-six pounds to Christabel. In March 1930, a statue of Britain's Gentle Amazon was unveiled in Victoria Square Gardens near the House of Commons. An observer wrote: "There are literal minds which suppose that Mrs. Pankhurst faced obloquy and prison to win votes for women. She did a greater thing than that. She suffered to remove from the mind of every young girl the sense that she is born to a predestined inferiority."

The Irish question proved more recalcitrant. The British hoped to resolve the centuries-old Irish problem with Home Rule—establishment of an Irish parliament. Asquith presented a Home Rule bill in 1912, but the Irish question inflamed passions, and Tory opponents shouted down proponents and the prime minister. This behavior encouraged resistance in Ulster, the Protestant and economically advanced northern part of Ireland. The northerners feared that deputies from the Catholic and agrarian South would swamp their interests in a parliament representing all Ireland.

The northerners organized militarily to fight home rule, and the government dispatched troops to Ulster. This policy caused opposition among the British themselves and even British army officers requested exemptions should military action prove necessary. When the government refused, they resigned in protest— a mutiny that extended to the War Office—and Conservative leader Bonar Law pledged to back Ulster. In response, southern Irish volunteers organized

Europe in 1900. In this map of Europe in 1900, the major trouble spots are shaded. The most important problems were a dispute over Alsace-Lorraine, which caused bad blood between France and Germany, and the Balkans. Before 1912–1913, Turkey still occupied most of this peninsula, which was the scene of contests among the small and large powers located in the area's proximity. Italy was unhappy about Austrian mistreatment of the Italians in historically Italian areas still held by Austria-Hungary (Trent, the Trentino, Trieste, and the Dalmatian coast). Ireland, occupied for centuries by Britain, still festered. Sweden and Norway were one country, but the Norwegians chafed at Swedish supremacy. However, in 1905, this was the only issue to be peacefully resolved.

themselves, and a new urban working-class movement under Jim Larkin emerged and pledged to seek Irish freedom. In 1913 a serious tramway strike broke out in Dublin, with militant workers joining Sinn Fein, a nationalist organization demanding independence from Britain. In 1914 the Irish dispute escalated when the British army that had ignored military activities in Ulster fired on southern volunteers in Dublin. In the meantime, the Lords utilized their few remaining powers to delay the home rule bill. The postponement had drastic consequences because, in the meantime, World War I broke out, stymied resolution of the problem, and further radicalized the Irish situation. Ireland seemed on the brink of civil war; the Irish refused to put aside their claims during the conflict.

By 1914 Britain presented a mixed picture. Significant reforms had been adopted, but agitation increased at all levels of British society. It has also been suggested that the increasingly serious disturbances encouraged the coming of war because sectors of British society believed it would increase patriotic sentiment and calm domestic differences. It has been argued that England had "offered the world a remarkable experiment in liberal, capitalist democracy," but, if so, World War I ended it.

France Muddles Through

In the late nineteenth and early twentieth centuries, France resolved the major political problems forcefully posed during the great revolution that had begun in 1789: power sharing between the executive and legislative branches, whether France should be a kingdom or a republic, and the role of the Catholic Church.

The Third Republic

A parliamentary crisis that began on May 16, 1877, ended in an understanding that cabinets would be responsible to a majority vote of the Chamber of Deputies elected by universal male suffrage. An indirectly elected Senate had little effective power, and the president was transformed into a figurehead.

The Third Republic had thus been established, but the fight between secularism and the Catholic Church continued. The church opposed liberalism and republicanism and was strongly allied to the forces in French society opposing both, especially the army, which resisted civilian control and supported the conservative forces in French society. The army favored a war of revenge on Germany and blamed the politicians for their failure to lead the country in a fight to recover the provinces of Alsace and Lorraine that had been lost to Germany in 1871 following the Franco-Prussian War.

In the 1890s the Dreyfus affair brought the struggle between conservatives and liberals to the fore. Captain Alfred Dreyfus, a Jew, was convicted by the army of betraying French military secrets to the Germans and was shipped off to Devil's Island. Supported by their conservative and clerical allies, military leaders eliminated Jews, Protestants, and republicans from influential army positions. These developments convinced Liberals, Radicals, Socialists, and anticlericals to unite in a Leftist bloc, and French society split on the issues of justice, authority, clericalism, anti-Semitism, political prejudice, and democratic rule. The struggle escalated when novelist Émile Zola published a famous letter in defense of Dreyfus. New evidence emerged demolishing the army's case against Dreyfus, but the military refused to reverse its decision. Dreyfus's innocence or guilt became irrelevant as different sectors of the French population staked out positions depending on their views of the future of French society

The battle's fortunes tilted in the Left 's favor with the constitution of a government of republican defense under René Waldeck-Rousseau, with Dreyfus's rehabilitation, and the electoral victory of the Leftist bloc in 1902. Ex-seminary student and anticlerical Émile Combes became prime minister, and the Left passed legislation against church congregations and favoring the army's republicanization, an intense period that culminated in 1905 with the separation of church and state.

The Rise of Nationalism

The Dreyfus affair finally resolved the political question of the church's position in France and reduced the French army's threat but did not end nationalist hatred for the Third Republic. Indeed, the Dreyfus case exacerbated French

Le Petit Journal
SUPPLÉMENT ILLUSTRÉ

LE TRAITRE

The famous Dreyfus case divided France at the end of the nineteenth and beginning of the twentieth century. Captain Alfred Dreyfus, a Jew, was convicted of betraying his country. In reality, this event brought to the fore domestic issues over which France had been fighting for a century: Church vs. State, Monarchy vs. Republic, Military vs. Civilian Control, rich vs. poor. This contemporary image shows Dreyfus receiving a dishonorable discharge from the French army after his conviction. He was later reinstated and fought in World War I.

anti-Semitism, probably the strongest in Europe, and stimulated the rise of a new, mystical, nationalism. Nationalists continued to accuse Jews of being disloyal: "There is not any likelihood that Dreyfus is innocent," they argued, "but it is absolutely certain that France is innocent." The champions of the new nationalism, Maurice Barrès and Charles Maurras, "felt that anti-Semitism filled a certain gap, supplied a need, and that without it nationalism could not survive." Maurras's *Action Française,* founded in 1899, pledged to end the evil Republic dominated by Jews, Freemasons, Protestants, and foreigners and argued that only restoration of the king could save France: "that is, *France* personified by the descendant and heir of forty chiefs who have made, enlarged, maintained, and developed it." *Action Française* presented itself as defending French tradition and accused the republic of destroying French culture by persecuting Catholics, corrupting French youths, and killing workers.

This last point illustrates how the nationalistic right appealed to the proletariat that it considered an integral part of the nation. Its leaders pledged to defend working-class rights by restoring the king, who alone could achieve social progress, maintain order, and "protect, organize and securely install the working class as his ancestors installed the bourgeoisie." Historian Zeev Sternhell described France during this period as a "laboratory in which the original political syntheses of our time were created" and maintained that this grafting of workers' rights onto traditional nationalist ideology was the beginning of a national socialist or Fascist ideology.

The "Modern Challenge" and France's Failure

This phenomenon gave rise to revolutionary syndicalism, which urged strikes and violent revolution because the workers' own political parties betrayed them. The rise of this movement illustrates the Third Republic's difficulty in responding to the "modern challenge."

Historian David Thompson defined the modern challenge as the task of resolving the issues "of the great present-day problems of unemployment and social insecurity, of industrial despotism and world economy, of aggression and international disorder." A solution necessitated fashioning a new compromise between the industrial elite and the proletariat, which the French proved unable to craft. During the first decade of the twentieth century, no durable agreement between these two forces emerged, despite an increase of per capita industrial production of 57 percent between 1901 and 1913, compared to a European average of 37 percent. The social basis for this failure was the Third Republic's domination by the petite bourgeoisie who were entrenched in the bureaucracy and the major parties—Republicans, Radicals, and Radical-Socialists, which were neither radical nor socialist. The political story of this failure played out amid the backdrop of momentous labor battles and epic oratorical duels in the Chamber of Deputies between France's most notable prewar politician, Georges Clemenceau—the Tiger—and Socialist leader Jean Jaurès over social legislation, strikes, and unionization.

As the new century opened, French Socialists were split into revolutionary and reformist parties. The revolutionaries, led by Jules Guesde, advocated taking power by violence, while the reformists, headed by Jean Jaurès, believed that socialism could be achieved gradually through parliamentary reforms. In 1905 these parties merged into the French Section of the Workers' International (SFIO), with Jaurès as its leader. Following the leftist victory in the Dreyfus affair, the Leftist bloc disintegrated, and the differences reemerged as Clemenceau responded to Jaurès's demand for collectivization: "The real France is founded on property, property, property."

BIOGRAPHICAL SKETCHES

Jean-Joseph-Marie-Auguste Jaurès
Martyr

Jean Jaurès, heroic figure of prewar French socialism, was born in Castres, France, on September 3, 1859. The son of an unsuccessful businessman, Jaurès attended the country's best school on a scholarship—the École Normale Supérieure. He taught at a lycée from 1881 to 1883 and lectured in philosophy at the University of Toulouse between 1883 and 1885.

In 1885 Jaurès won election to the Chamber of Deputies but was defeated for reelection in 1889. Following his defeat, he pursued graduate studies and earned a doctorate. He ran for Parliament again and won a seat from a working-class district in 1893. By this time Jaurès had converted to socialism, and when the Dreyfus affair touched off the greatest crisis in French politics and society before the 1930s Jaurès sought to reverse Dreyfus's conviction. This position contributed to his defeat in the 1898 elections, but it was his last loss, and Jaurès won reelection to the Chamber of Deputies in 1902, 1906, 1910, and 1914. Besides his political career, Jaurès devoted a great deal of time to scholarship, publishing a massive *Socialist History of the French Revolution, The Franco-German War,* and *The New Army.*

Jaurès belonged to a generation of remarkable Socialist leaders who believed in the gradual achievement of socialism through parliamentary reforms, but like most European Socialists of the age, the French split on this question. In 1904 Jaurès cofounded and edited *L'Humanité,* which helped spread his ideas. Jaurès dueled with Jules Guesde, leader of the revolutionary Socialist party, and Guesde's failure to garner much support set the stage for a merger in 1905 when the revolutionaries joined with Jaurès and, under his leadership, formed the SFIO. In Parliament, Jaurès became the champion of the working class and the great antagonist of Georges Clemenceau.

Besides his struggle for social reforms, Jaurès concentrated on foreign affairs. He feared above all the outbreak of a war in Europe, believing that French foreign policy—particularly its alliances with Russia and Britain—increased the danger of a conflagration and advocated international arbitration to assure continued peace. These views and what they perceived as a pro-German attitude brought violent extremist nationalist denunciations and a call for his assassination. In the summer of 1914, as Europe approached the outbreak of World War I, Jaurès threw his weight behind peace negotiations and argued that if France pressured Russia and the Germans pressed the Austrians, they could save the peace.

On the evening of July 31, 1914, Jaurès, some of his fellow Socialist deputies, and the *Humanité* staff dined at the Café Croissant in the Rue Montmartre—a popular meeting place for French and foreign journalists. Jaurès and his friends ate dinner seated on a bench with their backs to one of the restaurant's open windows. At about 9:30, just as he was finishing, a French nationalist who favored war with Germany pumped two pistol shots from the street through the window into the back of Jaurès's head. The Socialist leader died instantly.

The murder shocked France and Europe just as the conflict was breaking out. Jaurès's friend and Italian Socialist counterpart, Filippo Turati, expressed the feeling of many Europeans in his obituary that Europe could never have gone to war without first killing Jean Jaurès.

On March 14, 1906, Clemenceau became minister of the interior just as the largest French labor union, the Confédération Générale du Travail (CGT) adopted revolutionary syndicalist principles, which favored strikes and violence to overthrow bourgeois society. On May 1, 1906, the CGT planned a great demonstration in favor of the eight-hour day, and fear of the supposed imminent collapse of capitalism sowed panic in the hearts of the middle classes. Instead, Clemenceau arrested CGT officials, earning the undying enmity of Jaurès, who reproached him in Parliament for the next three years. At the same time, new elections produced a majority for a coalition of moderate Leftists and Centrists and a Clemenceau cabinet opposed to radical social or economic changes.

The Clemenceau government's performance turned out to be lackluster. Real wages for workers had lagged since 1902. The bill with the greatest potential for effecting social change would have established an income tax, but the government did not get it through the legislature until 1909, and implementation was delayed until 1914, then postponed again because of World War I. Another serious issue, women's rights, did not find a solution. Married women received control of their earnings in 1907, some acceptance in the bureaucracy, and the right to vote for professional bodies, but these steps left the women's movement unsatisfied because it demanded the right to vote in national elections. Efforts in Parliament to extend the vote to women got nowhere because France's largest party, the Radicals, and Clemenceau himself, resisted on the grounds that women would be influenced by priests to elect clerical candidates and jeopardize the republic.

Similarly, Clemenceau's government opposed union activities, especially in the public sector. When several public service unions joined the CGT in 1906 and 1907, Clemenceau fired their officers and proposed restricting unionization. This time Clemenceau came under fire for different reasons both by the Left and by conservatives who demanded he ban the CGT. Clemenceau refused, but the bitter debate with the Socialists over labor issues produced an irrevocable break. Several clamorous strikes, in which the police fired on the workers, killing six and wounding fifty, prompted an angry Jaurès to declare that there could be no rapprochement between the government and the Socialists. As a result, little in the field of social legislation had been accomplished by July 20, 1909, when the Clemenceau cabinet fell. By then foreign policy issues took precedence, and the opportunity to give France a modern social security system before the conflict had been lost.

France's inability to build an acceptable social security apparatus, to make the working class a partner in the government through meaningful collaboration with the Socialists, and to give workers a greater stake in the country caused the Third Republic to continue losing support among the proletariat. Reformist Socialists advocated participating in Parliament in order to share power, win reforms that would increase working-class living standards, and gradually achieve socialism, but an increasing number of workers agreed with intellectuals who charged that Socialist leaders had sold them out by participating in bourgeois politics that had robbed socialism of its revolutionary impetus. At the same time, the rightists beck-oned them toward nationalism. After World War I, both the leftist and rightist movements increasingly had international links to which many French workers had a stronger allegiance than to the Third Republic. The Third Republic's failure to retain the primary loyalty of important segments of the population contributed to its growing weakness and eventual demise.

ITALIAN DEMOCRACY IN THE MAKING

Unlike France and Britain, Italy was a new democracy. Its constitution, the Statuto, proclaimed by the king of Sardinia in 1848, established a parliament but reserved to the monarch the right to name and dismiss governments. With the proclamation of the Kingdom of Italy on March 17, 1861, the Statuto was extended to the new state. The Statuto had the advantage of evolving almost immediately into a liberal-democratic instrument, with a legislature that, in practice, mandated that cabinets win a vote of confidence in order to rule, and the influence of the directly elected Chamber of Deputies overshadowed that of the appointed Senate. Nevertheless, the Italian king retained important privileges that neither the British monarch nor the French president enjoyed, such as the capacity to name the war minister that often had serious indirect results.

Italian Constitutional Weaknesses

Italian conditions following unification limited the importance of the parliamentary system. The level of political participation was very low because gender, tax, and literacy requirements restricted the suffrage to about 2 percent of the population until 1882, when men who could read and write received the vote. Still, the elevated level of illiteracy (about 73 percent in 1870) presented a formidable barrier until 1912, when a new reform act introduced quasi-universal suffrage for men by giving illiterates the right to vote. Women could not vote, and devout Catholics refrained from doing so.

The Catholic question was particularly serious. Italian unification had taken place in opposition to the church's wishes and had destroyed its temporal power, but the church remained a powerful force in Italian society and challenged the new state's existence. In a decree called the *non expedit*, Pope Pius IX ordered Catholics to boycott national elections, a policy that prompted devout Catholics to question the idea of a unified Italy. In addition, the pope called on Catholic powers, such as France and Austria, to restore the papal state, causing the Italian government its most serious diplomatic problems before World War I and stimulating the Italians to respond by adopting anticlerical legislation.

When the church failed to break up the new state, it changed tactics. In 1898 a response to a serious rise in the cost of bread touched off riots; the government struck out violently against all opponents that challenged the state's existence, including Catholics, Anarchists, and Socialists. Stung by its identification with subversives, the church switched its policy to one of unofficial cooperation with the state against its leftist enemies, and relations between the church and state improved. When the country's first general strike in 1904 raised the specter of a Socialist electoral victory, Pius X sanctioned limited Catholic participation in the general elections of that year. The state in return did not enforce anticlerical legislation, and in 1909 the church extended participation.

In 1913 the first general election under male universal suffrage took place. Liberal Prime Minister Giovanni Giolitti understood that the participation of masses of peasants who could not read and write in the elections and the church's heavy influence had altered the political equation. Giolitti reached an unofficial understanding with Catholic leaders in order to ensure victory. The so-called Gentiloni Pact permitted collaboration between Catholic and governmental candidates that allowed the Catholics to enter the Italian political system in force—they subsequently claimed that more than half the deputies had been elected with their help.

In 1919 the pope repealed the *non expedit,* and the Catholics formed a powerful party that greatly increased the church's influence in Italian politics.

The state had less luck in integrating other political opponents into normal life. On the left, anarchism advocated the state's complete destruction by violent means. Italian anarchists threw bombs, attempted revolutions, and in 1900 assassinated the king. Anarchism was the dominant ideology among leftist intellectuals until the early 1890s, but had little popular appeal and lost its intellectual attractiveness.

Socialism replaced anarchism as the strongest movement on the left. In 1892 Filippo Turati, son of a former governmental official, and the Russian revolutionary Anna Kuliscioff established the Italian Socialist party (PSI), born of Marxism and pledged to overthrow the state. Turati and Kuliscioff were reformists who advocated political intransigence—that is, no cooperation with bourgeois political parties—but modified their views when the 1898 disorders shook the country. They argued that the PSI should collaborate with progressive political forces in order to fight conservatives who aimed to restrict civil and political rights and destroy the constitution.

The Rise of Extremism

This was a crucial change. In 1901 a Liberal government came to office with Giovanni Giolitti as its most influential member. Because of the delicate balance of political forces, a negative Socialist vote or abstention would have brought to power Sidney Sonnino, a politician who wanted to modify the constitution in a conservative direction, so the Socialist deputies led by Turati voted in favor of the government. This violation of explicit party orders set off a long-smoldering fight between reformists and revolutionaries in the PSI. Italian reformists (or revisionists) like Turati favored a gradual, parliamentary road to socialism, including case-by-case political alliances with progressive bourgeois forces, while the revolutionaries advocated political intransigence and violence.

The years between 1901 and 1903, the golden age of Italian reformism, brought significant improvements in wages and working conditions for northern industrial and rural workers. In 1903 this progress slowed significantly as the government altered its benevolent attitude because, as in France, strikes spread to the public sector. Giolitti formed a new government and offered Turati a post, but mounting party opposition forced the Socialist leader to refuse. To everyone's surprise, Giolitti formed a more conservative cabinet and went on to dominate the Italian political scene until 1914. Over the years, Giolitti and the Socialists played a cat-and-mouse game, occasionally hostile, sometimes friendly, but never collaborating as closely as they had in 1901, despite his successful support of important measures, such as old-age, sickness, and accident insurance; protection for women and children working in industry and for emigrants; land reclamation; legislation favoring malaria and pellagra-stricken areas of the country; reduction of the workday; longer weekends; and representative institutions that formed the basis of a Labor ministry. As in France, however, the working class as represented by the PSI never reached a position of power in the government. Giolitti and Turati, like

Clemenceau and Jaurès, failed to come to an agreement that might have stabilized the country.

While reformist fortunes declined, revolutionary ideology gained widespread support. In 1904 the first general strike paralyzed the nation and touched off a long wave of disorder. Within the PSI the ideological struggle continued, and in 1912 a young revolutionary, Benito Mussolini, came to the fore.

As a young Socialist, Mussolini wrote for a Milanese revolutionary syndicalist newspaper, denouncing electoral politics and advocating violence. He achieved local fame in his native Romagna region until his arrest for opposing Italy's war against Turkey in 1911–12, and his violent rhetoric, brought him to national prominence. Socialist inability to prevent the conflict produced a backlash against the reformists, and in 1912 delegates to the party congress hailed him and adopted his motion expelling some of the leading reformists. Mussolini's newfound fame allowed him to claim the editorship of the party's daily newspaper *Avanti!*, which gave him a platform to incite revolution. In June 1914, a revolt known as Red Week took place in his own Emilia-Romagna region. Mussolini hailed it as the beginning of the Socialist revolution, but its suppression destroyed Mussolini's faith in Marxism as an instrument for mobilizing the masses for revolution, and he looked around for other means. His open break with the party came after the beginning of World War I, when the PSI supported Italian neutrality and Mussolini advocated intervention as a means of stimulating revolution.

Mussolini's disillusionment with Marxism and his contacts with Italian Nationalist and Futurist groups drew him to the national socialist ideology that was being elaborated by Italian and French intellectuals. In Mussolini, this doctrine would find a leader well versed in the Socialist aspect of the dogma and with the political capacity to implement it.

Divisive Economic and Social Issues

Besides growing extremism, important economic and social questions confronted Italy in the new century. Because the country had practically no coal and iron, it lagged behind the other large European countries in industrialization. In 1878 and 1887, Parliament passed tariffs and other measures to create an iron and steel industry. This legislation spurred industrial and economic growth, which was mainly confined to the northern "industrial triangle" bounded by Milan, Turin, and Genoa and failed to reverse the disparity between the North and South. This failure spurred emigration, and in some years almost a million southerners left for other European countries and for North and South America in what became the largest mass migration in modern times.

Italy's southern problem had important political ramifications. Given the high illiteracy rate in the region, only a small proportion of southerners could vote, and only a relatively few ballots had to be changed for determined groups to secure election to the Parliament. This situation presented the government with too great a temptation not to intervene in favor of its candidates. In 1909, Socialist writer and historian Gaetano Salvemini published an influential tract describing the process, *Il ministro della mala vita* (The Minister of the Underworld).

Salvemini claimed that Giolitti allied with local elites and with the criminal associations endemic in the South to stuff ballot boxes, prevent political rivals from organizing, and stop opponents from voting. As a result of these tactics, Salvemini argued, Giolitti controlled almost the entire southern contingent in the Chamber of Deputies, which, when added to his northern supporters, gave him an unshakable majority. He advocated universal suffrage as a solution because otherwise the Socialists would never be in a position to pass important reforms in the Chamber of Deputies. Salvemini's desire to put the campaign for universal suffrage at the top of the Socialist agenda split the reformists because Turati and other reformist leaders believed that universal suffrage for illiterates would only increase the power of the Catholic church. The reformist split and Salvemini's withdrawal from the party favored the revolutionary takeover of the PSI.

The question of the vote for women was intimately linked to the debate on universal suffrage. The conditions of life for Italian women improved during the 1890s, and by 1900 hundreds of them had earned university degrees in the same fields as men. Women had begun working outside the home, although their jobs, such as teachers and telephone operators, paid poorly. Despite these improvements, however, Italian women suffered from an inferior legal, economic, and social status. Only women could be punished for adultery, and women needed their husbands' permission to open a bank account or administer their own property. Politicians acting in concert with the church regularly defeated divorce bills, claiming that they would destabilize society. In theory the Socialists favored the vote for women, and Salvemini made it a major component of his demand for universal suffrage, but other reformist leaders believed that it should be given a lower priority than winning the ballot for men because they feared that the women would vote for clerical candidates and strengthen the church's influence.

As a result of its weaknesses, Italy had a more fragile parliamentary system than either France or England despite the economic and social progress that occurred during Giolitti's tenure. Giolitti's political acumen allowed him to dominate the Italian political system for fifteen years, longer than any major European politician. In the process, however, Parliament practically became identified with him, transforming the fight his enemies conducted against the man into a denunciation of the parliamentary order. It is no coincidence that the major scholarly critics of the parliamentary system discussed in the previous chapter—Mosca, Pareto, and Michels—were either Italian or worked in Italy for many years. With every crisis came an attempt by his critics to shake Giolitti's hold on power without regard for the damage their methods might inflict on Parliament. Important instances of the confusion between unseating Giolitti and damaging Parliament came with the outbreak of the Libyan War against Turkey and culminated during the debate on whether Italy should intervene in World War I. The impact of the war on Italy completed the job of discrediting Parliament and made a major contribution to the rise of fascism.

Bibliographic Essay

There are many general books on modern Britain, but perhaps R. K. Webb's *Modern England* (New York, 1973), remains the most elegantly written, complete, and thoughtful work. The remark on the significance of Edward VII's reign is on p. 448, and Webb's citation of Lloyd George's remark about the cost of dukes may be found on p. 459. Other general histories that are still very useful include the classic work by R. C. K. Ensor, *England 1870–1914* (Oxford, UK, 1936); J. B. Conacher, *Waterloo to the Common Market* (New York, 1975); and a briefer account, James Butler, *A History of England 1815–1939,* 2nd ed. (London, 1960). For more specific topics, Gary Bryan Magee and Andrew S. Thomson's *Empire and Globalisation: Networks of People, Goods and Capital, 1850–1914* (Cambridge, UK, and New York, 2010), emphasizes economics, migration and investment. *Social Classes and Social Relations in Britain, 1850–1914* (Cambridge, UK, and New York, 1995), by Alastair J. Reid, discusses economics and social conditions. Free trade and its influence is examined by Frank Trentmann, *Free Trade Nation: Commerce, Consumption and Civil Society in Modern Britain* (Oxford, UK, 2009). Ernest P. Hennock, *The Origin of the Welfare State in England and Germany: 1850–1914* (Cambridge, UK, and New York, 2007), compares the social policies of both countries. On socialism in Britain, and changing views, consult Edward J. Bristow, *Individualism versus Socialism in Britain, 1880–1914* (New York, 1987). On Balfour, Kenneth Young's *Arthur James Balfour: The Happy Life of the Politician, Prime Minister, Statesman, and Philosopher* (London, 1963), the complete life, is based upon many unpublished documents. A more up-to-date biography is R. J. Q. Adams, *Balfour: The Last Grandee* (London, 2007).

A clear, concise account of the tenure and action of the Liberal government during the period discussed is Colin Cross, *The Liberals in Power (1905–1914)* (London, 1963). Good works on the major British politicians include John Wilson, *CB: A Life of Sir Henry Campbell-Bannerman* (London, 1973); this detailed biography argues that Campbell-Bannerman was an unusual personality to lead a great political party. A portrait of CB (in addition to those of many other British statesmen) may be found in Keith Laybour, *British Political Leaders: A Biographical Dictionary* (Santa Barbara, Calif., 2001). As might be expected, Asquith has received great attention, and there is an official biography written by J. A. Spender and Cyril Asquith, *Life of Henry Herber: Asquith, Lord Oxford and Asquith,* 2 vols. (London, 1932). Thirty years later, Roy Jenkins wrote *Asquith* (New York, 1964), using material opened to him by the family; this is a reasonable attempt to portray not only the man but the age. At any rate, the reader may also wish to consult a work independent of the family's possible influence: Stephen Koss, *Asquith: Portrait of a Man and an Era* (London, 1976). Interesting insights into how Asquith's cabinet worked are provided by the recollections of a member, Edward David, ed., *Inside Asquith's Cabinet: From the Diaries of Charles Hobhouse* (London, 1977). Given Lloyd George's continuing importance, there are many works on him. Emyr Price, *David Lloyd George* (Cardiff, 2006) is a general biography. An excellent and detailed description of Lloyd Georges's policy during the period covered in this chapter is John Grigg, *Lloyd George: The People's Champion 1902–1911* (Berkeley, Calif., 1978). A biography of Asquith is also in the Haus Publishers series on British prime ministers of the twentieth century, Stephen Bates, *H H Asquith* (London, 2006). The essay by H. C. G. Matthew, "The Liberal Age (1851–1914), in Kenneth O. Morgan's *The Oxford History of Britain* (Oxford, UK, 2009) analyzes some of the themes discussed in this chapter; the quotation that ends this section may be found on p. 581.

On the women's movement in Britain, Sandra Stanley Holton, *Feminism and Democracy* (Cambridge, UK, 1986), mentioned previously, a brief, well-organized work, is particularly interesting; it discusses how, in addition to sex equality, the movement became involved with class issues and the Labour party and argues that these themes became central. Cheryl R. Jorgensen-Earp examines the *Speeches and Trials of the Militant Suffragettes: The Women's Social and Political Union, 1903–1918* (Madison, N.J., 1999); she has also published a book on the WPSU, *The Transfiguring Sword* (Tuscaloosa,

Ala., 1997). Unusual aspects of the women's movement in Britain may be found in Krista Cowman, *Women of the Right Spirit* (Manchester, UK, 2007), which discusses paid functionaries of the WSPU between 1904 and 1918, and Mitzi Auchterlonie, *Conservative Suffragists* (London, 2007), which looks at women and the Tories.

There are many general histories of Ireland that have chapters on this period; consult, for example, Edward Norman, *A History of Modern Ireland* (Coral Gables, Fla., 1971). For particular themes, with good coverage of the Edwardian period, see D. George Boyce, *Nationalism in Ireland*, 3rd ed. (London, 1995); Lawrence J. McCaffrey, *The Irish Question*, 2nd ed. (Lexington, Ky., 1995); R. B. McDowell, *The Irish Administration 1801–1914* (London, 1964); and Eric Strauss, *Irish Nationalism and British Democracy* (New York, 1951). On social conditions, see Timothy Guinnane, *The Vanishing Irish: Households, Migration, and the Rural Economy in Ireland, 1850–1914* (Princeton, N.J., 1997).

On France, David Thompson, *Democracy in France Since 1870*, 5th ed. (London, 1969), a classic account, is stimulating and manageable; the citation regarding France and the modern challenge may be found on p. 171 of this book. Robert Stuart, *Marxism and National Identity: Socialism, Nationalism, and National Socialism During the French Fin de Siècle* (Albany, N.Y., 2006) touches on some of the issues raised in this chapter. D. W. Brogan, *France Under the Republic: The Development of Modern France* (New York, 1940), also a classic work, is a detailed. A brief account is Alexander Sedgwick, *The Third French Republic 1870–1914* (New York, 1968). Theodore Zeldin's *France 1848–1945,* 2 vols (Oxford, UK., 1973) is a social history that includes all aspects of French life during the period indicated and can profitably be utilized as a reference work. General works on economics also include a standard work, J. H. Clapham, *The Economic Development of France and Germany 1814–1914* (Cambridge, UK, 1921). Shepard B. Clough's *France: A History of National Economics 1789–1914* (Cambridge, UK, 1961) contains difficult-to-find information. Patrick O'Brien and Caglar Keyder, *Economic Growth in Britain and France 1780–1914: Two Paths to the Twentieth Century* (London, 1978), is a good comparative study. Peter Campbell, *French Electoral Systems and Elections since 1789* (Hamden, Conn., 1965) has an excellent section on the electoral organization of the Third Republic.

On some of the issues involved and their significance, see Frederic H. Seager, *The Boulanger Affair: Political Crossroad of France, 1886–1889* (Ithaca, N.Y., 1969), an important affair involving a possible military takeover. Many books have been written on the Dreyfus affair, including one by Dreyfus himself. Good introductions are Guy Chapman, *The Dreyfus Trials* (London, 1972), the complete story of the trials in clear prose, and Jean-Denis Bredin, *The Affair: The Case of Alfred Dreyfus* (New York, 1983), a detailed account that also discusses the implications of the case. The state of French Catholicism in relation to the Dreyfus affair was examined by Maurice Larkin, *Church and State after the Dreyfus Affair* (New York, 1974); this book looks at the issue in its wider historical and political context. The whole affair has been reexamined in a comprehensive manner by Ruth Harris, *Dreyfus: Politics, Emotion, and the Scandal of the Century* (New York, 2010). On the threat to French democracy at the end of the century, see Robert Kaplan, *Forgotten Crisis* (Oxford, 1995). Much has been written on anti-Semitism in France, and a good collection of essays on this theme may be found in Frances Malino and Bernard Wasserstein, eds., *The Jews in Modern France* (Hanover, Vt., 1985).

C. Stuart Doty wrote a good account of Barrès and his influence, including an account of his national socialism, *From Cultural Rebellion to Counterrevolution: The Politics of Maurice Barrès* (Athens, Ohio, 1976), on p. 162 of which is the citation on the nationalist view of the Dreyfus case. Charles Maurras's politics is considered by William Curt Buthman, *The Rise of Integral Nationalism in France* (New York, 1970), but this work is useful for all aspects of integral nationalism, from the reasons for its rise to an examination of its other proponents and their ideas. See also Michael Sutton, *Nationalism,*

Postivism, and Catholicism: The Politics of Charles Maurras and French Catholics, 1890–1914 (New York, 1982). On some of the other themes discussed with respect to Barres and Maurras, see *French Literary Fascism: Nationalism, Anti-Semitism, and the Ideology of Culture* (Princeton, N.J., 1994), by David Carroll. The quotations regarding Action Française principles are taken from a declaration of principles (March 23, 1908), translated by Leslie Derfler and published in an appendix to his excellent summary, *The Third French Republic 1870–1940* (Princeton, N.J., 1966). Michael Sutton, *Nationalism, Positivism and Catholicism: The Politics of Charles Maurras and French Catholics, 1890–1914* (Cambridge, UK, 1982), examines Maurras's links to Catholic tradition and to the French Catholics. Oscar L. Arnal argues that the church took a consistently conservative and defensive political and social line in *Ambivalent Alliance: The Catholic Church and the Action Française 1899–1939* (Pittsburgh, 1985).

As might be imagined, Clemenceau has received much attention because of his role in World War I (books on this aspect are cited in the appropriate chapter), but less attention is now given to his domestic politics. The most detailed work is David Robin Watson, *Georges Clemenceau: A Political Biography* (Plymouth, UK, 1974), sympathetic and well argued. Gregor Dallas *At the Heart of a Tiger: Clemenceau and His World, 1841–1929* (New York, 1993). Geoffrey Bruun, *Clemenceau* (Hamden, Conn., 1968), is a shorter treatment by a well-respected scholar. Hampden Jackson, *Clemenceau and the Third Republic* (New York, 1948), is also a brief, clear work. F. F. Ridley wrote about revolutionary syndicalism and the CGT during this period: *Revolutionary Syndicalism in France; The Direct Action of Its Time* (Cambridge, UK, 2008).

There are also several good biographies of Clemenceau's great Socialist antagonist; a detailed, well-constructed study is Harvey Goldberg, *The Life of Jean Jaurès* (Madison, Wisc., 1968), from which the Clemenceau quote on property is taken (p. 363); reprinted in a digital edition in 2005. Zeev Sternhell has discussed the developments in France that led to the elaboration of a Fascist ideology, a controversial topic. The reader will find this theory elaborated—especially with regard to the revolutionary revisionism of Marx and the revolutionary syndicalists—in his *The Birth of Fascist Ideology* (Princeton, N.J., 1994), previously cited, but the Israeli scholar made similar arguments earlier in *Neither Right Nor Left: Fascist Ideology in France* (Princeton, N.J., 1986); it is from this book that the citations on anti-Semitism (p. 46) and prewar France as a laboratory are taken (p. 14). Kenneth H. Tucker looks at revolutionary syndicalism from a different angle: *French Revolutionary Syndicalism and the Public Sphere* (New York, 2005). Edward J. Arnold's *The Development of the Radical Right in France: From Boulanger to Le Pen* (New York, 2000) includes an essay on this period.

General works on Italy during the approximate period covered in this chapter include a good summary by Salvatore Saladino, *Italy from Unification to 1919* (New York, 1970). René Albrecht-Carrié, *Italy from Napoleon to Mussolini* (New York, 1949), wrote under the influence of recent developments, fascism and World War II. Christopher Seton-Watson, *Italy from Liberalism to Fascism 1870–1925* (London, 1967), is a particularly detailed account. Denis Mack Smith, *Italy* (Ann Arbor, Mich., 1959), is a critical view of Italy's history. An interesting topic that is not usually covered but that was an important part of Italy during the prewar period is discussed in Frank Snowden, *The Conquest of Malaria; Italy, 1900–1962* (New Haven, Conn., 2006).

Spencer M. Di Scala, *Italy: From Revolution to Republic, 1700 to the Present,* 4th ed. (Boulder, 2009), is a more recent general account that brings in debates and has an extensive bibliographical essay that outlines the historiographical debate over various issues. Edward R. Tannenbaum and Emiliana P. Noether's *Modern Italy: A Topical History Since 1861* (New York, 1974) contains a series of still-useful essays. Richard Drake, *Byzantium for Rome: The Politics of Nostalgia in Umbertian Italy, 1878–1900*

(Chapel Hill, N.C., 1980), is a good study. The standard work on the Giolittian Era is A. William Salomone, *Italy in the Giolittian Era: Italian Democracy in the Making 1900–1914* (Philadelphia, 1960); he coined the phrase "Italian democracy in the making." The book includes a valuable introductory essay by Gaetano Salvemini; the quotation from that essay is on p. xxi. This edition of the book, originally published in 1945, contains a long section on a debate that the work and the essay generated: "Giolittian Italy Revisited." The best political biography of Giolitti is Alexander De Grand, *The Hunchback's Tailor: Giovanni Giolitti and Liberal Italy from the Challenge of Mass Politics to the Rise of Fascism, 1882–1922* (Westport, Conn., 2001). The all-imprtant topic of Catholicism has been examined by John F. Pollard, *Catholicism in Modern Italy: Religion, Society and Politics Since 1861* (London, 2008). Italian Socialist issues, with particular emphasis on Turati and the role of Giolitti, is the theme of Spencer Di Scala's *Dilemmas of Italian Socialism* (Amherst, Mass., 1980). On the Socialists in the Giolittian era, there is also James Edward Miller, *From Elite to Mass Politics: Italian Socialism in the Giolittian Era, 1900–1914* (Kent, Ohio, 1990). Good essays on different aspects of the Giolittian period may be found in the first part of Spencer M. Di Scala, ed., *Italian Socialism Between Politics and History* (Amherst, Mass., 1996). Alexander De Grand wrote the history of the Nationalist Association, *The Italian Nationalist Association and the Rise of Fascism in Italy* (Lincoln, Nebr., 1978). Futurism is discussed by Christine Poggi, *Inventing Futurism: The Art and Politics of Artificial Optimism* (Princeton, N.J., 2009). Charles Killinger published a life of Salvemini, *Gaetano Salvemini: A Biography* (Westport, Conn., 2002). An important but neglected social and legal thinker and the implications of his thought receives excellent treatment in Mary Gibson's *Born to Crime: Cesare Lombroso and the Origins of Biological Criminology* (Westport, Conn., 2002). Jonathan Dunnage concentrated on social issues in *Twentieth Century Italy: A Social History* (London, 2002).

Economics, with chapters on this period, are considered in Shepard B. Clough's *The Economic History of Italy* (New York, 1964); the more technical Vera Zamagni, *The Economic History of Italy* (Oxford, UK, 1993); and Gianni Toniolo, *An Economic History of Liberal Italy* (London and New York, 1990). The southern problem is put into perspective by Gustav Schachter, *The Italian South* (New York, 1965).

✍

CHAPTER 3

The Authoritarian States

CHAPTER OUTLINE

The German Empire: Greater Prussia • "That ramshackle realm": Austria-Hungary • Imperial Russia: "Institutions are of no importance"

BIOGRAPHICAL SKETCHES

Friedrich Wilhelm Viktor Albrecht of Hohenzollern, Failure • Karl Lueger, Mayor of Vienna

In 1900, the parliamentary systems of Germany and Austria-Hungary were not as fully developed as those of the liberal regimes previously discussed because governments were responsible to the monarch and could not be changed without their permission. Although the monarchs would have preferred to have the support of their parliaments, rather than be opposed by them, and did not wish to alienate them, they refused to give up any power despite the challenges of the representative bodies in their countries that wanted to emulate the Western parliamentary regimes. The German and Austrian monarchs' lack of accountability in government and foreign policy threatened European and world stability. Russia did not have a parliament until after the revolution of 1905, after which a parliamentary regime resembling that of the first two was set up.

THE GERMAN EMPIRE: GREATER PRUSSIA

The manner of German unification, completed in 1871, helps explain the weak position of Parliament in the German Empire. In contrast to Italy, unified during the same period, which has been described as a democracy in the making, Germany was a failed democracy despite the strong liberal tradition exhibited in that country during the revolutions of 1848. In 1862 a battle over the issues of popular representation, cabinet responsibility, and civilian control of the military raged in Prussia, the state that unified Germany. The regent who later became German emperor as Wilhelm I appointed the brilliant conservative Otto von

Bismarck as chancellor. Bismarck thwarted Liberal aspirations to introduce popular control over cabinets and the army, but he was much more than an old-fashioned reactionary. He understood Liberal yearning for a unified Germany and, more important, believed that Liberals would support unification even at the cost of their liberalism. Consequently, Bismarck managed to defeat the Liberals in the Prussian Diet, to strengthen the military, and to use that army to unify Germany. At the end of the process, Parliament itself blessed his action by passing a bill that sanctioned the expenditures had been made against the Diet's will.

The Constitutional Structure of United Germany

Bismarck pleased the Liberals by agreeing that the new German representative assembly (Reichstag) would be elected by universal male suffrage (aged twenty-five or older). Universal suffrage had long been a Liberal aim, but Bismarck conceived of it as window-dressing. The Reichstag had no control over chancellors, governmental ministers, or cabinets, a privilege reserved for the emperor, and German constitutional practice over the next half century did not substantially extend the Reichstag's power. The body could not question ministers (with the exception of the minister for war, whom the general staff kept uninformed for precisely that reason) and had a restricted role in economic, military, and foreign policy. The upper house, the Bundesrat (Federal Council), represented the different German states and could block legislation passed by the Reichstag. The Reichstag did possess powers, such as the right to vote on the budget and military appropriations, that, if further developed over the years, could have transformed Germany into a true parliamentary system. In the course of several crises up to World War I, the Reichstag might have been transformed into a Western-style Parliament, but the emperors always thwarted it.

Other flaws blocked Germany's evolution into a parliamentary democracy. These flaws included Prussia's special position in the empire as the largest German state containing two-thirds of Germany's population and, therefore, wielding enormous influence. However, Prussia's own constitution was undemocratic, with 15 percent of the population representing wealthy landowners and bourgeois ruling it through a Prussian representative assembly (the *Abgeordnetenhaus*), in which the highest taxpayers had two-thirds' representation (the three-class voting system). The Prussian king was also German emperor and appointed the imperial chancellor and the ministers. The imperial chancellor held the post of Prussian minister president and foreign secretary. The state of Prussia dominated both the Reichstag and the Bundesrat by electing 236 out of 397 Reichstag members and through its seventeen votes in the Bundesrat, with only fourteen needed to veto constitutional changes. Moreover, legislation could not be passed by the Reichstag alone but required the Bundesrat's assent.

There were other undemocratic features. In 1878, Bismarck instituted secretaries of state for various functions, bureaucratic administrators who oversaw specific departments. After his dismissal in 1890, his successors could not keep them under control. These secretaries had direct access to the kaiser, who could make decisions over which Parliament had little control. An outstanding example was Admiral Alfred von Tirpitz, father of the German navy, who went directly to

The career of Alfred von Tirpitz, father of the German navy, shows how the weakness of the German constitutional structure before World War I could be exploited for self-serving interests. When Tirpitz needed funds for his navy, he bypassed the Reichstag and went directly to the Emperor. Britain perceived the massive growth of the German navy as a direct challenge to its security.

Wilhelm II in order to gain support for a naval buildup that touched off an arms race with Britain, a principal cause of World War I.

The Tariff and Its Implications

Complex economic and social changes sweeping Europe in the late nineteenth and early twentieth centuries combined with German parliamentary weakness and had grave consequences for all Europe. In 1873 long-term improvements in transportation provoked a long-lived agricultural crisis because cheap American and Russian grain could be sold more inexpensively in Europe than the Europeans could grow it. This change produced demands for protection. In Germany, Bismarck dropped the free trade policies he had formerly supported and called for a protective tariff that passed in 1879. This tariff, which remained in effect after the agrarian crisis ended, protected the large landowners east of the Elbe River, the Junkers, but raised the price of food and consequently the wages that industrialists had to pay their workers. When the industrialists complained, the government compensated them by increasing its orders for military hardware. This deal between large landowners and industrialists resulted from *Sammlungspolitik,* supposedly the collaboration of national groups, but which can be more accurately described as a landowner-capitalist coalition to maintain the tariff and resist democratic reform.

A complex web of interests supported this arrangement. For example, a Navy League materialized to stimulate the popular demand for a bigger battle fleet necessary to win a large German colonial empire, but a larger navy boosted the profits of industrialists and talk of a world empire contributed to the British decision to defend their own possessions through new alliances. The tariffs, passed for seven years at a time, also had the effect of helping pay the Reich's bills and reducing parliamentary leverage over the budget.

German fiscal policy had deleterious effects throughout society. Import duties raised the price of food, while increased taxation for arms expenditures put further pressure on household budgets, causing more ordinary Germans to vote for opposition parties, especially the German Socialist party (*Sozialdemokratische Partei Deutschlands*, SPD). From 1900 to 1914 German industrial development reached unprecedented levels, but, because of the political and social domination of capitalists and landowners, the benefits barely filtered down to the population at large. Between 1890 and 1914, the growth of real wages in Germany has been calculated at 1 percent in comparison to 4 percent in Britain and France. Because of technological developments, the establishment of cartels, and governmental policies favoring industrialists and large landowners, German unemployment rates remained high, and economic growth was seriously unbalanced among different groups of workers, disparate regions, and rural and urban areas. The economic situation stimulated the entrance of wives into the workplace to make ends meet and an exodus from the land and the smaller cities to the large urban areas. This population shift from conservative rural areas to the cities did not result in a reapportionment of the Reichstag, however, and Junker influence remained strong as the least progressive areas of the country continued to be overrepresented in the legislature. In 1914, for example, a deputy from Berlin represented about 100,000 inhabitants compared to a rural Prussian deputy's approximately 24,000.

German Society

Conservative values appeared preeminent in prewar German society. They inculcated fierce loyalty to the Reich, militaristic attributes, and hatred for external and internal enemies. The family's authoritarian structure reinforced these attitudes by giving power to the father and transmitting an absolutistic image strengthened by other institutions, especially the schools. German secondary education did a good job of teaching literacy, but education generally did not improve one's social status; rather, the reverse. A student's social position usually determined his educational success. Moreover, the state mandated the teaching of patriotism and directed the schools to combat Socialist ideas.

While formal education generally ended with elementary school, some went on to an inadequate vocational education, and a small percentage successfully made it through the extremely difficult requirements for entrance to grammar school that opened the door to the university. Most grammar school students came from university-educated middle-class and civil service families, the lower classes rarely receiving a university education. Reflecting the generally limited access of Europeans to the academy during this period, the German university population in 1900 has been estimated at 34,000, out of a population of 56 million

(640 per million). German universities were renowned and universally imitated for their high standards, research, and scholarship, but imposed political conformity on students and faculty.

Because the universities shaped Germany's elite, strong mechanisms assured loyalty to the political and social system. Student fraternities and clubs imposed a neo-aristocratic code on boys of bourgeois origin, "inculcating them with norms and values intended to bind the potential representatives of future middle-class politics to the pre-industrial aristocratic ruling groups." Dueling societies encouraged fights, recalling medieval times, and students collected scars that, combined with an air of superiority, marked them as prestigious members of a learned elite. The successful graduate who avoided subversive ideas and a Jewish wife could count on an effective network that guaranteed him a good economic and social future.

German churches represented another powerful level of control. The dominant Protestant religion, Lutheranism, inspired the identification of church and state that deterred antigovernmental viewpoints and encouraged conservatism. Anti-Catholic prejudices that had their latest manifestation in the Kulturkampf (Bismarck's political struggle against the Catholics) were deeply imbued in German society. Bismarck ended the Kulturkampf in 1879 because he needed Catholic Center Party votes to pass the tariff, and that accommodation set the tone for future relations between Catholics and the state during the late nineteenth and early twentieth centuries. The Center Party, a highly disciplined organization with its base in Catholic southern Germany, provided crucial support for the government, which excluded overt political discrimination against Catholics. The Protestant majority, however, continued to include Catholics in an array of internal enemies not to be trusted, and Catholics never ceased regarding Protestant Prussia as the enemy. The Center Party and Catholic associations opposed liberalism, socialism, and modern trade unionism and hoped to dictate policy regarding education, the family, and social affairs in Catholic areas. Despite their dislike for each other, however, Germany's two most powerful religious denominations did not challenge the Reich's political or social structure.

Racism and Intolerance
The categorization of Catholics as enemies in the minds of many Germans revealed a common phenomenon linked to the authoritarian structure of society. Bismarck and his successors skillfully mobilized nationalist sentiment against foreign enemies, such as France, and against domestic outsiders, such as Catholics, Socialists, and national minorities, that were discriminated against in public employment and in the armed forces and singled out as actual or potential threats to the country. The largest pariah group in German society was the Jews. A great influx of Jews from Eastern Europe followed German unification. These new immigrants, along with longtime Jewish inhabitants, ran into a wall of intolerance encouraged by the idea of medieval Christianity that condemned the Jews for having killed Christ. This belief meshed with old economic and cultural myths—such as the image of the rapacious Jew using interest to exploit ordinary Germans or the Jew as incapable of being assimilated—reinforced by new ones. Anti-Semitism rose

sharply with increasing industrialization and the rise of socialism, with Jews being viewed contradictorily both as conspiratorial capitalists who exploited workers and as internationalist Socialist plotters who were out to destroy German culture. As in most of Europe, these notions cut across all German society and transformed the Jew into the scapegoat that many Germans needed to confirm their anti-Western ideas.

By the late nineteenth century, anti-Semitism had been transformed for many German thinkers (as well as for other Europeans) from the cultural to the biological variety. Writers advocated the purification of the German spirit by eliminating all things Jewish. A Völkisch culture emerged according to which race determined everything. The conception that people are the product of their heredity came into vogue. Mixing science with moral and cultural stereotypes of the Jew resulted for many Germans in the feeling that the Jewish character had certain permanent qualities. Racist writers attributed unfavorable characteristics to the Jewish "race" as a whole that conversion to Christianity or assimilation could not alter. By the early twentieth century, therefore, both cultural and biological anti-Semitism was widespread in Germany as in the rest of Europe. Although overtly anti-Semitic political parties did not attract large memberships, they did not probably because of the strength of anti-Semitism in the traditional political organizations. Such views favored ideas regarding biological predetermination and depersonalization of the Jews and, although present in other European countries, later served the Nazis well in their campaign to exterminate Jews and other groups.

Serious problems with other minority groups also troubled prewar Germany, especially the Poles who lived in Prussia. The Prussian Diet made German the official language in the Polish areas, including the schools, and created a mechanism to buy Polish land for German peasants. When the attempt failed, it adopted an expropriation law against the Poles in 1908, and German officials discussed expelling Poles wholesale from the areas they had occupied for centuries. As early as 1885, Bismarck had ordered the deportation of thirty thousand Poles (one-third of whom were Jews) from East Prussia, and in 1914 German war aims included a provision for clearing Poles from the areas they inhabited (the Frontier Strip) and turning the land over to German settlers. The smaller French and Danish minorities also experienced official discrimination.

German Women

Women similarly had difficulties in prewar Germany. The government lifted restrictions on women who wished to work in the universities only in 1909, but whether to educate them remained a question mark. Some German writers argued that it was racial suicide to educate women because women would leave the home for the professions, and the family's downfall would follow. One book that purported to prove the physiological feeblemindedness of women went into twelve editions. The editor of an encyclopedia offered to publish a scientific article by physicist Lise Meitner, who would later be the first to describe nuclear fission, and refused when he discovered that she was a woman.

In 1900 new legislation improved the situation of women slightly by removing the obligation for a wife to have her husband's consent to work, but a woman's property still became her husband's upon marriage, along with any property that came to her during the marriage. Husbands had the legal right to make decisions for the family and had control over the children, divorce was difficult to obtain, and in criminal cases women were considered unreliable witnesses. The state regulated prostitution, but only for the purpose of making it easier for young men to be initiated into the rites of sex.

After 1902 the number of women's associations, membership in them, and activity all increased, but women did not win the right to vote. Prussia and other states forbade women from engaging in political activity, but, as women defied them, they were relaxed after 1908. Disappointed with the lack of support even in leftist parties, German women linked up with similar movements in other countries, particularly Britain. The German women's movement, however, split between radicals and moderates and by 1914 was in turmoil. The political clout of feminism thus remained minimal.

German Socialism

The German Socialists presented the state with a more complicated picture. Bismarck had attacked them between 1878 and 1890, and discrimination followed after that year. Ironically, although SPD rhetoric remained revolutionary, in practice both the party and revisionist thinker Eduard Bernstein influenced the large unions affiliated with the SPD, and they both pursued a de facto policy of winning reforms to raise wages and improve working conditions. This policy did not change substantially after 1905, when, influenced by the atmosphere following the Russian Revolution of that year, growing dissatisfaction with the SPD majority produced a new radicalism that culminated in a formal split in 1917. The SPD had a proved capacity to appeal to voters, but an enlarged Reichstag SPD contingent held out little immediate promise for changing Germany's authoritarian political structure. The question was this: if the Socialists and their allies became a majority, would they be able to transform Germany into a parliamentary democracy?

This concern encouraged German governments to implement policies that historians have called social imperialism, an approach also found in other countries but was the clearest in Germany. "Social imperialism" is the attempt by conservatives to combat growing liberalizing movements by gaining popular support for imperialistic aims by convincing the common people that they have something to gain from those policies. Although traditional conservatives frowned on such notions, elections in 1912 favored candidates who held them. This development has been interpreted as amounting "to a definitive popularization of right-wing politics, and makes it possible to speak for the first time perhaps of a radical right." In this manner, Germany's increasing challenge to the existing world order was supposedly influenced by domestic considerations—the attempt of the German ruling class to defend its power by utilizing foreign adventure and an aggressive new, popular image of Germany's world role.

The Emperor

The continuing failure of the German political system to limit the executive branch's control of the government had a fundamental role in this development. The German constitution made the German emperor the most powerful man in the "world," and its flaws became glaringly obvious when the boastful and erratic Wilhelm II came to power as kaiser in 1888. Bismarck described the new kaiser's personality: "The Emperor is like a balloon," he stated; "if one did not hold him fast on a string, he would go no one knows whither." Two years later, the kaiser broke the string by dropping Bismarck as chancellor.

Although Wilhelm's swaggering and irrational statements have raised questions in the minds of historians as to his willingness to follow through on what he said, there is little doubt that he greatly influenced domestic and foreign affairs. Wilhelm favored the old-line Prussian Conservatives and large agrarian interests, both of whom remained entrenched in the bureaucracy and the army and who refused to make concessions to peasants and industrial workers. As for the liberal middle class whose presence increased because of the enormous growth of industry, its political clout diminished even while Wilhelm supported its economic aims.

The Failure of Reform

The German political scene in the years before World War I is littered with failed opportunities to reform the German Constitution and to adjust to changing social and economic conditions. Between 1894 and 1896, a crisis occurred between the kaiser and his own government. The dispute began over a legal issue but culminated in the question as to whether the emperor could refuse to dismiss a minister the cabinet wished to discharge, a fight the cabinet lost.

During the early years of the new century, the demand for constitutional reform gained momentum as middle-class opinion increasingly seemed to turn against Wilhelm and to favor the steadily advancing Social Democrats. If the Liberals, Social Democrats, and the Center had joined together, the support they enjoyed in the country might have produced a demand for a stronger Parliament, favored by the rise of the Center's left left wing led by Matthias Erzberger.

The year 1906 witnessed a constitutional crisis originating in a dispute between the Center Party and the chancellor, Bernhard von Bülow, because the Colonial Office refused to acknowledge any control by the Reichstag. The quarrel prompted the normally placid Center to vote against part of the financial assessment for German Southwest Africa. Since the Social Democrats supported the Center, the government found itself in the minority. Instead of resigning, Bülow dissolved the Reichstag, put together an electoral coalition consisting of the Conservatives, the middle-class National Liberals, and Progressives, and won the 1907 elections. However, this "Bülow bloc" proved unstable because the Conservatives wished to reestablish an alliance with the Center, a crucial division that made it impossible to revise constitutional procedures even though a new scandal created an opportunity to do so.

BIOGRAPHICAL SKETCHES

Friedrich Wilhelm Viktor Albrecht of Hohenzollern
Failure

Kaiser Wilhelm II hoped to outshine Bismarck and win a place in the sun for Germany, but history recognizes him as a failure.

Wilhelm, grandson of Queen Victoria of England, the son of her eldest daughter Princess Victoria and Crown Prince Frederick, was born in Berlin on January 27, 1859, with a useless, withered left hand. With training, he seemed to overcome this handicap, but observers speculated that it left psychological scars and contributed to his bombastic, vain personality. His parents gave Wilhelm a liberal education, but perhaps under the influence of Bismarck, he grew up a conservative who developed into an anti-Semite and militarist drawn to power politics. In 1881, he married Augusta Victoria, duchess of Schleswig-Holstein, and had seven children.

Wilhelm's father Frederick, a liberal whom Bismarck feared, became emperor in 1888 but died of throat cancer after three months in office. Although only twenty-nine when he inherited the throne, Wilhelm chafed at Bismarck's tutelage and dropped him as chancellor in 1890. Wilhelm believed that he had a right to rule with minimal input from Parliament, and his domestic policy contributed to Germany's failure to develop into a parliamentary democracy. In foreign affairs, he devalued the Russian connection that Bismarck held dear because it prevented a possible two-front war that he believed Germany could not win. When the Russians joined up with the French, the Germans sought a military solution to their encirclement with Wilhelm's approval. In addition, Wilhelm's diplomacy, noted for its clumsiness, alienated the other great powers.

During World War I, Wilhelm faded into the background as the army took effective control of the country and his popularity dropped. After four years of war, the Allies made it clear that Wilhelm himself was an obstacle to peace and, on November 9, 1918, his country in revolt, he abdicated. He fled to Doorn, in the neutral Netherlands, purchasing an estate where he lived until his death. The Dutch refused Allied demands to hand him over as a war criminal.

In exile, Wilhelm worked for his restoration and briefly flirted with Hitler when he thought the Nazis might accept him as emperor. His second wife, whom he married in 1922, was pro-Nazi, as was a son who joined the Nazi SA Storm Troopers. When France fell in 1940, the old kaiser sent Hitler a congratulatory telegram because the Fuehrer's generals had received their training under his rule, but relations remained cool. When Wilhelm's grandson died in combat, Hitler resented the show of sympathy that Berliners demonstrated at his funeral and secretly ordered all Hohenzollern relatives drummed out of the armed forces. When the Germans took over the Netherlands, the British offered him asylum, but Wilhelm refused. After the emperor died on June 5, 1941, Hitler hoped to hold a funeral in Germany for propaganda purposes, but Wilhelm's will stated that he should be buried at Doorn and that there should be no swastikas at the funeral. In retaliation, Hitler ordered that no German military officers attend the services and buried news of his death in the back pages of the newspapers.

Wilhelm II lies buried in a small mausoleum on his estate, now Dutch government property. He is the object of veneration by German monarchists who periodically visit, marching to military music and carrying banners. The old emperor awaits his return to Germany—as he ordered in his will—when the monarchy is restored.

On October 28, 1908, the kaiser released an interview to the British newspaper, the *Daily Telegraph,* that managed to alienate Britain, Japan, King Edward VII, and the Boers. Before its publication, Wilhelm sent a copy of the interview to Bülow who was too busy to read it. When the interview aroused a firestorm of criticism, the Reichstag, with Bülow's support, issued a timid statement criticizing Wilhelm, who promised to be more discrete in the future. Wilhelm was furious with Bülow but did not fire him because of the country's intense reaction to his bungled interview. Under the circumstances, the country seemed likely to have supported Bülow and the bloc if they had tried to take greater control over foreign policy and name a cabinet responsible to the Reichstag, thus bringing Germany closer to the West European parliamentary mainstream. It is doubtful that Bülow supported such a move, but at any rate the Conservatives feared liberalization and in 1909 seized on a minor difference with the government to desert the Bülow bloc and ally once again with the Center Party. Bülow resigned, ending the crisis and permitting Wilhelm to reassert his autocratic ways. Wilhelm appointed as chancellor a bureaucrat who was unlikely to challenge his authority, Theobald von Bethmann-Hollweg.

The *Daily Telegraph* affair's sorry end angered the liberal parties, who, unlike the Center, resolved to support the Social Democrats in reforming the German constitution. The Progressives and National Liberals joined a loose coalition with the Social Democrats in the 1912 elections, increasing their representation while the representation of the Conservatives and Center dropped. In 1913 to 1914, another constitutional crisis flared, and the Reichstag censured the government with little effect. Constitutional reform thus proved impossible in prewar Germany.

Major historical schools have interpreted these events differently. The older school, represented by historian Arthur Rosenberg, viewed the emperor's policies as serious errors. Wilhelm's stifling of reform had two results, he argued. The lack of control in foreign policy made it easier to blunder into a major war, and the impossibility of implementing reforms peacefully increased the chances of a revolution and the empire's overthrow. For Rosenberg, Wilhelmine Germany was on the road to crisis and revolution even if war had not broken out.

For historian Hans-Ulrich Wehler, the situation was more complex. Wehler argued for the continuity of German history through Hitler's atrocities. Wehler wrote that Germany's elites defended their privileges not only through internal resistance to reform—that at some point would have overwhelmed them—but primarily by turning to a policy of conquest that would divert the people's attention, arouse nationalistic support, and expand German power. Wehler concluded that the power and values of these elites remained in place after World War I and made Nazi policies possible.

Historians Geoff Eley and David Blackbourn cautioned against accepting Wehler's approach. They argued that German politics and society were much more complex and suggested that the "capitalist mode of production" favored a new structure for politics in which the bourgeoisie did not accept a subordinate role to the aristocracy. In addition, they argued, the peasants were not automatically subjected to the control of the landowners, that the relationship was complex, and that the focus should be on the specifics of that association and on compromise.

"THAT RAMSHACKLE REALM": AUSTRIA-HUNGARY

Germany's major ally, Austria-Hungary, appeared to be an anachronism at the beginning of the twentieth century. Consisting of territories collected by the Hapsburg dynasty over the course of centuries, throughout the nineteenth century it opposed nationalism and constitutionalism because it favored limited governments and the independence of national minorities—ideals that threatened a multinational empire held together by an absolutistic emperor and a German-speaking ruling class.

In 1867, the Austrians and Hungarians agreed on the Ausgleich (Compromise) that created the dual monarchy of Austria-Hungary that sanctioned the Austrian Germans' rule in Austria and Magyar control of Hungary, both of which contained many nationalities demanding equal rights.

A Complicated Constitutional Structure

The 1867 Compromise established separate parliaments for Austria and Hungary, along with a complicated system of coordination. Austrian Emperor Francis Joseph was also king of Hungary and had to give his consent for all major

Austrians and Hungarians. This map shows the Austrian and Hungarian populations of Austria-Hungary in 1910. Other nationalities that composed the empire ruled by these two national groups included Poles, Czechs, Slovaks, Serbs, Ruthenes, Croats, Romanians, Italians, and Ladins. Bosnia-Herzegovina included a large Muslim population. Note the presence of Austrians in a strategic area of what would become Czechoslovakia after World War I and would cause a major crisis during the interwar period.

decisions in both countries. Austria had a bicameral legislature (the Reichsrat) consisting of a hereditary House of Lords and a House of Representatives elected after 1907 by universal male suffrage. In matters affecting both Austria and Hungary, the Lords elected twenty delegates and the representatives forty; this "Austrian delegations" and a similarly elected Hungarian delegations met separately to express the views of their countries and to enact limited legislation. The Hungarian parliament consisted of a Chamber of Magnates and a Chamber of Deputies elected under a restricted and complicated electoral system, to which must be added forty deputies from Croatia during discussion of Croatian matters.

In order to run affairs common to both halves of the empire, the emperor appointed three common ministers who served at his pleasure—finance, foreign affairs, and war; otherwise, the countries had separate governments except for the same person as monarch. Ten-year treaties between Austria and Hungary regulated economic affairs, each country's contribution to the common budget, and customs issues. Negotiation also determined the number of conscripts from the two countries who would be drafted into the army. Complex crown councils conducted the empire's everyday affairs, subject to the king-emperor's approval. Disputes among the many nationalities, the unwieldy parliamentary structure, and a centralized German-speaking bureaucracy that resisted reform and concessions to the subject nationalities ensured the emperor's power.

The Nationalities Problem

Austria and Hungary faced similar problems during the early twentieth century with regard to the subject nationalities. In Austria, the Czechs were 23 percent of the population and led the cultural and political opposition to German domination. The Austrian government attempted to meet some of the Czech opposition's demands, but the measures alienated the Austrian Germans, and the government had to promulgate them by decree. The emperor had scarce regard for Parliament. In January 1900 he appointed as minister president a civil servant who resorted to emergency decrees, deals, and corruption when the government could not attain a majority for its legislation: "Parliament had ceased to have any effective voice in the government of the country," and, furthermore, the system curtailed the influence of parties, such as the Christian Socials and the Social Democrats, whose support increased as the result of a growing economy.

In the first decade of the twentieth century, the nationality question worsened. In 1908 the Czechs boycotted ceremonies celebrating Francis Joseph's sixty years in power, a state of emergency had to be called in Prague, and the local government suspended. The Ukrainians became increasingly attracted to Russia, and a pro-Russian Pan-Slav movement held a great congress in Prague. Ethnic divisions also permeated the Social Democrats, whose rank-and-file viewed the dictatorship of the proletariat as a centralized state run by German-speaking Austrian workers, despite the feelings of party leader Viktor Adler. In 1905 Czech workers split the party and trade union movement on the basis of nationality.

The Catholic Church was similarly affected even though it officially repudiated nationalism. It was rich, taught religion in the schools, told peasants whom to vote for through the parish priest, and underwent a political revival because of its influence in parties concerned with social issues. In 1891 several Christian currents that were concerned with social questions had joined together under the leadership of Karl Lueger to form the Christian Socials. Lueger's enormous popularity, the organization's support of social legislation, his skillful manipulation of anti-Semitism, and his efficiency in implementing municipal services as mayor of Vienna made the party a force to be reckoned with as its German base allied with traditional clerical forces.

Hungary versus Austria

Hungary faced similar problems, but the situation was exacerbated by the complicated relationship between the two countries. The question of whether to retain, modify, or terminate the 1867 Compromise with Austria dominated Hungarian political discourse until the empire's dissolution in 1918. During these years, pro-Compromise politicians Count Kálmán Tisza, his son Count Istvan Tisza, and Count Gyula Andrássy tried to ensure that the popular misgivings over the Austrian arrangement had little representation in Parliament, governmental agents intervened in elections, and political leaders who challenged the Compromise were made to understand that Francis Joseph would reject any modification.

BIOGRAPHICAL SKETCHES

Karl Lueger
Mayor of Vienna

Karl Lueger would not be a center of debate if the young Adolf Hitler had not spent time in the Austro-Hungarian capital and stated that he learned from the anti-Semitic techniques of the longtime Vienna mayor. Lueger led the Christian Social Party during the early twentieth century, the first political party in the country with mass appeal. Perhaps the country's most popular politician, he transformed anti-Semitism so that it became the basis of his vast political power. Lueger attained so much political influence that no prime minister could come to power without his unofficial approval.

Historians argue over the character of Lueger's anti-Semitism. Some observers, including Jews at the time, believe that it was not racist but that Lueger employed it only as an instrument for achieving and retaining power. This version is summarized in a famous statement attributed to him: "*I decide who is a Jew!*" A second interpretation holds that his anti-Semitism had a biological basis and that it foreshadowed Hitler's racism. Supporters of this view point to the writings and speeches of followers who called for the partial extermination or eradication of the Jews and predicted a time when they would be killed and burned. A statement attributed to Lueger seems to lend credence to this rendering: "I'll only be happy after the last Jew has disappeared from Vienna." Emperor Francis Joseph and the Austrian Catholic hierarchy both feared the extreme reactions his anti-Semitism elicited.

continued

continued

Regardless of the historical debate, it seems clear that Lueger's politics made anti-Semitism a strong force in Austria. Regardless of Lueger's personal feelings about the Jews, his anti-Semitic techniques inspired Hitler's admiration, and the Fuehrer not only mentioned him in *Mein Kampf* and in his table conversation, but carried around a medal with his portrait. Joseph Goebbels, Nazi propaganda minister, used Lueger's figure in one of his most infamous propaganda films.

In addition to anti-Semitism, Lueger skillfully used his influence with women to perpetuate his political power. He never married, perhaps because he realized that marriage would reduce his sex appeal and the devotion of the legion of women who worked for his success. "Lueger's Amazons" canvassed Vienna raising funds for him, built up preelectoral interest, and got out the vote. His rhetoric was legendary, and his ability to whip up enthusiasm among all classes is reminiscent of fascism.

Lueger had an active sex life, cherished good food, and dressed well, all elements that increased his popular appeal. According to his longtime mistress, he loved to eat caviar and crabs and drank fine wines and champagnes. He also enjoyed simpler fare and could go on for pages about the virtues of dumplings. His mistress reported, however, that he embarrassed her by closely scrutinizing the restaurant bills. He dressed elegantly and valued jewelry, such as gold watch chains, cuff links, and stickpins, although he did not like to spend money on such items and relied on gifts. In his administration of municipal funds, on the contrary, he was scrupulously honest, opposed corruption, and gave away half his salary.

Born on October 24, 1844, to a family of humble origin, Karl Lueger studied the law and was elected mayor five times before Francis Joseph consented to his installation. After twelve years in office, the much-loved mayor died on March 10, 1910, of complications from diabetes and nephritis. A million people attended his funeral, the greatest Vienna had ever seen. The city paid the expenses for Lueger's last illness, his funeral, and his tomb in Vienna's Central Cemetery, where the Lueger Memorial Church is a commanding presence.

Nevertheless, the dispute threatened the empire's internal structure. The Austro-Hungarian army wanted a larger contingent from Hungary to reflect the increase in population. The Hungarians, in turn, demanded that the units be made more Hungarian through changes in the language of command, the soldiers' oath, and the insignia. Francis Joseph vehemently objected to these requests, and in 1906 the fight ended in a victory for the emperor, which increased confusion and resulted in greater interference in the electoral process and an intensification of tensions between Hungary and Austria in other areas regulated by the Compromise. Francis Joseph's successful opposition to changes in the Compromise in Parliament increased radical opposition to the political system in the country. Strikes and disorders proliferated and culminated in strikes on the land and a general strike in 1912.

The Nationalities Question in Hungary

Hungary did not go its separate way because of the serious challenge that Hungarian domination faced from the subject nationalities. The Hungarian government followed a policy of forced assimilation. It "Magyarized" the civil service by requiring a degree from a Hungarian university, which could be earned only in the Magyar language; with few exceptions, Magyar was also the language of the primary schools. Only Hungarian speakers could enter the professions or even get menial jobs in the administration. State employees had to Magyarize their names, and the government did the same to the place names of areas inhabited by non-Hungarians. The assimilation policy succeeded only in preparing the ground for the later partition of Hungary.

Resistance to the Hungarians centered on the Romanians who were concentrated in Transylvania. The Romanians boycotted parliament, demanded full autonomy, circulated their grievances to all Europe, and established a vigorous cultural league with links to independent Romania, which they joined after World War I. The Slovaks and the Serbs united with the Romanians in calling for greater cultural autonomy, while the Croats frequently rioted. Self-determination might have been a productive way to respond to these problems, but the Hungarians responded by excluding prominent leaders of the subject nationalities from Parliament, arresting others, and intensifying their Magyarization campaign. The nationalities issue thus was even more explosive in Hungary than it was in Austria.

Economic Development and Its Effects
Had Hungary and Austria followed a more flexible policy toward the subject nationalities, the "ramshackle realm" might have survived. The empire was economically viable, and its development would have contributed to a positive resolution of its social problems. In both Austria and Hungary booms followed by busts followed by the loss of land by many Austrian peasants and subsequent emigration characterized the late nineteenth century. By 1900, the reduced population, technical improvements, and the cooperative movement brought economic renewal, while a new tariff encouraged industrialization. Almost 26 percent of the Austrian population earned its living through industry and mining, compared to 52 percent for agriculture; city populations expanded rapidly; and Vienna grew to 1.675 million people.

This economic progress favored the high and middle bourgeoisie, increased its political importance, and altered its composition. There was an influx of Jews, who concentrated in industry, the professions, finance, and the press. Anti-Semitism increased dramatically, especially among the petite bourgeoisie, who received the right to vote in 1882. Initially attracted to Georg von Schonerer's extremist anti-Semitic Germanic nationalist movement, they later switched to Karl Lueger's Christian Socials, only moderately anti-Semitic compared to the Nationalists.

The Christian Socials and the Social Democrats championed the growing number of factory workers, and between 1885 and 1887, the government adopted a series of social reforms that included limited working hours, protection for women and children, Sunday rest, factory inspections, and some sickness insurance. These measures were frequently evaded, however.

Social and economic change came slower to Hungary than to Austria. Economic activity increased during the early twentieth century, but slowly, so by

1914 Hungarian national wealth amounted to about half of Austria's, even though its population was only 20 percent less. Furthermore, Hungarian wealth was badly distributed among a few very rich families and a great number of poor people. Vast estates run by old families characterized the Hungarian countryside, with four thousand magnates owning 30 percent of the land. These magnates dominated Hungarian social and political life and supplied the country's minister presidents. The medium-to-large landholders (about ten thousand) were the bulk of the empire's supporters because the emperor had favored their acquisition of land following the 1848 revolution. However, most Hungarian peasants held very small plots, and rural life had undergone a decline after the 1880s when a depression in wheat prices prompted the introduction of machinery. In the early twentieth century, increasing industrialization siphoned off labor from the land to the cities and eventually mitigated the bad conditions.

The influx of labor into the urban areas depressed wages, working conditions, and living standards. A 1900 survey revealed that in the factories, men typically worked a twelve-hour day for very low wages, and women, paid proportionately less, nine to ten hours. In burgeoning Budapest, only about 6 percent of the people lived one or two to a room in 1910, while 10 percent resided ten or more to a room and others lived in caves, holes in the fields, and even in trees. Workers responded by joining unions and the Hungarian Social Democratic Party, which was not able to get many of its demands implemented because the government strongly opposed the party's internationalist ideology and its non-Magyar and Jewish leadership.

As in Austria, the growth of industry caused a large inflow of Jewish immigrants into the country. In 1900, Jews accounted for 8.5 percent of the total population but for 25 percent of Budapest's inhabitants. The newcomers achieved a near-dominant role in industry, trade, finance, the professions, the press, and the law. Jews were not well represented in Parliament, the civil service, or the army, but exercised considerable behind-the-scene influence on the government. The alliance of Jewish capitalists with Liberal party leader and Minister President Kálmán Tisza and other politicians who were anxious to spur rapid economic development produced a tolerant policy toward Jews and other religions, in contrast to Austria. In 1894 Hungary ended the Catholic Church's privileged position and declared all religions equal, required civil marriage, and recognized interfaith marriages.

Could Austria-Hungary Have Survived?
During the first decade of the twentieth century, the industrialization of Austria-Hungary became almost dizzy in its tempo. Between 1898 and 1913, industrial plants increased by 84 percent, employed workers by 76 percent, and the value of goods manufactured by 126 percent. Industry accounted for 27 percent of the national income. Factories in Austria grew by 40 percent, and workers who were employed by 49 percent. Real per capita income in both Austria and Hungary rose by about 40 percent. Austria-Hungary's commercial development suggests that its national and political problems, not its economic viability, account for its eventual destruction.

The tragic and long-reigning Emperor Francis Joseph occasionally took courageous stands but refused to renounce any part of his power or to reform the parliamentary system. He rejected meaningful autonomy for the subject nationalities and stubbornly followed the policies of centralization and absolutism handed down to him by his ancestors. Plans to restructure the empire by reaching agreement with other national minorities that would allow them to rule in their own areas, similar to the Hungarian Compromise, once the old emperor died were vague. The leader of this movement, heir presumptive Francis Ferdinand, a conservative with a liberal reputation because he had married outside a restricted noble circle, was rumored to have a plan to include Serbs and Croats in the governing groups; he seems unlikely to have made significant structural alterations even if had he not been assassinated on June 28, 1914.

IMPERIAL RUSSIA: "INSTITUTIONS ARE OF NO IMPORTANCE"

Russia suffered from mediocre leadership and outmoded institutions. The notion that leaders, rather than institutions, counted most in governing Russia became a mantra in the nineteenth and twentieth centuries. The failure of the autocracy to adapt to a changing world and the inability of Parliament to sink roots in the country conditioned Russia's modern history.

A Multinational Empire

In 1900 the Russian empire included one-sixth of the earth's landmass, stretching into Asia as far as Siberia. In central Asia the Russians dominated large and nationally diverse Muslim and Christian populations, some of whom resisted Russian domination by force of arms. In the West, they ruled over numerous European subjects, including Poles, Finns, Swedes, Baltic Germans, Romanians, Ukrainians, Letts, Lithuanians, and Estonians. With few exceptions, the Russians allowed the ethnic minorities no political autonomy, arousing resentment especially among the Poles, who revolted several times in the nineteenth century. Finland, linked to Russia through a personal union with the tsar, enjoyed some autonomy.

Religious problems exacerbated national ones. The Russian majority belonged to the Eastern Orthodox Church controlled by the tsars. The church performed governmental functions and received direct state subsidies. Other religious groups, Catholics, Lutherans, and Muslims, encouraged resistance to Russian rule and contributed to the growth of national feeling in the subject territories. The incorporation of Polish and other lands also brought large numbers of Jews into Russia, so that by 1897 they numbered 4 percent of the population. The Jews were forced to live in certain areas (the Pale) and were excluded from higher education and the professions, and restrictions were placed on their economic activities. Even if restrictions were gradually lifted, the Jews suffered from official anti-Semitism and pogroms that spurred emigration.

Russian economic weakness impeded the country's social progress and military potential. Tsar Peter the Great (1689–1725) had attempted to import Western technology, and periodic attempts of this kind set off disputes between the

Slavophiles—champions of traditional Russia who opposed foreign influences—and the Westernizers, who were ashamed at Russia's backwardness and wanted to import Western technology and a parliamentary government. Out of this contest, which lasted into the twentieth century, the intelligentsia emerged—well-educated persons who sought to modernize Russia according to creeds that ranged from moderate to revolutionary, from liberalism to socialism.

Insufficiency of Reform and Radicalization

Given the autocracy's complete control of the country, only the tsars could initiate reforms. They did so sporadically throughout the nineteenth century, instituting governing institutions but not a constitution. Probably the most important reforming tsar was Alexander II, who emancipated the serfs in 1861. However, emancipation produced such a complex situation that it prevented rapid progress on the land and impeded industrialization in the cities. The state compensated landlords for the loss of their lands but obliged the peasants to reimburse the treasury in annual installments for the next forty-nine years and created legal barriers to owning, selling, and leaving the land. This situation prevented the cities from importing the labor they needed and slowed Russian industrialization.

Contemporaneously, the failure to implement political reforms, such as parliamentary institutions, created resentment, alienated middle-class intellectuals, and radicalized the intelligentsia. The regime's opponents split into broad groupings: The Liberals, moderates who wanted a Parliament on Western European lines—and different shades of Socialists, who believed that parliaments were useless and wanted to overthrow the social and political order by violence. Russian authorities violently attacked both, alienating Liberals who were willing to accept a representative government and fostering terrorism.

Social discontent grew exponentially in the cities and on the land as the government's encouragement of industrialization to catch up to the West, unaccompanied by political reforms, contributed to urban disaffection. Finance Minister Count Sergei I. Witte instituted monetary reform, encouraged the building of railroads, extended tariff protection, and provided subsidies and guarantees to entrepreneurs. This policy stimulated the building of factories but resulted in the creation of an urban proletariat working under miserable conditions and to growing labor unrest. In the countryside, the peasants bitterly complained about the lack of land, but it was backward cultivation techniques, indebtedness as a result of emancipation, obstacles to freedom of movement, and the instability created by the village communes running the farms that accounted for the ills of Russian agriculture.

The Crumbling Autocracy

The absolute government of the tsars could not adapt to the complexities of modern life. Russia's last tsar, Nicholas II, refused to delegate decisions and was overwhelmed by insignificant trivia, such as approving the requests of pages for leaves of absence, that he could not devote appropriate attention to the major problems of his empire. The autocratic system also failed to produce

Sergei Witte had a distinguished political and domestic career. A reformer, he concentrated on building a railway network in Russia and labor reform. After the 1905 revolution, he became Russia's first "Prime Minister." Witte set the stage for the crucial reforms of Peter Stolypin. He is shown on the far left in this picture negotiating an end to the Russo-Japanese War in 1905 with the aid of Teddy Roosevelt in Portsmouth, New Hampshire.

high-quality rulers: Russians joked that they did not need a limited monarchy because Nicholas already was a limited monarch.

Ironically, the Russian autocratic system produced governmental anarchy. The tsar often named cabinet ministers who frequently pursued contradictory policies and warred with each another. This technique bolstered the tsar's power but made for inefficiency. Another serious governmental flaw: because ministers served at the tsar's pleasure, and the tsar controlled their salaries and privileges, they feared expressing their true opinions because they understood that they were the tsar's servants rather than his trusted advisers. Their obsequiousness toward the monarch and their poor salaries caused the public to hold them in low regard.

Despite some indication before his accession that he might change the autocratic system, Nicholas II proclaimed his intention to keep it intact. He continued his father's repressive policies, curtailed the rights of national minorities, and pursued an anti-Semitic policy. His refusal to change emboldened the opposition, helped as it was in the early twentieth century by the social changes fostered by industrialization. Liberals clamored louder than in the past for a constitution and representative government. They allied with *zemstvo* (elected local governmental officials) activists and professionals, found leaders in economist Peter B. Struve and historian Paul N. Miliukov, and in 1903 formed the Union of Liberation, the nucleus of the future Constitutional Democratic Party (Kadets). Socialist parties, such as the Russian Social Democratic Workers' Party (SDs)—a Marxist organization that demanded a revolution led by the industrial proletariat—grew in strength. This party split over whether there should be a transitional phase to socialism through the establishment of a bourgeois democracy (the Mensheviks, guided by Georgii V. Plekhanov), or whether a violent revolutionary elite should overthrow the government immediately (the Bolsheviks, led by Vladimir I. Lenin). Secret governmental agents attempted to combat the Marxists by infiltrating workers' associations and encouraging them to accept the ideas of Socialist revisionists, such as Eduard Bernstein. This strange experiment was known as police socialism, but it encouraged strikes and quickly ended. Another socialist organization, the Party of the Socialist Revolutionaries (SRs), appealed primarily to the peasants, demanded all land for the workers, and advocated terrorism.

The 1905 Revolution
Despite the confused political condition in which it found itself, Russia became embroiled in a disastrous war with Japan in 1904 and 1905. On January 9, 1905— "Bloody Sunday"—troops guarding the tsar's Winter Palace in Saint Petersburg fired on workers marching to redress grievances. The resulting massacre touched off mass demonstrations demanding a parliament, civil rights, and a reduction

The many problems of imperial Russia and the refusal of Emperor Nicholas II to concede meaningful political reform led to a revolution in January 1905 during the Russo-Japanese War that was a prelude to even more momentous events. Here is an illustration of the "Bloody Sunday" fighting at the Winter Palace that eventually led to the Bolshevik Revolution in 1917.

of the working day while a Soviet (council) of Workers' Deputies, consisting of Mensheviks, Bolsheviks, SRs, and revolutionary intellectuals, called a general strike that paralyzed the capital. As violence spread to the countryside, Nicholas was faced with the choice of instituting a military government or granting a constitution. On October 30, 1905, his promise of civil liberties and a democratically elected assembly defused Soviet calls for revolution and split the opposition. The Socialists demanded a republic and nationalization of the land, while the Liberals divided into the Octobrists, who thought the revolution had achieved enough, and the Kadets who demanded more liberties. However, the army remained loyal, and by the end of 1906 the government had quelled the disturbances.

The new constitution had a limited scope, and legislation creating the state Duma, the national representative body, instituted a complex voting system that granted the vote to males aged twenty-five years or over. Governmental ministers were responsible to the tsar, not the Duma, and the government did not need Parliament's approval for its actions. After February 1906 the Council of State—half of whose members were appointed by the tsar and half who were elected by privileged groups—had to give its assent, and no law could take effect without the tsar's permission.

Struggle in the Duma

The unsettled conditions after the war, land hunger, and universal male suffrage favored governmental opponents in elections and spelled the quick end of the first two dumas. Opposition groups in the first Duma elected in 1906 have been estimated at 55 percent, and the government proved unable to work with moderate groups. All parties demanded a cabinet responsible to Parliament, abolition of the Council of State, the cessation of extraordinary security measures, and expropriation of privately held lands for redistribution to the peasants. The government, led by Ivan L. Goremykin, rejected these provisions, and when the first Duma turned into a disorderly battleground, the tsar dissolved it in July 1906.

The energetic new prime minister, Peter A. Stolypin, implemented agricultural reforms and drafted a reform program for presentation to the new Duma. The elections increased the representation of opponents on both the left and the right, and when the new Duma rejected the government's program, Stolypin dissolved it. For the next elections, Stolypin and the tsar changed the criteria for representation by giving a greater voice to European Russia and to the propertied classes. The strategy worked. The third Duma met in November 1907, and while it was far from pliant, it had a working majority based on the Octobrists, a party dominated by the moderate nobility, commercial, and industrial interests. The third Duma passed major land, educational, judicial, administrative, and social legislation, lasted its full five-year term. and was regularly succeeded by the fourth Duma.

This increased stability did not resolve Russia's parliamentary weakness. Nicholas retained too much power, resorted to ruses to get his way, and regularly interfered in parliament's operations. The Kadets refused to support the government because the cabinet was not responsible to Parliament. This forced Stolypin to rely not only on the Octobrists, but on nationalist groups that favored the passage of objectionable legislation with regard to the national minorities. Moreover, Stolypin had problems with Nicholas, who was reluctant to work within the parliamentary system. The ascendance of Gregory Rasputin, a religious mystic with an unsavory reputation, increased Stolypin's difficulties at court. Rasputin convinced the empress that his special powers could stop the bleeding of her son and the heir to the throne, a hemophiliac, and wielded great political influence. When Stolypin complained to Nicholas, the tsar answered: "I agree with you . . . but it is better to have ten Rasputins than one of the Empress's hysterical tantrums." In 1911 Stolypin threatened to resign if legislation he presented favoring Ukrainian peasants over the Polish gentry that had been stalled by the Council of State did not go into effect. The tsar supported him, but only half-heartedly. The strained relations between the two men indicated that the prime minister was headed for dismissal when he was assassinated in September 1911.

By then, Nicholas regretted his institution of a parliamentary system. In the last years before World War I, constitutional reform in Russia seemed remote, and the tsar's excessive power caused increasing resentment. A historian observed: "First among the grave-diggers of Russia comes her last emperor."

Stolypin's Reforms

While Nicholas refused to concede a greater political voice to his people, he favored economic development that brought unparalleled advances. In November the government eliminated the redemption payments that the peasants still owed after their emancipation from serfdom. Over the next several years, Stolypin's government and the third Duma implemented crucial reforms that aimed at creating Western-style small peasant landholders, who would be free to buy and sell their land and to move about at will without the expropriation he considered unjust and inefficient, and at eliminating peasant support for the revolutionary parties. In order to achieve this goal, he set out to give individuals, instead of the village commune, legal title to the land and to allow peasants to move without passports and without forfeiting their holdings. In 1906 legislation instituted freedom of movement and established procedures by which peasants could obtain legal title to their land and consolidate scattered strips into single farms. By 1915 a quarter of the communal peasants had completed both steps.

This process brought greater inequality to the peasant villages than had previously been the case, but at least poorer peasants could sell their holdings and move to the cities with their capital and find work in the growing industrial sector. The governmental reforms raised the normal harvests for grains from 400 to 500 pounds per acre to 700 to 800, and the annual harvest increased from 54 million tons in 1900 to 97 million in 1913. The production of other crops saw similar increases, and the value of imported farm machinery rose from 28 million rubles in 1908 to 109 million in 1913.

Similar progress occurred in industry as the growth of cartels favored better use of capital and greater efficiency. Foreign investment flowed into Russia to finance industrialization, and native capital became progressively more important. Private entrepreneurs took their place beside the government as major investors in the country's modernization. Between 1909 and 1913, the pace of industrial increase outstripped Germany, France, and Britain. There were comparable increases in the commercial, banking, and trading sectors, and exports increased in value from 762 million rubles to over 1.5 billion between 1901 and 1913. The standard of living rose, and the largest Russian cities acquired modern services, such as electricity, water, and sewerage facilities.

Because Russia started from a lower base, it still trailed the industrially advanced European nations, but the pace of its growth on the eve of World War I pointed to the end of its economic backwardness.

Bibliographical Essay

An informative general history of Germany from the seventeenth century is W. M. Simon, *Germany: A Brief History* (New York, 1966) and Gordon A. Craig, *Germany, 1866–1945* (New York, 1978). Other informative, general histories with at least some coverage of the period discussed in this chapter include Martin Kitchen, *A History of Modern Germany, 1800–2000* (Malden, Mass., 2006); Stefan Berger, *Germany* (London, 2004), and Frank W. Thackeray, *Events that Changed Germany* (Westport, Conn., 2004), ten events, two of which occurred during the period under consideration. E. J. Feuchtwanger, *Imperial Germany, 1850–1918* (London, 2001) is a thorough history, but also look at Michael Sturmer, *The German Empire: A Short History* (New York, 2002).

Since the issue of how the process of German unification affected later history is so important, see the excellent work by Otto Pflanze, *Bismarck and the Development of Germany*, 3 vols. (Princeton, N.J., 1990). The same might be said about the most important character in that story, Bismarck, who has been the subject of numerous biographies. On Bismarck, see Erich Eyck, *Bismarck and the German Empire* (London, 1950); a standard work, Theodore S. Hamerow, ed., *The Age of Bismarck: Documents and Interpretations* (New York, 1973); and the more recent *Bismarck* (Harlow, UK, 2000), a through work. Readers should not neglect the delightfully written biography by A. J. P. Taylor, even while taking some of his interpretations with a grain of salt: *Bismarck: The Man and the Statesman* (New York, 1967). Jonathan Steinberg's *Bismarck: A Life* (New York: Oxford University Press, 2011) can now be considered the standard biography.

For particular issues, see Gordon A. Craig, *Politics and Culture in Modern Germany: Essays from the New York Review of Books* (Palo Alto, Calif., 1999), and Ann Goldberg, *Honor, Politics and the Law in Imperial Germany, 1871–1914* (New York, 2010). See also Peter Fritzsche's *Reading Berlin 1900* (Cambridge, Mass., 1996), a discussion of the German capital's cultural influence; Peter Alter, *The German Question and Europe: A History* (London, 2000), which goes up to 1990; *Modern Germany: Society, Economy, and Politics in the Twentieth Century* (New York, 1987), which includes a chapter on Wilhelmine Germany; Matthew Jefferies, *Contesting the German Empire, 1871–1918* (Malden, Mass., 2008), which raises new questions; and James N. Retallack, *Imperial Germany, 1871–1918* (New York, 2008), a collection by different scholars on important topics. Reappraisals by different scholars may be found in Jack R. Dukes and Joachim Remak, *Another Germany: A Reconsideration of the Imperial Era* (Boulder, Colo., 1988).

The classic work by Arthur Rosenberg, containing the view that the blockage of reform set a long road toward the revolution that took place in 1918, was originally written in 1928 and translated into English in 1931: *The Birth of the German Republic 1871–1918* (New York, 1962). This book stands the test of time very well. The quote about the German emperor being the most powerful man in the world is on p. 33. Hans-Ulrich Wehler's interpretations may be found in English in *The German Empire 1871–1918* (Providence, R.I., and Oxford, UK, 1991, 1993). This book may be slow going because it is replete with information and insights but will amply reward a careful reading. The quotes on how aristocratic values were inculcated into middle-class boys are on pp. 125–26, and the unwillingness of the ruling circles to adjust to changing conditions is on p. 245. Wehler's views raise the issue of the German problem in Europe; on this broader question, consult Louis L. Snyder, *German Nationalism: The Tragedy of a People* (Port Washington, N.Y., 1969), and David Calleo, *The German Problem Reconsidered: Germany and the World Order, 1870 to the Present* (Cambridge, UK, 1978).

The best book on the changes in the German Right and the growing influence of radical nationalism is Geoff Eley's *Reshaping the German Right: Radical Nationalism and Political Change after Bismarck* (New Haven, Conn., 1980). Eley's introduction is an admirable summary of some important historiographical issues, and Eley discusses the developments and changes in important associations on the right, such as the Navy League and the Pan-German League, with acumen. It is his judgment on radical nationalism, pp. 352–53, that is cited. Eley represents a different general view from that expressed by Wehler, as may be seen in the introduction; consult also David Blackbourn and Goeff Eley, *The Peculiarities of German History: Bourgeois Society and Politics in the Nineteenth Century* (Oxford, UK, 1984). The classic work on the German army, including an excellent treatment of this period, is Gordon A. Craig, *The Politics of the Prussian Army 1640–1945* (New York, 1964). Another important book for the understanding of German politics during this era is J. C. G. Rohl, *Germany Without Bismarck* (Berkeley, Calif., 1967). Some other works dealing with the constitutional crises include J. Alden Nichols, *Germany After Bismarck. The Caprivi Era 1890–1894* (Cambridge, Mass., 1958). Ekkehard-Teja P. W. Wilke, *Political Decadence in Imperial Germany* (Urbana, Ill., 1976) deals with the bureaucratic-political aspects of the crisis. Feminism during this period is covered by Richard J. Evans, *The Feminist Movement in Germany 1894–1933* (London, 1976).

There is a debate on the exact nature of Wilhelm II's role in German history. James N. Retallack, *Germany in the Age of Kaiser Wilhelm II* (Basingstoke, UK, 1966) is primarily a biography of the most important personage during the era. On him, consult as well Michael Balfour, *The Kaiser and His Times* (Boston, 1964), a readable biography; Thomas A. Kohut, *Wilhelm II and the Germans* (New York, 1991), which emphasizes Wilhelm's interaction with his people, from which (p. 5) Bismarck's description of the emperor is taken; and John C. G. Rohl, ed., *Kaiser Wilhelm II: New Interpretations* (Cambridge, UK, 1982), essays on important aspects of Wilhelm's reign.

George Dunlap Crothers, *The German Elections of 1907* (New York, 1968), provides an interesting account of the campaign and argues that these elections resulted in an increase of national sentiment. His position that Bülow's resignation had the result of somehow "involving the chancellorship in a kind of responsibility to the Reichstag," however, is weak and contradictory. Katharine Anne Lerman, *The Chancellor as Courtier: Bernhard von Bülow and the Governance of Germany, 1900–1909* (New York: 1990) is a biography. Konrad H. Jarausch has written a thorough study of Imperial Germany's last prewar chancellor: *The Enigmatic Chancellor: Bethmann-Hollweg and the Hubris of Imperial Germany* (New Haven, Conn., 1973).

The classic account of the SPD during this period is Carl E. Schorske, *German Social Democracy 1905–1917* (Cambridge, Mass., 1955). An interesting debate revolves around the attitude of German revisionist Socialists to German imperialism, a question raised in other countries as well. On this issue, see Roger Fletcher, *Revisionism and Empire: Socialist Imperialism in Germany 1897–1914* (London, 1984). See also Nicholas Stargardt, *The German Idea of Militarism: Radical and Socialist Critics, 1866–1914* (New York, 1994). For a detailed analysis of the role of religion in German politics, see Helmut Walser Smith, *German Nationalism and Religious Conflict: Culture, Ideology, Politics 1870–1914* (Princeton, N.J., 1995). Center Party policy is examined by Ellen Lane Evans, *The German*

Center Party, 1870–1933: A Study in Political Catholicism (Carbondale, Ill., 1981). A local study is David Blackbourn, *Class, Religion and Local Politics in Wilhelmine Germany* (New Haven, Conn., 1980). Richard J. Evans, *The Coming of the Third Reich* (New York, 2004), part of a trilogy, seeks to explain the seeds of Nazism.

The term "that ramshackle realm" to describe the Hapsburg Empire was used by David Lloyd George. Robin Okey's *The Habsburg Monarchy* (New York, 2001) is a general history from the eighteenth century to its end. An excellent brief history is A .J. P. Taylor's *The Hapsburg Monarchy 1809–1918* (London, 1948), which has a convenient appendix with figures for the different nationalities. Mark Cornwall discusses problems in the early twentieth century in *The Last Years of Austria-Hungary: Essays in Political and Military History, 1908–1918* (Exeter, UK, 1990) and *The Last Years of Austria-Hungary: A Multi-National Experiment in Early Twentieth Century Europe* (Exeter, UK, 2002). Steven Beller's *Francis Joseph* (London and New York, 1996) is an excellent attempt to recount the country's complex modern history in a short work; the book includes a good bibliography, maps, and a chronology. Longer biographies are Joseph Redlich, *Emperor Francis Joseph of Austria: A Biography* (New York, 1929); Jean Paul Bled, *Franz Joseph* (Oxford, UK, 1992); and Alan Palmer, *Twilight of the Hapsburgs: Life and Times of Emperor Joseph* (London, 1994).

A book that should be consulted for the scene it sets for the period discussed here is William A. Jenks, *Austria Under the Iron Cross 1879–1893* (Charlottesville, Va., 1965), which provides a full-scale analysis of an important period just before the one discussed.

The Hapsburg Empire's political and social structure has been well studied in a series of older major works; more recent scholars seem to be interested in the breakup of the empire rather than its functioning. The books include C. A. Macartney's meticulously detailed study of Austria and its possessions from the eighteenth century that is essential for its treatment of the twentieth, *The Habsburg Empire 1790–1918* (London, 1969). Macartney also published a more manageable and readable study on the same period, *The House of Austria: The Later Phase 1790–1918* (Edinburgh, 1978), from which the quotes on Hungary's industrial development and the Reichsrat's ineffectiveness may be found (pp. 233 and 249), as well as some of the statistics cited. Another superior work dealing with the issues in this chapter is Arthur J. May, *The Hapsburg Monarchy 1867–1914* (Cambridge, Mass., 1965). Robert A. Kann's *The Multinational Empire: Nationalism and National Reform in the Hapsburg Monarchy 1814–1918*, 2 vols. (New York, 1970) takes the story to another level of detail, examining in depth each of the different nationalities and their concerns. The nationalities question is examined in Paula S. Fichtner, *The Habsburg Empire: From Dynasticism to Multinationalilsm* (n.p., 1997) and in *The Nationalities Question in the Habsburg Monarchy* (Minneapolis, Minn., 1993), by Solomon Wank. Harold J. Gordon, Jr., and Nancy M. Gordon, eds., *The Austrian Empire: Abortive Federation?* (Lexington, Mass., 1974), provides interpretations on the question of whether the Hapsburg Empire was really an attempt to bring together different nationalities in one supranational unit, a debate that began much earlier. Laurence Cole and Daniel L. Unowsky examine another important question: *The Limits of Loyalty: Imperial Symbolism, Popular Allegiances, and State Patriotism in the Late Habsburg Monarchy* (New York, 2007). Oscar Jaszi, *The Dissolution of the Hapsburg Monarchy* (Chicago, 1929), asked the same question and concluded that the empire's breakup resulted from a long, organic, internal process, not from external causes.

The statement on institutions not counting in Russia is alleged to have been made by Konstantin Pobedonostsev, adviser of Alexander III and Nicholas II. Books on Russia with good chapters on the prerevolutionary scene include Ezra Mendelsohn and Marshall Shatz, eds., *Imperial Russia: State, Society, Opposition* (De Kalb, Ill., 1988), a series of essays in honor of Marc Raeff. W. E. Mosse, *Alexander II and the Modernization of*

Russia (New York, 1962), gives an overview of Alexander's policies and their effects. *Russia and the Russians* (Cambridge, Mass., 2001) is a general history.

Revolutionary movements against the Russian government during the late nineteenth and early twentieth centuries are well covered. Adam B. Ulam's *In the Name of the People: Prophets and Conspirators in Prerevolutionary Russia* (New York, 1977) is a detailed history of conspiracies in prerevolutionary Russia and the same author's *Russia's Failed Revolutions: From the Decembrists to the Dissidents* (New York, 1981) includes good chapters on the 1905 revolution and the years up to 1914. Avraham Yarmolinsky discusses radical movements in *Road to Revolution: A Century of Russian Radicalism* (New York, 1962). An account of Alexander III's reactionary policies and the bureaucracy's role in their implementation is Heide W. Whelan, *Alexander III and the State Council* (New Brunswick, N.J., 1982). The Jewish question is discussed in *Beyond the Pale*, by Benjamin Nathans (Berkeley, Calif., 2004).

Two classic works that consider all aspects of the period under discussion are Bernard Pares, *A History of Russia* (New York, 1958), and Richard E. Pipes, *Russia Under the Old Regime* (New York, 1974).

A brief introduction to Russia is Michael Karpovich's *Imperial Russia, 1801–1917* (New York, 1932); readers should be aware that Karpovich leans toward the thesis that the Bolshevik Revolution was probably unnecessary because of the empire's rapid modernization. A detailed and balanced history of Russia by a noted historian is Hugh Seton-Watson, *The Russian Empire 1801–1917* (Oxford, UK, 1967); Seton-Watson also wrote a shorter work concentrating on the later years of the empire, again at a high level, *The Decline of Imperial Russia, 1855–1914* (New York, 1952), from which the judgment of Nicholas II is taken (p. 378). Excellent books of moderate length include Sergei Pushkarev, *The Emergence of Modern Russia 1801–1917* (New York, 1963), which gives the view of a Russian expert and has an extremely useful bibliography; the quotation of Nicholas II on Rasputin is on p. 262. Edward C. Thaden, *Russia Since 1801: The Making of a New Society* (New York, 1971) emphasizes the development of Russian society. J. N. Westwood, *Endurance and Endeavour: Russian History, 1812–1971* (Oxford, UK, 1973) is particularly good on the period discussed. The same author also published a social history, *Structures of Society: Imperial Russia's "People of Various Rank"* (DeKalb, Ill., 1994).

Hans Rogger, *Russia in the Age of Modernisation and Revolution 1881–1917* (New York, 1983), takes a thematic approach and is excellent in his discussion of institutions and different social groups. Other books with a similar emphasis include another excellent contribution by Bernard Pares, *Russia Between Reform and Revolution* (New York, 1962), and Jacob Walkin, *The Rise of Democracy in Pre-Revolutionary Russia* (New York, 1962). Richard E. Pipes, ed., *The Russian Intelligentsia* (New York, 1961), is a series of essays on the intelligentsia in general, with some specific contributions for the period discussed in this chapter. Roberta Thomson Manning discusses *The Crisis of the Old Order* (Princeton, N.J., 1982), and Elise Kimerling Wirtschafter examines *Social Identity in Imperial Russia* (DeKalb, Ill., 1997) while Peter Gatrell looks at industrial development before World War I, particularly the armaments industry, and tsarist policies: *Government, Industry, and Rearmament in Russia, 1900–1914* (New York, 1994).

The 1905 revolution is covered in a thorough and scholarly manner by Abraham Ascher, *The Revolution of 1905*, 2 vols. (Stanford, Calif., 1988–92). Laura Engelstein's *Moscow, 1905* (Stanford, Calif., 1982) is a specialized work on the Moscow uprising with an emphasis on the social and political background and worker organization. The best general analysis of rural conditions before 1917 is Geroid T. Robinson, *Rural Russia Under the Old Regime: A History of the Landlord-Peasant World and a Prologue to the Peasant Revolution of 1917* (Berkeley, Calif., 1967). Andrew M. Verner looks at the role of the tsar in the revolution and its effects, *The Crisis of the Russian Autocracy* (Princeton, N.J., 1990).

Books that consider the policies of specific individuals are also valuable in getting at the history of a period. Mary Schaeffer Conroy, *Peter Arkad'evich Stolypin* (Boulder, Colo., 1979) is an impartial analysis of Stolypin's policies; George Yaney, *The Urge to Mobilize: Agrarian Reform in Russia, 1861–1930* (Urbana, Ill., 1982), is an extensive discussion of Stolypin's agrarian reforms, their implementation, and their effects. Books that discuss the wider significance of Stolypin's reforms include Abraham Ascher, *P. A. Stolypin: The Search for Stability in Late Imperial Russia* (Stanford, Calif., 2001); Stephen F. Williams, *Liberal Reform in an Illiberal Regime* (Stanford, Calif., 2006) which discusses the creation of private property in Russia during this period; and Judith Pallot, *Land Reform in Russia, 1906–1917* (Oxford, UK, 1999), which examines how the peasants reacted. The constitutional/parliamentary aspect is studied by Leonid Ivan Strakhovsky and Florence Strakhovsky, *The Era of Stolypin* (Portland, Maine, 2009) and by Alexandra Shecket Korros, *A Reluctant Parliament: Stolypin, Nationalism, and the Politics of the Russian Imperial Council, 1906–1911* (Lanham, Md., 2002). Richard Pipes's, *Struve: Liberal on the Left, 1870–1905* (Cambridge, Mass., 1970) and *Struve: Liberal on the Right, 1905–1944* (Cambridge, Mass., 1980) are sympathetic biographies of the Kadet leader. Edward H. Judge tells the story of a famous interior minister, assassinated in 1904, who sought to maintain the autocracy but who wanted it to adapt to changing conditions: *Plehve: Repression and Reform in Imperial Russia 1902–1904* (Syracuse, N.Y., 1983). Howard D. Mehlinger and John M. Thompson published *Count Witte and the Tsarist Government in the 1905 Revolution* (Bloomington, Ind., 1972), an uncommonly complete work with a valuable appendix of different drafts of the fundamental laws issued at the time. Sidney Harcave's *Count Sergei Witte and the Twilight of Imperial Russia* (Armonk, N.Y., 2004), is a good biography. Biographies of Nicholas II are easily obtainable; Dominic Lieven, *Nicholas II: Twilight of the Empire* (New York, 1993), is a manageable one. Raymond K. Massie, *Nicholas and Alexander* (New York, 1967), is the readable story of Russia's royal couple.

CHAPTER 4

❧

Foreign Policies

CHAPTER OUTLINE

Britain: Managing Decline • World Policy (*Weltpolitik)* • France's Lost
Provinces • Showdown in the Balkans • The Peace Emperor and the Balkan
Cauldron • Italy Searches for Security

BIOGRAPHICAL SKETCHES

Francis Joseph of Hapsburg, Unlucky • Théophile Delcassé,
Warrior Diplomat

The foreign policies of the European powers involved complex issues.
Germany's economic advance spurred it to become a world power, like
Britain. The Germans believed that a large colonial empire was necessary to
achieve that aim, but most of the colonial areas already belonged to the British
and the French. In Europe, Russia wanted to increase its influence in the Balkans
and the Turkish Empire, but the dominant power in the Balkans was Austria-
Hungary, Germany's major ally, and Germany was increasing its own influence
in Turkey. A clash appeared likely even to contemporary observers.

BRITAIN: MANAGING DECLINE

At the beginning of the twentieth century, Britain ruled the largest empire ever
seen. With an imperial population of 400 million, the country governed ten times
as many people as its closest competitor France. Britain, however, had fallen behind
Germany in the areas of industrial production that translated into economic and
military strength. Britain was forced to alter its foreign policy in order to manage
its relative decline and to confront Germany.

The German Challenge
The British Empire reached is peak in 1901 when South Africa came solidly under
its control as a result of the Boer War. The poor British performance in that conflict,

European Empires, 1914 (Population in 000's)

	AFRICA	ASIA	AUSTRALIA AND PACIFIC	AMERICA AND N. ATLANTIC	TOTALS
Belgium	15,000.0	–	–	–	15,000.0
Denmark	–	–	–	125.8	125.8
France	26,681.2	14,773.0	81.1	450.9	40,986.2
Germany	11,428.4	168.9	636.5	–	12,041.6
Great Britain	37,990.2	323,865.9	6,551.5	10,006.8	378,504.4
Italy	1,373.2	–	–	–	1,373.2
Netherlands	–	38,000.0	–	140.6	38,140.5
Portugal	8,243.6	895.8	–	–	9,139.4
Spain	235.8	–	–	–	235.8
				Grand Total	495,547.0

*Adapted from *Statesman's Year-Book*, 1914.

Source: From C. E. Black and E. C. Helmreich, *Twentieth Century Europe*, 2nd ed. (New York: Knopf, 1961), p. 24.

however, revealed military weaknesses and produced a debate over the empire's future. Technical changes could not resolve the military problems because British hegemony had been based upon industrial leadership and in recent decades, other countries, especially Germany, had outpaced it.

The seriousness of the German industrial challenge may be summed up in one astounding statistic: modern steel production. Before German unification, Britain produced twice as much steel as all the German states; forty years later, Britain manufactured only half as much. Germany's economic development and military efficiency held out the prospect that it could fight two great powers simultaneously and still have a reasonable likelihood of victory. According to historian Paul M. Kennedy, "Germany was not only growing out of its European 'skin' but was also acquiring the early attributes of a world power—booming overseas trade, political influence abroad, colonial acquisitions and an expanding fleet. All this necessarily implied a *relative diminution* in Britain's own commercial/colonial/ maritime position unless it in turn was able to export more, colonise more, and build more ships, so as to preserve the original relationship." Instead, Germany left Britain increasingly in the dust.

In the late 1890s, Germany embarked on a big navy program, an essential element of its drive to become a world power. Geography dictated that this buildup must take place in the North Sea, which automatically threatened Britain. Because it was an island, Britain could maintain a navy bigger than any of its rivals could afford in order to prevent an invasion, but only a small colonial army, while the continental powers had to split their economic resources between a large army and a navy. Before 1914, Germany's economic develop-

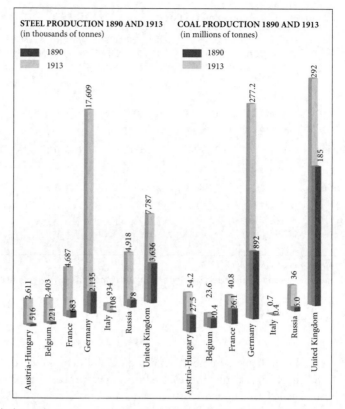

STEEL PRODUCTION 1890 AND 1913
(in thousands of tonnes)

■ 1890
□ 1913

COAL PRODUCTION 1890 AND 1913
(in millions of tonnes)

■ 1890
□ 1913

This graph shows the increases in production of steel and coal of the major European powers between 1890 and the eve of World War I. Note the German increases as compared with Britain.

ment held out the frightening prospect it could build a fleet that threatened the Royal Navy while retaining the capability of landing a superior army on the British Isles.

Technological advances worsened the situation. Navies took decades to build, and Britain possessed a lead in the number of ships that would be difficult to overtake. However, in 1906, the British launched the *Dreadnought*, a technological revolution in naval warfare. Pre-*Dreadnought* warships were now obsolete because big-gun dreadnought-class ships could easily sink them. The British faced the prospect of an evaporating lead as the Germans and others built dreadnought-class ships, stimulating an invasion psychosis in Britain that showed up in a war scare in 1909 and an insistence on the immediate construction of a large number of dreadnoughts; as a popular slogan of the year demanded: "We want eight, and we won't wait!" Dreadnoughts were extremely expensive to build, even for the Germans, but the British psychosis led to an overestimation of the dreadnoughts the Germans were building, and they went full steam ahead. The British estimated

Strategic materials produced by major powers. Note how Germany caught up with its rivals by 1900 and surpassed them by 1910.

		UNITED KINGDOM	FRANCE	GERMANY
Steel				
(thousands of metric tons)	1865	225	41	97
	1900	5,130	1,565	6,645
	1910	6,374	3,506	13,698
Pig Iron				
(thousands of metric tons)	1865	4,892	989	882
	1900	9,003	2,714	7,549
	1910	10,380	4,032	14,793
Coal				
(thousands of metric tons)	1860	80.0	8.1	12.3
	1900	225.2	32.7	109.3
	1910	292.0	40.9	277.3

*Adapted from S. B. Clough and C. W. Cole, *Economic History of Europe* (New York, 1941), pp. 538, 545.

SOURCE: C. E. Black and E. C. Helmreich, *Twentieth Century Europe*, 2nd ed. (New York: Knopf, 1961), p. 5.

The appearance of *Dreadnought* class battleships in 1906 revolutionized the arms race before World War I by making older battleships obsolete and giving Germany the possibility of catching up and surpassing Britain on the seas. This development, in turn, revolutionized diplomacy before 1914 by encouraging Britain to abandon its "splendid isolation" and join European allies. Here is a picture of the *Dreadnought* at sea in 1909.

that the Germans would have twenty-one by 1912, but the actual numbers were fifteen for the British and nine for the Germans. This furious naval arms race brought war closer.

Diplomatic Revolution

The arms race had revolutionary effects. The traditional British policy of "splendid isolation"—refusing to enter into permanent alliances because their island home was invulnerable to invasion—was now obsolete. Faced with an increasingly powerful Germany and their own relative decline, the British were forced to make agreements with continental powers, which were also faced with the possibility of German hegemony, a normal feature of their diplomacy.

The new British policy gave a new dynamism to foreign affairs. In 1902 the British reached an agreement with Japan in which the Japanese helped look after their Asian interests. This pact allowed them to transfer much of the Asian fleet to European waters to confront the growing German naval challenge. This arrangement strengthened the war party in Japan that advocated a war with its Asian rival Russia, a not-unwelcome outcome for the British, who considered the Russian expansionist dreams toward Britain's Mediterranean lifeline a dangerous threat. When the Russians lost the Russo-Japanese war (1904–05), Germany became the focus of British foreign policy. The British strengthened their ties with the French, who were at risk from a possible German attack. Britain agreed to French freedom of action in Morocco in return for a free hand in Egypt from the French, a deal that ignored German interests and contributed to German fears of isolation and to the series of international crises that preceded World War I.

The kaiser's blustering language and intimidations encouraged a belief that German expansion was unavoidable and that only the end of German economic prosperity could blunt the threat. In 1907, British naval war planners argued: "The country [Germany] has been launched on a road which has led to this enormous increase of material prosperity, and whether the authors of the policy would like to draw back now or not, they cannot do so. The expansion must go on until it meets a force stronger than itself, or until the policy directing the [German] State ceases to be of a sufficiently virile nature to stimulate growth and encourage prosperity."

Britain's new pro-French policy, framed in the context of preserving the European and world balance of power, was reinforced by military conventions with France. Even more than Britain, the French were vulnerable to the German threat because they shared a common border with the Germans. Germany's explosive economic growth produced great imperialistic ambitions, and geography dictated that to fulfill those ambitions, Germany had to threaten both the British and French homelands. This mortal threat united Britain and France, ancient enemies and declining powers, which understood that the defense of their homelands and colonial possessions was inextricably tied to their success in containing Germany.

WORLD POLICY (*WELTPOLITIK*)

The Germans had abandoned Bismarck's legacy in foreign affairs that he had elaborated following unification. Cognizant of French enmity and desire for

This map illustrates France's isolation by Bismarck.

retribution, Bismarck had attempted to nullify France's ability to wage a war of revenge by depriving it of allies. Bismarck especially feared an alliance between France and Russia, a two-front war that would force the Germans to split their army.

Collapse of Bismarck's System

By juggling the complex issues driving big-power diplomacy, Bismarck fulfilled his goal of isolating France. In 1879 Germany signed the Dual Alliance with Austria-Hungary in which each pledged to aid the other if attacked. In 1881 Bismarck concluded the Three Emperors' League joining Germany, Austria-Hungary, and Russia. In 1882, Germany, Austria-Hungary, and Italy signed the Triple Alliance, an agreement that was a result of Italy's search for allies. Bismarck also hoped for a British alliance. He fell short of this goal, but his efforts produced excellent relations with Britain because he agreed not to threaten Britain's hegemony at sea.

Bismarck's diplomatic system, however, contained deep flaws that quickly developed wide cracks after the kaiser fired him in 1890. Despite the Three Emperors' League, the Austrians had been clashing with the Russians in the Balkans and the Turkish-controlled Near East for centuries. The Russians were anxious to gain access to the Mediterranean Sea, which Turkish control of the Straits (Bosporus and Dardanelles) denied them. After Bismarck left the scene, the Germans favored the Austrians, which led the Russians to refuse to renew the

The Germans reacted to the breakdown of Bismarck's diplomatic system and the fear that they would have to fight against the French and the Russians simultaneously in case of a war by elaborating the famous "Schlieffen Plan." Here is its author, Alfred von Schlieffen, in his military uniform, sporting his medals.

Three Emperors' League in 1887. Likewise, the Austrian-Italian enmity hollowed out the Triple Alliance. After Italian unification, the Austrians still held Italian-speaking areas (the *Irredenta*) and mistreated the Italian minority there. This and other disputes actually brought the two allies close to war at different times.

Bismarck foresaw the likelihood of a Russian-French alliance if the link with Germany and Austria were broken, and in 1887 signed the Reinsurance Treaty with Russia, "reassuring" the Russians that if the Austrians attacked Russia, Germany would not come to Austria's aid. Bismarck did not consider this understanding a conflict with the Dual Alliance because that pact provided for German help to Austria only if another power attacked it, not if Austria attacked another country or provoked a conflict. The Reinsurance Treaty has been interpreted as Bismarck's attempt to moderate Austrian policy in the Balkans by warning it that if Austrian machinations there produced a conflict with Russia, Austria could not automatically count on German aid. However, his successors believed that a contradiction with Germany's commitments under the Dual Alliance did exist and let the treaty lapse in 1890. This decision signaled that Germany valued the Austrian alliance above the Russian connection and left the Russians free to link up with the French.

Over the next several years, the Russians and French negotiated a treaty and a military convention that left the Germans vulnerable to a two-front war.

The Schlieffen Plan

The Germans answered with the Schlieffen Plan. Instead of splitting their army into two equal parts to fight the French and Russians in the East and the West, they would concentrate most of their military might on the Western front to deliver a swift knockout blow against France. Having defeated the French, the German army would be shifted to the East and defeat Russia. This plan depended on an important factor without which it would not work: the different rates at which Germany, France, and Russia mobilized. Germany and France, modern industrial countries, mobilized rapidly, while industrially backward Russia did so slowly. The Germans would hold off the Russians in the East with small forces and make their right wing on the Western front invincible. To ensure its success, the Schlieffen Plan called for an invasion of France through Belgium (and the Netherlands, but this feature was dropped). The Germans would take the French by surprise because both countries had guaranteed Belgian neutrality in case of war; this combination would overwhelm the French, and the German army would deal with the Russians before they had fully mobilized.

A brilliant conception on paper, the scheme had unfortunate consequences. The plan obliged the Germans to attack France first if Russia ever became involved in a conflict, but what if France stayed out of a war involving Russia, Germany, and Austria-Hungary? In case of a Balkan war in which Russia became involved, Austria would need German help. Should the Germans agree to aid their allies, the Schlieffen Plan obliged them to attack France even if that country was not involved. Moreover, going through Belgium risked bringing in the British, who feared a big power occupying the European coast closest to their island homeland—or at least it would serve as a pretext to do so. Germany could not risk going to war against Russia while leaving France neutral and free to intervene once the German army was entangled in the East. The Germans did not have a contingency plan in which they would fight only Russia and not France, increasing the likelihood that a Balkan war would set off a general conflict in Europe.

Moreover, the Schlieffen Plan created a rigid mindset that favored war. Russia had embarked on a program of rapid industrial modernization that threatened to undercut the assumption that Russia would mobilize slowly. The Schlieffen Plan ran the risk of becoming obsolete very soon, contributing to a mindset among German officials that it was better to have a war sooner rather than later.

Several factors convinced many Germans that war was certain. They included the implications of social imperialism, the economic understanding between industrialists and large landowners already discussed, and the enormous growth of German industry. Many Germans assumed that a British decline would lead to Britain's colonial possessions being divided among the rising powers, for which they had to be prepared. Convinced that their impressive strength entitled them to a "place in the sun," already by 1897 the Germans embarked on *Weltpolitik* (World Policy). As Kaiser Wilhelm remarked: "Nothing must henceforth be settled in the world without the intervention of Germany and the German Emperor."

The Schlieffen Plan. This map shows the original plan, which was later modified so that the Germans would not invade the Netherlands or wheel around Paris. In addition, the right wing was weakened to bolster other fronts. The map demonstrates how the Germans planned to violate Belgium's neutrality, which the European powers—including Germany—recognized.

Making good on this promise, the Germans suddenly appeared as a force in China, Africa, and other parts of the world, where they clashed with the Russians and the British. In the Turkish Empire they built the Baghdad railway, a centerpiece of German influence, and sent advisers to train the Turkish army. Wilhelm offered German protection to the Muslims by posing as a defender of the weak against British and Russian imperialism. *Weltpolitik* also dictated construction of a big navy that incarnated the ideas of world policy, social imperialism, profits for industrialists, increased employment, and national pride. Historian Fritz Fischer contended that this mentality seized hold of the cultural and political elite and permeated German society.

Aggressive German posturing during the crises that led up to World War I spurred the other big powers to put into place a series of alliances to contrast with German power. German policy makers, in turn, interpreted these agreements as encirclement and as a desire to deprive Germany of its rightful position as the world's leading power. Germany increasingly felt that it could count only on a crumbling Austria-Hungary. Anxious to achieve world power status before time ran out, German statesmen played by the accepted diplomatic rules less and less, and German policy took on a blundering and upstart quality. The country's constitutional structure, which had few checks on policy makers who pursued reckless policies, worsened the foreign policy situation.

FRANCE'S LOST PROVINCES

Relations were especially bad with France, which continued to resent bitterly Germany's annexation of Alsace and Lorraine in 1871 after France lost the Franco-Prussian War.

The Poisoned Atmosphere

For the next 20 years Bismarck prevented the French from retaliating against Germany by keeping them isolated and deprived of allies. However, he also attempted to distract them by encouraging their successful efforts to win a large colonial empire in Africa and Asia. Bismarck was disinterested in colonies and hoped that a friendly policy would make France forget about going to war and perhaps even culminate in a Franco-German alliance. As he told the French ambassador, referring to his support for French colonial gains: "Renounce the Rhine and I will help you to secure everywhere else the satisfactions you desire."

The answer arrived from a French nationalist leader: "I have lost two children and you offer me twenty domestics." Despite a periodic warming of relations, French and German statesmen considered it just a matter of time before war broke out. In 1875 there was a war scare. Both countries increased military spending in 1886, 1887, and 1888. In 1892 demonstrations broke out when the German queen mother visited France, prompting Germany to implement the steps preliminary to mobilization.

France Emerges from Isolation

France fought Germany's growing power with an increasingly sophisticated diplomatic campaign. In 1894, it emerged from diplomatic isolation by concluding a mutual cooperation agreement with the Russians, the Entente Cordiale (Entente in French means understanding). Russia had had qualms about linking up with a republican regime with radical roots, but the Reinsurance Treaty's lapse left France as the only choice for an ally. At first, this alliance meant little in military terms, but in 1899 both countries transformed it into an active means of maintaining the European balance of power by tightening their diplomatic and military cooperation.

The person responsible for this new assertive French policy became foreign minister in 1898. Théophile Delcassé aimed to revive French influence by strengthening the Russian connection and by reaching agreements with Britain and Italy. He skillfully played on Italian resentment of Austrian policies and on the traditional Franco-Italian friendship. Although the Italians formally remained in the Triple Alliance, in 1902 both countries pledged not to attack each other in a treaty reminiscent of Bismarck's Reinsurance Treaty.

Delcassé's major goal, an agreement with Great Britain, caused him the greatest agony. Franco-British tensions caused by competing colonial interests remained high. In September 1898, a crisis erupted over Fashoda, in the Sudan, bringing the two countries close to war, and Delcassé had to exercise all his talents to avoid a rupture. The crisis, however, ended with an unexpected result: friendship. With the Germans increasing in strength on land and sea and threatening

This map shows France's success in emerging from isolation, the danger to Germany of a two-front war, and why the Germans feared "encirclement."

BIOGRAPHICAL SKETCHES

Théophile Delcassé
Warrior Diplomat

An ardent patriot, Théophile Delcassé believed that the Alsace-Lorraine problem made a war between France and Germany certain. As the French foreign minister from 1898 to 1905, he worked to end the isolation into which Bismarck had thrust France by strengthening the alliances with Russia and Britain and favoring a rapprochement with Italy. His policies irritated the Germans and alarmed the French political establishment, which feared a war. Delcassé reached an agreement with the British and stood up against the Germans in Morocco, but the French cabinet feared that in doing so, he would provoke a war with Germany. In a cabinet meeting on June 6, 1905, the French cabinet forced Delcassé out of office. The affair strengthened the German reputation as bullies.

It seemed that Delcassé was through, but his policy eventually triumphed because French public opinion believed that the government ousted Delcassé because of German pressure. During the next few years, a Franco-British-Russian entente for which Delcassé had laid the basis became a reality. At this point, historical accounts of Delcassé's role usually stop, but his subsequent actions may have had an even greater impact.

A serious gap existed between the strong foreign policy that Delcassé advocated and the country's military prowess. Particularly worrisome was the state of the French navy, plagued by neglect, scandal, and a series of accidents culminating on March 12, 1907, in the explosion of a warship that killed 118 men. A parliamentary commission headed by Delcassé reported that the French built battleships too slowly, that they lacked sufficient war supplies and ammunition, and that the country possessed only one shipyard capable of repairing them. In June 1911, Delcassé took over as navy minister until January 1913.

Delcassé believed that if France were to win a war against Germany, it must hold the Mediterranean with a strong navy. Only with the safe transport of men and supplies from the colonies to the western front could France ensure that it would obtain numerical superiority against the German army. Delcassé constructed more and better ships faster, reorganized the naval command structure, improved training for crews, modernized shipyards, gained the trust of the Socialist-influenced shipyard workers, built an efficient support structure for the ships, improved naval ammunition, and founded an air arm.

In addition, Delcassé negotiated a crucial agreement with Britain by which the British navy protected the coast of northern France while the French concentrated their power in the Mediterranean. This understanding morally committed Britain to enter a conflict on the French side in case of war with Germany. In February 1913, the government appointed Delcassé ambassador to Russia. Delcassé convinced the Russians to increase their preparedness for a war against Germany, which in 1914 resulted in a more formidable enemy for the Germans than they had expected. During World War I, he served as minister of war. Following that conflict, he opposed the Versailles treaty because he believed that it guaranteed France neither reparations nor security. He retired from public life in 1919.

continued

continued

Born on March 1, 1852, into a modest family, Delcassé early adopted the ideas of Léon Gambetta, the father of the Third Republic, and gained notoriety as a journalist. Because his wife was sickly and his son died following his release from a German prisoner-of-war camp in World War I, sadness marked his personal life. Théophile Delcassé died on February 22, 1923, received a state funeral, and lies buried at Paris's Montmartre cemetery.

their homelands, the British and the French could not afford a war over colonies. They pulled back from the brink of war and, over the next several years, worked out their outstanding colonial problems, particularly in Africa. France recognized Britain's paramount interest in Egypt, and England did the same for France in Morocco. In 1904 an Anglo-French accord, the Entente Cordiale, foreshadowed the Triple Entente, solidified in 1907 when France's allies England and Russia concluded an agreement.

These French successes irritated Germany. In the diplomacy of imperialism, countries planning to take over an area negotiated with all powers that had interests in a region and compensated them. When he moved on Morocco, Delcassé neglected to negotiate with Germany—blunder or provocation? Germany reacted strongly, typically going beyond a mere defense of its interests. In this case, the Germans were also motivated by a wish to test the strength of the new friendship between France and Britain and to discover how it would hold up in a crisis.

Violating diplomatic protocol, the kaiser visited Tangier in March 1905 and informed the sultan that Germany supported Moroccan independence, touching off a crisis in which the Germans threatened war. At a cabinet meeting on June 6, 1905, Delcassé made his case for resisting German demands, but his colleagues judged France unprepared for a conflict while its Russian ally had recently been defeated in a war with Japan. The cabinet then forced Delcassé to resign, a great victory for the Germans. This triumph turned into a debacle when the British strongly supported the French at an international congress held in 1906 at Algeciras and the other European countries isolated Germany.

Escalating Nationalism

The 1905 Moroccan emergency preceded a series of grave crises that shook Europe before 1914. Because these crises usually ended in diplomatic duels between France and Germany, they increased the stridency of French nationalism, which became more influential and steeled for war. The dramatic increase of French chauvinism favored the rise of hard-liners, such as Raymond Poincaré—the premier and later president—who rebuffed German offers of a rapprochement. The hardening of French public opinion strengthened Germany's fear of "encirclement," and in 1913 Germany undertook the largest increase ever in its army. Convinced of the inevitability of armed conflict, French diplomats had woven a tight web around their traditional enemy.

SHOWDOWN IN THE BALKANS

In the meantime, tensions increased between Russia and Austria-Hungary in the Balkan Peninsula and brought the area to the boiling point. The decline of the Ottoman Empire encouraged the Russians to push harder for the right of passage of their warships through the Straits into the Mediterranean and to increase their influence by strongly supporting the Slavic inhabitants of the area. These policies clashed with those of Austria-Hungary, long dominant in the peninsula, but slipping and fearful that strong Russian backing would encourage the Slavs in their empire to secede and threaten its very existence. The situation was radicalized because the diplomatic agreements with France and Britain had brought the Russians powerful new allies, while German support for the Austrians increased because they were the only reliable German allies.

Increasing Conflict

Already by 1903 the situation in the Balkans was on its way to becoming critical. Nationalists staged a palace coup in Serbia, a Russian protégé and the strongest independent Balkan State. This development increased tensions in Bosnia-Herzegovina, which had been under Austrian military occupation since 1878 but was not legally Austro-Hungarian. Serb nationalists hoped to end the Austrian occupation and eventually to annex the two provinces. The Serbs demanded autonomy for Bosnia-Herzegovina, giving rise to a new diplomatic crisis.

The Russians hoped to use the affair for their own purposes. In September 1908, Russian Foreign Minister Alexander P. Izvolsky and his Austrian counterpart Lexa von Aehrenthal struck a secret deal: the Russians agreed to formal Austrian annexation of Bosnia-Herzegovina provided that an international conference approved and that the Austrians supported Russian demands on Turkey. Because of internal Turkish developments, however, Austria suddenly annexed Bosnia-Herzegovina without waiting for a conference. When other powers objected to this unilateral change, a major crisis ensued, and Austria moved toward mobilization. The Serbs looked for aid from their Russian protector, but Russia, still weak from defeat in the Japanese war and the 1905 revolution and intimidated by Germany, backed down.

The Bosnian crisis stimulated Slavic nationalism and increased Russian sympathy for the Balkan Slavs. Moreover, Serb nationalists founded the *Narodna Obrana,* or National Defense, society to promote Slavic interests in Bosnia-Herzegovina. Pan-Slavic congresses in 1908 (Prague) and in 1910 (Sofia, Bulgaria) emphasized Slavic kinship and called for national liberation from the Austrians and Turks. Encouraged by this increased activity, the new Russian foreign minister, Sergei D. Sazonov, capitalized on the Libyan War that Turkey fought with Italy in 1911–12 by forging Serbia, Montenegro, Bulgaria, and Greece into an anti-Turkish coalition. In September 1912, those countries attacked Turkey and drove it out of the Balkans in the First Balkan War. The Second Balkan War saw the coalition break up as the former allies fought each other. The result of these wars was a huge gain in territory for Serbia followed by an Austrian ultimatum threatening war if Serbia did not withdraw from territory giving it access to the sea (the area of Albania, formally recognized as independent in 1913). Serbia turned to a still-weak Russia, which backed down in order to avoid a war. The Austrians aimed to prevent Serbia's transformation into a powerful pole of attraction for dissatisfied Slavs in the Dual Monarchy, but the affair increased tensions among the great powers.

The 1912–13 events left Russia embittered and Europe at the brink of war. Russia had suffered two humiliations and could not continue to be humbled without losing its great power status. Serbia still hoped to bring all the Slavs who lived in Austria-Hungary together in one state with Russian support, a goal that threatened Austria-Hungary's existence because it would embolden the other nationalities to secede. Convinced that Serbia must be eliminated as an independent state, the Austrians understood that they could not accomplish this aim without German help because Russia was unlikely to accept another diplomatic humiliation and would go to war. The Germans feared both the collapse of their Austrian ally and the long-term Russian economic and military potential, so a showdown between Russia and Austria-Hungary over the Balkans seemed destined to touch off a war that would bring in their allies.

Emperor Francis Joseph professed to oppose war. He said in November 1912: "I don't want war. I have always been unlucky in wars," but the nationalities question had made a general conflict likely.

ITALY SEARCHES FOR SECURITY

Italy's economic deficiencies made it the weakest of the great powers and severely conditioned its foreign policy. During the early twentieth century, Italy's long-term prime minister, Giovanni Giolitti, followed a prudent foreign policy, and Italian diplomats aimed at achieving security for the country.

The Troubled Triple Alliance

Giolitti and his foreign minister Antonino Di San Giuliano feared that Austria's Balkan policy would drag Italy into war. Both of them made clear to their partners on several occasions that the Triple Alliance was a defensive pact and that on no account would their country enter a conflict provoked by an Austrian desire to suppress Serbia. Italy also had friendly relations with Britain—publicly declaring with the agreement of its allies when it signed the Triple Alliance that it was not directed against Britain—and pursuing friendly relations with France during the early years of the twentieth century.

While relations with France warmed, those with Austria-Hungary cooled primarily because of the poor treatment of the Italian minority in Austria and conflicting interests in the Balkans. By 1908 tensions were so high that the chief of staff of the Austrian Army advocated an attack on Italy when a massive earthquake in Sicily made the country particularly vulnerable. Italian diplomats told their colleagues that only fear of war with each other kept Austria and Italy in the same alliance.

Italy fought Turkey for Libya, the last part of North Africa not colonized by a Western power, in 1911, thus threatening the European diplomatic equilibrium. It was the first war in which air power was used. The Italians were criticized for their brutal treatment of Libyan rebels; such treatment was typical, in varying degrees, of Western imperialism. This picture shows the execution of rebels during or shortly after the conflict.

BIOGRAPHICAL SKETCHES

Francis Joseph Of Hapsburg
Unlucky

Francis Joseph's characterization of himself as unlucky in war applied to his entire life. In fact, the only happy time he had was probably during his childhood, which ended early and abruptly.

Francis Joseph was born on August 18, 1830, the oldest son of the archduke and heir to the throne of Francis Charles and the Archduchess Sophia. His uncle, Emperor Ferdinand I, was mentally unfit to govern, leaving a regency council to rule the Austrian Empire. In 1848 revolutions shook Western Europe, including the Austrian possessions. Vienna came under the control of revolutionaries who were put down only by the ruthlessness of Prince Felix Schwarzenberg. Schwarzenberg forced the incompetent Ferdinand's resignation, and when Francis Charles refused to become emperor, Francis Joseph acceded to the throne on December 2, 1848, at age 18.

Francis Joseph had no governing experience and relied on Schwarzenberg's advice. After the prince's death in 1852, the young emperor was on his own as Austrian power declined precipitously. The Austrians refused to join the Russians against the British and French in the Crimean War (1853–56). Because of former close relations, the Russians considered this failure a betrayal and never forgave

continued

continued

it. Between 1859 and 1866, Austria lost its Italian possessions, and an unfriendly Italy emerged on its borders. In 1866 Prussia drove the Austrians out of Germany, uniting that country under its suzerainty. In 1867, in order to keep Hungary in the empire, Francis Joseph agreed to an arrangement that made Hungary practically independent (the Dual Monarchy).

Bismarck favored friendly relations with Austria-Hungary, and the two countries signed a treaty in 1879. However, because of strategic considerations, he was primarily concerned with placating the Russians rather than the Austrians. After Wilhelm II fired Bismarck in 1890, Austro-German relations became closer because the kaiser gave less weight to the Russian connection and because the two emperors had close personal ties. Francis Joseph's lack of independence from the German emperor contributed to the eventual breakup of the Hapsburg Empire.

Francis Joseph's bad luck in foreign policy extended to his personal and political life. In 1854 he insisted on marrying a sixteen-year-old Bavarian princess Elizabeth (Sissy), against his mother's opposition. His wife and his mother quarreled, and Sissy became more eccentric over the years. The couple had one son, Rudolf, the heir to the throne, born in 1858. Rudolf, more liberal than his father, constantly quarreled with Francis Joseph about politics. In 1889 the unhappy Rudolf committed suicide with his mistress at Mayerling outside Vienna. In yet another tragic occurrence, an Anarchist assassinated Sissy in 1898.

These were not the sum of his misfortunes. Francis Joseph had been particularly close to his younger brother Maximilian, who became involved in an ill-fated French attempt to take over Mexico and claimed its throne. The Mexicans revolted and, despite Francis Joseph's attempts to save him, executed Maximilian on June 19, 1867. In 1896 his other brother, Charles Ludwig, died on a pilgrimage to the Holy Land after he drank disease-laden water. With the deaths of his brothers and his son, the succession passed to Charles Ludwig's son Francis Ferdinand. The new heir did not get along with the old emperor, not the least because he insisted on marrying Sophie Chotek. Sophie did not belong to the restricted noble circle in which royalty married, and their children were ineligible to inherit the throne. On June 28, 1914, assassins killed Francis Ferdinand and his wife, touching off World War I despite the emperor's reluctance. Luckily he died on November 21, 1916, before his empire and dynasty ended. Transformed over the decades after his death into an Austrian national hero, Francis Joseph proved luckier in death than in life.

The Libyan War

The only exception to Giolitti's unadventurous foreign policy was Italy's declaration of war on Turkey in 1911. Italy had long sought colonies and, during the early years of the century, had staked its claim on Libya, the last available area in North Africa. When it seemed that other powers might move into the area if Italy did not act soon, a vociferous Italian Nationalist campaign mobilized public opinion against Giolitti and pressured the prime minister into taking action. For Giolitti, however, the main motivation for war was to make Italy more secure by preventing a takeover of Libya by a great power, possibly Germany, that would install itself on the Mediterranean shore opposite Italy.

The Balkan Peninsula Before the Wars of 1912–1913. The map shows the borders of the small states and the amount of land held by Turkey. With the expulsion of Turkey, the small states fought among themselves for the territory formerly held by the Ottoman Empire, involved the Great Powers, and set the stage for World War I.

In the course of defeating Turkey, Italy gravely weakened it. The Europeans had avoided armed conflicts with Turkey because of fears that it might fall apart and touch off wars for parts of its vast empire. The Libyan War led directly to the Balkan wars of 1912 and 1913 when the Russians brought together the feuding

Balkan states and convinced them to attack Turkey. The wars increased tensions among the big powers and set the stage for World War I.

Bibliographical Essay

Many of the books cited in Chapter 3 have chapters on foreign policy. Good, basic texts on diplomatic history, with coverage of this period include René Albrecht-Carrié, *A Diplomatic History of Europe Since the Congress of Vienna* (New York, 1958), a standard work, and Norman Rich, *Great Power Diplomacy 1814–1914* (New York, 1992). A. J. P. Taylor's *The Struggle for Mastery in Europe 1848–1918* (Oxford, UK, 1954) is a classic. For an understanding of the diplomatic history leading up to the period under discussion, see William L. Langer, *European Alliances and Alignments 1871–1890* (New York, 1950). Patricia A. Weitsman's *Dangerous Alliances: Proponents of Peace, Weapons of War* (Stanford, Calif., 2004) gives a more up-to-date examination of the major alliances during this period.

On the central question of this era, the best work is Paul M. Kennedy, *The Rise of the Anglo-German Antagonism 1860–1914* (London, 1980). This book stands out for its comprehensiveness, insight, and balanced judgments. Kennedy's 1907 citation from the British Admiralty's war plans may be found on p. 310; the quotation on the implications of Germany's economic expansion is on p. 465. A little collection of essays, Donald Read, *Edwardian England* (New Brunswick, N.J., 1982), is excellent on all aspects of British life of the period, but there are two outstanding essays on the armament and foreign policy issues discussed in this chapter: Michael Howard, "The Edwardian Arms Race" (pp. 145–161), and, of note for the sophisticated interpretations of the wider foreign policy of the period, J. A. S. Grenville, "Foreign Policy and the Coming of War" (pp. 162–180).

For more specialized views of Britain's relative economic decline discussed in this chapter, consult Bernard Elbaum and William Lazonick, eds., *The Decline of the British Economy* (Oxford, UK, 1986); the work contains an informative essay on the steel industry before World War I. The collection edited by Derek H. Aldcroft and Harry W. Richardson, *The British Economy 1870–1939* (New York, 1969), also includes illuminating studies, as does Derek H. Aldcroft, ed., *The Development of British Industry and Foreign Competition 1875–1914* (Toronto, 1968). Trade rivalry, a frequently mentioned issue of uncertain impact on the relations between Britain and Germany, is discussed by Ross J. S. Hoffman, *Great Britain and the German Trade Rivalry 1875–1914* (New York, 1964). Look also at the book of essays and interviews by Richard English and Michael Kenny, *Rethinking British Decline* (New York, 2000). Newer books tend to concentrate on the period after World War I to the present, but they usually have material related to the early twentieth century.

On Germany, see Andrew R. Carlson, *German Foreign Policy, 1890–1914, and Colonial Policy to 1914: A Handbook and Annotated Bibliography* (Metuchen, N.J., 1970). The book contains much valuable technical information about foreign and colonial policy and the domestic influences on it. The kaiser's remark on *Weltpolitik* is on p. 16. Ludwig Dehio's classic *Germany and World Politics in the Twentieth Century* (New York, 1959) argues that Germany's wars were in the European tradition of a struggle for continental hegemony and that Germany was preparing to succeed Britain in the early twentieth century. Dehio's book criticizes Germany's foreign policy even while putting it in a wider context, but Gordon Craig, *From Bismarck to Adenauer: Aspects of German Statecraft* (Baltimore, 1958), discusses the personalities involved during this period (usually harshly) and argues that German diplomats proved unequal to the task required by Germany's situation. Peter Alter wrote a history of the German problem in Europe from 1800 to 1990: *The German Question and Europe: A History* (London, 2000). The way the Germans and French saw each other is the subject of Michael E. Nolan, *The Inverted Mirror: Mythologizing the Enemy in France and Germany, 1898–1914* (New York, 2005). Mark Hewitson challenges accepted views in *National Identity and Political Thought in Germany: Wilhelmine Depictions of the French Third Republic, 1890–1914* (New York, 2000).

For Austria, there is Samuel R. Williamson, *Austria-Hungary and the Origins of the First World War* (New York, 1991).

Good studies of different lengths exist on French foreign policy. Frederick L. Schuman's *War and Diplomacy in the French Republic* (New York, 1970) is an excellent and detailed study of how foreign policy was controlled in France, along with accounts of the various crises, the politics influencing them, and how they were handled. The quotations from Bismarck and Paul Déroulède, the nationalist, on Alsace and Lorraine, are cited on p. 21 of the 1923 Creighton lecture by G. P. Gooch, *Franco-German Relations 1871–1914* (New York, 1967), an excellent, brief, and clear account. Charles W. Porter published a specialized, readable, account of Delcassé's aims and action, *The Career of Théophile Delcassé* (Westport, Conn., 1975), at its best when describing how Delcassé built the French relationship with Britain during a difficult period. One of Delcassé's most important collaborators was the French ambassador to England, Paul Cambon (not to be confused with his brother Jules, ambassador to the United States), whose career can be followed in Keith Eubank's *Paul Cambon: Master Diplomatist* (Norman, Okla., 1960). On the Entente Cordiale, see Antoine Capet, *Britain, France, and the Entente Cordiale Since 1904* (New York, 2006), which contains several essays on the period discussed in this chapter, and an examination of the agreement and the British King: *Edward VII and the Entente Cordiale* (London, 2004), by Ian Dunlop. The growth of chauvinism in France during this period is described very well by Eugen Weber, *The Nationalist Revival in France, 1905–1914* (Berkeley, Calif., 1968).

The standard diplomatic history of French and Russian diplomacy at the end of the nineteenth century is Wlilliam L. Langer, *The Franco-Russian Alliance 1890–1894* (New York, 1967), but see the book by Fiona K. Tomaszewski, *A Great Russia: Russia and the Triple Entente* (Westport, Conn., 2002). Michael Hughes's *Diplomacy Before the Russian Revolution* (New York, 2000) examines relations between Britain and Russia. Alan Sharp and Glyn Stone produced a book on British-French rivalry, *Anglo-French Relations in the Twentieth Century* (New York, 2002). A history examining a similar topic over a hundred years is Philippe Chassaigne and M. L. Dockrill, *Anglo-French Relations, 1898–1998* (New York, 2002). George F. Kennen's *The Fateful Alliance; France, Russia, and the Coming of the First World War* (New York, 1984) is a work by a famous American diplomat. *United Government and Foreign Policy in Russia, 1910–1914* (Cambridge, Mass., 1992) is an overview.

Barbara Jelavich's *A Century of Russian Foreign Policy 1814–1914* (Philadelphia, 1964) is a good survey of the topic, while the same author's *Russia's Balkan Entanglements, 1806–1914* (New York, 1991) puts the question into historical context. For an understanding of the Turkish situation in relation to big-power imperialism, see Edward Mead Earle, *Turkey, the Great Powers, and the Baghdad Railway* (New York, 1966). Ronald Park Bobroff's *Roads to Glory* (London, 2006) examines Russia and the Straits question.

Two works that address Austrian foreign policy in a scholarly and well-documented manner are F. R. Bridge, *From Sadowa to Sarajevo: The Foreign Policy of Austria-Hungary, 1866–1914* (London, 1972), and the brief treatment by Barbara Jelavich, *The Hapsburg Empire in European Affairs, 1814–1918* (Chicago, 1969).

Italian foreign policy during this period has not received much specialized treatment in English, and the interpretations frequently tend to be colored by later developments or by unreasonable assumptions. Spencer M. Di Scala's *Vittorio Orlando:*

Italy (Makers of the Modern World series) (London, 2010) offers a different view of prewar Italian diplomacy. Among the more objective treatments of the subject, see William C. Askew's chapter in Lillian Parker Wallace and William C. Askew, eds., *Power, Public Opinion, and Diplomacy: Essays in Honor of Eber Malcolm Carroll by His Former Students* (New York, 1968), "The Austro-Italian Antagonism, 1896–1914"—an outstanding overview of the subject. Askew also wrote the diplomatic history of the Libyan War's origins and impact, *Europe and Italy's Acquisition of Libya 1911–1912* (Durham, N.C., 1942). R. J. B. Bosworth, *Italy, the Least of the Great Powers* (London, 1979), is marred by too close an identification of this period with later ones. R. A. Webster's *Industrial Imperialism in Italy, 1908–1915* (Berkeley, Calif., 1975) is an examination of Italian industrial development and its connection to imperialism.

✍

CHAPTER 5

European Peripheries

CHAPTER OUTLINE

Scandinavia: An Ideal Unity • Different Roads: The Low Countries •
The Making of a Conservative: Switzerland • The Iberian States •
Southeastern Europe

BIOGRAPHICAL SKETCHES

Niels Henrik David Bohr, "Uncle Nick" • Émile Vandervelde,
Evolutionary Socialist

Although the smaller countries of Europe lacked the military power of the larger states, they had enormous influence on the continent's intellectuals, as the careers of Danish storyteller Hans Christian Andersen, the Swedish writer August Strindberg, and the Norwegian playwright Henrik Ibsen testify. Twentieth-century Scandinavia presented interesting new social democratic models of organizing modern society, while the Low Countries and Switzerland had a disproportionate impact in the economic and colonial areas. The Iberian states offered the lesson of once-great powers that languished in the modern age, only to conserve unsuspected energies that allowed them to flourish by the end of the century. The countries of southeastern Europe presented a different picture—restless, turbulent states whose resentments and ambitions critically affected the course of world history.

The states of the European peripheries thus presented a highly differentiated but important picture of the continent at the beginning of the twentieth century.

SCANDINAVIA: AN IDEAL UNITY

The independent Scandinavian states—Sweden, Norway, and Denmark—had been united in the Union of Kalmar from 1363 to1434, but even after this union ended, the cultural interchange and the idea of political collaboration remained strong and still characterizes the area.

The small countries of Europe, sometimes neglected, had a major influence on the continent's history in the twentieth century.

Swedish Democracy

Modern democracy in Sweden has it origins in the eighteenth century, when an era of strong, warlike kings ended with the death of Charles XII in 1718. An Age of Freedom followed, in which a seesaw political struggle between the kings and representative institutions occurred, and the Swedes adopted a constitution in 1809, Europe's oldest written document of its kind. The executive branch retained considerable powers, but the Riksdag (Parliament) voted taxes and exercised joint power with the king. The king appointed the government (Council of State), but it was accountable to the Riksdag. The constitution opened up offices to all social groups, but nobles still enjoyed tax advantages and the division of the Riksdag into four estates (nobility, clergy, peasant, and burgesses) gave greater representation to the privileged classes. By 1841, after the growth of an industrial middle class, a shift in the balance of power to the legislative branch had occurred. In 1865, the First Chamber, indirectly elected on a weighed vote dependent on income, and the Second Chamber, elected directly with a property qualification for voters, replaced the four estates, gave power to the urban middle class, but excluded the city workers and rural laborers. In 1889 the Social Democratic Party was founded and joined the Swedish trade unions in championing the demands of the growing ranks of workers produced by increasing industrialization. This situation led to more strikes during the early years of the new century and the government's passage of legislation regulating workers' safety, workers' compensation, diminished social strife, and an extension of the vote following a 1905 electoral victory for leftist groups. A compromise combined male universal suffrage and proportional representation for the Second Chamber and a more complicated proportional system for the First Chamber. Clearly delineated parties emerged, with farmers, industrialists, and the upper-middle class composing the Right and Liberal groups (urban radicals, small farmers, tradesmen) and Social Democrats (factory workers and the lower-middle class) making up the Left, with both open to collaboration. In 1911 the Social Democrats renounced orthodox Marxism and cooperated with Liberals in the Riksdag, while conservatives accepted reforms they believed inevitable and helped enact them into law. In 1919, the Swedes extended voting privileges to women.

Swedish Economic Progress
Economic progress paralleled political developments. The industrial revolution had created vast demands for lumber, which Sweden possessed in abundance, and the timber industry powerfully stimulated the economy, helped as well by free trade legislation. In 1858 a Swedish industrialist perfected the Bessemer method and opened up the age of modern steel. The need to haul products over long

Alfred Nobel, inventor of dynamite, was a businessman and a man of peace. He established the famous Nobel Prizes in five categories that are the most prestigious in their fields. The prizes include the Peace Prize, awarded in Oslo because at the time of their institution Sweden and Norway were a single country, while the other prizes are awarded in Stockholm.

distances stimulated construction of a railway network, built through the cooperative efforts of the state and private enterprise. People assembled everywhere "in countless numbers to gaze on the splendour" of the railway. Alfred Nobel, who later instituted the prizes named after him, patented dynamite, Lars Magnus Ericsson invented the table telephone and founded a company with worldwide sales, Alexander Lagerman built a machine to mass produce matches, and Sven Wingquist developed the modern ball bearing. Notable progress also occurred in agriculture. The Swedes resisted the protectionist policies adopted by many countries to confront the crisis of cheap American and Russian grains flooding Western Europe and switched to the production of dairy products and sugar beets and the machinery necessary to process them.

In the early twentieth century, the Swedish economy boomed with new technology, such as the invention of methods for making brown paper from wood pulp and for working Swedish iron ore, rich in phosphates. Sweden emerged as an important player in the new industries of the second industrial revolution: electricity, the telephone, and related products. This expanding economic activity led to the development of new credit institutions that helped change Swedish life. This impressive economic activity changed the nature of Swedish emigration. It remained sizable, but the new emigrants were better educated and prosperous than in the past.

Norwegian Democracy

A combination of democratic reform, social advance, and industrial growth also characterized Norway. The greatest problem at the beginning of the twentieth century was a union with Sweden, imposed by the Great Powers in 1814, by which the Swedish monarch ruled both countries. However, Norway already had a constitution and a unique parliament, the Storthing, which combined the characteristics of a unicameral and a bicameral legislature. Voted in by a restricted number of electors, the Storthing elected one-third of its members to a separate house, the Lagthing, while the remaining members constituted the Odelsthing. By July 1884 the Storthing sitting together gained the right to name the government.

End of the Union with Sweden

Despite its domestic independence, Norwegians chafed at their subordination to Sweden in foreign policy and Swedish control of the consular service. Norway possessed the world's third-largest merchant marine, and Norwegian captains and businessmen resented having to turn to Swedish consuls to handle their business matters abroad. Resolution of the dispute failed in 1905, and in June the Norwegians dissolved the union. Norway made military preparations to resist possible Swedish action, but instead a referendum resulted in the union's official end and the selection of a Danish prince as the new king of an independent Norway.

Important political reforms followed. Election to the Storthing was made direct, and in 1919 proportional representation was instituted in national elections. Women gained the right to vote sooner than in other countries. The leader of the movement, Frederikke Marie Quam, had supported the dissolution of the Swedish union by securing the signature of hundreds of thousands of women.

In 1907 women with high incomes, who in 1901 had been given the vote in local elections, secured that right in national contests. In 1910 all women received the vote on an equal basis with men in local elections and in 1913 in national elections.

Novel Economic Experiments
A combination of private initiative and state activity brought unprecedented prosperity to the country in the decade following 1905. Railroad building reached a fever pitch after 1908, and new steamship lines improved communication between coastal areas. The old sailing fleet rapidly converted to steam, and in 1910 the Norwegian American Line entered the Atlantic route. The Norwegian fishing fleet was rapidly modernized, a telephone network was built, and facilities for the extraction of nitrogen from the air and modern hydroelectric plants materialized. The enormous development of electricity from Norwegian waterways made the country one of the earliest to be sensitive to ecological matters. Between 1906 and 1909, the Storthing passed the first modern concession laws restricting the purchase and use of forests.

Norwegians addressed traditional social concerns under the guidance of the Liberal (or Left) Party. Between 1909 and 1915, a wave of social legislation established or strengthened accident insurance for industrial workers, health insurance, and aid for mothers and illegitimate children. Legislation established mediation of labor disputes and a labor court to settle differences over contracts. In agriculture, the government encouraged land ownership, a policy that produced a stunning increase in the number of small farms, and established agricultural schools to introduce and maintain the highest standards.

Denmark's Anguished Politics
Once the most important Scandinavian country, Denmark's proximity to the big powers made its political and foreign affairs history more turbulent as it became embroiled in French Revolutionary affairs and in the wars for German unification.

The modern Danish constitution has its origins in the 1848 revolutions that forced the Danish king to issue the June Constitution that guaranteed freedom of the press and of religion and established a Rigsdag (Parliament). Composed of the lower house (the Folketing), elected by men aged thirty and older who were not on relief, and an upper chamber (the Landsting), indirectly elected by property owners at least forty years of age, the Parliament shared the legislative power with the king. In July 1866, however, a new, more conservative constitution that ensured the government a perpetual majority in the upper house came into force and precipitated a political struggle between the Left and Right for the next thirty years. In 1901 the conservative parties were defeated, and the king appointed a government that had the confidence of the majority party in the Folketing, opening up an era of parliamentary democracy.

In 1905, radical townspeople and poorer rural inhabitants founded the Radical Left Party, which supported the breakup up of large estates, the cession of land to landless peasants, and reduced military expenditures. This party, in alliance with the Social Democrats, emerged supreme in 1913 and remained a staple of Danish politics for the next fifty years. The coalition favored constitutional changes, and in June 1915 the constitution was liberalized and power was shared. Men and women over age twenty-five would elect the Folketing, while conservative control of the Landsting was assured by indirect elections and a higher age requirement.

Danish Economic and Social Change

Steady economic and social progress occurred in Denmark from the mid-nineteenth century with the application of steam-engine technology to the manufacturing sector, the growing ability of peasants to own their land free and clear, the end of trade monopolies once enjoyed by urban areas, and end of guild control of manufacturing. The government reduced tariffs and fees on seaborne traffic, measures that helped the Danish merchant fleet to convert to steam and stimulated its rapid growth. Industrial development encouraged construction of a railway network to connect vital parts of the country, and the development of iron and steel manufacturing, food processing, and porcelain production.

Growing industrialization brought with it an expanding proletariat, a Social Democratic Party, social legislation, and labor organizations. In 1903, laws facilitated entrance into higher schools. The tax system was modernized with the abolition of church tithes and the institution of general property, progressive income, and wealth taxes. Women won the right to vote in local elections in 1908. During the early twentieth century, strikes and lockouts agitated the country but labor unions and employers defined the conditions for strikes and agreed on procedural rules for resolving disputes that lasted until 1960. In 1907, the state began paying subsidies to trade unions for their unemployment funds and for poor relief. These compromises resulted in the doubling of real wages for Danish workers in the forty years before 1914.

The major innovations in the Danish economy came on the land. The cheap American and Russian grain that flooded Europe beginning in the 1870s threw European agriculture into crisis and forced most countries to impose high tariffs, but the Danes turned away from cereal growing and towards lucrative dairy and cattle production. The invention of appliances necessary for the working of dairy products encouraged farmers to band together and spurred creation of producers' and consumers' cooperatives that collaborated in the exportation of bacon and eggs to the English breakfast table. Specialized schools and the Folk High School Movement spread knowledge of the new agricultural techniques, and Danish cooperatives became a model for Europe.

The World Center of Quantum Physics

The Danish capacity for innovation during the early twentieth century is illustrated in the transformation of its capital, Copenhagen, into one of the world's most important centers of science. The Danish physicist, Niels Bohr, had gone to Manchester, England, to study with British physicists J. J. Thompson and Ernest Rutherford in 1911 and 1912. Bohr, a graduate of the University of Copenhagen,

The gates of the Carlsberg Brewery in Copenhagen, Denmark. It was on these grounds that Niels Bohr eventually took residence and where major advances in quantum physics were made—all financed with the proceeds from the sale of Carlsberg beer.

became intrigued with Rutherford's model of the atom and in 1913 published a fundamental paper on its quantum structure.

When Bohr returned to Copenhagen, the Royal Danish Academy of Science financed an institute for theoretical physics for him. The academy granted fellowships to physicists from all over the world to study atomic physics with Bohr. The roster of physicists who arrived in Copenhagen reads like a who's who of the giants of modern physics: Germans, Italians, Americans, Belgians, Swedes, Dutch, Japanese, Russians. Among them, Bohr's "children," the proudest boast was: "I used to work with Bohr."

Bohr's story has an interesting connection with Danish economics and cultural outlook because the Carlsberg Brewery made much of this scientific activity possible. The founder of the brewery willed the academy the income from the proceeds of the business. In the 1930s, with the death of the previous occupant of a mansion built for the brewery's founder on the grounds of his establishment, Bohr and his family took up residence in it. The sales of Carlsberg beer built Bohr's institute, paid for the fellowships to visiting scientists, and had a crucial role in the development of atomic theory that changed the world.

DIFFERENT ROADS: THE LOW COUNTRIES

Like the Scandinavian countries, the Low Countries—the Netherlands and Belgium—once had the same ruler. Unlike Scandinavia, language, culture, and religion caused serious problems and hardened divisions. The Dutch language pulled the Netherlands into the German cultural orbit, while French civilization attracted the French-speaking Belgians. Also living in Belgium were the Flemish, who were closer to the Dutch. Belgium was thus an ethnically divided land and has remained so. Religious differences accentuated the linguistic-cultural split in the Low Countries. In the sixteenth century Spain ruled both countries, but the Dutch revolted and established Calvinism as the predominant religion while Belgium remained predominantly Catholic. In 1815 the Congress of Vienna gave Belgium to the Kingdom of the Netherlands, but the Belgians successfully revolted in 1830. Between 1830 and 1839 the European powers recognized Belgium's independence and agreed to its neutralization.

BIOGRAPHICAL SKETCHES

Niels Henrik David Bohr
"Uncle Nick"

Niels Bohr, one of the most influential physicists of the twentieth century, was born in Copenhagen on October 7, 1885. His father taught physiology at the University of Copenhagen, where Niels and his younger brother Harald, a famous mathematician, both studied. Their mother Ellen Adler was the daughter of an assimilated Jewish politician. The Bohr family's intellectual activities gave the children a deep respect for learning, and Niels received a doctorate in physics in 1911.

Bohr won a Carlsberg foundation grant to study with J. J. Thompson in Cambridge, England, but left in March 1912 to work with Ernest Rutherford. During the next year, he published three fundamental papers, presenting the now-familiar model of the atom with electrons orbiting around the nucleus. He indicated that each successive orbit could contain more electrons than the inner ones and that atoms gave off radiation when electrons jumped to different orbits—the "quantum leap." Bohr applied the quantum theory to atomic structure, becoming a leader in the elaboration of the quantum mechanics that revolutionized physics in the 1920s and winning the Nobel Prize in 1922. Bohr's theories, including the "liquid drop" model of the atomic nucleus, proved essential for the explanation of fission and the development of the atomic bomb.

Bohr received a chair in theoretical physics at the University of Copenhagen in 1916 and began planning for his celebrated physics institute that opened in 1921. He remained its director until he died. With Bohr's institute, Copenhagen became the world center of quantum studies, hosting famous physicists from all over the world. "Bohr's Boys" reported him to be a slow thinker with a low-key style and a voice so soft it frequently could not be heard. At conferences brilliant young physicists would explain complicated theories that everybody immediately understood and applauded, except for Bohr. He would stubbornly request explanations of a simple point. Soon no one understood anything anymore, except for Bohr, who began to understand. In the end, what he got from the lecture was different from what everyone else had understood, and correct, while the lecturer was frequently wrong. In addition to physics, Bohr loved sports and westerns. His favorite films included *The Gun Fight at the Lazy Gee Ranch* and *The Lone Ranger and a Sioux Girl*. He would cajole his friends into going to the movies with him and ask constant questions about the plot during the show, annoying the audience. He developed a scientific theory of why the good guy always wins gunfights, tested it with his students using toy guns, and turned out to be right.

Bohr remained in Denmark when the Germans occupied the country during World War II. His favorite student Werner Heisenberg, in charge of the German atomic bomb project, visited him. The two had a long conversation that remains mysterious and controversial, but relations between the two scientists were cold from then on. When resistance operatives informed the part-Jewish Bohr that the Germans were about to arrest him, a Danish fisherman rowed him to the Swedish shore, where a British Mosquito bomber flew him to Britain. Bohr occupied the tail gunner's position and could communicate only by intercom. Over the North Sea the pilot asked how he was but could get no answer. Distressed, he rushed to the tail section after he landed—to find Bohr fast asleep.

Out of the Nazi clutches, Bohr participated in the building of the atomic bomb under the alias Nicholas Baker—"Uncle Nick." In 1944 he wrote to President Franklin Delano Roosevelt urging international cooperation for the control of nuclear weapons, and after the war became a powerful voice advocating peaceful uses for the atom. In 1957 he received the first Atoms for Peace Award given by the United States. On November 18, 1962, in his beloved Copenhagen, Niels Bohr died of a heart attack.

ECONOMIC PROGRESS

Dutch Economic Development

Splitting off from the more industrially advanced South stimulated the growth of industry in the Netherlands. Glass and porcelain manufacturing, cloth production, railways, shipbuilding, electricity, and chemicals all boomed, helped by the coal and oil reserves of the Dutch East Indies. Postal and currency reform, an extensive canal system, and the telegraph strengthened communications; Amsterdam, Rotterdam, and The Hague all expanded greatly. In agriculture, the Netherlands became the major producer of butter and margarine, while traditional sources of income, such as the diamond industry, flourished.

Political and religious problems made it difficult to address the growing problem of workers' discontent that accompanied industrialization. Originally the Dutch constitution reserved most power for the monarch, and in the constitutional debate, Liberals backed by Catholic groups fought against Calvinist conservatives linked to the Dutch Reformed Church. The crisis ended in a victory for Parliament in 1868 and in 1898, females were allowed to succeed to the throne in the person of William's daughter Wilhelmina.

The Influence of Dutch Socialism

Constitutional alterations allowed the Netherlands to confront the growing discontent caused by expansion of the factory system, low wages, and long working days that led to bad diet, poor sanitary conditions, low life expectancy, and alcoholism. In 1881, Ferdinand Domela Nieuwenhuis founded the Social Democratic Union (SDB) that favored revolution, but in 1894 the Dutch revisionists organized themselves into the Social Democratic Labor Party (SDAP) and defeated the Nieuwenhuis faction.

In the meantime, the Liberal-run government tried instituting social reforms to slow the growth of socialism. By 1901, Parliament had prohibited the employment of children under age twelve, limited women's working hours, implemented factory inspections, and made accident insurance mandatory for all workers. Between 1900 and 1905, the state established compulsory education and gave the local authorities the power to set minimum housing standards. Intervention in the medical field culminated in a 1912 law providing medical services to the poor.

These reforms left the Dutch Socialists unsatisfied, and when a conservative cabinet came to power in 1901, labor disturbances increased and culminated in a great rail strike in 1903. Fortunately, the period from 1903 to 1914 brought economic prosperity and moderate conservative businesspeople supported reform. In 1907, labor contracts brought employment under the purview of the States General; the fifty-eight-hour workweek for women and children arrived in 1910; between 1905 and 1913, secondary and university education was reformed; and in 1917 the stated mandated equal subsidies for public and private schools.

The voting system was also reformed. In 1917 Socialist-championed universal male suffrage arrived, along with proportional representation. Women won the right to be elected but, strangely, not the vote. However, in a struggle spearheaded by Wilhelmina Drucker and her Free Association of Women, women won full voting rights in 1922. Dutch women made important progress during the early twentieth century. In 1901 legislation ensured that a woman's property did not automatically become her husband's, and in 1909 women gained the right to file paternity suits.

The Dutch had an active foreign policy. They fought a long war against Indonesian rebels to maintain their control of the area, but in Europe they stood out for their peace efforts. They remained unofficially neutral and gained notoriety as the host of the First International Peace Conference, held at The Hague in 1899. This conference was a celebrated attempt to implement international law conventions. Dutch support of the Afrikaners (Dutch immigrant descendants in South Africa) during the Boer War won world attention. Because of their close cultural affinity and empathy for the Germans, Dutch diplomats talked about an alliance with them to avoid invasion in case of war and rebuffed a Belgian request to coordinate military measures in case of a German attack.

Divided Belgium

The progressive nature of Belgian politics and the region's intense and rapid industrialization following the 1830 revolution contrasted with the Netherlands. The country had a strong constitutional tradition but struggled with the reality of its division into two conflicting language and cultural groups and the power of the Catholic Church.

The Belgian Constitutional Tradition

The Belgian constitution of 1831 was a model for European Liberals. The document mandated a cabinet responsible to Parliament consisting of two houses—the Chamber of Representatives and the Senate—both directly elected.

In the early twentieth Century the Dutch worked hard to formulate international laws regarding the conduct of war, despite the excessive force they sometimes employed to maintain their colonial rule in Indonesia. Here is a street scene in The Hague, the Netherlands, probably in 1910, location of the first international peace conferences. Note the pedestrians dressed in Indonesian attire.

Although property qualifications limited the electorate, it was still the largest in terms of the proportion to the population. The constitution guaranteed fundamental liberties, including freedom of speech, the press, assembly, and association, and severely limited arbitrary state action. These were unusual features at the time. In practice, weak cabinets had difficulty confronting energetic kings, who successfully exercised greater authority than the constitution gave them, but the constitution's flexibility and a national consensus that the parliamentary system was the best means of resolving intractable problems made it a work in progress. For example, Belgium introduced compulsory universal male suffrage in 1893, although it was conditioned by plural voting dependent on property and education, which was rectified only in 1899. The record was poor when it came to the vote for women; women gained limited suffrage in 1921 and full voting rights in national elections only in 1948.

An Industrial Powerhouse
Belgium was the first country to which the industrial revolution spread—along with the steam engine and the railroad—in the early nineteenth century after its introduction in England. It very quickly became an industrial powerhouse diffusing the new technology. By 1900 Belgium ranked as one of the most heavily industrialized areas in Europe, building railroads and developing modern enterprises all over the world: "Belgian locomotives, railway tracks, tramlines, gas, electrical and coal-mining plant and steelworks combines could be found from Siam to Spain and from Russia to South America."

This rapid industrialization brought social problems in its wake: low wages, long working hours, strikes, and the growth of socialism. Unions and workers' cooperatives emerged, and in 1885 the Belgian Labor Party was founded. In 1893 the Socialists called a great general strike in support of universal male suffrage. Led by their noted leader Émile Vandervelde, they also demanded free education, shorter working hours for women and children, the legalization of trade unions, and an income tax. With Socialist encouragement, Belgium became a model for the European cooperative movement. Alongside the Socialists, a strong Christian Democratic movement demanded social justice in line with Pope Leo XIII's landmark 1891 encyclical *Rerum Novarum*. This activity spurred the passage of laws to protect workers, including the restriction of working hours for women and children, housing for workers, workers' insurance, and pensions.

Struggle with the Church
The development of the industrial sector did not resolve the deep divisions in Belgian society. Belgium suffered from a typical nineteenth-century malady that lasted well into the twentieth: the Catholic-Liberal schism. The governing Liberals favored a secular state, while the Catholics, conditioned by Pope Pius IX's hostility to liberalism, rejected the Liberal constitution. Combat between the two concepts took place mainly in education, culminating in the 1878 School War. The Liberals attempted to reverse a law that had established secular schools in the cities and Catholic ones in rural areas, both at state expense, by mandating nonchurch schools controlled by the state for all communes. For many Belgians, the legislation violated religious precepts and local autonomy, and they protested by transferring their children from the state schools to newly established Catholic institutions.

In 1884 the Catholics defeated the Liberals and retained control of the government until World War I. They mandated compulsory religious instruction in all schools and authorized local officials to provide subsidies to Catholic schools. This policy resulted in serious underfunding of non-Catholic schools in Catholic communes, while suppression of the ministry of education and the weakening of state oversight of education lowered standards. In 1910, the illiteracy rate was estimated at 10 percent, causing concern and prompting King Leopold II to intervene to check Catholic extremists.

The Flemish Problem
In addition to the serious challenge of the religious issue, the Flemish problem threatened to dismember the state. Dominated by the French-speaking Walloons, the Belgian government made French the official language of the country following independence. Local governmental officials and the primary schools used Flemish, but French was the language of the law, the army, and higher education. Flemish suffered from de facto discrimination because higher officials could not understand it, and Flemings had to learn a second language if they wished to go on to higher education and advance in the bureaucracy and political life.

BIOGRAPHICAL SKETCHES

Émile Vandervelde
Evolutionary Socialist

Despite many splits in the prewar European Socialist parties before 1914, the prevailing theory advocated the gradual achievement of socialism through parliamentary reforms. Émile Vandervelde, born in Ixelles, Belgium, on January 25, 1866, was a universally respected theoretician of this ideology, in addition to a skilled practitioner.

Having joined the Belgian Workers' Party in 1889, Vandervelde quickly assumed a leading role in the party. He received a doctorate in social sciences in 1891 and in 1894 won election to Parliament as a Socialist. He favored peasant cooperatives, contributed articles to the most influential European Socialist journals, and published several books expounding his Socialist ideas. He led the battle for universal male suffrage in Belgium, granted in 1914.

Vandervelde's writings and avid participation in international Socialist affairs made him one of the best-known leaders of his time. He won election as president of the Socialist (Second) International in 1900 and remained its head until 1918. This organization of Socialist parties was supposed to coordinate their action, but it collapsed when it failed to prevent World War I from breaking out. When the Germans invaded Belgium in 1914, Valdervelde joined the cabinet and remained in the government throughout the war. Following the conflict, he participated in the talks leading to the Versailles treaty and obtained the inclusion of a clause advocating the eight-hour workday and other measures favorable to labor. As minister of justice in 1919, he implemented a series of penal reforms and a law that greatly reduced alcoholism in the country. Throughout the postwar period, he remained an active and visible participant in international Socialist politics.

In 1925, Vandervelde became foreign minister in a Socialist-Catholic coalition government following the success of the Workers' Party in the elections of that year. As foreign minister, he helped negotiate the Locarno Pact of 1925, an agreement among Germany, France, Britain, Belgium, and Italy that promised a new era of peace. He resigned his post in 1927 when the opposition criticized him for his antimilitarism and for advocating the reduction of compulsory military service to six months. Vandervelde rejoined the Belgian cabinet from 1935 to 1936 as a minister without portfolio and from 1936 to 1937 as the minister of public health. On January 29, 1937, he resigned in protest against the government's neutral stance in the Spanish Civil War that pitted the Fascist and Nazi-backed rebellion of Generalissimo Francisco Franco against the legitimate government of the second Spanish republic.

Since 1924 Vandervelde had held a chair at the University of Brussels. After he left public life, he devoted his time to teaching law. Émile Vandervelde died in Brussels on December 27, 1938.

Besides the language issue, the Flemish areas of Belgium failed to keep pace with the country's economic development and were increasingly dominated by the French-speaking bourgeoisie. A study showed that fewer than 10 percent of Flemings knew French and that of Belgium's 382 high civil servants, only 22 were Flemish. Popular discontent after an 1866 incident in which the state executed two Flemings after a trial conducted in French, which they did not understand, led to a series of laws that were designed to improve the Flemish condition. This legislation was frequently not enforced, but with the extension of suffrage in 1893, the Flemish population gained more political clout because Liberals, Catholics, and Socialists vied for their votes. In 1898, Parliament decreed the legal equality of Flemings and Walloons.

Far from calming the waters, this success encouraged demands for ethnic favoritism in Flanders and bilingualism in government, which, in turn, led to the proliferation of French-speaking Walloon defensive associations bent on preserving their position. The Walloon-Flemish split defied resolution, and a Walloon politician informed the king of the "enormous and horrifying truth: there are no Belgians. . . . You are reigning over two different peoples." Events during World War I—ethnic unrest in the Belgian army and German attempts to exploit it—and following World War II confirmed that harsh judgment.

Belgian Foreign Affairs

Belgium's strategic position in Europe and its African possessions gave it an importance disproportionate to its small size, and its foreign policy stands out for the role of its kings. In 1885, King Leopold II successfully gained control of the

King Leopold II of Belgium, whose rule in the Belgian Congo was so vicious that it qualified as the first genocide of the twentieth century. He owned the Congo personally and made a vast fortune from it. Eventually the Belgian Parliament had to take away control from him because his brutal methods there aroused international indignation.

Congo Free State, a central African territory eighty times the size of Belgium. Even though the Congo belonged to him and not to the country, this vast mineral-rich area brought numerous economic benefits to the Belgians. Leopold's shameless use of slave labor and mass killings to enrich himself and enforce his rule gave rise to "the first great international human rights movement of the twentieth century" and forced the Belgian Parliament to intervene.

Another area in which the kings took an active role was in preparing for the danger of an invasion despite the country's neutralized status. Belgian monarchs unsuccessfully tried to convince Parliament that in case of war, the Germans might try to outflank the French by going through Belgium. In order to prevent Belgium from being quickly overrun, however, the Belgians either had to abandon their neutrality or reinforce their defenses. The first choice was impossible; the second unpopular. Only in 1913 did the Belgians agree to increase the size of the army and bolster their fortifications—too late. In 1914 the Belgian armed forces fought the German invasion bravely but unprepared and alone.

THE MAKING OF A CONSERVATIVE: SWITZERLAND

Besides Belgium, the other European neutral, Switzerland, also struggled to maintain its neutrality, recognized on March 20, 1815, in the face of periodic pressure from the great powers. The country adopted a novel organization of its armed forces, the "armed nation" by which its citizens received military training and took their rifles home with them. This and the rugged mountainous terrain was enough to discourage attacks by larger powers. Switzerland's trust in its citizens made it a darling of European radical movements, but with increasing prosperity came greater conservatism, unfriendliness to exiles, and a shrewd capacity to profit from neutrality. The country of democracy-obsessed, freedom-loving mountaineers emerged in the twentieth century as a haven for funds sent by unsavory rulers who were threatened by their subjects. By the end of the century, these distasteful aspects would characterize Switzerland for many foreigners.

Swiss Direct Democracy and Its Involution

The origins of Swiss direct democracy can be traced back to the thirteenth century, when leaders from Switzerland's forest, mountainous, and plateau areas banded together in common defense against the Holy Roman emperors. After securing their formal independence in 1648, the cantons set up a system to arbitrate differences among themselves and established a weak confederation with a Diet possessing few powers in order to maintain maximum local autonomy. After the centralizing efforts of the French Revolution, in which Switzerland was involved, the Swiss adopted the Pact of 1815 by which the cantons regained their sovereignty and the central state lost practically all its powers. During the nineteenth century, wars between Protestant radicals and Catholic conservatives ended with a Catholic defeat and the promulgation of a new constitution on September 12, 1848, that created a unique balance between federalism and centralism by the creation of a bicameral legislature consisting of the National Council elected by men aged twenty and older representing the nation as a whole and the Council of States, modeled on the American Senate, representing the cantons. In setting up the executive branch, however, the Swiss rejected the American presidential model because they believed it would foster monarchy or dictatorship. They opted for a seven-man executive, the Federal Council, voted in by the legislature. The legislature also elected a Supreme Federal Court.

In 1874, the Swiss introduced the popular initiative and the referendum, institutions that promoted the famous image of Swiss direct democracy. In fact, however, these institutions had a major impact on the country's political orientation by ensuring that major changes in policy would only occur very slowly if at all. The requirement that the people be consulted meant effective and frequent use of the referendum to block progressive measures. Swiss direct democracy paradoxically encouraged the country's drift in an increasingly conservative direction as Switzerland became more prosperous and sought to keep outsiders from sharing its wealth. The Swiss had continual problems with minorities, even before a large number of persons immigrated to the country later in the twentieth century, and in 1866 Switzerland was the last Western European country to grant civil rights to the Jews, primarily for trade reasons and under French pressure. The Swiss stubbornly refused to grant women the right to vote in federal matters, and, despite a strong suffrage movement, women received voting rights in some cantons only in the latter years of the twentieth century.

A positive aspect of the Swiss constitution was its suitability for a country that was composed of different linguistic groups and religions. Switzerland has three official languages, German, French, and Italian, with only 1 percent of the population speaking Romanche, the other national language. The population is evenly divided between Protestants and Catholics who once fiercely opposed each other.

Economic and Social Development

The Swiss economy followed general European trends. In agriculture, the Swiss offset the price decline that affected grains beginning in the 1870s by increasing production from pasture and dairy farming, especially cheese, and these activities remained lucrative into the twenty-first century. Cotton weaving and silk production prospered, and Switzerland maintained its domination of the watchmaking craft. The country participated in the industrial boom touched off by railway building, initially run by private enterprise and later taken over by the state. Locomotives, electric power plants, and different types of machinery headed a long list of exports that, along with tourism, helped pay for the resource-poor country's imports. Banking, the activity that would become synonymous with Switzerland, was not a major activity in the early twentieth century, but grew dramatically during and after the two world wars.

The rise of industry stimulated the rise of a Socialist party and demands for social legislation, which was initially enacted by the cantons and later by the federal government. In the late nineteenth and early twentieth centuries, legislation limited the workday, restricted women and child labor, and introduced factory inspections, health regulation, and industrial accident, unemployment and old age insurance.

The social and economic development of Switzerland, Scandinavia, and the Low Countries thus followed general West European trends, but in the South and Southeast it was a different story.

THE IBERIAN STATES

Spain and Portugal both confronted the twentieth century with a heavy legacy of greatness and decay.

Spain

Political Chaos in Spain

During the seventeenth century, Spain had dominated Europe and constructed a vast empire in the New World, but Spanish monarchs rapidly squandered the wealth, and the country became the "sick man" of Europe. During the next century, Spain remained divided between liberal and conservative forces, entrenched in different geographic areas that fought over whether the king or the legislature would have political power into the mid-twentieth century. A liberal constitution implemented in 1876 brought some stability, but in 1902 King Alfonso XIII implemented personal rule.

Social Disintegration

By the twentieth century, political and economic turbulence in Spain had resulted in large landholders greatly increasing their possessions while smaller holdings shrank. Pauperization of the rural population and massive emigration to the cities was widespread, and an oversupply of unskilled labor, depressed wages, and unemployment characterized them. Because of extreme poverty, the Spanish population was in no position to stimulate a demand for new products. Industrial growth consequently faltered, and Spain could not successfully absorb the increased population. Railroad building arrived late, investment remained in the hands of foreigners and wealthy Spaniards, and wealth was badly distributed. As modern problems exacerbated the old, the nobles, bourgeoisie, and large landowners maintained their economic and social domination through a tacit understanding between the Liberal and Conservative parties that alternated in government and did not adopt measures that might change the social situation. Spanish cabinets favored private entrepreneurs and passed social legislation only late and under the pressure of demonstrations. The political compromise brought a false political stability and allowed Alfonso XIII to make a sham of parliamentary institutions. Most important, it resulted in an abiding distrust of politics and forced opponents to act outside the discredited political system.

Leftist Violence and Rightist Reaction

This disenchantment produced disorder. The Anarchists dominated labor organizations and leftist politics into the 1930s, its labor federation counting four times as many members as its Socialist counterpart. In 1879 the typesetter Pablo Iglesias founded the Spanish Socialist Workers' Party, hoping to channel workers'

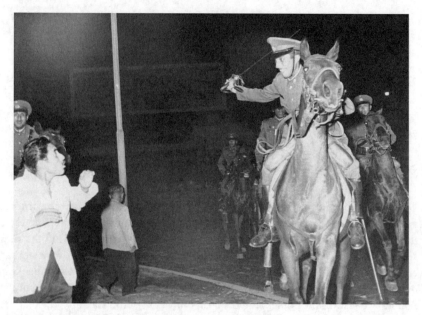

The Guardia Civil, military guardian of Spanish order, would be unleashed against government opponents during the frequent conflicts of the early twentieth century that beset the country. This picture from 1953 of a Guardia Civil horseman attacking a civilian illustrates why adversaries feared them.

demands into peaceful legal methods, but Anarchist violence and direct action had a greater appeal for the disaffected Spanish workers. Waves of strikes, bombings, and assassinations marred Spanish life, and voting rates remained low. Revolutionary syndicalism also attracted a peasant following—another anomalous and unusual development. In 1911, Anarchist unions united in a national labor federation, the CNT, whose membership outstripped the Socialist union, the UGT. The government did not propose reforms but employed the dreaded Guardia Civil to suppress disorders, suspended constitutional liberties, and called out the army instead of proposing reforms.

In June 1909, Catalonia erupted in revolt following Conservative Prime Minister Antonio Maura's request for military credits to suppress a revolt in Morocco. A major target was the Catholic Church, the prime factor in maintaining Spanish social conditions in a backward state. The church's political arm, Catholic Action, waged war on anarchism and on secular influence in all phases of Spanish life, reactionary Catholic capitalists sabotaged social initiatives fostered by their Liberal coreligionists, and the number of nuns and priests tripled in the fourteen years before 1900. The government suppressed the Catalonian outbreak and executed the anticlerical school reformer, antimilitarist, and former Anarchist Francisco Ferrer. The execution touched off a wave of protest all over Europe. Like the Dreyfus case in France, the Ferrer affair split Spanish society on the question of whether Spaniards should accept the status quo or fight to overthrow it. Moreover, Catalonia demanded regional autonomy and the Basque country demanded separation, increasing the fear of Spanish rightists.

Spanish neutrality during World War I, the tremendous demand for goods during the conflict, and the influx of foreign capital brought the possibility of change, but with a great acceleration in Spanish industrial growth came increased turmoil. In 1917 disturbances broke out, and a sharp economic downturn at the war's end provoked more disorders in an increasingly dangerous situation. The "tragic week" of June 1909 had brought the army back into the fore of Spanish politics after a hiatus of some years, and its presence increased ominously before and after World War I. The 1906 Moroccan revolt led to an increase in the army's resources and a conviction by the king and the conservatives that the military was the last bastion of order against a rising tide of violence and disorder. The army's strengthened role in Spanish society and the increased opposition to the government set the stage for civil war in the 1930s.

Portugal

Portuguese Upheavals

If anything, the state that shared the Iberian Peninsula with Spain suffered greater instability and political disorder. Portugal followed an evolution similar to that of Spain during the nineteenth century, with a great struggle between liberal and conservative forces and an even more complicated dynastic contest. In 1834 "Miguelism," the Portuguese counterpart of conservative Spanish "Carlism," (support for conservative pretenders to the throne) went down to defeat and a constitution established a two-house legislature—one elected by limited suffrage, the other appointed—that remained the basis of Portuguese constitutions until 1910.

Miguelism's defeat produced rule by upper and upper-middle class Liberals, the growth of Freemasonry, and an attack on the church. Church lands were sold but wound up in the hands of the wealthy, industrialization advanced slowly, and agriculture remained stagnant. During the 1890s, economic development accelerated but remained handicapped by the lack of raw materials, capital, and technicians. Furthermore, foreign capital, especially British, received favors and dominated the country. Fewer changes came to Portuguese society than to any other part of Europe, except perhaps the Balkans, and poor working conditions and the decline in the real wages of urban workers encouraged the rise of Socialist and Anarchist working-class organizations. As in Spain, political power alternated between conservative and liberal groups, a system called *rotativismo*, and the compromise remained in force until the rise of Portuguese republicanism.

The Portuguese Revolution

The Portuguese Republican program demanded political freedom, equality, separation of church and state, the right of association, the right to strike, and the repeal of regressive indirect taxes. Support for the Republican movement was concentrated in the larger towns, and it also enjoyed the support of a large radical nationalist secret society, the Carbonária. The government reacted to the Republican challenge by strengthening the crown's powers, but in 1900 the rotativist system began to break down with the defection of one of its leaders,

Joao Franco, who institution rule by decree. In 1908, the government suppressed a Republican-inspired army revolt, and the Carbonária assassinated King Carlos I and his heir in Lisbon. Carlos's inexperienced second son became king, and Portugal descended into chaos as cabinets rapidly succeeded each other, the monarchists split into warring groups, strikes increased dramatically, and radicals took over the republican movement. In October 1910, a military revolt overthrew the monarchy and established a republic.

The new Republican regime acted immediately; it adopted radical measures, curbed the power of the church, and announced new social policies favoring workers. On the whole, however, the middle class and the bureaucracy dominated the new republic and prevented it from implementing drastic measures on behalf of the population. The Republicans did little for women and, although they instituted a voting system approximating universal male suffrage in 1911, they cut the electorate in half in 1913. Republican fiscal policy tripled the already large Portuguese deficit and caused severe inflation. In 1912 the most serious wave of strikes in the country's history shook the country, protest demonstrations escalated, and radical army officers attempted to overthrow the government. The republic thus failed to resolve Portugal's economic backwardness, social problems, and political instability.

SOUTHEASTERN EUROPE

While turmoil in the Iberian Peninsula remained isolated, the political and territorial ambitions of the southeastern European states affected Europe and the world. Having gained their independence from the Ottoman Turks after centuries of domination, all the southeastern states hoped to gain territory from a rapidly declining Turkey and maneuvered between the dominant regional powers— Austria-Hungary and Russia. In these fights, the wild cards were Russian Pan-Slavism, the common Eastern Orthodox faith that all these states shared with the tsarist colossus, and Austria's German ally. This last factor meant that regional issues had the capacity to trigger a wider European war.

Romania

The Romanian King

The great powers helped carve independent states in the region from Turkish territory even while taking a generous helping of territory for themselves, and in 1858, they pressured the Ottomans into allowing the previously formed principalities of Moldavia and Wallachia to choose their own rulers. Proponents of Romanian unity selected the popular Alexandru Cuza as the ruler for both areas, and in 1861 Cuza united both principalities as Romania and issued a constitution.

Five years later a coup led by radical liberals removed Cuza and issued a constitution that lasted until World War II. Although the constitution created a bicameral legislature that had substantial powers on paper, it failed to achieve a Liberal regime because of the country's weak middle class and limited franchise through favoring the wealthy. Peasants, the vast majority of the population, elected only a

Extreme poverty characterized the situation of most Romanians in the early 20th century. The condition was especially dire and did not improve much until after World War I. Here is a picture of Romanian vendors in 1916.

few representatives to the Chamber of Deputies. Under these circumstances, the monarch had a preponderant role in the government until after World War I by allowing the alternation in power of liberal and conservative political parties that did not threaten the status quo.

Economics and Society

Romania's first king, Charles I, was a sophisticated member of Prussia's ruling family who ruled from 1866 until his death in 1914. He hoped to industrialize the country on the Western capitalist model through protective tariffs and subsidies for large and medium enterprises. These measures produced a concentration of capital and production in a relatively small number of industries, along with serious gaps and foreign domination of the important oil-refining sector. In 1914, along with lumber and food processing, oil refining accounted for almost 75 percent of the country's production.

Working conditions were very poor as immigration from the countryside into the cities ensured an oversupply of inadequately compensated labor and long working days ranging between twelve and sixteen hours. Wages stayed low, and enterprises preferred to hire women and children who were paid from 20 to 50 percent less than men. The weakness of the Romanian Socialist party ensured that no social legislation protected workers. Dissolved in 1899, the party struggled to rebuild itself in the early years of the twentieth century.

The peasantry formed the backbone of the Romanian population and economy, and agriculture still accounted for two-thirds of the country's production and for most of its exports in 1900. Reforms in the late nineteenth century had freed the peasants and granted them property rights, but the lack of sufficient land to make a living kept them in extreme poverty and bound to the landlords through rents paid in the form of labor services. Large landlords and the state owned 70 percent of the land, in contrast to Romania's neighbors Bulgaria and Serbia. These conditions and the peasants' exclusion from the government led to a serious revolt, in February 1907. The government quelled the uprising at the cost of 11,000 lives, after which it passed a series of ineffective reforms. Conditions on the land remained static until a wholesale reform was implemented after World War I.

The "Jewish Question"

Another serious social problem in Romania was the influx of Jews, primarily from Russia. By 1900, Jews accounted for over half Romania's urban population. Periodic anti-Semitic riots were a common feature because Romanians feared economic domination by the Jews, and Article 7 of the Romanian constitution restricted naturalization to Christians. This treatment of Romanian Jews prompted the intervention of French Jewish groups, which applied economic pressure and created difficulties when the government floated foreign loans. In 1879, under French and German compulsion, Romania modified Article 7, but it adopted implementing legislation that made it practically impossible for Jews to become citizens; Jews did not obtain full rights until after World War I.

Foreign Policy

Romanian recalcitrance on the Jewish question affected the country's international economic position, but King Charles's German heritage and control over foreign policy secretly brought Romania into the Triple Alliance because he aimed to secure a German guarantee of Romania's territorial integrity against potential Russian aggressiveness. There was a contradiction in Romania's adherence to the Triple Alliance because Austria-Hungary owned Transylvania, a Romanian-inhabited area coveted by Romanian nationalists. During the Balkan War of 1913, Romania attacked Bulgaria and won territorial concessions. The Balkan wars, the friendly French and Russian attitude, and Hungary's policies against its Romanian minority completed the country's alienation from the Triple Alliance, and the country entered World War I on the allied side after the death of King Charles.

Bulgaria

Bulgaria's Political Fragility

Bulgaria's past resembled Romania's. The Bulgarians lived under Muslim tutelage for five hundred years, maintaining their national identity and Orthodox faith. What was more remarkable, the Bulgarian peasants and nobles also survived Ottoman rule, and the typical Bulgarian peasant emerged from Turkish rule as a small proprietor who was able to support his family on his own land. A national revival occurred in the early and mid-1800s, and, as a result of a victorious Russian war with Turkey in 1878, a large independent Bulgaria reemerged. The new country included parts of Macedonia, a disputed region that destabilized the entire area.

In 1879 the Bulgarians adopted a liberal constitution that set up a complex unicameral legislature (the Subranie), enfranchised men over age twenty-one, invested power jointly in the executive and legislative branches, and granted wide individual rights to the citizens, but Liberal leader Stefan Stambolov, in league with the Russians, circumvented it. In 1894, Ferdinand fired Stambolov and ruled Bulgaria by manipulating the different liberal and conservative groups who were operating in the country. Before World War I, the Bulgarian parliamentary system failed to function according to the constitution, and neither the urban working class nor the peasantry looked to the established parties to address the grievances that arose from economic growth. In 1899, the peasants formed the Bulgarian Agrarian National Union, which advocated reforms and the establishment of a peasant republic.

Bulgarian governments favored industrialization through foreign loans, protectionism, an expanded transportation system, a solid banking system, direct intervention, and the promotion of new agricultural methods. Economic growth continued strong until 1912, with the number of industrial plants increasing from 36 to 345 between 1887 and 1911. This development was financed by an enormous increase in the national debt that by 1912 resulted in interest payments eating up 20 percent of the budget. The resulting high taxes and corruption led to resentment and revolts, especially in 1905 after the Russian Revolution of that year. In 1906 a rail strike and anti-Greek rioting over Macedonia shook the country. In 1907 the prime minister was assassinated, and in 1908 more rioting occurred, revealing the great fragility of Bulgarian institutions.

Foreign Dissatisfactions

Besides these internal problems, the Macedonian problem created serious domestic and international difficulties. The Internal Macedonian Revolutionary Organization, demanded the liberation of Macedonia from the Turks through violence and terrorism and its annexation to Bulgaria. The problem was complicated because Greece and Serbia also claimed parts of Macedonia, and partisans of the different countries clashed there. In 1912 the Bulgarians participated in the first Balkan War against Turkey but the resulting disagreement among the victorious powers over Macedonia encouraged the Bulgarians to attack Serbia in 1913. This provoked a counterattack by Serbia, Greece, Romania, and Turkey that resulted in a Bulgarian defeat. The war ended with Bulgaria in possession of only a small part of Macedonia—an outcome that incensed Bulgarian nationalists. More importantly, in attacking Serbia, Bulgaria had ignored Russian warnings, worsening the already tense relations between the two countries. Bulgarian foreign policy, shifted toward the Central Powers and it would join them during World War I.

Greece

Instability and Corruption

Like Bulgaria, Greece also suffered hundreds of years of Turkish domination and retained its national identity through its Eastern Orthodox faith. Following independence won between 1821 and 1833, Greece came under British influence and established a monarchy under a young German prince who ruled as Otto I.

His new state included under a million people and left the most prosperous Greeks within Ottoman borders. Greek peasants were mostly landless, and the banditry and disorder that afflicted rural areas induced many Greeks to flee the country. Two Greek constitutions floundered on primitive social conditions and corruption. After Otto was driven out, corruption, factionalism, and instability characterized the reign of the new Greek King George I. During the 1880s and 1890s, however, King George became convinced that rule by a parliamentary majority would lead to political coalitions and stability, and two politicians, Charilaos Trikoupis and his rival Theodore Deliyannis, alternated in power, but corruption and instability remained serious problems despite the passage of some reforms, especially by Trikoupis. Trikoupis improved education and the state administration, curbed banditry, and bolstered the armed forces. Cotton and woolen mills were constructed, railway building achieved modest success, a telegraph line was built, and the basis of the Greek merchant marine, one of the twentieth century's largest, was laid. The Greek economy, however, remained backward, and its few exports were mostly agricultural and highly subject to market fluctuations. Greece borrowed heavily to finance its industrial development and by 1893 was bankrupt in everything but name.

The "Great Idea"

Greek domestic and foreign affairs were closely linked. Following independence, the Greek state hoped to bring the "unredeemed" Greeks living in the Ottoman Empire into Greece, a policy known as the "Great Idea." At first the Greeks concentrated on Crete, which constantly revolted against the Turks, and in 1897 Greece went to war with Turkey with disastrous results.

In 1908 more Cretan unrest and an economic crisis produced a revolt by disgruntled army officers who were upset at restrictions on promotion and favoritism. In 1909 they formed a military league and threatened to march on Athens if the government did not accept their demands for military, economic, and tax reforms. When the government responded unsatisfactorily, the league threw its support to a politician from Crete who had not been compromised by the corrupt ruling elite—Eleftherios Venizelos. In December 1910, Venizelos won a large majority in Parliament but did not drastically alter the 1864 constitution.

The energetic Venizelos improved the civil service, established free and compulsory primary education, introduced a progressive income tax, and set minimum wages for women and children. Legislation recognized trade unions and banned company unions. Because of the reforms, in 1910 and 1911 the country ran a budget surplus after many years in the red. Venizelos oversaw the reorganization of the army and the navy by bringing in British and French experts. Military reconstruction and the political unity that Venizelos achieved account for the important Greek military successes during the Balkan wars, which advanced the Great Idea.

In 1912 Greece joined in the first Balkan War against Turkey, and in the second helped defeat Bulgaria and was rewarded with a substantial slice of the ancient Greek province of Macedonia. In 1913, the Great Powers recognized Greek sovereignty over Crete. Greece did not completely achieve its Great Idea of

THE BOILING POINT.

Although the Balkans were a peripheral part of Europe politically and economically, their international squabbles affected Europe and the world and would touch off World War I. Here is a cartoon from 1912 from *Punch* magazine that shows the large powers of Europe desperately trying to contain the "Balkan Cauldron" from exploding.

redeeming all Greeks, but the country did amazingly well and increased both its territory and population by 70 percent. These gains, however, put a large number of Slavs and Turks under Greek control, and in 1913 another event occurred that presaged trouble ahead: George I fell to an assassin. George I left a successor who lacked his flexibility and commitment to constitutional rule.

Serbia

Instability and Assassination

Serbia had even vaster ambitions for the conquest of unredeemed territory and a greater impact on Europe's future.

Under the Turks, the Serbs had maintained their Eastern Orthodox faith and a measure of local self-government. In 1878 an independent Serbia appeared as a country of small but politically subservient landholders, and in 1882 it became a full-fledged kingdom. In contrast to Western parliamentary states, in which the executive needed the confidence of the legislature, "in Serbia it seemed as though the parliament had to enjoy the confidence of the government." In 1889 a new constitution was promulgated (called the constitution of 1888, from the Julian calendar). The fruit of a compromise between the Radicals, who pushed for a full-fledged parliamentary regime, and King Milan Obrenovic, the new instrument increased the assembly's prerogatives and introduced the concept of sharing power between the executive and the legislature. However, politically burned out and shaken by personal problems, the king abdicated.

A regency council ruled for his son Alexander and ushered in increased confusion. The years from 1889 to 1892 witnessed a Radical ascendancy that encouraged the growth of disorder and banditry. Austria and Russia became involved in Serbia's internal affairs by supporting different plots and counterplots. Complicating the political situation, Alexander took as his mistress a woman of disrepute and, to make matters worse, married her. This marriage, his purging of officials who disapproved, her inability to have children, and rumors that her brother might succeed Alexander outraged the country. In 1901, the king promulgated yet another constitution contrary to the established procedure, but his main goals were to allow a female to succeed him should he have no male progeny, to make his wife regent in case of his death, and to acquire popular support for the monarchy. In 1902 and 1903, political opposition increased; between demonstrations and attempted coups, the army's disaffection became clear.

On June 10–11, 1903, army conspirators invaded the royal palace and brutally butchered Alexander, his wife, the prime minister, and other officials. They installed a rival dynasty under Peter Karadjordjevic. A Western European-type liberal, the new king promulgated a constitution that established a unicameral legislature, extended its powers over finances, strengthened civil rights, and provided for a strong executive. The new regime then set out to modernize the army and reform Serbian society and national life.

The disorders delayed Serbian economic development. Industrialization remained slow until 1906, when a tariff war with Austria-Hungary caused the economy to loosen its dependence on imports from its giant neighbor and stimulated industry. The government strengthened credit institutions and attracted foreign investment that went primarily into mining, railway building, meatpacking, and electrification. In 1910 some social legislation was passed to address the most egregious problems of the workers.

Destabilizing the Balkans

The 1903 revolution reoriented Serbian foreign policy. The Serbs believed that they had the historic mission of freeing the South Slavs from Austrian and Ottoman domination and unifying them under their leadership. These principles had the strong support of the Serbian people, and the conviction that Alexander had not furthered the mission was part of the reason for the army's revolt in 1903.

With the new regime, Serbia turned definitively against Austria-Hungary and toward Russia. The Serbian desire for economic independence from Austria and political opposition to Austria contributed to the tariff war of 1906 to 1911. The Bosnia-Herzegovina crisis from 1908 to 1909 further exacerbated relations between the two countries, provoking popular demonstrations against the Austrians and an enraged reaction by the Serbian government. The crisis escalated, and the Austrians threatened war. Nationalist feelings led to the founding of secret organizations that pledged to achieve South Slav unification by revolutionary action and by influencing Serbia's governmental policy—ideas with strong army support. The Balkan wars, in which Serbia made enormous gains, brought the issue of Greater Serbia to a new plateau by expelling the Turks from Europe and by making Austria-Hungary the focus of Serbian action to free the Slavic inhabited lands possessed by Austria-Hungary. Austrian statesmen understood that Serbian success in this endeavor would logically lead to the empire's breakup, and they determined to eliminate Serbia as a threat.

Bibliographical Essay

Wayne C. Thompson, *Nordic, Central, and Southeastern Europe, 2008* (Harper's Ferry, W.Va., 2008) is a general history of many of the regions covered in this chapter.

Modern Scandinavia as a whole—including the areas that were not independent and therefore not covered in this chapter—is analyzed in separate chapters of the massive Jorgen Bukdahl et al., eds., *Scandinavia Past and Present: Through Revolutions to Liberty* (Copenhagen, n.d.). The separate articles also consider the arts and humanities. Tony Griffiths, *Scandinavia*, 8th ed. (New York, 2004) is a concise general introduction that also discusses intellectuals. T. K. Derry's *A History of Scandinavia: Norway, Sweden, Denmark, Finland, and Iceland* (Minneapolis, Minn., 1979) is a standard work. H. Arnold Barton's *Essays on Scandinavia History* (Carbondale, Ill., 2009) gives a grounded background on the 18th and 19th centuries. Two books of essays that look at different aspects of Scandinavian economic and social experience are Susanna Fellman, *Creating Nordic Capitalism* (Basingstoke, UK, 2008) and Niels Finn Christiansen, *The Nordic Model of Welfare: A Historical Reappraisal* (Copenhagen, 2006).

On Sweden, general works with good coverage of the period discussed include Neil Kent, *A Concise History of Sweden* (Cambridge, UK, 2008), combining social, economic, and cultural history, and Byron J. Nordstrom, *The History of Sweden* (Westport, Conn., 2002), which discusses the emergence of the democratic system in the country. See also Franklin D. Scott, *Sweden: The Nation's History* (Minneapolis, Minn., 1977), subsequently republished with an epilogue by Steen Koblik. Andrew A. Stromberg, *A History of Sweden* (New York, 1970), is a more detailed, older work originally published in 1931 that is particularly useful for intellectual, constitutional, and social issues. Ingvar Andersson, *A History of Sweden*, 2nd ed. (New York, 1970), the translation of a work by a noted Swedish observer, is a particularly engrossing account; the citation on the Swedish railways is on p. 356. For readers seeking a more concise history, Irene Scobbie, *Sweden* (New York, 1972), is a good choice, emphasizing economic and social affairs. More specialized works on Sweden's economy include Eli Heckscher, *An Economic History of Sweden* (Cambridge, Mass., 1954), and Carl G. Gustavson, *The Small Giant: Sweden Enters the Industrial Era* (Athens, Ohio, 1986), an industrial history. Swedish politics over a hundred-year period are the topic of Leif Lewin, *Ideology and Strategy: A Century of Swedish Politics* (Cambridge, UK, 1988). Books on interesting topics include Jan-Erik Nylund et al., *Forest Tenure in Sweden: A Historical Perspective* (Uppsala, Sweden, 2007), which demonstrates Swedish interest in a topic mentioned in this chapter; and Eva Ahren, *Death, Modernity, and the Body: Sweden 1870–1940* (Rochester, N.Y., 2009), which discusses an unusual topic in the coming of modernity.

For Norway, see Hjalmar Hjorth Boyesen, *A History of Norway From the Earliest Times* (n.p., 2007). Karen Larsen published a full and interesting general account: *A History of Norway* (Princeton, N.J., 1948). For a very detailed and complete history that also pays attention to the arts, see Knut Gjerset, *History of the Norwegian People* (New York, 1969, published originally in 1932). T. K. Derry produced two good general works: *A History of Modern Norway, 1814–1972* (Oxford, UK, 1973), good not only on economic, political, and social affairs, but on Norwegian emigration, and the shorter but still useful *A Short History of Norway,* 2nd ed. (London, 1968). On the important Norwegian shipping industry, see *Norwegian Shipping* (Oslo, 2007), a history of technological innovation.

For Denmark, see Knud J. V. Jespersen's *A History of Denmark* (New York, 2004), a general history including material on the modern period. Stewart Oakley, *The Story of Denmark* (London, 1972), is an excellent source. Another useful work is W. Glyn Jones, *Denmark: A Modern History* (London, 1986). Both books go into ample detail on modern Danish history, with the first being more complete. On Niels Bohr, there is the volume edited by Stefan Rozenthal, *Niels Bohr: His Life and Work as Seen by His Friends and Colleagues* (Amsterdam, 1967). For information on his institute, see George Gamow, *Thirty Years that Shook Physics* (New York, 1966). The citations are from p. 51.

On Holland, there is the excellent, compact, and clear work by Gerald Newton, *The Netherlands: An Historical and Cultural Survey, 1795–1977* (London, 1977), which covers the modern period very well. Another good survey is Frank E. Huggett, *The Modern Netherlands* (New York, 1971). Mark T. Hooker, *The History of Holland* (Westport, Conn., 1999), is another survey. A very brief survey is A. J. Barnouw, *The Making of Modern Holland: A Short History* (London, 1948). Bartholomew Landheer, ed., *The Netherlands* (Berkeley, Calif., 1943), offers specialized essays on different aspects of Dutch affairs. Amry Vandenbosch, *Dutch Foreign Policy Since 1815: A Study in Small Power Politics* (The Hague, 1959), is a meticulous examination of the subject. J. W. Schot examines the role of technology beginning in the period discussed in this chapter: *Technology and the Making of the Netherlands* (Cambridge, Mass., 2010). Luxembourg, connected dynastically with the Netherlands, is the subject of James Newcomer's *The Grand Duchy of Luxembourg* (London, 1984).

E. H. Kossman wrote a very detailed parallel history of the Netherlands and Belgium, *The Low Countries 1780–1940* (Oxford, UK, 1978). Similar treatments are Paul Arblaster, *A History of the Low Countries* (New York, 2006) and J. C. H. Blom and Emiel Lamberts, *History of the Low Countries* (New York, 1999). *A House Divided* (Lanham, Md., 1997) discusses the Flemish problem in relation to the Catholics and Socialists in the 19th century. Margot Lyon, *Belgium* (London, 1971), is an excellent short history; Lyon quotes the statement about the king ruling two peoples on p. 58. Bernard A. Cook, *Belgium* (New York, 2002) is a general history. Stephen B. Wickman, ed., *Belgium: A Country Study* (Washington, D.C., 1985), primarily concerns the period after the one discussed in this chapter, but has an excellent introduction and chronology. Another way to understand Belgium during the years covered is through biographies of its monarchs. In this respect, consult Barbara Emerson, *Leopold II of the Belgians: King of Colonialism* (London, 1979), which also devotes considerable attention to his imperialistic activities. The older book by John de Courcy MacDonnell, *King Leopold II: His Rule in Belgium and the Congo* (New York, 1965, but originally published in 1905), is still useful for its wealth of detail. The best account of Leopold's rule in the Congo is Adam Hochschild's *King Leopold's Ghost: A Story of Greed, Terror, and Heroism in Colonial Africa* (Boston, 1999); the quote on the first international human rights organization is on p. 2. Martin Ewans discussed the topic and its ramifications in detail in *European Atrocity, African Catastrophe: Leopold II, the Congo Free State and Its Aftermath* (London, 2002). There is also a biography of Leopold's successor by Evelyn Graham, [pseud. for Lucas Netley], *Albert King of the Belgians* (New York, 1929).

The best manageable history of Switzerland, noted for its balanced viewpoints and its rich detail, is E. Bonjour, H. S. Offler, and G. R. Potter, *A Short History of Switzerland* (Oxford, UK, 1952). George Arthur Codding, *The Federal Government of Switzerland* (Boston, 1965), is an excellent examination of the Swiss government in relation to the land, people, and history. Other general histories that can be profitably consulted are

Wilhelm Oechsli, *History of Switzerland* (Cambridge, UK, 1922), and, for its particular outlook on Swiss direct democracy dating from the years covered in this chapter, Henry Demarest Lloyd, *A Sovereign People: A Study of Swiss Democracy* (New York, 1907). *Peace, Freedom, Security* (Bern, 2003) discusses Swiss defense policy over two centuries. Matthieu Leimgruber, *Solidarity Without the State?* (Cambridge, UK, 2008) examines the Swiss welfare system.

The historical literature on Spain is abundant, although readers will have to glean out the material covered in this chapter. Salvador de Madariaga's *Spain: A Modern History* (New York, 1967) is a classic account that exhaustively discusses the major themes of Spanish history. Mary Vincent's *Spain 1833–2002* (New York, 2007) is a general history that concentrates on politics and culture. Eléna de La Souchere, *An Explanation of Spain* (New York, 1964), is excellent for the clarity of its interpretations; the quotation on Spain in the text is taken from p. 106. Some particularly useful general histories are Raymond Carr, *Modern Spain 1875–1980* (Oxford, UK, 1980), a concise work with three excellent chapters on the period discussed and a valuable chronology and glossary that allow readers to keep developments clear; George Hills, *Spain* (New York, 1970), particularly valuable for chapters on the constitutional monarchy and the African war and its political effects; and Richard Herr, *Spain* (Englewood Cliffs, N.J., 1971), which contains a series of essays by a noted historian.

There is also good literature on specialized topics. These works include Adrian Shubert, *A Social History of Modern Spain* (London, 1990), which investigates important sectors of the economy and social development. Earl R. Beck's *A Time of Triumph and of Sorrow: Spanish Politics During the Reign of Alfonso XII, 1874–1885* (Carbondale, Ill., 1979) is an account of the reign of Alfonso XII arguing that the king failed in modernizing Spain because of the opposition of entrenched customs, traditions, and political groups. The church has been a focus of investigation in the historical literature, but a clear, concise, and balanced treatment of the institution with material on this period is Frances Lannon, *Privilege, Persecution, and Prophesy: The Catholic Church in Spain, 1875–1975* (Oxford, UK, 1987). Joan Connelly Ullman studied the Catalan revolt of 1909 in its historical and anticlerical dimensions in *The Tragic Week: A Study of Anti-Clericalism in Spain, 1875–1912* (Cambridge, Mass., 1968). Joseph McCabe, *The Martyrdom of Ferrer* (London, 1909), is a contemporary account illustrating the international echo of the affair. Carolyn P. Boyd, *Praetorian Politics in Liberal Spain* (Chapel Hill, N.C., 1979), examines the army's role in Spanish politics primarily after 1917, but includes two chapters on earlier years.

Portugal is not nearly as well covered in the literature as is its larger Iberian neighbor, but Stanley G. Payne's *A History of Spain and Portugal,* vol. 2 (Madison, Wisc., 1973), includes a comprehensive and clear account of Portuguese history of this period, in addition to Spanish affairs. A. H. de Oliveira Marques, *History of Portugal,* vol. 2 (New York, 1972), discusses the constitutional monarchy and the republic in detail, including the African colonies and their vicissitudes. H. V. Livermore, *A New History of Portugal* (Cambridge, UK, 1966), includes two chapters on the same topics. Douglas L. Wheeler, *Republican Portugal: A Political History, 1910–1926* (Madison, Wisc., 1978), is a history of Portugal from 1910 to 1926. V. de Bragança-Cunha, *Revolutionary Portugal* (London, 1937), an examination of Portuguese republicanism, pronounces the republic a disappointment. Two general books are worth looking at: M. D. D. Newitt, *Portugal in European and World History* (London, 2009), and Richard Alan Hodgson Robinson, *Contemporary Portugal* (London, 1979).

On the Southeastern European states, Romania is fortunate to count some impressive works. Keith Hitchins, *Rumania 1866–1947* (Oxford, UK, 1994), is a thorough, balanced, and well-informed work with a good bibliography. Hitchins also published *The Identity of Romania* (Bucharest, 2009). Lucian Boia concentrated on *Romania: Borderland of Europe* (London, 2001). The older book by R. W. Seton-Watson, *A History of the Romanians* (New York, 1963), is very detailed, well written, and clear. Valuable briefer accounts include Vlad Georgescu, *The Rumanians: A History* (Columbus, Ohio, 1984), and Georges Catellan, *A History of the Rumanians* (Boulder, Colo., 1989). On specialized topics, see the account of the crucial early years of independence, Gerald J. Bobango, *The Emergence of the Romanian National State* (New York, 1979). Philip Gabriel Eidelberg contends that the 1907 peasant revolt resulted from fights between political parties supporting or opposing industrialization: *The Great Rumanian Peasant Revolt of 1907: Origins of a Modern Jacquerie* (Leiden, the Netherlands, 1974).

Although there is material on post–World War I and Communist Bulgaria, Bulgaria has not attracted as much scholarly attention as Romania for the time period discussed in this chapter. Luckily, however, a clearly written, balanced, thorough, and scholarly work exists: Richard J. Crampton, *Bulgaria 1878–1918: A History* (New York, 1983), from which the quote on the effects of the Stambolov regime is taken (p. 158). The same author also wrote *A Short History of Modern Bulgaria* (Cambridge, UK, 1987), with a brief chapter on the period covered in this chapter, and *A Concise History of Bulgaria* (New York, 1997). An older work is useful for its thematic approach: George Clenton Logio, *Bulgaria: Past and Present* (Manchester, UK, 1936). For an example of Communist historiography on Bulgaria, see D. Kossev, H. Hristov, and D. Angelov, *A Short History of Bulgaria* (Sofia, 1963). John Macdonald's *Czar Ferdinand and His People* (New York, 1971, but reprinted from an older account of an unspecified date), is a romantic account.

As is the case of many areas with a glorious ancient past, modern Greece has suffered from some neglect. Richard Clogg's *A Short History of Modern Greece* (Cambridge, UK, 1979), however, is a very good study. C. M. Woodhouse, *Modern Greece: A Short History* (London, 1991), has several good chapters on the period covered here. Douglas Dakin, *The Unification of Greece 1770–1923* (London, 1972), goes into more detail, and Dionysios A. Zakythinos, *The Making of Modern Greece* (Oxford, UK, 1976), and John K. Campbell and Philip Sherrard, *Modern Greece* (London, 1968), emphasize social history. Less scholarly but informative treatments include Jane Perry, Clark Carey, and Andrew Galbraith Carey, *The Web of Modern Greek Politics* (New York, 1968); David Holden, *Greece Without Columns: The Making of the Modern Greeks* (London, 1972); and D. George Kousolulas, *Modern Greece: Profile of a Nation* (New York, 1974). Thomas W. Gallant, *Modern Greece* (London, 2001) is a survey. On the most remarkable Greek politician of this period, see Herbert Adams Gibbons, *Venizelos* (Boston, 1920). Theodore A. Couloumbis et al., *Greece in the Twentieth Century* (Portland, Ore., 2003) is a book of essays on important modern topics.

On Serbia, an essential starting point is Michael Boro Petrovich, *A History of Modern Serbia 1804–1918,* 2 vols. (New York, 1976), from which the quote on the 1869 constitution is drawn (vol. 2, p. 369). Stevan K. Pavlowitch, *Serbia; The History of an Idea* (New York, 2002), is a detailed survey; Alex N. Dragnich, *Serbia Through the Ages* (Boulder, Colo., 2004) is less detailed. The early twentieth century is covered by Wayne S. Vucinich, *Serbia Between East and West: The Events of 1903–1908* (New York, 1968). David MacKenzie, *The Serbs and Russian Pan-Slavism: 1875–1878* (Ithaca, N.Y., 1967), discusses the relationship between Russia and Serbia in the late nineteenth century, while his *Serbs and Russians* (Boulder, Colo., 1996) has more material on the period discussed in this chapter. Charles Jelavich's scholarly study *Tsarist Russia and Balkan Nationalism: Russian Influence in the Internal Affairs of Bulgaria and Serbia, 1879–1886* (Berkeley, Calif., 1962), examines Russian influence in Serbian (and Bulgarian) internal affairs and draws an implicit comparison to the post–World War II situation in the same region.

PART II

End of Hegemony

CHAPTER 6

✍

World War I

CHAPTER OUTLINE

Imperialism and Diplomacy: From Crisis to Crisis • History of a History:
Causes of World War I • Combat! • The Home Fronts • The War Ends

BIOGRAPHICAL SKETCHES

Henry Gwyn Jeffreys Moseley, A Casualty of War • Erich Maria Remarque,
"But now, for the first time, people learned what it was really like"

At the height of their political and economic influence in 1914, Europeans
went to war lightheartedly. Film footage shows troops from the different
nations smiling and waving to ensure that they would be filmed for posterity.
The last major European war had ended a hundred years before, writers and poets
had glorified combat, and most expected that a modern war could not last long.

Instead, the Great War turned into a global conflict, lasting four years, killing
millions, bankrupting countries, and ending Europe's world hegemony.

IMPERIALISM AND DIPLOMACY: FROM CRISIS TO CRISIS

In 1900 Europeans believed that imperialism had contributed to the prosperity
of the colonial powers by providing raw materials and markets. The desire of the
powers to increase their colonial possessions was a major cause of the war.

German Imperialism

Given Bismarck's disinterest in colonies, Germany possessed only a few African
territories and some islands in the Pacific. In the late 1890s, however, Germany
made a bid for more colonies as an aspect of its drive for world power, but found
the colonial world dominated by Britain and France, which Germany considered
declining powers. As a result, one school of historical scholarship to be discussed
later argued, German rulers wanted to acquire sufficient resources to guarantee

their country's "place in the sun"—not only colonies, but domination of the European continent. The German drive for power was the most important factor in the crises leading to World War I.

An Entangled Web

In 1904 Britain and France had sealed the Entente Cordiale by a colonial deal recognizing each other's interests in Egypt and Morocco. This bargain alienated Germany, which demanded an international conference to discuss colonies. Germany's bellicosity led to its diplomatic isolation at the 1906 Algeciras conference and prompted conversations between the British and French military staffs. In 1907, fearing that a war might break out with Austria-Hungary backed by Germany over the Balkans, the Russians resolved their imperial differences with the British and reached an understanding with them. Because the Russians already had an agreement with the French, the Triple Entente was born.

These developments confirmed the German fear of encirclement, and the Schlieffen Plan—the means by which the Germans hoped to win a two-front war—became an article of faith: "The German General Staff, indeed, the whole German officer corps (with negligible exceptions) regarded this plan as the infallible recipe for victory. This is all the more significant because the political leaders (before, during, and even after the war) also accepted this plan as sacrosanct or at any rate did not question it." The Schlieffen Plan came to dominate German foreign policy because it envisioned a German attack on France in case of a crisis involving Austria and Russia, even if the French were not directly involved, thus ensuring that a war in the Balkans would not remain localized. Moreover, the Germans had a sense of urgency about applying the plan because they calculated that Russian modernization would enable the Russians to mobilize as quickly as the Germans and make the Schlieffen Plan obsolete by 1917.

The Schlieffen Plan convinced the Germans that they could simultaneously defeat both France and Russia, but what would happen if the British intervened? It was likely that the British would intervene in any war to prevent France's destruction and Germany's domination of the continent and to protect Belgium. The Germans hoped for a British alliance or, at least, neutrality, offering to slow down the naval buildup that threatened British security, a condition that their *Weltpolitik* (world policy) made impossible. Nevertheless, they convinced themselves that the British would remain neutral if they could blame the Russians for a war that forced them to defend a superior Anglo-German civilization against the "inferior" Slavs. Consequently, according to historian Fritz Fischer, the Germans pushed the Austrians to maneuver the Russians into mobilizing first in order to justify a German attack on France, through Belgium, in the naive assumption that Russian mobilization would ensure British neutrality.

Diplomatic Crises

These considerations, combined with the German need to bolster Austria-Hungary, produced a series of diplomatic crises before 1914. In 1908 and 1909 it took an Austrian show of force that risked war to resolve the Bosnia-Herzegovina crisis. The Austrians consulted carefully with Germany. German Chief of Staff

Helmuth von Moltke offered his full support, while Wilhelm II noted in the margins of a military attaché's report: "Such a favorable opportunity for disciplining the unruly Serbs will not come again soon." On March 19, 1909, Austria sent Serbia an ultimatum demanding Serbian recognition of Austrian annexation of the two provinces. Three days later the Germans sent one to the Russians, demanding clear acceptance of the annexations and warning that the responsibility in case of refusal would fall exclusively on them. Not yet recovered from war and revolution, the Russians complied. Both Austrian and German officials lamented that diplomacy had deprived them of a golden opportunity to settle the Balkan question.

In 1911 the second Moroccan crisis flared when the French exploited local disturbances to extend their control of the area. The Germans reacted more vigorously than they had during the previous Moroccan crisis of 1905–06, perhaps because domestic public opinion had been upset with the kaiser's failure to make gains then. The Germans dispatched the gunboat *Panther* to the Moroccan port of Agadir—the "*Panther* leap." They demanded exorbitant compensation for recognizing the French protectorate: western Morocco or the entire French Congo. Afraid that French weakness would change the balance of power in Europe, the British strongly backed their ally, and David Lloyd George issued a stern warning the Germans. The kaiser frequently blustered and then retreated when war actually threatened, and he did so now.

"Wilhelm the Timid's" acceptance of worthless territory in the French Congo deluded all sectors of German society. It contributed to the German government's electoral losses in 1912 and, more ominously, to establishment of a conservative pressure group, the Army League, that took its place alongside the Navy League. Both these organizations aimed to mobilize the nation in favor of imperialism and more armaments. In 1912 the Germans expanded their peacetime army to 544,000 soldiers and, in 1913, to 661,000, forcing less populous France to increase the term of conscription to three years.

The Balkan wars of 1912–13 cast the German and French moves in an ominous light. Impressive Serbian territorial gains increased Austrian fears that the Serbs constituted a powerful pole of attraction for Slavs living in the Dual Monarchy and threatened its existence. On October 18, 1913, after securing a pledge of assistance from the Germans should the Russians intervene, Austria ordered the Serbs to evacuate territory on the Adriatic Sea that they had won during the conflict. The ultimatum carried an eight-day deadline, after which the Austrians would declare war. The Serbs conferred with their Russian allies, who once again counseled Serbia to back down. A disappointed Austrian Chief of Staff, Franz Conrad von Hoetzendorf had wanted war to eliminate the Serbian nuisance, but his German counterpart Moltke told him that "this was only a postponement and not a solution."

German Aims

In 1961, German historian Fritz Fischer published a controversial book citing German war aims as proof that the Germans were responsible for World War I. He argued that by 1914, the Germans were desperate to achieve their goal of

German Chancellor, Theobold Bethmann-Hollweg, shown here at the beginning of World War I in his military uniform, played an important part in the developments leading to the conflict and has been viewed as both a moderate wishing to avoid war and an aggressive leader whose actions during the final crisis favored it.

becoming a world power. However, despite growing German industrial and military power, the British and French succeeded in blocking them. Germany hoped to join Britain and the United States in the rank of world powers by reorganizing Europe according to its Mitteleuropa (Middle Europe) policy. The exact shape that Mitteleuropa would take was under constant discussion among representatives of powerful economic, social, and political groups, but as expressed in 1914 and later, Mitteleuropa meant that Germany would annex vast stretches of European territory and strategic areas and would create a customs union that would unite the entire continent economically. This discussion raged into the opening weeks of World War I when Chancellor Bethmann-Hollweg adopted the September Program, officially accepting Mitteleuropa as a German war aim. The program was stunningly ambitious in its complex whole of annexations, including economic, military, and political details that would have permanently destroyed France and eliminated Russia as a European power. At the same time, the Germans aimed at creating Mittleafrika from French and Belgian colonies, the African counterpart to Mitteleuropa, to guarantee a steady supply of raw materials for German industry.

Although the crises before 1914 were settled at the last minute, Germany's search for a place in the sun meant threatening Britain and destroying French and Russian power. At the same time, the Germans believed that time was running out on them because Russia was modernizing and Austria-Hungary would break up if it did not eliminate Serbia; Austria could not do so without fighting a war with Russia that required German support—and a two-front war.

HISTORY OF A HISTORY: THE CAUSES OF WORLD WAR I

On June 28, 1914, the Bosnian Serb nationalist Gavrilo Princip assassinated Francis Ferdinand, heir to the Austrian throne, and his wife on a visit to the Bosnian capital Sarajevo. The subsequent investigation of the crime revealed a conspiracy by the Black Hand, a Serbian terrorist organization, and the possible involvement of Serbian officials but never demonstrated direct governmental responsibility.

On the surface, the reason for war was the assassination of the archduke and the Austrian desire to eliminate Serbia as a threat. The Austrians obtained German support for a possible Russian reaction and for an ultimatum to Serbia, deliberately framing it so that if the Serbs accepted it, they would lose their sovereignty. On July 23, 1914, the Serbs received an ultimatum and two days to answer it. British Foreign Minister Edward Grey remarked that he had never seen such a "formidable document" sent to an independent state. The ultimatum demanded that the Serbians accept ten points, two of which, points 5 and 6, would have effectively ended Serbian independence. Point 5 would have required the Serbs to accept the collaboration of Austro-Hungarian officials in suppressing "the subversive movement directed against the territorial integrity of the Monarchy." This point was dangerous for Serbian sovereignty, but the Serbs agreed to it consistent with international law. However, they could not accept Point 6, which demanded that "delegates of the Austro-Hungarian Government will take part in the investigation" of the assassinations because acceptance would have severely limited Serbia's sovereignty. When Austria-Hungary declared war, the Russians mobilized, and the Germans implemented the Schlieffen Plan by attacking France through Belgium, which brought Britain into the war.

This explanation would make the outbreak of World War I the result of prewar diplomacy gone haywire, but the victors of World War I charged the Germans with war guilt. The origins of the war took on greater significance because of the German rejection of blame and the role it had in bringing Adolf Hitler to power in 1933. The causes of the World War I are still debated.

The Fay Hypothesis and Its Impact

American historian Sidney B. Fay best represents the school that attributed the outbreak of war to prewar conditions, which provided the tinder for it. His 1928 book *The Origins of the War* minutely examined the diplomacy and actions of the different powers and cataloged errors on the Austrian, British, French, Russian, and Serb sides, as well as the German. Fay cited the conflict's multiple causes—diplomatic entanglements and alliances, the arms race, the irresponsible conduct of newspapers, and surging nationalism. He rejected the notion that Germany deliberately provoked a war and maintained that Germany made belated efforts

Sir Edward Grey, British Foreign Secretary, in 1914. He has been accused of favoring the outbreak of World War I by failing to make clear to Germany that if it started a war Britain would intervene against it.

to avoid the conflict. According to Fay, Germany made a mistake in giving Austria a "blank check" in the form of unconditional support in case of war, a policy that allowed the Austrians to call the shots in the Balkans. Confident in the support of Germany, Austria used the blank check to pull Germany into the conflict in support of its policies. Fay concluded: "[T]he verdict of the Versailles Treaty that Germany and her allies were responsible for the War, in view of the evidence now available, is historically unsound. It should therefore be revised."

Fay's analysis confirmed the German thesis of the war's outbreak and had a major impact on the way in which many observers viewed the war's causes. His interpretation reinforced British misgivings soon after the war's end about how the Germans had been treated and added to the criticisms of the economic clauses of the 1919 Treaty of Versailles already made by British economist John Maynard Keynes. Furthermore, conditioned by balance-of-power ideas, the British suspected the French of wanting to dominate the continent following Germany's defeat; well protected by the English Channel, the British did not share French fears of a German resurgence. Confirmation from non-German historians that the conflict had resulted from general conditions, that Germany had been punished too harshly, and that its objections to the peace settlement were justified encouraged the British to support what they considered legitimate German requests for revision of the Versailles settlement that would normalize international relations, exorcise the specter of a new conflict, and restore the balance of power on the continent. This attitude would later contribute to a policy of appeasement that was a factor in the coming of World War II.

The Fischer Thesis

German historian Fritz Fischer contradicted the idea that the war was a result of ordinary prewar diplomacy in two books that used previously unknown archival material: In *Germany's Aims in the First World War* (1961, English translation 1964) and *War of Illusions: German Policies from 1911 to 1914* (1969), Fischer blamed the war on Germany because its goal of dominating the European continent forced Britain, France, and Russia to defend themselves. In the first book, Fischer concentrated on Germany's vast war aims and on German diplomatic manipulations during the final crisis. Far from Austria pulling Germany into the war, the Germans exploited the Austrians so that they could serve as the catalyst that forced the Russians to mobilize and the Germans to implement the Schlieffen Plan. The vociferous controversy that Fischer's book aroused forced him to write *War of Illusions,* detailing exactly how German policies led to the war.

All the European powers had resentments, contingency war plans, and objectives they wanted to achieve in case of war, but for Fischer, Germany had the strongest motives—the quest for world power and the conviction that it was fighting against time. German society agreed with the country's rulers: *Weltpolitik* required specific territorial and economic gains that could never be achieved peacefully. Reinforcing the appeal of world power, the undemocratic structure of German government made an expansionist policy necessary to divert the attention of the lower classes who were increasingly turning against the ruling class.

Fischer wrote that German officials decided for war in a council held on December 8, 1912. Soon thereafter, the kaiser approved a press campaign to prepare his people for war. Aiding this conditioning was the belief in empire as essential for a nation's economic success and Social Darwinism—proving the natural supremacy of some races over others through war as an element determining the survival of the fittest. This idea permeated European society and intellectuals, expressed it habitually and with great conviction; this attitude helps explain the genocides that occurred before, during, and after World War I. In 1900 the Englishman Karl Pearson admonished his countrymen that they had to prove themselves fit to survive: "The dependence of progress on the survival of the fitter race . . . gives the struggle for existence its redeeming features; it is the fiery crucible out of which comes the finest metal." Despite the lightheartedness regarding war, not all sectors of German society favored it. It was imperative for the German government to gain the Social Democratic Party's (SPD's) support in any conflict because of the party's influence over the masses—and because the SPD considered wars as conflicts between capitalists. German officials plotted to gain SPD support, according to Fischer, by portraying the Russians as repressive Asiatic aggressors against whom the German workers had to defend their hard-earned gains.

Fischer's work had vast implications. If the Germans had provoked the war, their complaints against the war guilt clause had no basis, and they were not absolved of the responsibility for Hitler. Fischer's account imparted a sense of continuity to German foreign policy and even domestic affairs, from before World

War I through the Nazi period, including the idea of racial imperialism. Fischer's work led to a historical debate and criticism of its interpretation of foreign and internal affairs, but it has strongly affected scholarship on the causes of World War I.

COMBAT!

The Germans implemented the Schlieffen Plan on August 6, 1914. The German railway system, developed under military tutelage, ran 550 trains daily to the western front, and 11,000 trains transported 3,120,000 soldiers. The trains of the other combatants did likewise. Historian A. J. P. Taylor labeled it "war by timetable."

Failure of the Schlieffen Plan

Schlieffen had envisioned an irresistible attack on France by the German right wing west through Belgium. In the meantime, the weaker German left wing in Alsace-Lorraine would be a tempting target for the French, who would force it to retreat and bring the French out of their fortresses in hot pursuit. The right wing would smash into France in the north, wheel around Paris, and attack the French army in the rear, out in the open, without the protection of its forts, and caught between the right and left wings. In order to function properly, the right wing had to be made invincible. Schlieffen's dying words were supposed to have been: "Don't weaken the right wing!"

Not surprisingly, the trenches took on the national characteristics of the soldiers who built them. This photo shows French soldiers on the Western front enjoying dinner during a lull in the fighting. Note the tablecloth and the flowers.

The Schlieffen Plan Misfires. This map shows the limit of the German advance in 1914 and the German inability to score a military breakthrough or to take the French capital.

Schlieffen's successor Moltke and the kaiser balked at the thought of French troops on German soil and strengthened the left wing by adding to it eight of the nine divisions that became available between 1905 and 1914, weakening the right wing. Schlieffen had also accepted the likelihood of a Russian invasion of Germany because the army on the eastern front would be weak, but because the Russian army could not mobilize quickly and could not attack in force, it would quickly be driven out after the expected rapid German victory on the western front. But the kaiser did not want Russian troops on German territory and reinforced the Russian front, again at the expense of the right wing in the West.

The weakened right wing proved unable to complete the task that Schlieffen had assigned to it. Belgian resistance slowed it down, and by the time it smashed into France, the forewarned French stopped it at the Battle of the Marne (September 5–12, 1914). The war of movement that was supposed to win victory in three or four months turned into one of position as both sides dug trenches that allowed them to resist withering enemy fire.

Trench Warfare

Both sides dug deep narrow trenches to present a difficult target for enemy artillery. In wet areas, the trenches had earthen ramparts reinforced by sandbags. In dry terrain, the trenches went deeper, some German trenches as deep as 30 feet. In snow-covered mountain areas, the trenches rose higher in winter and fell lower in the spring and summer as the snow melted. The armies dug several lines of parallel trenches. Two hundred yards or so behind the front line, there would be a support line, with reserve trenches 400 yards behind it, but no consistent pattern because the trenches shifted as armies retreated and advanced. Traverses—kinks designed to minimize artillery hits—periodically broke the straight lines of the trenches. Communication trenches, which allowed interaction among the soldiers, tired troops to go to the rear, and reserves to reach the front, ran at right angles to the main trenches. Saps projected from the main trenches into the "no man's land" between the lines of the different armies. Barbed wire, invented by American ranchers, surrounded the trenches, thinly at first but progressively denser. The trench system resembled a maze in which soldiers easily got lost. In the east the trench system was thinner because of the lower ratio of troops to space, and communication lines were frequently above ground.

The casualties were enormous, and the fighting cost Europe an entire generation of men. The war did not spare artists and scientists who could have given much to the world, including the poet Wilfred Owen, killed on the western front a week before the war ended, and Henry Mosely, an eminent physicist who died during a British offensive against Turkey in 1915.

Wartime propaganda portrayed the trenches almost as resort hotels, but reality differed. British troops rose at 4:30 A.M. and got ready to meet a possible dawn attack. If no attack came, they prepared breakfast, cleaned their weapons, made repairs, got shelled by enemy artillery, tried in vain to get the lice off themselves, brought up supplies, answered questions posed by bureaucrats, wrote letters, or slept. At night the men worked outside the trenches under enemy fire, conducted patrols, and launched raids.

Historian Paul Fussell described the trenches' national styles: "cynical" for the French, "amateur" for the British, and "clean, pedantic" for the Germans.

The machine gun drastically changed the nature of war, forcing troops to dig trenches for protection. Usually soldiers had to be fortified with alcohol to induce them to "go over the top" toward an almost certain death. This photograph graphically portrays why soldiers were so reluctant to leave the trenches during World War I.

This photo illustrates the horror of World War I. In the so-called "No Man's Land" between enemy trenches it was too dangerous to recover the remains of fallen soldiers. Their bodies eventually decayed and their skeletons remained fully clothed, to the point that it was possible to identify when they were killed by the changes that had taken place in the design of the uniforms since their deaths. The photograph shows dead French soldiers in one of the many No Man's Lands that characterized all the fronts of World War I.

The terrain determined the nature of the trenches. In the West, the Germans were frequently fortunate enough to occupy dry, high land. The British, engaged in a wet, rainy sector, waded in water up to their waists—one soldier remarking that the navy would come to their aid. Lice infested all the troops, and all attempts to get rid of them failed miserably. Rats rummaged everywhere, growing fat on the food the men ate and on their dead bodies. They became increasingly bold, attacking the men while they slept but were a source of amusement: soldiers dipped them into gasoline, set them afire and threw them over no man's land; enemy soldiers, believing an attack had begun, would fire on the suffering and wriggling animals.

BIOGRAPHICAL SKETCHES

Henry Gwyn Jeffreys Moseley
Casualty of War

Henry Moseley's story gives a taste of the tragedy and losses for humanity caused by World War I. Born on November 23, 1887, at Weymouth, England, Moseley grew up in a household with two scientists as parents. He received his secondary education at Eton, Britain's elite private school, and then attended Trinity College, Oxford, in 1906. He graduated in 1910 with a degree in the natural sciences.

From Oxford, Moseley went to the University of Manchester, where he collaborated with Britain's premier physicist Ernest Rutherford. In 1912 he left teaching for full-time research, and in 1913, using X-rays, he noted that there was no relation between the atomic weight of atoms and the wavelengths of the elements, but that there was one with the atomic number.

continued

continued

Moseley had made a fundamental discovery. Scientists had believed that the position of elements on the periodic table describing their chemical characteristics depended on their atomic weights, not their atomic number (the number of protons in the nucleus of an atom). This error had made it difficult to explain certain inconsistencies in the periodic table, but Moseley's work clarified them, predicted the position on the periodic table of yet-to-be identified elements, and enabled chemists to analyze the composition of materials in hours instead of years. Besides chemistry, Moseley's work had important implications for physics because his discovery had a close relationship to Niels Bohr's model of the atom, also elaborated in 1913. Moseley's research demonstrated that there could be no element lighter than hydrogen and that no element could exist between hydrogen (atomic number = 1) and helium (atomic number = 2). Scientists had postulated both possibilities.

In 1914 Moseley returned to Oxford, but World War I intervened, and he volunteered to join the Royal Engineers. Despite the efforts of Rutherford and other prominent scientists to protect him from danger, he insisted on doing combat duty. He participated in Winston Churchill's ill-fated operation at Gallipoli against the Turks and, on August 10, 1915, a sniper's bullet killed the young man who will always be remembered as the person who "numbered the elements."

Scientists agree that Moseley could have advanced the cause of science much more had he not become a casualty of war at age 27. His death contributed to the decision of the British government to exempt scientists from combat duty in World War II.

The troops feared "no man's land," a relatively narrow, deadly, area 200 to 300 yards wide on the western front, but sometimes only 25 yards. On the eastern front, the width of no man's land might be 3,000 to 4,000 yards. Because fire from the opposing army prevented the men from rescuing their wounded comrades, they died a horrible death from their wounds and lack of water. The best gift a friend could give comrades in that situation was a bullet in the head. Successive waves of offensives left thousands of dead bodies in no man's land to putrefy and turn into skeletons.

Under the circumstances, the men drank the hard liquor all armies generously provided. They would not normally go out of the trenches without being fortified with rum or cognac because it meant almost certain death. Soldiers could usually tell if an enemy offensive was imminent because the smell of alcohol on the breaths of enemy soldiers reached them or if they received an increased supply of alcohol when their side was planning an attack. A British soldier testified that rum won the war.

German Successes in the East

In the West neither side made much headway for four years, but the story was different in the East. Given the German engagement in the West, on the eastern front Austrians and Russians fought the big initial campaigns. The Austrians made headway in late August and early September but were pushed back by the Russians whose war industry overcame the early shortages of materiel.

The Russians invaded Germany, but the Germans, under generals Erich von Ludendorff, Paul von Hindenburg, and August von Mackensen, struck back, defeating the Russians in the battles of Tannenberg and of the Masurian Lakes. The Germans and Austrians linked up, but, given German involvement on two fronts, they were unable to knock the Russians out of the war.

A Widening War

The war widened considerably with Turkey's entrance in October and November 1914. The Germans had wielded considerable influence in the Ottoman Empire, reorganizing the Turkish army and building important projects, and the Turkish-Russian rivalry reasserted itself with the outbreak of war. When reflagged German ships fired on Russian cities, the Russians declared war, followed by Britain and France. The Turks attacked in the Caucasus but made little headway. In April 1915, alleging that the Armenians living in the empire helped the Russians, Ottoman authorities began roundups and deportations, accompanied by massacres, quickly leading to genocide.

European Stalemate. When World War I broke out the Schlieffen Plan proved unable to resolve Germany's two-front dilemma. The shaded areas show the extent of the different armies at different dates. Even after Germany defeated Russia, it did not obtain a breakthrough on the Western Front.

The war spread to North Africa when the Turks attacked Egypt. The campaign failed, but the Turks pinned down many British troops, preventing them from intervening on the western front. The British, Russians, and Turks also clashed in Asia, where their empires or spheres of influence bordered each other. In sub-Saharan Africa, the outmanned Germans lost most of their possessions to British, French, and South African attacks, but in some cases were still in the field when the war ended. The Germans lost their Pacific Ocean possessions to the Japanese, who entered the conflict on August 23, 1914.

Despite the conviction of Allied commanders that victory would come on the western front, the war there remained hopelessly stalemated in 1915, despite a series of great offensives that gained insignificant amounts of territory at the cost of hundreds of thousands of casualties. These failures led the Allies to consider other options. Some British planners, especially Winston Churchill, championed a strike against Turkey. Despite the objections of Sir John French and Joseph Joffre, British and French commanders on the western front, a force that included Australian troops sailed for the Dardanelles with the objective of taking the Turkish capital of Constantinople. Tenacious Turkish resistance defeated the attempt despite heroic fighting by the Australians at Gallipoli. Churchill resigned and did not reemerge as an influential leader until World War II.

The most important event of 1915 was Italian intervention. Italy had long regarded the change in the defensive nature of the Triple Alliance with alarm and had warned its allies several times that it would not follow them into an aggressive war. After the Austrian ultimatum to Serbia led to war, the Italians declared their neutrality and, under the terms of the alliance, requested compensation from the Austrians for the changes they had made in the Balkans. They hoped to gain the Italian-speaking area of Austria, the Irredenta, in return for their continued neutrality, but the Austrians refused until it was too late. The Entente, anxious to secure Italian intervention hoping that it might tip the scales in their favor, offered the Italians the Irredenta and other gains in case of victory. On April 26, 1915, Italian foreign minister Sidney Sonnino negotiated the Pact of London, which called for Italian entrance into the war within three months, and Italy declared war on Austria-Hungary on May 23, 1915, citing the Irredenta as the reason.

Italy's weight was not decisive, but it was influential because it opened up a major new front and tied down hundreds of thousands of enemy troops. The Italian front was the most difficult of the war—it was mountainous and stony, and the Austrians occupied all the mountain crests. The Italian war effort quickly bogged down as had the one on the Western front, and, like their allies, the Italians made little headway despite enormous casualties.

The Bleeding of Armies

Both the Allied and German commanders hoped to reach a decision on the western front in 1916, which instead was noted for its great battles, horrific human losses, and military futility. German General Erich von Falkenhayn opened the Battle of Verdun on February 21, hoping to achieve a breakthrough by bleeding the French dry. He chose a small area of the front and attacked it in a battle that holds the record for length because it ended only on December 15. Verdun cost

The Battle of Verdun was one of the bloodiest of the war. This pile of the bones of dead soldiers gives a graphic idea of the battle's ghastly cost.

both sides 700,000 casualties for no substantial gains. "It was France's supreme sacrifice and her supreme triumph, and to the splendor of her achievement all the world paid homage." French losses, however, drastically reduced the country's ability to contribute to a great offensive led by the new British commander, Sir Douglas Haig. The Battle of the Somme lasted from July to November 1916 and witnessed the first appearance of tanks, but it accomplished little beyond a million casualties on both sides. The Russians also launched an offensive that achieved few strategic results.

In the Balkans the Austrians had been unable to defeat the Serbs, and both camps maneuvered to secure the intervention of other Balkan states on their side. In 1914 the Russians had promised the Romanians large gains in Transylvania, and the death of their pro-German King Charles on October 14, combined with a massive Russian offensive that began in June 1916, convinced the Romanians to enter the conflict on the Allied side on August 27. The Allies had hoped to entice Bulgaria to intervene on their side with the assurance of important gains, but the Central Powers outbid them because Bulgaria's geographic position threatened Serbia. On September 6, 1915, Bulgaria signed an alliance with Germany and Austria and attacked Serbia, which fell under the control of the Central Powers. The Russian failure in the June 1916 campaign allowed the Central Powers to defeat Romania, most of which the Central Powers occupied by January 1917. This victory allowed them to take control of Romanian wheat and oil reserves that they desperately needed for their war effort. The Greeks also bargained with the Entente, but could not decide whether to intervene until the Allies forced the abdication of King Constantine and Venizelos brought his country into the war on June 26, 1917.

With Serbia and Romania controlled by the Central Powers, 1917 began on a bleak note for the Entente and worsened as it progressed. On the western front, the siege-battles continued throughout the year with huge losses and scant results. The continuous slaughter caused mutinies to break out between May and June in the French army affecting sixteen corps as soldiers refused to leave the trenches to fight the enemy. "If the Germans had a better information service, and had attacked at that moment, they would have inflicted upon the French army a defeat which would perhaps have been irreparable." Strikes also broke out in the country protesting war profiteering and high prices. The French named a new commander, Philippe Pétain, who had to implement army reforms and renounce offenses for a year.

In the East and the South, the situation was worse. War weariness and defeat brought about a revolution in Russia in March 1917, after which Tsar Nicholas II abdicated. Russia became a republic, and the country's new rulers vowed to remain in the war. They unleashed a new offensive that failed. The failure turned into a collapse when the Bolshevik Revolution took place in November 1917, the Russian army dissolved, and the Russians agreed to an armistice on December 15. On March 3, 1918, the Bolsheviks signed the Treaty of Brest-Litovsk and handed over large stretches of territory in Eastern Europe to German control. The Germans reorganized the territory, which included Russia's most productive areas, under their direct or indirect rule. The most important result of the Russian defection was that a large number of German troops were freed up for use on the western front.

The Germans also responded to the pleas of their Austrian allies to knock Italy out of the war. Repeated Italian offensives had failed to gain much territory but had brought Austria to the brink of collapse, and the Austrians doubted they could resist the next one. A powerful German force caught the Italians by surprise at Caporetto and broke through. For a period, the Italian retreat took on the aspects of a rout, but the Italians halted the attack on the Piave River and began a steady recovery. The Italian commander General Luigi Cadorna blamed the defeat on subversive Socialist propaganda, but the real reasons were war weariness, surprise, and his own harsh disciplinary measures, and he was replaced. The most important result of the German intervention, however, was its failure to knock Italy out of the conflict.

Weapons and Tactics

The industrialization of war accounted for the appalling slaughter of World War I and the failure of either side to break the military deadlock. Before World War I, most commentators believed that it would be impossible for society to support a long modern war because of the enormous costs in men and materiel.

Instead the belligerents replaced the incredible amount of war material swallowed up by the conflict, railroads delivered the material and troops to the front, the troops endured much more punishment than ever considered possible, and medical services proved adequate. The tremendous capability of modern industry may be illustrated by one statistic: during a German offensive on May 27, 1918, 6,000 guns fired 2 million artillery rounds in about four hours.

In addition, few understood the impact of new weapons. In the decade before 1914, the French developed an accurate, rapid-fire 75mm field gun that set the artillery standard for other European armies. Magazine rifles came into general use. Above all, the previously unwieldy machine gun was streamlined and became easy to manage, prompting European armies to equip their forces with it between 1905 and 1908, even though they did not know exactly how to utilize it. The Russo-Japanese War of 1904 to 1905 should have taught the Europeans the machine gun's potential. For example, French military observers reported:

> The [Russo-Japanese] war has shown the incontestable value of machine guns. . . . It was above all in the defensive that these weapons displayed their terrible effectiveness, particularly at the point when, with the two adversaries being a few hundred meters from each other, the men become nervous and aim too high, although their fire could be more effective if it were properly adjusted. In these circumstances machine guns, soulless devices without nerves, literally mow down the attackers.

But the military planners drew the wrong conclusions. They downplayed the enormous casualties caused by machine guns and commented that Japanese bayonet charges carried the day in spite of heavy losses. Despite their observations regarding the power of the defense, military observers concluded "that the Japanese performance had proved, up to the hilt, the moral and military superiority of *the offensive.*" European generals later sent millions of their soldiers to their death in futile offensives because they admired bayonet attacks, which, they thought, proved the moral superiority of the society whose soldiers employed bayonets and because these attacks coincided with their philosophical precepts. European military academies emphasized Bergson's élan vital, which they interpreted to mean that moral strength counted more than material conditions. The offensive embodied this concept. Instead, the machine gun tragically proved the military superiority of the material to the moral during World War I.

Besides the adoption of the machine gun, several other important changes occurred in European armies in the early years of the new century. Military experts realized that bright colors made good targets and recommended neutral colors for their uniforms, except for the French, to their regret. Powerful field glasses extended an army's vision. In theory the telephone should have enabled commanders to communicate more effectively with their troops, but in practice huge batteries were needed, and the wires were frequently cut. Mass battles and the inability to communicate except through runners contributed to the high casualty rate. Trucks made armies more mobile and allowed supplies to be brought right to the theater of operations that railroads could not reach.

The internal combustion engines also revolutionized aviation. Balloons had been flying since the eighteenth century, but in the twentieth century, the new

Military planners missed the significance that the machine gun would play in future wars. Here is a picture of British machine gunners wearing gas masks in action at the Battle of the Somme in 1916. It is estimated that 60,000 soldiers were lost on the first day of that July offensive.

The airplane played a romantic role during World War I in which the pilots were essentially transformed into the knights on horseback of old. However, the new weapon was not decisive. Here is American Ace Eddie Rickenbacker riding his trusty steed, an airplane.

engine made possible different types of dirigibles that were useful for warfare, pioneered by the French. In 1907 Prime Minister Georges Clemenceau and his war minister generated enormous enthusiasm for the new airship when they flew in a balloon. Germany trailed France but pulled ahead, thanks to the efforts of Count Ferdinand von Zeppelin, who pioneered a rigid design. From the military viewpoint, however, airships had major disadvantages: they were very expensive, needed complex ground support to take off and land, could easily be blown off course in adverse weather, were slow, made wonderful targets, and frequently exploded because they used hydrogen gas. The dirigible's disadvantages and the development of reliable engines made airplanes more attractive. Once again, the French led the way. In 1909 Louis Blériot's flight across the English channel and a weeklong air show at Rheims drove public enthusiasm for the airplane to fever pitch, the German emperor endorsed them, and the Italian pacifist Socialist leader Claudio Treves became an enthusiastic supporter of air power after he was taken up in a plane.

In World War I the airplane demonstrated its great potential for reconnaissance, but the difficulty of flying the machine severely limited the pilot's capability in this area. The pilot had to take along an observer to examine what was happening below and then had an arduous time communicating with the ground regarding the observations. Dogfights developed early but were also limited by the risk of pilots shooting off their own propellers. When the Germans invented a synchronized machine gun that fired through the propeller, they gained temporary control of the skies until the Allies got hold of a downed plane and copied the invention. Thereafter, air battles captured peoples' imaginations, but despite the visibility of air aces, such as Manfred von Richthofen—the "Red Baron," with eighty kills—the airplane did not alter the fortunes of war between 1914 and 1918.

Three weapons potentially had the ability to end the military stalemate, but the combatants used them prematurely. Properly used, poison gas might have changed the course of the war. First employed by the Germans at the Second Battle of Ypres (April–May 1915), the surprise use of poison gas opened up a large hole in the Allied lines as the troops holding the sector were incapacitated or fled. The Germans could have poured their forces through this gap, but the troops concluded it was a trick and stopped. From then on, both sides used poison gas, but both had more- or less effective gas masks. The tank met the same fate. Championed by Winston Churchill, this supersecret British weapon had the capacity to crash through enemy lines, but the British utilized it in insufficient numbers at the Battle of the Somme. Instead of being employed at night, making it more difficult for artillery to see them, and in large numbers, only forty-nine tanks saw action the first time they appeared, on September 16, 1916. Nine broke down, German artillery hit ten, and five did not advance. "My poor 'land battleships,'" lamented Winston Churchill; "they have been let off prematurely and on a petty scale." The Germans played the submarine card. The submarine had the potential of starving the British Isles and preventing fresh supplies and troops from reaching Allied lines in France, but its employment raised moral issues. Because submarines were considered sneaky, international law obliged them to surface before sinking merchant ships, announce themselves, and let the crew off safely. The British took advantage of the law to arm their merchantmen and blow the German submarines out of the water when they surfaced. As a result, submarines abandoned the rules, but then they encountered moral condemnation. When the Germans sank the *Lusitania* in 1915 with the loss of 1,198 civilians, including 139 Americans, the United States threatened war if the Germans did not desist. Unwilling to draw in such a powerful enemy, the Germans complied. In desperate straits by 1917, however, they reinstituted unrestricted submarine warfare and provoked American intervention. The Germans calculated that the Americans could not send enough soldiers to Europe to make a difference in the war, but thanks primarily to the convoy system, not a single American soldier who came over to fight the war was lost to the German submarine.

Political Changes

Even though the British believed that they could carry on business as usual, the belligerents had to organize their societies around the war effort. This made World War I the first total war and had an impact on all areas of civilian life.

In the Allied countries, politics changed. The political conflicts that marked prewar societies could no longer be tolerated in public, although antagonism continued behind the scenes. Politically, this harmony found expression in coalition governments, the enormous strengthening of the executive power, and the emergence of powerful personalities. France established the "sacred union" coalition, and in November 1917, Georges Clemenceau formed a strong cabinet in response to the army mutinies and political divisions that led France to victory and lasted until 1920. In England, the Asquith government created a coalition in May 1915. As in France, an inner cabinet group supervised military operations, and the government tightened its control over the production of munitions. The British had attempted to meet the war's manpower demands through a volunteer army that raised a million soldiers. By the end of 1915, volunteers no longer sufficed, and in January 1916, Parliament instituted conscription. In April, the British reacted harshly to the German-supported Easter Rebellion in Ireland by executing the rebellious leaders, but the shock and the mounting crisis produced a war cabinet headed by the energetic Lloyd George. In Italy on June 16, 1916, the nondescript Paolo Boselli headed a cabinet that replaced the existing government that had gotten Italy into the war. The trauma of the Caporetto defeat produced a new, more effective coalition cabinet headed by Vittorio Emanuele Orlando on October 25, 1917, to guide the country successfully through the last year of war. In all three countries, the military was a concern, but the governments kept it under control.

In the authoritarian countries, the monarchs made changes but refused to give their populations a greater political voice, which might have helped the war effort. In Germany, by 1917, the army effectively ran the country in the persons of generals Hindenburg and Ludendorff. Even though insistent demands for political reforms divided the country, the kaiser promised only abolition of the three-class voting system in Prussia. In Austria-Hungary the imperial government made no substantial concessions to the empire's different nationalities. The new emperor, Charles, who succeeded Francis Joseph after his death on November 21, 1916, issued a manifesto transforming the state into a federation of nationalities on October 16, 1918, but it was too late. The other autocratic state, Russia, stubbornly refused to concede significant reforms, which, along with its military failure, led to two revolutions in 1917.

THE HOME FRONTS

When hostilities first broke out, World War I enjoyed an enormous amount of popular support. Socialist ideology vociferously opposed war, but with the exception of the Russians and the Italians, the major European parties voted for funds to support the war. Parties, unions, and workers put their demands on the back burner for the war's duration even though past grievances were not resolved and new ones surfaced because of the economic strains.

Governmental relationships with industrialists were different as the combatants abandoned the gold standard, suspended gold payments, and ended the convertibility of currencies. The involution of trade and the difficulties producing armaments and supplies forced the belligerents to restructure their economies and confront the labor shortages that resulted from the great expansion of armies and the high number of casualties. All the warring countries imposed controls on wages, prices, raw materials, and freedom of movement.

Industrial Reorganization and the Civilian Population in Germany

In Germany the Prussian war ministry controlled the raw materials necessary for the manufacture of arms, and private industry produced them at enormous profits. By August 1916, the demand for war materiel became critical, and the army proposed the Hindenburg Program calling for compulsory labor service for the entire population, including women, and the utilization of all men ages fifteen to sixty in the armed forces or in arms manufacturing. All suitable factories were to be converted to war production, and, in a reversal of previous policy, enterprises that could not be so transformed were to be closed.

The dire need for workers would have drastically restricted freedom of movement for workers before it was modified, but the Germans still faced labor shortages. The Germans hoped to end the labor shortages by recruiting Polish and Belgian workers who had been left unemployed by the German occupation of their countries. When the Belgians, in particular, did not respond, in October 1916 German soldiers began rounding up Belgian workers for deportation to Germany, transporting them under harsh conditions and herding them into concentration camps until they could be distributed to industries. It was difficult for the Germans to force them to work, however, and protests by neutral countries ended the program in February 1917.

Unions initially supported their governments by renouncing wage increases, but because of excessive profits and inflation, real wages plunged. In Germany, cooperation between unions and employers' associations ended as the war dragged on and real wages declined sharply because of the inflation caused by steep increases in governmental expenditures. The Allied naval blockade created shortages of basic commodities, along with a decline in quality. Luxuries disappeared, and the supply of butter, potatoes, and vegetables dwindled. The consumption of eggs and fish declined by half, and coffee disappeared. The civilian population was malnourished, and their homes were poorly heated. These conditions increased mortality rates, with that of German women increasing in 1917 by 30 percent over the prewar period. The black market flourished, making a mockery of governmental statistics. Officially, the cost of living rose 200 percent in Germany, but black market prices for important commodities increased from 300 to 700 percent, while average wages for men went from 4.84 marks daily in March 1914 to 10.26 in September 1918, when a pound of butter on the black market cost 24 marks. Women fared even worse, their average daily wage rising only from 2.27 to 5.41 marks.

By 1917 sporadic protest strikes became extensive and turned into political instead of economic actions that involved the armed forces as the navy mutinied. In April 1917 the Independent Social Democrats split from the official Socialist party and demanded peace without annexations. In July, the Reichstag passed a resolution favoring such a peace. In September, however, the Supreme Army Command and leaders of heavy industry demonstrated that a large part of the German people still favored the war effort by founding the Patriotic Party, but these events illustrated the country's deep divisions.

Class Divisions in Britain

In Britain the prewar class divisions remained, but a grave crisis did not develop during the conflict because of the ability of the ruling class to compromise. The government met workers' demands more successfully than in Germany, and most labor leaders collaborated with it. The major labor problem was "dilution"—the employers' policy of replacing skilled workers who had gone to the front with unskilled labor. In February 1915, dilution and rapidly rising prices provoked a severe wildcat strike in the Clyde River valley, an important industrial complex producing iron, steel, and chemicals. The government settled the strike by imposing compulsory arbitration and pledging to limit employers' profits. The Munitions War Act gave the government wide latitude to restrict workers' freedom of movement, but it usually gave in to wage demands, and the unions temporarily obtained the right to define a skilled worker. In January 1916 the government instituted the conscription of single men. In order to meet the resulting shortage of skilled workers, the government determined who would be conscripted, and in April 1917, the unions could no longer define who was skilled.

The labor issue was just one aspect of the British government's escalating ability to control British life. As a result of a national debate on the quality and quantity of British arms, the government instituted controls over the armaments industry through the munitions ministry, originally under the energetic Lloyd George. When unrestricted submarine warfare begun by the Germans in 1917 threatened the food supply, the government instituted price-fixing to check rapidly rising prices and rationing to control distribution. By then, rationing had become a fixture of all belligerents.

In Britain and all belligerent countries, wages did not keep up with rising prices. The wages of skilled workers rose to a lesser degree than did those of unskilled workmen—less than 100 percent as compared to 100 percent to 125 percent between July 1914 and July 1918. Women, who moved in large numbers into traditionally male jobs such as armaments production, saw their wages rise in comparison by an average of 150 percent, but their wages did not reach parity with those of men.

Social Resentment

The conflict exacerbated the social struggle among the classes, to various degrees, in all the countries that participated in it. The frontline soldiers resented anyone who was exempted from military service or was stationed in the rear. Exemptions for essential skilled workers antagonized the unskilled workers. The peasants and urban workers, who were disproportionately represented in the armies and in the casualty lists, were especially resentful. The enormous losses—10 million dead soldiers, 20 million wounded—brought postwar bitterness between people who had fought in the trenches and those who had not, considered by the soldiers as deserters and war profiteers.

The rancor was not only in one direction. The peasants ate better than did the urban dwellers, who could not escape rationing, and withheld food in order to drive up prices. In the cities, declining real wages increased strife between the workers and capitalists, who profited inordinately from the war. The Liberals, who had formerly accepted badly distributed wealth in the belief that capitalism created enough riches for all and who looked forward to their more equitable distribution, watched the war eat up their countries' treasure and the police repress civil rights in the name of unity. After the conflict, many of them would turn to communism, which blamed the war on the capitalists.

The war's insatiable appetite for weapons, ammunition, artillery shells, trucks, airplanes, and ships set off what amounted to a new industrial revolution in both the established and emerging industrial powers. The engineering industry in Russia quadrupled between 1914 and 1916, and the production of chemicals doubled. This expansion enabled Russian industry to increase its production of shells by 2,000 percent, rifles by 1,100 percent, and artillery by 1,000 percent, but in all countries, the expansion set the stage for a postwar economic crisis and labor disorder when it came time to convert wartime industry to peacetime uses.

Women at War

Unprecedented industrial growth created a great demand for new labor, partially supplied by the entrance of more women into the labor market. Many women moved from domestic or other work activity to war-related work, where the proportion of women rose in various degrees in the combatant countries. The number of women in the British workforce increased approximately 1.5 million between 1914 and 1918. The number of French women employed in the metals industry went from about 17,700 in 1914 to 104,600 in mid-1916, and the

During World War I, women moved into jobs held by the men fighting on the front. This happened not only in the armaments industry but in other occupations as well. Of course the prejudices against women persisted. This illustration shows a woman taxi driver who has crashed and demolished five lampposts and was consequently given the nickname of "The Tank."

proportion of women working in the industrial labor force increased from 29.8 percent in 1914 to 37.1 percent in 1917. Despite this increase, social attitudes against women working in all the belligerent countries changed little. The Germans and Austrians preferred to use prisoners of war and foreign workers to meet the increased demand for labor. In countries, such as Italy and France, whose economies had large agricultural components, fewer women went into industry, but with their husbands away, women took over on the land and became heads of households, which altered traditional mentalities.

In most countries, the entrance of more women into the labor force decreased the differential between wages earned by women and men, but equal pay for women remained elusive. The female presence in labor unions and in strikes for higher pay and better working conditions increased. Many women considered work a temporary expedient and left their jobs after the war. Others resisted returning to less desirable activities and hoped to continue their jobs, but following the war, society was less welcoming and interpreted the desire of women who wanted to remain in the labor force as selfishness because they took jobs away from returning veterans.

After the conflict, most countries considered marriage a bar to working, with the British excluding married women from receiving benefits in 1922. Such measures effectively forced women to stop working once they married.

Besides joining the war effort by serving in the workforce, women contributed in other ways. In general, the belligerents expected women to act in traditional ways: help in recruiting, staying home to keep the birth rate up, encouraging the men to fight. The armies considered women valuable as nurses, cooks, drivers, and clerks. The British organized the Women's Army Auxiliary Corps (WAAC), which numbered 41,000 in 1918, many of whom served in France as cooks, and the navy and in the air force similarly utilized them. In Germany and Austria-Hungary, women had comparable roles.

Except for a Russian combat battalion in 1917 and for some Polish women fighting in the Austro-Hungarian army, women did not generally engage in combat. The sight of women in uniform (as in the WAAC), even in noncombat roles, aroused hostility. In part, this reaction was due to women freeing up men who served in noncombat positions for combat roles, partly because of class distinctions, and partly because of the perception that women were appropriating the role of men. Women in uniform were particularly susceptible to charges of immorality. The increased illegitimacy rate (from 9 percent to 14 percent in France from 1914 to 1918 and from 10 percent to 13 percent in Germany), as well as increased allegations of adultery as a cause for divorce, reinforced this perception.

Interpretations of the effect of World War I on gender relations differ—from an increasing division because men fought and women did not, to increasing solidarity as women served as nurses and in other auxiliary positions. In either case, the war did not alter the traditional perception of women's role in European society.

State and Society

Total wars, of the kind World War I was the first, demand that the entire society participate in the drive to outproduce and defeat the enemy. This necessity leads to the tremendous growth of state power because governments control and coordinate the economies and society itself.

Governments in the states at war passed emergency legislation that gave them sweeping emergency powers. Parliamentary elections were postponed, and, in practice, legislatures surrendered their right to criticize the government or to act as a check on it, although representative institutions in the democratic countries showed life when war-related crises occurred. Governments set goals for the production of war materiel, allocating resources, and regulating labor through many newly created ministries, commissions, and agencies and controlled the railways, the major means of transportation. They regulated wages and prices, provided welfare, and organized food supplies.

The combatants accepted censorship, once intolerable, as normal. Governmental propaganda urged the people to work hard and to support the governments and their allies. They utilized posters, the press, and the movies—but also parlor games, jigsaw puzzles, and toy soldiers. They published official books to reinforce their viewpoints (which took their name from the colors of their covers). Italian poet Gabriele D'Annunzio dropped propaganda leaflets from the sky for the first time. The belligerents used truths and half-truths to whip up the feelings of their people; some of the stories about German atrocities in Belgium were true, but others were not. Allied propaganda proved more effective than that of the Central Powers, as the campaign against German submarine warfare and attacks on people of German descent in various countries demonstrated. Churches generally supported their governments, as did the Catholic and Protestant churches in Germany. The German Protestants emphasized a war against Catholic France and Orthodox Russia. German Jews were attacked for purported war profiteering and draft dodging. Italian and French Catholics supported the war effort despite Pope Benedict XV's call for peace in January 1915.

The greatly expanded role of government during World War I created enormous difficulties in the postwar period, despite the attempt of some governments to reduce their presence in society, touching off the conflict over governmental interference that characterized twentieth-century Europe.

War and Science

Science benefitted from governmental support. The Germans organized the Raw Materials Section and other entities after September 1914. They hoped to develop substitutes for substances that were needed by the army but were denied them by the Allied blockade. Fritz Haber, the first person to synthesize ammonia from its elements, allowed the Germans to continue their war effort after the blockade cut off this compound necessary for explosives and worked on developing poison gas. Ironically, Haber, a Jew who won the 1918 Nobel Prize for chemistry, resigned his position as director of the Berlin-Dahlem Institute for Physical and Electrochemistry in 1933, following Hitler's anti-Semitic legislation and, heartbroken, left Germany. In Britain, the Zionist Chaim Weizmann made a great contribution to the British war effort with a new process for producing acetone, necessary for munitions, and was a factor in the Balfour Declaration of 1917 that envisioned Palestine as a possible Jewish homeland.

Considerable progress also occurred in medicine. The trenches made soldiers more susceptible to disease, including gangrene, tetanus, and trench fever (caused by lice excrement dug into the skin because of scratching), which the development of new antiseptic preparations and anesthetics helped. The Austrians discovered an early diagnostic procedure for typhus, a chronic disease of soldiers at war. The French perfected a vaccine against typhoid fever, and the British developed one against dysentery. Blood transfusions became normal during the war, and, because of this and other advances, soldiers were much more likely to survive their wounds than in previous wars.

These improvements contrasted with the little that scientists could do against a deadly disease aided by the conflict: Spanish influenza. Although not caused by the war, influenza may have been fostered by the overcrowded conditions in military camps and by the transfer of soldiers to all parts of the world. By 1918 influenza had developed into a pandemic that killed 21 million people, and estimates run as high as 100 million.

THE WAR ENDS

The Germans had attempted to use their submarine weapon effectively in 1915, but the threat of American intervention had dissuaded them. Discussions on reactivating the submarine campaign continued among German planners only because of the deadlock on land and the stalemate at sea, illustrated by the inconclusive Battle of Jutland (May 31–June 1, 1916). The military standoff and British implementation of a successful blockade of Germany led to a change in strategy.

American Intervention

By the end of 1916, the Germans calculated that they could win the war in five months if they instituted unrestricted submarine warfare by designating a zone in which any ship could be sunk without warning and by destroying 600,000 tons of Allied shipping a month. The campaign would prevent food and war material from being shipped to England and prevent the landing of an American Expeditionary Force in France should the United States make good its threat to enter the war because of the submarine campaign. In fact, the Germans exceeded their target but still failed to achieve their objective. A greatly increased British shipbuilding program made good and even exceeded the losses, and the new convoy system reduced the initially high damages to less than 1 percent. The development of depth charges and the use of airplanes against submarines also contained the submarine threat. The United States intervened with its enormous resources on April 6, 1917, making American shipbuilding capacity available to the British and a great number of new troops available for fighting.

Germany's inability to stop American troops and supplies from reaching Europe spelled defeat for the Central Powers. Although the war was generally expected to last into 1919, Germany's allies began to collapse in the fall of 1918. The Bulgarian and Turkish fronts collapsed. The Italians routed the Austrians at Vittorio Veneto, and, on November 4, the war in the South ended with an armistice. The Austro-Hungarian army dissolved, and with it, the empire. Emperor Charles abdicated, Austria and Hungary proclaimed themselves separate republics, and the different nationalities became independent or joined other countries.

On the western front, powerful German offensives in the spring and summer of 1918 failed. Large-scale Allied assaults followed (the Battles of the Argonne and Ypres). Ludendorff insisted that the government begin armistice negotiations as hopelessness triumphed among his troops and as war weariness and the bleak military situation paralyzed Germany. On November 3 naval crews mutinied at Kiel, and the disorders spread rapidly. Revolution broke out in Munich on November 7 and 8. On November 9, Wilhelm II abdicated and fled to Holland, while the Socialists announced the establishment of a German republic and requested an armistice. The fighting was over.

Strategic and Cultural Issues

American intervention and emergence from isolation had worldwide significance. Before 1914, Europe had dominated the world, but the military stalemate demonstrated that the Europeans could not settle their own affairs and had to depend on an outside force to do so.

BIOGRAPHICAL SKETCHES

Erich Maria Remarque

"But now, for the first time, people learned what it was really like"

The author of the most famous antimilitarist war novel *All Quiet on the Western Front* was born Erich Remark on June 22, 1898, in Lower Saxony, Germany, but reclaimed the French spelling of his name used by his ancestors. Because he was the child of an artisan family, the school system barred him from taking humanities courses, but he read widely. He joined with several other youths who were taken with art and literature in a club they called the Dream Circle, where he encountered an older poet and painter who became his mentor.

On November 21, 1916, the army drafted Remarque. At the front he carried a comrade wounded by shrapnel to safety, a soldier transformed into a character in *All Quiet*. A long-range British artillery shell severely wounded him behind the lines, and he became a pacifist during an extended hospital stay. The conflict over, Remarque worked for a magazine as the publicity director and editor, moved on to sports journalism, and wrote novels. He traveled widely and became addicted to hard drinking and beautiful women even after he married. On January 31, 1929, his third novel appeared: *All Quiet on the Western Front*.

According to Remarque, he wrote the novel during a six-week period at night after he returned home from the office. Unsatisfied with the work, he did not submit it for six months, and then the publisher turned it down because no one would be interested in a war novel ten years after the war. A new publisher agreed to bring it out, first serializing it as the biographical work of a nonprofessional writer. The novel confounded the publishing world, selling 1.5 million copies in its first German edition, going through numerous editions worldwide, and making its author rich.

Observers have maintained that despite his claim to have written the work in a hurry, Remarque planned *All Quiet on the Western Front* for years, perhaps while he lay wounded in the hospital. Since he saw little action, he asked friends to describe their wartime experiences and used people he knew as his characters. The manuscript apparently contained explicit pacifist portions that he modified at his publisher's insistence.

In 1930 a film made from the novel attained success everywhere but in Germany, where the Nazis opposed its antimilitarist tone. At its premiere in Berlin, Nazi head Joseph Goebbels and his followers released bevies of white mice, threw stink bombs and beer bottles, and shouted "Germany Awake!" Such tactics blocked its screening in Germany. In the early hours of January 29, 1933, with Adolf Hitler poised to become chancellor, a friend warned Remarque to flee Germany, and he fled across the Swiss border in his Lancia. His novels joined other proscribed books in Nazi bonfires. Ironically, when two storm troopers who were sent to guard his agent's house during the book burnings asked for reading material, they chose to read *All Quiet* and another Remarque novel.

With the royalties from *All Quiet*, Remarque had previously purchased a villa in the Italian part of Switzerland and had sent his money there. He began collecting art with the help of one of his lovers, and the paintings he purchased later were worth millions. When he was later invited to return to Germany, Remarque remarked: "What? Sixty-five million people would like to get away and I'm to go back of my own free will? Not on your life!" He led a pleasant life in the Swiss cafés, had a penchant for movie stars, and had a long affair with Marlene Dietrich. In April 1951 he fell in love with Paulette Goddard, the actress launched by Charlie Chaplin in his classic *Modern Times* and who was formerly married to him. Remarque and Goddard married on February 22, 1958. Remarque wrote twelve other novels but never duplicated the success of *All Quiet on the Western Front*. He died of heart failure on September 25, 1970, and is buried at his villa in Ronco, Switzerland.

In addition, in 1917 the conflict changed character. Imperialist ambitions caused the war, the hope of aggrandizement enticed other powers to enter it, and dreams of gain kept it going. But by 1917 the huge toll of the fighting convinced people that no gain could compensate them for the losses they had sustained. Enter the United States—which claimed to fight only for a principle, to make the world safe for democracy. Democracy would end war and was well worth the price, so World War I was reborn as the "war to end all wars." In 1917 as well, the Bolsheviks seized power in Russia. also claiming to fight for moral principles—to end capitalist exploitation, to transform the world, and to achieve social justice. From 1917 until 1989, communism and liberal democracy, represented by the Soviet Union and the United States, shared the world stage as protagonists.

The experience of the war's main characters, the soldiers, emerged in novels, memoirs, plays, poetry, and films. Perhaps the best-known novels are Erich Maria Remarque's *All Quiet on the Western Front,* from the German side, and Ernest Hemingway's *A Farewell to Arms,* based on his experiences as an ambulance driver in Italy. Robert Grave's *Goodbye to All That* stands as a classic. Former soldiers brought their wartime experiences in the trenches to the general public, and the concrete descriptions of the fighting contrasted with the pompous wartime propaganda.

One important area in which the traditional persevered was in the mourning in which all combatants engaged and that became a central theme. The anguish over the loss of so many loved ones graphically demonstrated the common cultural tradition of the continent. Throughout Europe, commissions searched for the millions of missing soldiers, established new cemeteries, collected bones, and built monuments to the dead. The millions in mourning shared common images, icons, and symbols. The response to the slaughter of World War I produced shock waves in European culture that could be heard into the 1980s, as the French film *Life and Nothing Else But* illustrates. Europeans pursued a suitable diction of bereavement and turned to traditional religious or romantic topics that that emphasized the common character of Europeans, defeated or victorious, and illustrated that the war had been a true civil conflict.

Bibliographical Essay

For more detail on the important economic and foreign policy issues facing the different powers before World War I, refer to the books cited for Chapters 2, 3, and 4.

There are a number of good general treatments of the causes of World War I. James Joll and Gordon Martel, *The Origins of the First World War* (Harlow, UK, 2007), is an excellent diplomatic history. Richard F. Hamilton and Holger H. Herweg, *The Origins of World War I* (New York, 2003), contains essays by distinguished scholars. Laurence Lafore, *The Long Fuse*, 2d ed. ((Philadelphia, 1971), is useful as an introduction, as is David Fromkin's engagingly written *Europe's Last Summer* (New York, 2004). Ian F. W. Beckett's *The Great War 1914–1918* (Harlow, UK, 2001) is as complete a history in one volume as anyone could wish; it examines social, political, and military elements of the conflict, while Miranda Carter's *George, Nicholas and Wilhelm* (New York, 2010) focuses on the three most important monarchs. Eric Dorn Brose's *A History of the Great War* (New York, 2010) is a general account, as is H. P. Wilmott, *World War I* (New York, 2003). William Kelleher's Storey's *The First World War* (Lanham, Maryland, 2012) is a global military history that includes an examination of environmental factors on the war, a discussion of non-European people, and an analysis of the conflict's global impact. As a magisterial treatment considering the issue in minute detail but keeping the whole in perspective, Luigi Albertini's *The Origins of the War of 1914*, 3 vols. (Oxford, 1952–1957), is unlikely to be surpassed.

The English-language translations of Fischer's books were published as *Germany's Aims in the First World War* (London, 1967) and *War of Illusions: German Policies from 1911 to 1914* (New York, 1975). In this latter work may be found the quotations regarding the widespread acceptance by German politicians and military commanders of the Schlieffen Plan, p. 389; of Moltke, p. 214; and the citations of Bethmann-Hollweg on the September Program, p. 536. The debate on the Fischer thesis may be followed in Fritz Fischer, *World Power or Decline: The Controversy over Germany's Aims in the First World War* (New York, 1974), and the excellent, brief John A. Moses, *The Politics of Illusion: The Fischer Controversy in German Historiography* (London, 1975). Woodruff Smith's *The Ideological Origins of Nazi Imperialism* (New York, 1986) is a balanced discussion of Fisher and the "social imperialism" thesis and the relationship of Wilhelmine foreign policy to Hitler's. The idea that the war came out of general conditions before World War I is best argued in Sidney B. Fay, *The Origins of the War* (New York, 1928). Fay's conclusion, quoted in the text, is taken from the second edition, revised, *After Sarajevo: The Origins of the World War*, vol. II (New York, 1966), p. 558. Harry Elmer Barnes, *The Genesis of the World War* (New York, 1970, originally published in 1926), is a more aggressive attempt to blame the war on the general situation, not on Germany. Niall Ferguson's *The Pity of War: Explaining World War I* (New York, 1999) is a revisionist view that sees the war as unnecessary. The historiographical debates are summed up in Annika Mombauer, *The Origins of the First World War* (New York, 2002), and in J. M. Winter and Antoine Prost, *The Great War in History* (New York, 2005).

Walter Laqueur and George L. Mosse, eds., *1914: The Coming of the First World War* (New York, 1966), contains excellent essays on different problems from the perspective of the large and small powers. George F. Kennan, *The Fateful Alliance: France, Russia, and the Coming of the First World War* (New York, 1984), is a thorough examination of the relationship between France and Russia, the counterpart to the Austro-German connection. There is not much in English on Italy's entrance into the war, but see the treatment in Spencer M. Di Scala, *Vittorio Orlando: Italy* (Makers of the Modern World series) (London, 2010), and William A. Renzi, *In the Shadow of the Sword* (New York, 1987). On the general diplomatic issues, see the older but still useful previously cited books by A. J. P. Taylor, *The Struggle for Mastery in Europe* (Oxford, UK, 1954); and René Albrecht-Carrié, *A Diplomatic History of Europe* (New York, 1958); and the more recent Norman Rich, *Great Power Diplomacy, 1814–1914* (New York, 1992). Imperialism is given a good general treatment, including an analysis of the economic and political factors and interpretations, in

Woodruff D. Smith, *European Imperialism in the 19th and 20th Centuries* (Chicago, 1982). Isaiah Friedman wrote a book on British policy in the Middle East during and after the war: *British Pan-Arab Policy, 1915–1922* (New Brunswick, N.J., 2010).

On the arms race before World War I, there is the excellent David G. Herrmann, *The Arming of Europe and the Making of the First World War* (Princeton, N.J., 1996), which compares the armies of all the great powers and their development from 1904 to the war's outbreak; the citations on the lessons learned from the Russo-Japanese War and the 1909 ultimatum are found on p. 68 and p. 126, respectively. Paul M. Kennedy, ed., *The War Plans of the Great Powers 1880–1914* (Boston, 1985), also discusses the thinking behind the plans.

There are many works on the military progress of the war, but Captain B. H. Liddell Hart's *The Real War 1914–1918* (Boston, 1930) remains a classic of its kind; the judgment on the Battle of Verdun is found on p. 215. John Keegan's *The First World War* (New York, 2000) is the most accessible military history in one volume. Michael Howard, *The Lessons of History* (New Haven, Conn., 1991), has several excellent essays on the prevailing mentality before World War I and on military affairs; the Karl Person citation is reported on p. 110. The quote on the French mutiny of 1917 is in the opening chapter of Gaetano Salvemini's *The Origins of Fascism in Italy* (New York, 1973), p. 14. While concerned with Italian Fascism, this book has a good treatment of the misconceptions regarding Caporetto. The full story of the French mutiny and its impact may be found in John Williams, *Mutiny 1917* (London, 1962). Martin Gilbert's *The First World War: A Complete History* (New York, 1994) is a blow-by-blow military history oriented toward the general reader but has surprising gaps; the Churchill citation on tanks is on p. 286. Robert B. Asprey's *The German High Command at War: Hindenburg and Ludendorff Conduct World War I* (New York, 1991) is an excellent account of how the Germans ran the war. The eastern front is covered in scholarly detail by Norman Stone, *The Eastern Front, 1914–1917* (New York, 1975). The best book in English on the Austro-Italian front is John R. Schindler, *Isonzo: the Forgotten Sacrifice of the Great War* (Westport, Conn., 2001); there is also Mark Thompson, *The White War: Life and Death on the Italian Front* (London, 2008). On the war in Africa, an unusual topic, see Edward Paice, *World War I: The African Front* (New York, 2008).

The horrors of trench warfare (and their "literary" repercussions) are detailed by Paul Fussell, *The Great War and Modern Memory* (New York, 1975), invaluable also because of his discussion of the conflict's literary impact. The quotes regarding the national style of the trenches is on p. 45. Marc Ferro, *The Great War 1914–1918* (London, 1973), emphasizes the social aspects of the fighting. Neil M. Heyman, *Daily Life During World War I* (Westport, Conn., 2002), focuses on life both in the trenches and at home. The conduct of the German occupiers of Belgium has long been debated; Larry Zuckerman's book *The Rape of Belgium: The Untold Story of World War I* (New York, 2004) presents evidence on the brutality of the occupation. On the Armenian genocide, see Tanaer Akcam, *A Shameful Act: The Armenian Genocide and the Question of Turkish Responsibility* (New York, 2006). Jennifer D. Keene, *World War I* (Westport, Conn., 2006), describes the lives of the American soldiers.

Developments in the home fronts may be followed in Gerd Hardach, *The First World War 1914–1918* (London, 1977), which is good in discussing international ramifications of the war in all fields, Britain and Germany, especially, and various other countries. Arthur Marwick, *The Deluge: British Society and the First World War* (New York, 1970), is a good general history of British society during the war, as is E. Sylvia Pankhurst, *The Home Front: A Mirror to Life in England During the First World War* (London, 1932), the reminiscences of a radical Englishwoman. Germany is covered in detail in two excellent works by Gerald D. Feldman, *Army, Industry, and Labor in Germany, 1914–1918*

(Princeton, N.J., 1966), and Robert B. Armeson, *Total Warfare and Compulsory Labor: A Study of The Military-Industrial Complex in Germany During World War I* (The Hague, 1964). Jean-Jacques Becker examines the French experience in *The Great War and the French People* (New York, 1986). On Austria-Hungary, see the essays in Robert A. Kann, Bela K. Kiraly, and Paula S. Fichtner, eds., *The Hapsburg Empire in World War I* (Boulder, Colo., 1977).

On women munitions workers in England, there is Angela Woollacott, *On Her Their Lives Depend: Munitions Workers in the Great War* (Berkeley, Calif., 1994), and the more general work by Arthur Marwick, *Women at War 1914–1918* (London, 1977).

Finally, two brief general works may be cited. Jack J. Roth, ed., *World War I* (New York, 1967), argues that World War I was a turning point, and A. J. P. Taylor, *From Sarajevo to Potsdam* (London, 1965), takes the story beyond the war.

On the cultural impact, see Fussell, cited earlier, and Jay Winter, *Sites of Memory, Sites of Mourning: The Great War in European Cultural History* (Cambridge, UK, 1995), which emphasizes the role of mourning and challenges some of the standard interpretations. Some of Fussell's themes are continued by Samuel Hynes, *A War Imagined: The First World War and English Culture* (London, 1991).

CHAPTER 7

✍

The War's Immediate Impact:
The Russian and other Revolutions

CHAPTER OUTLINE
War and the Russian Revolutions • The German Revolution • Revolution in Austria • The Hungarian Revolution • Continuous Rebellion: Artists and Scientists

BIOGRAPHICAL SKETCHES
Vladimir Ilych Ulyanov, A Sealed Train • Rosa Luxemburg, Marxist Martyr

World War I had enormous immediate and long-term repercussions for both the losers and the victors. In the authoritarian countries, revolutions broke out with the goal of establishing liberal or social democratic governments, and fierce struggles raged among the Liberals, Socialists, and Communists. In the parliamentary democracies, economic dislocations, resentment, and radical ideologies caused severe unrest.

WAR AND THE RUSSIAN REVOLUTIONS

In Russia the assassination of Francis Ferdinand and the ensuing diplomatic crisis had touched off popular demonstrations in favor of Serbia, and leading observers predicted a revolution if the tsar failed to protect that country. Nicholas hoped that a Russian victory would build national unity, bolster his popularity, and increase his personal authority.

Russian Military Deficiencies
The Russians had contingency plans only for a short war, and the tsarist regime proved too inflexible, inefficient, and authoritarian to confront the hardships of modern war. The Russians had some competent commanders, but the army suffered from the lack of a general plan of operations and a clear command structure. According to one general, the strategy was "order, counter-order, disorder."

In theory, Russia had an inexhaustible reserve of manpower, but Russian officials mobilized less than half the percentage of its population than did the Germans and less than a third of the French and had poorly trained reserves. When spectacular defeats decimated the standing army and the immediate reserves, untrained recruits replaced them.

The war ministry had no wartime production plan and placed orders in foreign countries, causing long delays in delivery, complicating the integration of weapons, and causing problems with the low quality of foreign purchases. The army ordered its soldiers to fire only ten bullets a day and, when they had no rifles, to wait until they could pick up those of their fallen comrades. The shortages of munitions, clothing, food, and medicine soon became critical and contributed to the spread of deadly diseases in the ranks. The scarcity of railways, trucks, telephones, and telegraphs hampered mobility and impeded communications. Eventually, Russian industry responded better to the enormous demand for war materiel, but too late. The increasing carnage caused by spectacular German victories broke the army. A million soldiers surrendered, and disorderly troops became bandits behind the lines.

Although Russian industry started off slowly in meeting the enormous demands of war and its production of war materiel greatly accelerated during the course of the conflict, it was too late to change the outcome. This poster illustrates a woman working in a war factory; it proclaims "All for the War!"

The February Revolution

Defeat, demoralization, and disorganization ultimately brought down the regime. In July 1915 pressure from critics, including some ministers, small businessmen, and dissident generals, forced the tsar to call the Duma into session. Two-thirds of the members of the Duma joined the Progressive bloc, made up of parties whose political orientation went from the moderate right to the moderate left, that demanded a cabinet that could win the people's support. Paul Miliukov, the leader of the Progressive bloc, asked about the war effort: "Is this stupidity or is it treason?" Ten governmental ministers came out in support of the bloc when Nicholas suddenly announced that he would leave St. Petersburg and assume personal command of the armies at the front.

Panic resulted because Nicholas's plan gave effective control of the capital to the empress and Rasputin. On September 2, 1916, the tsar dissolved the Duma; reaffirmed confidence in his loyal but ineffective prime minister, Ivan Goremykin; and tongue-lashed the rebel ministers. The two-day general strike that followed failed to convince Nicholas to reconvene the Duma, and he fired the Liberal ministers, replacing them with allies of Rasputin. The tsar also tightened police control, extended censorship, fanned anti-Semitism in order to gain popular support, and banned public meetings. When Nicholas left for the front, Empress Alexandra's influence increased dramatically. Rasputin determined the hiring and firing of governmental ministers, causing instability and confusion. Rasputin replaced Goremykin as prime minister with the even more incompetent Boris Stürmer, while the empress consistently misinformed Nicholas about the true situation at home and swayed military decisions by a continuous stream of letters.

The public turned against the tsar, openly criticizing him, discussing his abdication, and accusing the tsarina and Rasputin of sexual misconduct and pro-Germanism. Opposition to the monarchy became synonymous with patriotism, and conspirators talked about how to force the tsar's abdication, arrest the tsarina, and murder Rasputin. On December 16, 1916, young aristocrats lured Rasputin to one of their homes, where they poisoned, shot, and dumped him into a river until he finally died. They had hoped to change Nicholas's politics by this act, but the tsar strengthened his opposition to reform.

By early 1917, the Russian domestic situation had reached a crisis. An exceptionally cold winter exacerbated the food shortages that afflicted the capital. On March 8,[1] International Women's Day, women in St. Petersburg demonstrated for equal rights. Women strikers protesting the bread shortage joined them, and their men came out in support. The government called out the Cossacks, but they hesitated when ordered to fire on the crowds, and the rioting turned into protests against the tsar and the war. Nicholas ordered the military commanders to suppress the uprising, but the soldiers joined the demonstrators. Themselves peasants and workers, the troops went over to the crowd, fought with the police, and

---

[1]The dates used in this account are according to the New Style (Western calendar). As a result, the February Revolution occurred in March, and the October Revolution, discussed in the next section, took place in November.

mutinied. The soldiers occupied strategic points in the capital and transformed the disorders into a revolution. Insurgents raised red flags, commandeered motor vehicles, rushed from one part of the city to the other, attacked the police, and destroyed the symbols of imperial authority. Fifteen hundred people died in the fighting, and 6,000 were wounded. On March 12 the revolutionaries formed the Petrograd Soviet [Council] of Workers' Deputies, dominated by the moderate Socialists (Mensheviks and Social Revolutionaries), and three days later adopted the name Soviet of Workers' and Soldiers' Deputies because of the soldiers' role.

Unfortunately for the revolution, there were two centers of power, the Soviet and the Duma, both of which hesitated to assume command. The Soviet had authority over the revolutionaries but declined to accept formal governing responsibility. It feared that the people might turn on it if it tried to rule and wavered because the revolution had not spread from the capital to the rest of Russia. It also feared an attack from frontline troops headed by the tsar and believed that a government formed by the Duma would reassure the tsar and prevent counterrevolution.

Most of all, the Soviet got caught up in squabbles over doctrine. The idea that Russia must pass through an obligatory bourgeois revolution before it could

The February Revolution overthrew the Tsar and set up a de facto republic but did not end the story. The continued fighting provoked hardship and increasing disorder before the Bolsheviks carried out their coup d'etat in November 1917. This photograph from May 1917 shows Petrograd (St. Petersburg) residents burning coats of arms torn away from buildings.

institute socialism strengthened the idea that the Duma should form a government, but the Duma hesitated because it had little influence in the streets. The result was ironic: the Duma set up a provisional government that had legal power but no real authority; the Soviet, which had authority, did not want legal authority. Finally, the Soviet agreed to support the provisional government, but only if it implemented Soviet principles—rejecting formal command but preventing the provisional government from ruling.

This dual power resulted in paralysis, as illustrated by the Soviet's Order Number One. The order acknowledged the Soviet's authority but provided that the provisional government's military orders be obeyed only if they did not contradict the Soviet's. Order Number One established elected soldiers' committees in army units that undermined the authority of officers and encouraged the breakdown of army discipline, indirectly contributing to the Bolshevik takeover.

The Tsar Abdicates

When the disorders that threatened his throne began, Nicholas attempted to return to his capital, but the revolutionaries diverted his train from Petrograd to Pskov. His most senior advisers informed him that it was too late to put down the revolution and convinced him to abdicate. Nicholas first indicated his son as successor, then his younger brother Michael. This plan might have saved the monarchy but proved impossible to implement. Riots broke out when the tsar's action was announced, and, at any rate, Michael rejected the job. As a result of these developments, Russia became a de facto republic.

Following Nicholas's abdication, the revolution quickly got out of hand. The people rejoiced, then destroyed the symbols of tsarism and attacked the rich. The peasants took matters into their own hands and expropriated the gentry's property. The provisional government had not condoned this move, its inaction helping to account for the decline of its authority and the rise of the Bolsheviks. As violence and looting spread throughout the country, the intellectual demolition of the old regime began. Pamphlets and plays about the royal family's supposedly degenerate lifestyle proliferated. At the front, the officers lost control of their troops. The soldiers desired peace and to return home to participate with their fellow-peasants in the expropriation of land owned by the gentry. Between March and October 1917, a million Russian soldiers deserted. They accelerated the revolution that had already begun on the land. Bolstered by frontline troops, the peasants first forced the gentry to accept long lists of concessions, then confiscated their land and went on a rampage of killing and looting. Local peasant Soviets proliferated and legalized the land takeovers. The administrative structure of the old regime collapsed overnight.

The land and the cities erupted into full revolt. Workers struck for higher wages, the eight-hour workday, better working conditions, and equal pay and maternity leave for women. The spiraling inflation, layoffs, and employers' resistance induced many workers to join labor unions and to make political demands, including governmental control or nationalization of factories and elected factory committees to oversee all phases of production. Workers formed armed Red Guard units to protect the workplaces. As the situation became more chaotic, the moderate Socialist majority of the Soviet sought to oppose the demands of the radical workers. Because moderate Socialists also predominated in the labor unions, these institutions became frontline opponents of the Bolsheviks, who demanded radical changes. Their control of the factory committees and the Red Guards gave the Bolsheviks an enormous influence in the cities that they skillfully exploited in their drive to achieve power. Bolshevik popular support grew rapidly and was substantial by September 1917.

The provisional government proved helpless to confront the revolutionary situation. It endorsed full civil rights, universal, equal, secret, and direct suffrage, and called for a constituent assembly. Because of the different parties' maneuvering for position, voting for this body was finally held only on November 12—too late. A cabinet crisis occurred when Foreign Minister Miliukov avowed that the country would demand the annexation of Constantinople in case of an Allied victory. This declaration touched off a dispute with the Soviet, which advocated peace without annexations. Demonstrations against the government forced Miliukov to resign, and the government followed his example.

A new cabinet came to power. Its strongest member was War Minister Alexander Kerensky, a Socialist Revolutionary (SR), and it included representatives of the Soviet. This government supported continuation of the war and attempted

Seen here saluting his troops, Alexander Kerensky was the strongest and most visible political leader in Russia during the period after the Tsar's fall and the Bolshevik takeover. Many Russians blamed his ineptness for allowing Communism to take over their country. After his defeat he fled to the United States where he did research and lectured. He died in New York in 1970 at age 89.

to stop the breakdown of order. The Soviet representatives went along with both aims, alienating the rest of the body. The majority in the Soviet moved toward the left, while other political forces in the capital reacted by strongly supporting the bourgeoisie and the restoration of order. This polarization of the Russian political situation caused more confusion and helped the Bolsheviks, the only political force with a clear idea of its goals and the will to achieve them.

The October Revolution

Bolshevik chief Vladimir Ilych Lenin had returned to Russia from Swiss exile in a sealed train, courtesy of the Germans. The Germans brought him home because he favored immediate peace, but secured the train because he was a dangerous revolutionary who might infect German workers with his ideology.

Once home, Lenin enunciated the April Theses that he believed would lead to a second revolution. Like the Mensheviks, he had to grapple with Marxist ideology, which mandated that agricultural countries such as Russia would have to traverse a bourgeois phase because socialism could be implemented only by an industrial society. He neatly resolved this issue by maintaining that the February revolution had simultaneously implemented a bourgeois dictatorship and a revolutionary democratic dictatorship of the proletariat and peasantry, which had taken the guise of the provisional government and the Soviet. He then addressed the practical question: the Bolsheviks must proceed directly to the Socialist revolution, which he defined as the rule of the workers and the poor peasants. The Bolsheviks had to do so through the Soviet, Lenin believed, despite its domination by the moderate Mensheviks and SRs. The Bolsheviks should push the Soviet into seizing power and then transform it into a class-conscious (Bolshevik) institution. All production would then come under Soviet control, and all the land would be nationalized and subsequently collectivized. The peasants would not be allowed to hold land privately, except perhaps on a temporary basis.

In implementing these ideas, the Bolsheviks had a great advantage—they were backed by strong armed forces—revolutionary sailors at Kronstadt, the machine gunners of the Petrograd garrison, and the radical workers of the capital's Vyborg district. These shock troops champed at the bit, but Lenin had little popular support. This lack of popular support caused a problem illustrated by the "July days." In an attempt to change the fortunes of war, Kerensky launched an offensive that cost the Russians 400,000 casualties and a like number of deserters. These losses touched off popular demonstrations in the capital, followed by a military revolt by Bolshevik units. This mutiny was spontaneous, had little direction, and quickly failed. The government reacted by arresting key Bolshevik leaders, although Lenin escaped.

The government's show of force against the Bolsheviks, interpreted by the Soviet as a counterrevolution, backfired. Soviet protests led to a government reshuffling. Kerensky emerged as the prime minister with a moderate Socialist majority in the cabinet. He was at the height of his prestige because of his links to the Soviet and the Duma and because of the support he had among the people, the bourgeoisie, and the military leaders. These advantages prompted Kerensky to shift to the right in an attempt to restore calm and to strengthen the country's war effort. His government reduced Soviet influence, reinstated the death penalty for indiscipline at the front, diminished the authority of soldiers' committees, and restricted public gatherings. Kerensky also appointed General Lavr Kornilov, a political rightist and proponent of continuing the war against the Germans, as the commander in chief of the army.

BIOGRAPHICAL SKETCHES

Vladimir Ilych Ulyanov
A Sealed Train

The man who led the Bolsheviks to victory in Russia using the pseudonym Lenin was born on April 22, 1870, in Simbirsk. His father taught school and rose to the position of a provincial school inspector. His mother, Maria Aleksandrovna Blank, a doctor's daughter, devoted her life to her six children.

As a child, Lenin was unruly, noisy, and given to temper tantrums. He is alleged to have had a cruel streak, and his parents punished him more frequently than they did the other children. An intelligent boy, Lenin learned to read at age 5 and excelled in literature, history, and languages at school. He read Latin and Greek and could speak and read several modern languages, including German. In 1887, he graduated from secondary school with a gold medal for excellence in his studies.

Particularly attached to his older brother Alexander, Lenin participated in sports and played chess with him despite their personality differences. Alexander was reserved and studious and, as a child, had his toys broken by his raucous younger brother. The brothers and the other Ulyanov children learned to despise the reactionary social system of tsarist Russia and turned to subversive activities. When Lenin was 17, the police arrested and executed Alexander for plotting to murder Tsar Alexander III. This event was a turning point in the young Lenin's life and filled him with a visceral hatred of tsarism.

After secondary school, Lenin decided to study law at the University of Kazan, but the police arrested and banished him to his grandfather's home village for taking part in a demonstration protesting the lack of freedom. In the fall of 1888, he returned to Kazan but was not readmitted to the university. In September 1889 the family moved to Samara, and in the spring of 1890, Lenin was permitted to resume his studies as an external student at the University of St. Petersburg: He could study for his law degree, but not attend courses. Lenin completed his requirements in eighteen months, passing the final examination in November 1891. He then practiced law in Samara in 1892 and 1893, taking up the causes of poor clients and building up more hatred for the political and legal establishment.

During the time he spent in Samara, Lenin undertook a vast study of Marxist texts and gained a reputation as a formidable theoretician. In August 1893, he moved to the capital of St. Petersburg, continuing his activities as a defender of the poor and a Marxist thinker. During this time, he met his future wife and coworker, Nadezhda Konstantinovna Krupskaya, who taught school for factory workers. Two years later, he was exiled to Siberia, where he remained until 1900. He then left Russia to continue his activities abroad.

Lenin lived and breathed Marxism, attempting to convince people that revolutionary Marxism was still alive despite the assertions of revisionists that Marx had been wrong about the imminent coming of the revolution. His most influential publication from this early period is probably the pamphlet *What Is to Be Done?* (1902). Lenin wrote prodigiously, earning the nickname "the Old Man" at age 23 because of his intensity. He insisted that an elite vanguard dedicated only to the revolution should lead the workers' movement—and he practiced what he preached. It is said that he once rejected a lover because she was not a Social Democrat; she answered that he was "only a Social Democrat" and left him.

Lenin returned to Russia during the revolution of 1905 and left in 1907. When World War I broke out, he was in Switzerland. Lenin believed that war brought a great revolutionary opportunity, and he was right. A revolution occurred in Russia in March 1917, but the country did not withdraw from the war. Because Lenin advocated that the Russians abandon the imperialist conflict, the Germans gave him passage home, but in a sealed train so he could not contaminate their compatriots. Back in Russia, Lenin successfully guided the Bolshevik revolution to victory.

These changes led to the murky Kornilov affair that weakened Kerensky and smoothed the Bolsheviks' road to power. Kerensky and Kornilov hoped to use each other to bolster their own power, jockeyed for position, and got their signals crossed. Kornilov moved troops toward the capital in the mistaken belief that Kerensky had asked for protection from the Bolsheviks, but Kerensky feared being ousted and denounced Kornilov for attempting a coup d'etat. The Soviet reacted by mobilizing, an action that revealed its dependence on Bolshevik military might.

Kerensky's influence declined after the Kornilov affair because the right resented his treatment of Kornilov and the left suspected him of plotting with the general. The episode further radicalized the urban areas and contributed to the process by which the Bolsheviks took over the Soviet in Petrograd, which drove events to take a more radical turn in other major Russian cities during August and September. The Bolsheviks won over the executive bodies of the Soviets, and the Bolshevik leaders, who were arrested during July, were released. These Bolshevik leaders included Leon Trotsky, a subtle strategist, tireless activist, and a spellbinder of crowds.

City elections confirmed the Bolsheviks' increasing importance when the party won an absolute majority in Moscow. At the same time, the moderate Socialist Mensheviks and SRs collapsed. Factory workers had been going over to the Bolsheviks in the spring of 1917, and the trend intensified in the fall because the younger, more militant Bolshevik leaders appealed to them more than did the indecisive Mensheviks and SRs. By late July, Bolshevik party membership swelled to 250,000 members and by October, 350,000. A great increase in industrial strikes and an acceleration of the peasant revolution also took place. What accounted for the growth in Bolshevik popularity was their clear demands: radical social revolution, expropriation of property, peace, and power to the Soviets.

Kerensky continued to hold formal power but became increasingly isolated as the people ignored the government's decrees. The government marked time until a constituent assembly could be elected and produce an executive that had national support. Lenin, however, cut the Gordian knot by convincing his party to organize a revolution before the assembly could meet. He rejected the thesis of Bolshevik leaders who wanted to wait until the outcome of a Soviet congress, which was scheduled for late October, on the assumption that a Soviet government with a strong Bolshevik component would emerge from it. Reasoning that the Bolsheviks would be only one faction of the government, he demanded sole power for his party.

On November 7, 1917 (October 25, old style), a Bolshevik coup took place. Portrayed as a grand occasion in Sergei Eisenstein's classic film *October,* the event was instead described by observers as a small affair that people had almost come to expect. The Kerensky government offered only slight resistance at its seat, the Winter Palace. As Bolshevik troops careened in trucks to take control of the city's strategic areas and buildings, performances at theaters went on as scheduled, patrons drank coffee in cafés, and streetcar traffic was normal. The October Revolution "was in reality such a small event, being in effect no more than a military coup, that it passed unnoticed by the vast majority of the inhabitants of Petrograd."

Consolidation of Bolshevik Power

The next day, at the Soviet congress, the Bolsheviks announced the government's arrest (except for Kerensky, who had escaped). Some resistance now materialized, but Lenin deflated it with a manifesto promising peace, bread, and land. As the Bolsheviks moved to seize the machinery of government, the first signs of division appeared. Strikes broke out, especially among the civil servants who considered the new government illegal. Few believed that the new Bolshevik government would endure because Lenin's drive for complete control had divided the party and isolated it from the rest of the revolutionary movement.

Several factors worked in Lenin's favor. First was his determination to seize power and hold onto it from the bottom up. Lenin energized the Soviets at the local level, the factory organizations, and the soldiers' committees by giving them full support to destroy the existing power structure. This technique undermined local support for his most dangerous competitors, the SRs, and reduced backing for a constituent assembly by making the Soviets the organs of direct democracy. This method eradicated the old political system, a prelude to the building of a new state through a Bolshevik dictatorship. The Bolsheviks also gained the support of the ethnic nationalities by giving them the right to break away from Russia should they wish to do so. The Bolsheviks made a bid for the support of women by repealing laws favoring inequality with men, calling for equal pay for equal work, and supporting the liberation of women from household drudgery.

The Bolsheviks' opponents underestimated them by failing to organize a serious resistance on the assumption that the elections for the constituent assembly would be a national referendum that would end Bolshevik power. In fact, Lenin opposed the elections because he was convinced that the Bolsheviks would lose them. He argued that the direct democracy of the Soviets negated the need for a constituent assembly, but the Bolsheviks' previous propaganda and the national support for the body proved impossible to counter, and the Bolsheviks won only 24 percent of the seats. However, Lenin had no intention of surrendering power.

The Bolsheviks intimidated the assembly's officers, outlawed the Kadet party, and arrested Menshevik and SR leaders. When Bolshevik opponents organized a series of nonviolent demonstrations against these tactics, the Bolsheviks ordered the troops to fire on them and dissolved the constituent assembly after its first meeting in January 1918.

The people did not rise to save the assembly because Lenin pursued a successful campaign to weaken its popular support. Local Soviets approved takeovers of the gentry's holdings, thus satisfying the peasants' centuries-old hunger for land. Lenin encouraged the action of the revolutionaries as "looting the looters." The result was an orgy of despoliation, degradation, and murder perpetrated against the gentry, the bourgeoisie, and the Orthodox Church.

At the same time, Lenin constructed a police state that systematically terrorized its enemies. The Cheka, headed by Felix Dzerzhinsky, was the prime instrument of this campaign. Dzerzhinsky, who had spent half his life in tsarist prisons, created a vast police apparatus of 250,000 people and organized a network of prisons, concentration camps, and torture chambers. The murder of the ex-tsar and his family during the night of July 16–17, 1918, eliminated the threat of a restoration and signaled the beginning of this Red Terror. By then a "White" volunteer army had taken the field to overthrow the "Reds" in a civil war that lasted until 1921. The Allies sent in small detachments to protect their interests, and the Whites hoped that these soldiers would support their efforts, but they did little. The civil war, the Whites' propensity to return land to the gentry in the regions they liberated, and the urgency of organizing a Red Army to fight the Bolshevik enemies increased the terror. The Whites also conducted a vicious terror campaign. These events stiffened the resolve of the Bolsheviks to remain in power. The Cheka greatly extended its activities, and its victims, representing a cross section of Russian society, numbered in the hundreds of thousands.

Bolshevik Policies

Besides a confused domestic situation and civil war, the Bolsheviks still faced the German army. The Bolsheviks supported immediate peace with no annexations or indemnities, but when the Germans continued the conflict, many Bolshevik leaders advocated a revolutionary war on the grounds that the Russian peasants would fight to defend the gains they had made. Lenin disagreed and advocated an immediate separate peace because the Bolsheviks needed time to consolidate their revolution and feared that army remnants would overthrow them if peace were not concluded. The Bolshevik leadership rejected these arguments and adopted Trotsky's idea of withdrawing from the war without signing a peace treaty. The Germans ignored them, attacked, and moved forward 150 miles in five days, forcing the Bolsheviks to sign the peace of Brest-Litovsk on March 3, 1918. This treaty practically pushed Russia out of Europe, with the Russian republic losing 34 percent of its territory, 32 percent of its agricultural land, and 54 percent of its industry. The Ukraine, one of the richest areas of Russia, became a German puppet state.

The disastrous peace nevertheless allowed the Bolsheviks to translate their ideology into action. In 1918 they attempted to organize collective farms, but failed. Even worse, the irate peasants refused to sell their grain at prices fixed by the government because of the rampant inflation and the hope for greater profit. The government thereupon organized committees of poor peasants to seize the stocks of peasants with surplus grain but dropped this policy by the end of the year. The attempt caused great confusion and disorganization that caused a drastic decline in agricultural production. In 1921 and 1922, deaths from famine and disease surpassed the combined total casualties suffered in World War I and the civil war.

Industry was easier to dominate than agriculture because it employed far fewer people and was limited to the cities where the Bolsheviks had greater influence. The Bolsheviks pushed the workers to take over the factories but ran into such strong resistance from former owners and managers that the attempt severely handicapped production. During the summer of 1918, the Bolsheviks responded by nationalizing industry and centralizing its operations under a supreme economic council, a move that failed to eliminate the disorganization and inefficiency. By 1920 industrial production had dropped to 20 percent of the 1913 level. Other areas of the economy, including trade and banking, collapsed as well as the Bolsheviks nationalized them. The economic situation was so desperate that many areas of the country resorted to barter while revolts on the land and in the cities shook the regime.

The NEP

Given this disastrous situation, Lenin backtracked. In 1921, the Bolsheviks officially recognized the private enterprise that had spontaneously revived in various parts of the country and implemented trade liberalization. This New Economic Policy (NEP) had immediate benefits. It increased the volume of trade and reinvigorated agriculture, and state concessions to peasants who wanted to own their own farms greatly bolstered production. Peasant farms increased 65 percent over the prewar figure during the NEP period, but it was an important defeat for the Bolsheviks because the rich and poor reappeared. The NEP was a tactical withdrawal signifying that for the moment the Bolsheviks had renounced their attempt to implement socialism in the agricultural sector, the largest part of the economy. The Bolsheviks were more successful in the much smaller industrial sector, which remained under state control and slowly returned to the 1913 level of production by 1927.

In July 1918 the Bolsheviks announced a new constitution. This document formalized the system of government by Soviets. It created a federation of republics based on the Soviets, the Union of Soviet Socialist Republics (USSR), of which the Russian Socialist Federated Soviet Republic (RSFSR) was the largest. The constitution mandated that the Soviets meet twice a year in the All-Russian Congress of Soviets. This body, in turn, elected the All-Russian Central Executive Committee that voted for the Council of Commissars or government. All citizens aged 18 and older could vote, including women, but the vote was weighted in favor of city workers.

World War I had thoroughly revolutionized Russian politics and society. The monarchy had disappeared, and a Socialist federation had been created.

Most important, the Bolsheviks had demolished the country's entire social, economic, and political structure down to the smallest administrative level of local government. They hoped that the Socialist revolution would spread to the entire world, as Marx had predicted, but when this revolution failed to occur, Bolshevik policy reaffirmed Russian national interests. Nevertheless, in 1918 and 1919, the Bolshevik Revolution's success stood in stark contrast to the other revolutions provoked by the world war.

THE GERMAN REVOLUTION

The revolution that broke out in Germany during the last days of the war was more limited than the Bolshevik Revolution.

Disorders engulfed Germany as the Germans sued for peace. In October a massive strike demanded food, the abolition of martial law, and an end to the three-class Prussian system of voting that propped up conservative rule. The strike was not limited to the antiwar left and Bolshevik sympathizers but drew on the deep dissatisfaction of workers throughout the political spectrum.

End of the War in Germany

Sniffing imminent military disaster, Ludendorff called for the introduction of a parliamentary regime in October 1918. Such a change might get better peace terms from the Allies and would make civilian politicians responsible for the defeat. A new chancellor, Prince Max von Baden, established a parliamentary government that included representatives of the SPD because the prince was a liberal and because the conservative parties were excluded. On October 28 at the Kiel naval base, sailors defied orders to put to sea and mutinied. They raised the Red flag, elected sailors' councils, and demanded the kaiser's abdication. "Fear and hatred ruled the day in Germany." The disorders culminated in Berlin on November 9. The army withdrew its support from Emperor Wilhelm, forcing him to abdicate, and SPD leader Philipp Scheidemann proclaimed a republic. SPD leader Friedrich Ebert replaced Prince Max as chancellor and installed a cabinet consisting of three SPD and three USPD representatives and called for a constituent assembly.

The Struggle for Power

These events touched off a struggle for power between diverse revolutionary centers. The German revolution had been essentially spontaneous, but it took on a more radical character as it progressed. The previous state governments dissolved, and the resulting vacuum encouraged the rebels to elect workers' and soldiers' councils on the Russian soviet model and to proclaim world revolution. The SPD joined the revolution by participating in the election of the councils but was most concerned with preventing chaos and civil war. Consequently, moderates predominated in the revolutionary councils and dampened calls for the nationalization of property. The USPD (which had broken off from the SPD) and the Spartacists, Bolshevik sympathizers, tried to make the German Soviets the revolutionary instruments of government. The lines in Germany were clearly drawn between moderates favoring a parliamentary regime and radicals advocating the implementation of socialism by revolutionary councils.

Because neither side could immediately achieve its objective, they compromised. The constituent assembly would be postponed, the SPD hoping to regroup and the USPD aiming at a consolidation of rule by councils. The compromise turned out to be a defeat for the radicals. On November 12, Ebert eliminated martial law, censorship, and labor restrictions and decreed an amnesty. He promised an eight-hour working day; unemployment assistance; and secret equal voting rights for persons over age 20, including women. The government pledged to nationalize enterprises, consistent with continued production and the protection of property. Because these reforms satisfied the country's desire for democracy and the army's demobilization seemed to end the militarist problem, a large majority of the German people supported a parliamentary government rather than revolutionary socialism. In reality, the government's nationalization program encountered insuperable practical problems and a fear of Bolshevism, and on November 25 a conference of the prime ministers of the German states overwhelmingly voted against nationalization of the banks and in favor of a constituent assembly. The executive committee of the workers' councils objected that any decision on convening the constituent assembly should be delayed until a December 16 meeting of the Congress of Workers' and Soldiers' Councils, but it received a rude shock when the delegates endorsed a constituent assembly.

A sailors' revolt following the meeting was quickly repressed, causing the USPD to withdraw from the cabinet and producing a break between it and the Spartacists. The extreme left concluded that their radical program could be realized only by force before the constituent assembly convened, as had happened in Russia. Consequently, the Spartacists constituted themselves as the German Communist Party (KPD) on December 30, 1918. The KPD's most visible leader and most notable theoretician, Rosa Luxemburg, favored caution but published inflammatory statements in the party newspaper that had the opposite effect. The revolt began when the government dismissed the Berlin chief of police, supported by the Communists, but it lacked a strategic plan.

The government deputized SPD leader Gustav Noske to quell the revolt. He aimed to destroy the KPD, but the army was demobilized, so Noske turned to the Freikorps—restless, conservative, elite, intensely anti-Communist volunteer ex-soldiers who were committed to protecting Germany's eastern frontier against Russians and Poles. Freikorps units brutally suppressed the Spartacists and murdered Luxemburg and Liebknecht. By employing the Freikorps, the government set a precedent for later paramilitary action.

Foundation of the Weimar Republic

Balloting for the Constituent Assembly occurred on January 12, 1919, with women voting for the first time. The democratic parties won a majority: the SPD, the Center party, and the Democrats (the old Progressives). The election ended the German revolution despite the continuation of disorder over the next few years. In the winter and spring of 1919, there were several Communist uprisings, but the Friekorps suppressed them. Strikes and uprisings continued into the early 1920s because of the severe economic crisis. In March 1921 and October 1923, Communist revolutions were attempted and failed. The extreme right attempted two failed putsches that occurred under Wolfgang Kapp in March 1920 and Adolf Hitler in November 1923.

BIOGRAPHICAL SKETCHES

Rosa Luxemburg
Marxist Martyr

A prolific writer, Rosa Luxemburg earned a lasting reputation as a major Marxist theoretician. She was born in Russian-controlled Poland on March 5, 1871, to an assimilated Jewish family. Rosa's father ran a timber business and frequently traveled to Germany. He had been educated in Germany, and German culture predominated in the home. The family paid little attention to the active local Jewish community.

As a young woman, Luxemburg became attracted to socialism and took an active part in the Socialist debates in Poland. She established a reputation as an independent thinker and as a tenacious defender of her ideas. Both in her youth and in later years, she engaged in spirited fights with famous European Socialists, including the Russians Vladimir Lenin and Georgii Plekhanov and Austrian Socialist leader Viktor Adler. Besides her intellectual capacities, Luxemburg's appearance commanded respect from adversaries and colleagues. A fastidious woman, she wore expensive but plain clothes and never appeared in disarray. Because of time served in prison, Luxemburg suffered from ill health, and her hair turned white. She had a rigid personality, which contributed to her difficulties in getting along with people, especially her intellectual inferiors. Luxemburg disliked some people easily and quickly, not necessarily on ideological grounds. Addicted to walking, for example, she detested colleagues she considered physically lazy. Her German collaborator Clara Zetkin managed to work with her because she acknowledged Luxemburg's intellectual preeminence.

Upon graduation from the University of Zurich, Luxemburg moved to Berlin in May 1898, obtaining a residence permit by concluding a sham marriage with the son of a Polish friend living in Germany. In Berlin, she lived in an apartment that faithfully reproduced her meticulous personality —filled with old, well-preserved furniture, carpets, and favored gifts. She methodically marked everything, neatly stored her books, and carefully put away her manuscripts so they would be easy to find if she requested friends to do so.

Once established in Germany, Luxemburg rose to prominence in Socialist circles. In February 1914, the authorities tried her because she publicly called on German soldiers to refuse to fire on their French brethren in case of war. When the trial ended, she made a speech that became legendary in German Socialist annals, but, her appeals exhausted, the police arrested her in early 1915 and shipped her off to prison.

In the last weeks of the war and during the revolutionary crisis immediately following the conflict, Luxemburg and Karl Liebknecht led the Spartacists, a revolutionary Communist league. This organization sparked a revolution, and Luxemburg went along despite her misgivings. The Freikorps put down the

continued

continued

revolution in blood and arrested both leaders on January 15, 1919. The Communist leaders were brought in for questioning, but the soldiers had already made plans to kill them. The soldiers beat Luxemburg and took her to a waiting car where an officer shot her through the head. The killers dumped the body in a canal and gave out the story that a mob had kidnapped her. Luxemburg's body resurfaced on May 31. The murders of Luxemburg and Liebknecht, shot "while trying to escape," led to widespread protests in Germany and outside the country, but except for the left, the German press considered the killings a natural consequence of the attempted revolution.

On June 13, 1919, Luxemburg was buried alongside her fallen comrades who had been entombed earlier. Supporters dedicated a memorial to the fallen martyrs of 1919 on June 13, 1926, but the Nazis later demolished it. The East Germans rebuilt it after World War II.

On February 11, 1919, the Constituent Assembly, meeting in the city of Weimar, chose Friedrich Ebert as the republic's first president and on July 31 adopted a Liberal constitution. The Weimar Republic would last only twelve years. The German Socialists allowed the empire's authoritarian bureaucratic structure, its social structure, and its powerful army to remain intact, and these were the Achilles' heel of the new democratic republic.

REVOLUTION IN AUSTRIA

In Austria, the Social Democrats (SDs) played a role similar to that of their German counterparts in defeating attempts to revolutionize Austrian society. During the war, the SDs supported the war effort on the grounds that Russia was an autocracy, but with the Bolshevik Revolution, this rationale dissipated, and resentment against the war increased.

The Austrian Uprising

As Austria-Hungary spiraled toward defeat, an ethnic and social revolution loomed. Strikes broke out, and different subject minorities plotted to secede. On May 30, 1917, the government called Parliament back into session after a three-year break in order to defuse the discontent. Instead the Socialists recognized the right of Slavic peoples to self-determination and looked forward to a democratic republic, socialism, and union with Germany if the empire broke apart.

In January 1918, a wave of strikes hit the country, and a Socialist manifesto exhorted the workers to fight for peace without annexations. The strike movement spread to Hungary, and the first revolutionary workers' councils were established. The SDs, however, did not push for revolution because the Czechs were heading toward succession and the Germans appeared ready to invade. The strike ended with the government's acceptance of a set of workers' demands, but had important political consequences. It hastened the breakup of the empire by touching off mutinies in the armed forces and encouraged the Slavs to prohibit the export of food and strategic materials to Austria. This action prompted the SDs to demand

Socialist head Karl Renner was instrumental in preventing a social revolution in Austria and instituting reform in a democratic context, as was Friedrich Ebert, his German counterpart. He became the first Chancellor of the new Austrian Republic in 1918 and the first President of the Second Republic in December 1945.

a separate German Austrian parliamentary republic and, in concert with other Austrian parties, declared that the German Austrian deputies constituted a provisional national assembly. On October 24, 1918, the final Italian offensive that destroyed the Hapsburg armed forces began, and between October 28 and 31, the empire dissolved. The subject territories declared their independence, the Austrians issued a republican constitution, the emperor abdicated, and the Political Council of the provisional national assembly took control. Returning Austrian soldiers formed Red Guards, seized armories and food stores, and ran amok.

The Austrian revolution quickly turned into a social uprising. A new SD-led cabinet took power and raised a military force based on a preexisting Socialist network, the Volkswehr, composed primarily of factory workers returning home from the war. This force included soldiers who had witnessed the revolution in Russia and who were anxious to spread it to Austria.

The Revolution Winds Down
Like their German colleagues, the Austrian Socialists opposed a Bolshevik type revolution and faced a dilemma. The Entente maintained its blockade against

Austria as the war wound down and vowed to lift it only if peace and order were maintained. The SDs understood this policy to mean that the Allies opposed the spread of Bolshevism and supported the establishment of a bourgeois democracy. The Allies could starve any radical revolution into submission—a revolution that, at any rate, had little popular support outside Vienna. The peasants favored a republic only because of the hardships of a long war, but they rejected government-imposed price controls and condemned the nationalization of property.

The SDs concluded that the dictatorship of the proletariat demanded by radical Viennese workers would lead to a bloody civil war and emphasized reform in a democratic context. On February 16, 1919, they won 69 out of 150 seats in elections for the National Assembly. Led by Karl Renner, they became the dominant partners in a coalition cabinet with the progressive wing of the Catholic (Christian Social) party. The government implemented a series of social reforms, including unemployment relief, forcing employers to hire new workers in a set proportion to their existing personnel, and prohibiting them from dismissing employees. On December 17, 1919, a law established the eight-hour workday and on July 30, annual vacations. Other legislation instituted workers' committees in factories and other enterprises.

After these reforms, the passion for revolution cooled off because of fears of a Communist takeover and the bourgeoisie's recovery of confidence. An Austrian Communist party was founded on November 3, 1918, and the spring of 1919 brought the establishment of a Soviet republic in Hungary, a Hungarian request for Austrian support, and an SD refusal. The Hungarians fomented Austrian revolutions on April 18 and June 15, both put down by the Volkswehr.

By the summer of 1919, the Austrian revolution had run its course, with even the SD considered too far to the left. On October 17, 1920, the Catholics won a majority in the National Assembly and formed a new cabinet without the SDs. A currency crisis and the financial restrictions necessary to resolve it completed the return of the bourgeoisie to power. As in Germany, the Social Democrats succeeded in instituting important reforms but not in altering Austrian society.

THE HUNGARIAN REVOLUTION

The Hungarian part of the former Dual Monarchy followed a different course. Hungary was the only country to which the Bolshevik revolution spread, if only briefly.

Opposition to the War
In Hungary dissatisfaction, strikes, and sabotage increased as World War I dragged on. In the fall of 1917, supporters of the Bolshevik revolution organized workers' councils on the Russian Soviet model, and in January 1918, a massive strike movement hit Budapest when news of the Brest-Litovsk negotiations and the Austrian protest strikes arrived. The Hungarian Socialists endorsed the strike, but only on a limited basis. The government's backtracking on a series of promises favored the emergence of an extreme left and polarized the Socialist movement. In June

a second major strike wave rocked the country, and a determined Communist group began taking shape.

Béla Kun and the Hungarian Communists

The Communist hard core consisted of a group of Moscow-trained Hungarian prisoners of war, led by former Social Democrat Béla Kun, who had participated in the Bolshevik revolution. The Communists returned to Hungary with Lenin's blessing with the goal of establishing a Hungarian republic of Workers' and Soldiers' Councils. Kun arrived in Budapest on November 7, 1918, and by November 24 had convinced opposition elements in the Social Democratic opposition to secede and form the Communist Party of Hungary. Kun built a centralized party organization on the Russian example and recruited members among the unemployed, the poor, and former prisoners of war.

In October 1918, opposition leader Mihály Károlyi formed a liberal democratic government with Social Democratic participation. By then Hungary had lost half its territory, the economic situation was desperate, and demands were made to set up a popular republic. Social Democratic membership in the cabinet limited the party's political choices and favored Kun's intransigent Communists as workers seized factories, peasants attacked landed estates, workers' councils replaced city administrations, and unruly soldiers roamed the streets. On March 19, 1919, the Entente sent Hungary an ultimatum requiring it to form a neutral zone on its eastern frontier and to withdraw its army behind it, further radicalizing the masses and resulting in a Socialist withdrawal from the government. The Socialists then reached an agreement with Kun and the Communists that effectively merged their two organizations. Thus, the Hungarian Soviet Republic came into existence because of Kun's Russian connections and Allied blundering.

The Hungarian Soviet Republic

The Hungarian Soviet Republic, born in April 1919, had a brief life of 133 days. Two fatal illusions and two ideological fallacies condemned it. The illusions were that the Russians would send help and that the Socialists and Communists would cooperate; the fallacies were that socialism could be installed rapidly in Hungary and that the revolution was part of a worldwide wave.

The Hungarian Soviet Republic's governmental structure consisted of an executive, the Revolutionary Governing Council (RGC), and, wielding the ultimate power, the Budapest Council of Workers' and Soldiers' Deputies. Both institutions had Socialist not Communist majorities. As time went on, the Socialists became more restless with the alliance, and the Communists proved unable to garner much mass support in the country. Despite their minority status in the government and the country, the Communists initially had great influence because of Kun's presence in the cabinet and because the RGC passed reform measures, including the eight-hour workday, higher wages, and lower rents.

Other, more specifically Communist, actions proved less successful or alienated the population: the abolition of conscription, a volunteer army composed exclusively of proletarians, and collectivization of the land. The Communists also failed to keep support in the cities because extremist Communists controlled the

Although Béla Kun's Communist regime in Hungary following World War I was relatively brief, its success and its policies alarmed Europe and he was overthrown. However, its historical impact was considerable and its memory remained strong. The photo shows a Soviet-era rendering of the Hungarian Revolution of 1919.

secret police and utilized terror against the Revolution's enemies through the "Lenin Boys"—leather-jacketed thugs and criminals—who specialized in break-ins and kidnapping. The Socialists ended the Lenin Boys' activities, won control of the police, and reversed Communist influence.

End of the Soviet Republic

On April 17, the Romanians attacked Hungary after Kun turned down yet another Allied ultimatum, and the Hungarian Soviet Republic descended into chaos as the population turned against the postwar disorder, Jewish Communist leaders, and a governmental anticlerical campaign. On June 24 the Socialists resigned from the RGC, resulting in a new wave of Communist violence. Czech and Romanian forces converged on Budapest, and on August 1, 1919, Kun resigned and fled the country.

The balance sheet of the Hungarian Soviet Republic was unimpressive. Its brief tenure did not alter Hungarian society, and the reaction to it paved the way for an authoritarian regime.

CONTINUOUS REBELLION: ARTISTS AND SCIENTISTS

World War I encouraged not only political and social but also cultural revolutions that had antecedents in prewar Europe; the conflict removed all restraints on them. In the case of science, the fundamental research conducted before the war came into full fruition during the 1920s, 1930s, and thereafter, culminating in the development of the atomic bomb and in nuclear energy.

Dada and Revolution

While in exile in Zurich, Lenin lived at Spiegelgasse number 12. Across the street, on February 5, 1916, a young German couple opened the Cabaret Voltaire, which had "the object of becoming a center of artistic entertainment. The Cabaret Voltaire will be run on the principle of daily meeting where visiting artists will perform their music and poetry." While the staid and cold Lenin studied and plotted revolution, Hugo Ball, a poet and theater director who had fled Berlin during World War I, played the piano while his future wife, Emmy Hennings, sang for the patrons. The new café began quietly as a literary adventure but quickly escalated into a boisterous nuisance that instigated many complaints by the public. It is easy to understand why: "Total pandemonium. The people around us are shouting, laughing, and gesticulating. Our replies are sighs of love, volleys of hiccups, poems, moos, and miaowing. . . . Tzara is wiggling his behind like the belly of an oriental dancer. Janco is playing an invisible violin and bowing and scraping." The sedate but now irate neighbors called the police, who shut down the cabaret but ignored Lenin. While Lenin read Marx, the Cabaret Voltaire gave birth to the extraordinary literary and artistic movement known as Dada.

The émigrés who flocked to the club included Tristan Tzara, the tiny but aggressive Romanian poet who invented the word *Dada* and electrified audiences with his iconoclastic readings; Dr. Richard Huelsenbeck, whose riding whip whistled in the air during his performances—"metaphorically—onto the public's behind: Shalabenshalabei-shalametzomai"—and the artists Hans Arp, Marcel Janco, and Max Oppenheimer. Dada fights, abuse, and audience provocations, copied from Italian Futurism, became their trademark and its iconoclasm an instant sensation. The proponents of Dada opened a gallery in Zurich in January 1917, where Ball read abstract sound poems that discarded traditional language, "devastated and ravaged by journalism." Arp tore up one of his drawings, let the pieces flutter to the ground, and glued them back together again in the chance arrangement in which the pieces had fallen: Dadaists contended that they had discovered in chance the "'mobilization of the unconsciousness."

The Dadaists mutinied against the nineteenth-century belief in progress, but in contrast to futurism, Dada was apolitical: a "state of mind," "a force of nothingness," above all "a protest against the civilization that had led to the war. . . . " The conflict proved the total bankruptcy of European civilization, and its adherents claimed that they wanted to destroy its moral and social assumptions through a savage anti-middle-class program. That strategy seemed to be working when, at the war's end, Dada spread like wildfire to revolutionary Germany, Italy, Hungary, and other countries where old political systems were breaking down. Dada was the counterpoint to political revolution, spreading rebellion against art and authority.

In 1918 Dada's center shifted to Paris, where prewar avant-garde movements and disgust at the war had prepared a fertile ground. In late 1919, Tristan Tzara arrived to wild acclaim to organize Dadaist activities in the French capital. André Breton, his main contact there, had been converted to Dadaism by his wartime experiences. In 1918 he founded the review *Littérature* in which disillusioned former French warrior intellectuals aimed to tear down the restraints of bourgeois society and attracted Tzara's attention. On January 23, 1920, the *Littérature*

Dada and Surrealism were the two revolutionary artistic movements that shook
Europe during and following World War I. In this 1932 photograph, the most famous
exponent of Dada, Tristan Tzara, is in the center, and Paul Breton, founder of Surrealism,
is on the left.

group organized the first Parisian Dada manifestation. By this time, ironically,
the bourgeois society that it vilified had accepted Dada, and Dada acknowledged
this critical acclaim. Consequently, Parisian exponents of Dada, including Breton,
condemned the movement for having become stagnant and orthodox and started
a new artistic movement.

Surrealism

Like Dadaism, surrealism demanded the destruction of art and a return to chaos
in order to recover the subconscious and believed that the automatic method of
writing could achieve that aim. While Dadaism stressed destruction, surrealism
declared that a new art would emerge from the unconscious, from the irrational, and from the uncontrolled regions of the mind. In this sense, the surrealists
accepted psychoanalytical notions and methods and discovered a second reality
fused with but different from ordinary reality. This conception influenced important novelists writing at the time, such as James Joyce and Franz Kafka, "who,
although they have nothing to do with surrealism as a doctrine, are surrealists in
the wider sense, like most of the progressive artists of the century."

Unlike Dada, a sense of wonder was linked to surrealism, and surrealism
appeared as a fundamentally optimistic movement. It represented a first attempt
to heal from the horrors of war and paralleled the winding down of revolutionary
activity in politics. Surrealist ideas may be seen in the paintings of Salvador Dali,
who introduced and mixed the most incongruous realistic items, such as a

donkey's dead body on a piano. Superficially, Dali's paintings are absurd, but they are really "the expression of a desire to bring unity and coherence . . . into the atomized world in which we live."

As the war receded, revolutionary artistic developments were gradually absorbed into the mainstream to become, along with death, destruction, and upheaval, the common European heritage of World War I.

Revolutionary Developments in Physics

The search for unity in the arts paralleled events in science. Since its first expression in 1900, the quantum theory had produced stranger and stranger notions of reality. In 1925 German scientist Werner Heisenberg elaborated the uncertainty or indeterminacy principle according to which the observer, far from being neutral, changed reality. Experimenters, for example, could not simultaneously determine both the velocity and position of an atom's electron because doing so would alter the variables involved. In the hidden subatomic world, the rules changed, nothing could be known for certain, and weird and contradictory states coexisted. This uncertainty resembled the unconscious that was so important in modern art. Just as the surrealists believed in a second reality, light had a dual nature, and scientists Werner Heisenberg and Niels Bohr contended that in the subatomic world, "there are two truths rather than one alone." In 1919, an important confirmation of Einstein's relativity theory arrived when an experiment conducted during a solar eclipse showed that gravity bent light. Relativity, which had "disintegrated common sense," was accepted, and Einstein became famous. After World War I, science kicked out the intellectual underpinnings of European society with even greater effect, perhaps, than art.

Bibliographical Essay

The historical literature on the Russian revolutions of 1917 is extraordinarily rich and generally includes discussions of the old regime; the reader, however, should beware of interpretations based on ideology. Interestingly enough, these viewpoints have varied not only according to ideology but also to periods. Moreover, it is likely that different perspectives will emerge on the entire Communist experience because of the Soviet Union's demise in 1991 and as previously closed archives are combed by historians.

Richard Pipes wrote two extraordinarily detailed and scholarly works that are basic to an understanding of events, *The Russian Revolution* (New York, 1990), and *Russia Under the Bolshevik Regime* (New York, 1993). Orlando Figes produced a detailed and well-documented but very accessible history, *A People's Tragedy: The Russian Revolution, 1891–1924* (New York, 1996); it is from this book that the quotations on the lack of a general plan for the Russian army in World War I (p. 259) and the description of Petrograd on October 25 (p. 484) are taken. The role of Russian peasants in the years up to and including the revolutions and later is examined by Aaron B. Retish, *Russia's Peasants in Revolution and Civil War: Citizenship, Identity, and the Creation of the Soviet State, 1914–1922* (Cambridge, UK, 2008). Alexander Rabinowitch published a good account of how *The Bolsheviks Came to Power: The Revolution of 1917 in Petrograd* (New York, 1978) and one on how they maintained power during the crucial first year, *The Bolsheviks in Power* (Bloomington, Ind., 2007). An idea of the different terrors may be found in

The Red Terror in Russia (London, 2008), by S. P. Mel'gunov, and *White Terror: Cossack Warlords of the Trans-Siberian* (New York, 2005) by Jamie Bisher. Sean McMeekin discusses the "looting" of Imperial Russia's riches by the Bolsheviks in *History's Greatest Heist* (New Haven, Conn., 2008). All these works pay great attention to social as well as political and intellectual matters. A classic eyewitness account is John Reed, *Ten Days That Shook the World* (New York, 1967); another eyewitness description is Nikolai N. Sukhanov, *The Russian Revolution, 1917: Eyewitness Account,* 2 vols. (New York, 1962). A brief but well-done overview of the revolution is Sheila Fitzpatrick's *The Russian Revolution* (Oxford, UK, 1982). Another good, short book is Theodore H. Von Laue, *Why Lenin? Why Stalin? A Reappraisal of the Russian Revolution, 1900–1930,* 2d ed. (Philadelphia, 1971).

Bruce W. Menning's *Bayonets Before Bullets: The Imperial Russian Army, 1861–1914* (Bloomington, Ind., 2000) is a general history, while the agony of the Russian army and its role with respect to the revolution is minutely examined by Allan K. Wildman, *The End of the Russian Imperial Army,* 2 vols. (Princeton, N.J., 1980–87). The standard work on Brest-Litovsk is John Wheeler-Bennett, *Brest-Litovsk: The Forgotten Peace, March 1918* (New York 1971).

Good studies of the working class in major Russian cities include S. A. Smith, *Red Petrograd: Revolution in the Factories, 1917–1918* (Cambridge, UK, 1983), a thorough examination of factory organization and the workers during the revolutionary period. David Mandel, *The Petrograd Workers and the Soviet Seizure of Power: From the July Days, 1917 to July 1918* (London, 1984), looks at the role of the workers between those dates. Diane Koenker does the same for Moscow in *Moscow Workers and the 1917 Revolution* (Princeton, N.J., 1981). The situation on the land is amply discussed in the previously cited books, but see also a work dedicated to the SRs and their fate, Oliver H. Radkey, *The Agrarian Foes of Bolshevism: Promise and Default of the Russian Socialist Revolutionaries, February to October, 1917* (New York, 1958). Robert Vincent Daniels, *The Conscience of the Revolution: Communist Opposition in Soviet Russia* (New York, 1960), examines the disputes on various issues within the Bolshevik party itself. On a different social class and its role, see Matthew Rendle, *Defenders of the Motherland: The Tsarist Elite in Revolutionary Russia* (New York, 2010). The civil war's course is considered in detail by David Footman, *Civil War in Russia* (New York, 1961).

Biographies of the major characters are plentiful and easily available, but two may be mentioned here: Robert Service, *Lenin: A Political Life,* 2 vols. (Bloomington, Ind., 1985–91), is a complete life, and the first volume of Issac Deutscher's classic biography, *The Prophet Armed: Trotsky, 1879–1921* (New York, 1955), covers the period considered in the text while *The Prophet Outcast* (New York, 1963) covers his later life. Robert Service takes a different view from many historians in his *Trotsky: A Biography* (Cambridge, Mass., 2009). Raymond K. Massie tells the story of what happened to the bodies of the royal family and their servants after their murder and explains how DNA evidence was used to identify their remains in a fascinating study, *The Romanovs: The Final Chapter* (London, 1995).

F. L. Carsten discusses the German, Austrian, and Hungarian revolutions in an excellent work, *Revolution in Central Europe 1918–1919* (Berkeley, Calif., 1972). Pierre Broue, *The German Revolution, 1917–1923* (n.p,, 2006) is a general work. The German Socialists and their action during the revolution of 1918 are examined in a well-argued and detailed work by A. J. Ryder, *The German Revolution of 1918: A Study of German Socialism in War and Revolt* (Cambridge, UK, 2008). The first volume of Richard J. Evans, *The Coming of the Third Reich* (New York, 2004) discusses Germany right after the end of World War I; the quote on the fear that prevailed is on p. 78. Richard A. Comfort,

Revolutionary Hamburg: Labor Politics in the Early Weimar Republic (Stanford, Calif., 1966), concentrates on labor politics in an important city. The most thorough work on Rosa Luxemburg and her influence is J. P. Nettl, *Rosa Luxemburg* (New York, 1975). Werner T. Angress, *Stillborn Revolution: The Communist Bid for Power in Germany, 1921–1923* (Princeton, N.J., 1963), analyzes Communist attempts to take power in Germany between 1921 and 1923.

Mark Cornwall discusses the Austro-Hungarian war effort and the end of the empire in his *The Undermining of Austria-Hungary* (New York, 2000). The Austro-Hungarian Empire's breakup is considered in detail in Z. A. B. Zeman, *The Break-Up of the Hapsburg Empire* (New York, 1977); Leo Valiani, *The End of Austria-Hungary* (London, 1973); and the second volume of Arthur J. May's *The Passing of the Hapsburg Monarchy 1914–1918* (Philadelphia, 1966). The chapter on Austria-Hungary in Sir Lewis Namier's *Vanished Supremacies: Essays on European History, 1812–1918* (London, 1958) can still be read for its remarkable insights. A manageable and surprisingly objective account of the revolution in Austria and the interplay of the various nationalities, by an important participant, is Otto Bauer, *The Austrian Revolution* (New York, 1970). John C. Swanson, *The Remnants of the Habsburg Monarchy* (Boulder, Colo., 2001) examines the end of the empire and the creation of the new states up to 1922.

Rudolf F. Tökés, *Béla Kun and the Hungarian Soviet Republic: The Origins and Role of the Communist Part of Hungary in the Revolutions of 1918–1919* (New York, 1967), is an excellent account of the roles of the Communists and Socialists during the Hungarian revolution and a good general history of that event; it is also valuable for its reproduction of documents and other appendixes. Tibor Hajdu, *The Hungarian Soviet Republic* (Budapest, 1979), is a good complement to the previous work because of its archival sources and treatment of social and cultural issues, although it takes a rather narrow approach. Howard Morley Sachar, *Dreamland: Europeans and Jews in the Aftermath of the Great* War (New York, 2002) has a chapter on Kun. A reprint of a 1924 work, Oscar Jaszi, *Revolution and Counter-Revolution in Hungary* (New York, 1969), is still useful for its detail.

Some books that analyze the themes with relation to the arts discussed in this chapter include Irving Howe, ed., *The Idea of the Modern* (New York, 1967), which primarily deals with literature. The reader will find interesting essays on Dadaism, surrealism, and other modern movements; the citations on surrealism and surrealist painting are on pp. 231 and 232. A good idea of Dadaism's nature can be gained by reading Tristan Tzara's *Seven Dada Manifestos and Lampisteries: Documents of the International Dada Movement* (London, 1977). Hans Richter published *Dada 1916–1966* (Munich, 1966), which includes art reproductions and documents; the quote on Huelsenbeck's performance is on p. 3, and the idea of the mobilization of the unconscious is on p. 7. Hugo Ball's diary, *Flight Out of Time: A Dada Diary* (New York, 1974), features an excellent introduction; the description of activities at the Cabaret Voltaire is on p. xxiii. Kenneth Coutts-Smith, *Dada* (London, 1970), is a brief overview that reprints the advertisement quoted in the text on p. 9 and uses the term "savage anarchism" on p. 22. Histories of Dadaism include Dietmar Elger and Uta Grosenick, *Dadaism* (Los Angeles, 2004), and Rudolf E. Kuenzli, *Dada* (London, 2006), a wider treatment. Ruth Hemus, *Dada's Women* (New Haven, Conn., 2009) assigns a more important role to women in Dadaism than was previously thought. J. H. Matthews, *An Introduction to Surrealism* (University Park, Penn., 1965), is an excellent starting point for understanding the movement, while Mary Ann Caws, *Surrealism* (London, 2004), is a general history. See also Nahma Sandrow, *Surrealism: Theater, Arts, Ideas* (New York, 1972), for the remark on Einstein's disintegration of common sense, p. 13. The discussion of Einstein,

Heisenberg, and quantum theory may be followed in Denis Brian, *Einstein: A Life* (New York, 1996); the citations regarding the uncertainty principle and its implications are on pp. 162 and 163 (see also Einstein's remark regarding quantum theory on p. 199). Galvin Parkinson describes the connections between physics thinking and art during the period in *Surrealism, Art, and Modern Science: Relativity, Quantum Mechanics, Epistemology* (New Haven, Conn., 2008).

CHAPTER 8

❦

The Consequences of the Peace

CHAPTER OUTLINE

The Paris Peace Conference • The Territorial Consequences • Economic
Consequences • The Moral Consequences • The League of Nations

BIOGRAPHICAL SKETCHES

Georges Clemenceau, Tiger • Sidney Sonnino, Failed Diplomatist

The Paris Peace Conference that convened on January 18, 1919, to hammer
out peace terms and ensure future peace, had as its model the Congress of
Vienna, held in 1814 and 1815, at which "the boundaries of almost every state
in Europe were remodeled; reparations were inflicted upon the dominant military power; colonial territories were redistributed; new international organizations were erected; and even schemes for the perpetuation of world peace were
considered."

In fact, the Vienna precedent did not hold for several reasons. In Paris the
representatives had to consider popular opinion, which demanded revenge against
the Germans, and to confront a new factor, the overwhelming power of the United
States, which had rescued the Allies and did not sympathize with their values.

THE PARIS PEACE CONFERENCE

In a speech to the U.S. Congress on January 8, 1918, American President Woodrow
Wilson issued the Fourteen Points as the basis for ending the war and concluding a lasting peace. Open agreements "openly arrived at" must replace traditional
diplomacy and secret treaties, he said, as he enunciated his points: freedom of the
seas as defined by international law; elimination of trade barriers; arms reduction;
and giving native colonial populations equal weight with imperial governments.
His concrete proposals included the autonomous development of the nationalities
of the Austro-Hungarian and Turkish empires; the formation of an association
of nations to guarantee peace; and German withdrawal from Russian, Belgian,

French, Romanian, and Serbian territory. Very important for Wilson and the Europeans was the establishment of an independent Poland with access to the sea to ensure its economic viability; the return of Alsace and Lorraine to France; and the rectification of international borders, such as the Italian, along clearly recognized lines.

Contentious Issues

When American intervention and acceptance of the Fourteen Points by the Germans ended the war and Wilson toured the continent, the people received him with wild enthusiasm, but the Allies tried to water down the proposals that most affected their own national interests. They bargained with Wilson before the peace conference met and compromised his principles, especially with regard to British and French requests, to gain support for his cherished League of Nations. The British did not want their own freedom of action on the seas limited by international law because it would hamper them in wartime; they objected, and Wilson relented. Moreover, existing treaties negotiated after the war broke out limited Wilson's freedom of action and caused problems. Alsace-Lorraine had been promised to France, Constantinople to Russia, and the head of the Adriatic to Italy. No one disputed France's claim, Russia had forfeited its rights, and Wilson's opposition to Italian demands caused a crisis.

Boundary issues in Western Europe were child's play when compared to those in Eastern Europe, where frontiers based on national lines meant little because different nationalities had lived in mixed areas for centuries and where often a city was predominantly of one nationality and its hinterland of another. Nationality conflicted with strategic considerations, historical claims, centuries-old ethnic and racial hatreds, and contrasting Allied promises. The victorious powers could either sanction the expulsion of national minorities from areas in which they had lived for centuries or impose guarantees of minority rights on the small Eastern European states, which they did. However, the clauses they imposed in the peace treaties mandating respect for minority rights caused fierce resentment and opposition that sowed the seeds of dissension, war, and expulsion of the minorities. In addition, the great weakness of the Versailles system was the absence of Russia, which, when it recovered from the war's devastation, reasserted its ambitions in Eastern Europe.

In the Middle East, Africa, and Asia, the Allies coveted the German and Turkish colonial possessions, but thanks to Wilson's Fourteen Points annexation of the colonies was impossible. The problem was solved by a "mandate" system that allowed them to govern the areas under the authority of the newly created League of Nations in order to bring the native peoples closer to democracy and to prepare them for independence. The scheme classified the former German and Turkish possessions "A" mandates; colonies fairly close to independence, "B" mandates—unlikely to achieve independence anytime soon—and "C" mandates to be ruled as if they were part of the mother country. The mandate system did not resolve the problem of colonialism, and the mandates did not gain their freedom until the general decolonization movement after World War II. In principle, the league had widespread support but major difficulties in practice. The Allies distrusted the league's capacity to keep the peace and relied on alliances and on economic means, particularly reparations, to ensure that Germany would never again threaten them.

Reparations

In theory, reparations would force Germany to pay for the material devastation and financial costs of war that they had provoked. French Prime Minister Georges Clemenceau was most adamant in utilizing them not only as repayment for the enormous costs of the conflict but as a means of keeping Germany permanently weak. British Prime Minister David Lloyd George had a softer attitude, but he had gone on record that he would make the Germans pay "until the pips squeaked." This common goal gave some unity to British and French policy, but the French feared above all a future German attack, while the British, more secure behind the English Channel, were less anxious. The United States, even farther away, was less concerned about a German military revival.

BIOGRAPHICAL SKETCHES

Georges Clemenceau
Tiger

Georges Clemenceau was determined and opinionated from the time of his youth. Born in the Vendée, the poor region in the west of France, on September 28, 1841, he grew up as a solid Republican like his father. His views got him into trouble with Emperor Napoleon III's regime, and he spent a period of about two months in jail. Clemenceau studied to be a physician and went to New York after he got his degree. He admired the freedom he found in the United States and contemplated settling there. He found a job as a teacher in Stamford, Connecticut, and eventually married one of his students. In 1869, after seven years' residence in the United States, he returned to France to practice medicine in the Vendée.

In 1870 the Franco-Prussian War broke out. Napoleon III was quickly defeated, and a republic was established. Clemenceau moved to Paris, where he was elected to the Chamber of Deputies in February 1871 as a radical Republican. His aggressive debating and writing style earned him the nickname of "The Tiger." Accused of being paid off by the British in a scandal involving a French attempt to build a canal across the Isthmus of Panama, Clemenceau lost a reelection bid in 1893. He then turned full time to journalism, which he had practiced in the past. Clemenceau contributed daily articles to newspapers and in 1900 founded his own newspaper, *Le Bloc*. The newspaper defended Alfred Dreyfus, a Jewish military officer who was falsely accused of treason.

In 1902 Clemenceau returned to Parliament as a senator. In contrast to his earlier politics, he was now a nationalist. In 1907 he became prime minister in a cabinet that lasted until 1910 during which he fought bitterly with the French unions. His oratorical duels in Parliament with Socialist leader Jean Jaurès over social reforms became legendary. When World War I broke out, he edited a newspaper, *L'Homme Libre,* which criticized the government's conduct of the war.

continued

continued

His objections to Joseph Joffre as the commanding general of the French army and accusations of pacifism against important members of the government led to the suppression of his newspaper.

At the height of the French crisis during the war in November 1917, Clemenceau became prime minister at the head of a coalition government and minister for war. He brooked no criticism and had prominent politicians arrested for treason. Clemenceau successfully revived French morale and reinvigorated the flagging war effort. He persuaded the Allies to create a unified command under Marshal Ferdinand Foch in order to achieve victory. His view of war was cynical. "War," he said, "is a series of catastrophes that results in a victory."

At the Paris Peace Conference, Clemenceau—strongly anti-German from the time of his youth—took on both Woodrow Wilson, whom he considered too idealistic, and British Prime Minister David Lloyd George, who thought that Clemenceau's tough stance toward Germany would provoke another war. Clemenceau got Alsace-Lorraine restored to France, but his strategy to contain Germany failed.

Ironically, considering his charges that the Americans and the British were too lenient toward Germany, he lost the January 1920 presidential election because the French thought that the Versailles treaty was soft on the Germans and blamed him. After his loss, "The Tiger" retired from politics to write his memoirs and to warn of a renewed conflict with Germany. Georges Clemenceau died in Paris on November 24, 1929.

In addition, the Bolshevik revolution; the uprisings in Germany, Austria, and Hungary; and the disorders in the Allied states provided a dramatic backdrop to the Peace Conference. The Allies were furious with the Bolsheviks because they had pulled Russia out of the war with Germany, had published the secret treaties signed before World War I, and had repudiated the enormous debts the country owed the Western powers. The Germans argued that they should be treated well because they had established a democratic republic; the Austrians maintained that the Hapsburgs should be held responsible for the war, not they; and fighting continued to rage over the boundaries of the new states in East Europe.

These issues could not be resolved in the six months that the conference met, and negotiations continued long afterward. The territorial, economic, and military terms are embodied in five instruments signed between 1919 and 1920: the treaties of Versailles with Germany, June 28, 1919; St. Germain with Austria, September 10; Neuilly with Bulgaria, November 27; Trianon with Hungary on June 4, 1920; and Sèvres with Turkey, August 20, 1920. The allies presented a reparations bill of 132 billion gold marks to Germany on April 27, 1921, but disputes over reparations continued into 1924—and the bad blood for much longer.

THE TERRITORIAL CONSEQUENCES

The general principle that the new European frontiers should follow ethnic lines guided the victors, but they also considered strategic factors and the

The Polish Corridor. This strip of land served as a pretext for the outbreak of World War II on September 1, 1939.

rectification of past injustices. The losers protested against the decisions and argued that vengeance drove them.

German Losses

The new German boundaries caused problems that were not resolved. In the West, Germany lost Alsace and Lorraine to France, a foregone conclusion that the Germans did not accept because they demanded a plebiscite. A plebiscite held in Schleswig resulted in the predominantly Danish northern part opting for Denmark. The Allies required Germany to cede some small strategic areas to Belgium.

The disposition of the left bank of the Rhine river strained the relations among the Allies. The French demand for paramount influence in the area to create a buffer against German invasions ran into stiff British and American opposition because they feared that it would create a new problem that would poison future European relations. Clemenceau accepted a compromise: a demilitarized Rhineland occupied by an Allied force for fifteen years and an Anglo-American pledge to sign a treaty with France guaranteeing aid to France in case of an unprovoked German attack, a promise the Americans did not fulfill. The French also backed off their demand to annex the strategic, coal-rich Saar basin, which they claimed as compensation for German destruction of French mines. France agreed to having the rights to the area's coal, sovereignty exercised by a League of Nations commission for fifteen years, and a plebiscite that in 1935 restored the Saar to Germany.

The Germans objected to these changes on their western borders, but were enraged by those in the East. An independent Poland with secure access to the sea was one of Wilson's basic points, but there were formidable practical problems. German statesmen considered the maintenance of Germany's eastern borders a condition of its continuation as a great power, and Poland's revival of Poland earned undying German enmity. Moreover, the Germans had systematically encouraged immigration into Polish-speaking areas for 150 years after the Polish partitions of the eighteenth century, resulting in an intermixture that made it impossible to draw clear-cut lines on the basis of nationality and inflamed tensions during the interwar period.

The nationality issue guaranteed that any solution to the problem of Polish access to the Baltic Sea would fail because no access to the sea meant economic "strangulation" for Poland. The Allies created a "Polish Corridor" that split East Prussia from the rest of Germany and put a sizable German minority into Poland. Danzig, a German city of 300,000 and the main port in the area, became a free city protected by the League of Nations within a Polish customs union. In 1939, World War II began in Danzig.

The Polish Corridor was only the tip of the eastern iceberg. Plebiscites were ordered in other German districts, leading to bloody confrontations with the German paramilitary Freikorps. The Germans objected to Polish annexation of Upper Silesia, an important industrial area, after they won a plebiscite on March 20, 1921, but after which the Poles with French support annexed the principal industrial and mining districts. In all, Germany ceded an area of 16,750 square miles to Poland with a population of 1 million Germans and 1.8 million Poles. German losses did not cripple the country or significantly reduce the country's industrial capacity, but they inflamed German emotions and set the stage for World War II.

Germany's Losses. Shown here is the territory Germany lost after World War I. The country's core and its productive capacity, however, remained intact.

The Polish Problem and Russian Losses

Reconstituting Poland also caused many difficulties in settling the new state's boundaries with Russia. In principle the Russians accepted an independent Poland to include regions having an indisputable Polish ethnic majority, but in a large zone it was impossible to determine the ethnicity of the majority population. In December 1919, experts at the Paris Peace Conference drew a provisional eastern boundary that included incontrovertibly Polish areas, the Curzon line, that could be extended farther east with the determination of relevant facts. The Poles refused to accept this solution and insisted on boundaries based on the 1772 frontiers, when Poland was a large state. After the Russian refusal, the Poles with French support attacked them in April 1920 and won large gains because of the turmoil caused by the Russian civil war. At the Treaty of Riga, March 18, 1921, the Russians agreed to large territorial losses and the placement of a large number of Ukrainians and White Russians in Poland. This solution alienated the Russians and disregarded geography. The Poles estranged two temporarily weakened big powers that had common borders with them, thereby helping create the conditions for a new partition in 1939.

In addition to the territory the Russians lost to the Poles, Finland and the Baltic States (Estonia, Latvia, and Lithuania) won their independence from the Bolsheviks. More territory went to Romania. Because of the German military collapse, Russia recovered most of the territory lost at Brest-Litovsk, but, with the exception of Austria-Hungary, it was the biggest loser of World War I.

The Breakup of Austria-Hungary and Its Consequences

Former Austro-Hungarian lands accounted for all or a great portion of the territories acquired by Czechoslovakia, Poland, Yugoslavia, and Romania. This Balkanization of Eastern Europe caused bitter border disputes and increased nationalism, the incorporation of restless minorities by small states, and economic difficulties. The Poles incorporated eastern Galicia, along with 3.5 million Ukrainians, and claimed the rich coal mining area of Teschen that the Allies awarded to Czechoslovakia. The continual bad blood between the two countries resulted in Polish occupation of the area in 1938 during the infamous Czechoslovak crisis. In another complicated dispute, the Poles absorbed Vilnius, the ancient Lithuanian capital, on the basis of its slight Polish majority, producing a state of war until 1927 and acrimonious feuding thereafter.

Czechoslovakia also presented a major problem. The Allies took care to give it defensible frontiers, but this meant incorporating the mountainous Sudetenland inhabited by 3 million disgruntled Austrian Germans, who in 1938 became the focus of a crisis between Czechoslovakia and Germany. Luckily, Czechoslovakia inherited the old empire's industrial heartland, but this did not prevent it from incorporating Hungarian-inhabited areas on economic grounds.

The Hungarians were the most unfortunate of the East European losers. Like Austria, Hungary emerged as a separate state, but while most of the prewar German-speaking population was part of Austria, the peace settlement put large Hungarian minorities into the neighboring states, particularly Romania, causing Hungary to attempt to overthrow the Versailles system. Romania also

Russian Losses. The shaded areas of the map show the enormous amount of territory lost by Russia. These losses provoked the country to try to make them good once it got on its feet again. The Russians were very interested in regaining the Baltic States and areas of the new Poland that were inhabited by White Russians and Ukrainians.

The End of Austria-Hungary. After the war, major portions of former Austro-Hungarian territory went to Czechoslovakia, Poland, Romania, and Yugoslavia.

tried to annex a southern Hungarian district of mixed population (the Banat of Temesvar), but had to split the area with Serbia, which created bad relations between them. Finally, Bulgaria was forced to cede territory to Greece and lost its access to the Aegean Sea.

The peacemakers did not authorize the expulsion of national minorities as happened after World War II but instead forced the East European states to protect minorities by inserting clauses into the treaties with them and assigning enforcement to the League of Nations. Hostility to the minority clauses helped undermine the postwar settlement in Eastern Europe.

Southeastern Europe

In southeastern Europe, the Serbians had difficulty uniting the south Slavs in the new South Slave state it had dreamed about. On December 4, 1918, the Kingdom of Serbs, Croats, and Slovenes (later, Yugoslavia) was proclaimed. The new state faced serious domestic difficulties because the Croats and Slovenes were Roman Catholic and had a Western orientation while the dominant Serbs were Orthodox Christians with Eastern roots. These problems emerged as a never-resolved struggle between the Serbian demand for centralization and the federalism desired by the other Slav groups in the area. Centralization won out in a constituent assembly held in 1919, but the struggle continued until Yugoslavia's violent breakup in the 1990s.

Yugoslavia faced serious questions on the foreign front as well. President Woodrow Wilson supported Yugoslavia against Italian claims for the city of Fiume at the Paris Peace Conference, causing a rift with the Italians. The question dragged until January 27, 1924, when a treaty signed with Benito Mussolini of Italy ratified Italian annexation of the city, but this settlement failed to calm the Duce's determination to undermine the peace settlement or his hostility toward Yugoslavia.

Left to right: Prime Minister David Lloyd George of Britain, Prime Minister Vittorio Emanuele Orlando of Italy, Prime Minister Georges Clemenceau of France, and President Woodrow Wilson of the United States. Although Wilson was the most prominent participant at the Peace Conference, Clemenceau and Lloyd George managed to get what they wanted from him, frequently in violation of his ideals and of his famous Fourteen Points. Orlando, representing the weakest power and with a divided government behind him, received less than his people and political opponents demanded.

ECONOMIC CONSEQUENCES

When the Germans requested an armistice, they agreed to Wilson's point specifying that they would pay for the war damages caused to the Allied civilian populations, but the reparations question was the most troublesome at the peace conference and after.

The Allies and Reparations

No matter what their sympathies, American experts who studied reparations concentrated on a practical question: how could the world return quickly to a sound financial footing and restore the prewar trade regime? They suggested that $15 billion was a realistic sum based on the German capacity to pay, profoundly disappointing the British and French. Clemenceau and Lloyd George objected that such a low figure would cause their governments to fall and interrupt the peace conference until new elections could be held.

The dispute revolved around two central points—whether an amount should be fixed at Paris or later, and what expenses should be included in the reparations bill in order to calculate a definitive sum. Clemenceau and Lloyd George argued that it would be politically unwise to agree on a sum at the conference because the British and French people would consider any sum too low. The American delegation argued that a fixed figure would permit the Allies to receive a maximum amount from the Germans immediately, allow France and other countries that were partially dependent on German payments to balance their budgets right away, and encourage Germany to work out methods to meet a specific payments goal. On this issue, however, Wilson supported Lloyd George and Clemenceau.

The other rancorous reparations question involved the categories to be included in the calculations for reparations. Damage to civilians and their property had been the basis on which the belligerents had agreed to end the conflict, but the British, with French support, insisted that this amount include war costs because these costs ultimately had to be paid by the civilian population. This reasoning allowed the inclusion of anything remotely connected to the war. For example, the British included as a legitimate war cost the price of a mortgage taken out by an Australian shepherd on his house as a result of the disruption of trade caused by the war. An alarmed Wilson informed his colleagues that the Allies had offered peace on the basis of civilian damages only and that including war costs in the reparations bill would be unjust. The American president won his case, but then the British and the French argued for the addition of separation costs and war pensions, also stiffly opposed by the American delegation. The South African delegate Jan Smuts responded that while the costs of arming and supporting troops were military expenses, the funds spent on citizens and their families before and after their military service were civilian expenses. This reasoning convinced Wilson, who shouted down his American advisers when they objected to the faulty logic: "Logic! Logic! I don't give a damn for logic. I am going to include pensions!" This inclusion doubled the German bill to $30 billion.

BIOGRAPHICAL SKETCHES

Sidney Sonnino
Failed Diplomatist

Italy's foreign minister during World War I and at the Versailles Peace Conference was Sidney Sonnino. The son of a wealthy Jewish banker and a Welsh woman, Sonnino spent his early childhood in the family home in Alexandria, Egypt, and was reared in the Anglican faith of his mother. His unusual circumstances did not harm his political career in Giolittian Italy as much as his rigid personality. He served in local and national politics and became prime minister in 1906 and 1909, the country's first Protestant chief executive of Jewish descent. Sonnino passed through a conservative phase but developed a reputation as a reformer. Nonetheless, his tenure in office lasted only a total of two hundred days.

continued

continued

An early opponent of Italian colonial expansion in Africa, Sonnino was not much interested in colonial gains after World War I but hoped to win Italy a position as a major power in the Mediterranean. Named foreign minister in November 1914 following the death of neutralist Antonino Di San Guiliano, Sonnino negotiated Italy's entrance into World War I in 1915 through the Pact of London with the Allies. Following this agreement, he and Prime Minister Antonio Salandra successfully maneuvered to bring the country into the conflict despite the opposition of the majority of the people and their representatives. Under Sonnino's leadership, Italy missed the opportunity afforded by the United States's entrance into the war to jump on the moral bandwagon against the Central Powers, unlike Georges Clemenceau and David Lloyd George. Consequently, the country remained identified with the unfortunate maxim under which Salandra said it had entered the conflict, *Sacro Egoismo* [Sacred Egoism]. This slogan and Sonnino's diplomacy conveyed the impression that Italy had exploited the precarious Anglo-French situation of 1915 to exact its pound of flesh and was still determined to do so at Versailles. Sonnino's failure to correct this perception demonstrated an amazing lack of understanding of the altered world atmosphere following World War I.

The major problem for the Italians at Versailles was their demand for territory that American President Woodrow Wilson believed should go to Yugoslavia. Wilson argued on the basis of self-determination, while the Italians sought a secure frontier. The dispute with Wilson provoked the Italian delegation to leave Versailles and withdraw from the negotiations for a time. Wilson and the Italians then struggled for the hearts and minds of the Italian people.

When the government of Vittorio Emanuele Orlando resigned in June 1919, Sonnino withdrew from political life. Lamentably, the unresolved territorial dispute with Yugoslavia had poisoned the Italian political atmosphere. Resentment at being ill treated welled up in the country, and public opinion condemned the Allies and Italians who accepted the principle of self-determination. Many Italians identified self-determination with renunciation of the country's gains made at the cost of a great number of casualties and the enormous expenditure of economic wealth. These feelings fueled the rise of extremist movements, especially Benito Mussolini's Fascist party, which destabilized the country and came to power in 1922.

Besides his diplomatic and political activity, Sonnino excelled as a scholar. In Parliament, he wrote influential political articles and coauthored a famous sociological study on poverty in Sicily that made the country aware of the scope of the southern problem. He was also an avid student of Dante's poetry. Born in Pisa on March 11, 1847, Sidney Sonnino died in Rome on November 24, 1922. He is buried by the sea at his castle near Livorno.

This latter figure was the American delegation's estimate, but the British estimate was $120 billion, and the French refused to give one. When the experts failed to resolve their differences, Allied representatives worked out guidelines and charged a permanent reparations commission to come up with a figure and method of payment by May 1, 1921. In the meantime, they directed the Germans to come up with $5 billion immediately, hand over their merchant fleet to make good British losses, deliver large quantities of coal to France and Italy, and give a great number of farm animals to the Allies. Eventually the total that Germany had to pay was set at $56 billion (current dollars) over a forty-two-year period.

The Criticisms of John Maynard Keynes

Although some Allied experts considered this sum reasonable, economist John Maynard Keynes, a peace conference participant attached to the British Treasury, objected in a very influential book published in 1920. In *The Economic Consequences of the Peace,* Keynes argued that Germany would be unable to pay the stated amount and backed his argument with a series of impressive statistics. Other economic clauses of the Versailles peace treaty—tariff restrictions, confiscation of the merchant marine and railroad stock, and the delivery of German coal—ensured that Germany would be unable to pay the reparations imposed by the Allies, he wrote. The interest would mount faster than Germany's ability to pay, so that the debt would increase despite the payments, and thus the treaty obliged Germany "to hand over to the Allies the whole of her surplus production in perpetuity." Keynes's estimate for reparations was under $9 billion.

Keynes believed that the Allies had deliberately set out to demolish Germany by destroying the three foundations of its economic prosperity because they threatened the British: its overseas trade, which required the healthy merchant marine it had been forced to surrender; its ability to manufacture high-quality, reasonably priced manufactured goods, which challenged the British in their overseas and home markets; and its growing foreign investments, which competed with the Allied investments. The Allies had not reconstructed Europe's fragile economic prosperity, Keynes maintained, but had dealt it a deathblow by wrecking its most vibrant economy.

Whether or not Keynes was correct, his book had an extraordinary influence as economic events seemed to vindicate his opinions. The Germans defaulted on reparations payments in 1922, which led to French and Belgian occupation of the industrial Ruhr valley in March 1923. This occupation touched off hyperinflation in Germany that crippled the middle class and later contributed to the rise of Adolf Hitler. In late 1923, the Dawes Plan revised reparations downward, worked out a new payment schedule, and offered the Germans a loan. In 1929, the Young Plan reduced the total bill to $8 billion, close to Keynes's suggestion, to be paid over fifty-eight years at 5.5 percent interest. These plans calmed the economic waters and seemed to vindicate the British economist, but Keynes thought that they did not correct the economic distortions caused by reparations and suggested either the cancelation of reparations and war debts or the lowering of Allied tariff barriers so that the Germans could sell their goods and earn the funds necessary to pay reparations.

The Americans rebuffed cancelation of the war debts, and the Allies refused to grant unrestricted German access to their markets because of the competition that the efficient German industry presented for their firms. An artificial and serendipitous economy resulted: only American loans, seemingly for other purposes, allowed the Germans to pay reparations to the Allies, which permitted them to pay war debts, which, in turn, enabled the Americans to lend more to the Germans to pay reparations. When the Great Depression arrived, the Americans stopped lending money to the Germans, who defaulted on reparations, which caused the Allies to default on their war debts to the United States. By the early 1930s, countries were paying installments on neither sum.

Although the collapse of Europe's postwar economy seemed ultimately attributable to the factors denounced by Keynes, the British economist came in for serious criticism. Observers noted that Keynes's book poisoned American and British opinion against the Versailles treaty and encouraged German resistance to it. Keynes's contention that Germany lacked the capacity to pay the reparations assessed by the Allies has also been challenged. Some historians have revised the view of a prostrate Germany unable to reimburse a hard-nosed and vindictive France, replacing it with the picture of a recalcitrant country capable but unwilling to pay.

THE MORAL CONSEQUENCES

Despite the efforts of the statesmen at Paris, the peace settlement following World War I had more negative than positive results. Besides the economic issues, the word *reparations* itself condemned Germany and its allies for deliberately instigating the war. Following past conflicts, the victors frequently assessed indemnities on the losers, but these had no moral connotations; the Versailles treaty made German guilt explicit.

The "War Guilt" Clause
Article 231 of the Versailles treaty forced Germany and its allies to accept exclusive blame for the war, a condemnation that appeared as the first article in a section entitled "Reparation" that describes how Germany will make atonement through monetary and in-kind compensation. According to a moderate member of the American Peace Commission: "While the causes of the war may still be in dispute, we cannot reconcile ourselves to any theory but that Germany's aggression was responsible." The Allies forced the Germans to agree, but the Germans never accepted exclusive blame for the war, greatly resented the charge, and launched a campaign to prove their innocence. Eventually, writers in the Allied countries agreed with them. The "war guilt" clause fueled nationalistic desires for revenge, failed to sap Germany's might, and was a factor in Hitler's rise to power.

The Disarmament Clauses
Finally the Allies disarmed the Germans, limiting their army to a volunteer professional force of 100,000 and their navy to a coast guard without submarines, and denying them an air force. Because a general aversion to war had already begun among their own populations, the Allies justified these provisions by saying that German disarmament would "render possible the initiation of a general limitation of the armaments of all nations." Talks discussing disarmament between the wars took place in Geneva, but went nowhere. The Allied contention boomeranged because it provided Hitler with a pretext to rearm, since the other European countries had not fulfilled their pledge.

The Allies repeated their errors with Germany's defeated associates, inspiring in them a desire for vengeance without following through on effective

Former Viceroy for India and postwar Foreign Secretary, the British statesman Lord Curzon was responsible for drawing up an equitable boundary between Russia and Poland, the "Curzon Line."

enforcement. Reparations worsened the precarious Austrian and Hungarian economic situations, and the two countries pleaded that the Hapsburg monarchy, not the successor states, was responsible for the war. The Allies responded that they could not shirk responsibility by a technicality and fanned resentment by blaming their populations for not having resisted Hapsburg militarism.

The Specter of Anschluss

The Allies also handled the Austrian desire for union (Anschluss) with Germany poorly. The Austrians utilized Wilson's nationality principles to argue that they should be in the same nation with their German brethren. Had the Allies agreed, however, Germany would have become the paramount European power, so they flatly refused. In short order, the Germans became the champions of Anschluss and inserted an article into the Weimar constitution defining how Austrians would participate in German affairs before and after union. The Allies blocked this procedure but acted slowly, allowing Anschluss to develop into a major emotional issue that came back to haunt them.

THE LEAGUE OF NATIONS

The Allies responded to the desire for Anschluss by agreeing to alter Austria's international status if the Council of the League of Nations agreed. Since Britain

Brainchild of American President Woodrow Wilson and forerunner of the postwar United Nations, the League of Nations had serious flaws that doomed it to ultimate failure. The greatest lack was the refusal of the Americans to join the League. Shown here is a campaign song sponsored by the Democratic National Committee trying to solicit popular support for the new organization.

and France dominated the League of Nations, however, it ruled that Austria must remain a sovereign state, but only in late 1922. The decision did not settle the question because everyone recognized that the League of Nations was controlled by the victorious powers.

Structure of the League

President Wilson championed the creation of an international organization to prevent future conflicts. He called for an association of nations in his Fourteen Points, and the Paris Peace Conference named a commission headed by Wilson himself to draft a covenant that was adopted on April 28, 1919. The League of Nations came into being in January 1920. It is interesting to consider the league's structure because it both explains its weakness (and that of similar organizations like the United Nations) and because it was suggested as a model for European unification in the 1920s.

The League of Nations had a permanent secretariat located in Geneva. A council consisting of the big powers and four nations representing the small ones constituted the executive. All member states had one vote in the general assembly. The members agreed to submit their quarrels to inquiry or arbitration and, if unsatisfied, to refrain from war until after a cooling-down period of three months. They agreed to respect the territorial integrity of all members and, in case of aggression, to support each other. If members went to war with each other in contravention of the rules, the other members could impose sanctions and take military action—but the absence of a league military force made this impossible.

The question of giving the League of Nations an armed force was the subject of a crucial debate among the Allies. The French insisted on the establishment of an international military force under the league's command, but this meant the partial surrender of national sovereignty to the international organization. The United States and Britain, both geographically immune to a German threat, refused. The Americans returned to their isolationism, and the British suspected that France would dominate a League of Nations army. The U.S. Senate rejected the Versailles treaty, but with regard to the League of Nations, the senators refused the international commitments required by the league's covenant because they feared that the league would interfere in domestic affairs.

Consequences of the League's Weakness

The League of Nation's stillbirth had major consequences for world affairs. The league failed to resolve the disarmament question because of resistance by the big powers, which generally ignored it. It had jurisdiction over the clauses guaranteeing minority rights in Eastern Europe, but this emotional issue constantly embarrassed the organization, which had no effective authority in the matter. The League of Nations' minor diplomatic successes did not counterbalance its structural defects, and the powers continued to use traditional diplomacy to defend their interests.

During the 1920s, the French set up a new diplomatic order on the European continent. First, they torpedoed German membership in the League of Nations and attempted to make Poland a strong power as an eastern counterweight to Germany. As was already seen, this policy required supporting Polish claims against Germany and favoring its expansion against Bolshevik Russia. The French also signed alliances with the countries of Eastern Europe that had profited from the postwar settlement (Czechoslovakia, Romania, and Yugoslavia) in order to establish a front to Germany's east and a wall blocking Soviet influence in the West, in addition to defending the Versailles settlement. This policy had the major flaw of being based on weak countries that could never balance the military potential of Germany and the USSR while alienating both and driving them into each other's arms.

The League of Nations was consequently unable to keep the peace. Its real legacy was its establishment of a forum for discussion and its social policies, both of which foreshadowed the United Nations, and its inspiration of a plan for a European Union presented in 1930 (see chapter 17). Women leaders from different nations urged the league to broaden its horizons to nonpolitical issues by extending the principle of international cooperation to areas, such as health; labor; and the suppression of the arms, opium, and white slave traffic. The League of

Nations created specialized agencies to deal with these issues that became part of the United Nations structure after World War II.

At the Congress of Vienna, the French delegate had exploited allied differences to his country's advantage; influenced by this historical tidbit, the Allies prohibited German representatives from taking part in the Paris discussions. On May 7, 1919, they delivered a copy of the Versailles treaty to the German delegation and allowed the delegation to make only written comments. The Germans vehemently protested that the treaty did not keep faith with the Fourteen Points and that Germany could never fulfill its provisions. The Allies made some insignificant modifications and threatened to resume the war if Germany did not sign. On June 28, 1919, German representatives affixed their signature, but the Germans never accepted the peace.

Bibliographical Essay

The most complete and detailed work on the Paris Peace Conference that all serious students should consult is the classic by Arno J. Mayer, *Politics and Diplomacy of Peacemaking: Containment and Counterrevolution at Versailles, 1918–1919* (New York, 1967). Mayer emphasizes the relationship between internal and foreign politics and sees the conference as influenced by reactions to the Bolshevik revolution. The comparison with the Congress of Vienna was made by Charles K. Webster, quoted on p. 4 of Mayer's book. Harold Nicholson, *Peacemaking 1919* (London, 1943), is a classic work on the topic. Margaret MacMillan, *Paris 1919: Six Months that Changed the World* (New York, 2002), is a detailed work. Although the emphasis of historians has been placed on the Paris Peace Conference and the Treaty of Versailles, this is only part of the story because the conferences continued long afterward and a series of treaties were signed. A major new series on these events by London's Haus Publishing has resulted in the publication of 32 volumes, published between 2008 and 2011: "Makers of the Modern World: The Peace Conferences of 1919–23 and Their Aftermath." Erik Gosstein, *The First World War Peace Settlements 1919–1925* (Harlow, UK, 2002) is a one-volume treatment.

Good older and briefer books that are worth consulting are F. S. Marston, *The Peace Conference of 1919* (London, 1944), and Paul Birdsall, *Versailles Twenty Years After* (Hamden, Conn., 1962).

A superb source is the collection of articles illuminating a variety of problems and the complexities of peacemaking by the American delegates: Edward Mandell House and Charles Seymour, eds. *What Really Happened at Paris: The Story of the Peace Conference, 1918–1919, by American Delegates* (Westport, Conn.,1976); Wilson's exclamation about logic is on p. 272, and the citation on Germany's war guilt is on p. 288. Good books containing essays on the most varied themes at the conference include M. L. Cockrill and John Fisher, *The Paris Peace Conference, 1919: Peace Without Victory?* (New York, 2001); Conan Fisher and Alan Sharp, *After the Versailles Treaty: Enforcement, Compliance, Contested Identities* (New York, 2008); and a book dedicated to a distinguished scholar, Gaynor Johnson, *Peacemaking, Peacemakers and Diplomacy, 1880–1939: Essays in Honour of Professor Alan Sharp* (Newcastle, UK, 2010).

Given the enormous impact of the results of Versailles, the question of their impact in the future has been an object of great discussion. David Andelman's *A Shattered Peace* (Hoboken, N.J., 2008) discusses "the price we pay today," while Sally Marks examines the "illusions": *The Illusion of Peace: International Relations in Europe, 1918–1933* (New York, 2003).

Readers may better understand the postwar settlement by considering the policies, problems, and diplomacy of individual countries at the peace conference and after. Luckily, there are a number of good studies they may consult. Michael L. Dockrill and J. Douglas Goold, *Peace Without Promise: Britain and the Peace Conference, 1919–1923* (London, 1981), examines Britain's role; W. M. Jordan, *Great Britain, France, and the German Problem, 1918–1939: A Study of Anglo-French Relations in the Making and Maintenance of the Versailles Settlement* (London, 1971), discusses the major problems. A. Lentin, *Lloyd George and the Lost Peace: From Versailles to Hitler, 1919–1940* (New York, 2001), examines the role of an important participant from an interesting perspective. Seth P. Tillman analyzes the relationship between Americans and British in *Anglo-American Relations at the Paris Peace Conference of 1919* (Princeton, N.J., 1961). René Albrecht-Carrié's *Italy at the Paris Peace Conference* (New York, 1966), is the standard work on the subject. Spencer M. Di Scala, *Vittorio Orlando: Italy* (Makers of the Modern World series) (London, 2010) consulted little-known archival sources that shed more light on the Italian position. Dragan R. Zivojinovic analyzes one of the thorniest problems of the peace in *America, Italy and the Birth of Yugoslavia* (New York, 1972). Yugoslavia's policies are presented by Ivo J. Lederer, *Yugoslavia at the Paris Peace Conference: A Study in Frontiermaking* (New Haven, Conn., 1963). John M. Thompson argues that European affairs could not be resolved without considering Russia and discusses the Bolshevik problem in *Russia, Bolshevism, and the Versailles Peace* (Princeton, N.J., 1966). The Belgians are discussed by Sally Marks, *Innocent Abroad: Belgium and the Paris Peace Conference of 1919* (Chapel Hill, N.C., 1981). Kay Lundgren-Nielsen wrote *The Polish Problem at the Paris Peace Conference* (Odense, Denmark, 1979). Another problem with fateful consequences is the subject of an excellent study by Francis Déak, *Hungary at the Paris Peace Conference: The Diplomatic History of the Treaty of Trianon* (New York, 1972). The complicated legacy of Hungary in terms of minorities, economics, and boundaries as a result of the Treaty of Trianon is spelled out in C. A. Macartney's *Hungary and Her Successors: The Treaty of Trianon and its Consequences, 1919–1937* (London, 1937). Hungary suffered most unjustly from the peace settlement; see the lectures delivered by former Hungarian Prime Minister Count Stephen Bethlen, *The Treaty of Trianon and European Peace* (New York, 1971). Romanian policy is analyzed in *Rumania at the Paris Peace Conference: A Study of the Diplomacy of Ioan I. C. Bratianu* (New York, 1962), by Sherman David Spector. The politics of the smaller powers is the subject of Stephen Bonsal, *Suitors and Suppliants: The Little Nations at Versailles* (New York, 1946).

The story of the Germans at the conference is told by Alma Luckau, *The German Delegation at the Paris Peace Conference* (New York, 1971). On the ramifications of the desire of Austria and Germany to unite, see Alfred D. Low, T*he Anschluss Movement, 1918–1919, and the Paris Peace Conference* (Philadelphia, 1974).

On the disarmament question, see Lorna S. Jaffe, *The Decision to Disarm Germany* (Boston, 1985), and Gerda Richards Crosby, *Disarmament and Peace in British Politics, 1914–1919* (Cambridge, Mass., 1957), a succinct study of the issue. James F. Willis, *Prologue to Nuremburg* (Westport, Conn., 1982), analyzes the war criminal problem after World War I.

On colonial questions, see the work by George Louis Beer, American representative on the territorial section committee for Africa, *African Questions at the Paris Peace Conference* (New York, 1923). Consult also William Roger Louis, *Great Britain and Germany's Lost Colonies 1914–1919* (Oxford, UK, 1967). Quincy Wright presents a full discussion of the origins and development of the mandate system in *Mandates Under the League of Nations* (Westport, Conn., 1968).

On reparations, see how the clauses were arrived at in a book by the chief American representative on the Reparations Commission, Bernard M. Baruch, *The Making of the Reparation and Economic Sections of the Treaty* (New York, 1970). John Maynard Keynes's brilliant 1920 classic *The Economic Consequences of the Peace* has been reissued many times; there is a good Penguin edition with a readable introduction by Robert Lekachman that puts his ideas into context (New York, 1971); Keynes's statement on reparations quoted in the text is on p. 167. Keynes published a sequel to this book in which he considers events since the original publication of his work and fleshes out his ideas, *A Revision of the Treaty* (London, 1922). Don Markwell's *John Maynard Keynes and International Relations: Economic Paths to War and Peace* (New York, 2006) has interesting material on the period covered. An important rebuttal of Keynes is Etienne Mantoux, *The Carthaginian Peace or the Economic Consequences of Mr. Keynes* (Pittsburgh, 1965). British economic war aims and foundations of reparations are the subject of Robert E. Bunselmeyer, *The Cost of the War 1914–1919* (Hamden, Conn., 1975). A major issue at the peace conference was how much Germany could pay, analyzed in Harold G. Moulton and Constantine E. McGuire, *Germany's Capacity to Pay: A Study of the Reparation Problem* (New York, 1923). Reparations are also considered in Carl Bergmann, *The History of Reparations* (Boston, 1927), and by the revisionist Marc Tractenberg, *Reparations in World Politics* (New York, 1980).

There are many sources on the League of Nations. A good survey is F. S. Northedge, *The League of Nations: Its Life and Times, 1920–1946* (Leicester, UK, 1986), while F. P. Walters produced a longer account, *A History of the League of Nations* (London, 1960). For a view from a particular perspective, see the book by Alfred E. Zimmern, *The League of Nations and the Rule of Law, 1918–1935* (New York, 1969).

CHAPTER 9

✍

Hard Landings: From Crisis to False Prosperity

CHAPTER OUTLINE

Britain: Back to 1914 • France's Quest for Security • Italy: From Red Biennium to Fascism • Weimar's Three Original Sins • The USSR: The Crisis of NEP

BIOGRAPHICAL SKETCHES

John Maynard Keynes, Savior of Capitalism • Benito Amilcare Andrea Mussolini, Young Rebel

In stating that the world must return to normal following the devastation of World War I, American President Warren G. Harding made a grammatical error by using the word *normalcy*. This word stuck, but the former belligerents had a very difficult time getting back on track because the costs of the conflict produced severe economic and social crises for victors and vanquished alike. Many soldiers who were used to fighting could not readjust to peaceful civilian lives and developed a strong bond—a "trenchocracy"—that contributed to the rise of fascism. Economic conditions worsened as the people in all countries demanded rapid demobilization. This demobilization created mass unemployment because millions of soldiers came onto the labor market when industry was shedding wartime jobs and converting to peacetime production, and the need to pay war debts and reparations contributed to inflation and hyperinflation.

BRITAIN: BACK TO 1914

In 1917 in Britain the ministry of reconstruction planned for an orderly demobilization and the reorganization of health services, housing, transportation, and relationships in the workplace in order to achieve greater equality.

Economic Problems
The planners had feared the unemployment that rapid demobilization would bring but could not resist the popular desire to see the soldiers return home.

Demobilization did not create as many problems as were feared at first because Britain had not suffered any destruction, British industry was poised to take advantage of the pent-up postwar demand for civilian goods, and an economic boom created plenty of jobs. But the boom proved short lived, and a downturn that occurred in 1920 turned into a depression in 1921.

By 1923, the economic crisis had killed hopes about improving the social conditions of the lower classes. Parliament watered down bills extending the length of secondary education, building subsidized housing, and reorganizing the electric and transportation industries. Health and transport ministries were created, but they lacked the clout to make a difference. Joint industrial bodies, called Whitley Councils, which were created to encourage collaboration between capital and labor, failed to change conditions in the country's major industries. The economic slump prompted the government to curtail activities even in areas where its action had been moderately successful, such as housing; caused breakdowns in social insurance; and led to the detested dole.

Political Questions and Ireland

In the political arena, Britain alternated between movement and stagnation. In 1918, the country held elections for the first time since 1910, with women aged 30 and older granted the right to vote. The Labour Party withdrew from the wartime coalition, and a Conservative-Liberal coalition won 484 seats. Lloyd George remained prime minister, but trouble loomed ahead because, although defeated, Labour was on its way to replacing the helplessly divided Liberals and, in the future, would regularly alternate with the Conservatives in power. Furthermore, the Lloyd George government was hamstrung by the prevailing economic belief in austerity during slowdowns, which caused unemployment to skyrocket.

Added to the weak economy, Britain's Irish dilemma threatened the stability of Lloyd George's cabinet. A home-rule provision had been put on hold during the war, but by 1918 resentment caused by executions following the Easter Rebellion had made it irrelevant. In the 1918 elections, Sinn Fein (Ourselves Alone), an Irish party supporting independence, won seventy-three seats, all but four outside Ulster. This party proclaimed an Irish parliament, declared independence on January 2, 1919, and created the Irish Republican Army (IRA). A guerrilla war, complete with terror, broke out, pitting the IRA against the Black and Tans, auxiliary British forces.

In December 1920 the British established parliaments in both northern and southern Ireland, with a council coordinating them. Ireland remained part of the United Kingdom. In May 1921, elections took place. Northern Ireland agreed with the British plan, but the southerners, under Eamon de Valera, Michael Collins, and Arthur Griffith, favored independence. Amid continuing violence, negotiations produced an Irish Free State as a dominion of the British Empire in December 1921. The Irish Parliament ratified this solution, but a civil war broke out between the "Regulars," who supported Parliament, and the "Irregulars." By 1923 the Irish government had suppressed the Irregulars, but sporadic acts of violence continued for many years.

Irish events and foreign policy problems brought Lloyd George down in October 1922. Conservative leader Bonar Law replaced him, and new elections resulted in a Conservative majority. In May 1923 Law resigned because of ill health and was replaced by Stanley Baldwin, his chancellor of the exchequer, and, in Winston Churchill's characterization, "a man of the utmost insignificance."

Rise of the Labour Party

The early 1920s brought a rise in the Labour Party's fortunes, stimulated by workers' unrest, the Liberal Party's decline, an internal reorganization, and a sharpened Socialist ideology. Labour's program, elaborated by Fabian Socialist Sidney Webb, *Labour and the New Social Order,* advocated a minimum standard for social services, full employment, higher taxation, a capital tax to shrink the national debt, and democratic control of industry that aimed at the nationalization of industry and land.

In 1922 Labour doubled its popular vote and in January 1924 got its opportunity after the Conservatives lost their majority in the December 6, 1923 elections. Labour received the second-largest number of seats, allied with the Liberals, and came to power under Ramsay MacDonald. Inexperience and dependence on Liberal votes weakened MacDonald, and he fell because of his friendliness to the Soviet Union and his refusal to prosecute a Communist journalist who was accused of political interference. During the intense electoral campaign of 1924, the forged "Zinoviev Letter" from Moscow, purporting to give British Communists instructions to work for a Communist revolution, might have affected the outcome in favor of the Conservatives. Baldwin returned to power and succeeded in passing some reforms.

BIOGRAPHICAL SKETCHES

John Maynard Keynes
Savior of Capitalism

Contradictions marked the life of John Maynard Keynes, the most famous economist of the twentieth century. Keynes worked at the British Treasury during World War I, where he labored to prevent his country's economic collapse under the strain of the conflict. A pacifist who disagreed with Britain's avowed aim of Germany's unconditional surrender, he prayed for an absolute financial crash, yet strove to prevent it. A practicing homosexual, he married ballerina Lydia Lopokova in 1925 in a happy union. An economic liberal, he successfully blended liberal values and state intervention. He despised capitalism, but his economic theories saved it.

Born on June 5, 1883, in Cambridge, England, Keynes grew up in an academic family. His father Neville was a scholar and administrator at the University of Cambridge. Florence, his mother, a minister's daughter, was an early female Cambridge graduate. Maynard enjoyed a happy childhood, attending Eton, the elite private school, where he achieved both academic and social success.

continued

continued

In 1902, Keynes entered Cambridge University, where he garnered even more success. He joined the Bloomsbury Circle, a famous group that included the most influential British intellectuals who dominated cultural life during the 1920s. He joined the civil service after graduation and wrote a treatise on Indian finance. He began teaching at Cambridge, joining the Treasury Department in 1915, where he became an influential personage. He accompanied David Lloyd George to Versailles, became disillusioned with the peace process, and published the book that made him famous, *The Economic Consequences of the Peace.*

Keynes returned to teaching at Cambridge in October 1919 and remained there until 1937. His light teaching load allowed him to devote himself to writing. Keynes gave eight lectures a year, the early drafts of books that attracted hundreds of listeners, and supervised a small number of students at his house on Fridays or Saturdays before dinner. On Monday evenings he presided over the Keynes Club in his drawing room, where members listened to his papers or others by distinguished guests. He financed his lifestyle through his journalism and investments, which he directed while having breakfast in bed. He gained and lost several small fortunes and fared poorly in the stock market crash of 1929.

Keynes freely gave the British government advice on public policy. He criticized its return to the gold standard in 1925 and fretted about the consistently high unemployment rate. When the Great Depression arrived in 1929, governments confronted the slump by restricting spending. Keynes denounced this policy and argued in favor of increasing both private and public spending. In a famous radio broadcast on January 15, 1931, he advised British homemakers that their patriotic duty lay in spending their money and in taking advantage of the cheap prices, not in saving. He likewise urged the government to undertake public works, at the cost of accepting deficit spending, in order to create employment. In 1936 his most influential work appeared: *The General Theory of Employment, Interest, and Money.*

Keynes stood previous liberal economic theory on its head by arguing in favor of state intervention in the economy through public works and subsidies when lowering interest rates did not work. In order to reverse severe economic downturns, governments must accept budget deficits. Keynes convinced his colleagues and governments of the correctness of his stance, and after World War II the Western democracies accepted them. This reversal of their previous economic beliefs helped capitalism adapt to the modern world.

Keynes participated in important economic decisions during and following World War II, but died soon after it ended on April 21, 1946, in Firle, Sussex, England.

Return to the Gold Standard

British reinstitution of the gold standard on April 28, 1925, in an attempt at a return to pre-1914 economics, was disastrous. The United States was economically dominant, and British industry could no longer successfully compete with more modern and aggressive foreign industry. Oil and electricity replaced coal, a major British revenue source, as fuel. Returns from British investments had fallen off considerably and could no longer pay for the gap created by high imports and low exports. With the return of the gold standard and reinstatement of the pre-war exchange rate with the dollar, the British pound became overvalued and hurt

British exports. British industrialists tried to reduce costs by lowering wages, which provoked strikes. In June 1925, mine owners announced lower wages and longer work hours. The T.U.C. (Trades Union Congress) General Council and the government opened talks, but on May 2, 1926, the government ended them. A general strike resulted but failed on May 13 when the government called out the army. The strike's failure on May 13 left a bitter taste for workers, who straggled back to work as new legislation weakened the unions. The government's victory was short-lived as Baldwin's popularity steadily declined, and he lost the next election held in May 1929. Even though it did not win a majority, Labour emerged as the largest party, and Ramsey MacDonald returned as prime minister. In October the New York stock market crashed, signaling the Great Depression. British export markets collapsed, and by the end of 1930, British unemployment reached 2.5 million.

British Foreign Policy in the 1920s

Paralleling domestic developments, British postwar foreign policy was nondescript. MacDonald encouraged the negotiations that produced the Dawes Plan, which seemed to resolve the thorny issue of reparations and supported the Geneva Protocol that promised to achieve security for France, resolve defaults, favor collective security, bolster the League of Nations, and promote a general European peace, but it was not ratified before his cabinet fell. MacDonald recognized the

Stanley Baldwin, British Prime Minister during the later 1920s, ran a humdrum administration that failed to confront the country's problems in any meaningful manner. Winston Churchill labeled him a man of the "utmost incompetence." Here he is speaking on the radio, a new instrument that permitted politicians of the era to speak to their citizens directly.

Soviet Union and aimed to resolve outstanding issues with it, but Baldwin did not continue this policy.

Baldwin's administration agreed to the 1925 Locarno Treaty, in which the Germans recognized their western borders with France and, along with Italy, guaranteed them. This treaty was important for the moral pledges made by the countries involved and for accepting Germany's entrance into the League of Nations, and it initiated a period of goodwill known as the "Spirit of Locarno." In 1927, however, Baldwin denounced the treaties that the Labour government had signed with the USSR because of Soviet subversive activities.

FRANCE'S QUEST FOR SECURITY

Not surprisingly France embarked on a painful quest to recover the confidence it had lost during the war, a quest made difficult by political instability.

The "Red Menace"

Bolshevik influence had a major impact on France. The French government's intervention in the Russian civil war and its refusal to consider legislation favorable to workers contributed to increased radicalism that culminated in a failed general strike in May 1920. This strike resulted in the firing of more than 20,000 workers and in workers' hostility for the next fifteen years.

Politically, the "Red Menace" had incalculable results. On December 30, 1920, the Socialist SFIO split because its congress at Tours voted to join the Third (or Communist) International controlled by the Bolshevik government. The majority of SFIO leaders founded the French Communist Party (PCF), and a minority continued in the old organization, severely weakening the Socialists who, despite the split, did not resolve the old question of whether they should pursue revolutionary or reformist policies. The continuing divisions among the Socialists hindered their political action in the 1920s and 1930s, while the PCF followed Russian Bolshevik directives.

In addition to the Socialist split, the Red Menace frightened the middle class into supporting the Bloc National (National Bloc), a coalition of right and center groups whose candidates ran on a conservative platform and supported demands to make Germany pay for the war. The Bloc National won the elections of November 1919 by such a large majority that the resulting Chamber of Deputies was called the "Blue Horizon" Chamber because so many of the former soldiers who were elected showed up wearing their blue uniforms. The chamber was so conservative that it rejected Clemenceau as president of the republic because it considered the Versailles treaty too lenient.

Politics and Economics

The Bloc National coalition followed a conservative course in economic affairs as well as in politics. It refused to raise the income tax rate, held down during the war, in order to pay for reconstruction and relied on short-term bonds that favored privileged bondholders. Although German reparations helped balance the budget and maintain the franc's value for a while, the French currency began a precipitous fall during 1923. Worth 20 U.S. cents in January 1919, it slipped to 4 cents in 1926, causing a severe inflation. Governmental policy also alienated the middle class that, during the war, had patriotically traded gold for war bonds paying 6 percent. In addition to the erosion caused by inflation during the 1920s, while gold kept its worth, the government reduced the interest rate to 4.5 percent.

In 1923 French Prime Minister Raymond Poincaré occupied the Ruhr Valley because the Germans defaulted on reparations and further alienated French public opinion by raising taxes 20 percent in order to pay for the operation. Combined with the National Bloc's determined pro-Catholic Church policy (the resumption of diplomatic relations with the Vatican and Joan of Arc's sanctification), the occupation galvanized Leftist parties into action. Radicals and Socialists were the primary components of the Cartel des Gauches (Cartel of the Left) that won a large majority in the 1924 elections.

The Cartel des Gauches had built-in weaknesses that doomed it to failure. On the one hand, its decisive victory stimulated the rise of extreme right nationalist groups in response, but on the other the cartel was badly split. The leftist rhetoric of the Radicals contrasted with their desire to protect existing privileges and caused friction with their Socialist allies. The leftist roots of the Radicals and their objection to the conservative policies of the rightist parties drove them to ally

Raymond Poincaré was an activist French President who played an important role in the lead- up to World War I. In 1923 he occupied the Ruhr Valley, which touched off German hyperinflation. In the later 1920s he stabilized the volatile French political and economic situation.

with the Socialists, but Socialist policies frightened them and they pulled back toward the center and the right. The Socialists demanded higher taxes on the rich, which they knew their allies opposed. These contradictions destabilized the cartel governments and set the stage for a reversal of alliances as the weak cartel cabinets proved unable to resolve the grave postwar financial crisis. Moreover, the Socialist demand for higher taxes on the wealthy caused the rich to dump governmental bonds and send their capital abroad, and the franc sank ever further. In 1925 six governments followed one another, and in 1926 the cartel disintegrated.

Poincaré returned as prime minister. He had learned his lesson from the Ruhr occupation disaster and turned foreign affairs over to Aristide Briand, who was willing to make up with Germany, and concentrated on domestic affairs. Poincaré skillfully balanced the cabinet between the Radicals and rightists, practiced budgetary restraint, kept labor in line, coaxed French money back home, and attracted foreign loans. He inspired confidence at a time when a worldwide economic recovery began and in 1928 stabilized the franc at one-fifth its prewar value. Stabilization at this low rate made French goods more competitive on the world market and stimulated exports, but it ruined holders of fixed-rate obligations, governmental bonds, and insurance policies, while landlords who had leased their property long term suffered severe losses.

Elections in April 1928 gave Poincaré's the National Union a comfortable majority. When ill health forced Poincaré to resign on July 27, 1929, France appeared confident and serene, but the 1930s demonstrated the extreme fragility of the structure that had been built during the previous decade.

A Real Peace?

During the 1920s, foreign affairs and a search for security were high on the French agenda. In the early postwar years, the French followed a harsh policy toward Germany that culminated in the occupation of the industrial Ruhr Valley in January 1923 when Germany defaulted on reparations. When the occupation touched off hyperinflation in Germany that threatened to ruin the European economic system, France found itself isolated and criticized even by the British and was forced to compromise. Negotiations eventually led to the Treaty of Locarno, which recognized France's border with Germany, and sent disputes to arbitration. The "Spirit of Locarno" seemed to bring real peace to Europe and security to France for the first time since World War I. French evacuation of the Rhineland five years before the term specified at Versailles, the Young Plan giving Germany better payment terms for reparations, and a plan for a federal European union culminated on August 28, 1928, in the Kellogg-Briand Pact, which outlawed war and called for a system of compulsory arbitration in case of disputes.

However, Germany refused to recognize its eastern borders with Poland and saw the French alliances in Eastern Europe as tightening the Versailles noose around it; France emphasized collective security against aggression and continued to conceive of the League of Nations in an anti-German light and, despite the Kellog-Briand Pact, began construction of the Maginot line in 1929 to repel an attack across the same borders that Germany had just guaranteed.

ITALY: FROM "RED BIENNIUM" TO FASCISM

Italy was not attacked in 1914 but entered the conflict ten months later out of fear that if the Central Powers won, they would dominate the continent; a longing to take over the Italian-speaking areas of the Austro-Hungarian Empire; and a desire to win new territory. During its period of neutrality, a debate raged between opposing political forces that wanted to keep the nation neutral and those who advocated intervention—neutralists and interventionists. The neutralists included Giovanni Giolitti, the major Liberal politician, the Catholics, and the Socialists, while the king and prime minister were interventionists. The neutralists either opposed war on principle or believed that it would be too much of a strain for the country; the interventionists hoped for glory and territory or wanted to defend democratic ideals.

The Troubled Postwar

Instead of ending, the national debate escalated after the war. Despite the Italians' best military effort, the dispute over Fiume and other areas at the Paris Peace Conference convinced many that that they had won a "mutilated victory." The disruptive economic and social effects of the war raised the level of the controversy. Although the conflict contributed greatly to the modernization of Italy's industrial base, industry had a difficult time adjusting to peacetime. The cost-of-living index soared to 268 in 1919 from a base of 100 in 1913, the lira dropped from 19.30 U.S. cents prewar to 4.97 U.S. cents in 1920, and the budget shot completely out of balance. The Socialists, who had opposed the war, saw membership in their labor union (the CGL) explode from 249,000 in 1918 to 1.2 million in 1919 and to 2.3 million in 1920. Man-days lost to strikes increased from 906,000 in 1918 to a record 14.1 million in 1919.

The country also suffered social unrest. Returning peasant soldiers, promised land to keep them fighting, invaded large estates and began working vacant land. In the cities, workers demanded an eight-hour workday and factory councils on the Soviet model that would have a dominant voice in management. Strikers attacked former soldiers who frequently had no other clothes to wear but their old uniforms. Future Communist Party founder Antonio Gramsci declared Italy ripe for Bolshevism.

The "Red Biennium"

At its 1919 Bologna Congress, a Bolshevik-influenced Italian Socialist Party (PSI) revoked its 1892 program and endorsed violence as a means of taking power, but it still emerged severely split. The majority Maximalists, led by Giacinto Menotti Serrati, rejected the extreme left's demand to abstain from elections and to organize a revolution, pushing the extreme left to break off in 1921 and found the Italian Communist Party (PCI, originally PCd'I). At the same time, Maximalist revolutionary rhetoric antagonized the moderate Socialists, paralyzed the party, and frightened the middle class, which sought salvation on the right.

In contrast to Britain and France, Italian resentment against the results of the Paris Peace Conference led to the triumph of the left, not the right, in Italy in the first postwar elections of 1919. The Socialists tripled their vote and became the largest party in the Chamber of Deputies with 156 seats. The next largest party, the new, left-leaning, and Catholic Italian Popular Party (PPI), led by sociologist priest, Don Luigi Sturzo, won 100 seats. A Socialist-Catholic alliance would have given Italy a stable majority, but these forces hated each other, and the Bolshevik-influenced Socialists would not cooperate with any other party. Making matters worse, proportional representation, implemented in 1919, permitted many min-iscule groups to win representation in the Chamber of Deputies. The old Liberals, also badly divided, barely collaborated with the Catholics to give Italy a series of weak and highly unstable governments.

In this situation, Parliament turned to the country's senior statesman Giovanni Giolitti, who attempted to reestablish fiscal soundness by increasing levies on the rich, imposing a war profits tax, and registering stocks and bonds in owners' names so they could be taxed. This program alienated the bourgeoisie and the Catholic party, which, combined with lack of Socialist support, sabotaged it. In the meantime, increasing disorder in the country provoked a response. In August and September 1920, 600,000 workers occupied the factories and tried to continue production. Giolitti wisely refrained from using force, correctly believ-ing that the movement would soon fall apart, which it did. Giolitti next tried to reduce Socialist representation in Parliament by calling new elections for May 1921, and when the elections failed to do so, he resigned on June 27. His departure worsened governmental instability, and rightist groups started taking matters into their own hands.

The Fascist Reaction

If the danger of a Bolshevik revolution in Italy had ever existed, historians agree that it dissipated after the failure of the factory occupations. In 1921 man-days lost to strikes dropped by more than half in industry and by over 90 percent on the land, and a backlash began. Former revolutionary Socialist Benito Mussolini established the Fascist movement in Milan on March 23, 1919. Mussolini had ini-tially agreed with the Socialist party line and supported neutrality, but his belief in the war's revolutionary potential led him to advocate intervention, after which, in an emotional meeting, the party expelled him. Mussolini saw action in the war and after the conflict joined bands of ex-soldiers, nationalists, and futurists in attacking former neutralists. He emphasized a common bond among soldiers who had fought in the war and who hated those who had opposed it, especially Social-ists and Bolsheviks. Mussolini's innovation was to proclaim his movement both Socialist and nationalist and to organize it into *Fasci di combattimento* [combat groups]—members of which were called "Fascisti"—consisting of war veterans, former revolutionary interventionists, Republicans, and dissident Socialists.

In 1919 the Fascists issued a program that made radical demands similar to those of the Socialists: universal suffrage, lowering the voting age to 18, the right of women to vote and hold office, abolition of the conservative Senate, the election of a constituent assembly, an eight-hour working day, a minimum wage, workers' participation in industrial management, lowering the retirement age from 65 to 55, nationalization of arms factories, a heavy graduated income tax, the confiscation of property belonging to religious congregations, the expropriation of 85 percent of war profits, and a republic. The Fascists, however, could not compete with the more established and better organized Socialist party and failed to elect anyone to the Chamber of Deputies in 1919.

This failure, Fascism's strong nationalist component, and the national backlash against the "Reds" combined to drive the Fascists to the right and to abandon the radical 1919 program. On the land, where anti-Socialist resentment predominated, the agrarian bourgeoisie financed armed Fascist action squads that destroyed property belonging to peasant leagues, leftist parties, and working-class institutions. Lacking central direction, the peasant labor organizations succumbed to the Fascist onslaught while the local authorities, alienated by the leftists, turned a blind eye. Hammered by the Fascist offensive, the Socialist party split in 1921, the left wing forming the Italian Communist Party, and in 1922, the Maximalists expelled the reformists, who established a separate competing party.

BIOGRAPHICAL SKETCHES

Benito Amilcare Andrea Mussolini
Young Rebel

Mussolini's background would not have led anyone to predict his political future as Il Duce of Fascism. His father Alessandro, a Socialist with anarchistic tendencies, named his son after Mexican revolutionary Benito Juarez and two Italian Anarchists, Amilcare Cipriani and Andrea Costa. Alessandro published articles in local Socialist newspapers and read sections of Marx's *Capital* and other Socialist literature to his children (Benito had a brother and a sister) and, like his son, was committed to violent revolution. Mussolini freely acknowledged his father's influence, stating that his fate would have been much different without him.

Alessandro, a blacksmith frequently out of work, spent a good deal of time at the pub and left the details of running the house to his wife, Rosa Maltoni, an elementary school teacher. Alessandro's unreliability intensified the family's poverty. Benito recalled daily meals of vegetable soup and turnips eaten out of a common dish, with some meat broth on Sundays. Benito, born on July 29, 1883, at Predappio, in the Romagna region of northeast Italy, uttered inarticulate sounds and hardly spoke until age 3. He was wild as a boy, roaming the fields at the head of a gang of young boys, fighting, and stealing fruit from trees. Periodically, he went off by himself, a habit he continued into adulthood. He liked music and played the violin, which always had a soothing effect on him, and his musical talent was transferred to one of his sons who became a jazz pianist.

Worried about her son, Rosa sent him to a Catholic boarding school. Mussolini bitterly resented the discipline and the class distinctions that forced him to eat bread teeming with ants with the poorest children. He had few friends, and the school asked him not to return when he stabbed a fellow student in the hand during a fight. Mussolini finished school nevertheless and in 1901 received his diploma as a teacher. In February 1902 his father's Socialist connections got him

continued

continued

a job as a substitute teacher for the second and third grades in a small town, but his contract was not renewed because of his scandalous love affair with a woman whose husband was away in the army—one of many liaisons. Faced with the prospect of returning to his hometown, and boredom, Mussolini left Italy for Switzerland on July 9, 1902.

The Swiss experience was decisive because Mussolini became a politician there. He took a job in construction, but the work was too hard, and he only lasted a week. He went to Lausanne and made contact with emigrant Italian Socialists, writing articles for their newspapers and giving lectures. His talents as a journalist and orator emerged during this period. Returning to Italy in late 1904, Mussolini had success as a newspaperman, wrote a novel *(The Cardinal's Mistress)*, and rose in the local Romagna party hierarchy because of his participation in the peasant struggles against big landowners. In 1911 he gained national notoriety because of his violent opposition to the Libyan War and for his denunciations of the reformists who headed the Socialist party. Mussolini was a firebrand who did not believe in voting but in violent revolution. At the party congress of 1912, he delivered a violent speech against the reformists. Mussolini belonged to a radical group that gained control of the organization, bullied his way into the editorship of the party's daily newspaper *Avanti!*, and used the newspaper as a platform to call for violent revolution. In June 1914 this revolution seemed to have arrived with violent disorders in the "Red" region of Emilia. However, the defeat of the movement by the army dashed Mussolini's hopes.

Mussolini changed. In the past he had called for revolution to attain socialism; now he revealed himself as more interested in violent revolution for its own sake. This attitude helps explain his abandonment of the party's official position at the beginning of World War I opposing Italian entrance into the conflict. Mussolini reversed himself because, among other reasons, he believed that the war would hasten a revolution. The Socialists expelled him from the party, and Mussolini founded a new movement called fascism.

The Fascist Dictatorship

The Socialist splits prevented them from stopping the Fascist drive to power, while the Liberals and Catholics underestimated the danger. On October 28, 1922, Fascist squads staged the March on Rome in the midst of a governmental crisis. The king refused to declare martial law because, he later said, he feared civil war. The monarch asked Mussolini to head a government even though the Fascists held only 35 of the 525 seats in the Chamber of Deputies. Mussolini formed a coalition cabinet in which Fascist members were a minority and received a vote of confidence on November 17. Italian non-Fascist politicians voted in favor of it, believing that it might be able to restore calm and assuming that they could vote Mussolini out of office at any time— a fatal error because Mussolini's squads controlled the streets.

In April 1924, Mussolini held elections under the "Acerbo law," which modified proportional representation in an effort to create political stability by making it easier to win a majority in Parliament. According to the new law, two-thirds of the seats in the Chamber of Deputies would go to the electoral coalition receiving the most votes, provided it was at least 25 percent of those cast, the remaining seats to be divided proportionately. Governmental interference and Fascist violence ensured that the Fascist-led coalition received almost 65 percent of the vote despite heavy opposition in the North, where the Fascists did not receive a majority.

The magnitude of the violence during the campaign prompted Giacomo Matteotti, a reformist Socialist deputy, to protest publicly and to demand new elections. On June 10, 1924, Matteotti disappeared and was later found beaten to death. The resulting crisis seriously threatened Mussolini as the country and even Fascists turned against him. The opposition boycotted Parliament hoping to force the king to intervene, but Victor Emanuel III was convinced that he would have to replace Mussolini with a Socialist prime minister, and he merely reshuffled the cabinet by putting trusted advisers in key posts.

As the crisis dragged on, extremist Fascists, concerned that they would be tried for their crimes if the government fell, pressured Mussolini to take action. On January 3, 1925, in the Chamber of Deputies Mussolini accepted moral responsibility for the Matteotti murder and defied his opponents to remove him. Mussolini's supporters then passed repressive legislation, made easy because of the boycott. Measures passed between January 1925 and the end of 1926 instituted governmental control of the press, gave the police new powers to arrest citizens, outlawed all parties except the Fascist, and jailed Fascist adversaries—many of whom fled into exile. Mussolini also reorganized the government's machinery by extending executive control over the legislature; solidifying his dominance of the

As soon as they assumed took over in Italy in 1922, the Fascists instituted a dictatorship, even though the actual contours of the fascist state assumed form only in the years following the assassination of Socialist leader Giacomo Matteotti in 1924. Here is an illustration of the Italian police conducting mass arrests of Communists in Trieste in 1923.

executive branch; purging the bureaucracy; and giving party institutions, such as the Fascist Grand Council, governmental functions. Mussolini had organized a one-party dictatorship complete with secret police in the heart of Western Europe, becoming both Il Duce (leader) of the party and of the country.

The rise of the Fascists signaled a dangerous new trend. Mussolini's opponents characterized his regime by inventing a new term: *totalitarian*. Although the monarchy, the church, and other traditional institutions of Italian society resisted and sometimes limited it, fascism replaced democracy with a revolutionary party that imposed a new form of mystical, expansionistic nationalism whose aim was to change the Italians into an organic, unified community of single-minded conquerors. Such tendencies had existed in Italian and European society before World War I, although it is unlikely that the Fascists would have come to power anywhere without the disruptions and dislocations caused by the conflict. In the 1920s, fascism appeared to European observers a peculiarly Italian phenomenon, but under the economic and social pressures of the Great Depression of the 1930s, it spawned similar movements throughout Europe—although each with their national variations. In 1933, Nazism, the movement that copied Mussolini's style most closely, came to power in Germany and altered Europe's destiny.

Fascist Policies in the 1920s

The first real test of the Fascist regime's stability came in the economic field. Mussolini benefited from the policies of earlier postwar cabinets that had begun to turn around Italy's dismal economic predicament. Following the normal postwar pattern, during the 1920s Mussolini favored less governmental intervention and restrained the workers, policies that brought him international praise. Between 1922 and 1925, a free trader, Alberto De Stefani, held the post of minister of finance. De Stefani's low tax, privatization policies, and continued aid to banks and industry, pleased large industrialists and the church. Combined with low wages and the low value of the lira, these measures allowed Italy to take advantage of a European recovery, and Italian exports and productivity jumped.

In 1925 the lira dropped precipitously because of international speculation and caused inflation, the erosion of real wages, and labor agitation. In 1926 Mussolini artificially pegged the lira at a high value and choked credit. The costly lira made Italian goods expensive, and exports fell. Large firms weathered the deflation crisis because the government, foreshadowing future policy, intervened to help them, but small firms and the workers suffered. In 1927 the government implemented a 20 percent wage reduction on the grounds that lower prices compensated workers for the cut, but by 1929 real wages had fallen considerably.

On the labor front, the Fascists had destroyed the independent unions shortly after they came to power, but there were Fascist labor unions whose leaders were genuinely committed to helping workers and who had helped Mussolini come to power. These labor unions counted on Mussolini's help to strengthen their movement, but the industrialists pressured Mussolini to immobilize it. Il Duce did so between 1923 and 1927. The government issued a "Labor Charter" in 1927, but this charter turned out to be a pious statement of principles. There was an internal debate over Fascist "corporativism"—restructuring the country's economy—an interesting intellectual concept that Mussolini also defeated.

In the 1920s, Mussolini also campaigned to make Italy self-sufficient, especially in foodstuffs. He launched the "Battle of the Grain" with great fanfare in 1925, succeeding in increasing grain production, but at an enormous cost to the treasury and to other crops more suited to Italian conditions. Fascist industrial polices favored heavy industry and modernization, and by 1929 the country had made economic progress at the expense of the weakest sections of society.

Mussolini's preoccupation with consolidating his power and economic development prevented him from following through on his pledge to pursue an active foreign policy during the 1920s. He resolved the Fiume dispute with Yugoslavia and in 1923 occupied the Greek island of Corfu in retaliation for the murder by Greek bandits of Italian officials marking the Albanian border for the League of Nations. This issue was settled quickly, however, after which Mussolini's foreign policy entered a quiescent phase. Nevertheless, Mussolini chafed at French dominance of the continent and harbored ambitions that would produce radical changes in Italian foreign policy in the 1930s.

WEIMAR'S THREE ORIGINAL SINS

During the 1920s Germany seemed to take the opposite road of Italy by implementing a democratic regime. The Weimar Republic retained the empire's federalist structure, with the states (Länder) represented in a Reichsrat. Unlike the prewar Bundesrat, however, the states could not veto legislation passed by the popularly elected Reichstag, which could override the Reichsrat's rejection of its bills by a two-thirds majority. In addition, the constitution imposed restrictions on the states' areas of competence and on Prussian representation. A president elected by the people rounded out the constitution's democratic structure.

The reality of Weimar, however, differed from the appearance. Three factors threatened its success: its structural continuity with the Empire, the legacy of Versailles, and hyperinflation.

Structural Continuity

While federalism had benefits, it also had disadvantages in the German postwar context. Prussia, whose size and importance had dominated the Empire, was weakened but not broken up into several administrative units as some reformers had suggested. However, the SPD-Center coalition that ran Prussia from 1920 to 1932 made that state a "bastion of Weimar democracy," and it was a great blow to democracy when Nazi leader Hermann Goering became Prussian president in 1932. Germany's regional character, with states having different social and political traditions, contributed to radically different politics and threats of secession in the Rhineland, Bavaria, and other areas. This disparity occasioned continual conflict between the central and state governments, and the danger posed by possible secession helped secure passage of the constitution's Article 48, which effectively gave the president the right to rule by decree under emergency conditions. This provision would contribute to Hitler's rise.

The perpetuation of other aspects of the Empire also weakened Weimar. The November revolution had retained the bureaucratic structure and personnel nurtured during the Empire. Judges punished violent action by rightists against the Republic leniently—such as when Hitler tried to overthrow the government in 1923—and reserved harsh treatment for leftist opponents. Like the bureaucracy, large German industry and large landholdings in the eastern part of the country survived practically intact, allowing both to resist the notion of trade unions as equal partners in economic discussions and in the formulation of policy. Even though organized labor and the SPD had important responsibilities in the country, industrialists, Junkers, and large sections of the population looked at them with a suspicion that conferred a vaguely illegitimate air on the Republic. Many Germans viewed Weimar as a consequence of defeat and as essential to bargain with the Allies, not the result of the people's desire for a republic. The middle class yearned for traditional values, which the war and inflation had swept away. Despite passage of a democratic constitution, historians, from Arthur Rosenberg to Fritz Fischer to Hans-Ulrich Wehler, concurred that Germany did not change in a fundamental way after World War I.

The Versailles Legacy

This outline puts the complex events of Weimar into perspective. By 1920 right-wing extremism had become a serious problem. Furious nationalists condemned the government for accepting the Versailles treaty even though it had no choice. In March, the government fled before a nationalist coup effort led by Wolfgang Kapp. The army refused to intervene, and only a Socialist strike ended the attempt. When radical workers tried to transform the movement into a revolution, however, the army suppressed them.

Elections on June 6, 1920, validated this shift to the right. Parties supporting Weimar lost votes when compared to the 1919 elections, the SPD dropping from 37.9 percent to 21.6, later settling at about 25 percent until the 1930s in large measure because it its inability to shed its Marxist ideology. Its Center party ally went from 19.7 to 13.6 percent after a split. A third important liberal component of the Weimar coalition, the German Democratic Party (DDP), which was primarily responsible for the constitution, went from 18.6 to 8.4 percent. In contrast, Weimar's most determined enemy, the German National People's Party, or Nationalists (DNVP), rose to 15.1 percent from 10.3. The Nationalists were the heirs of the prewar Conservatives . Reactionary and anti-Semitic, they had the support of the old ruling class—large landowners, army officers, and industrial and middle-class elements. Weimar's enemies on the left, the Communists, received 2 percent of the vote in 1920, but they engaged in obstructionist tactics that reinforced the right. The 1920 elections revealed a rightist national trend away from the parties supporting Weimar; between June 1920 and November 1922, minority cabinets ran the country.

In May 1921, the Allies set a final figure for reparations and threatened retaliation if the Germans did not pay. This threat increased disorder in the country.

In Weimar Germany persons who favored a policy of "fulfillment" of the terms of the Versailles Treaty were targeted for assassination. Such was the case of moderate liberal Walter Rathenau, a Jew and a German patriot who had put the country on a war footing during World War I. He was brutally assassinated on June 24, 1922, a few short months after becoming Foreign Minister.

The Minister for Reconstruction and later Foreign Minister Walter Rathenau, a Jewish industrialist, supported a policy of fulfillment on the grounds that French intransigence would alienate its Allies; enraged anti-Semitic Nationalists brutally murdered him on June 24, 1922. Public outrage against reparations would subside when economic conditions improved, but the reparations played an important role in the Nationalist and Nazi propaganda against Weimar.

In November 1922, a cabinet of experts came to power in order to deal with reparations, but on January 9, 1923, Germany's default caused France and Belgium to occupy the highly industrialized Ruhr Valley.

Hyperinflation

The German government responded by calling for passive resistance. Workers struck, and industrialists refused to cooperate with the occupiers. The government paid workers and reimbursed the industrialists, putting a severe strain on German finances. These events have frequently been cited as the major reason for the hyperinflation that followed, but this does not seem to be the case. All governments had relied more on borrowing than on taxation to finance the war, causing postwar inflation, but Germany had done so more than the others, assuming it would win and the losers would pay the debts. The financial effort to meet the Ruhr occupation tipped the scales into hyperinflation because it added to the enormous debt left over from the conflict. The story of the German hyperinflation can be summarized by a few figures. The exchange rate of the mark to the dollar stood at 76.7 in July 1921. When the Ruhr invasion began in January 1923, the rate was 17,972. By September 1923, it stood at 98.8 million, and at the mark's lowest point, November 1923, the exchange rate was 4.2 trillion to the dollar.

Hyperinflation devastated German society as the savings of the middle class were wiped out, and heavy debtors profited handsomely. Industrialists who had borrowed heavily to finance their activities paid off their debt in worthless currency. Streetcar conductors collected fares at the end of a trip because, in the interval, the mark lost even more value. A monthly streetcar ticket cost 12 million marks in August 1923. A woman who put her currency in a basket to buy bread forgot her money outside the bakery; she ran out and was shocked to discover that someone had dumped out the money and stolen the basket. Newspapers published a list of daily prices and multipliers for goods and services that necessitated complicated arithmetical operations for ordinary daily tasks. Taking a cab required multiplying the stated fare by 600,000, and buying a book meant multiplying the published price by 300,000. Workers rioted if they were not paid daily and used wheelbarrows to carry their wages home.

The hyperinflation accelerated the corrosion of the nation's traditional values that occurred during the war by contributing to sexual promiscuity and to the family's breakdown. Daughters scoffed at their mothers' advice that they should get an education, work, and get married only when a couple had attained economic security: "Earn money! Ridiculous! Our money isn't worth earning!" Women no longer had dowries necessary to set up a solid household, and the men coming back from the war had nothing to offer. If they had to wait for security, daughters argued, they would be too old to marry. Consequently, many women left their families, with their restrictive, obsolete, morals. "The first man who offered a chance [to get away from their families] was the one with whom they went away, either marrying him or not."

The loss of savings that families had built up over a lifetime also increased the despair of the postwar situation as hyperinflation and the economic crash made it difficult to put food on the table, added to the specter of starvation, and increased political disorder. On August 13, 1923, a great coalition cabinet, headed by Gustav Stresemann, tried to end the crisis by implementing fulfillment of the Versailles treaty, but did not immediately stop the disturbances. In October, workers' outrage revived left-wing radicalism in Saxony, Thuringia, and Hamburg. Industrialists reduced the gains previously won by workers and forced out several opponents from the cabinet demanding that the army be used to quell the unrest. In the South, Bavaria became a hotbed of rightist and anti-Semitic activity. In Munich in November 1923, Adolf Hitler attempted a revolution known as the Beer Hall *Putsch*. Badly organized, it failed miserably, but his subsequent trial and the publication of *Mein Kampf*, written in jail, made him a national figure.

These events shifted the political axis to the right. Angered by the government's bias against the left, the SPD toppled Stresemann's government. The ensuing crisis and elections weakened the Socialists, and a more conservative cabinet that included DNVP representatives took power. In 1925, the election of World War I hero Paul von Hindenburg as president accentuated the conservative trend.

Foreign Policy and Its Domestic Effects

The saving grace was that Stresemann remained in the cabinet as foreign minister. Stresermann's policy of fulfillment brought Germany out of diplomatic isolation so it could profit from a worldwide economic recovery between 1925 and 1929. Hyperinflation subsided with the substitution of the inflated currency by a new one backed by a "mortgage" on all German land and industry, the Dawes plan establishing a repayments schedule for reparations, and a foreign loan. By 1927 German production surpassed that of 1913, and, at Locarno, Germany accepted its western frontiers, thus recognizing Alsace-Lorraine as French. In September 1926, Germany was admitted to the League of Nations with a seat on the Council. Despite these hopeful developments and other signs of thawing, however, Germany still refused to accept its responsibility for the war and conducted an "innocence" campaign that was designed to demonstrate that it had not caused the war and to fight against reparations. In a September 18, 1927, speech President von Hindenburg formally rejected the notion of German culpability for the war. Simultaneously, Germany conspired with the USSR to develop new weapons that evaded the Versailles treaty's disarmament terms and helped lay the basis for the rapid rearmament under Hitler. The army seemed to become more integrated into the Republic, but its officers were antirepublican, nationalist influenced, and recalcitrant to civilian control.

With the easing of the economic crisis in the mid-1920s, these troubling aspects of the new Germany remained hidden. The internal peace and good economy brought political stability as right-wing violence and assassinations declined. In May 1928, the parties supporting the constitution won an electoral victory, and the extremist parties took only 30 percent of the vote. Socialist ministers joined the cabinet for the first time since 1923, and an SPD member became chancellor.

However, the moderate victory would be short lived. The anti-Weimar Nationalists had reluctantly participated in cabinets despite internal divisions, but their severe defeat in the 1928 elections made them accept antirepublican industrialist and newspaper magnate Alfred Hugenberg as their new leader and financier. Under Hugenberg's leadership, the party virulently opposed the Republic. Its opposition to the Young Plan, which in August 1929 lightened reparations and set a new payment schedule, embodied this policy. Believing that the plan would undermine Germany's will to resist the war guilt idea and to nullify the Versailles treaty, Hugenberg campaigned against the Young Plan in concert with other right-wing groups, including the Nazis, in a December 1929 referendum. Although the referendum failed miserably, this campaign brought the Nazis to the forefront of German politics.

Between 1925 and 1929, the Weimar republic enjoyed stability and economic progress along with the rest of Western Europe, but it never overcame its original sins. It failed to develop sturdy institutions on which it could rely in times of crisis and did not change the nation's social structure and mentality. With the strain of the Great Depression, the Weimar republic's fragile structure came down.

THE USSR: THE CRISIS OF THE NEP

In Soviet Russia, the New Economic Policy (NEP) turned out to be an important economic success that allowed agricultural production to regain its prewar level in 1926. Livestock production, for example, rose by 3 percent to 4 percent a year between 1924 and 1928—faster than before World War I. However, the NEP cost the Communists their ideological consistency by introducing a market economy into Soviet agriculture.

The NEP Debate

The NEP's economic success contradicted Communist theory by allowing the reemergence of capitalism on the land and economic differentiation within the peasantry, but because the Bolsheviks remained committed to state planning, industrialization, modernizing agriculture, and transforming society, a dispute emerged among the leaders. The majority on the Communist Party's most important organ, the Politburo, consisting of an alliance between Josef Stalin and Nikolai Bukharin, argued that Communist objectives could be achieved *through* rather than *against* the market by governmental guidance. However, Bukharin believed that socialism could be achieved by increasing the wealth of the peasants, so he therefore favored more economic differentiation on the land, tax reductions, and the allocation of more resources for consumer goods; Stalin viewed the increased standards of living as Socialist accumulation, available for the implementation of communism, and eventually turned against Bukharin. Lenin's death in 1924 weakened the NEP and set the stage for a battle for succession that Stalin would win. Against the majority opinion, the Bolshevik left, led by Trotsky, Lev Kamenev, and Grigorii Zinoviev, believed that the party had made too many concessions to petty bourgeois landowners by allowing private trade and favoring rich peasants. It argued in favor of proceeding full speed ahead with rapid industrialization, a policy that Stalin would eventually adopt.

The Peasant Challenge

Relations between peasants and the government were filled with tension. The socialized sector of agriculture accounted for only about 2 percent of production. Ninety percent of households belonged to peasant communes (*mirs*) that periodically redistributed land as they had before the revolution. The Bolshevik Revolution had broken up the large private estates, redistributed land in a more or less equitable manner, and supplied peasants with farm implements and draught animals, but otherwise agriculture continued as before.

The Bolsheviks rejected this result and saw the peasants as divided into four categories: rich peasants, or kulaks, who hired labor and therefore exploited it; middle peasants, who cultivated their own land; poor peasants, who owned very little land and hired themselves out for part of the season; and proletarians with no land who worked the land of others. This characterization led Communist ideologues to target the kulaks when the government decided to proceed with rapid industrialization and the creation of large collective farms and to turn the poorer peasants against the richer ones, with varying success. The Communists also targeted the middle peasants because owning land went against their ideal of common ownership of the means of production.

These considerations set the stage for suppression of the peasants because communism could not be implemented through the NEP. Good harvests lowered the price of grain, but governmental subsidies kept the cost of industrial goods high; peasants refused to buy these goods until the government reduced the price. The situation worsened with bad harvests, as in 1924. In theory, agricultural prices should have risen, but the government refused to pay more, and the kulaks withheld their products in the hope of selling them in the expanding private market. The government doubled the price of grain, but this development made a mockery of Communist theory. In 1927 shortages of consumer goods and speculation brought about a governmental crackdown on private enterprise just at the time when Politburo advocates for rapid industrialization won their case because the defeat of the Chinese revolution and a dispute with the British brought home the USSR's urgent need to defend the Bolshevik Revolution.

The End of THE NEP

Because of these domestic and foreign developments, the Leftists escalated their criticism that the moderate policies pursued under the NEP endangered the gains of the October revolution and won their case. They abandoned their conciliatory attitude toward the kulaks and prepared an assault against them; in December 1927 the XV party congress accepted the conversion of small farms into collectives as the party's main task.

The Bolsheviks immediately ran into resistance from the peasants. Between October and December 1927, the peasants sold only half as much grain to state collection agencies as they had before because the government's prices were too low and they preferred to store their grain instead of selling it for cash that they could not spend on industrial goods that were in short supply anyway. Whereas the party had accommodated the peasants in the past, this time it refused to increase prices for grain, insisted on its push for industrialization, and seized the peasants' products. As the peasants obstructed collections, the government tried them for hoarding and speculation and called on the poorer peasants for support. The government's actions ignited a debate in the party. The alliance between Nikolai Bukharin and Stalin collapsed; Bukharin opposed the policy while Stalin favored it, strengthening his own political position. The party raised taxation for the kulaks to intolerable levels, raised collection quotas, confiscated land, and escalated punishments for resisters by sending them to prison or internal exile. Fearful of being labeled kulaks, the most efficient and prosperous farmers reduced the amount of land they farmed and sold or slaughtered their animals. The results were a drastic decrease in production, severe food shortages, rationing in urban areas, intensified state control of the countryside, requisitioning, the closing of private shops, and the expansion of state farms.

During the civil war, the Bolsheviks had requisitioned grain and other agricultural products that were necessary to win, but the policies of 1928 and 1929 signified that the party was determined to collectivize the peasantry and forcibly implement communism on the land. The normalcy that the NEP had brought to Russia had been more apparent than real and, as happened in the rest of the European continent, the 1930s ushered in more repression than Russia had previously experienced.

Bibliographical Essay

Raymond J. Sontag, *A Broken World 1919–1939* (New York, 1971), considers the period discussed in this chapter and the next. Good general works on the first postwar decade include Charles S. Maier, *Recasting Bourgeois Europe: Stabilization in France, Germany and Italy in the Decade after World War I* (Princeton, N.J., 1975), which is concerned with the attempt to stabilize those countries. Zara S. Steiner, *The Lights that Failed* (New York, 2005), is a comprehensive history of the attempt to reconstruct Europe in the 1920s. Dan P. Silverman, *Reconstructing Europe after the Great War* (Cambridge, Mass., 1982), concentrates on economic issues. Dirk Berg-Schlosser and Jeremy Mitchell, *Authoritarianism and Democracy in Europe, 1919–1939* (New York, 2002), is a comparative analysis.

The most complete work on Britain after the war is Charles Loch Mowat, *Britain Between the Wars 1918–1940* (Chicago, 1963). A. J. P. Taylor, *English History 1914–1945* (Oxford, UK, 1965), has chapters on this period filled with details and insights. Roy Jenkins wrote *Baldwin* (London, 1995). On different aspects of the Baldwin period, see the essays collected by John Raymond, ed., *The Baldwin Age* (London, 1960). For an analysis of Ramsay MacDonald, see Benjamin Sacks, *J. Ramsay MacDonald in Thought and Action* (Albuquerque, N.M., 1952). On the ramifications of the Zinoviev Letter, see Gill Bennett, "A Most Extraordinary and Mysterious Business: the Zinoviev Letter," *Historians LRD,* N. 14 (London 1999). Two useful works on British foreign policy are Anne Orde, *Great Britain and International Security 1920–1926* (London, 1978), and David Carlton, *MacDonald versus Henderson: The Foreign Policy of the Second Labour Government* (New York, 1970). Keith Erick Neilson, *Britain, Soviet Russia and the Collapse of the Versailles Order, 1919–1939* (Cambridge, UK, 2006), argues that the intellectual inability to maintain the order established in 1919 contributed to the outbreak of World War II. *The Morbid Age: Britain Between the Wars* (London, 2009), by the distinguished historian Richard J. Overy, is an examination of intellectual life during the period.

France during the 1920s has not been a popular topic. Nathaniel Greene's brief *From Versailles to Vichy: The Third French Republic, 1919–1940* (New York, 1970), covers the entire interwar period. Another general history, Charles Sowerwine's *France Since 1870,* 2d ed. (New York, 2009), discusses culture and society and has a chapter on interwar France. Allan Mitchell, *A Stranger in Paris: Germany's Role in Republican France, 1870–1940* (New York, 2006), is a wide-ranging discussion of the relationship between the two countries. A good biography of the most important French statesman during this period is J. F. V. Keiger, *Raymond Poincaré* (Cambridge, UK, 1997); Keiger states that Poincaré was the only French politician to have exercised a decisive influence in both the first and second halves of the Third Republic. Stephen A. Schuker's *The End of French Predominance in Europe: The Financial Crisis of 1924 and the Adoption of the Dawes Plan* (Chapel Hill, N.C., 1976) presents a thorough analysis of both domestic and foreign affairs up to 1924. Piotr S. Wandycz, *France and Her Eastern Allies 1919–1925* (Westport, Conn., 1974), is a detailed look at French and Eastern European diplomacy of the period.

Spencer M. Di Scala, *Italy: From Revolution to Republic, 1700 to the Present,* 4th ed. (Boulder, Colo., 2009), includes a detailed treatment of twentieth-century Italian history. H. James Burgwyn discusses the concept of the mutilated victory in *The Legend of the Mutilated Victory: Italy, the Great War, and the Paris Peace Conference* (Westport,

Conn., 1993). Books that focus on the "Red Biennium" in English are scarce, while those that concentrate on Italian Communist Party founder Antonio Gramsci are plentiful. See John Cammett's *Antonio Gramsci and the Origins of Italian Communism* (Stanford, Calif., 1967); Martin Clark, *Antonio Gramsci and the Revolution that Failed* (New Haven, Conn., 1977); and Richard Bellamy and Darrow Schecter, *Gramsci and the Italian State* (Manchester, UK, 1993). A classic work on the Red Biennium and the coming of Fascism was written by the (then) Communist Angelo Tasca, *The Rise of Italian Fascism, 1918–1922* (London, 1938). Historian Gaetano Salvemini wrote two polemical but classic accounts of the rise of Fascism: *The Origins of Fascism in Italy* (New York, 1973), previously cited, and *The Fascist Dictatorship in Italy* (London, 1928). Alexander De Grand published a parallel history of the Italian Socialist and Communist parties with good coverage of this period, *The Italian Left in the Twentieth Century: A History of the Socialist and Communist Parties* (Bloomington, Ind., 1989). The period of the Red Biennium and the rise of fascism has been examined by Donald Sassoon, *Mussolini and the Rise of Fascism* (London, 2007), and Dalia S. Elazar, *The Making of Fascism:Class, State, and Counter-Revolution, Italy 1919–1922* (Westport, Conn., 2001). Adrian Lyttelton, *The Seizure of Power: Fascism in Italy, 1919–1929* (New York, 1973), is a thorough work on the subject. Spencer M. Di Scala's *Renewing Italian Socialism: Nenni to Craxi* (New York, 1988) includes a chapter discussing the early exile movement, and his previously cited *Italy: From Revolution to Republic, 1700 to the Present*, 4th ed. (Boulder, Colo., 2009) has a comprehensive chapter on the rise of fascism.

Fascism's love affair with violence is discussed by David Forgacs, "Fascism, Violence and Modernity," in Jana Howlett and Rod Mengham, *The Violent Muse: Violence and the Artistic Imagination in Europe, 1910–1934* (Manchester, UK, 1994). Alexander De Grand's essay "Bolshevik and Fascist Attacks on the Liberal State, 1919–1922" in Frank J. Coppa, ed., *Studies in Modern Italian History: From the Risorgimento to the Republic* (New York, 1986), is a good account of agrarian fascism. Anthony Cardoza's *Agrarian Elites and Italian Fascism: The Province of Bologna, 1901–1926* (Princeton, N.J., 1982) links agrarian and commercial fascism. Cardoza also published a good brief biography of Mussolini: *Benito Mussolini: The First Fascist* (New York, 2006). Discussions of fascisms in different parts of the country include Paul Corner, *Fascism in Ferrara 1915–1925* (London, 1975), and Alice Kelikian, *Town and Country under Fascism: The Transformation of Brescia,1915–1926* (Oxford, UK, 1986). H. James Burgwyn, *Italian Foreign Policy in the Interwar Period 1918–1940* (Westport, Conn., 1997) is a good book on a neglected topic.

On economic issues, see Douglas Forsyth, *Monetary and Financial Policy and the Crisis of Liberal Italy* (New York, 1993), and on diplomacy, see Alan Cassels, *Mussolini's Early Diplomacy* (Princeton, N.J., 1970).

Good general histories of Weimar Germany include Detlev Peukert, *Weimar Germany: The Crisis of Classical Modernity* (New York, 1992), and Paul Bookbinder, *Weimar Germany: The Republic of the Reasonable* (Manchester, UK, 1996). Stephen J. Lee's *The Weimar Republic* (New York, 2010) is a wide-ranging introduction. A. J. Nicholls, *Weimar and the Rise of Hitler* (London, 1968), is an excellent short work. Richard Bessel and E. J. Feuchtwanger, *Social Change and Political Development in Weimar Germany* (London, 1981), collects a number of good essays on the social history of the period. Richard Bessel has also published a detailed history of the immediate aftermath of the war, *Germany After the First World War* (Oxford, UK, 1993). Two contemporary accounts of the Weimar republic that can still be read with profit are Elmer Luehr, *The New German Republic* (New York, 1929), and James W. Angell, *The Recovery of Germany* (Westport, Conn., 1972). Annika Mombauer, *The Origins of the First World War: Controversies and Consensus* (London, 2002) is an excellent account of the controversies swirling around the question of whether Germany was to blame for the outbreak of the war and of the official attempt to establish German "innocence."

On the German hyperinflation, the most complete and detailed work is Gerald D. Feldman's massive *The Great Disorder: Politics, Economics, and Society in the German Inflation, 1914–1924* (New York, 1993). Feldman also published a study of heavy industry and its antiworker politics, *Iron and Steel in the German Inflation 1916–1923* (Princeton, N.J., 1977). A good short work is Fritz K. Ringer, *The German Inflation of 1923* (New York, 1969), which includes a good introduction and interesting readings; the citations in the text are taken from p. 135. Adam Fergusson's *When Money Dies: The Nightmare of the Weimar Collapse* (London, 1975, 2d ed., 2010) is a readable account of inflation's consequences. Constantino Brescian-Turroni's *The Economics of* Inflation (London, 2003) examines the depreciation of German currency and the hyperinflation between 1914 and 1923. Bernd Widdig, *Culture and Inflation in Weimar Germany* (Berkeley, Calif., 2001), analyzes the traumatic effects and permanent scars on German culture. A German view of reparations and of the Versailles settlement in general can be gleaned from Hjalmar Schacht, the man credited with planning the end of the hyperinflation, *The End of Reparations* (London, 1931), while Leonard Gomes, *German Reparations, 1919–1932* (New York, 2010), is a complete survey.

The crucial role that American loans played in Weimar's economic recovery is analyzed by William C. McNeil, *American Money and the Weimar Republic* (New York, 1986).

On particular personalities, institutions, and parties, see David Felix, *Walter Rathenau and the Weimar Republic* (Baltimore, Md., 1971), which concentrates on the crucial issue of reparations. Gene Smith, *The Ends of Greatness* (New York, 1990), has a good general account of Rathenau's fate (and those of other World War I characters). Henry L. Bretton, *Stresemann and the Revision of Versailles* (Stanford, Calif., 1953), is a good treatment of Stresemann's attempt to change the Versailles settlement peacefully. More disturbing is Hans W. Gatzke, *Stresemann and the Rearmament of Germany* (Baltimore, Md., 1954), which reveals German attempts to evade the disarmament clauses of Versailles, especially in collusion with the Soviets. Lewis Hertzman, *DNVP: Right Wing Opposition in the Weimar Republic, 1918–1924* (Lincoln, Nebr., 1963), examines a pivotal political party; this book should be consulted in conjunction with John A. Leopold's *Alfred Hugenberg: The Radical Nationalist Campaign Against the Weimar Republic* (New Haven, Conn., 1977), which puts the Nationalist leader and his campaign against Weimar under a microscope. Hermann Beck, *The Fateful Alliance: German Conservatives and Nazis in 1933* (New York, 2008), examines the complex relationship between the two. Germany's attempt to regain the military attributes of a great power is discussed more fully by Gaines Post, Jr., *The Civil-Military Fabric of Weimar Foreign Policy* (Princeton, N.J., 1973). A more general discussion of foreign policy, reparations, and Versailles is Royal Jae Schmidt, *Versailles and the Ruhr: Seedbed of World War II* (The Hague, 1968), and F. L. Carsten provides a full treatment of army policy in *The Reichswehr and Politics 1918 to 1933* (Oxford, UK, 1966). John Wheeler-Bennett's *The Nemesis of Power* (New York, 2005) looks at the German army in politics between 1918 and 1945. The coverage of Weimar in the first volume of Richard J. Evans, *The Coming of the Third Reich* (New York, 2004), is excellent; the quote on Prussia is on p. 89.

On the USSR during the NEP period, see Sheila Fitzpatrick, ed., *Russia in the Era of NEP* (Bloomington, Ind., 1991), which includes essays on various aspects of the NEP; so does R. W. Davies, *From Tsarism to the New Economic Policy* (Ithaca, N.Y., 1991). Gregory L. Freeze, ed., *Russia: A History* (New York, 1997), contains an essay by Daniel Orlovsky on the experiment. Fitzpatrick's more general work, *The Russian Revolution* (New York, 2008) includes a chapter on the NEP. See also Vladimir I. Lenin, *The New Policies of Soviet*

Russia (Chicago, 1921), with writings of protagonists. The discussion of the NEP crisis is usually covered by works that discuss the later collectivization effort as well. Two excellent works that look at the period examined in this chapter, as well as the 1930s, are R. W. Davies, *The Socialist Offensive: The Collectivization of Soviet Agriculture, 1929–1930* (New York, 1980), and Steven F. Cohen's *Bukharin and the Bolshevik Revolution: A Political Biography, 1888–1938* (New York, 1973). Christopher Read's *The Making and Breaking of the Soviet System* (New York, 2001) is a comprehensive history of the period, including the implications of the NEP, the struggles that brought it to an end, and ensuing events.

PART III

An Age of Dictators

CHAPTER 10

✑

The Great Depression and the Liberal Democracies

CHAPTER OUTLINE

The Great Depression • British Democracy • Troubled France • Scandinavia: Toward Social Democracy • Marking Time: The Low Countries and Switzerland

BIOGRAPHICAL SKETCHES

James Ramsay MacDonald, Labour's Nonperson Prime Minister • Léon Blum, Popular Front

Economic dislocations of the Great Depression's scope, intensity, and duration profoundly challenged Europeans to maintain or revamp their democratic traditions in the face of social and political disorder.

THE GREAT DEPRESSION

In October 1929 the U.S. stock market collapsed and touched off a Great Depression that stunned the leaders of the advanced industrial nations who believed that they had successfully overcome the dislocations caused by World War I.

The Long Wave

Despite the economic progress that characterized most of the 1920s, warning signals, such as the weak state of agriculture, were apparent. The rising grain prices during World War I had encouraged farmers to put more land into production, but the end of hostilities brought about a reduced demand and falling prices. The decline hit the small countries of Eastern Europe the earliest, and in the mid-1920s the strong peasants' parties forced governments to enact tariff barriers against imported agricultural goods—the first shots in an economic war that would engulf the world. A similar crisis affected coal, the basis of British prosperity since the industrial revolution and now being rapidly being displaced by oil.

Greater economic interdependence, symbolized by American loans to Germany and mistaken governmental policies, increased the severity and length of the 1930s economic downturn. The Germans paid reparations to the European allies partly with American funds, who used them to pay war debts to the Americans, who then had more money to lend to the Germans—and so on. When Wall Street crashed, American investors withdrew their loans, and the process stopped. European banks faltered, capped by the clamorous failure of the Kreditanstalt in Vienna in May 1931 that intensified the financial panic and led to more bank closings, industrial failures, and layoffs.

As for the governments, their insistence on the gold standard and balanced budgets when the crisis began made things worse by contributing to a deflationary spiral. When unemployment increases, people reduce their spending, and the decreased purchasing power reduces demand. Producers cannot sell their products and lay off more workers, which reduces demand, production, and prices even more. Severe deflation ignited social and political unrest, especially in the most highly industrialized countries where production fell about 37 percent and unemployment reached 25 percent.

The Great Depression increased the appeal of communism because it seemed to confirm the hypothesis of Karl Marx, who predicted that capitalism would collapse in a gigantic final crisis of overproduction that would cause the proletariat to revolt, overthrow capitalism, and implement socialism. Many leftists took the Soviet Union as a model, provoking a serious backlash even in countries with well-developed democratic traditions. In countries where democracy did not have a long tradition, the reaction against communism encouraged the rise of dictatorial regimes.

A Downward Spiral

Combined with the American stock market crash, trading difficulties had lethal effects. In June 1930, the United States adopted the Smoot-Hawley tariff that touched off a new round of protectionism that worsened the economic downturn. The crash wiped out the savings and jobs of millions of Americans and Europeans. The greatly diminished purchasing power caused production to drop and business confidence and investment to slip as the increased risk of business failures caused investors to sell stocks and call in mortgages and loans. With the tightening up of credit, Germany could no longer pay reparations, and the British and French defaulted on their war debts to the United States. High unemployment rates led countries to close their borders to imports to keep as many of their own citizens employed as possible. The decline of international trade caused more unemployment, which caused increased governmental expenses and decreased tax revenues. Governments had to provide benefits to more people but had a limited ability to raise taxes because people were less able to pay them. They borrowed to make up for the shortfall, but lenders demanded further cuts to ensure that they would be paid back, and more borrowing caused a run on currencies as citizens tried to exchange currency for gold.

In the past, agriculture had served as a buffer against economic disaster, but this time no relief arrived. The bountiful harvests of 1929 and later years worsened the agricultural crisis of the mid-1920s. Prices kept falling because major world producers of wheat and cereals lacked enough storage facilities, forcing them to

The Great Depression that followed the American Stock Market Crash of 1929 had its origins in the mistaken policies of the major countries. They followed restrictive economic policies and remained on the gold standard, thus worsening the recession that followed that event. This picture shows a protest march of the unemployed in London.

sell their products quickly, and the USSR increased wheat exports hoping that the revenues would help fund its policy of rapid industrialization.

Governmental Policies

After World War I, governments insisted on reinstituting the gold standard as a means of anchoring national currencies and preventing wild fluctuations in exchange rates that would result in inflation and social disorder. For example, in 1925, the British responded to balance-of payments deficits by contracting their economy in order to reinstitute the gold standard. Because they imported too many goods and paid for them in gold, however, the precious metal flowed out of the country, and British monetary authorities tried to reduce the outflow by restricting people's ability to buy goods.

The classic way of reducing consumer buying is to increase unemployment, but in times of severe crises, this policy can set off a dangerous downward spiral. The gold standard made it impossible to address balance-of-payments deficits by devaluing the currency, which reduces the price of a country's products on the world market and increases exports and, consequently, employment. According to Peter Temin, bad monetary policy, not structural causes, precipitated, prolonged, and deepened the Great Depression.

The gold standard was not the only reason for the severe downturn. In times of crisis, governments of the period cut expenses and raised interest rates, the exact opposite of what was needed, according to British economist John Maynard Keynes, who advocated increased governmental spending and lower interest rates to stimulate the economy during economic crises. Keynes wrote during the depression, but monetary officials did not accept his ideas until the post–World War II period. Governments, such as that of German Chancellor Heinrich Bruening, followed restrictive financial policies and adopted harsh budgets to decrease the deficit, and the Americans increased interest rates and shrank their economy. The British followed similar policies until 1931, when they pursued a policy of mild expansion that brought some relief.

BRITISH DEMOCRACY

During the Great Depression, the liberal democracies of northern Europe retained their democratic structures despite difficult and sometimes dramatic circumstances.

Britain Confronts the Crisis

In Britain, Ramsay MacDonald's second Labour government (May 1929–August 1931), in office when the Great Depression began, needed Liberal support to remain in power and forced him to confront the emergency with classic economic, not Socialist, solutions.

BIOGRAPHICAL SKETCHES

James Ramsay Macdonald
Labour's "Nonperson" Prime Minister

Born to Anne Ramsay out of wedlock in Lossiemouth, Scotland, on October 12, 1866, Ramsay MacDonald shared the stigma of an illegitimate birth with two other famous British Labour leaders, Keir Hardie and Ernest Bevin. Education was MacDonald's ticket to success. At age 15, his appointment as a "pupil teacher" took him out of the fields and gave him an excellent grounding in English literature, Latin, and Greek. This education—unusual for political leaders of his class—inclined him to leadership.

In 1885, MacDonald went to Bristol and then London, working in humble jobs. He joined the Fabian Society, inspired by Beatrice and Sidney Webb, who believed in achieving socialism gradually. MacDonald championed equal opportunities for women and married Margaret Gladstone, a leader in the struggle. A meeting of local workers congratulated "Mrs. J. R. Macdonald in having won the esteem of Comrade J. R. Macdonald which in due time matured into love and it further resolves that she is one in a thousand."

Margaret's private income gave MacDonald a measure of economic security and aided his rise to political prominence. MacDonald became the first secretary of the Labour Representation Committee, the forerunner of the Labour Party, in 1900. In 1906, he won election to Parliament, along with twenty-eight other members of the organization, and in 1911 became its parliamentary leader. A traditional

Socialist pacifist, in 1914 MacDonald opposed Britain's entrance into World War I because he believed that the conflict did not threaten the country. The Labour parliamentary delegation disagreed with him and voted war credits, prompting him to resign his leadership post. His popularity plummeted, and in 1918 he lost his seat.

Recovering from this defeat, MacDonald won reelection and led the Labour opposition. Following the 1923 elections, the Liberals supported MacDonald as prime minister in a coalition government. Despite some successes, his first term ended on a sour note on November 4, 1924, because of the botched prosecution of a Communist newspaper editor for his opinions. In the 1929 elections, Labour became the largest British party, allowing MacDonald to return as prime minister. He named as minister of labor the first woman to hold cabinet rank, Margaret Bondfield. This governmental experience proved a failure because the cabinet did not resolve the problems of the depression. MacDonald resigned on August 24, 1931, but, believing a national government necessary to confront the crisis, agreed to head a cabinet that included Liberals and Conservatives. In reality, MacDonald had little real power, and Conservative Stanley Baldwin led the cabinet. MacDonald relinquished the prime minister's post on June 7, 1935, but stayed on until May 29, 1937. Exhausted and lonely, he departed for a South American tour and died of heart failure at sea on November 9 aboard the steamship *Reina del Pacifico*. His body was taken back to Scotland, cremated, and interred with that of his wife, who had died of blood poisoning in 1911.

Although MacDonald was the first Labour prime minister, the party treated him as an embarrassment and ignored him because it considered him a traitor for not implementing Socialist policies, for his decision to stay on as prime minister in 1931, and for being an impractical dreamer. In fact, MacDonald lacked a majority to achieve a Labour program, and no other leader handled the depression satisfactorily. In treating him as a nonperson, the Labour Party and its historians disregarded the successful efforts that MacDonald made to construct a Labour Party organization and to win public acceptance as a replacement for the Liberal Party.

When unemployment shot up from 10 percent to 16 percent and the country's exports declined by one-half in two years, MacDonald had no choice but to extend the dole to an increasingly greater number of the unemployed—2.5 million by the end of 1930. As tax receipts fell precipitously because fewer people could afford to pay taxes, MacDonald and his unimaginative Chancellor of the Exchequer Philip Snowden could do no better than implement austerity. In July 1931, economic experts recommended sharp increases in taxation and drastic spending cuts for the country to qualify for new loans and to remain on the gold standard. They suggested a 10 percent cut in unemployment benefits and prohibiting the embattled unemployment insurance fund from borrowing more money. In August, the American J. P. Morgan Bank declared that it would not lend any more money to the Bank of England unless the Labour government went along with the cuts, which were bound to increase unemployment. MacDonald and Snowden saw no alternative because they feared that the pound would lose value if they did not comply. MacDonald brought the question before the cabinet, which split on the question and resigned.

The National Government

Instead of resigning when he consulted with the king, MacDonald unexpectedly secured a mandate for a national government from the monarch. He believed that the crisis required a unified, nonpartisan cabinet, but his own Labour Party objected and expelled him. MacDonald's new National Government cabinet included Conservative leader Stanley Baldwin, who quickly overshadowed the prime minister. It reduced relief and governmental salaries and attempted to balance the budget, measures that alleviated neither the financial nor the social crisis. Investors continued to dump pounds for gold, and salary reductions provoked antigovernment riots. Realizing that strikes and social disorder would intensify if it continued on its deflationary course, the government abandoned the gold standard.

Almost immediately the pound fell to 70 percent of its old exchange rate with the dollar—less than observers had expected. MacDonald then called for new elections to ask a mandate from the voters. On October 27, 1931, the elections gave the National Government a large majority of 497 seats, but the mandate went to the Conservatives, not MacDonald, by decimating the Labour Party and making MacDonald more dependent on Baldwin. Labour retreated to reorganize itself, but it would take power again only in 1945. The National Government cabinet, with Baldwin as its real star, enjoyed a large majority to take decisive action. Fortunately for Britain, abandonment of the gold standard by reason of popular discontent stimulated the British economy because the pound's devaluation made British goods cheaper on the world market.

The electoral campaign had been fought primarily over the question of whether the country should reverse its traditional free-trade policy and protect essential industries, and protection won out. In 1932 the government imposed a 10 percent general duty and intervened in the private industrial sector by fostering mergers and nationalization in areas such as cotton and steel production, eliminating weaker companies, and giving it the ability to control prices. It also nationalized London transport, subsidized shipbuilding and important agricultural products, and imposed import quotas, all of which helped stimulate growth. In 1934 the government embarked on a public works program and made grants to the country's most depressed areas, where, despite the country's economic improvement, unemployment remained distressingly high.

Political Challenges

Despite the economic crisis, the British political system proved remarkably stable and successfully confronted challenges from both the right and the left.

A native Fascist movement under Sir Oswald Moseley, a former Conservative Member of Parliament from an old distinguished family, as well as an ex-Socialist, took root. As a minor official in the MacDonald government, Moseley had presented a radical proposal for emergency action to the cabinet, but after its defeat, he turned sharply right, embraced fascism, and formed the raucous British Union of Fascists. This organization created a commotion in the country, but never won enough followers to make a difference in British politics.

On the left, one of the most important Labour party affiliates, the Independent Labour Party (ILP), seceded in 1932. ILP members included influential young leftist intellectuals who revolted against old-line trade union Socialists and founded the Socialist League. Influenced by Harald Laski, a political science professor at the London School of Economics, and John Strachey, scion of a celebrated literary family, and attracted by Marxism, they denounced fascism and the rightward drift of the Labour Party. They advocated a Popular Front alliance with the Communists, believing that the Labour Party should institute a temporary dictatorship to impose a Socialist revolution. The ILP had great cultural appeal in England, and in 1935, the publication of a new book that was favorable to the Soviet Union by Sidney and Beatrice Webb—*Soviet Russia: A New Civilization?*—boosted their cause. The ILP's influence, however, remained cultural, and the Labour Party remained firmly under the control of Clement Attlee, who succeeded George Lansbury in 1935, and Ernest Bevin, a trade union leader who distrusted intellectuals.

Unlike Labour, the Conservative Party under Stanley Baldwin weathered political uprisings with little difficulty. These revolts included Churchill's denunciation of the British dominions' drift toward de facto independence that resulted in Ireland effectively becoming a republic in 1937 and India's increasing shift toward the independence that occurred after World War II. More important, Churchill advocated resisting Hitler's demands and unsuccessfully opposed the appeasement policies of Baldwin, after he became prime minister in 1935, and of his successor Neville Chamberlain.

TROUBLED FRANCE

The 1930s were years of crisis for the other major European democratic power, France, which saw a rapid growth of nationalistic and quasi-fascist organizations after the victories of the Cartel des Gauches coalition of Radicals and Socialists in 1924 and 1932. The economic crisis of the 1930s and the seeming success of Fascist Italy and the growth of Nazism in Germany emboldened French Fascist-leaning organizations.

France and the Depression

Despite the growth and increased efficiency of French industry during the 1920s, France remained a country based on small business and an inflexible mentality. The Great Depression struck later than in other countries because of its self-sufficiency and large number of small companies and independent landowners. Investors trading their currencies for gold also preferred Paris as a refuge for their wealth, which gave the impression that France had immunity from the economic crisis. The French, leaders of the "gold bloc," stubbornly refused to go off the gold standard and followed deflationary policies longer than other countries. This policy caused a drop in industrial production of 27 percent between 1930 and 1932, rising unemployment, increased expenses, and revenue shortfalls.

The country's steadily worsening economic situation radicalized workers, peasants, and the middle class. The workers increasingly supported Socialist and Communist organizations. On the land, the peasants joined right-wing and leftist organizations that were hostile to the republic because of a fall in revenue of 40 percent between 1931 and 1934. The middle class, its security gone, favored right-wing groups advocating the government's overthrow. Owners of small businesses, themselves caught by the crisis, tenaciously resisted workers' demands for improved wages and working conditions. Popular support for the Third Republic seemed to evaporate.

Political Disorder

In this situation, the French political system failed. In 1929 and 1930 André Tardieu, the most energetic premier after Poincaré, proposed massive construction projects, electrification, industrial and agricultural renovation, and increased social insurance, but the right opposed him because it favored the lower classes, and the left feared political competition. Pierre Laval replaced Tardieu and followed a deflationary economic policy that gave rise to a new Cartel des Gauches that won the 1932 elections. The new union suffered from the same weakness as the old one—a fundamental incompatibility between the Socialists and the Radicals. The Socialists demanded a forty-hour workweek and nationalization of the armaments industry, but the Radicals opposed them, and the cartel then fell apart; six cabinets followed each other in rapid succession between June 1932 and February 1934.

In February 1934 the Stavisky scandal set off serious street disorders. It had been rumored that high governmental officials had protected Serge Stavisky, a financier who had been involved in many questionable dealings. When Stavisky died under mysterious circumstances, his victims protested because they believed that the police had killed him to cover up the involvement of his highly placed partners. Radical Prime Minister Édouard Daladier took a strong stand against the disturbances by firing the Paris police chief, and rightist groups sympathetic to Fascist Italy and Nazi Germany reacted by leading riots in Paris on February 6, 1934, that left 14 dead and 263 wounded. Daladier resigned—the first time in the Third Republic's history that a cabinet left office because of riots. A national union cabinet replaced Daladier and followed deflationary economic policies that failed to resolve the economic and political tensions.

The French leftists interpreted the disorders as a Fascist conspiracy to overthrow the republic, demonstrating and calling a general strike to protest the growing threat from the right. At this point, the Communists, who had previously rejected cooperation with the Socialists, decided to negotiate with them because of the rise of Hitler in Germany and the Nazi threat to the USSR. The talks produced a unity-of-action pact that brought closer relations between them, and the agreement was enlarged in 1935 with the adherence of the Radicals. In January 1936 the parties joined in a common program known as the Popular Front.

Right and Left: A Mortal Struggle

Challenging the left were fascistic groups that had an important cultural impact and would reach their zenith after the French defeat by the Nazis in 1940. The rightist leagues had absorbed the popular nationalism of Maurice Barrès and Charles Maurras (see Chapter 1), denouncing French political decadence and exhorting the nation to strive for excellence and heroism. Although they might cooperate as they did in the February 1934 riots, they did not speak with a unified

France was struck by corruption and disorders during the Great Depression. The riots in Paris that resulted from the financial embezzlements of Serge Stavisky in 1934 left many dead and wounded and resulted in the government's fall.

voice. The Action Française, the Camelots du Roi, and the Croix de Feu were ultra-nationalist, antiparliamentarian, and authoritarian, but were not in the Fascist tradition; the Jeunesses Patriotes, the Solidarieté Français, and later the Cagoulards admired Fascist Italy and Nazi Germany. In the 1930s French fascism was highly visible but failed to attract a mass following. Georges Valois's Le Faisceau collapsed in 1928. Marcel Bucard's Françistes, founded in 1933, received Italian subsidies but remained small. Jacques Doriot's Parti Populaire Français (French Popular Party, PPF), created after the Popular Front's electoral victory of 1936, was a partial exception. It grew rapidly for a time but declined even faster in 1938 and 1939 when apprehension that the leftists would take over France faded.

The Popular Front and Its Failure

The struggle between the right and the left became fiercer following the Popular Front's electoral campaign and victory in May 1936, which polarized the country as never before. The Socialists emerged as the largest French party, with 146 seats in the Chamber of Deputies, and the Radicals followed with 116. The most spectacular result, however, was the increase in Communist seats—from 10 to 72. For the first time, a Socialist leader, Léon Blum, became prime minister, increasing fears that the Popular Front would lead to a Communist dictatorship and confiscation of private property, and eliciting expressions of anti-Semitism because Blum was Jewish. The likelihood of a Communist dictatorship was slim because the Communists refused to enter the cabinet and restricted their support to parliamentary votes. The Radicals joined the cabinet, but they opposed the social and economic reforms advocated by their Socialist and Communist partners.

BIOGRAPHICAL SKETCHES

Léon Blum
Popular Front

The most important French politician of the 1930s, Léon Blum, was born in Paris on April 9, 1872, into a Jewish family from Alsace. Blum graduated with honors in law in 1894 from the Sorbonne and became a literary critic. Scandalized by the Dreyfus affair, Blum went into politics, joined the French Socialist Party in 1899, and helped Jaurès found the leading Socialist newspaper *L'Humanité*. Blum won election to the Chamber of Deputies in 1919.

Blum had a crucial role in French Socialism in the 1920s and 1930s. After the Bolshevik revolution in Russia, the Communists founded the Third International (Comintern) and circulated a list of twenty-one conditions. Parties that wanted to join the Comintern had to accept all of them for membership in the new organization, a demand that threw the postwar European Socialist parties into crisis. In France on December 20, 1920, a majority of the Socialist Party agreed to all the conditions. The Communist faction thus gained control of the party machinery, funds, and newspaper and changed the party's name. The Socialists had to rebuild their movement from its foundations, and Léon Blum guided the process.

Blum directed Socialist Party policy after its reconstitution. In 1924 he supported the Cartel des Gauches that won the elections of that year. In the 1928 elections, the Socialist Party won 104 seats. Blum's bid for reelection failed, but he was returned the next year.

Faced with the challenge of rising right-wing agitation at home and increasing Fascist aggression abroad, Blum elaborated a program in 1932 emphasizing the battle against unemployment. After the Stavisky riots of February 1934, Blum worked hard to build a left-wing coalition to fight fascism. Despite internal party opposition, he successfully formed the Popular Front electoral alliance with the Radicals and the Communists. In the national elections of April and May 1936, the Popular Front swept to victory with 376 seats in the Chamber of Deputies.

As the architect of the Popular Front, Blum became French premier in June 1936. His background as France's first Jewish and Socialist prime minister, his program, and his activism raised the hostility of the right. He forced industrialists to grant a forty-hour workweek, vacation time, and other concessions to the workers and nationalized the Bank of France and the munitions industry. In foreign policy, he responded positively to the Spanish government's request for aid against the Fascist-supported attempt to overthrow it, but then backtracked under pressure from the British and from members of his own cabinet to adopt a policy of nonintervention. However, the bitter hostility of French business to Blum's plans to confront the deepening depression doomed the government. When the Senate refused to grant him emergency powers to counter the economic crisis in June 1937, Blum resigned.

The heroic period of Blum's life was over. Blum served as vice premier in 1937 and briefly returned as prime minister from March 13 to April 10, 1938. After France's defeat by Germany in World War II, the Vichy government arrested and tried him with other leaders of the Third Republic in February 1942. It accused them of having caused France's collapse. The trial ended without a verdict because of the strong arguments of the defense and the outlandishness of the charges, but Blum remained in jail until the Germans shipped him to a concentration camp. Allied troops liberated him in May 1945, and Blum resumed his Socialist politics. He negotiated an important financial agreement with the United States in which the Americans forgave French debts and lent the country money for postwar reconstruction.

Blum headed a month-long cabinet in December 1946 and retired from public life after the fall of 1948 to his estate of Jouy-en-Josas. He died there on March 30, 1950.

Bad feelings between the Socialists and Communists divided the Popular Front coalition. The Communists had previously alienated the Socialists by labeling them "Social fascists." Moreover, the Socialists aimed at salvaging the Third Republic, while the Communists wanted its destruction. In 1934, Communist policy changed because of Stalin's fear that Hitler would invade the USSR, and in 1935 Stalin signed an alliance with France directed against a possible German attack. The agreement would become worthless if the right took over in France, so Stalin ordered the French Communists to reverse course, and they entered the Popular Front coalition.

The dramatic change in Communist tactics did not end the differences. The Communist trade union rejoined the Socialist-influenced CGT, from which it had split in 1920, but ideological problems quickly appeared between the old Socialist leadership, oriented toward economic reforms, such as a reduced workweek and paid vacations, and the revolutionary orientation of the Communists who were joining the union. Ideology also polarized the Socialist Party. Blum and other leftist Socialist Party leaders supported a Communist alliance after the February 1934 Stavisky riots, but Socialist leaders, such as general secretary Paul Faure, distrusted the Communists. The Socialists also split on foreign policy: Faure was a convinced pacifist, while Blum was willing to use force against Germany.

The Popular Front government took office on June 5, 1936, and trouble began immediately. A massive wave of sit-in strikes by workers demanding immediate reforms shook the country, with 2 million strikers participating in Paris alone. Blum coerced the employers into accepting measures known as the Matignon Accords, named after the prime minister's residence. These agreements granted workers a general wage increase, a forty-hour workweek, and paid vacations and provided for the reorganization and ultimate nationalization of the Bank of France. The workers claimed victory, but bitter members of the bourgeoisie sent their money out of the country to the tune of 30 billion gold francs. The slogan "Better Hitler Than Blum" summarized their view of the prime minister after this incident.

The government's hopes that the Matignon agreements would stimulate the economy quickly evaporated. The shorter workweek was an obstacle to this goal and was later lengthened. The improved social legislation raised costs and resulted in increased prices, stagnant production, and fewer exports. The nationalization of the Bank of France raised fresh fears of the confiscation of property and increased the outflow of capital. By March 1937 the economic crisis had intensified to the point that the government unsuccessfully requested decree powers to block the flow of currency out of the country. Blum resigned, and the Popular Front experiment officially ended in 1938 with the withdrawal of the Radicals from the coalition.

The Popular Front's failure may be attributed to a variety of causes. The workers were concerned with increasing their wages and reducing working hours, not finding solutions to the country's economic ills. The Communists did not believe in the Third Republic's capacity to reform itself. The Radicals, as usual, were not willing to make drastic changes. Finally, the bourgeoisie crippled the Popular Front by sending its money outside France, depriving the country of investments. In the end, the Popular Front exacerbated French divisions.

A series of weak governments followed Blum's resignation. In foreign affairs, they proved incapable of stopping Hitler from marching troops into the Rhineland or from taking over Austria. In domestic affairs, the economy improved after April 1938 after the franc's devaluation and after Parliament granted Radical Prime Minister Daladier the power to rule by decree.

In the 1930s the French republic was less able than other industrial democracies to confront the economic emergency and passed through unprecedented tumults, political upheaval, and loss of confidence. At the beginning of World War II, France found itself polarized and unequal to the task of defending the country against a resurgent Germany.

SCANDINAVIA: TOWARD SOCIAL DEMOCRACY

In the Scandinavian area, the most industrially developed country, Sweden, served as a model. The individual countries were faced with disorders, labor problems, inflation, and political instability after World War I, despite their neutrality. In general, single parties did not win absolute majorities, and the countries were ruled by coalitions.

Postwar Unrest and Reform

Neutrality during World War I brought Scandinavia economic benefits, but their uneven distribution allowed Bolshevism to make strong inroads. In Sweden, Norway, and Denmark, strikes and demonstrations demanded the creation of workers' and soldiers' soviets. The Norwegian Labour Party joined the Communist International, but the appeal of communism quickly faded for the Norwegians. In Finland, which achieved independence from Russia in 1917, the Finnish Communist Party remained an important presence. In Sweden, workers' sympathy for the Bolsheviks did not translate into political support. The Social Democrats, the largest Swedish party, were Marxists, but they backtracked when they discovered that they lost votes when they moved toward socialism and ended up as a moderate party with a strong social consciousness.

The Swedish government responded to postwar unrest with sweeping electoral reform. In 1922, reforms eliminated voting restrictions based on tax payments, gender, and property, making Parliament's conservative First Chamber more democratic. Other Scandinavian countries also responded to demands for reform: Denmark embarked on a program of social legislation and land reform that continued into the 1920s; Norway introduced the eight-hour workday (forty-eight-hour workweek); Finland allowed agricultural workers to buy the land they held at 1914 prices and conceded generous state loans that by 1930 permitted tenants to buy 90 percent of all the rented farms.

Like the rest of Europe, the Scandinavians fought postwar inflation by orthodox economic methods. They implemented deflationary policies that, by the 1920s, allowed them to reestablish the gold standard. These policies caused difficulties, but prosperity returned, as in the rest of Europe, during the decade. Norway witnessed a great expansion of its fishing industry, and the Norwegian fleet resumed its prewar position as the world's fourth largest. In Denmark, the gold standard produced greater disruption than in the rest of Scandinavia, with 30 percent unemployment and numerous strikes, but by 1928, good times had returned. An economic boom driven by exports to Britain followed Finland's successful struggle for independence. By 1928, Finland exported 56 percent more than it had in 1913, and the value of its industrial production increased by 33 percent.

Confronting the Depression

The Scandinavian countries coped better than the other democracies with the end of the 1920s prosperity and the depression of the 1930s. Governing coalitions based on Social Democrats emerged as the central Scandinavian political force. In Sweden and Denmark, governmental coalitions based on the Social Democrats presented programs to strengthen social legislation. In 1932 the Social Democrat–Agrarian coalition in Sweden confronted high industrial and

The Swedish modern style that had its origins during the Great Depression has exerted an enduring influence on modern design. Here is an example from 1956.

agricultural unemployment and strikes by acting on two fronts: economic policy and social welfare.

In economics, Sweden became one of the first countries to apply the theories of John Maynard Keynes, advocating more governmental spending, not less, during economic slowdowns. The Swedish government devalued the krona and stimulated the economy by increasing spending for public works and unemployment relief. Its policies doubled Swedish exports between 1932 and 1936. In the social sphere, Swedish housing cooperatives constructed affordable housing in partnership with the state and private industry and established their own bank. The housing program emphasized efficiency and utilitarian design in construction and decoration and made "Swedish modern" world famous. In keeping with the country's tradition of social welfare, the cooperatives planned housing with both working wives and husbands in mind, including labor-saving devices that they hoped would help reverse the declining birth rate. The Scandinavian countries also cooperated with each other in combating the depression by aggressively encouraging cooperatives and extending their influence at the national and international levels with the aim of combating international cartels, high prices, and capitalist excesses. Sweden encouraged the formation of mixed public-private firms to protect its national resources. These policies resulted in greater industrial efficiency and an unusually rapid Scandinavian recovery from the depression.

Swedish governmental intervention in daily life in the 1930s came about as the result of a compromise among the parties and was emulated in the other Scandinavian countries. The Swedish Social Democrats renounced socialism and emphasized welfare; the conservatives criticized and modified social legislation but did not block it. The Danish government embarked on a program of public works and direct intervention in the economy, and in 1933 the Danish parties reached a compromise similar to the Swedish understanding, the *Kanslergade* agreement. This agreement sanctioned the social reform policy advocated by Social Democrat leader Karl Kristian Steinche, according to whom social legislation was a right not a charity. Steinche's program "was a thorough tidying-up of Danish social legislation, which then remained unaltered for some forty years." In Norway the Labour party supported strengthening social legislation—unemployment insurance, protection of workers, employee consultations, and compensation for dismissal. Finland passed significant social legislation and encouraged a robust cooperative movement. Finnish women made important progress and actively participated in politics. Finland had been the first country to recognize the equality of men and women, and during the interwar years the Scandinavian countries enacted over a dozen laws strengthening the position of women. This legislation defined the status of unmarried mothers, freed children who were born out of wedlock from legal disabilities, and gave Scandinavian women the vote before other countries in Western Europe.

Foreign Affairs

Despite the successful Scandinavian response to postwar unrest and the economic downturn, several parties modeled on the Nazis appeared in Sweden, Denmark, and Norway, but even at the height of their influence, they received only

2.2 percent of the vote. The most important Scandinavian Fascist organization was Vikdun Quisling's National Unity Party in Norway. Quisling cooperated with the Nazis during the World War II occupation, and his name became a synonym for traitor. Finland, facing strong leftist labor agitation and disorder, witnessed a long period of illegal violence against the Communists but overcame the crisis.

The small Scandinavian countries had a greater influence in foreign affairs than was warranted by their small population. They supported the rule of international law, and one of them always occupied a nonpermanent seat on the Council of the League of Nations. The Scandinavians were most concerned about preserving their neutrality against the pretensions of the big powers. Finland faced the most serious problems because of a territorial dispute with Sweden, the existence of an influential Swedish minority, and the USSR's eye on Finnish territory. Denmark, which had received North Schleswig from Germany following World War I, feared the revived German claims to the area after the Nazis came to power. Militarily, only Sweden supported a strong armed force.

MARKING TIME: THE LOW COUNTRIES AND SWITZERLAND

The different experiences of Belgium and the Netherlands during the war marked their immediate postwar history. The Germans had occupied Belgium, causing a great deal of destruction and world sympathy. The Netherlands had remained neutral, and the Allies thought that it tilted toward Germany, a suspicion confirmed in their minds when, after the war, the Netherlands gave asylum to the former German kaiser and refused to hand him over for trial.

The Low Countries

Impact of the War
Belgium received a small amount of territory and reparations from Germany after the war, but not enough to pay for the country's reconstruction, which took until 1928 to complete. The Belgians devalued the franc, stimulated the economy, and returned to the gold standard in October 1926. In contrast to the Dutch, they also implemented significant social legislation after the war. Economically, the Dutch were better off after the war until 1939 and returned to the gold standard before Belgium in April 1925.

Postwar Politics
There were curious similarities and differences in the politics of the two countries. In the Netherlands, male universal suffrage and proportional representation produced a proliferation of political groups that did not occur in Belgium. In the Netherlands, governmental stability prevailed despite frequent cabinet changes because the same persons kept their old positions despite shifting governments. Religious parties dominated the country during the interwar years, with the Dutch Catholic Party seeking at all costs to maintain Catholic unity by avoiding severe conflict with its partners. This concern made it swallow the unpalatable Hendrick

Colijn, head of the Protestant Anti-Revolutionary Party (ARP), as the country's leader. In Belgium the opposite occurred. Although Catholics, Socialists, and Liberals continued to dominate Parliament, Belgian cabinets did not reflect this stability. Prospective prime ministers could not conciliate the disparate demands of party factions, and numerous cabinets followed each other.

The acute divisions between the Walloons and Flemings described in Chapter 5 continued to dominate Belgian politics during the interwar years, and the Flemish question flared up during the 1920s. The election of eleven members of the Flemish nationalist Front party to Parliament in 1929 made the government open to compromise. In 1932 it attempted to resolve the language problem by dividing the country into two separate linguistic regions and by imposing the use of the Flemish language in the public administration, schools, and courts of the Flemish regions, but relations between the Walloons and the Flemings remained tense despite these concessions.

The Depression's Impact

When the Great Depression hit the Low Countries in 1931, both the Belgians and the Dutch implemented deflationary measures in an unsuccessful attempt to counter it. Failure forced Belgium off the gold standard in March 1935, followed by the Netherlands in September 1936. In both countries, currency devaluation of over 20 percent, public works projects, and unemployment assistance brought some relief, but in both countries, the economic downturn favored the growth of fascist-type organizations on the Italian model. In Belgium, Léon Degrelle's ultra-Catholic Rexists, formed in 1935, advocated authoritarianism and corporativism (see Chapter 12). The Rexists received Italian support, won 12 percent of the vote and 22 parliamentary seats in the elections of 1936, but were defeated in 1937 by Prime Minister Paul van Zeeland. Besides the Rexist threat, groups sympathizing with fascism also appeared in the Flemish areas, but they were concerned with the ethnic question, as illustrated by Verdinaso, an organization that advocated a federation of the Low Countries. In the Netherlands the Dutch National Socialist movement won 8 percent of the vote in 1935 but lost half its electoral support in 1937.

Switzerland

Swiss Anxieties

In Switzerland, fascistic organizations made little headway despite unrest following the war and during the depression.

The Swiss had made money during the conflict by supplying war materiel to the belligerents, but this activity distorted the economy by stimulating war-related industries. Moreover, the country had mobilized to defend its neutrality, greatly increasing the national debt and setting the stage for postwar economic difficulties and unrest. The Swiss Social Democratic Party demanded reform and, after a threatened general strike in Zurich in November 1918 that the government repressed, a forty-eight-hour workweek and proportional representation for National Council elections were implemented.

Economic dislocations caused by the depression increased agitation and favored the rise of Fascist groups. In November 1932 demonstrations in Geneva left twelve demonstrators dead. Fascist organizations appeared in each of the different language areas, prompting a widespread governmental crackdown on extremist groups in May 1933. This repression reduced the danger posed by Fascist groups, but support for these groups had already dwindled because of German and Italian claims to Swiss territory. These threats rallied the Swiss, and in October 1933, the government was empowered to rule by decree in economic affairs, and the country adopted the banking secrecy laws for which it later became famous.

In foreign policy, the Swiss concentrated on their neutrality and security. They agonized over the question of whether joining the League of Nations meant relinquishing their neutrality, but ultimately joined the League, whose headquarters were located in Geneva, and the International Court of Justice at The Hague. With the rise of Nazism, Switzerland reiterated its commitment to absolute neutrality, and the League of Nations exempted it from certain obligations, but recent evidence has suggested that during World War II Swiss foreign policy was more pro-Nazi than neutral.

During the interwar years, Scandinavia, the Low Countries, and Switzerland confronted difficult economic times and witnessed the rise of groups advocating fascistic answers to the Great Depression, but they all maintained their democratic structures.

Bibliographical Essay

Peter Temin produced an excellent overview of the Great Depression, drawing its lessons for contemporary economic policy: *Lessons from the Great Depression* (Cambridge, Mass., 1989). His *Did Monetary Forces Cause the Great Depression?* (New York, 1976) is a more detailed work. Charles P. Kindleberger, *The World in Depression, 1929–1939,* rev. and enlarged ed. (Berkeley, Calif., 1986), is a standard general account, as is the readable Goronwy Rees, *The Great Slump: Capitalism in Crisis, 1929–1933* (New York, 1970). Ben Bernanke's *Essays on the Great Depression* (Princeton, N.J., 2000) is a technical work. Good general books that are quite thorough include Patricia Calvin, *The Great Depression in Europe, 1929–1939* (New York, 2000); Charles H. Feinstein, Peter Temin, and Gianni Toniolo, *The World Economy Between the World Wars* (Oxford, UK, 2008); Theo Balderston, *The World Economy and National Economies in the Interwar Slump* (New York, 2003), a book of essays; and Timothy J. Kehoe and Edward C. Prescott, *Great Depressions of the Twentieth Century* (Orlando, Fla., 2002). Patricia Calvin's, *The Failure of Economic Diplomacy* (New York, 1996), Thomas Emerson Hall's and J. David Ferguson's *The Great Depression* (Ann Arbor, Mich., 2001), and Nikolaus Wolf, *Europe's Great Depression* (London, 2010), focus on the international dimension.

For the economic history of specific countries during this period, consult Robert Skidelsky, *Politicians and the Slump: The Labour Government of 1929–1931* (London, 1967), for England, and *The Slump: Britain in the Great Depression* (Harlow, UK, 2010), by John Stevenson and Chris Cook. Developments in English political history may be followed in Charles Loch Mowat, *Britain Between the Wars 1918–1940* (Chicago, 1955), and economic affairs in H. W. Richardson, *Economic Recovery in Britain, 1932–9* (London, 1967). See also Stuart Ball, *Baldwin and the Conservative Party* (New Haven, Conn.,1988), and Noreen Branson and Margot Heinemann, *Britain in the 1930s* (New York, 1971). For Germany and the Great Depression, see Mark Weder, *Some Observations on the*

Great Depression in Germany (London, 2003), and Harold James, *The German Slump* (Oxford, UK, 1986).

France in the 1930s has received greater attention than Britain. David A. Irwin, *Did France Cause the Great Depression?* (Cambridge, Mass.,, 2010) asks whether the hoarding of gold by France caused the depression. Eugen Weber's *The Hollow Years: France in the 1930s* (New York, 1994) is an excellent treatment. Julian Jackson, *The Politics of Depression in France 1932–1936* (Cambridge, UK, 1985), pays particular attention to economic affairs. Philippe Bernard and Henri Dubief, *The Decline of the Third Republic, 1914–1938* (Cambridge, UK, 1985), is a scholarly summary of the major issues. On the Popular Front in general, see Julian Jackson, *The Popular Front in France* (Cambridge, UK, 1990). The French Socialists during the Popular Front era are examined by Nathaniel Greene, *Crisis and Decline: The French Socialist Party in the Popular Front Era* (Ithaca, N.Y., 1969). Peter J. Larmour's *The French Radical Party in the 1930s* (Stanford, Calif., 1964) is a thorough study of the party's structure, policies, and personnel. Susan B. Whitney, *Mobilizing Youth* (Durham, N.C., 2009), considers the Communist and Catholic youth movements. John Bulaitis, *Communism in Rural France* (New York, 2008), looks at the complex relationship between the French Communist Party and rural France during the Popular Front. Jessica Wardhaugh published a study of left- and right-wing organizations during the Popular Front: *In Pursuit of the People: Political Culture in France, 1934–9* (Basingstoke, UK, 2008). Books on the international dimensions of the Popular Front include Nicole Jordan, *The Popular Front and Central Europe* (New York 2005), and *Leon Blum, French Socialism and the Popular Front*, by Helmut Gruber (New York, 1986). Biographies of Léon Blum include Joel Colton, *Léon Blum: Humanist in Politics*, 2d ed. (New York, 1987), and Jean Lacouture, *Léon Blum* (New York 1982). James Joll's *Three Intellectuals in Politics* (New York, 1961) has a portrait of Blum and, as an added bonus, of Rathenau and Marinetti. Zeev Sternhell wrote a major work on the ideology of French fascism, *Neither Left nor Right* (Berkeley, Calif., 1986), while Robert Paxton, a distinguished historian of France, takes a different view and concentrates on fascism as practice rather than as ideology in *The Anatomy of Fascism* (New York, 2004).

On Scandinavia, see Marquis Childs, *Sweden: The Middle Way* (New Haven, Conn., 1963), which describes the cooperative movement in Sweden, and *Welfare Peripheries* (New York, 2007), by Steven King and John Steward, which has material on the Scandinavian countries. The quotation on Danish social legislation may be found in W. Glyn Jones, *Denmark: A Modern History* (London, 1986), p. 141. Another informative work is W. R. Mead, *Finland* (New York, 1968). Concise histories of the Scandinavian countries, usually beginning in ancient times, include Neil Kent, *A Concise History of Sweden* (Cambridge, UK, 2008); Byron J. Nordstrom, *The History of Sweden* (Westport, Conn., 2002); Hjalmar Hjorth Boyesen and Charles Francis Keary, *A History of Norway from the Earliest Times* (n.p., 2007); Knud J.V. Jespersen, *A History of Denmark* (New York, 2004); John H. Wuorinen, *A History of Finland* (New York, 1965), the most comprehensive book on Finland; D. G. Kirby's *Finland in the Twentieth Century* (Minneapolis, Minn., 1979), which concentrates on modern history, and his *A Concise History of Finland* (New York, 2006); and Jason Edward Lavery, *The History of Finland* (Westport, Conn., 2006), a book of essays.

Information on Scandinavian fascism, as well as fascism in the other countries discussed in this chapter, as well as in Italy and Germany, may be found in Stanley G. Payne's comprehensive *A History of Fascism 1914–1945* (Madison, Wis., 1995). Payne's book is important for its nuanced and balanced treatment of the issue of just what constituted Fascist movements. On a Danish organization, see Henrik Lundbak, *Danish Unity: A Political Party Between Fascism and Resistance 1936–1947* (Copenhagen, 2003).

Hans Rogger and Eugen Weber, eds., *The European Right: A Historical Profile* (Berkeley, Calif., 1966), contains excellent essays on the rightist movements, including those in some of the small countries. See also Martin Blinkhorn's book of essays on different countries, *Fascists and Conservatives: The Radical Right and the Establishment in Twentieth-Century Europe* (London, 2003).

E. H. Kossman's *The Low Countries 1780–1940* (Oxford, UK, 1978), previously cited, has a detailed discussion on developments in Belgium and the Netherlands during this period. Concise histories of the Low Countries are Paul Arblaster, *A History of the Low Countries* (Basingstoke, UK, 2006); J. C. H. Blom and Emiel Lamberts, *History of the Low Countries* (New York, 2006); Paul F. State, *A Brief History of the Netherlands* (New York, 2008); and Bernard A. Cook, *Belgium: A History* (New York, 2002). On Switzerland, there is John Wilson, *The History of Switzerland* (New York, 2007).

In addition, on individual countries, consult the works cited in Chapter 9, or, in the case of the smaller countries, Chapter 5, which usually include sections on this period.

CHAPTER 11

✍

The Crisis of Democracy in Eastern and Southern Europe

CHAPTER OUTLINE

The Victors of the Versailles Settlement • The Versailles Settlement's Losers •
The Aegean and the Adriatic • Iberia

BIOGRAPHICAL SKETCHES

Josef Klemens Pilsudski, Polish Dictator • Thomas Garrigue Masaryk,
European Democrat

Most of the nations of Eastern and Southern Europe installed authoritarian regimes during the postwar period. There was nothing inevitable about this trend. Liberal traditions existed in both areas, but most Eastern European countries faced impossibly difficult situations following World War I. The new nations had to create an administrative and political structure while absorbing a great deal of territory and sizable minorities and confronting foreign threats. For most of the countries in the East and the South, the Great Depression was the last blow to democratic ideals.

THE VICTORS OF THE VERSAILLES SETTLEMENT

The Versailles settlement left the countries of Eastern Europe facing major border disputes, national minorities of 19 million out of a total population of 98 million, and poor economic circumstances. Eastern Europe quickly became polarized between groups advocating political systems according to ideological schemes of the right or left that promised greater economic justice and efficiency than democracy, and a similar trend emerged in the South.

In examining Eastern and Southern Europe following World War I, one can roughly group the countries into those that benefited from the postwar settlement and those that lost.

The Baltic States

The Baltic states—Lithuania, Latvia, and Estonia—had been part of the Russian Empire and won independence after World War I.

The weakest state, Lithuania, had a serious border dispute with Poland over Vilnius, which the Lithuanians claimed as their capital. Lithuania was overwhelmingly Catholic, while the majority of Estonians and Latvians were Lutheran. All the states contained significant minorities of Germans, Poles, Jews, and Russians, and, in the 1920s, Lithuania had a significant problem with anti-Semitism, while the German minority caused serious difficulties for Lithuania and Latvia.

The Baltic population was mostly peasant, and all three states had large agrarian parties that favored land reform that led to a strengthened agricultural sector between 1918 and 1931, while industries in all three countries lacked raw materials, capital, and markets.

Between June 1920 and August 1922, the Baltic states adopted democratic constitutions but were unable to achieve political stability, and right-wing dictatorships took over. In Lithuania in 1926, party infighting and political instability provoked a military coup on December 17 with the support of Nationalist leaders Antonas Smetona and Augustinas Voldemaras and of elements of the Christian Democratic bloc. Smetona dissolved Parliament and promulgated a constitution providing for a strong president. Voldemaras, head of a secret pro-Nazi paramilitary organization, Iron Wolf, challenged him, but Smetona cracked down on the German minority and Nazi organizations.

Right-wing regimes came to power in Estonia and Latvia in 1933 and 1934 as the result of the depression and parliamentary instability. In Estonia, Nazi-influenced nationalists won a referendum establishing a strong presidency. The Agrarian Party leader Konstantin Pats, installed as the temporary chief executive with emergency powers, liquidated Parliament. In Latvia, the Nazi-influenced Thunder Cross fought leftist groups that were accused of planning a Communist coup. Karlis Ulmanis, head of the Farmers' Union, assumed emergency power on May 15, 1934, outlawed political parties, dissolved Parliament, and arrested political opponents.

Smetona, Pats, and Ulmanis ran "largely nonideological arbitrary governments of a predominantly rural, conservative nationalist character, restrained by the leaders' self-imposed limitations and by the old social pluralism" until the absorption of the Baltic states into the USSR in 1939.

Poland's Reemergence

One of the biggest gainers from the war, Poland had major weaknesses. Victory over Soviet Russia in 1919 and 1920 put 6 million Ukrainians and Belorussians into the state, in addition to the Polish Corridor and 800,000 hostile Germans. This situation encouraged the formation of separatist movements and made it easy for the USSR and Nazi Germany to partition Poland in 1939.

Poland struggled to reunite the different parts of the country dominated by foreigners for 150 years, ruled by a hodgepodge of diverse laws, subject to different customs unions, and separated by different railway systems and political traditions. At the same time, Poland's enormous war debt and defense expenditures (one-third of its budget) to guard against a possibly resurgent Germany and Russia drained resources that were urgently needed for economic development.

The Rise of Pilsudski

Economic problems and political divisions touched off hyperinflation that sent the exchange rate of the Polish mark (the zloty was introduced later) with the dollar to 20 million in January 1924. On April 26 the Socialists resigned in protest from a coalition government that proposed measures that would reduce the real income of workers. The resulting crisis produced a coup d'état by Marshal Josef Pilsudski supported by the army.

Pilsudski, a strong personality with left-wing connections, had been a powerful contender for president following Polish independence. The assumption that he would win induced his right-wing opponents who controlled the Sejm (Parliament) to adopt a constitution modeled on that of the Third French Republic, with a very weak president. Pilsudski thereupon refused to run for president and retired as chief of the general staff. In the next three years, the inflation crisis forced the Sejm parties to give wide powers to a reforming cabinet led by Wladaslaw Grabski, but Parliament lost support because of its inability to revise the constitution, galloping inflation, strikes, rioting, and bloodshed, and Pilsudski took over.

Pilsudski had the support of Socialists, Radical Peasants, and Communists to implement social and economic reforms. Pilsudski declared that he was neither a leftist nor a rightist but favored social equilibrium. He governed through prime ministers and held elections but brooked no opposition. Over the years Pilsudski shifted to the right with the support of industrialists and large landowners. The strong peasant parties lost influence, and land reform was delayed. After Pilsudski's death in May 1935, strikes, violence on the land, and serious opposition in elections confronted his successors.

Polish Economic Stabilization

Pilsudski curbed inflation by ending cost-of-living increases for state employees, budget cuts, American loans, higher taxes, and scaling back costly social programs. The Polish state intensified its regulation and intervention in the economy, and Polish industry increased efficiency by organizing stronger cartels. In 1924 the government introduced a new gold-backed currency, the zloty. These policies resulted in a recovery beginning in 1928, but the good times ended with the Great Depression that dealt the overwhelmingly agricultural country a severe blow by decimating the value of its exports. The government worsened matters by stubbornly sticking to its deflationary policies and to the gold standard until April 1936. Abandonment of the gold standard and the introduction of centralized planning that was designed to industrialize the country improved economic conditions.

BIOGRAPHICAL SKETCHES

Josef Klemens Pilsudski
Polish Dictator

Between World War I and World War II, Marshal Josef Pilsudski was an Eastern European fixture. The hero of Polish independence, Pilsudski was looked upon by Polish Americans as their George Washington, and even now squares and roads in Poland bear his name.

Pilsudski's adventurous life, travel, and war experiences were similar to those of other Eastern European national leaders of the period. Pilsudski was born on December 5, 1867, at Zulow, near present-day Vilnius in Lithuania, at the time part of Russia. His parents, from old well-known and well-off families in the area, had twelve children. His mother was a Polish patriot who read Polish books that were banned by the Russians and instilled in her children a love of the Polish language. When Pilsudski attended high school, he was obliged to speak only in Russian, his defiance of which got him into trouble.

In June 1885, Pilsudski attended medical school, became marginally involved in the same conspiracy to assassinate Tsar Alexander III that cost Lenin's brother his life, and was sentenced to five years' exile in Siberia. After his release in April 1892, Pilsudski joined the Polish Socialist party (PPS) and wrote for its clandestine newspaper *Robotnik*. His articles dealt with Socialist themes and called for Polish independence from Russia. He traveled to London and Paris in 1896 to gain international support for his position but failed. On July 15, 1899, converted to Protestantism, he married Maria Juskiewicz, called "the beautiful lady": a Protestant, divorced, and with a daughter. The couple continued to publish *Robotnik* together until February 1900, when the police arrested them. Pilsudski, by now an essential member of the PPS, was freed in a plot by which Pilsudski pretended to be insane. Transferred from prison to a less secure hospital, he escaped.

By now, war was changing the political landscape of Europe, and Pilsudski saw in the conflicts an opportunity to win Polish independence. When the Russo-Japanese war broke out in 1904, Pilsudski traveled to Japan to offer a Polish legion to help the Japanese defeat the Russians. The Japanese refused the offer, but Russian losses contributed to the revolution of 1905 and to disturbances in Poland. Pilsudski took charge of creating a Polish armed force and, with the reestablishment of Russian control, turned to raids on governmental establishments to raise funds for his cause. His most famous exploit was a daring attack on a night train carrying tax money on September 19, 1908. Pilsudski also trained an armed force under cover of rifle associations, and in 1914 he commanded Polish soldiers fighting with the Austrians against the Russians. Pilsudski achieved the rank of brigadier general, but was arrested by the Germans when he refused to cooperate with them against the allies after Russia's defeat.

The Germans released him in November 1918, and he negotiated their withdrawal from Poland. After the war Pilsudski successfully created a large Poland, incorporating millions of Ukrainians and White Russians. This annexation brought him into conflict with the Bolsheviks, but he successfully defended the country against them in 1919 and 1920. Pilsudski had gained supreme control of Poland, but he respected the constitution and resigned as chief of state in December 1922.

continued

continued

However, unhappy with the workings of Parliament, he staged a coup d'état in May 1926. He established a dictatorship and served in several offices, including prime minister, from 1926 to 1928 and again in 1930. In foreign affairs, he followed a policy of friendship with both Russia and Germany, unaware that his annexationist policies had doomed his country.

In his last years, plagued by ill health, Pilsudski left the details of government to his trusted lieutenants. He died in Warsaw on May 12, 1935, spared the knowledge that his country would be dismembered when World War II began in 1939.

Poland after Pilsudski

On May 12, 1935, Marshal Pilsudski's death left "the dictatorship without a dictator." Different contenders competed for power, and the government veered from right to left and back again to confront growing opposition from the peasants and Socialists. The government feared communism and created the Camp of National Unity (OZN) to capitalize on the anti-Semitic and Nazi appeal illustrated by the success of the National Radicals (Naras) and other rightist groups that the regime had closed down. When the OZN leader called for a totalitarian Poland, alarmed governmental moderates restrained it in 1938, but by then domestic politics took a backseat to the approaching war.

BIOGRAPHICAL SKETCHES

Thomas Garrigue Masaryk
European Democrat

The career of Thomas Garrigue Masaryk demonstrates that strong democratic personalities operated in Eastern Europe between the wars, despite the problems of the region.

Thomas Masaryk was born in the Moravian town of Hodonin on March 7, 1850. His Slovak father worked on Emperor Francis Joseph's estates, while his mother, from a Germanized Moravian family, was a domestic servant. His mother insisted that he get a good education in order to avoid the manual labor of the parents. Masaryk attended a German school, since no Czech schools existed in Moravia at the time. While at this school, he came to doubt the prevailing anti-Semitism because of his contact with a Jewish student. In 1864, he worked with a locksmith and later with a blacksmith before he returned to school at Brno and then Vienna. He had the good fortune to meet a schoolmate whose father, later the chief of police in Vienna, befriended and employed him to tutor his son. In 1872, he began to study at the University of Vienna and received his doctor's degree in philosophy in 1876. In the hope of securing a university position, he published his first book, which criticized the existing social structure.

Masaryk moved to Leipzig, where he met the daughter of a Dane who had immigrated to America, Charlotte Garrigue, a former pupil of Franz Liszt who was studying at the conservatory. Together they read English philosophers and fell in love. Masaryk proposed and followed her to America, where they married on March 15, 1878. Happily married for fifty years, he added her name to his.

Masaryk began teaching at the University of Vienna in 1879 and, despite opposition from the archbishop of Prague to his philosophical writings, was named professor at the University of Prague. He chastised capitalism and wrote on the Czech Reformation and the Czech cultural revival of the nineteenth century. He examined the strains between Czechs and Austrians, which he had encountered as a student in Vienna. In 1889 Masaryk turned to politics and was not afraid to risk unpopularity. He unmasked two supposedly medieval Czech poems as forgeries and in 1899 fought the anti-Semitism aroused by the Hilsner case, in which a Jew was falsely accused of ritual murder. He considered anti-Semitism a superstition and a danger to the Czech people and hoped to eradicate it.

Elected to the Austrian Parliament, he denounced Austria-Hungary's alliance with Germany and its Balkan policies. With the outbreak of World War I, Masaryk fled to the West and cooperated with British, French, and Italian leaders. He advocated the breakup of Austria-Hungary on ethnic lines and the creation of an independent, democratic Czech-Slovak state. After the revolution of February 1917 in Russia, he organized the Czechoslovak Legion—formed by former prisoners of war. He left for the United States after the Bolshevik takeover, working with Czech and Slovak groups to obtain American support for Czechoslovak independence. At Pittsburgh he promised the Slovaks ample home rule, which turned out to be a source of later disputes.

In June 1918 Czechoslovakia came into being along the lines envisioned by Masaryk. The newly independent country rewarded him by electing him president on November 14, 1918, at age sixty-eight, reelecting him another three times. The people recognized him as a hero and as their liberator. Despite all the problems of the new multinational state, Masaryk tried to ensure that it would respect minority rights. He was one of the first statesmen to fear for Eastern Europe's future after the Nazis came to power in 1933. On December 14, 1935, he resigned as president and died on September 14, 1937. After World War II, his son Jan became foreign minister and died under mysterious circumstances just before the Communist takeover of his country.

Birth of Czechoslovakia

Poland's neighbor Czechoslovakia faced similar economic and political problems but had the advantage of having inherited the industrial heartland of the old empire. It also had great liabilities: bad blood between its two major ethnic components, Czechs and Slovaks, and large minorities that handed its neighbors convenient claims to part of its territory.

Czechoslovakia's success in the early years was due, in great measure, to the leaders of its independence movement, Thomas G. Masaryk and Edvard Benes, respectively, its first president and its longtime foreign minister. Fighting during the war destroyed the Czech economy and led to shortages, high postwar inflation, and unemployment. Disorder followed, with workers clamoring for a Bolshevik-type social revolution and the peasants seizing land.

Masaryk's government fought inflation by introducing a new currency, the Czechoslovak crown; by following deflationary policies, such as reducing the circulation of notes and imposing a high tax on the property of wealthy persons; and by encouraging foreign investment. The state took an activist role in the economy and acquired important parts of the country's infrastructure, including the railways and the electric, telephone, and telegraph industries, while cities took over municipal services. Parliament passed wide-ranging social legislation: the eight-hour workday; accident, sickness, and unemployment insurance; pensions for widows and children; and workers' participation in management and profits. It implemented land reform by breaking up large estates and by making funds available to peasants who wanted to buy land. It also invested in education; during the next twenty years, the number of elementary schools increased by 300 percent.

These measures revived the economy and diminished the appeal of Bolshevism, but strong social tensions and rioting returned with the hardships caused by the Great Depression. In 1934, the government helped farmers by establishing a grain monopoly that had the exclusive right to purchase and sell agricultural products and to regulate their importation and exportation. In industry, a 1935 law regulated the circumstances under which employers could close factories or lay off more than 10 percent of their workers, and in 1936, legislation expanded collective bargaining.

Dilemmas of Czech Democracy

The Czechoslovak experiment in democracy was the most successful in postwar Eastern Europe, but it faced serious problems. In 1920, the country adopted a constitution setting up a Parliament and guaranteeing liberty and equality, but the existence of numerous parties and proportional representation encouraged splintering. Five-party coalitions were the norm for cabinets, and they rarely had focused programs.

The major parties included the leftist Social Democrats and National Socialists (no relation to the Nazis), agrarian parties, and organizations representing the large German minority in the Sudentenland. In 1921, the Communist Party of Czechoslovakia (CPC) was founded and briefly became the second-largest party, but its subservience to Moscow, which opposed Czechoslovakia's existence, brought about its decline. On the extreme right, the Nazi Sudeten German Party, under Konrad Henlein, had 60 percent support from the large German minority in the Sudetenland. As the second-largest ethnic group after the Czechs and 23 percent of the population the Sudeten Germans were a mortal threat because they also inhabited the only defensible frontier against Germany and favored annexation to the Reich after Hitler came to power.

Besides the German problem, Czechoslovakia could not satisfy the contrasting demands of its different national minorities or fully integrate them into the democratic system. The Czechs, constituting only half the country's population, dominated political and economic life, which caused constant friction not only with the German, Polish, Hungarian, and Ruthenian (Ukrainian) minorities, but also with the Slovaks, who were supposedly their partners. The Slovaks chafed at Czech bureaucratic and political domination, and there were religious differences as well: Catholicism in Slovakia was more conservative than in the Czech areas, and the Slovaks resented the inroads that Protestantism had made among the Czechs. The real basis for Czech influence over the country, however, was economic. Slovakia was a predominantly agricultural economic backwater with an ill-educated population possessing few technical skills, while the Czech area was

Konrad Henlein, the Nazi leader of the Germans living in the Sudetenland, Czechoslovakia on May 13, 1938, shown here leaving Winston Churchill's house. The Sudetenland had never been a part of Germany and was ceded to the new Czechoslovak state after World War I because the Sudeten Mountains provided the new country with a defensible frontier against a possible German attack. Henlein's movement was important because if it succeeded in uniting with Germany it would in effect make the country a German satellite. Henlein illustrates both the major weakness of Czechoslovakia—ethnic minorities that resisted Czech rule—and Hitler's technique of utilizing Europe's German-speaking minorities to further his foreign policy aims.

highly industrialized. Resentment against the Czechs by the Catholic peasants of Slovakia threatened unity because the peasants supported the authoritarian Slovak People's Party that demanded autonomy and then separation. Following the Munich Conference that dismembered Czechoslovakia in September 1938, Slovakia gained full autonomy under Monsignor Joseph Tiso and declared its independence the following March. Czechoslovakia's nationalities problems gave foreigners the idea that the country was "a medley ruled by a minority" (*The Observer,* March 6, 1938) destined to fall apart.

The Aggrandizement of Romania
The national question that destroyed the Czechoslovak state also threatened Romania. The country doubled in size and population after World War I by annexing Transylvania and the Bukovina, formerly Austro-Hungarian, and Bessarabia

from Russia. In order to safeguard their gains, the Romanians joined Czechoslovakia and Yugoslavia in the French-sponsored "Little Entente" alliance.

The gains brought all ethnic Romanians into the country, but also hostile minorities that amounted to 30 percent of its population: Hungarians (9 percent); the hated Jews (almost 5 percent); and sizable numbers of Germans, Ukrainians, and Bulgarians. Disputes over land reform, the press, education, and religion among these minorities immediately caused trouble. Finally, the enormous increase in the country's size disrupted the traditional prewar parties and politics.

King Ferdinand I introduced mass politics into Romania by granting universal male suffrage, and political instability resulted. The 1919 elections did not produce a majority, but two parties based on strong personalities dominated the political scene. The National Liberal Party, controlled by the Bratianu family, advocated strong administrative centralization, while the National Peasant Party (PNP), headed by Iuliu Maniu, championed land reform.

The threat of Bolshevism encouraged the passage of important agrarian reform legislation in June 1921 that increased the average size of farms, but dwarf holdings continued to proliferate and large estates did not disappear. Yields remained low, capital short, and living standards one of the worst in Europe. Furthermore, many large landowners were ethnic Hungarians who blocked reform by appealing to the League of Nations under the terms of treaties safeguarding minority rights; this process led to years of disputes and litigation.

The Royal Dictatorship

The National Liberals were in power between 1922 and 1928. They favored industry by passing antiunion measures and banning the Romanian Communist Party. The pace of industrial development quickened, but when the depression struck in 1930, industry still represented only 10 percent of the gross national product. National Liberal policies that had produced sporadic strikes in the 1920s escalated into violence during the depression, and the industrialists called on the army to intervene. A new king, Carol II, took over on June 8, 1930, and for the next several years he alternated among the main political parties to help him rule the country. In 1937, National Liberal influence declined, and King Carol entrusted the government to the extreme right anti-Semitic Christian National Party. Within a month, this party had outraged international public opinion by implementing a savage anti-Semitic policy, and Romanian bankers and industrialists, fearing economic retaliation from the international financial community, called upon Carol to intervene.

On February 10, 1938, the king imposed a dictatorship. He proclaimed martial law, issued a new constitution that gave him control of Parliament and the judiciary, dissolved all political parties, and established his own political organization, the National Renaissance Front. In economic policy he worked with a small group of bankers and industrialists to spur state investments and increase production.

Carol's was a conservative, not a Fascist, dictatorship marked by anticommunism and fierce nationalism. Carol particularly feared the anti-Semitic virulence that marked Romanian fascism because of its rapid spread after Mussolini's March

Cornelieu Zelea Codreanu was the most important Fascist theoretician in Eastern Europe. He was also a practical leader whose "Legion of the Archangel Michael" threatened the government. The Romanian security police murdered him while he was in their custody, along with his most important associates. The picture shows Romanian and German officials at his funeral in December 1940.

on Rome. The most successful Romanian Fascist organization was the Legion of the Archangel Michael, established in 1924 by Cornelieu Zelea Codreanu—called "the Captain." The legion presented a serious threat because it emphasized ortho-dox Christianity and Rumanian peasant values and had a strong peasant electoral base in addition to competent middle-class leadership. Adding to the danger was its powerful and violent paramilitary organization, the Iron Guard. Carol's gov-ernment ordered the legion dissolved, setting off a deadly battle during which the Iron Guard assassinated the prime minister.

The king could not win a decisive victory. Every time the government dis-solved the legion, it returned more sympathetic to the Nazis under an assumed name. In 1937 the movement won 15.5 percent of the vote, making it the coun-try's third-largest political force. Carol tried to negotiate with Codreanu but failed. In April 1938, the police arrested "the Captain" and several thousand followers. Codreanu was sentenced to ten years in prison, but on November 30 the state security police murdered him along with thirteen associates. Codreanu's death made him a martyr, and the brutal battle continued with the Iron Guard assas-sinating another prime minister.

Yugoslav Factionalism

Yugoslavia (called the Kingdom of the Serbs, Croats, and Slovenes), another Versailles "winner," traveled a similar path. The new country concretized the Serb dream of creating a large south Slav state from the Slav-inhabited territory of the old Austro-Hungarian Empire, but national divisions favored a royal dictatorship.

Because of their desire for control, the Serbs could not conciliate the different Slavic groups, and they engaged in a struggle for control over the other nationalities, complicated by religious differences. The combatants included the Kosovo Albanians and the Bosnian Moslems who inflamed Balkan passions until the end of the twentieth century. The Serbs controlled the country's administrative machinery but proved unable to run a state three times the size of prewar Serbia. The main conflict was fought between the supporters of federalism and the supporters of centralization (which, in practice, meant Serb control) that would end in the breakup of Yugoslavia after the fall of communism.

The King Takes Over

The divisions among Slavic groups surfaced immediately after the war. Peasant leader Stephen Radic won the 1920 Croatian elections for a constituent assembly on a platform advocating federalism and a republic. In June 1921, however, the assembly adopted a constitution that established a strong central government favoring the Serbs. This constitution alienated the Croats and the Slovenes and

Croatian Fascist leader Ante Pavelic (left), shown here with German Foreign Minister Joachim von Ribbentrop in 1941, was a nationalist who hoped to break Croatia off from Yugoslavia. He spent some time in exile in Italy but relations with the Italians were poor and he turned to the Germans. During World War II he organized a Croatian State, a Nazi satellite. Pavelic's organization, the Ustase, committed so many brutal atrocities against Jews, Serbs, and Gypsies that they shocked even the Germans. Pavelic escaped after the Nazi defeat and spent a long exile in several countries, finally dying in Spain on December 28, 1959.

provoked terrorist activities. Parliament then passed repressive legislation, and several years of political confusion followed.

On June 20, 1928, a deputy sympathetic to the Serbs shot and killed Radic and his nephew in Parliament. On January 6, 1929, King Alexander dissolved Parliament and political parties, abolished the constitution, suppressed the press, and assumed complete power; the police imprisoned and tortured Croat leaders and other opponents.

Despite the confused political situation, during the 1920s Yugoslavia made economic progress. The decade saw the recovery of agriculture, railway building, and stabilization of the dinar. When the depression hit, however, credit collapsed, banks failed, and foreign loans dried up. The government was forced to buy up the 1932 wheat crop at above market prices, declare a moratorium on peasant debts, cut administrative salaries, and increase taxes. The slump heightened political tensions, and on October 9, 1934, Croat separatists assassinated King Alexander in Marseilles. A regency council ruled the country for his young son, but the government remained authoritarian.

The most virulent Croat separatist movement was the anti-Semitic Ustasha, whose agents killed Alexander. The organization's head, a lawyer from Zagreb named Ante Pavelic, fled the country and took refuge in Mussolini's Italy. Pavelic gained international prominence during World War II as the head of a puppet, German-controlled Croatia. He ran one of the most brutal regimes of the period and set up a concentration camp, known as the Auschwitz of the Balkans, that specialized in exterminating Serbs and Jews.

THE VERSAILLES SETTLEMENT'S LOSERS

By the end of the 1930s, dictators ruled three of the four Eastern European victors of World War I; the losers fared even worse.

Hungary's Rightist Regime

The biggest East European loser in World War I, Hungary, lost two-thirds of its territory and population. After the fall of Béla Kun's Communist regime, Admiral Mikós Horthy, former commander of the Austro-Hungarian navy, took over the country.

Horthy instituted a rightist regime. He restored the old social system by returning large landed estates, banks, industrial, and commercial concerns to their former owners and by giving jobs or land grants, in proportion to their social status, to 350,000 former members of the old landowning class who returned to Hungary after the war.

Hungary's decrease in size fueled anti-Semitism because Jews as a percentage of the population increased, and the success of Jewish professionals fueled resentment. The government harassed the Jews, restricted the number allowed to attend universities, and practically excluded them from the bureaucracy and other state jobs.

In political life Horthy wielded supreme power and ruled through cabinets headed by leaders of different political factions. In the 1920s, he appointed as prime minister Count István Bethlen, a moderate reactionary who made some room for liberty. In October 1932, he installed General Gyula Gombos, a radical rightist who sympathized with Mussolini and Hitler, as premier.

Officially the government condemned trade unions and social democracy but in practice tolerated both. Industrial activity increased, with national income from manufacturing rising from 21 percent to 28 percent while income from agriculture declined from 54 to 43 percent. In the rural areas only about a third of the peasantry had enough land to sustain themselves, and the rest led a miserable existence with starvation always part of the landscape. Between 1934 and 1937, the Hungarian economy became more dependent on Germany, but the increased activity smoothed Hungary's transformation into a semi-industrialized country by the late 1930s.

Hungarian Fascism

The Great Depression and its aftershocks spurred the development of fascism. The most successful of a great variety of Fascist organizations was Ferenc Szalasi's green-shirted Arrow Cross. Szalasi theorized a Hungarian-dominated East European federation but repudiated Nazi racial ideas and favored Jewish emigration. Horthy and his surrogates opposed the Arrow Cross, suppressed it several times, and attempted to steal its thunder by strengthening governmental power, ratcheting up their own anti-Jewish program, and creating a quasi-Fascist party. Nothing worked. In the 1939 elections, the middle class, workers, and peasants awarded the Arrow Cross 25 percent of the vote.

The Political Struggle in Austria

Austria never settled down after its defeat in World War I. Although the Social Democrats had blocked Bolshevism, many Austrians identified Socialists with Communists, and Austrian nationalists founded paramilitary groups—particularly the *Heimwehr*—to fight them. The disproportion between "Red" Vienna, with about half the country's population, and the conservative Catholic countryside complicated politics. When powerful Socialist groups gained control of working-class districts in the cities, the industrialists subsidized nationalist units, and bloody street fighting between nationalists and leftists followed.

Austrians were hopelessly divided by politics and a bad economy. Many favored a union with Germany (*Anschluss*), prohibited by the peace treaties; blamed the Socialists for signing the peace treaty; were terrified of Marxism; and rejected the republic. The postwar economic recovery stumbled. Between 1922 and 1926, only a large loan granted by the League of Nations under onerous conditions enabled Austria to survive. Between 1925 and 1929, unemployment averaged between 10 percent and 15 percent. In 1931, the French vetoed a proposed customs union with Germany, fueling resentment during the depths of the depression. In May 1931 a major bank in Vienna, the Kreditanstalt, collapsed and led to runs on banks in Germany and Eastern Europe.

Struggle with the Nazis

The depression radicalized Austrian politics. *Heimwehr* leader, E. R. von Starhemberg, had close links to Mussolini, who actively interfered in Austrian politics. In 1932, the Austrian Nazis won over 16 percent in local elections and staged demonstrations against the government of anti-Nazi Christian Social leader Engelbert Dollfuss. Dollfuss opposed both Anschluss and Nazi racism, as did Mussolini (who at this time opposed Hitler), and suppressed the Nazis, which produced tensions with Hitler. In March 1933 Dollfuss instituted a dictatorship with *Heimwehr* support, creating a fatherland front and dissolving all other political organizations. This step provoked a Socialist uprising in Vienna in February 1934 that the government suffocated in blood, destroying the only domestic force capable of blocking a Nazi takeover.

In May, Dollfuss promulgated a new conservative Catholic constitution instead of the Fascist one he had promised Mussolini. Nevertheless, Mussolini considered Dollfuss a protégé, and he favored the Austrian leader because of his usefulness as a partner in his attempt to revise the Versailles settlement in Eastern Europe. What was most important, an independent Austria served as a buffer between Italy and Germany. This combination of ideology and reality explains Mussolini's action when the Austrian Nazis attempted a coup d'état on July 25, 1934. The *Putsch* failed, but the Nazis shot Dollfuss and left him to bleed to death. When it appeared that Hitler might intervene militarily, Mussolini rushed six divisions to the Austrian frontier, and Hitler backed off—the only time anyone called his bluff before World War II.

Dollfuss's lieutenant Kurt Schuschnigg succeeded Dollfuss, with *Heimwehr* leader Starhemberg serving as the vice chancellor. By 1936 the two had fallen out over Schuschnigg's anti-Nazi vigor, and the government dissolved the *Heimwehr*. Schuschnigg persisted in his efforts to crush the Nazis, but their popular support

The "losers" of World War I were led by Italy, a country that won the war but that remained unsatisfied with its results. This picture shows Benito Mussolini (center) with Englebert Dollfus (left), Austrian Chancellor who established a sort of "Catholic" Fascism, and Hungarian President Gyula Gomboss. Dollfuss died in an attempted Nazi coup in 1934, when relations between Mussolini and Hitler were still poor.

grew. By March 1938 the party counted proportionately more members than the German Nazis had before they took over Germany. Schuschnigg, however, blocked their road to power until Mussolini allied with Hitler and withdrew his opposition to Anschluss.

Bulgaria: From Defeat to Dictatorship

The losses suffered by Bulgaria did not compare with either Austria's or Hungary's, but they caused lasting bitterness and terrible consequences. Besides leaving an estimated 16 percent of Bulgarians outside the mother country, mostly under Greek control, Bulgaria lost access to the Aegean Sea and had to pay heavy reparations. Inflation, starvation, and revolt caused King Ferdinand to abdicate in favor of his son, Boris III, on October 1, 1919. The Agrarian party (BANU), led by Alexander Stamboliisky, won the most seats in new elections. The Communists came in second but were not a decisive factor during the interwar period.

Stamboliisky followed a radical program. On the land, he encouraged the formation of cooperatives and attempted to legislate equality by reducing larger holdings, a policy that increased the size of very small farms but that ultimately failed. The government revamped education by constructing new schools, changing the content of the curriculum, and making teachers accountable. Finally, Stamboliisky reformed the electoral system, which greatly benefited his party and successfully defeated a series of domestic opponents. He seemed headed for personal rule, but, ironically, his success contributed to his downfall.

During the interwar period, the Macedonian Revolutionary Organization (IMRO) conducted a brutal terrorist campaign to make Yugoslavian Macedonia part of Bulgaria. Stamboliisky, however, favored improved relations with Yugoslavia as a way of bringing Bulgaria out of its diplomatic isolation and in March 1923 reached agreement with it to combat terrorism. The pact united Stamboliisky's enemies against him. In June, they revolted, hunted him down, cut off his ears and hands, decapitated him, and sent his head to the capital in a box.

Following Stamboliisky's death, shifting, heterogeneous coalitions of nationalists, army elements, and bourgeois parties ruled Bulgaria, and the country seemed to fall apart. IMRO was a state within a state and continued its terrorist campaign. The economy was saddled with high reparations payments, hit by price declines for its crucial tobacco crop, and ruined by the gold standard that made Bulgarian exports too expensive on the world market. The economic decline brought political fragmentation, the growth of communism, and the army's return to politics.

In April 1935, the instability prompted King Boris to ban parties and to take power through civilian politicians and government-dominated elections. Notable features of Bulgaria were Boris's concession of the vote to married women and widows and the lack of a large role for anti-Semitism because the merchant class was Greek, not Jewish.

THE AEGEAN AND THE ADRIATIC

As in Eastern Europe, democracy did not survive in the South during the interwar period.

The Greek Labyrinth

Extreme instability, characterized by a bewildering array of coups, countercoups, failed coups, cabinet changes, and constitutional revisions, characterized Greece between the wars. Greece had made important gains in Thrace after World War I and, following Turkey's defeat, attempted to complete the Great Idea policy of incorporating all Greeks into the motherland by invading Asia Minor. The Turks under Kemal Ataturk routed them and then expelled the Greek minority, after which 1.5 million destitute refugees flooded into Greece—25 percent of its population.

The collapse of the Great Idea had important political, social, and economic consequences. A revolt of army colonels signaled the entry of the army into politics. It forced King Constantine to abdicate in favor of his son George. In April 1924, a republic was proclaimed, followed during the next four years by short-lived governments, attempted military coups, a dictatorship, and the restoration of parliamentary government; the fight was between Eleftherios Venizelos, who favored a republic, and supporters of the monarchy.

In 1928, Venizelos returned to power at the head of a large parliamentary majority. He expropriated large estates, protected small-scale industrialists and merchants, built schools, and instituted public works projects. Venizelos financed his reforms with international loans, but corruption scandals brought Venizelos down, and political instability forced him to flee the country. In November 1935, the army restored King George.

The Refugee Problem

The other consequence of the Great Idea's collapse was socioeconomic instability. On July 24, 1923, the Treaty of Lausanne provided for the compulsory exchange of populations with Turkey. Unable to handle the great influx of refugees, Greece negotiated large loans under League of Nations auspices in 1924 and 1927, handed over administration of the refugees to the Refugee Settlement Commission, and tried to give the refugees land. The government obtained land from the expropriation of large estates and from state holdings, so that by 1930 large landholdings practically ceased to exist and almost 146,000 refugee families had been settled on the land. These measures alleviated Greece's refugee problem. In addition, new crops, such as tobacco, were introduced, and the value of agricultural products doubled between 1922 and 1932.

Refugees who settled in the overcrowded cities had a harder time, but some had managed to bring money, jewelry, and other movable wealth with them. Aided by Greece's protectionist tariff, many of them established commercial and industrial enterprises. Industry, which contributed only marginally to the national income in 1918, accounted for 18 percent in 1940.

Depression and Dictatorship

With the collapse of agricultural prices during the depression, the refugee problem became explosive. Because they were not committed to the existing political structure, many joined the Communist Party (KKE), which grew rapidly as hundreds of strikes and demonstrations shook the country. The January 1936 elections were a draw between the monarchists and republicans, which gave the Communists the balance of power in the formation of coalition governments. However, the army refused to accept Communist participation in the government, which led King George to institute a dictatorship under General John Metaxas on August 4, 1936.

Metaxas was convinced that only the suppression of political parties and a strong government could save Greece, so he dissolved Parliament, eliminated press freedom, and jailed his opponents. Otherwise, Metaxas ran a fairly efficient and honest government. He regulated the economy and trade unions and banned strikes, but protected workers through compulsory arbitration of disputes and minimum wages. Metaxas talked about creating a third Greek civilization based on classical and Byzantine society. His administration adopted some of the Fascist trappings of power common to the age, including a youth movement (EON) that attracted a million members, but was not a Fascist.

Isolated Albania

Greece's neighbor to the northwest, Albania, was the least advanced part of Europe. It possessed few schools or roads, a tribal social organization in large parts of the country, and an armed populace. Deep regional divisions increased the strong divisions between remote Catholic tribes of the north who were seeking governmental largesse, Muslim landowners employing their influence to increase their holdings, and Eastern Orthodox southerners complaining about economic exploitation. The tensions between peasants and large landowners who owned over half the arable land was expressed in antagonism between the landowner-backed conservative Progressive Party and the Democratic, or Popular, Party, headed by an Eastern Orthodox Bishop, Harvard-educated Fan Noli.

International disputes had resulted in Albanian independence in 1913, but contending forces fought over it during World War I. After the conflict, disputes broke out with Greece and Yugoslavia, which claimed different areas of ethnic Albania. In 1921, the Allies awarded Kosovo to Yugoslavia despite documented Serbian atrocities. Albanian-inhabited territory that went to other countries caused trouble throughout the interwar period and up to the end of the twentieth century.

Instability and the Albanian Dictatorship

Albanian conditions fostered instability and revolts that probably no parliamentary system could have survived. In the 1920s, Fan Noli and Muslim leader Ahmed Zogu emerged as the most important personalities. In June 1924, a revolution put Noli at the helm with a program of radical agricultural, legal, and administrative reform that alienated the landowners without gaining the peasants' support. Backed by Yugoslavia and financed by the British (who hoped to find oil in Albania), Zogu took over as president on January 31, 1925. Zogu declared himself Zog I, king of the Albanians, on September 1, 1928. He had absolute power through a new constitution supported by large landowners and others favoring the status quo. Zog could at times be moderately progressive, as in 1937 when he attempted to force the unveiling of Muslim women, ban men from wearing national costumes, and discourage peasants from sleeping on the floor by promoting beds.

Zog maintained his rule through a system of paying pensions and salaries to tribal leaders—effective but expensive. Because the Yugoslavs could not afford to keep subsidizing him and the international financial community refused to consider loans, Zogu turned to the Italians. Albania's proximity to the Italian coast and Mussolini's desire to extend his influence in the Balkans made Italy the only large power with an important stake in the country. The Italians granted loans, set up a credit system and a currency, made investments, signed friendship pacts, and widened their influence over Albanian civilian and military life. However, Zog chafed under Italian tutelage, and Mussolini invaded the country in April 1939. Italy's King Victor Emanuel III thereupon became the king of Albania as well.

IBERIA

On the opposite end of Europe, the Iberian Peninsula also came under the control of dictators.

Failure of the Portuguese Republic

The Portuguese republic, established in 1910, promised progress and social justice but was characterized instead by anticlericalism, financial failure, factionalism, instability, and the army's interference in politics. Portugal entered World War I

Antonio Salazar, shown here in 1959. Salazar established a state that had Fascist elements but was authoritarian rather than totalitarian. He kept Portugal neutral during World War II and his regime lasted until September 1968 when a fall incapacitated him.

in 1915 on the Allied side; when the war ended, inflation, strikes, disorder, terrorism, and leftist demands for revolution followed. The military took over in June 1926 and sought loans that the international financial community would not give because of the country's disastrous economic situation. The military then called on a professor of political economy at the University of Coimbra, Antonio de Oliveira Salazar, to put Portuguese finances in order.

Salazar's "New State"

Salazar cut expenses, increased the efficiency of tax collection, and balanced the budget. These accomplishments made him the strong man of the regime. In May and June 1930, when the depression devastated Europe, Salazar stated that he would transform Portugal into a corporate republic based on Catholic thought and patriotic unity—the "New State"—and in 1933 issued Europe's first corporate constitution. Corporativism, an important component of Italian Fascism, was supposedly based on the peaceful collaboration of all classes and social and economic groups.

The constitution's major innovation was a consultative corporate chamber chosen by economic groups and cultural and professional societies. The government orchestrated elections and established the "National Union" to aid in this task. As in Italy, the regime banned strikes and lockouts and regulated relationships between workers and employers. The new organization did little to spur the economy, and static agriculture, slow industrial progress, and high illiteracy continued to characterize Portuguese society.

Salazar's regime was authoritarian rather than Fascist. In fact, the Fascists, organized in 1932 as the National Syndicalists or Blue Shirts, wanted to graft elements of Portuguese Catholicism onto a movement of the Italian type. Salazar condemned their emphasis on Fascist values, such as the cult of youth and direct action, and dissolved them on July 29, 1934. In foreign policy, Salazar supported Francisco Franco during the Spanish Civil War by allowing the Spanish rebels to use Portuguese facilities. Portugal remained neutral in World War II, although it favored the Allies after 1943. Salazar's careful foreign and domestic policies allowed the regime to survive until 1974.

Military Dictatorship in Spain

Another long-lived authoritarian regime emerged in Spain, albeit in a more dramatic and bloody fashion.

Spain was neutral during World War I, but the conflict still affected it. Industry grew rapidly because of the war-related demand from the Allies, but in 1917 a wave of strikes led by the Socialist trade union, the UGT, demanding social and economic reform hit the country. Continuing disorders between 1918 and 1920 and a revolt in Morocco discredited the parliamentary government and resulted in a military dictatorship under General Miquel Primo de Rivera on September 13, 1923. Primo de Rivera resolved to restore order, deal with Spain's financial chaos, win in Morocco, and save Spain from its politicians.

The dictatorship succeeded in all these goals except the last. Between 1920 and 1930, the percentage of the industrial labor force rose from 22 percent to

26.5 percent and the service sector from 20.8 percent to 28 percent, while agricultural labor declined from 57.2 percent to 45.5 percent; illiteracy fell; the number of university students doubled; and greater economic opportunities for women materialized. However, Primo de Rivera failed to create a political constituency, and his illness weakened his regime. In January 1930, the peseta's fall, rising unemployment, and an unbalanced budget convinced King Alfonso XIII to request his resignation.

Despite Spain's rapid progress, its economic and social development lagged far behind the advanced industrial countries, and Spanish society was unready for the Liberal leftist governments of the 1930s.

The Republic and the Polarization of Spanish Politics

Alfonso aimed at a gradual return to a parliamentary regime, but strong republican opposition materialized. Manuel Azaña's Republican Action Group, formed in 1925, combined with other republican societies on August 17, 1930, to create the umbrella Republican Committee and to set up a provisional government that included the Socialists. Disorders and a victory in the local elections of April 1931 encouraged the provisional government to demand the monarchy's end. When huge crowds supported the end of the monarchy and the army refused to back Alfonso, the king left the country without abdicating on April 14.

The provisional government proclaimed a republic and attacked the church. Over a hundred church buildings were torched without Azaña discouraging the destruction. The violence, burnings, killings, and atrocities caused resentment and demonstrated that the Republicans had lost control of public order.

A republican constitution, adopted in 1931, instituted a parliamentary form of government, guaranteed civil rights, and granted women the vote and equal rights in marriage and divorce. The constitution decreed the separation of church and state, but while it guaranteed freedom of conscience, it dissolved religious orders and confiscated their property. Between 1931 and 1933, Azaña undertook a vigorous reform program that brought mixed results. The state alienated Catholic parents by closing their schools, while the construction of new schools faltered. The lack of local compliance often negated labor legislation giving workers new benefits and a voice in management. The new land reform was complicated and underfunded and failed to resettle many families. Finally, the breakdown of public order made it difficult to implement the reform measures.

By late 1933, mounting unemployment, strikes, and strains in the republican coalition forced the Azaña government to resign. The left's radical policies encouraged more unity on the right and spurred the growth of the CEDA (Confederation of Autonomous Rightist Groups), headed by a university professor, José Maria Gil Robles, that, with the addition of several Catholic groups, grew into the largest Spanish party. In addition to the CEDA, the right included business groups; radical right monarchists, headed by Mussolini admirer José Calvo Sotelo; and the Fascist Falange, led by José Antonio Primo de Rivera—son of the former dictator.

The right staged a comeback in the 1933 elections, and the leftist parties responded by uniting in a Popular Front coalition on the French model in

Spain experienced political unrest during the early 1930s, with violent struggles between the right and the left. The elections of 1936 established a Popular Front government that implemented radical measures for which the country was unprepared and set the stage for a civil war during the 1930s that has been seen as a prelude to World War II. In this photograph, posters go up during the turbulent electoral campaign of 1936.

preparation for the upcoming elections of February 16, 1936. The balloting produced a big victory for the Popular Front, and Azaña returned as prime minister. Emboldened by the triumph, the left undertook radical land distribution that included sanctioning land seizures and expropriation through taxation. Between May and July 1936, strikes, demonstrations, arson, and killings directed mainly against the right escalated. This violent period culminated in the murder of Calvo Sotelo by leftist police officers.

The Spanish Civil War

These events produced a rightist military revolt in mid-July 1936. The conspirators envisioned a quick victory and a regime modeled on the Portuguese New State, but their plans went awry when they encountered major opposition in the areas that supported the Popular Front. The military effort bogged down and developed into a civil war. Both sides called for foreign help. Italy and Germany intervened in favor of Francisco Franco, leader of the nationalist forces, while Soviet-backed Communists dominated the left. The Civil War turned into an internecine struggle between the international Fascist and anti-Fascist forces.

The opponents of fascism formed the International Brigades and fought alongside the Spanish republicans, while the Italians and the Germans presented their thinly disguised military intervention as an anti-Communist crusade. The struggle—a milestone on the road to World War II—lasted until 1939 and caused a million casualties before Franco finally won.

In April 1937, Franco took over the Falange and turned it into the official state party, but watered it down at the same time that he gave his regime some of the Fascist trappings that were typical of 1930s authoritarian governments. More than Fascist, Franco's Spain has been interpreted as "a Catholic, corporative, and increasingly demobilized authoritarian regime."

Bibliographical Essay

The statement on the nature of the dictatorships in the Baltic states is taken from V. Stanley Vardys and Romuald J. Misiunas, eds., *The Baltic States in Peace and War 1917–1945* (University Park, Penn., 1978), an excellent collection of essays (pp. 77–78). The Information Department of the Royal Institute of International Affairs, *The Baltic States* (London, 1938), is packed with information on the economies, social situation, and politics of the Baltic states. John Hiden and Patrick Salmon, *The Baltic Nations and Europe*, rev. ed. (London, 1994), brings the story up to the present. There are several concise histories of the Baltic States; they include Kevin O'Connor, *The History of the Baltic States* (Westport, Conn., 2003), a narrative from ancient times, and Andres Kasekamp, *A History of the Baltic States* (New York, 2010), which deals with all three of the countries.

Economics in Eastern Europe between the wars is covered thoroughly by M. C. Kaser and E. A. Radice, eds., *The Economic History of Eastern Europe 1919–1975*, Vol. 1 (Oxford, UK, 1985). *A Low Dishonest Decade* (New York, 2002) by Paul N. Hehn considers the role of the great powers in economics and the origins of World War II. A book of essays that discusses more specialized business topics is Christopher Kobrak and Per H. Hansen, *European Business, Dictatorship, and Political Risk, 1920–1945* (New York, 2004). The most thorough general work on all Eastern Europe during this period remains Hugh Seton-Watson, *Eastern Europe Between the Wars 1918–1941*, 3rd ed. (New York, 1962). Anta Prazmowska's *Eastern Europe and the Origins of the Second World War* (New York, 2000) analyzes the complex dilemmas of the East European states. Alexander V. Prusin's *The Lands Between* (New York, 2010) has ample material on the period under consideration. The previously cited book by Zara Stein, *The Lights that Failed* (New York, 2005), is a thorough history of international affairs between the wars with much material on Eastern Europe.

Ferdynand Zweig, *Poland Between Two Wars: A Critical Study of Social and Economic Changes* (London, 1944), neglects the minority question but otherwise is a very good study of the social and economic situation. Economics is more fully discussed by J. Taylor, *The Economic Development of Poland 1919–1950* (Ithaca, N.Y., 1952). A good general history is Norman Davies, *Heart of Europe: A Short History of Poland* (Oxford, UK, 1984). Aleksander Gieysztor et al., *History of Poland*, 2nd ed. (Warsaw, 1979), is a thorough work on the entire sweep of Polish history, seen from the East. Bernadotte E. Schmitt, ed., *Poland* (Berkeley, Calif., 1947), contains perceptive essays on all aspects of modern Poland. On the important Polish Jewish community, consult Israel Gutman et al., eds., *The Jews of Poland Between Two World Wars* (Hanover, New Hampshire, 1989) *Anti-Semitism*; on the Catholic Church in Poland during the interwar period, see *Rome's Most Faithful Daughter* (Athens, Ohio, 2009) by Neal Pease.

Mark Cornwall et al., *Czechoslovakia in a Nationalist and Fascist Europe, 1918–1948* (New York, 2007), is a collection of essays on the dilemmas of democracy in the country during the interwar period. Josef Korbel, *Twentieth-Century Czechoslovakia: The Meanings of its History* (New York, 1977), is a clearly written account, sympathetic to the Czechs, that includes much information on the period discussed. William V. Wallace's *Czechoslovakia* (Boulder, Colo., 1976) is an excellent, more detailed work. Essays on particular themes and problems may be found in Victor S. Mamatey and Radomir Luza, *A History of the Czechoslovak Republic, 1918–1948* (Princeton, N.J., 1973). Georges Castellan's *A History of the Romanians* (New York, 1989) has a good chapter on the interwar period. David Mitrany's study on land reform, *The Land and the Peasant in Rumania: The War and Agrarian Reform, 1917–21* (New York, 1968), originally published in 1930, gives a complete picture. Dejan Djokic, *Elusive Compromise* (New York, 2007), is a history of interwar Yugoslavia. Stephen Clissold, ed., *A Short History of Yugoslavia: From Early Times to 1966* (Cambridge, UK, 1966), includes an excellent chapter on interwar Yugoslavia. On Hungary, the most scholarly work is C. A. Macartney, *A History of Hungary 1929–1945* (New York, 1956). Paul Ignotus, *Hungary* (New York, 1972), has the passion of a participant. Another participant in the events, Oscar Jaszi, wrote about an important transition, *Revolution and Counter-Revolution in Hungary* (New York, 1969).

The Fascist movements in Hungary and Romania are analyzed by Nicholas M. Nagy-Talavera, *The Green Shirts and the Others: A History of Fascism in Hungary and Romania* (Stanford, Calif., 1970). A good idea of the Austrian situation may be gained by looking at C. E. Edmondson, *The Heimwehr and Austrian Politics* (Athens, Ga., 1978); F. L. Carsten, *Fascist Movements in Austria from Schonerer to Hitler* (London, 1977); and Gordon Brooke-Shepherd, *Dollfuss* (London, 1961). A comparative study of the Heimwehr and the Nazis is offered by John T. Lauridson, *Nazism and the Radical Right in Austria 1918–1934* (Copenhagen, 2007). See also Gottfried-Karl Kindermann, *Hitler's Defeat in Austria, 1933–1934* (London, 1988). For details on Bulgaria during this period, consult R. J. Crampton, *A Short History of Modern Bulgaria* (Cambridge, UK, 1987).

For the rise of Fascist-type organizations during the latter part of the period discussed, see Béla Vago, *The Shadow of the Swastika: The Rise of Fascism and Anti-Semitism in the Danube Basin, 1936–1939* (London, 1975).

On Greece, see John Campbell and Philip Sherrard, *Modern Greece* (London, 1968). On the economic details, there is Mark Mazower, *Greece and the Inter-War Economic Crisis* (Oxford, UK, 1991); on Metaxas, consult J. V. Kofas, *Authoritarianism in Greece: The Metaxas Regime* (Boulder, Colo., 1983). Miranda Vickers, *The Albanians: A Modern History* (London, 1995), provides a succinct account of Albanian developments.

Portuguese events can be followed in T. Gallagher, *Portugal: A Twentieth-Century Interpretation* (Manchester, UK, 1983); R. A. H. Robinson, *Contemporary Portugal* (London, 1979); and Hugh Kay, *Salazar and Modern Portugal* (New York, 1960). On Portuguese corporativism, see H. J. Wirda, *Corporativism and Development: The Portuguese Experience* (Amherst, Mass., 1977). Much more has been written on Spain and the Spanish Civil War. The most comprehensive work on the republic is Stanley G. Payne, *Spain's First Democracy: The Second Republic, 1931–1936* (Madison, Wis., 1993), from which the statistics on Spain's economic progress are taken (p. 24). The best book on agrarian reform is Edward E. Malefakis, *Agrarian Reform and Peasant Revolution: Origins of The Civil War* (New Haven, Conn., 1970), while the resurgence of the right is discussed by Richard A. H. Robinson, *The Origins of Franco's Spain* (Plymouth, 1970). The quotation on Spain's political evolution under Franco comes from Payne, *Fascism,* previously cited (p. 267). Books on the Civil War are cited in the bibliography to Chapter 14.

On two important topics discussed in this chapter, see Matthew Feldman et al., *Clerical Fascism in Interwar Europe* (New York, 2008), a book of essays on the topic, and

Civil War and World War in Spain, Yugoslavia and Greece, 1936–1949 (New York, 2008), by Philip B. Minehan.

Much has been written on the Spanish Civil War and the conditions leading up to it. Hugh Thomas's *The Spanish Civil War* (New York, 2001) is a classic that has been brought up to date. Paul Preston wrote both a general history of the conflict, *The Spanish Civil War: Reaction, Revolution and Revenge* (New York, 2007), and the acclaimed *Franco: A Biography* (New York, 1994). Antony Beevor's *The Battle for Spain: The Spanish Civil War 1936–1939* (New York, 2006), a complete history, and *The Spanish Civil War* (New York, 2001) are good sources. Andrew Durgan's *The Spanish Civil War* (New York, 2007) has the added bonus of surveying the recent literature on the topic. Hilario M. Raguer Suñer and Gerald Howson's *Gunpowder and Incense* (New York, 2007) is a study of the Catholic Church's role in the Spanish Civil War.

✍

CHAPTER 12

Mussolini's Fascism

CHAPTER OUTLINE

Fascist Practice • Fascist Ideology

BIOGRAPHICAL SKETCHES

Edmondo Rossoni, Fascist Labor • Margherita Sarfatti, "Dictator of the Figurative Arts"

Fascism's economic policies during the 1920s were similar to those described in Chapter 8 for other European countries, but the implementation of a dictatorship was a radical departure from Italian tradition. Mussolini's seizure of power convinced opponents that industrialists and big landowners were behind the takeover, but, although Mussolini did have support in both groups, Fascism was a highly complex phenomenon whose significance transcended economics. (Used with a capital letter, *Fascism* refers to Italy; *fascism* in lower case refers to the generic movement). Because of the contradictions within Fascism, it is important to examine both its practice and ideology.

FASCIST PRACTICE

Fascism's opponents described it as a jumble of ideas. The Fascists themselves claimed that they disdained the quibbling of intellectuals and favored "action," that theory did not interest them because they lived for the moment, and that their movement was based on youth. In fact, at age 39, Mussolini and was the youngest prime minister in Italian history, and the movement attracted the young. Fascism's formal systemization came only after the Fascists had been in power for a decade.

The Government

After Mussolini consolidated his regime in 1925, he got rid of the non-Fascists in his cabinet and replaced them with party stalwarts known for their support of the monarchy and their personal closeness to the king. He had previously opposed the monarchy, and after the Matteotti affair, he thought it essential to mollify the king by reducing the influence of Fascist left-wingers who noisily advocated a second wave of revolution to sweep away existing Italian social and political institutions. Mussolini transformed the National Fascist Party (PNF) into a mass organization that ordinary Italians were obliged to join if they wanted to accomplish the tasks of everyday life. Membership in the PNF, in contrast to the Soviet Communist or German Nazi parties, meant little.

Mussolini blended traditional and new organizations, which consolidated his power and made his rule more attractive abroad. His compromises with existing Italian institutions allowed him to rule easier, but Mussolini never gained complete power over Italian society and frequently could not enforce important measures. Ironically, when the Duce tried to make Italy more Fascist, he ran into greater passive opposition.

Structure of the Dictatorship

In 1925 and 1926, the government took control of the independent press, suppressed opposition parties and associations, expelled opposition deputies from the Chamber of Deputies, and created a special tribunal to try crimes against Fascism. The regime also gave the police broad new powers to arrest persons merely on suspicion of conspiring against the political and social order. Lina Wertmüller's film *Love and Anarchy,* for example, tells the loosely based-on-truth story of an anarchist who was executed because he was plotting to kill Mussolini, although he never made the attempt. Officials received the right to cancel passports, to fire on people who were attempting to flee the country, and to deprive opponents of the regime who were living abroad of their citizenship and property.

Fascist legislation deprived Parliament of any power. In December 1925, parliamentary control over cabinets evaporated with the transformation of the prime minister into a head of government responsible only to the king. The Chamber of Deputies lost its power to select individual cabinet ministers, to be chosen in the future by the Duce subject to the king's approval. Mussolini's control of the agenda of the Chamber of Deputies eliminated Parliament's legislative initiative. In January 1926, the government removed Parliament's power over the state administration by implementing decisions after consultation with the Council of State. Later in 1926 and in 1928, the government instituted control over local affairs by substituting elected officials by appointees from Rome.

The Fascists merged party and state institutions, although this phenomenon did not go as far as in the USSR or in Nazi Germany. In 1927, the Fascist Grand Council (the Fascist Party executive) changed the method of electing the Chamber of Deputies by drawing up a slate of 400 persons who were recommended by employer, employee, and other associations and presenting the list to the voters, who either accepted or rejected it. The Grand Council later gained a voice in the succession to the throne and in naming an eventual successor to Mussolini. The Duce asserted his control of the Grand Council by calling it into session only rarely. Ironically, when Italy was being defeated during World War II, the Fascist Grand Council ousted Mussolini from power in 1943 by asking the king to resume command. The event demonstrated how, despite all the changes, Italian

This February 1922 photograph of Pope Pius XI shows the Pontiff at the time of the March on Rome that brought Mussolini to power. Pius's policies helped the Duce, and the 1929 Concordat, in the minds of many people, signified that the Church approved of the regime. Mussolini did not intend to relinquish power and quickly attacked the Church, but after his fall the Concordat gave the Church great power in the new Italian Republic.

institutions retained the capacity to strike back at the Fascists: unlike Nazi Germany or Soviet Russia, Italy retained a constitutional official who could dismiss the Duce.

Uneasy Peace with the Church

The powerful Catholic Church had an ambiguous role when it came to Fascism. Mussolini understood the church's great influence and tried to gain its support. On February 11, 1929, the Duce and the Vatican signed the Lateran Accords ending the dispute between the church and state that had resulted from confiscation of papal territory in 1861 and 1870 during Italian unification. The Lateran Accords created the independent state of Vatican City in Rome, paid the church a large sum as compensation for the annexed territories, regulated religious affairs in the country, and instituted salaries for the clergy. Because Italy paid the money in state bonds, the Catholic Church acquired a large stake in the stability of the Fascist regime. In the concordat that was part of the accords, the state relinquished control over matrimony to the church, allowed religious instruction in public secondary schools, and gave the church censorship powers over free expression in the Holy City. This agreement ended the possibility of divorce in the country (until 1970) and, by making Catholicism the official state religion, put other religious denominations in an inferior position. The Lateran Accords contributed to Mussolini's international prestige and were the last important step in the consolidation of Italian Fascism.

Immediately after signing the Lateran Accords, the Duce curbed the church's political and social influence over the country's youths by attacking Catholic Action. The campaign ended in 1931 with a victory for Mussolini. At least until the anti-Semitic laws of 1938, the church supported the regime in domestic and foreign policy. Mussolini had achieved stability at home and respect abroad.

Labor Policy

The normalization of the Fascist state after the postwar disturbances accounted for Mussolini's appeal to foreigners. Indeed, the Fascists attained this peace by suppressing the Socialist and other independent trade unions. Nevertheless, Fascism professed to be a strong friend of labor even while it opposed the excessive strikes and violence that had marked the Red Biennium. Fascist trade unionists had won a large following, but because the powerful industrialists had thrown their support to the Duce, the question after 1922 was how they would influence labor policy. The desire of Fascist labor leaders to empower workers conflicted with Mussolini's need to solidify his regime by reaching agreement with the employers. Fascism's contradictory aims touched off an internal debate between the Duce and the Fascist union leaders.

Edmondo Rossoni, the Fascist labor movement's strongest advocate, aimed to strengthen the General Confederation of Fascist Unions by absorbing the Socialist and Catholic labor unions. Rossoni, a former member of the Socialist International Workers of the World (IWW) in the United States and an experienced labor organizer, hoped to win recognition for his organization as the only representative of labor. On December 19, 1923, the employers established a privileged relationship with the Fascist unions but put off creating corporations—institutions in which both employers and employees would have representation. During the next two years, tensions escalated as the standard of living for workers declined and provoked strikes by both the Fascist and non-Fascist unions. Alarmed by labor's activism, the Duce ordered wage increases but resolved to tame the Fascist labor movement.

On October 2, 1925, representatives of the industrialists' association (the Confindustria) and the Fascist unions signed the Palazzo Vidoni pact recognizing each other as representatives of employers and employees. This agreement seemed favorable to the workers, but a series of measures over the next two years achieved Mussolini's aim. Because only Fascist unions could legally negotiate and enforce contracts, all previous contracts were voided, and the independent unions were disbanded in 1926 and 1927. At the same time, the Confindustria became Fascist, and its president and secretary entered the Fascist Grand Council. In 1926, legislation drawn up by Nationalist theoretician Alfredo Rocco prohibited both strikes and lockouts. In 1928, the government further weakened Rossoni's labor movement by splitting his Confederation of Fascist Unions into six organizations.

The Nationalists had merged with the Fascists in 1923 and hoped to foster national unity by reducing labor conflict through the formation of corporations, which Rocco's legislation mentioned for the first time. In order to gain labor support in a climate of increasing tension, in 1927 the government issued a declaration of workers' entitlement to good wages, working conditions, and social security, known as the Labor Charter. Private enterprise was the most efficient means of serving the country's interests, but state intervention in the economy was promised, if necessary. The Great Depression soon put the government's assurance to the test.

The Depression, Industry, and Autarky

The economic crisis struck Italy when the country had not completely digested the effects of the revaluation crisis discussed in Chapter 8. The government responded to the slump by decreasing salaries, rationalizing and expanding social security, and undertaking a vast public works program that included land reclamation, building new cities, road building, and rural electrification. It also discouraged the movement of the rural unemployed into the cities, although it did not achieve this goal.

BIOGRAPHICAL SKETCHES

Edmondo Rossoni
Fascist Labor

Edmondo Rossoni's career paralleled Benito Mussolini's, although Rossoni remained more faithful to his principles. Born in Tresigallo in the province of Ferrara on October 6, 1884, Rossoni joined the Italian Socialist Party at an early age. He became attracted to revolutionary syndicalism, a Socialist faction that preached the supremacy of workers and their unions and considered the general strike the prime weapon for implementing socialism. He took part in strikes on the land and in 1904 moved to Milan, the stronghold of the revolutionary syndicalists. His activities attracted the attention of the police, and in 1908 he fled the country. Rossoni went to France and Brazil before going to New York in 1910. In New York, he wrote for the revolutionary newspaper *Il Proletario* and joined the IWW. In 1913, he returned to Italy, again engaged in revolutionary activities, was arrested and released, and again left for New York City. When World War I began, he advocated Italian intervention, and in May 1916, he returned to Italy and volunteered for combat.

On June 9 and 10, 1918, Rossoni and his friends resurrected the Unione Italiana del Lavoro (Italian Union of Labor, UIL), which represented revolutionary syndicalists who had supported the war. The UIL adopted Rossoni's slogan: "Do not deny the nation; conquer it." The UIL advocated fighting for workers' control of production and distribution. In March 1919, the union occupied a large steel plant outside Milan, an action that Mussolini supported. In 1920 the UIL urged the expropriation of land that was not under direct cultivation, thus increasing its appeal for the landless peasants and the returning peasant-soldiers.

In January 1922, Rossoni agreed to head the Fascist unions, mistakenly believing that Mussolini would support workers' increased power through mixed unions with employers. Although the corporative state later included elements of these institutions, industrialists and landowners resisted Rossoni's demands, and the Duce withdrew his support. In November 1928 the government broke Rossoni's Fascist Confederation of Labor Unions into several separate organizations, signaling his definitive defeat and that of Fascist labor.

Rossoni had little power as undersecretary for the presidency of the Council of Ministers (1932–35) and minister of agriculture (1935–39). He was a member of the Fascist Grand Council and voted for a motion that removed Mussolini from power on July 24 and 25, 1943. This act earned Rossoni Mussolini's enmity, and he had to take refuge in the Vatican when the Germans occupied Italy in September 1943. In 1944, Mussolini's puppet Italian Social Republic held trials in Verona for the Grand Council members who had betrayed the Duce, and Rossoni received a death sentence in absentia. After the war, a court sentenced him to life imprisonment for his role in suppressing Italian liberty during the Fascist era, but Rossoni fled to Canada.

In 1947, the sentence revoked, Rossoni returned to Italy, where he lived peacefully until his death in Rome on June 8, 1965.

The slump produced long-range changes in industry and commerce. As the economic situation deteriorated, Mussolini turned for advice to a non-Fascist banking expert, Alberto Beneduce. After the creation of new agencies that were empowered to make loans to ailing companies proved insufficient to stem the crisis, the government founded the Institute for Industrial Reconstruction (IRI) to arrange for the long-term financing of failing firms. The idea was for IRI to buy up depressed companies in the portfolios of the banks and liquidate them; instead IRI acquired the commercial and industrial holdings of the major banks and achieved control of the companies and of the banks themselves. Although IRI was supposed to sell its holdings when recovery came, its acquisitions had become too big and valuable to do so. Moreover, as Mussolini embarked on a series of wars, the state wanted to keep basic industries in its hands.

These considerations led to the reorganization of essential economic sectors in which IRI companies were active, such as steel, communications, and shipbuilding. By 1937 IRI had evolved into a modern holding company under public control employing the most advanced private-sector techniques. Through IRI and other public companies, the Fascist state owned and managed a greater proportion of Italian industries than any other European state except the USSR.

In 1935, preparations for the Ethiopian War, the combined cost of the conflict, public works, and increased interest payments produced large budget deficits that forced Mussolini to devalue the lira in October 1936 to keep it in line with the dollar and the pound. Prices rose despite governmental controls, and unions obtained salary increases in 1936, 1937, and 1939. A general economic recovery, accompanied by increased industrial production, occurred during those years.

In 1936, Mussolini instituted a policy of autarky, or self-sufficiency, in response to League of Nations sanctions imposed after his invasion of Ethiopia. The policy, however, had its origins earlier in the Great Depression and in the collapse of free trade and intensified under the pressure of war. Mussolini instituted currency controls, austerity, the substitution of Italian products for imported ones where possible, and curbs of imported raw materials by large firms and state agencies. The government also became involved in developing new products and processes, in regulating all phases of manufacturing, and in searching for new sources of energy. Among the most important of these newly created state agencies was the Italian General Firm for Petroleum (AGIP). Both AGIP and IRI survived the fall of Fascism, IRI closing only in the year 2000 and AGIP becoming part of a large state hydrocarbon combine.

Fascist economic policies counted both successes and failures. The deficiencies came primarily in agriculture and the poor performance of real wages. The accomplishments included stimulation of important modern industries, such as electricity, steel, engineering, chemicals, and artificial fibers, so that Italy's profile began to resemble that of a modern European country. This success contributed to the economic miracle after World War II. Up to the time that Mussolini embarked on his warlike adventures, Fascism's policies and ideology appeared brilliant and, for many depression-era Europeans and Americans, a model to emulate.

In attempt to make Italy self-sufficient in food, the Mussolini government began a huge propaganda effort to encourage farmers to grow more wheat. The campaign succeeded in doing this, but the economic impact of the effort showed mixed results. The Duce was always hands-on in his propaganda efforts. This picture shows him giving a hand with the grain harvesting.

Agriculture

Fascism achieved less-impressive results in the agricultural field. Relations between the Fascist unions led by Rossoni and the landowners' organization were poor and, despite his rhetoric, Mussolini threw his weight against the peasants.

In 1925 the Duce announced the "Battle of the Grain," one of the regime's more spectacular and successful propaganda efforts. For reasons of prestige and self-defense in case of war, Mussolini aimed to make the country self-sufficient in foodstuffs by encouraging investment and improvements to increase grain production. The government hoped to achieve its goal by increasing the yield per acre without reducing the production of other crops. The campaign cut Italy's grain imports substantially, and Mussolini claimed victory. However, bringing more land into production and shifting production away from other crops, not more yield per unit, accounted for the increase and caused the production and export of more lucrative products, such as wine, to suffer. Moreover, the collapse of international food prices forced farmers to kill off more of their animals and to introduce tractors and modern chemical fertilizers. Many small landholders who had contracted debts to pay for their land fell behind on payments and lost it. This development reversed a previous trend toward small landholding. The plight of agricultural laborers remained poor and was worsened by legal measures preventing them from leaving the land for urban areas. In contrast, the large landholders, who enjoyed close ties with the government, consolidated their position because their wealth made them better able to adapt to the changes. Because of this situation, Italian farmers had a difficult time participating in the economic recovery of the late 1930s.

FASCIST IDEOLOGY

In the 1930s the Duce tried to give his movement a clear ideological formulation to contradict the claim of anti-Fascists that fascism had no ideology and that its intellectual structure was a façade for exploiting workers. Historians have been debating these issues ever since. Some writers, such as Zeev Sternhell and Emilio Gentile, have pointed out that the Fascists were not the only ones whose ideology demonstrated discrepancies when compared to practice.

Since the international movements that professed to be Fascist had disparate ideologies, historians have attempted to identify specific characteristics that marked so-called generic fascism even while using Italian Fascism as a model. There is agreement on certain characteristics, such as nationalism, the paramount role of the leader, and perhaps corporativism, but not on all the elements of what has become a very long list. Although during the early years of his regime Mussolini did not consider his movement suitable for export, later the Fascists paid more attention to the international dimensions of the movement and subsidized groups, such as the Cagoulards in France and the Rexists in Belgium. Despite these activities, the Italians did not devote a great deal of effort to spreading the Fascist gospel, and the influence it had abroad came primarily from spontaneous emulation.

The "Third Way"

In the 1930s, sophisticated thinkers, such as philosopher Giovanni Gentile and Nationalist theoretician Alfredo Rocco, with contributions from Mussolini, undertook the task of systematically explaining fascism to the rest of the world. Judging from the regime's actions, this ideological framework functioned primarily as window dressing for conservative economic and social policies, but to conclude that the ideology had no importance for the Fascists would be inaccurate. Moreover, the ideas expressed during the frequently passionate internal debates among Fascists are helpful for understanding the inner mechanisms of the movement, the inconsistencies of the regime, and Italian Fascism's attractiveness outside Italy.

In a comprehensive statement in the *Enciclopedia Italiana* (Italian Encyclopedia), written with Gentile in 1932, Mussolini condemned communism as an absurd delusion. He also denounced liberalism and democracy, which he lumped together with socialism because they emphasized the individual over the community. According to the Duce, these doctrines reduced society to a mere "sum of individuals" that generates communism and submerges the individual within the community. The Fascists believed that their movement represented an alternative to liberalism and communism, the "Third Way," because it recognized the community as supreme but left ample space to individual initiative. Unlike the other ideologies, Fascist ideology held that individuals were naturally *unequal* and emphasized heroism and sentiment. Fascism, its adherents claimed, combined the superiority of the state with enhancement of the individual without the false freedom of democracy or communism.

These statements and the Duce's revolutionary Socialist roots suggested to some historians that Fascism had leftist origins. In the 1960s, Italian historian Renzo De Felice argued that the development of Mussolini's ideology was a subject worthy of serious consideration. His contention set off a furious debate, with some leftist observers accusing him of being a veiled Fascist. Over the next thirty years, however, De Felice continued to develop his ideas, stating also that, for a certain period, Fascism had the consensus of the Italians. After De Felice, other historians described Fascism in a variety of ways that have contradicted the contention of leftists that the movement had no coherent philosophy. They viewed Fascism as a developmental dictatorship and as a leftist revision of Marx by revolutionary syndicalists (see Chapter 1).

The Corporate State

The Fascists adopted principles that were derived from the prewar Italian Nationalists, who merged with the Fascist party (PNF) in 1923. They projected the Marxist class struggle onto the international plane as the struggle between rich and proletarian nations, of which Italy was the chief representative. Italian Nationalists believed that the international class struggle between proletarian and rich nations would culminate in a revolutionary war led by Italy. The Italian Fascists embraced this idea and updated it into a fight between the "Have-Nots" and the "Haves." In order to prepare for the coming conflict, the Italians had to achieve internal unity, the Nationalists believed. This concept had important repercussions and contributed to a fundamental Fascist principle, the Corporate

State, that had an influence outside Italy. Alexander J. De Grand defined it as "a system of institutional arrangements by which capital and labor are integrated into obligatory, hierarchical, and functional units (corporations) recognized by the state, which become organs of self-government for issues relating to the specific category as well as the basis for participation with other corporatively organized interests in policy decisions affecting the whole society (corporative parliament)." This idea required the creation of concrete institutions (corporations) in which workers and employers would be represented and work out disputes between capital and labor by negotiation.

The Corporate State dates from 1926, when a law alluded to the corporations, but because of employers' opposition, the government did not institute them. With the Great Depression, Fascist unionists pressed for their formal introduction and clear definitions of their structure and function. Between 1930 and 1934, a vigorous debate on the corporations occurred in which important Fascist intellectuals viewed them as the concrete embodiment of the "Third Way." Leftist Fascist Ugo Spirito argued that the corporations should integrate the workers as full-scale partners in production, transform existing entrepreneurs into managers, and assume ownership of the firms. Spirito believed that making the corporations owners of the means of production would end the class struggle and fulfill Fascism's promises. These ideas got Spirito denounced as a Bolshevik, and conservative Fascists won the fight.

On February 5, 1934, legislation created twenty-two corporations in all sectors of production—agriculture, commerce, services, and industry. On the surface, this law embodied the ideas of the Revolutionary Syndicalists, who saw the future Socialist society as being organized by unions dominating different areas of production. It is important, however, to distinguish the theory of the corporations from the facts of their operation. Employee and employer organizations had equal representation in the corporations, or *sindacati*, despite the numerical superiority of workers. This was a clear discrimination against labor. In theory, the corporations brought together representatives of employers and employees to determine production and settle differences in the presence of delegates representing governmental interests, as the Nationalists had preached. In reality, the corporations had little power and normally ratified governmental proposals generated by the employers' associations.

Completing the Corporate State, a 1938 law abolished the Chamber of Deputies and substituted for it the Chamber of Fasces and Corporations, composed of Fascist Party officials and members of the National Council of Corporations. People became members of this new chamber by virtue of their office, eliminating the need for elections. The Corporate State thus modified the basis of representation from the individual to the productive members of society. This change supposedly fulfilled the Fascist view of economic self-government and national unity that had its origins in revolutionary syndicalism and Nationalism. In practice, a PNF-business alliance ran the country.

Mobilizing the Masses
In seeking to determine the characteristics of Fascist regimes, historians emphasize mobilization of the masses in support of the government and its goals and to give

people a sense of nationalism, identity, and security. Italian Fascism provided a model for the rest of Europe with its organizations and strong symbolism. Fascists wore black shirts, used the Roman salute (outstretched arm, open palm, facing downward), adopted the ancient Roman Fasces (bundle of rods) as their symbol of discipline, and established a paramilitary militia—the squads—that beat up their enemies. According to historian Emilio Gentile, they founded a secular religion with its symbols and mythology. Fascists all over Europe followed their example.

The Fascists created organisms of mass mobilization in the 1920s, but these organisms increased in importance during the next decade as Mussolini embarked on a series of wars. The Fascists attempted to regiment the country's youths in order to create the new Fascist man and woman. The Opera Nazionale Balilla (ONB) organized boys and girls ages 6 to 21 in seven youth organizations. These young people wore uniforms, marched, and participated in common activities. To influence future intellectuals, university students were obliged to join the Gioventù Universitaria Fascista (GUF), but higher education remained relatively free from political interference despite the requirement that university professors sign loyalty oaths. The regime also substantially failed to fascistize secondary education despite a 1923 reform, but propagandized the primary schools very heavily by inculcating students with Fascist principles and overtly glorifying the Duce. The Opera Nazionale Dopolavoro (OND) rounded out the Fascist socialization network. This leisure-time organization arranged discounts for theaters and cinemas and provided vacations, tours, and sports events at reduced prices. The OND engaged millions of workers and was the regime's most successful establishment of this kind, but was of doubtful utility in making Fascists. Italian institutions served as models for similar organizations in Nazi Germany.

By the 1930s, even the Fascist Party emphasized socialization and mass mobilization, despite its retention of some of its revolutionary attributes. Fascist revolutionaries in the early, unruly PNF had caused Mussolini difficulties, and he was determined to tame them. In 1930 he reduced the PNF to a bland and unthreatening body. By the early 1930s, membership in the party was required for all activities, diluting the organization to the point that it meant very little to the average citizen. This development helps explain why the party did not come to Mussolini's aid when he fell in 1943.

Propaganda

The 1930s also witnessed the greater use of technological innovations for propaganda. The radio, favored by the regime but of slow diffusion in the 1920s, profited from the government's help during the next decade, although the number of sets still trailed far behind those in Britain, Germany, and the United States. Nonetheless, the radio carried Mussolini's speeches to all the main piazzas of Italy, and the population gathered there while loudspeakers blared out the Duce's most important speeches.

From its beginnings Italian Fascism billed itself as a movement of the youth. Another of its important characteristics was that it concentrated on mobilizing the masses. That is, citizens had to support the state actively, could not remain passive with regard to it and had actively to support its policies. These photographs illustrate a combination of the two principles. The State created a vast youth movement designed to whip up enthusiasm for Fascism and propagandize the young who represented the future of the State and the movement. The Italian Fascist youth movement served as a model for other countries during this period, especially Germany.

BIOGRAPHICAL SKETCHES

Margherita Sarfatti
"Dictator of the Figurative Arts"

Born into a comfortable Venetian Jewish family on April 8, 1883, Margherita Grassini Sarfatti was exposed to feminism and socialism while still a teenager. She published in Socialist and feminist newspapers, cofounding and writing for *La Difesa delle Lavoratrici* (Defense of Women Workers) with Anna Kuliscioff and Angelica Balabanoff, Russian émigrés who were prominent in the Italian Socialist movement. She moved to Milan, where she worked with young firebrand Benito Mussolini, then editor of the Socialist Party's daily newspaper. When Mussolini advocated Italian intervention in World War I and left the party, Sarfatti and her husband Cesare followed his lead and joined the fledgling Fascist movement.

A refined art critic, Sarfatti became art editor for Mussolini's new newspaper, *Il Popolo d'Italia* (The People of Italy). During the Duce's rise to power, she greatly influenced Mussolini's actions, and the two became lovers. Mussolini made her editor of his ideological journal, *Gerarchia* (Hierarchy), in 1921, and in 1926 she published a famous biography of Mussolini, *Dux,* for which the Duce wrote a preface. Sarfatti used her connections to write newspaper articles favorable to Mussolini that helped establish his reputation abroad, particularly in the United States. It was in the arts, however, that she exerted a paramount influence.

Sarfatti's link to the Duce as his mistress and confidante, her extensive political connections, and her artistic sophistication allowed her to mold Italian cultural life before the anti-Semitic laws were passed in 1938. Sarfatti greatly esteemed and favored modern art, which, largely because of her influence, won the regime's official sanction. Italian art of this era substantially escaped the stultifying trends that characterized the figurative arts in Soviet Russia and Nazi Germany.

Sarfatti promoted modernism in art and literature through her membership on governmental committees that determined the course of cultural affairs, by sponsoring individual painters and architects, and through the Novecento (Twentieth Century) movement. Besides Sarfatti, Novecento counted painter Mario Sironi—in addition to other former Futurists—among its adherents and published an influential journal. Novecento aimed at a revolutionary reconciling of traditional, particularly Roman, elements with international modernism in order to provide Fascist Italy with a new cultural dynamic. On February 14, 1926, at the height of Sarfatti's influence, Mussolini addressed the opening of a major Novecento exhibition and gave his views on the intimate relationship between art and politics.

In the 1930s, Sarfatti's star declined, although she continued to travel on cultural assignments to the United States and Europe. The Novecento style had set off disputes among Fascist Party officials, and by 1934 Sarfatti and the Duce were no longer lovers. She kept on writing extensively until passage of the anti-Semitic laws when the government suppressed her articles, which Sarfatti fiercely contested.

In 1939, Mussolini ordered that Sarfatti be given a passport so she could leave Italy. The "Jewish mother of Fascism" went to Argentina, then to France, and later to the United States, where she lived until World War II ended. Margherita Sarfatti then returned to Italy and continued to pursue her artistic interests until her death at her villa on Lake Como on October 30, 1961.

The cinema, a field in which the country had once excelled, languished behind foreign and especially American films, which dominated at the box office. In 1931, a new law encouraged domestic production under governmental supervision, and later the Cinecittà studios were built. These developments stimulated the film industry and set the conditions for future development, but it remained behind in its own market. Ironically, censorship seemed to have little effect, and this period was the seedtime of the postwar flowering of Italian directors. In addition, although officials discussed using film for propaganda, the movie industry made few such films. The regime preferred to use the weekly newsreel—in whose editing Mussolini personally participated—as its primary propaganda vehicle. In 1935 the press and propaganda affairs, radio, cinema, and other means of communication came under a new ministry of popular culture.

In literature and art, the regime exercised only a weak censorship and did not crack down except in cases of blatant opposition. The government never adopted an official artistic style, exercising indirect control over artists through a combination of labor unions, governmental purchases, and regional and national exhibitions. Architecture, heavily dependent on public construction projects, was most susceptible to governmental influence, but building design ranged from classical to the most modern international styles. In the art world, until the anti-Semitic campaigns of the late 1930s, Mussolini's Jewish mistress Margherita Sarfatti served as the regime's unofficial dictator of culture. Sarfatti championed modernistic trends in cultural life until she left Italy because of the racial laws.

Fascism and Women

Sarfatti's prominence illustrates the ambivalence of Fascism toward women. The Fascist outlook disdained females and femininity, assigned women a subordinate position, and emphasized a masculine life of action and danger, while women were supposed to stay home to bear and look after children.

In practice, the reality of women did not differ to a great degree from that in the democratic countries. During the 1920s, the Fascists praised women and argued for recognizing their rights and duties within the nation, as they did for men; created parallel institutions to mobilize them; and expanded maternity leave and other social security benefits. During the 1930s, the depression and the wars made the policy on this issue more congruent with the Fascist style. Since the Duce required more soldiers and a larger population to allow him to claim more territory, he encouraged women to stay home and have more babies, giving them medals if they had many children. To increase productivity and profits, the government tolerated single women working at low wages, but tried to force them into the home as they got older. Fascist propaganda discouraged viewing work or the professions as a means of liberation for women and passed legislation to curtail the number of women working in state and private offices in order to reduce the unemployment of men during the depression. Despite such measures, however, women represented over a quarter of the nation's workforce in the 1930s.

The Fascists tried to increase the birth rate through propaganda and by giving subsidies for workers who had larger families and other economic incentives similar to those taken in France. The government also imposed a tax on bachelors. The ironic result: the birth rate fell.

Ordinary Lives

In attempting to create a feeling of community, the Italian Fascists borrowed heavily from poet Gabriele D'Annunzio, who, during the occupation of Fiume in 1919, staged parades, invented bizarre cries, developed symbols, and dressed his followers in distinctive uniforms. The Duce improved upon these techniques, which the Nazis would later perfect, by haranguing crowds from the balcony of his office in the Palazzo Venezia.

In private life, the Fascists impinged on the lives of ordinary citizens the least of the three major totalitarian regimes. Aside from attending rallies, applauding the Duce's speeches, and submitting to a constant barrage of propaganda, the ordinary person found that the regime exercised little control over his or her life when compared to Nazi Germany and the USSR. The Fascists emphasized sports and exercise and compelled teenagers to work out in the piazzas on Saturdays (the *sabato fascista*). The regime pushed physical fitness in newsreels, where the Duce appeared working with a bare chest in the fields while his paunchy subordinates were put through their paces.

Although Mussolini was not as bloodthirsty as Hitler, his secret police acted brutally against his enemies abroad. In 1937 the OVRA incited a French Fascist organization to murder two of his opponents, Carlo and Nello Rosselli. Here is the body of Carlo, who had fought against the regime in the Spanish Civil War, shortly after his murder. The fact that brothers were Jews helped convince the Duce that the Jews opposed him and had a role in the institution of the anti-Semitic campaign. The murders served as the basis for Alberto Moravia's famous novel, *The Conformist*.

Overt political opponents of Mussolini could not operate in Italy and had to go into exile if they wished to participate in politics. There they were subject to surveillance by the OVRA, the Fascist secret police. OVRA operatives infiltrated exile organizations, fomented splits, and sometimes resorted to assassination. The most spectacular killings—the basis for Alberto Moravia's compelling novel *The Conformist*—occurred in France, where the Fascists engineered the murder of opponents Carlo and Nello Rosselli. In Italy, even prominent people who had opposed the Duce enjoyed relative personal freedom provided they renounced politics. The regime generally limited persecution to job discrimination and constant surveillance—with a few days in jail when Mussolini came to town. It was unwise for citizens to speak ill of the Duce in public. Mussolini's sayings appeared on the outside of buildings, and his stern image stared at students from their textbooks. The regime also attempted to change language, mandating Italian terms for foreign ones in current use (*coda di gallo* for cocktail) and the second person plural *voi* for the polite *Lei*. The regime praised a vigorous masculine lifestyle and persecuted known homosexuals, as illustrated in the film *A Special Day*. There was no official anti-Semitism in the movement.

The Anti-Semitic Laws

The Duce had compromised in order to remain in office, but in the 1930s he attempted to increase his personal power. Mussolini chafed at the king's constitutional supremacy, talked about establishing a republic, transferred potential rivals to lesser jobs, and became more nationalistic. Slogans like "Mussolini is always right" and "Believe, Obey, Fight" covered Italian buildings as his cult, *ducismo*, intensified. However, Mussolini perceived that Fascism was flagging and searched for a means of reviving its spirit. By the late 1930s, also because he had linked up with Hitler, he settled on anti-Semitism as a means of reinvigorating his movement and of strengthening the German alliance.

These factors help explain why Mussolini turned to a policy that had roots neither in Italian society nor in the Fascist movement: even if minor personages did favor anti-Semitism, they had little influence. Italian Jews numbered only about 45,000 and were well integrated into Italian society. Jewish Fascists had helped Mussolini come to power, and their numbers were proportionately greater in the Fascist movement than they were in the Italian population. Mussolini had publicly condemned and ridiculed Hitler's anti-Semitism and made Italy a refuge for German Jews. In 1937 and 1938, however, an anti-Semitic current, consisting of Fascist hierarchs who wanted to increase their influence by cementing Italian-German relations and of leftist Fascists who identified Jews variously with the bourgeoisie, liberals, Socialists, or Communists, formed in the Fascist Party. Mussolini initially refused to sanction an anti-Semitic campaign, but after May 1938, he changed his mind. Several factors seem to have motivated him: Hitler's visit to Italy that month, the existence of prominent Jewish anti-Fascists, a feeling that Italians fraternized with the local population in their African colonies and were not behaving as conquerors, and, above all, a sense that the Fascist movement was flagging and could be reinvigorated with a new goal.

In September 1938, the Fascists passed the racial laws prohibiting foreign Jews from entering Italy, banning Jews from the teaching profession, and excluding them from receiving an education in public secondary schools. More serious provisions followed in November, including a ban on intermarriage, exclusion from the army and public jobs, and a limit on Jewish economic activities. A host of confusing exceptions accompanied the laws, allowing many individuals to escape their worst effects, and concentration camps were not established.

Contrary to the Duce's expectations, a wave of disgust and passive resistance followed the enactment of the anti-Semitic legislation, despite acceptance by party hacks and some intellectuals. The Jewish community set up separate secondary schools, and state commissions continued to give the required examinations that conferred official state recognition of diplomas. Frequently, although Jews had to give up their professional licenses, employers continued to allow them to work. Many foreign Jews, who were supposed to leave within six months, remained in the country.

The laws harmed the country by provoking the emigration of prominent scientists, such as Enrico Fermi, whose wife was Jewish, and Emilio Segrè. Both men, Nobel Prize winners, and other Italian nuclear scientists did fundamental work on the development of the atomic bomb in the United States. Intellectuals in other fields immigrated to the United States, where they used their energies to turn the American government against Mussolini. The anti-Semitic campaign prompted significant segments of the population to turn against the regime, and popular rejection of the anti-Semitic campaign heralded the growing disenchantment with the regime.

In the late 1930s, internal opposition to Fascism was primarily passive. The exile movement plotted against the regime, but the Fascist secret police kept its activities in check. By 1940, however, increasing isolation from the nation marked Mussolini's Fascism.

Bibliographical Essay

There have been attempts to understand what elements make up the general phenomenon of Fascism. One of the most successful is that of Stanley G. Payne, *Fascism: Comparison and Definition* (Madison, Wis., 1980). George L. Mosse published *The Fascist Revolution: Toward A General Theory of Fascism* (New York, 1999). This book is mainly concerned with Germany but includes excellent essays on Italy and France. A controversial book that compares Italy with Germany and France is Ernst Nolte's *Three Faces of Fascism: Action* Française, *Italian Fascism, National Socialism* (New York, 1965). Roger Griffin's *The Nature of Fascism* (New York, 1993) is an examination of the phenomenon with a political science emphasis. Griffin's *Modernism and Fascism* (Basingstoke, UK, 2007) analyzes the relationship with modernization. Two books that summarize how Fascism has been interpreted include Renzo De Felice, *Interpretations of Fascism* (Cambridge, Mass., 1977), and A. James Gregor, *Interpretations of Fascism* (Morristown, N.J., 1974). Alexander De Grand, *Italian Fascism*, 3rd ed. (Lincoln, Nebr., 2000), and Alan Cassels, *Fascist Italy*, 2d ed. (Arlington Heights, Ill., 1985), are good brief treatments of the Fascist phenomenon. R. J. B. Bosworth, *The Italian Dictatorship* (New York, 1998), also focuses on interpretations.

On ideology, the best work is Emilio Gentile, *The Origins of Fascist Ideology, 1918–1925* (New York, 2005). Renzo De Felice's massive and controversial biography of

Mussolini is unavailable in English, but his brief interview, *Fascism: An Informal Introduction to Its Theory and Practice* (New Brunswick, N.J., 1976), edited by Michael Ledeen, is not to be missed. For an assessment of De Felice's impact, see the special issue of the *Italian Quarterly*, edited by Spencer M. Di Scala, *Renzo De Felice and the Problem of Italian Fascism*, 36: nos. 141–142 (Summer–Fall 1999). See also Borden W. Painter, "Renzo De Felice and the Controversy over Italian Fascism," *American Historical Review* 95, no. 2 (April 1990): 391–405. David D. Roberts, *Historicism and Fascism in Modern Italy* (Toronto, 2007) is a collection of articles by the author that examines the link between fascism and intellectuals. A. James Gregor takes the question head-on in *The Ideology of Fascism: The Rationale of Totalitarianism* (New York, 1969), and in *Italian Fascism and Developmental Dictatorship* (Princeton, N.J., 1979), and there is an excellent chapter in his *The Fascist Persuasion in Radical Politics* (Princeton, N.J., 1974). The idea of the Fascist mystique may be found in Adrian Lyttleton, ed., *Italian Fascisms from Pareto to Gentile* (New York, 1973). Important documents are published in Benito Mussolini, *Fascism: Doctrine and Institutions* (New York, 1968), while Roger Griffin's *Fascism* (New York, 1995) contains original writings. Palmiro Togliatti, *Lectures on Fascism* (New York, 1976), presents the Marxist viewpoint of the 1930s. The issue of origins is discussed in Zeev Sternhell's *The Birth of Fascist Ideology: From Cultural Rebellion to Political Revolution* (Princeton, N.J., 1994), cited in Chapter 1. A. James Gregor argues as well that fascism had a rational ideology and examines the contributions of different intellectuals to it in his *Mussolini's Intellectuals: Fascist Social and Political Thought* (Princeton, N.J., 2005).

Biographies are always important and especially so when it comes to Fascism. The best is still Ivone Kirkpatrick's *Mussolini: A Study in Power* (New York, 1964). The most noted biography in English, Denis Mack Smith's *Mussolini* (New York, 1982), has a polemical tone that reduces its value. Laura Fermi, *Mussolini* (Chicago, 1961), is readable but of little scholarly value. Paolo Monelli, *Mussolini: An Intimate Life* (New York, 1954), presents an interesting view of his personality. R. J. B. Bosworth, *Mussolini* (New York, 2002), has a section that traces his influence after his death. Peter Neville's *Mussolini* (New York, 2004) is a thorough work and Anthony L. Cardoza's *Benito Mussolini: The First Fascist* (New York, 2006) is an excellent short biograhy.

Good views of the Fascist regime may be found in the classic works of Gaetano Salvemini, an old enemy, *The Fascist Dictatorship in Italy* (New York, 1967), and *Under the Axe of Fascism* (New York, 1936). Adrian Lyttleton described the regime's consolidation in *The Seizure of Power* (New York, 1973). Philip Morgan, *Italian Fascism 1915–1945* (New York, 2004), is a concise general history. Doug Thompson, *State Control in Fascist Italy: Culture and Conformity, 1925–43* (Manchester, UK, 1991), discusses the transition from violent coercion during the early phase of fascism to nonviolent control of the country through legislation, mass organizations, and propaganda. On a similar theme, Emilio Gentile, *The Sacralization of Politics in Fascist Italy* (Cambridge, Mass., 1996), examines in detail the transformation of Fascism into a secular religion. Good treatments of how the regime mobilized the masses are Tracy Koon, *Believe, Obey, Fight: Political Socialization of Youth in Fascist Italy* (Chapel Hill, N.C., 1985), and Victoria De Grazia, *The Culture of Consent: Mass Organization of Leisure in Fascist Italy* (New York, 1981). On popular culture, consult Edward Tannenbaum's *The Fascist Experience: Italian Society and Culture, 1922–1945* (New York, 1972). The interpretation of cinema during this period has changed, thanks to Marcia Landy, who argued that the postwar cinema had its origins in the Fascist era, in *Fascism on Film* (Princeton, N.J., 1986), and to James Hay, *Popular Film Culture in Fascist Italy* (Bloomington, Ind., 1987), who sees a realistic culture in the films of the period. A book that argues that Italian cinema of this period reveals a fundamentally conservative view toward its role is Marga Cottino-Jones, *Women Desire, and Power in Italian Cinema* (New York, 2010). A good idea of radio's role can be gleaned from Philip Cannistraro, "The Radio in Fascist Italy," *Journal of European Studies* II, 2 (June 1972): 127–54. A excellent work on economics is the brief but incisive *Italian Fascism* (Harmondsworth, UK, 1974) by Giampiero Carocci. Fascist relationships with industry are explored by Roland Sarti, *Fascism and the Industrial Leadership in Italy, 1919–1940* (Berkeley, Calif., 1971). The complexity of censorship during the regime is analyzed by George Talbot, *Censorship in Fascist Italy, 1922–43* (New York, 2007).

The Corporate State is an issue that deserves greater attention but has been neglected; Carl T. Schmidt's *The Corporate State in Action* (New York, 1973), originally published in 1939, is now inadequate. The Fascist Party also has not received much attention in English, the only full-length study being Dante Germino's *The Italian Fascist Party in Power* (Minneapolis, Minn., 1959). On the idea of spreading Fascist doctrine and its implications, there is Michael Ledeen, *Universal Fascism: The Theory and Practice of the Fascist International, 1928–1936* (New York, 1972).

Fascism's view toward women received attention in Alexander De Grand, "Women under Italian Fascism," *The Historical Journal* 19 (1976): 647–88; Philip Cannistraro and Brian Sullivan, *Il Duce's Other Woman* (New York, 1993), a biography of Margherita Sarfatti and her influence on culture; Victoria De Grazia, *How Fascism Ruled Women: Italy, 1922–1945* (Berkeley, Calif., 1992); and Perry R. Willson, *The Clockwork Factory: Women and Work in Fascist Italy* (New York, 1994). Willson also published *Peasant Women and Politics in Fascist Italy: The Massaie Rurali Section of the PNF* (New York, 2002). See also Gigliola Gori, *Female Bodies and Italian Fascism: Submissive Women and Strong Mothers* (London, 2004). The term "The Jewish mother of Fascism," referring to Sarfatti, is the title of an article published in the Israeli newspaper *Ha'aretz* on June 17, 2008.

The relationship with the church is set in a wider context by Richard A. Webster, *The Cross and the Fasces* (Stanford, Calif., 1960). Two other books on the same important theme are J. F. Pollard, *The Vatican and Italian Fascism, 1929–1932* (Cambridge, UK, 1985), and, on the international reaction to the Lateran Accords, P. Kent, *The Pope and the Duce* (London, 1981). John F. Pollard, *The Vatican and Italian Fascism,1929–1932: A Study in Conflict* (New York, 2005), describes the relationship between the two after the signature of the Lateran Accords.

On the complicated issue of Fascism and the Jews, see Meir Michaelis, *Mussolini and the Jews: German-Italian Relations and the Jewish Question in Italy, 1922–1945* (Oxford, UK, 1978). A comparative view is emphasized in Ivo Herzer, ed., *The Italian Refuge* (Washington, D.C., 1989). Aaron Gilette's *Racial Theories in Fascist Italy* (New York, 2002) discusses early anti-Semitism and argues that racial theories did not reinvigorate the movement. Alexander Stille, *Benevolence and Betrayal* (New York, 2003), discusses the histories and fate of five Jewish families during the period. Michele Sarfatti takes a more revisionist, negative view about the Italian record, but in this author's opinion, has not proved his case. His book, originally in Italian, was translated as *The Jews in Mussolini's Italy: From Equality to Persecution* (Madison, Wis., 2006).

CHAPTER 13

◢◣

Stalin's Communism

CHAPTER OUTLINE
Communist Ideology • Communist Practice

BIOGRAPHICAL SKETCHES
Nikolai Ivanovich Bukharin, Communist Theoretician • Alexandra
Mikhaylovna Kollontai, "Red Rose of the Revolution"

Although the New Economic Policy (NEP) had yielded important practical results and had strong supporters, as pointed out in Chapter 9, by 1929 the stage was set for its termination. By the end of the decade, the Soviet Union had reached an impasse between Bolshevik ideology and the bourgeois practices that the NEP represented. Stalin had decided to go full-speed ahead to build communism and had begun his drive for absolute power, and the debate over the NEP became an important part of his campaign. Whether Stalin perverted Lenin's ideas and methods in constructing his dictatorship or was his worthy successor is still debated, but his rule embodied communism for the world from then on.

COMMUNIST IDEOLOGY

Unlike Italian Fascism, where practice preceded a coherent ideological statement, Soviet Communism claimed a long ideological pedigree and Lenin as Marx's successor.

Lenin's Concept of the Party
The Bolshevik Party's authoritarianism began with Lenin and culminated with Stalin. Lenin justified violence against the bourgeoisie and extended the principle to dissidents in 1921 when he put down internal party opposition and a mutiny of sailors at the Kronstadt naval base. Lenin contended that allowing the formation of factions within communism threatened party unity. He began with the

premise that, as the sole party of the working class, the Bolsheviks must educate the advance guard of the proletariat and organize the working masses. Consequently, Lenin attacked both the right and the left wings of Bolshevism, as Stalin would in the future.

Lenin criticized the right wing by contending that the revolutionary victory had deprived the unions of their primary task of defending the workers from capitalist exploitation. He denounced the leftist revolutionaries in *"Left Wing" Communism: An Infantile Disorder,* drafted in April 1920, because they objected to a centralized party structure. A truly revolutionary party delegated leadership to a few authoritative persons, he declared. The Bolsheviks had to be secure at the helm of the movement so it could destroy capitalism and attain recognition of the Soviet system as the revolutionary model for all countries. Lenin believed that allowing the formation of political currents in the party of the proletariat meant permitting backward groups of workers to cave in to the wiles of false Socialists who were planning to destroy communism.

Party congresses held in April 1920 and March 1921 debated these principles. With the defeat of capitalist intervention against the revolution (the Civil War), the Bolshevik Party had as its major tasks destroying the old social order, creating a new one, and building a Socialist state by means of an iron discipline. The party could not tolerate internal dissension; it could discuss policy, but then unanimity must follow because factions threatened unity.

Thus Lenin championed a single unified party in which minorities having different viewpoints would either conform or be silenced because party discipline, justified by the working class's superior interests, took precedence over freedom of expression. Lenin's concept of the party guided Communist Party organization and particularly inspired Stalin. (The older term *Bolshevik* gradually gave way to the more cosmopolitan *Communist* after the regime consolidated itself and began to export the revolution.) The Executive Committee of the Communist Party possessed the instruments to control central Soviet activities, and public authorities and party institutions absorbed state institutions. Within the Executive Committee, a political office (the Politburo) directed political affairs, but the party's command center was the Secretariat, the true decision-making organ of the Executive Committee and the Politburo. The Communist Party's combined political, economic, and social functions allowed it to impose its authority over every state institution and regulate the lives of its citizens. This centralized organization helped communism survive in Russia.

Josef Stalin headed the Workers' and Peasants' Inspection Commission, the party's most powerful control organism, and gradually accumulated other functions. As Stalin concentrated important tasks in his hands, his colleagues worried that he was gaining too much power. Lenin, however, did not act against Stalin and demurred only after he was too sick to have much influence.

Stalinism

Stalin's control of different party organs overwhelmed the strong tendencies toward collective leadership within early Bolshevism and allowed him to win the struggle for power by 1929. After Lenin's death on January 21, 1924, a committee that included Stalin succeeded him. Stalin presented himself as the dead leader's ideological successor in two works, *Foundations of Leninism* (1924) and *Problems of Leninism* (1926). In these books, Stalin defended Lenin's concept of party hegemony, condemning factions because they could not oppose an organization (the Communist Party) that personified the dictatorship of the proletariat and downplayed the possibility that party leaders might seize power with his argument that the Communist Party could guide the proletariat only by delegating the task of destroying world capitalism to some of its leaders.

Stalin's views set the stage for his absolute power and the internal purges of the 1930s, which he believed were nothing less than a necessary law of development for the prevention of party deviations. In sum, Stalin decreed the infallibility of the party, which had proved its worth by successfully making the revolution. He claimed for himself the right to liquidate all opposition because it endangered the social gains achieved by the working class.

Socialism in One Country

Stalin undoubtedly appears as a true Bolshevik, sincerely committed to implementing what he conceived as socialism; but his thinking also included a crucial international dimension. Concerned with the final victory of communism, Stalin believed that the capitalist countries would strike at the USSR when the opportunity arose. In the 1920s, he interpreted Russia's isolation as encirclement by the capitalist powers. He claimed that to defend the Communist revolution, Socialist encirclement had to replace capitalist encirclement. This concept meant that the nations surrounding the USSR must be transformed into Socialist countries, become Soviet allies, and dedicate their resources to protecting the Socialist fatherland, the USSR. Stalin viewed world revolution—spontaneous revolutions occurring in advanced capitalist countries because of industrialization—in neither traditional Marxist nor Leninist terms but in strictly territorial terms. Marx had argued that socialism grew out of increasing industrialization, and Lenin had expected that communism would quickly spread to the West. When successful Communist revolutions did not occur in the advanced Western countries, Soviet leaders concentrated on the need to defend communism in the USSR. Stalin hoped to do so by gaining control of neighboring countries. This view has produced the interpretation that Stalin viewed himself as both a true Bolshevik *and* as a classical Russian statesman: a National Bolshevik.

A consequence of this reasoning was the need to strengthen the USSR's power and influence. Russia had two important advantages in achieving this goal: The countries surrounding it were small and weak, and in the Western democracies, strong Communist parties favored close collaboration with the Socialist Fatherland. Stalin counted on Soviet diplomacy and the Third International's dominance of foreign Communist parties to exploit the differences among capitalist countries and to foster war among them. Such conflicts would exhaust capitalist nations and provide the USSR with opportunities for a revolutionary march into bordering areas. However, during the late 1920s and 1930s, Stalin had bungled events in Germany, and Hitler came to power. He then shifted his attitude toward France, encouraged the Popular Front, and sought a French alliance. These events demonstrated the flexibility on strategy that Stalin would demonstrate on numerous occasions in the future.

Agricultural Collectivization

Stalin's thesis had fundamental implications for Soviet domestic policy. Because Stalin assumed that war with the capitalist countries was unavoidable, the USSR had to expand its industrial capacity—vital for rearmament and the implementation of socialism; preparing for a major conflict with the capitalist powers required the creation of an immense, war-oriented heavy industry. This policy required the USSR's rapid transmutation from an importer of industrial products into a major world producer of heavy industrial goods. Without the country's transformation, both it and the revolution would be overwhelmed. This problem posed the urgent question of where the resources would come from to accomplish this ambitious goal. Because the USSR was a Communist country shunned by the capitalist industrial nations, it had to rely most heavily on its own assets.

At this point, Stalin, the Bolshevik, and Stalin, the Russian statesman, merged. He advocated rapid agricultural collectivization as a means of gathering wealth for the intensive industrialization effort he believed essential for the survival of communism, to guarantee grain deliveries at low prices, and to encourage the emigration of labor to the urban areas where industrialization would occur. Moreover, it made sense to combine the push for industrialization with a new offensive to implement socialism when Communist leaders decided to end the NEP that had represented a retreat for the Revolution. Already in the 1920s, Stalin had noted that merely encouraging the development of cooperatives in the countryside did not create socialism, and he favored their implantation with the help of peasant allies. When he referred to cooperatives, Stalin did not mean consumer or credit cooperatives favored by moderate Bolsheviks, but collectivization, which meant a radical departure from the NEP. Because the resistance of peasant landowners to collectivization would be tremendous, the state had to use force to implement it.

BIOGRAPHICAL SKETCHES

Nikolai Ivanovich Bukharin
Communist Theoretician

Probably the most attractive, humane, and flexible of the "Old Bolsheviks," Nikolai Bukharin was born in Moscow on October 9, 1888, the son of a schoolteacher. Bukharin entered political life early as an opponent of the tsarist regime. In 1906, still a university student, he joined the Russian Social Democratic Party's Bolshevik faction, rising to head the Moscow Bolshevik organization in 1908. In 1911 he left the country for the United States after being arrested for his political activity. Bukharin traveled to the West Coast; eventually, he settled in New York City, where he edited the revolutionary newspaper, *Novy Mir* in 1916. He established himself as a leading theoretician and returned to Europe to work on the party newspaper *Pravda* with Lenin. In August 1917, Bukharin was back in

Russia and later participated in the Bolshevik revolution. When Lenin advocated signing a separate peace with the Germans to end Russia's involvement in World War I, Bukharin disagreed and unsuccessfully sought to transform the conflict into a worldwide revolutionary war.

Before Stalin achieved absolute power, policy debates in the Bolshevik camp were common, without persons necessarily losing their influence or their lives because of their opposition to the ideas of other leaders. Although Lenin's line won out, Bukharin remained his good friend and a prominent member of the Bolshevik inner circle, holding important positions. He edited *Pravda* from 1918 until 1929 and *Bolshevik,* the party journal, between 1924 and 1929. Bukharin became a full member of the Politburo in 1924 and chair of the Communist International (Comintern) in 1926. During this period, he also published a number of major works, including *Economy of the Transitional Period* (1920), *The ABC of Communism* (1921), and *The Theory of Historical Materialism* (1921).

In the years following Lenin's death in 1924, a struggle occurred among the Bolsheviks for power that led to Stalin's supremacy. Because of the economic and social devastation caused by civil war and the attempt to impose communism in Russia, Lenin initiated the NEP. This policy allowed the economy to recover, but it delayed the implementation of communism. An ideological debate on whether to modify or end the NEP was part of the fight. Bukharin advocated gradual rather than rapid collectivization and industrialization, opposing Stalin, who favored the speedy accomplishment of both. The battle over this question and others ended in Stalin's triumph by 1929.

The end had begun for Bukharin. Accused of heading the "right deviation" faction, Bukharin lost his posts on the Politburo and the Central Committee and was expelled from the party. In 1934 he briefly edited another party newspaper, *Izvestia,* but was dismissed. Arrested in January 1937, Bukharin was a major victim in a show trial, known as the Trial of the Twenty-One, in March 1938. Accused of scheming to overthrow the state, Bukharin "confessed" and was shot on March 13, 1938.

The government also persecuted Bukharin's young wife Anna Larina. Arrested after her husband's trial, she spent twenty years in a Siberian labor camp but remained dedicated to her husband's memory. After her release, she worked to rehabilitate his reputation. She succeeded in 1988, when, under Mikhail Gorbachev, the Soviets sought to demonstrate that there was an alternate communism to Stalin's brand. The Soviets rehabilitated Bukharin and posthumously restored his party membership. In addition, the opening of Stalin's own archives revealed philosophical writings by Bukharin, poetry, and an autobiographical novel, *How It All Began,* published in 1994. Larina told her story and that of Bukharin in an award-winning 2001 documentary, *This I Cannot Forget.*

In 1926, Stalin declared: "Building socialism in the USSR means overcoming our own Soviet bourgeoisie by our forces in the course of a struggle." This struggle would occur primarily against the upper and middle strata of the peasantry, but it would transform the USSR into a world industrial power capable of confronting the capitalist countries, implement socialism, save the country, and create the premise for Soviet expansionism. By combining collectivization in agriculture with industrialization, Stalin linked Communist principles and economic development. He allied Lenin and Peter the Great.

COMMUNIST PRACTICE

The crisis of the NEP at the end of the 1920s provided Stalin with the opportunity to implement communism, industrialize the country, and increase his personal power. Stalin's alliance with Bukharin broke down in 1928 and he defeated Bukharin between February and April 1929, giving him control of the USSR.

Collectivization

Collectivization—the expropriation of peasants, the destruction of private property, and the creation of collective farms over which the state had complete control—set the stage for rapid industrialization. Collectivization had been encouraged earlier, but by 1928 collective farms had attracted only about 1 percent of the rural population. Most important, NEP had created a large reservoir of "middle" peasants who strongly resisted collectivization.

Given these facts, Stalin moved cautiously to create the political, psychological, and ideological preconditions for collectivization. Already in 1926 and 1927, Stalin exploited friction in foreign policy to argue that the USSR was in imminent threat of attack from the capitalists surrounding it. The next year witnessed the first show trial on a favorite theme: Russian counterrevolutionaries in league with foreign and counterrevolutionary capitalists in a conspiracy to wreck the Soviet economy. Then came the drastically reduced ability of state grain-purchasing agencies to purchase grain after the 1927–28 harvest at the desired prices. The government responded by closing the grain markets and a campaign of coercion—searches, confiscation of grain, and arrests—was followed by food rationing in February 1929. The peasants resisted, and disorders took place. The party moderates suggested resolving the conflict by offering higher prices, but Stalin argued that the needs of industrialization precluded any price increases, that the problem was not economic, and that the real issue was kulak opposition to the Soviet regime; the solution to this political opposition was a class war.

Given the importance of dogma in the Soviet context, Stalin justified his position from an ideological standpoint by recalling Lenin's description of the peasants as a vacillating class that would flock to collectivization when educated about its benefits and by concluding that peasant irresolution would end when the state demonstrated that only dire misfortune awaited them outside collectivization.

Stalin's collectivization campaign started in November 1929 with an article in the party newspaper *Pravda*. According to Stalin, Russian peasants had rushed to collectivization, opening a new historical chapter. If this accelerated collectivization continued, the USSR would become one of the world's largest grain producers. Combined with a five-year plan for industry, this development would rapidly produce a Socialist society. In fact, collectivization combined with swift industrialization would constitute a second revolution, from above.

Stalin's article depicted the USSR as being at a crossroads in the establishment of socialism, but it misrepresented reality. According to Stalin, collectivization had been so successful that the time for a final push had arrived. In reality, the state would achieve this aim by defining *kulak* (the supposedly well-off peasant) in such a manner that anyone would qualify and by treating the kulak in such a brutal fashion that no one would want to be considered one. Stalin's henchman and future foreign minister Vyacheslav Molotov put the matter succinctly: "We must deal the kulak such a blow that the middle peasant will snap to attention before us." By making an example of the kulak and his family of what would happen if anyone resisted, Stalin hoped to terrorize the peasants into accepting collectivization.

The subsequent development of the campaign seems to confirm this view. At the beginning the definition of *kulak* was ambiguous. The Communists applied the term to all who made the least objection to collectivization and proceeded to expropriate their property and to punish them. A commission that was charged with drawing up specific plans on how to collectivize the peasants originally suggested allowing the kulaks to join collectives and retain some small animals under certain restricted conditions, but Stalin overruled the idea. Stalin simply slated the kulaks for elimination as a class. Consequently, the state did not permit them access to collective farms under any circumstances, transferred ownership of their property to the collectives, and deported them and their families to distant areas under abominable conditions.

Besides socialism, the state aimed to achieve specific economic goals through confiscation and deportations. Slaughtering farm animals was a prime means of resisting collectivization, so harsh punishments and complete confiscation would prevent the killing of livestock and provide essential capital for the collectives. Expropriation also contributed to the enormous sums the USSR allocated to pay foreign technicians, attracted as a result of the lack of work in the West.

Stalin initiated the drive for collectivization because of his desire to institute Communism after the NEP had stalled the drive to do so, in his opinion, and to increase production. Collectivization became policy in 1929, and although many families were forced into collectives, resistance remained strong. This somewhat idyllic picture shows peasants having lunch together on a collective farm near Kiev in August 1936.

Furthermore, the five-year plan, which was adopted at the same time, mandated the building of large industrial plants. In order to protect the new factories from possible foreign invasion—in addition to industrializing different parts of the country—the state located them away from the western borders in undesirable areas. This wisdom of this policy was confirmed during World War II, but the sites attracted few volunteer workers and increased the demand for forced labor.

By the beginning of 1930, about half the USSR's families had been forced into collectives, which were required to hand over specific amounts of crops to the state (about 40 percent) and to accept low payments that had to be split among the members according to the work they did. Resistance became widespread. In January 1930, the Soviet secret police reported 402 mass demonstrations of peasants against collectivization and dekulakization and 1,048 in February and 6,528 in March. These uprisings caused agricultural production to nosedive and induced Stalin to backtrack. In March Stalin made some concessions to the peasants, such as allowing them to have individual garden plots. According to Stalin, the Communists implemented these changes because they were "Dizzy from Success," as expressed in the famous title of one of his articles. This pause in collectivization reduced the number of revolts, but the secret police noted that 2.5 million peasants participated in 14,000 revolts during the year. The peasants demanded that their property and that of the kulaks be restored, that churches be reopened, that deportees be allowed to return home, and even that the Bolsheviks give up power. The ones who suffered the most in these battles with the state were the women, whom the peasants sent ahead in the front lines in the vain hope of moderating the reaction of the police.

Having come so far, however, Stalin had little choice but to press ahead with his campaign after a brief interlude. The deportation of large numbers of peasants to remote regions where new factories were being built—and to other inhospitable areas with important raw materials—provided a large labor reserve. These unfortunate people did the most strenuous physical work at subsistence wages under police supervision, making a major contribution to the rapid industrialization of the Soviet Union. Besides peasants who served as unskilled labor, the government also arrested engineers and technicians who had been educated before the revolution, tried them, and sentenced them to work in the camps. The inmate population swelled from an estimated 30,000 in 1928 to approximately 2 million in 1931 and had to be organized under a separate Chief Administration of Corrective Labor Camps (GULAG), grippingly described by writer Alexander Solzhenitsyn. The inmates built roads, canals, and railroads and mined coal, gold, and other essential raw materials. Because prisoners had their sentences prolonged upon completion or otherwise remained within the camps' orbits, the camps were a means of systematizing vast amounts of slave labor. Combined with the government's imposition of an internal passport system, the arrangement was a Soviet version of serfdom that peasants called the "second serfdom."

Estimates of the number of people who were displaced during collectivization run to about 7 million, with half them being deported to labor camps or exile colonies in Siberia and other inhospitable areas. In the winter of 1932–33, the confusion and disruption of dekulakization and forced collectivization

This photograph shows the dark side of collectivization. Stalin ordered the expropriation of the "wealthy" peasants, the Kulaks, and their forcible integration into the collectives. A massive government campaign murdered or put them into forced labor camps after they resisted and hid their meager possessions. Here members of the Communist Youth are digging up bags of grain that Kulaks hid in a cemetery near Odessa.

precipitated a widespread famine, particularly in the grain-producing regions, such as the Ukraine, where estimates run to 3 million deaths in 1933. The peasants were convinced that the government caused the famine because they resisted collectivization, but from the government's viewpoint, the operation succeeded. By 1937, 93 percent of the households had been collectivized, the state had gained control over grain production and distribution, and a steady, low-cost supply of grain to industrial workers was assured.

Collectivization was not a spontaneous movement but a party and police-directed operation, with the cooperation of city dwellers, against rural Russia. Despite its efforts, the state failed to enlist substantial support from poor peasants, so shocked by the brutality that many did not participate in the expropriations.

The Five-Year Plan and the Personality Cult

The five-year plan to convert the USSR from an agricultural into a great industrial power was part and parcel of the collectivization and socialization effort. Formally adopted in April 1929, the plan called for an annual increase in industrial output of 20 percent. Stalin duly proclaimed the great success of the five-year plan in four years and implemented others. Indeed, if one looks at the bottom line, the USSR created industries that had hardly existed before, acquiring a substantial capacity to produce automobiles, aircraft, tractors and other agricultural machinery, textiles, and iron. It vaulted from a trailing to a leading position in coal and petroleum production. Total national output attributable to industry rose from 48 percent to 70 percent of the total between 1928 and 1932. This swift buildup of Soviet heavy industry permitted the doubling of the Soviet armed forces in less than ten years and made the USSR better able to resist Nazi Germany in 1941. Combined with the results of later five-year plans, the USSR increased its industrial production up to six times and eventually became the world's second-largest industrial power, behind the United States. At a time when the depression in the West decreased production and caused massive unemployment, the Soviet Union increased its industrial output and imported labor.

When observed closely, however, the five-year plan had wide implications beyond the numbers that are cited. Constant shifts in the production goals of heavy industry caused disruption and inefficiency in supplies and the production of materials necessary to meet those aims. Western economists have maintained that the Soviets could have accomplished similar impressive results without the millions of deaths or labor camps. Nor can it be argued that collectivization and the five-year plan furthered socialism, even according to Stalin's doubtful definition. Despite regimentation of the peasants in collective farms, by the end of the 1930s, Soviet society found itself more stratified than before, and with a depressed standard of living. Most of the population was overworked and hungry most of the time. Fifteen million persons lacked shelter. Peasants could be shot if they stole even insignificant amounts of grain from the collectives to help feed their children. The starving children of deported kulaks roamed the villages, with peasants afraid or unable to help them and with the state exploiting them as extra-cheap labor. At the same time, functionaries received important privileges from the government that permitted them to live relatively comfortably and distinguished them from ordinary people, with higher-level functionaries enjoying greater privileges.

This was only one area in which Socialist egalitarianism suffered a setback. Stalin reestablished ranks throughout Soviet society, replacing persons who had been purged and establishing a new Soviet citizenry that was completely committed to him. Stalin publicly glorified workers who produced more than their quotas or set new records by intensifying their pay differentials and by officially recognizing workers, such as Alexei Stakhanov, a coal miner who exceeded his quota by 1,400 percent. Stakhanov's example led to contests in which workers tried to outperform their quotas, which led to higher quotas that they resented. Stalin reestablished an aristocracy of merit through various orders—the Order of Lenin for special merit in Socialist construction, the Order of the Red Star for distinction in the defense sector, and the Red Banner of Labor. He reinstated officer ranks and insignia in the armed forces and uniforms for schoolchildren. The rewards included special privileges, such as lower rents, special consideration for the children of awardees in admission to schools, and free transportation on streetcars. Stalin promoted unknowns and young people and insisted on opening up careers to nonparty members on a par with party loyalists. The regime supported higher education to graduate technicians for industrialization, tripling the number of students and doubling those of working-class origins. In extending opportunities to all levels

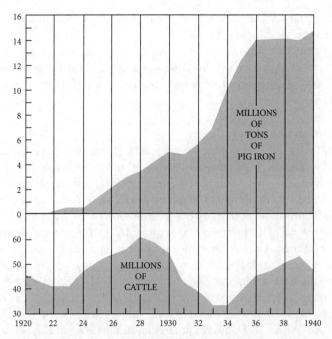

This chart illustrates how agriculture was made to serve the interests of industrialization during the Communist regime. The revolution, disorganization, and the civil war explain why Russia produced almost no pig iron in 1920. By the end of the decade, production had risen to pre-1914 levels, while the number of cattle grew significantly under the NEP. During collectivization, this number fell disastrously at the same time that pig iron production grew tremendously. By 1940, Russia produced more pig iron than Germany, Britain, or France. By the same year, however, numbers of cattle had risen only to the level of 1920.

This photograph illustrates the tremendous effort the USSR made during the Five-Year Plan to catch up to the West. Industrial production and unquestioning loyalty to Stalin combined with the constant threat of an attack from the capitalist world, which Stalin inflated, produced the brutal suppression of all possible enemies. They were the major instruments the Soviet dictator used to maintain his power. This is a picture of a Soviet metal plant in 1930.

of Soviet society, Stalin returned to the notion of a service nobility that had existed in prerevolutionary Russia.

Stalin's modifications made the state supreme. The state grew enormously by absorbing private property, building monumental new projects, multiplying central planning organs, and increasing centralization. High state functionaries constituted a new Soviet elite.

A Revolution in Culture

Rounding out these developments, a cultural revolution purged intellectuals and attacked historical figures whom Stalin did not believe fit in with his current thinking in an area—no matter how indirectly. Historical interpretation depended on what Stalin was thinking at the moment, and he took full advantage of cultural trends and authors for his own benefit. In the late 1920s and early 1930s, he favored leftist cultural movements, as represented by the Russian Association of Proletarian Writers, because he wanted to combat the right. In 1932, he dissolved the organization when his policy changed and set up a new writers' union that was charged with advocating the Soviet cause. In 1931, Maxim Gorky, Russia's greatest living writer, returned to live in Russia. Stalin celebrated him but, when the purges began, put him under virtual house arrest to prevent him from speaking out. When Gorky died in June 1936, rumors swirled that Stalin had him killed. From the mid-1930s, Soviet culture became decidedly conservative, with the state imposing Socialist realism in art, promoting the revival of traditional Russian folk culture, and slowing the campaign against religion. Stalin's supporters oversaw the rewriting of Bolshevik history to glorify his role, Cossacks sang traditional melodies for him in theaters, and the state printed his books in millions of copies.

The Bolshevik revolution had held out the promise of liberation for women, an ideal that faded under Stalin's rule. Few women were among the "new men" that Stalin groomed to replace the previous generation of leaders. Ideas of sexual freedom and free love, best represented by Alexandra Kollontai, evaporated. Communist theory held that the bourgeois family subjugated women, so in theory this family would disappear and the state would raise children, thus liberating women. In practice, it proved impossible to remove children from the family. Despite the Bolshevik conception of marriage as confining and bourgeois, a 1920s survey indicated that more than 90 percent of women believed in love and marriage instead of free sex, as did more than 80 percent of men. The disruptions and hardships caused by the revolution made both men and women less interested in free love and longing for traditional relationships.

This attitude was probably a reaction to the freedom in sexual matters that followed the revolution, when young Communists avoided even mentioning the word *love*, when marriage and family were considered restrictive, and collective love was thought of as revolutionary. However, this attitude frequently meant leaving women alone to raise children because the men left for other partners as soon as the women became pregnant and looked upon by men as finished. In short, men looked upon sex as a natural urge that women should fulfill.

BIOGRAPHICAL SKETCHES

Alexandra Mikhaylovna Kollontai
"Red Rose of the Revolution"

Born the daughter of a tsarist general, probably in April 1872, Alexandra Kollontai became widely known for her feminism and her endorsement of the widest possible sexual experiences for women. She participated in the Bolshevik Revolution with Lenin, became the first Soviet woman minister, and died a distinguished diplomat.

Rebellious and drawn to politics during her early teens, Alexandra Mikhaylovna Donontovich married her cousin at age 16, but the couple soon separated. She attended the University of Zurich, where she studied political science. Already attracted to socialism, on her return to Russia she actively participated in the movement, organizing workers and women. In 1908, the government exiled her for criticizing its Finnish policies. Abroad she continued her Socialist activities in several countries, leading strikes in Paris, organizing coal miners in Belgium, lecturing in Bologna, participating in political fights in Finland, and writing books on economic and social issues. In Switzerland she plotted with other Russian revolutionaries to overthrow their government. She also became a leading feminist who was concerned with society's proper recognition of motherhood.

When World War I broke out, she traveled extensively throughout Europe working for peace. In 1916, she visited eighty-one cities in the United States and lectured on socialism and pacifism. With the fall of the tsar in 1917, she returned to Russia, where the Kerensky government imprisoned her. Released, she won election to the Bolshevik Central Committee. On November 10, 1917, with her appointment as commissar (minister) of welfare, she became the first woman to hold cabinet rank. During her tenure, which ended on March 24, 1918, she helped write much of the legislation that regulated the status of women.

A well-known advocate of free love and the author of several famous books on the relationship between the sexes, Kollontai became the subject of many anecdotes. According to one of them, Kollontai had a passionate affair with a Bolshevik naval hero, during which they forgot about the revolution and went off to the Crimea. The Central Committee judged this action harshly, and its members demanded their execution. Lenin rose to speak and commented that death would be too good for them. He presented a motion condemning the lovers to faithfulness to each other for five years. The Central Committee, not known for its sense of humor, broke into laughter and dropped the matter, but Kollontai held this incident against Lenin well into the future.

In late 1922, Kollontai embarked on a distinguished diplomatic career. Named plenipotentiary representative to Norway in 1923, she became minister to that country when it recognized the Soviet Union in 1924. The appointment made her the world's first accredited woman envoy and aroused strong enthusiasm among women. Two years later, she became ambassador to Mexico, but the Americans refused to let her pass through the United States because they considered her a revolutionary. The Mexicans gossiped about her past loves and her supposedly fabulous jewelry collection. Kollontai returned to the more hospitable Norway after she suffered incidents of official disrespect. In 1930, she became minister to

continued

continued

Sweden, a country that had imprisoned her sixteen years earlier, with the Swedes graciously revoking the order exiling her. In 1943, she became Soviet ambassador to that country until she retired because of ill health two years later. During her tenure in Sweden, she conducted negotiations with the Finns that resulted in the end of the Russo-Finnish war in 1940. Rumor had it that she had negotiated to end the conflict between Russia and Nazi Germany, but she denied the allegation. Diplomats considered her one of the most brilliant practitioners of their profession and credited her with being "the diplomatic star of the Bolshevik world."

Alexandra Kollontai died on March 9, 1952.

Concerning divorce, a major demand of European leftists, a December 1917 decree permitted dissolution of the marriage bond for incompatibility if only one spouse requested it from the court—making Soviet Russia the first country to do so. The Bolsheviks also adopted advanced legislation on abortion; although they did not initially legalize it, they attempted to remedy the dangerous conditions under which abortions were performed. In 1920, legislation provided free abortions on demand if done by doctors in hospitals.

Stalin reversed this relative freedom in social relationships. In 1936, the government banned abortion as mentally and physically harmful to women and took measures to strengthen family life, including making divorce more difficult. A switch occurred from sexual freedom to a conservative policy with the banning of contraception and sex education. Women could not get safe abortions and resorted to illegal ones at the risk of their lives. Kollantai had already fallen out with the revolution, and Stalin had the adherents of her movement executed, although he found it inconvenient to eliminate Kollantai herself.

Leninist Antecedents

With regard to the initially tolerant cultural policy of the Bolshevik revolution, already under Lenin Bolshevik ideology favored state domination of cultural life. Because Marxists considered culture a manifestation of economics in which art reflected the social status of the artist, they had assumed that destruction of the bourgeoisie would produce revolutionary changes in culture. But this assumption raised the question of exactly how much freedom an artist should have, given the Bolshevik view that with the changes in property relations, mechanized collectivism would replace individualism. Communist theory thus eventually forced intellectuals to work within the guidelines established by the new ruling class and placed political constraints on them that suffocated the freedom that characterized the revolution's early years.

Leading this development, Lenin established the Commissariat of Enlightenment (*Narkompros*) that, with its affiliated Proletarian Cultural (*Proletkult*) movement, blanketed the Soviet countryside with its local organizations. Despite his respect for earlier culture, Lenin feared that the bourgeoisie could use its cultural advantages against the workers and considered culture a propaganda weapon to be used against the bourgeoisie. His relatively relaxed Narkompros commissar, Anatoli Lunarcharskii, agreed and implemented the censorship that Lenin advocated. The artistic world quickly turned against the Bolsheviks, who were supported by novelist Maxim Gorky and the Russian Futurists and supported by party hacks. The Bolsheviks liquidated the daily and periodical press and assumed control of book publishing. In June 1922, a newly established cultural censorship office began bringing all the arts under its wing and arresting and exiling intellectuals it considered disgruntled or unorthodox. The regime also banned the importation of suspect foreign literature and newspapers and intensified its control of the schools and universities.

The Communists tried to win support through extensive use of the Agit-prop Theater. Actors traveled to the smallest towns and produced plays out of trains, streetcars, and trucks. The plays dealt with simplistic themes and featured stereotyped characters representing pure good or pure evil, as determined by their social status, their relationship with the regime, and their place in the Soviet ideological scheme. The audiences emotionally expressed their hatred for their enemies, frequently becoming uncontrollable.

As in Fascist Italy, the regime attempted to change language usage. Russians greeted each other as Comrade, avoided discredited words, invented euphemisms to signify arrest or execution, and showed a penchant for acronyms. As in other totalitarian countries, they used the schools to indoctrinate the young and encouraged students to rebel against the politically unreliable faculty. The government created youth organizations, such as the Pioneers, which included children younger than fifteen who could graduate into the Union of Communist Youth (*Komsomol*), which had a more overtly political and propagandistic function than did the Pioneers. Because ideology took precedence in the educational field, however, the Soviets did not achieve their goal of bringing universal literacy and education to Russia. Communist ideas on eliminating the family and the dislocation of Russian society contributed to the millions of homeless children who gathered in gangs and roamed the country rather than going to school. By the end of the 1920s, the literacy rate did not rise appreciably compared with tsarism's last years. In higher education, Soviet policy on affording the poor an equal opportunity changed because the need for more engineers and technicians for industrialization favored the heirs of the middle class; the number of women attending universities dropped as well, and ideology conditioned science.

Stalinism and Science

Stalin's word reigned in science as well as society at a time when science made spectacular advances. Hitler divided science into "Jewish" and "German," while Stalin considered it either "capitalist" or "proletarian." The renowned Russian physicist George Gamow wrote: "It became a crime for Russian scientists to 'fraternize' with scientists of the capitalistic countries, and those Russian scientists who were going abroad were supposed to learn the 'secrets' of capitalistic science without revealing the 'secrets' of proletarian science."

In his memoirs, Gamow tells how the Physico-Mathematical Institute of the Soviet Academy of Sciences set up a "jury of machine shop stewards" to judge physicists guilty of defending Einstein's relativity theory, condemning them to harsh punishments. Eventually the state prohibited scientists from traveling abroad, depriving them of the contact that is the lifeblood of scientific progress. It prevented the talented physicist Peter Kapitza from returning to Cambridge, where he had worked, and Russian scientists who were lucky enough to go abroad— including Gamow himself —refused to return.

In the most notorious case of state interference in science, Stalin backed Trofim Lysenko, who championed an early nineteenth-century theory of genetics regarding the inheritance of acquired traits because it allowed for the biological inheritance of the social alterations made by the Communist regime. Lysenko's opponents lost their positions, were jailed, or disappeared forever. Russian genetics did not recover until the 1960s.

The Purges

There was criticism against Stalin's policies toward high-level Communists, because of the old Bolshevik political culture based on collective leadership, and even attempts to sabotage them. In August 1932, a Moscow Communist official drafted an appeal condemning Stalin's collectivization and industrial policies and accusing him of setting up a dictatorship. The discord even affected Stalin's immediate family as his wife turned against him; in November, she reportedly killed herself, but there still is strong suspicion that Stalin shot her.

On December 2, 1934 party leader Sergei M. Kirov was assassinated. Stalin used the murder as a pretext to initiate a great wave of terror and to purge his own movement in a successful attempt to consolidate his power. There is strong evidence that Stalin himself was behind the assassination. This picture shows Stalin (on the right) and other high Communist officials carrying Kirov's bier to the Kremlin wall for internment.

The disfavor swirling around him convinced Stalin that a vast conspiracy against him existed. Historians have argued that he considered himself a hero of the revolution and a political genius and could not understand how others could believe that he had made serious mistakes. Considering himself Lenin's legitimate successor, he especially resented his unpopularity among the prestigious Old Bolsheviks with whom he had made the October Revolution in 1917. When the secret police confirmed the objections to his policies, Stalin acted slowly but deliberately and in great depth.

First, he justified the power of the state in contrast to Marxist theory that predicted that the state would wither away. In January 1933, he asserted that the revolutionary state could not disappear until it had obliterated the dying classes. He affirmed that counterrevolutionaries had infiltrated the Communist Party, which now had to be purged, and entrusted the purge to a specially created commission that he controlled, while gaining the loyalty of the police, increasing the privileges of those who supported him, and reducing the economic pressure on the civilian population in order to gain popularity. On December 2, 1934, the murder of Sergei M. Kirov, a popular rival of Stalin, touched off five years of purges. In 1956, Nikita Khrushchev indicated that Stalin and his secret police (NKVD) trumped up the conspiracy and had Kirov eliminated.

The terror proceeded in waves. Between January 1935 and the summer of 1936, a quiet terror lopped off the bottom rungs of the Soviet Communist Party with little publicity. In all regions of the USSR, black NKVD cars, called ravens and carrying secret police operatives, prowled the night, and Soviet citizens who considered themselves possibly vulnerable dared not sleep between 11:00 P.M. and 2:00 A.M., when the NKVD usually made its arrests. Arrests, exile, and banishment to labor camps followed expulsion from the organization. From May to December 1935, the party expelled an estimated 190,000 members as spies or suspected spies. Stalin exploited this phase of the purges to tighten his control of the secret police and to claim that a vast plot, directed by Trotsky and the Fascists, aimed to overthrow him and destroy the revolution. A Soviet agent assassinated Trotsky, who was in exile in Mexico. Because Stalin's goal was to overthrow the Bolshevik political culture that impeded his control of the country, he required his former comrades to "confess" publicly to their misdeeds. The police obtained these confessions through mental torture, promises of release, and threats against the defendants' families. In mid-1936, the show trials and executions of the Old Bolsheviks began with those of leftists Grigori Zinoviev and Lev Kamenev. Neither the left nor the right wings were safe, and the purges culminated in 1938 with the trial and execution of Bukharin and twenty others.

Along with the elimination of the Old Bolsheviks, Stalin's purge decimated the Red Army's command structure. Although Stalin played up the imminence of a conflict for internal ideological reasons and probably did not foresee a war with Hitler soon, the real reasons for the military purges remain obscure. Documents released after the fall of communism show that Stalin counted on a conflict between the capitalist powers that would exhaust them, after which the Soviets could expand westward. In 1939, Stalin reached an accommodation with Hitler that encouraged the Germans to begin a war with the Western powers. Stalin's calculation proved erroneous because, instead of a long debilitating struggle, the Germans quickly defeated France in 1940, but it helps explain why he did not worry about the immediate implications of weakening the Red Army. However, domestic reasons also help explain Stalin's actions. Mikhail Tukhachevsky, civil war hero and first-class military thinker, along with other army commanders, had served under Trotsky, were too independent and had protested against collectivization. Stalin claimed to see a German-inspired Trotskyist plot against him in the army and tried about a thousand high officers. The purge of the army command weakened the capacity of the armed forces to fight, as demonstrated in the war against Finland in 1939 and 1940, and encouraged Hitler to attack the Soviet Union in 1941. The army's defeat removed the last obstacle to Stalin's establishment of a totalitarian regime. It is estimated that between 1937 and 1938, the Great Purge resulted in the arrest of between 4.5 to 5.5 million. Of these, 800,000 to 900,000 were executed, and the rest ended up in slave labor camps with an average life expectancy of six months.

Stalin's Triumph

By the end of the 1930s, Stalin had destroyed Bolshevik political culture, established his personal rule, collectivized agriculture, and industrialized the country. He had replaced the old generation of leaders with a new one formed under the USSR, too young to remember prerevolutionary times, and that he had promoted and schooled. Unlike the situation in capitalist countries, no one lacked employment, and youngsters rapidly advanced to high-level jobs at a fast pace. However, Stalin also destroyed the ability of this new generation to build on the experience of the old. He communized and industrialized the USSR but failed to modernize it. By instilling in the Soviet population the habit of blindly obeying a highly centralized and rigid party and state structure, he ensured the later demise of Soviet communism.

Bibliographical Essay

Many works have been written on the events described in this chapter, and the reader will have little trouble finding sources. Some of the books cited in Chapter 9 and biographies of Stalin include discussions of the events considered here. Sheila Fitzpatrick, *The Russian Revolution* (New York, 2008), asks when the Russian Revolution ended and, in the process, provides an excellent short history of the entire event. For an examination of the debates on Stalin's rule, see Chris Ward, ed., *Stalin's Russia,* 2d ed. (New York, 1999). Robert C. Tucker, *Stalin in Power: The Revolution From Above 1928–1941* (New York, 1990), is one of the best books on the period, replete with sources and bibliography; the quote on building socialism in the USSR is on p. 58, and Molotov's statement on the kulaks is cited on p. 139. Robert Service's *Stalin: A Biography* (Cambridge, Mass., 2005) gives a more complex vision of the man and his polices than is usually the case. Simon Sebag Montefiore, *Stalin: The Court of the Red Tsar* (New York, 2004), describes the atmosphere and people surrounding him. Another interesting biography that can be profitably consulted is Dmitri Volkogonov, *Stalin: Triumph and Tragedy* (New York, 1991). Statistics of such enormous events are disputed but may be found in Tucker and in the works cited later. Richard Pipes's *Russia Under the Bolshevik Regime* (New York, 1993) ends earlier but is very good on Soviet society. Two books take a close look at everyday life in Stalin's USSR: Orlando Figes, *The Whisperers* (New York, 2007), and Sheila Fitzpatrick, *Everyday Stalinism (New York, 1999)*. On Soviet women, see Feiga Blekher, ed., *The Soviet Woman in the Family and in Society* (New York, 1979), which is a good collection of essays on the topic; the information about women who had children being considered finished is on p. 29. For a wider consideration of Russian women up to 1930, see Richard Stites, *The Women's Liberation Movement in Russia: Feminism, Nihilism, and Bolshevism, 1860–1930* (Princeton, N.J., 1978).

Alex Nove, *The Stalin Phenomenon* (London, 1993), emphasizes Stalin's achievements. Chris Ward, ed., *The Stalinist Dictatorship* (New York, 1998), looks at Stalinism from three different perspectives. Steven F. Cohen published an excellent biography of Stalin's most important rival of the period, already cited, *Bukharin and the Bolshevik Revolution* (New York, 1973).

R. W. Davies is best on the early period of collectivization, *The Socialist Offensive* (London, 1980), previously cited. Robert Conquest, *The Harvest of Sorrow: Soviet Collectivization and the Terror-Famine* (New York, 1986), graphically describes the terror of collectivization. Roberta Thompson Manning reexamines the causes that led to collectivization in *The Rise and Fall of "the Extraordinary Measures," January–June 1928* (Pittsburgh, 2001). Lynne Viola, *Peasant Rebels Under Stalin* (New York, 1999), discusses the peasants' resistance to collectivization, while Sheila Fitzpatrick describes the postcollectivization village in *Stalin's Peasants: Resistance and Survival in the Russian Village after Collectivization* (New York, 1994). The plight of the peasants during the period is also examined by Lynne Viola et al., *The War Against the Peasantry, 1927–1930* (New Haven, Conn., 2005). The Ukrainian famine is the focus of Andrea Graziosi's *Stalinism, Collectivization and the Great Famine* (Cambridge, Mass., 2009) and *Causes of the Holodomor*, by Frederic P. Miller et al., (n.p., 2009). Analyses of industrialization may be found in Donald Filtzer, *Soviet Workers and Stalinist Industrialization: The Formation of Modern Soviet Production Relations, 1928–1941* (London, 1986); R. W. Davies, Mark Harrison, and S. G. Wheatcroft, eds., *The Economic Transformation of the Soviet Union* (Cambridge, UK, 1994); and William G. Rosenberg, *Social Dimensions of Soviet Industrialization* (Bloomington, Ind., 1993). See also Hiroaki Kuromiya, *Stalin's Industrial Revolution: Politics and Workers, 1928–1932* (New York, 1988), and Michael Reiman, *The Birth of Stalinism: The U.S.S.R. on the Eve of the "Second Revolution"* (London, 1987). O. V. Khlevniuk gives the history of an essential institution in this and later periods of Soviet history: *The History of the Gulag: From Collectivization to the Great Terror* (New Haven, Conn., 2004).

For culture, consult the relevant chapters in Richard Pipes, *Russia Under the Bolshevik Regime* (New York, 1993). Richard Stites, *Russian Popular Culture: Entertainment and Society Since 1900* (Cambridge, UK, 1992), presents an introduction to Soviet entertainment and popular culture. Sheila Fitzpatrick analyzes cultural domination by the state in *The Commissariat of Enlightenment* (Cambridge, UK, 1970) and also published *The Cultural Front* (New York, 1992). Robert C. Tucker's *Stalin in Power: The Revolution from Above 1922–1941* (New York, 1990), previously cited, has some good insights on culture. George Gamow, *My World Line: An Informal Autobiography* (New York, 1970), is an autobiographical account centering primarily on his years in his native Russia; the excerpt regarding capitalistic and proletarian science is on p. 93.

Good works on the terror and the debate on its effects are Robert Conquest, *The Great Terror: A Reassessment* (London, 1990), and J. Arch Getty and Roberta Manning, *Stalinist Terror: New Perspectives* (Cambridge, UK, 1993). Anne Applebaum, author of *Gulag: A History* (New York, 2003), discusses the origins and development of the Soviet camps and concludes that they were an organic component of Soviet Communism. Hiroaki Kuromiya, *The Voices of the Dead: Stalin's Great Terror in the 1930s* (New Haven, Conn., 2007), tries to give faces to all the categories of victims and describes how they were arrested and died. Martin Amis, *Koba the Dread: Laughter and the Twenty Million* (New York, 2002), compares the Soviet camps to the Nazi ones.

CHAPTER 14

The Nazi Assault on Weimar

CHAPTER OUTLINE

Weimar's Crumbling Support • Ascent of the Nazi Party • The Collapse of
Weimar • Installing the Dictatorship

BIOGRAPHICAL SKETCHES

Adolf Hitler, Down and Out in Vienna • Franz von Papen, Politico

In Germany, old mentalities, beliefs, and resentments remained strong despite
the change of political form from Empire to Liberal Republic. Bitterness pervaded the bureaucracy, industry, farmers, the bourgeoisie, and, most important,
the German people, who never fully accepted the Weimar Republic despite its
achievement of political stability and a measure of economic success between 1925
and 1929. As in 1919, they condemned Weimar for surrendering to the Allies,
accepting the Versailles treaty, and the hyperinflation.

WEIMAR'S CRUMBLING SUPPORT

The Great Depression facilitated the growth of extremist parties and paved the
way for Adolf Hitler and the Nazis.

The Radicalization of Agriculture and Big Business

The slump intensified the crisis of German agriculture that had been evident
since the 1920s. The Weimar government signed agreements with the new East
European countries in order to encourage industrial exports, and the country
paid the price by allowing the importation of cheap agricultural goods that caused
German farm prices to drop precipitously. With the depression, the agricultural
crisis merged with the economic slump, to which German farmers responded by
accentuating their rightist tendencies. The agricultural associations supported

radical organizations, such as the Nazis; demanded governmental relief; and advocated for preferential tariffs, quotas, and autarky. The Junkers, large landholders in the eastern part of the country who were hostile to Weimar, increased their political influence and successfully defended subsidies for big Prussian landowners (the *Osthilfe*).

The large industrialists also intensified their hostility to the republic during the depression. Big business detested everything Weimar stood for: social welfare policies, governmental intervention in labor-management affairs, and democratic politics. During the postwar period, the industrialists had greatly increased their concentration of wealth, making the opposition of business to the government more effective. When the government attempted to implement social measures to confront the depression, the industrialists insisted on cost-cutting procedures, such as reducing unemployment insurance. This fierce resistance presented the government with three unpalatable alternatives: replenish the unemployment fund from other governmental programs, raise taxes, or reduce payments to workers.

President Paul von Hindenburg, a stout Junker supporter, blocked the switching of funds from the *Osthilfe*, while the people vigorously opposed new taxes. Borrowing became harder because American bankers refused new loans unless the government balanced the budget. These circumstances forced Chancellor Mueller's coalition cabinet to reduce unemployment subsidies, which alienated the unions. In March 1930, the unions forced his resignation, an event that paralyzed parliamentary government and set the scene for Hitler's rise to power.

The Unemployed and the Welfare System

Besides increasing the opposition of the moneyed interests, the depression sapped popular support for the republic. Weimar's welfare organization and its humiliation of unemployed workers who were living in precarious conditions help explain this development.

To receive benefits, unemployed workers had to show up at the labor exchanges once a week. To ensure that workers would be available in case work materialized, workers could never come on the same day of the week or at the same hour as previous visits to collect their benefits. This process shamed and outraged desperate people and ensured that they could not organize their already disrupted lives. Unemployed workers spent long hours in overcrowded offices dealing with overburdened, irritable clerks. Tension, fights, demonstrations, arrests, beatings, and killings resulted. In one instance, a police officer told a civilian to move along. When he responded "Why, of course," the enraged officer asked what he meant by "of course," threw him into the paddy wagon, and took him to the police station where the police beat him up. Writer Christopher Isherwood summed up the general situation in Berlin: "Hate exploded suddenly, without warning, out of nowhere; at street-corners, in restaurants, cinemas, dance-halls, swimming baths; at midnight; after breakfast, in the middle of the afternoon."

Both Communist and Nazi political agitators converted exasperated workers into street fighters, but the Nazis excelled. While Communist ideology saw the middle class as "proletarianized" by the depression, the Nazis blamed the Versailles settlement, Jews, and Weimar traitors for their problems and gained a greater following among people who did not see themselves as losing social status.

ASCENT OF THE NAZI PARTY

The desperate circumstances of depression Germany and the declining support for the Weimar Republic translated into greater electoral support for extremist parties, especially the Nazis, with their simplistic explanations, fierce nationalism, charismatic leader, previous prediction of economic collapse, and clear remedies.

Hitler and the Nazis

The Nazi Party originated as the Munich-based German Workers' Party (DAP), founded by political unknown Anton Drexler. The organization glorified German workers, advocated their elevation to the middle class while favoring employers who did not abuse their privileged position, and featured strong anti-Semitism. In 1919, the DAP came to the army's attention, and the army dispatched one of its operatives, Adolf Hitler, to spy on it. Hitler converted to its ideas, left the army, and joined the organization.

Born in Braunau am Inn (near Linz), Austria, on April 20, 1889, Adolf Hitler was a lonely youth who had failed in his dream of becoming an artist. Poor but not destitute, he spent several years in Vienna imbibing nationalistic and anti-Semitic ideas, in addition to a distorted racial outlook based on pamphlets purporting to explain Darwinian ideas and to apply them to society. By the time he left for Munich, Germany, he had made no mark in Austria. When World War I broke out, he joined the German army, served with distinction, and was promoted to corporal. In 1918, he suffered temporary blindness by gas that is sometimes attributed to hysteria. He had a revelation that he would save Germany: "When I was confined to bed, the idea came to me that I would liberate Germany, that I would make it great. I knew immediately that it would be realized." Hitler felt that he was under divine protection: one day, while in the trenches eating his rations, a voice told him to move away. A few seconds later, a stray shell killed the group with whom he had been eating. Throughout his career Hitler never wavered in his faith that God guided him.

Hitler felt fulfilled in the army and accepted the assignment to investigate the DAP after the conflict. After he joined the party, he emerged from his former insignificance by exhibiting a great talent for oratory and bringing in funds through his fiery speeches and his ability to charm bourgeois observers, including the daughters of wealthy families. At his rallies, he sent speakers to warm up the audience, had a band play military marches, and strode in decisively at the proper psychological moment to the platform through columns of uniformed supporters looking neither to the right nor to the left but straight ahead. His speeches began haltingly as he sized up the audience. Then he heated up to the point that "every one of his words comes out charged with a powerful current of energy."

BIOGRAPHICAL SKETCHES

Adolf Hitler
Down and Out in Vienna

The history of the young Adolf Hitler gives no idea of his future career. Hitler's customs inspector father was restless and hot-tempered and moved several times before settling down in Leonding, a village outside Linz, Austria, in November 1898. Adolf attended the local elementary school, where he was an undistinguished student. He enjoyed reading stories of the American West written by popular author Karl May and recalled them later in life. In September 1900, he entered a secondary school that emphasized scientific over humanistic studies. He repeated the first year and frequently retook exams. His dream of becoming a great artist led to fights with his father, who wanted him to work at a steady job in the civil service.

Hitler's father died in January 1903. After 1905 Adolf convinced his doting mother that he should not go on to a technical school, and during the next two years, he led a comfortable life reading, painting, taking piano lessons, and daydreaming. He slept late and spent evenings at the opera listening to his favorite composer, Richard Wagner, and haranguing a friend about Wagner, art, architecture, and his own abilities. He contemptuously turned down all suggestions that he work, telling everyone that he intended to be a great artist.

Before his mother Klara died in December 1907 of breast cancer, Hitler went to Vienna and applied for admission to the Art academy, which promptly turned him down. Despite this blow to his pride, he became convinced that he would become a great architect. In Vienna, he roomed with a friend in town to study music. Thanks to a small inheritance, a small pension, and occasional contributions from his Aunt Johanna, he continued his leisurely existence. He ate poorly if at all and lived in a miserable room—but went to the opera. To the other merits he attributed to himself, he added writing and opera composition. He started plays and an opera but never got far. Aside from the opera, Hitler took no part in Vienna's lively cultural life. He is unlikely to have engaged in sex during his time in Vienna; in fact, sex seems to have repelled him. The politics of Mayor Karl Lueger impressed him, and, at some point, he became an anti-Semite and a biological racist. He had already been attracted to extreme nationalism in Linz.

In the summer of 1908, his money low and his friend gone, Hitler fell on hard times. By the autumn of 1909, he was homeless and slept in the open or in shelters. Reports have him unshaven, emaciated, infested with lice, wearing tattered clothes, and in the company of tramps. He moved to a hostel for the poor, where he could get a bed at night, a bath, some soup, and bread, but was expected to work during the day. Finally putting his artistic qualities to use, Hitler teamed up with another resident in a small business. He painted scenes of Vienna, while his partner sold them. He had Jewish partners in this endeavor and seems to have gotten along with them.

The money the painting business brought in was little, but it enabled the future Fuehrer to survive. By February 1910, Hitler lived in a men's home, where conditions were tolerable. He discussed get-rich-quick schemes with his partner, but preferred to pontificate on political subjects to the other residents—Social Democratic decadence, the decay of the Austrian Empire, German greatness. Eventually, Hitler quarreled with his partner over money, and they went their separate ways. He remained an embittered, disconnected man who criticized his own paintings and chafed at society's rejection of him. He hated Vienna and dreamed of going to Munich to study art. His failure to register for military service in 1909 because he hated the empire provided another incentive to leave, but he stayed because after April 20, 1913, his twenty-fourth birthday, he became eligible to receive an inheritance from his father. When he received the money, he packed his belongings in a black suitcase and, to the good-byes of his fellow-residents at the men's home, left for Germany.

Hitler built up and dominated the DAP. In February 1920, he changed its name to the National Socialist German Workers' Party (NSDAP), Nazi for short, issued an anticapitalist and anti-Semitic program consisting of twenty-five points that expressed the grievances of the lower classes, and in 1921 demanded dictatorial powers over it. He instituted a paramilitary organization, the SA (*Sturmableitung*), or Storm Troopers, to prevent enemies from interfering with his inflammatory discourses. The SA specialized in the street fighting essential to the Nazi rise to power. Hitler emphasized uniforms, symbolism, and rallies to mobilize the masses. In November 1923, he attempted to seize the government but failed miserably. The results: a short jail term, during which he wrote *Mein Kampf*, and a conviction to follow the legal road to power taken in Italy by his hero Benito Mussolini.

After 1924, Weimar recovered economically, and Germany seemed on the road to European reintegration. Prosperity made Hitler's predictions of disaster because of the Versailles settlement seem absurd, and the Germans ignored his violent preaching. Nazi support dwindled, and, in the 1928 elections, the Nazis won only twelve seats in the Reichstag

Revival of the Nazi Party

The depression catapulted the NSDAP to the political forefront. The Nazi recovery was aided by changes in the Nationalist Party (DNVP) after its takeover by the ambitious and politically inept newspaper magnate Alfred Hugenberg. As a protest against reparations, Hugenberg challenged the government's acceptance of the Young Plan that reduced payments and, in order to increase his chances of success, organized a right-wing front that included the Nazis. Certain that he could control the Nazis, Hugenberg gave them full access to his newspapers and increased their visibility and respectability.

The Nazis transformed the campaign against the Young Plan into a sweeping condemnation of the Weimar Republic. Their denunciation of the Versailles treaty as the source of Germany's troubles increased their popular support as the depression deepened and panic spread. The middle class feared losing its economic status as had happened in the catastrophic hyperinflation, fueling resentment

The paramilitary SA or Storm Troopers were essential to the rise of the Nazi Party. They protected Hitler during his public appearances and engaged in the street fighting that eventually made the movement paramount in the country. Here is SA leader Ernst Roehm in his uniform. Hitler gave the order to dismantle the SA and to assassinate Roehm during the "Night of the Long Knives" because the Army felt threatened by the SA and Roehm was too revolutionary. Hitler made a pact guaranteeing that the Army would be the only armed force in the nation, but, as usual, he did not keep his word.

and increasing support for the Nazis. In addition, the Nazi alliance alienated the moderate nationalists and split the DNVP, a schism that gave the NSDAP supremacy on the right.

In the meantime, the ruling coalition broke up, and the parties failed to agree on a new government. The lack of a majority in the Reichstag triggered Article 48 of the Constitution, which effectively allowed the president to rule by decree if a parliamentary majority did not exist. Because no chancellor could rule if the president refused to sign the decree laws, the center of power shifted from the Reichstag to President Hindenburg and his narrow circle of advisers. The new chancellor sanctioned by Hindenburg, Heinrich Bruening, dissolved Parliament and scheduled early elections for September 1930 in the hope that a majority would emerge.

THE COLLAPSE OF WEIMAR

Combined with these political developments, the economy's continued plunge sealed Weimar's fate. By 1932 German industrial production had fallen by 44 percent, unemployment skyrocketed to 6 million or 40 percent, and the unemployment fund was bankrupt.

The Electoral Breakthrough

The Nazis ran emotional electoral campaigns that denounced the "November criminals" who supported the republic and the Jews who were supposedly responsible for Germany's troubles. They used powerful theater, including the pioneering use of the airplane—swooping down from the sky and making dramatic entrances into cities where Hitler addressed mass rallies. Hitler's rhetoric made short shrift of political moderates as he demanded the destruction of the Versailles treaty and the Weimar Republic. The economic catastrophe brought the Nazis new support from groups that would not ordinarily have voted for them, including unemployed workers, women, and young people who never had held a job. By July 1932, 30 percent of Berlin's workers were voting for the NSDAP, and they made up over half the membership of the capital's Storm Troopers.

The women's vote was particularly important because women participated in elections in larger numbers than before. Women voted for the Nazis less often than did men, but the Nazis did better among them than did the Communists, despite the KPD's (Communist Party of Germany) advanced platform on women's issues. Helping to explain this ironic consequence, the Nazis were not too far out of line with the general thinking in late Weimar Germany by believing that women should devote their energies to their homes, husbands, and children. However, because the Nazis argued that radicals and Jews dominated the women's movement, rejected women candidates for the Reichstag, and maintained that feminism enslaved women, why did they have so much success among women voters? There seem to be two major reasons: Most women accepted the view of German society that cast them in the role of wives and mothers, and they believed that Hitler would cut unemployment and put the family's primary breadwinners back on the payroll.

The economic situation helps explain the stunning Nazi victory in the 1930 elections. The Nazis increased their votes to more than 18 percent from 2.6 percent, and their seats in the Reichstag soared from 12 to 107. Of the other parties, only the KPD increased its percentage, but only from 10.6 to 13 percent. The Catholic Center Party remained stable at 15 percent, but the SPD lost votes, and the left as a whole declined 4 percent. What was most significant, the Liberals and the People's Party, mainstays of the Weimar coalition, lost about half their votes.

The Nazi increase came primarily from the center of the political spectrum and new voters. The unemployed, the never employed, small businessmen, farmers in distress, and civil servants who were worried about their jobs contributed heavily to the Nazi tide. The young accounted for a substantial proportion of the Nazi tally, and the 1930 Reichstag was the youngest ever.

Parliamentary Paralysis and Increasing Disorder

The outcome of the 1930 elections was a turning point. No parliamentary majority emerged, confirming Hindenburg and his circle as the arbiters of

ARBEITER

WÄHLT DEN FRONTSOLDATEN

HITLER!

The Nazis came to power not only through violence, but primarily through shrewd campaigning. While the economic situation was good they were not an important political factor, but their electoral support increased dramatically with the onset of the Great Depression. Here is a Nazi electoral poster: "Workers choose Hitler!"

German politics. Parliamentary business was paralyzed because the parties supporting Weimar had 40 percent of the seats, while Nazi and Communist opponents of the republic controlled 32 percent. The 1930 elections transformed the NSDAP into a mass party with roots in the urban and rural middle class, and violence increased as the SA recruited adherents by offering pay, excitement, and the prospect of beating up leftist opponents. Street brawls killed three hundred people in a single year. The government did not ban the SA until April 1932 when it was too late.

Encouraged by the party's growing popular support, Hitler challenged the popular Hindenburg in the March 1932 presidential election. He did not win, but he performed impressively by outpolling the Communist and Nationalist candidates and forcing Hindenburg into a run-off election. Because of the president's advanced age, Hitler's showing established him as the person to contend with in German politics.

Because the president had become the focus of power, intrigues aimed at influencing him dominated German politics. In May 1932, he forced Chancellor

Bruening to resign because he was dissatisfied with his strategy in the recent elections.

The Drive to Power

Hindenburg replaced Bruening with a conservative Catholic noble Franz von Papen, who had little support in the country but had the backing of General Kurt von Schleicher, who represented the army. Papen installed a "barons' cabinet" consisting of army officers, including Schleicher as defense minister, and senior civil servants. He attempted to get Hitler's support by making two goodwill gestures: lifting Bruening order outlawing the SA and dismissing the Social Democrat-led government of Prussia, which was hostile to the Nazis. Hitler responded by remaining intransigent and by stepping up SA violence. Papen now feared that the Reichstag would condemn his policies and obtained Hindenburg's consent to hold new elections in July 1932.

The Nazis emerged from the new balloting as the Reichstag's largest party, with over 37 percent of the vote and 207 members, but there was still no majority. Papen hoped to resolve the situation by bringing the Nazis into a cabinet— but Hitler turned him down. Papen then followed a policy of attempting to weaken the Nazis by holding frequent elections because he judged that Nazi support had peaked and that losses would make the party more malleable. In the elections of November 1932, the Nazi vote total dropped about 4 percent, probably signaling a backlash against Nazi violence, and created a crisis in the NSDAP.

Far from weakening Hitler's position, however, Papen's maneuvering set off a new round of intrigue. General von Schleicher turned against Papen because he feared that the chancellor would install an authoritarian regime and provoke a civil war. Schleicher sought to get Hindenburg to withdraw his support of Papen, but the president had taken a personal liking to the chancellor. Schleicher then informed the president that he, Schleicher, could put together a cabinet that would obtain a vote of confidence in the Reichstag. Because of the Nazi electoral decline, Schleicher hoped to split the Nazi Party by assuming that a substantial part of the Nazi Party would revolt against Hitler and support a cabinet that he would lead. This plan failed miserably.

Papen responded by going straight to Hitler to cut a deal. He had the backing of heavy industry and agricultural and banking interests, while Hindenburg's advisers tried to soften up the old general who personally opposed the Nazi leader. The army feared that Schleicher's intrigues might turn the president against it and abandoned him. Papen offered Hitler the vice chancellorship in a new government, but Hitler demanded that he become chancellor and Papen, vice chancellor. Papen agreed, and on January 30, 1933, Hitler became chancellor in a coalition cabinet that included only three Nazis. Papen and his supporters believed that they had boxed in the Nazi leader so he could not do much harm and that they could eventually remove him, but they were wrong.

BIOGRAPHICAL SKETCHES

Franz von Papen
Politico

A wily politician, Franz von Papen was born into a noble Catholic family on October 29, 1879, in the Westphalia region of Germany. He led a very agreeable life before marrying into a wealthy industrial family in 1905. His wife's connections provided him excellent links to big industrialists and rightist political circles during the waning years of the Weimar republic when Adolf Hitler came to power.

Papen's background favored him in his chosen military career even though he was inattentive to details, devious, and willing to take chances. In 1911 Papen was assigned to the general staff and, in January 1914, became military attaché at the German Embassy in Washington, D.C. The Americans shipped him back to Germany in 1916 because they charged that he had conspired to disrupt war production. Affidavits also stated that Papen had an open relationship with an American girl in New York and organized wild parties with secret agents and their girlfriends. Back in Germany, he fought on the western front, where he won the coveted Iron Cross (First Class). Transferred to the Middle East, he fought well and attempted to foment revolution among Muslims under British control.

After World War I, the progress of the Communists and Socialists alarmed him, and, as a Center Party member, he disagreed with Chancellor Heinrich Bruening's policy of alliance with the Social Democrats. His links with powerful industrialists and the army kept Papen in the political loop among rightist circles, although he devoted much time to farming and horse breeding on his family estates.

With Bruening's fall, General Kurt von Schleicher introduced Papen to President Paul von Hindenburg. The witty and urbane Papen charmed the aging president, who gave him a mandate to form a government. Papen's rightist Barons' cabinet had no majority in Parliament and no support among the people. Because Hitler had strong popular support, Papen thought to co-opt the Nazis by bringing Hitler into a Conservative governmental coalition. Papen believed that entangling the Nazi leader in practical politics would make Hitler more moderate. As Nazi influence increased in the country, Papen negotiated harder to lure Hitler into the government, also as a means of sabotaging his new rival, Schleicher. When Hitler refused to enter a cabinet except as chancellor, Papen struck a deal with him and convinced Hindenburg to appoint Hitler chancellor while he took the position of vice chancellor. Because the Nazis had only three cabinet posts, Papen believed their influence on governmental policies would be strictly limited. Papen hoped to counter Hitler's radicalism by the application of Christian principles and make him reasonable. He also thought that he had restored state authority based on ideals, which he admired, that had existed during the kaiser's time.

Papen stayed in Hitler's cabinet until July 1934. He bravely protested against Nazi terror in a speech on June 17, 1934, to no effect. On the Night of the Long Knives, June 30, the Nazis killed two of his assistants, and Papen himself narrowly escaped death. Papen nevertheless cooperated with Hitler. Appointed as ambassador to Austria, he helped undermine the Austrian regime and aided the German takeover in 1938. He served as ambassador to Turkey from 1939 to 1944. The Nuremberg tribunal acquitted Papen of war crimes, but in 1949 a German denazification court sentenced him to eight years' hard labor, which he did not serve. In 1953, he published a set of exculpatory memoirs.

Franz von Papen died on May 2, 1969, immortalized as the person who put Adolf Hitler in the driver's seat.

INSTALLING THE DICTATORSHIP

The Nazi revolution began once Hitler became chancellor. On February 23, 1933, the Reichstag building burned down. The arrest of a feeble-minded Dutch Communist seemed to confirm Nazi charges of a Communist conspiracy to take over the country.

The Elections of March 1933

In response to the burning of the Reichstag, Hindenburg declared a state of emergency under Article 48 of the Weimar Constitution, authorizing the government to implement necessary action to "restore public order and public security" by restricting the freedom of assembly, press, and expression. The decree provided the legal basis for Nazi terror during the campaign for elections scheduled for March 5, 1933. The Nazi police spied on private communications, conducted search and seizure operations with impunity, and arrested Nazi opponents without charging them with specific offenses. Despite the terror campaign and governmental interference in the voting, the Nazis won under 44 percent of the vote and had to rely on the DNVP's 8 percent for a parliamentary majority. The voting followed earlier patterns, with the Nazis receiving the greatest support from small urban centers, Protestant agricultural areas, the lower middle class, voters who had formerly abstained, and new voters and losing in the Catholic and working-class regions of the country.

Following the elections, on March 23, two-thirds of the Reichstag adopted the Enabling Act. This measure, voted by the Nazis, Nationalists, and Center Party members and opposed by the Social Democrats (the government had already imprisoned the Communists and some Socialists), gave Hitler power to promulgate laws for the next four years.

Results of the Enabling Act

The Enabling Act allowed Hitler to establish his dictatorship. On July 14, 1933, the government dissolved all parties except the Nazi Party and ended the separation of powers of the different branches of government. Hitler formalized this situation after Hindenburg's death on August 2, 1934, upon which he assumed the powers of the presidency, and German officials swore loyalty oaths personally to Hitler as Fuehrer (leader).

The Nazis also implemented a leveling process (Gleichschaltung) that subjugated the individual German states, the administration, and German society. Through terrorism, decrees, and political pressure, the Nazis eliminated the legal basis by which German states could offer resistance to the central government.

Many officials of Weimar were former officers of the German Empire, and their support for the Republic was questionable. President Paul von Hindenburg, for example, was the general who had led Germany during World War I. This lukewarm support from high and not-so-high authorities of the Republic, combined with the economic disaster of the Great Depression, undermined Weimar, and the rise of extremist movements and constitutional weaknesses finally did it in. Although Hindenburg did not like Hitler personally, he gave the go-ahead for him to become Chancellor. The photograph shows Hindenburg riding with Hitler shortly after naming him Chancellor in January 1933.

They did away with the *Reichsrat*, or upper house representing the states, and appointed officials to run them. The destruction of the rights of the individual states ended Germany's traditional federal makeup and established the central government's supremacy.

The only organization capable of opposing Hitler, the army, made a deal with Hitler: when the aged Hindenburg died, the army promised not to oppose Hitler's addition of the president's functions to those of chancellor; Hitler agreed to recognize the army as the strongest armed force in the nation. This promise meant eliminating the army's principal rival, the SA, led by Hitler's old friend Ernst Roehm. The Nazi drive to power had swollen the ranks of the organization, which insisted on revolutionizing German society and on invading the army's sphere of competence. On the Night of the Long Knives, June 30, 1934, Hitler kept his side of the bargain by brutally ordering the killing of Roehm and his top lieutenants; for good measure, other people who had crossed him, including Schleicher and Gregor Strasser, a Nazi leader who had considered a deal with Schleicher in 1932, were also killed.

The Nazis eliminated all opponents from the civil service, in addition to the Jews they had excluded in April 1933. They took control of the police and the judiciary and crushed the trade unions and professional organizations, creating economic and cultural organizations to supervise and mobilize the masses—the German Labor Front and the Reich Cultural Chamber.

Although the army acquiesced in Hitler's takeover, it was ambivalent toward the Nazi regime. Its leaders sympathized with some Nazi goals, such as restoring German power through rearmament and perhaps eventual expansion in the East, but resented Hitler's continued attempts to control the armed forces. Hitler removed General Werner von Blomberg, the minister of war, and Chief of Staff General Werner von Fritsch, but failed to establish complete control over the armed forces. In 1938, at the height of the Czech crisis, rumors flew that the army might try to remove him from power, and during World War II, it chafed at his interference in military affairs. In 1944, some army officers attempted to assassinate Hitler, allowing him to destroy his enemies and finally gain domination over the army.

Nazism's Rise in Retrospect

In attempting to explain the triumph of Nazism, historians have concentrated on two aspects: Hitler's personality and German conditions.

Kurt von Schleicher led the German Army during the Weimar period, but his political maneuverings unintentionally aided Hitler's rise to the Chancellorship. Hitler had the former Foreign Minister and Chancellor murdered, along with his wife, on the "Night of the Long Knives" that consolidated his power.

Hitler dominated Nazism to such an extent that many biographies analyzing his family background, youth, frustrations, sexual proclivities, psychological makeup, and talents continue to be published. This very informative literature provides clues about why he succeeded in taking over and ruling a sophisticated modern country. Most important, biographers have concentrated on the magnetic force of his personality, his talents as an orator, and his ability to create a myth of himself that kept together the party and the country. During the infancy of mass communication, when only newspapers, radio, and film were available, Hitler used the mass meeting to gain converts and win elections. He proved himself a master at staging dramatic events and winning over audiences according to the precepts he outlined in *Mein Kampf*. Hitler's personal popularity made his triumph and rule possible. Even in the last days of World War II, when Germany was reeling and the Nazi Party lost its support, Germans continued to support the Fuehrer.

Nevertheless, it seems unlikely that one man alone could have caused the collapse of the Weimar Republic, no matter how many "talents of tyranny" he possessed. The result of the March 1933 elections, in which the Nazis failed to secure a majority, demonstrated this fact. Most obviously, historians have pointed out the weaknesses of the Weimar Republic, its inability to establish legitimacy, and the catastrophic economic conditions that weakened it. According to this view, the Nazis had a great probability of success because they assaulted a vulnerable political construction during a time of great crisis, whereas they had failed when conditions were less desperate.

Despite Hitler's failure to win an electoral majority, the Nazis did become the largest party; this fact has led historians to analyze the electoral results of this voting. They have concluded that the Nazis had important backing beyond the lower middle class and socially marginal groups that had lost their status because of the depression and could count on significant support among farmers, shopkeepers, artisans who feared that they would lose their economic and social positions. Probably this empathy signaled discontent with the long-term trends of German economic and social development favoring industrialization and increased workers' rights. The Nazis also had support among upper-class constituencies, including students and civil servants who were fearful of Marxist gains and unhappy with their careers and future prospects. Despite its appeal to anti-Marxists, the Nazi Party had important backing among workers in small industry who were not well integrated into the large unions. The female vote for the Nazis possibly exceeded the male vote in the last free elections. In addition, the Nazi Party appealed in great measure to older people, but it also drew support from young people. Catholic voters and industrial workers were most recalcitrant to Nazi influence.

Bibliographical Essay

The Coming of the Third Reich (New York, 2004) by Richard J. Evans, previously cited, is the most complete work on the rise of Nazism. Karl Dietrich Bracher's *The German Dictatorship: Origins, Structure and Effects of National Socialism* (New York, 1970) is a classic work on the rise of Hitler and the intimate nature of his regime. Another excellent work is Martin Broszat, *Hitler and the Collapse of Weimar Germany* (New York, 1987).

A good document collection is Jeremy Noakes and Geoffrey Pridham, eds., *Documents on Nazism 1919–1945*, 2 vols. (Exeter, UK, 1989). Geoffrey Pridham, *Hitler's Rise to Power: The Nazi Movement in Bavaria, 1923–1933* (New York, 1973), emphasizes the context of the Weimar republic. Allan Todd discusses Hitler's coming to power in the context of the rise of the other European dictatorships discussed in this part: *The European Dictatorships* (Cambridge, UK, 2002).

Biographies of Hitler are crucial to an understanding of the man, and readers will find many works of different quality on the subject. Ian Kershaw's *Hitler*, 2 vols. (New York, 1999–2000), is the most comprehensive biography. The same author wrote *The "Hitler Myth": Image and Reality in the Third Reich* (New York, 1987), a study of Hitler's image. A classic work that is still worth reading is Alan Bullock, *Hitler: A Study in Tyranny* (New York, 1995). See also his *Hitler and Stalin: Parallel Lives* (London, 1991). Good and detailed biographies include Joachim Fest, *Hitler* (New York, 1973); John Toland, *Adolf Hitler* (Garden City, N.Y., 1976); and William Carr, *Hitler: A Study in Personality and Politics* (New York, 1979). More recent biographies include John Lukacs, *The Hitler of History* (New York, 1998). As may be expected, psychological biographies of Hitler have also been written to understand his actions. An early one, written for the OSS in 1943 but published much later, is Walter Langer, *The Mind of Adolf Hitler* (London, 1974). The citations on Hitler's revelation that he had divine support and on his speaking style are on pp. 37 and 52. Another classic work along these lines is Robert G. L. Waite, *The Psychopathic God: Adolf Hitler* (New York, 1977). Other relevant works include Rudolph Binion, *Hitler Among the Germans* (De Kalb, Ill., 1984). The psychiatrist Fritz Redlich, *Hitler: Diagnosis of a Destructive Prophet* (New York, 1998), concludes that although a variety of physical and psychological ailments afflicted Hitler, they do not explain his behavior.

Economic developments that helped provoke Weimar's end may be studied in Harold James, *The German Slump: Politics and Economics 1924–1936* (Oxford, UK, 1986). Goronwy Rees, *The Great Slump: Capitalism in Crisis, 1929–1933* (New York, 1970), previously cited,, is a general history with good material on Germany. Edward W. Bennett, *Germany and the Diplomacy of the Financial Crisis* (Cambridge, Mass., 1962), analyzes the Young Plan, along with the relationship of Germany to Europe and the United States. Henry Ashby Turner, Jr., examines the relationship between Hitler and big business, *German Big Business and the Rise of Hitler* (New York, 1985). See also the story of I. G. Farben by Peter Hayes, *Industry and Ideology: IG Farben in the Nazi Era* (Cambridge, UK, 1989).

A. J. Nicholls, *Weimar and the Rise of Hitler*, 2d ed. (New York, 1972), is a good, brief and still valuable general survey on the last days of the Weimar Republic. E. J. Feuchtwanger, *From Weimar to Hitler: Germany 1918–1933* (New York, 1993), is a complete and detailed history. R. T. Clark, *The Fall of the German Republic* (New York, 1964), is an older, still useful, work that focuses on politics. Richard Bessel and E. J. Feuchtwanger, *Social Change and Political Development in Weimar Germany* (Totowa, N.J., 1981), and Michael N. Dobkowski and Isidor Wallimann, eds., *The Social and Economic Collapse of the Weimar Republic* (Westport, Conn., 1983), contain a series of excellent essays on Weimar themes that help explain the republic's failures. For the role of an important politician, see William L. Patch, Jr., *Heinrich Bruening and the Dissolution of the Weimar Republic* (Cambridge, UK, 1998).

A series of books have analyzed the people who voted for the Nazis. Among the best are Thomas Childers, *The Nazi Voter: The Social Foundations of Fascism in Germany* (Chapel Hill, N.C., 1983), and, by the same author, *The Formation of the Nazi Constituency* (London, 1986). Richard Hamilton, *Who Voted for Hitler?* (Princeton, N.J., 1982), examines the support of both the upper and lower middle class. Robert Gellatly, *Backing Hitler* (Oxford, UK, 2001), examines the issue of "consent and coercion" in Hitler's coming to power and during his regime. Peter Fritzsche, *Germans into Nazis* (Cambridge, Mass., 1998) rejects the conventional explanations of why people voted for the Nazis and points to democratization. Local support is discussed in the excellent William Sheridan Allen, *The Nazi Seizure of Power: The Experience of a Single Town* (Harmondsworth, UK, 1989), and Rudolf Heberle, *From Democracy to Nazism: A Regional Case Study on Political Parties in Germany* (New York, 1970).

CHAPTER 15

✍

Hitler's Nazism

CHAPTER OUTLINE

Foundations of Nazism • Nazi Theory and Practice • Everyday Life

BIOGRAPHICAL SKETCHES

Gertrud Scholtz-Klink, Unrepentant! • Hermann Goering,
Nazi Chieftain

H itler moved cautiously after he took over the state. Many Germans did not vote for him in 1933, and it is impossible to establish with certainty how many opposed his ideas. Nevertheless, as the Nazi regime established itself, it seems clear that most Germans believed in his ability to restore Germany to its former greatness.

FOUNDATIONS OF NAZISM

Nazism's underpinnings may be found already fully developed in *Mein Kampf,* which the Fuehrer penned while in prison for his failed 1923 Beer Hall Putsch. Biological racism was the centerpiece of the book, and Hitler tried to implement it.

Anti-Semitism

There is a distinction between Nazi anti-Semitism and the Nazi theory of racism. Although the Nazis believed in a superior race, the "Aryans," and inferior races, they reserved a special place for the Jews, who they saw as biologically inferior and warring on the Aryans in order to destroy the superior race. According to the Nazis, the Jews waged a subtle and disreputable campaign against the Aryans through divide-and-conquer techniques. Nazis viewed socialism, communism, capitalism, trade unions, feminism, and democratic ideas as Jewish conspiracies to split the "Aryan" community into antagonistic classes; they were inferior, evil, and cunning. Hitler believed that without the immediate implementation of urgent

Adolf Eichmann served in a number of capacities during the Third Reich. A major participant in the Holocaust, he coordinated the deportation of Jews to death camps and ghettoes in which they died of malnutrition and abuse. He fled to Argentina after the war but the Mossad tracked him down and brought him to Israel to stand trial for his crimes. Convicted by a civilian court, he was executed on May 31, 1962.

measures against the Jews, the fight would be lost. For the Nazis, the Jew served as the pervasive enemy and focus of hatred that totalitarian regimes require.

The Nuremberg Laws

When they came to power, the Nazis unleashed terror tactics against their leftist opponents and seized the occasion to include Jews in the attack. The Nazis initially tried to deprive Jews of the means to earn a living, not to extirpate them. In March 1933, violent demonstrations against Jewish businesses and professionals began, and on April 1, the Nazi Party organized a boycott of Jewish stores. Uniformed SA and SS thugs scared off customers and led noisy demonstrations while members of the Hitler Youth handed out leaflets. These efforts were not wholly successful, since non-Jews pointedly shopped in Jewish stores despite the intimidation. During the same month, a law to cleanse the civil service of Nazi opponents effectively removed most Jewish civil servants and excluded most Jews from the professions. Other measures in the spring and summer completed the work and established a quota for Jewish students. The Nazis hoped to force the Jews to emigrate and leave their property behind. Although 40,000 Jews emigrated in 1933, the effort failed; most of the 537,000 German Jews could not bear to leave their homeland, and the Nazi tactic of depriving them of funds made emigration more difficult.

On September 15, 1935, following a summer of boycotts and violence, the Nazis systematized their oppression of the Jews, and the police took a greater role in the persecution. The Nuremberg Laws deprived Jews of citizenship and prohibited sexual relations between Jews and non-Jews. Implementing legislation centralized Jewish matters under the Gestapo and the SD (Security Service). Adolf Eichmann became deputy chief of a new Jewish affairs section within the SD to reduce Jewish influence in German society and encourage emigration. With the passage of the laws, it became essential to define exactly who was a Jew. There was a difference of opinion between the party, which considered a Jew anyone with a drop of Jewish blood, and state officials, who argued for a distinction between pure and mixed Jews. Legislation in November 1935 defined a Jew as anyone with three or more Jewish grandparents, although under certain circumstances, a person could be considered a Jew with only two Jewish grandparents. Persons who did not qualify under the stated conditions or had only one Jewish grandparent comprised the *Mischlinge* (persons of mixed race), although arguments continued on a definition of this category as well.

Kristallnacht

The regime's desire to project a good image to the outside world during the Berlin Olympic Games made anti-Semitism less obvious during 1936 and 1937, but the pressure on Jews to sell their property cheaply to Aryans and leave the country intensified.

In November 1938, following the murder of a German diplomat in Paris by a Jew, the Nazis organized a widespread pogrom called *Kristallnacht* (the "Night of Broken Glass," November 9, 1938). Nazi thugs broke Jewish storefronts all over Germany and devastated Jewish homes, businesses, and synagogues. They arrested Jews en masse and herded many to the Dachau concentration camp. The government held all German Jews responsible for the murder and forced the Jewish community to pay for any losses and a heavy fine.

In early 1939, the state completed the measures that excluded Jews from all sectors of German business life. Employers could fire Jewish workers on short notice, and Jewish workers lost their rights to pensions and unemployment compensation as well. Courts shipped Jews off to concentration camps for minor infractions. Many Jews sold their property or businesses under duress to Aryans for a pittance, hoping to use the meager funds to emigrate, but few Jews made it out of the country before World War II.

Racial Imperialism

Although the Jews were the initial target, racism dominated the Nazi worldview. According to *Mein Kampf,* wherever there were Aryans, progress resulted; wherever there had been progress, there must have been Aryans who were responsible for it; wherever there was cultural decline, it resulted from the mixing of Aryan blood with those of inferior races. As evidence for the circular reasoning, Hitler claimed that Aryans could be identified by their physical characteristics, which were those of the ideal Nordic European —blond, fair-haired, blue-eyed, and slim. Ironically, the top Nazi leadership lacked these physical characteristics, except for the brain behind the SS state and SD head, Reinhard Heydrich, who perhaps had Jewish antecedents.

Hitler argued that Aryans always constituted a small proportion of the population of any given area. Therefore, their superior qualities were particularly subject to corruption through interbreeding, which led to the decline of culture and to the leveling off and end of progress. It is an error to believe that Hitler identified Germans and Aryans because Germans had themselves interbred and because Aryan blood had survived in other areas. Because of race mixing, it was necessary to purify Aryan blood and to prevent further defilement—hence, the Nazi racial laws that outlawed intermarriage with inferior races and euthanasia for persons with mental and physical handicaps, a program (discussed later) that foreshadowed the "final solution" of the Jewish problem.

Besides Jews, the Nazis vented their rage against the German Gypsies (Rom), both "pure" and "mixed." In Germany and in other countries, the Gypsies bore the stigma of being social outcasts. Under the 1935 Nuremberg laws, the Nazis

Once the Nazis came to power, they acted immediately to put their anti-Semitic policies into place. Besides instituting new laws against the Jews, they physically attacked them. On November 9, 1938, following the murder of a German diplomat in Paris, the Nazis destroyed Jewish property and conducted massive arrests of Jews. These events, known as Kristallnacht, or the "Night of Broken Glass" were an early demonstration of the brutal anti-Semitic nature of the Nazi State. Here a man shovels broken glass from a Jewish shop destroyed the night before.

conducted research that was aimed at identifying Gypsies of mixed blood in order to register them and put them into camps where they would be unable to inter-marry with other Germans. The Germans killed off a large percentage of Europe's Gypsy population in the extermination camps of World War II.

Hitler's racism had wide implications. Because the Aryans determined the progress of humanity, Hitler argued that they should dominate over other races and control their raw materials, land, and labor—in fact, had a duty to do so. He was convinced that Aryan control would ensure even the advance of the subject peoples: for example, the Slavs would achieve their greatest happiness working for the Germans. The Nazis established a hierarchy of races, and during World War II attempted to apply their racial doctrines in Eastern Europe: racial imperialism constituted the core of Nazism and mandated an aggressive foreign policy. They enslaved and eliminated millions of Poles, Russians, and other Slavs, in addition to Jews.

The Nazis did not intend to get rid of inferior people immediately but hoped to use their labor while implementing measures to increase the Aryan population that could occupy their land in the future. They were consistent in their folly, as witnessed by their campaign in Germany, to sterilize or eliminate Germans with mental and physical handicaps on the grounds that persons with such character-istics should not propagate undesirable characteristics to future generations. They persecuted gay people, shipping them to concentration camps, and, when conve-nient, used false charges of homosexuality to defeat their opponents.

"Life Unworthy of Life": The Nazi Euthanasia Program

Nazi brutality was a consequence not only of racial imperialism, but of the goal of creating a national community based on blood and race that had to be free of political undesirables, asocial elements, and persons with other genetic handicaps. Political undesirables included persons who actively opposed, or had opposed, Nazism; these persons either remained under a cloud of suspicion or ended up in concentration camps. "Asocials," persons whose behavior deviated from the norm, were similarly treated. In September 1933 and periodically thereafter, the police rounded up beggars, tramps, and homeless people and either put them to work or shipped them to concentration camps, where a black triangle identified them. Prostitutes, pimps, and other criminals met a similar fate. Because the Nazis con-sidered criminal degeneracy to be biologically determined, legislation permitted the arrest of anyone deviating from national community standards and a physical examination to determine biological abnormalities. The law applied pseudoscien-tific biological principles to persons with genetic diseases, which might include active or former membership in the Communist Party, and sterilized them on the grounds of preventing them from passing on their undesirable characteris-tics. Estimates of people who were sterilized between 1934 and 1945 range from 320,000 to 350,000.

Besides sterilization, the Nazis instituted a program for the killing of men-tally ill patients in asylums; these persons could include homosexuals or people who were consigned to asylums by police officers after traffic incidents who judged their behavior to be strange. In order to whip up feeling against mentally ill persons, Hitler ordered the making of propaganda films on the theme of mental illness for viewing by Nazi youth organizations and the public, and the Nazis conducted organized tours of asylums where they displayed patients who were the most ill.

Besides murdering the mentally ill, Hitler sanctioned the killing of severely ill and malformed children. This program allegedly began with a request to Hitler from the parents of an ill child and mushroomed into a large enterprise. In August 1939, the regime required doctors and midwives to register "idiot" children and those with Down's syndrome and a variety of other conditions, including physical deformities. This was the "T-4" program, named for its address in Berlin and organized by a physician, Dr. Leonardo Conti. The Nazi elimination campaign included physically handicapped persons who were considered to be present and future burdens on society. Nazi euthanasia was influenced by late nineteenth-century German thinkers who began with the concept of voluntary euthanasia and ended with the idea of the forced killing of what they considered "life unworthy of life." Economic arguments clinched the rationale for the campaign: "5,000 idiots costing 2,000 RMs [reichsmarks] each per annum = 100 million a year. With interest at 5% that corresponds to a capital reserve of 200 million. That should even mean something to those whose concept of figures has gone awry since the period of inflation." Capping the campaign, the Nazis informed Germans that, in only 120 years, the unfit would hopelessly outnumber the persons with valuable attributes.

The implementation of the T-4 program required the recruiting and training of a large number of professionals, such a doctors, nurses, and lawyers, and experimentation with the most efficient means of murdering patients. These methods varied from lethal injections to gas chambers, complete with the use of crematoria to get rid of the victims' bodies. The organizers took care to spread the responsibility for the killings so that everyone who committed them was equally guilty. Doctors sized up the victims before killing them and determined the cause of death from a standardized list of sixty-one diseases complete with symptoms. After cremating the victims, the doctors randomly collected the ashes and, in bureaucratic letters describing the illness and carefully noting the symptoms, informed the relatives of the deaths and offered to send the urns to them for interment. The euthanasia program was important in the training of personnel and in the determination the most efficient killing methods for later use in the extermination camps of World War II.

The deception linked to the euthanasia campaign did not work. In some cases, multiple urns arrived or a letter referred to a sick organ, such as the appendix, that the victim had had removed years earlier. Protests culminated in a public sermon against the program by Clemens August Graf von Galen, bishop of Muenster, on August 3, 1941, and discussion in diocesan churches. Following the sermon, Hitler agreed to a temporary halt for the duration of the war, although he specifically excluded children. Bishop Galen's sermon alone did not account for the pause in the euthanasia program, which has been explained by the increased demand for personnel in the extermination camps of the East. The Nazi euthanasia program

The Nazi euthanasia program—originally aimed at Germans—was stopped in Germany by internal opposition. Had Hitler won the war, he probably would have restarted it on a massive scale. As it was, it claimed hundreds of thousands of victims inside and outside of Germany and was a training ground for the Holocaust. Here is an exhibition held in January 2012 in Berlin commemorating the child victims of that program.

took at least 200,00 lives, including those within the occupied countries, during World War II.

NAZI THEORY AND PRACTICE

In theory the Nazi Party constituted a community of the elect that upheld moral values and aimed to regenerate political life. Consistent with the Communist and Fascist tendency to fuse party and state, in a law of December 1, 1933, the Fuehrer embodied the NSDAP's constitution, the repository of the German idea of the state.

The Party

The party was a public agency whose leaders assumed high-state functions. Their primary tasks: to explain National Socialism and transform the German people into a tight-knit community, goals that would permit the development to the fullest of the moral and heroic German man. German women instead, "mothers" of the people, had the duty of increasing the birth rate after a long period of decline as their special contribution to Nazi society. As one German official stated: "The German woman belongs in the kitchen!" Citizens could join the party, but only members of the German race could obtain

The SS was the core of the Nazi State and was the organization on which the future of Nazism was to be based. The organization had a major role in the Nazi euthanasia program and in the organization of the concentration camps. After a Nazi victory in World War II, they were to have the role of settling the East by returning to the soil and populating the region with racially pure Aryans. This picture shows an SS guard playing his trumpet at a rally. Note the skull and crossbones.

citizenship, so Jews could be neither German citizens nor party members. As the party's head, the Fuehrer concentrated all the powers of the state in his person, so state and party were one, and its task was to achieve racial purity.

The SS and the Nazi State

As Nazi practice developed, the SS (Security Guards), headed by Heinrich Himmler, increasingly tended to absorb the state, a development that had no real basis in Nazi theory. The SS penetrated and undermined existing institutions with the aim of creating an SS state. An observer wrote: "Fundamentally there was no sphere of public life upon which the SS did not make its competing demands: the economic, ideological, military, scientific and technical spheres, as well as those of agrarian and population policies, legislation and general administration."

The SS was the major instrument of Nazi racism. Himmler, with a degree in agronomy and a short stint as a chicken farmer, sought to apply to human genetics principles similar to animal breeding. Besides killing off subhumans so they could not pass on their undesirable traits, Himmler favored eliminating monogamy as a means of passing on desired Nordic features with less interference from society. He calculated that by applying Nazi genetic principles, only 120 years would be required to reestablish the authentic German look in the country. He waxed poetic about how the SS would return to the soil as peasant-warriors and entertained other romantic visions. Himmler prided himself on his own and on Germans' tenderness toward animals and condemned hunting as pure murder. It was ironic that such a person claimed to value honesty, boasting that the SS had very high standards and threatening to execute without mercy SS men who stole anything from the Jews they murdered. Even though the SS had a duty to eliminate the Jews as the chief enemy of the German race, he stated that "We have no right to enrich ourselves by so much as a fur, a watch, a mark, or a cigarette or anything else."

EVERYDAY LIFE

Most ordinary Germans accepted the Nazi regime and believed in National Socialism. Because most were not Jews, leftists, or members of religious sects that the Nazis targeted, such as the Jehovah's Witnesses, they had little contact with the authorities. The dreaded secret police, the Gestapo, could not have controlled the population if the regime did not have at least the tacit consent of the people.

Ordinary Germans

Germans during the Third Reich generally went about their own business and making a living. They knew that the Nazis persecuted Jews and political opponents, but the terror did not affect their own lives. There are even indications that a majority of Germans frowned on the violence and brutality of Kristallnacht and that public opinion, after hearing talk of gassings during World War II, criticized the practice. Germans told jokes about their leaders, including Hitler. Theoretically, the dissemination of such humor could result in severe punishments, but later surveys indicate that people did not expect to receive such punishment. Certainly, jokes, grumbling, and the like did not threaten the regime, nor did people intend them to do so. With the economy going well and with Germany respected internationally, most Germans felt satisfied. Most of them esteemed Hitler, even if they did not agree with all aspects of the regime.

Resisters who were ashamed of Nazism did appear in Germany, but generally restricted their activities to discussions. Perhaps the most famous, the Kreisau Circle of James Helmuth von Moltke, aimed to restore a decent German government once Hitler fell from power. This dangerous activity resulted in the execution of von Moltke, but no armed resistance or strong exile movement materialized.

On some social issues the Nazis demonstrated an ambivalent attitude. Some opposed bourgeois values, Hitler himself being the epitome of this outlook. In its relationship with most Germans, however, the party supported a bourgeois lifestyle. This approach won out with the enforcement of nineteenth-century behavioral norms and attitudes toward sex.

A similar ambivalent view emerged toward homosexuals. The number of homosexuals who were arrested and condemned to prison is unknown, although historians seem to accept 50,000 as a reasonable figure. Nazi authorities sent some of these prisoners to concentration camps, where they suffered about a 60 percent death rate, higher than the political prisoners. Nevertheless, with Nazi leaders estimating the number of gay people in Germany at 2 million, the arrests represented a limited number. In contrast to their views on race, the Nazis considered homosexuals curable because they supposedly had been seduced. Hitler himself had declared the homosexuality of his colleague Roehm a private matter, even if he used it against Roehm and the SA during the "Night of the Long Knives" and willingly exploited the charge against other enemies. After June 1934, the government stepped up the persecution of gays, but the campaign remained limited because, according to scholar Harry Oosterhuis, a widespread crackdown would have devastated the ranks of Nazi organizations.

BIOGRAPHICAL SKETCHES

Gertrud Scholtz-Klink
Unrepentant!

The daughter of a surveyor, the future chief of the Nazi Women's Group (NSF) was born Gertrud Treusch in Adelsheim (Baden), Germany, on February 9, 1902. In 1920 she married Friedrich Klink, future Nazi district leader of Offenburg.
She did social and propaganda work for the party, and in March 1930, her husband died of a heart attack during a demonstration. Spurred by a desire for revenge, her involvement with Nazism increased, and she took the lead in organizing the women of Baden in support of the Nazi cause. In 1932 she married Gunther Scholtz, a country doctor.

In 1931, the Nazis established the NSF as the central women's organization. Scholtz-Klink had been rising in the ranks of the Nazi women's movement and, following the Nazi takeover in 1933, she headed the National Women's Labor Corps. Her administrative talents, skill in cooperating with Catholic women, and Aryan appearance brought her to the attention of national Nazi leaders. Her close collaboration with Erich Hilgenfelt, director of national welfare, allowed her to overcome more accomplished rivals and led to persistent rumors that they were lovers. In February 1934, Adolf Hitler named Scholtz-Klink national women's leader of the Third Reich. German propaganda successfully portrayed her as one of the most important personalities in the Nazi leadership, and on a visit to England in 1939, the British press called her "the Perfect Nazi Woman." In 1940, two years after her divorce from Scholtz, she married an SS general. Before the marriage, an investigation of her background for four generations revealed that she did not have any Jewish blood.

Frequently seen in Hitler's company on public occasions, Scholtz-Klink had little influence on policy. Understanding that she would probably lose her position if she showed initiative, she was docile, downplayed ideology, and concentrated on everyday administration. She responded to allegations that she had no clout by stating that this was because Nazi leaders expressed their wishes orally. She claimed absolute independence for the Nazi women's movement because "No man ever represented us in the outside world. We spoke for ourselves." She insisted that she ran her organization in a democratic manner because, since it was a big happy family, the women ironed out their problems over tea. Even top Nazis were confused about her position in the state.

During the last days of World War II, Scholtz-Klink suffered depression and frequently failed to perform her official duties. Following Berlin's fall, the Russians captured her, but she escaped. She and her husband hid out in a small village as Heinrich and Maria Stuckebruck and worked as bakers. They were denazified under these false names in 1948 but were soon found out. A French court sentenced them to eighteen months in jail on April 14, 1948, for using false documents. In 1949, a German court sentenced Scholtz-Klink to eighteen months for having been the NSF leader, but commuted the sentence because she had already served the time. In 1950, an appeals court categorized both Scholtz-Klink and her husband as having been major criminals during the Nazi regime. The court condemned her to thirty months in a work camp, prohibited her from working as a teacher or journalist for ten years, and excluded her from political activity for life. Scholtz-Klink lived quietly until 1978, when she published her autobiography. Consisting primarily of speeches and articles written during the Third Reich, the book is an administrative report, rather than a reflection on her life. In interviews she praised the glory days, defended the Third Reich's most extreme policies, and reveled in her own role. More than forty years after its fall, Gertrud Scholtz-Klink remained an unbroken, enthusiastic, and unrepentant supporter of Nazism.

Nazi theory and practice toward women was also fundamentally ambiguous. Although the Nazis saw women as having their major role in the home, producing children, in 1931 they created the NSF. This was a centralized organization that was designed to regularize the auxiliary work—such as establishing soup kitchens, providing medical help to Nazi fighters, mending uniforms, and sewing flags and banners—provided by many local Nazi women's organizations. Between 1932 and 1933, the women's organization lost most of its important functions, especially as the vehicle attracting the young to the movement. In February 1934, the unimaginative Gertrud Scholtz-Klink became NSF head. The NSF did not easily reconcile itself to its loss of prestige and status but, given the primacy that the Nazis assigned to the male organizations and the competition that the NSF faced from women's organizations that were affiliated with the traditional religions, little could be done to restore its former reputation.

Ironically, the scant interest the Nazis had for women's organizations allowed these organizations greater freedom. In contrast to other parties that gave them greater importance but then limited their scope when they went off in directions the male leaders did not approve, the Nazi women's organizations could plan their activities with considerable flexibility. This liberty included interpreting the Fuehrer's thoughts, supervising mass marches and rallies, administering funds they collected, making speeches, and responding to rivals. The ideas of Nazi women may have been reactionary, but women expressed them in their own way, and, despite the official rhetoric, as Claudia Koonz pointed out, they never believed that they would return exclusively to homemaking and sought to open different areas of public life to their gender.

Cultural Aspects

In the cultural field, the Nazi government took over all areas of life. Education at all levels came under its control, and it imposed its racist thinking on intellectual discourse. A centralized Reich Chamber of Culture, established by Joseph Goebbels in September 1933, ran arts and leisure. Divided into subchambers for the different arts, this organization enrolled artists and professionals on a compulsory basis, weeded out what it considered dangerous elements and movements, and promoted "healthy" ones. The regime thus quickly took control of the country's writers, university professors, and other intellectuals and held it until 1945.

Submission also characterized German religious organizations. The Protestant churches objected more to Himmler's undermining of sexual mores in attempting to create a purified race than to the implementation of the more brutal features of Nazi racial policy. Hitler unified the Lutheran churches, traditionally close to the state, under a single authority controlled by the government and jailed opposition religious leaders. The Catholic Church, potentially less subservient to Nazi authority because it came under the pope's jurisdiction, feared subjugation to the Nazis and to the state's power. In July 1933, it signed a concordat with the state that prohibited priests from participating in politics and giving the regime a role in naming bishops. As in the Italian case, observers construed the concordat as moral approval for the regime, and Hitler apparently considered it significant in the struggle against the Jews. The extent to which Papal Nuncio Eugenio Pacelli, future Pope Pius XII, gave in to Hitler on these issues remains controversial. Although the Catholic hierarchy made some attempt to defend Jews who had converted, neither the Catholic nor the Protestant churches issued powerful rebukes against the Nazi racial policy, and the government did not hesitate to send any clergy or religious opponents to concentration camps.

The propaganda machine, which Goebbels created and ran, was instrumental in creating a consensus for the regime. The son of a Rhineland Catholic working-class family, Goebbels had a club foot that hampered him physically and psychologically. During Nazism's early days, his infirmity subjected the "little doctor" to ridicule from the muscular, well-built but unintelligent party specimens of the Aryan race. In 1926, Goebbels had demanded Hitler's expulsion from the party, but he grew to adore the Fuehrer and worked diligently to imbue the leader with a mystical quality. He orchestrated public spectacles favoring the regime, with the great marching columns, the flags, banners, searchlights, fanfares, and the coordinated shouting of slogans illustrated in Leni Riefenstahl's film *The Triumph of the Will*. Goebbels aimed to dissolve the individual into the mass and to induce the mindlessness that numbed the nation for the greater power of Hitler.

To organize leisure time, the Germans created the Strength Through Joy movement, modeled after the Italian *Dopolavoro*. This organization allowed workers to attend movies and live theater, to travel, and to participate in a host of activities. After World War II, German workers frequently cited the economic security of the Nazi era and their trips to the theater as the highlights of their lives.

Youths

The Nazis concentrated on indoctrinating and regimenting the country's young people aged 10 to 18 by incorporating them into the Hitler Youth, made compulsory between 1936 and 1939. Boys and girls aged 10 to 14 belonged to the German Young People and to the Young Girls League. Afterward, they graduated to the Hitler Youth and to the League of German Girls.

Boys and girls reveled in the camaraderie and feelings of power that came from membership in an association, uniforms, and a military atmosphere. Girls especially enjoyed the experience of time away from their stifling home lives. However, rebellious teenagers grew restive against the obligation to conform to the rules of the Nazi youth organizations. Hitler Youth leaders kept boys and girls strictly separate and prohibited them from smoking, drinking, having sex, or even from going out at night. Girls who dared wear makeup, high-heeled shoes, or short dresses had their heads shaved.

The rigidity and separation of the sexes that characterized the Nazi youth organizations encouraged the formation of rival groups that the regime frowned upon. Edelweiss Pirate groups consisted of boys and girls aged 14 to 18, mainly working class, who met during their leisure time with the avowed aim of escaping control by the Hitler Youth. They packed their gear during weekends, went to the countryside to camp together, and met with like-minded bands from other villages. They either avoided Hitler Youth patrols or attacked them, depending of the circumstances, according to the slogan: "Eternal War on the Hitler Youth." These adolescents experimented with subjects the Hitler Youth considered

Hitler wished to better the economic and social life of the Germans. This included fostering the development of an automobile ordinary Germans could afford, the "People's Car," or Volkswagen. A design of this car was sent to Pininfarina, the Italian automotive designer. He pronounced the design perfect, but suggested the addition of the rear side windows. Here is a photo of Hitler opening a Volkswagen factory on May 27, 1938.

taboo, especially sex, and the Nazi authorities viewed their exploits as delinquency.

The Swing Youth also sought to escape the conformity and rigidity of the Hitler Youth. This movement consisted of urban middle-class teenagers who rebelled against the bland music sanctioned by the regime, jitterbugging in city dance halls to the sound of jazz rhythms that the government frowned upon as "Negro" and foreign. These adolescents had more means and education than the Edelweiss Pirates; knew a smattering of a foreign language, usually English; and could afford to frequent dance halls, buy records, pay the fees to attend concerts given by foreign bands, and meet in homes big enough to hold large groups. Starting from traditional jazz music still played in Germany, they radicalized it and danced in ways the authorities considered sexually suggestive and sleazy. Although apolitical, the activities of the Swing Youth struck at the heart of the regime's philosophical core because its adherents had grown up during the Nazi regime and should have served as a showcase for it. The Nazis denounced the supposedly loose morals of the Swing Youth and discussed sending its leaders to concentration camps.

Reorganizing the Economy

Once in power the Nazis adopted new economic policies that spurred a recovery and prepared the country for war.

The Nazis quickly took on the powerful labor unions and their leftist political allies. In 1933 and 1934 they destroyed the labor unions through a terror campaign and by imposing strict controls on the labor force. They eliminated the possibility of striking and dismissed Socialist and Communist workers and shop stewards. Wages leveled off even as rearmament proceeded, but wages did not go up even when the economy improved dramatically because of the need to absorb large numbers of unemployed people, government-imposed controls, and the lack of unions.

In order to ensure their control over workers, the Nazis organized labor in the German Labor Front (DAF), led by Robert Ley, that industrial workers were obliged to join, and eliminated the influence of Nazi labor organizers. This arrangement symbolized the ideological unity of the Germans. Fearing too much concentration of power, employers and the government agreed that the DAF would not be the vehicle through which to settle the everyday issues of German industrial life. In November 1933, the employers joined the organization. Industry was considered to consist of industrial communities with a Fuehrer and followers. Consequently, industrial enterprises had to agree to councils that would advise administrators. Employers did not like this idea, but their return to profitability induced them to accept it.

In order to put people back to work and accelerate production for the coming war, the Nazis drew up a Four-Year Plan directed by *Luftwaffe* (air force) head Hermann Goering. The plan envisioned increasing governmental authority over workers, including the control of wages and production, and measures restricting job mobility. The government hesitated to implement these measures because of a labor shortage, and it anticipated workers' resistance. The authorities drafted workers for jobs on war-related enterprises in June 1938, but felt confident enough to institute wage and price controls only after the outbreak of war.

The government took pains to appear neutral in the relationship between labor and capital because a substantial number of workers had supported the Nazis and belonged to the party. The regime actively involved workers in its political accomplishments, subsidized leisure activities through the Strength Through Joy movement, and developed a "people's car," the Volkswagen, to increase the workers' personal mobility. Leisure activities included organized tourism, concerts by symphony orchestras at the factories, visits to theaters, participation in and attendance at sports events, and the creation of factory libraries (no subversive literature). Despite these activities, the workers lacked real power, and conflicts with their bosses smoldered under the surface.

BIOGRAPHICAL SKETCHES

Hermann Goering
Nazi Chieftain

Hermann Goering was probably the most visible and popular leader of the Third Reich besides Hitler. The son of a judge who had represented Bismarck in South West Africa, Goering had an aristocratic background that set him apart from the other prominent Nazi leaders.

Born on January 12, 1893, in Rosenheim, Germany, Goering fought in World War I as an infantry lieutenant and combat pilot. In 1918, he commanded Manfred von Richthofen's fighter squadron after the Red Baron's death, shooting down twenty-two enemy airplanes and winning two prestigious medals. After the war, he piloted planes for air shows in Denmark and Sweden, where he met his future wife. His love of adventure drew him to the Nazi party, and in 1923 he participated in the abortive Beer Hall putsch. Wounded, he fled to Sweden, where he had a mental breakdown and developed a life-long addiction to morphine. He returned to Germany in 1927 after an amnesty.

Goering's access to military, conservative, business, and aristocratic circles proved valuable for the Nazis, as did his organizational abilities. He was credited with the dramatic Nazi electoral victory of July 31, 1932, and was elected president of the Reichstag. When Hitler became chancellor in January 1933, Goering took over the Prussian Interior Ministry. Prussia, the biggest German state, played a crucial role in establishing effective Nazi control of the country. Goering purged the Prussian police force and, with Heinrich Himmler and Reinhard Heydrich, set up the first concentration camps. After passage of the March 1933 emergency decree, he eliminated the remnants of civil liberties in Prussia, imprisoned Nazi opponents, and destroyed the left-wing press. He also directed the "Night of the Long Knives," June 30, 1934, that destroyed his rival Ernst Roehm and the SA.

Goering amassed more power, offices, and wealth than any other Nazi chieftain. Appointed commander of the air force on March 1, 1935, he oversaw its rapid expansion. In 1936, he ran the Four-Year Plan that gave him effective control of the country's economic life. The Hermann Goering Works, established in 1937,

continued

continued

created a private industrial empire that employed 700,000 workers and allowed him to become fabulously wealthy. He lived in spectacular quarters in Berlin and in a hunting lodge outside the city, where he organized ostentatious parties and hunts. He collected art masterpieces and, during the war, stole many of them from all over Europe. However, Goering did not let his luxurious life interfere in the politics that had allowed him to attain it. He plotted against rivals who might have threatened him and worked out the details of Nazi actions against the Jews. He was so successful that in September 1939, Hitler named him his successor.

Goering had exaggerated pretensions to military greatness that proved his undoing during World War II. He made egregious errors that produced the German failure to defeat Britain from the air and contributed to the inability to defend Germany from Allied bombers. Hitler blamed him for these failures and came to hate him—more so because, compromised by the favors he had bestowed on him, he could not get rid of him. Aware of his sinking prestige, Goering withdrew into a world of denial. Just before Germany's final defeat, Goering misinterpreted Hitler's statement that he would stay in his bunker until the end and declared he would take over Germany. Hitler stripped him of his posts and had him arrested, but on May 9, 1945, the Americans captured him. The Nuremberg Tribunal found him guilty of war crimes and sentenced him to death. On October 5, 1946, two hours before his scheduled execution, Goering cheated the hangman by biting down on a cyanide capsule he had hidden in his mouth.

Nazism and Capitalism: Arms and Autobahns

Despite anticapitalist Nazi rhetoric and measures that appeared contrary to capitalist interests, the Nazis implanted capitalist policies to accelerate Germany's economic recovery and rearmament. The government attacked the high unemployment rate by launching a large road-building program—the *Autobahns*. When rearmament began full force after 1935, the government instituted a complex system of controls over the economy, including planning boards and governmental ventures into strategic industrial sectors that were necessary for arms production, including the massive Hermann Goering Steel Works. Large private enterprises, such as Krupp and I. G. Farben, profited handsomely from rearmament, but small businesses were unable to compete with the large private and state industries that enjoyed cozy arrangements with the Nazi Party. By spending enormous amounts on public works and rearmament, the Nazis eradicated the unemployment of the depression era, and governmental controls avoided inflation.

The Germans paid a heavy cost for governmental policies in the form of higher prices. Because the government reoriented the German economy away from consumer items and banned the importation of some goods, they paid higher prices for substitutes, wages failed to keep pace with production, and war-oriented state enterprises came with a high price tag. War preparations created a vicious economic circle: rearmament encouraged aggressiveness, which created a greater need for arms. Despite the great progress made by German industry, the country's war potential still fell short of the demands that Hitler made in preparation for the coming conflict. When World War II broke out, Germany was short of arms, food, fuel, and raw materials. The rapid conquests that were made during the early months of the war allowed Germany to make up the shortages, as Hitler had envisaged, but only temporarily.

The Nazis singled out agriculture as the inspiration for a romanticized and racist ideology and promised good times for this sector. Through the SS, the Nazis, in an ideal world, would return to the soil that they believed had nourished their race. This idea and promises of economic improvement had won the Nazis crucial support in rural areas, but they did not fulfill the Nazis' assurances. The government's halfhearted agricultural measures failed to stop the flight of the peasants from the land into the cities, whose population increased dramatically during the first five years of Nazi rule. Although the Nazis instituted a policy of restricting imports and firming up prices, rural income failed to keep pace with national income, and fewer people established farms during the Nazi era than during the Weimar period. Owners of small- and medium-sized farms sank deeper into debt, and peasants could not afford to make needed technological improvements. The Nazi emphasis on industry as a necessary facet of war preparedness makes it hardly surprising that governmental aid to farmers proved inadequate.

Social Ramifications

Nazi industrial policy had unintended effects that contradicted theory. The Nazis believed that women should remain at home producing more children for the master race, discouraging them from entering the labor market, politics, and the universities. The Nazis introduced measures, such as marriage credits, bonuses for children to combat earlier feminist demands for emancipation and to keep German women at home. With the booming economy and the resulting labor shortage caused by its rearmament policy, the government gradually reintegrated women into the workforce without admitting it. Women were paid less for their work than men and found it difficult to advance, but the number of women working outside the home increased from less than 4.25 million in 1933 to 5.2 million in 1938. Despite their ideology, the Nazis favored a trend that would accelerate during World War II and the postwar era.

Similarly, the Nazis advocated revolutionizing the existing society but implemented the idea only superficially. They claimed to aim at the creation of a people's community in which everyone would be equal under the leader; the people were national or "Volk" comrades. The Nazis scorned the existing society; derided the old bourgeoisie, capitalists, and intellectuals; glorified peasants and workers; and established a pervasive youth movement. The "people's community" had to act as one, especially on special holidays. On these occasions, the Nazis organized mass demonstrations with the emphasis on slogans epitomizing their ideals—"Blood and Soil" for the peasants, "Brawn and Brain" for the workers. Regimentation increased dramatically, and beginning in 1935, "labor soldiers"—workers—had to sign up at labor offices and be subject to the needs of rearmament.

The despised capitalists represented the old regime, but, contradicting this image, capitalists who cooperated with Nazism belonged to the "good" variety. The government favored charitable societies to aid less fortunate comrades and mobilized the population to raise money for the poor. On occasion, it used these events to humiliate the groups they despised, such as intellectuals. In 1937, the Nazis sent Leipzig professor and Nobel Prize-winning nuclear physicist Werner Heisenberg out onto the cold city streets to beg funds to aid the urban poor. Ironically enough, by knocking over class barriers, in the end National Socialism contributed to the modernization of German society, a goal that Nazi ideology professed to oppose.

Bibliographical Essay

Richard Evans's *The Third Reich in Power* (New York, 2006) is the most complete book on this period and beyond. A good general work that discusses the topics considered in this chapter is Martin Broszat, *The Hitler State: The Foundation and Development of the Internal Structure of the Third Reich* (London, 1981). More recently, there is Michael Burleigh, *The Third Reich: A New History* (New York, 2000).

The social impact of Nazism is examined by David Schoenbaum, *Hitler's Social Revolution: Class and Status in Nazi Germany, 1933–1939* (New York, 1997), who examines broken pledges to farmers and the lower middle class. William Allen Sheridan, *The Nazi Seizure of Power* (New York, 1984), discusses the events and social impact in a single town. David Crew, *Nazism and German Society: 1933–1945* (London, 1994), emphasizes interpretations. Timothy W. Mason concentrates on labor in *Social Policy in the Third Reich* (Providence, R.I., 1993) and in a series of essays (that also include Fascist Italy), *Nazism, Fascism, and the Working Class* (Cambridge, UK, 1995). Proving your Aryan blood was important; on this issue, see Eric Ehrenreich, *The Nazi Ancestral Proof* (Bloomington, Ind., 2007). Three works that explore the ordinary German's world during this period are Bernt Engelmann, *In Hitler's Germany: Everyday Life in the Third Reich* (London, 1988); Elaine Halleck, *Living in Nazi Germany* (San Diego, Calif., 2004); and Detlev Peukert, *Inside Nazi Germany: Conformity and Opposition in Everyday Life* (Harmondsworth, UK, 1989), which also discusses the issue of racism in everyday life. Eric A. Johnson's *Nazi Terror: The Gestapo, Jews, and Ordinary Germans* (New York, 1999), is an excellent detailed work on the everyday interactions of Germans, the Gestapo, and Jews. Volume 1 of Saul Friedlaender's *Nazi Germany and the Jews* (Cambridge, Mass., 1997) examines the period discussed in this chapter. Richard Bessel, ed., *Life in the Third Reich* (New York, 1987), discusses how Germans perceived the actions of their government during this period. Sarah Gordon published a nuanced book on *Hitler, Germans, and the "Jewish Question"* (Princeton, N.J., 1984). John Cornwell, *Hitler's Pope: The Secret History of Pius XII* (Harmondsworth, UK, 1999), is a controversial interpretation of Eugenio Pacelli's role during this period and as pope.

Elimination of the Jews in the Reich has been interpreted both as stemming from a design and as gradually evolving. Lucy Dawidowicz, *The War Against the Jews, 1933–1945* (Harmondsworth, UK, 1990), and Karl A. Schleunes, *The Twisted Road to Auschwitz: Nazi Policy Toward German Jews* (Urbana, Ill., 1990), take different positions on this subject. Robert Gellately's *The Gestapo and German Society: Enforcing Racial Policy, 1933–1945* (Oxford, UK, 1991) shows the public's reaction to the dreaded secret police and its operations.

Nazi women are discussed by Claudia Koonz, *Mothers in the Fatherland: Women, the Family, and Nazi Politics* (New York, 1987). Jill Stephenson examines the origins, development, and functions of women's groups associated with the party from the 1920s to 1945 in *The Nazi Organisation of Women* (London, 1981).

Biographies of Hitler's subordinates can also lead to an understanding of the Nazi phenomenon. Joachim C. Fest gathered a series of short sketches that serve as an excellent introduction to these subalterns: *The Face of the Third Reich: Portraits of the Nazi Leadership* (New York, 1970), from which the citation on the SS state and Himmler's statement on the duty of SS soldiers to be honest are taken (pp. 117 and 118). On Himmler, see Willi Frischauer, *Himmler: The Evil Genius of the Third Reich* (Boston, 1953), and Richard Breitman, *The Architect of Genocide: Himmler and the Final Solution* (Hanover, N.H., 1991). Another of Hitler's subordinates described Himmler's plans, Albert Speer, *The Slave State: Heinrich: Himmler's Masterplan for SS Supremacy* (London, 1981). Anthony Read, *The Devil's Disciples* (New York, 2004), is a book on Hitler's inner circle.

On the SS itself, consult Adrian Weale, *The SS: A New History* (London, 2010), a complete history from its rise to its fall. Gerard Reitlinger, *The SS: Alibi of a Nation* (New York, 1968), includes a discussion of the relationship with the SA, and Helmut Krausnick et al., *The Anatomy of the SS State* (London, 1982). Biographies of Hitler's other lieutenants include Ralf Georg Reuth, *Goebbels* (San Diego, Calif., 1994); Helmut Heiber, *Goebbels* (New York, 1972); and the earlier Curt Riess, *Joseph Goebbels* (Garden City, N.Y. 1948). Take a look also at *Joseph Goebbels* (New York, 2009). Leonard Moseley has written a comprehensive biography of Hermann Goering, *The Reich Marshal* (Garden City, N.Y., 1974); see also Richard J. Overy, *Goering: The Iron Man* (London, 1987). Joachim von Lang published an extensive biography of Hitler's influential secretary, *Martin Bormann* (Garden City, N.Y., 1974).

Books on more specialized issues include one on birth control and abortion: Atina Grossmann, *Reforming Sex* (New York, 1995). Michael Burleigh, *Death and Deliverance* (London, 2002), is an excellent work on the Nazi euthanasia program and some of its antecedents; the quotation on the cost of maintaining patients is on p. 99. Henry Friedlander makes the connection between Nazi policies on euthanasia and the final solution in *The Origins of Nazi Genocide: From Euthanasia to the Final Solution* (Chapel Hill, N.C., 1995). For some of the other groups discussed, see Richard Plant, *The Pink Triangle* (New York, 1986), for the Nazi attack on homosexuals; Sylvie Graffard and Michel Reynaud, *The Jehovah's Witnesses and the Nazis* (New York, 2001); M. V. Seeman et al., *The Holocaust and the Mentally Ill* (Armonk, N.Y., 2006); Suzanne E. Evans, *Forgotten Crimes: The Holocaust and People With Disabilities* (Chicago, 2004). On the Rom during this period, there is a chapter by Ian Hancock, "The Roots of Antigypsyism: To the Holocaust and After," in C. Jan Colijn and Marcia Sachs, eds., *Configuring the Holocaust* (Lanham, Md., 1997).

Dietrich Orlow, *The History of the Nazi Party,* 2 vols. (Pittsburgh, 1969–1973), analyzes the impact that the achievement of governmental power on the NSDAP. The army's role is analyzed by John W. Wheeler-Bennet, *The Nemesis of Power,* 2d ed. (London, 1980), the standard work, and Klaus-Jurgen Muller, *Army, Politics, and Society in Germany, 1933–1945* (New York, 1987). Ian Kershaw, *The "Hitler Myth": Image and Reality in the Third Reich* (Oxford, UK, 1989), previously cited, discusses public opinion during the Nazi period.

The debate about the extent to which the German people supported Hitler's policies against the Jews has always stirred historians. Two opposing views may be found in Daniel Goldhagen, *Hitler's Willing Executioners: Ordinary Germans and the Holocaust* (New York, 1996), and in the diary of a Jew who lived in the Third Reich, Victor Klemperer, *I Will Bear Witness: A Diary of the Nazi Years,* 2 vols. (New York, 1998). For an examination of Goldhagen's impact, see Geoff Eley, ed., *The Goldhagen Effect: History, Memory, Nazism—Facing the German Past* (Ann Arbor, Mich., 2000), and Robert R. Shandley, ed., *Unwilling Germans? The Goldhagen Debate* (Minneapolis, Minn., 1998).

On social issues, consult David Schoenbaum's *Hitler's Social Revolution: Class and Status in Nazi Germany 1933–1939* (London, 1966). A book of essays, Richard Bessel's *Life in the Third Reich* (Oxford, UK, 1987), previously cited, includes valuable treatments of important social issues. M. L. Thornton, *Nazism 1918–1945* (Oxford, UK, 1966), a general treatment of Nazism, has several useful chapters. Paul Brooker's *The Faces of Fraternalism* (Oxford, UK, 1991) examines consensus in Germany and Italy. See Chapter 12 for works on Italy.

On the churches, see Ernst Christian Helmreich, *The German Churches Under Hitler* (Detroit, 1979), and J. S. Conway, *The Nazi Persecution of the Churches* (London, 1968).

Good discussions of Nazi economic policies and their impact are in Avraham Barkai, *Nazi Economics: Ideology, Theory, and Policies* (New Haven, Conn., 1990), and Richard J. Overy, *The Nazi Economic Recovery, 1932–1938,* 2d ed. (Cambridge, UK, 1996).

Books emphasizing different interpretations of the Nazi phenomenon include Ian Kershaw, *The Nazi Dictatorship: Problems and Perspectives of Interpretations,* 3rd ed. (London, 1993). Thomas Childers and Jane Caplan, eds., *Reevaluating the Third Reich* (New York, 1993), is a series of excellent essays that discuss important themes regarding the history of the Third Reich and that illustrate some new thinking about Nazi Germany.

George L. Mosse has written many works on the ideas that eventually flowed into Nazism. Most relevant for this chapter is *Nationalism and Sexuality: Respectability and Abnormal Sexuality in Modern Europe* (New York, 1985). This book explains how such stereotypes as healthy, degenerate, normal, and abnormal could end up in the persecution of Jews, Gypsies, homosexuals, and the handicapped. Mosse also wrote *The Fascist Revolution: Toward A General Theory of Fascism* (New York, 1999), which is primarily concerned with Nazism but has interesting essays on Italy and France.

After the fall of Nazism, a debate took place on whether it had deep roots in German society and whether the country followed a "special path" that led to Hitler. This is known as the *Sonderweg* debate. For the ramifications of this debate, see Hans-Ulrich Wehler, *The German Empire, 1871–1918* (New York, 1985), and the essay "The German Identity and Historical Comparison," in Peter Baldwin, ed., *Reworking the Past* (Boston, 1987). See also Charles S. Maier, *The Unmasterable Past: History, Holocaust, and German National Identity* (Cambridge, Mass., 1988), and David Blackbourn and Geoff Eley, *The Peculiarities of German History: Bourgeois Society and Politics in Nineteenth- Century Germany* (New York, 1984).

CHAPTER 16

✐

Interwar Society and Culture

W orld War I caused many changes in European society and culture. The
sorrow caused by so many deaths dampened the European zest for living.
Gigantic ossuaries containing soldiers' bones sprouted over the European landscape; hyperinflation destroyed the savings of Germans; fascism took over in Italy;
war, boundary disputes, ethnic divisions, anti-Semitism, and incipient dictatorships disrupted East European life. Nevertheless, at least in the West, the middle
class had come to expect leisure time and social welfare as a right. During the
1920s and the depression, European states passed legislation guaranteeing their
citizens paid free time and other benefits, while technological changes improved
the lives of ordinary people, and quantum mechanics revolutionized modern life
and attitudes.

SOCIETY

World War I created a more subdued atmosphere in Europe, but the need for war
supplies and labor improved the economic position of many people, and, on good
days, British vacationers on the southern coast could hear the report of shells fired
on the battlefield.

Private Lives
After 1918, the toned-down lifestyle of ordinary Europeans appeared in more subdued leisurely activities, such as reading books and daily newspapers, that became

an ingrained habit by 1920 in Britain. Advertising came into its own, contributing most of the newspaper revenue and exercising an important impact on economics and society.

The results of the conflict revolutionized social habits during the 1920s and 1930s on the continent. In Germany hyperinflation removed the restraints from young bourgeois women to run off and get married without waiting for the financial security or the socially appropriate bridegroom that prewar attitudes demanded. Bolshevik Russia witnessed an extraordinary emancipation of women from the sexual mores of the prerevolutionary era. In Italy a new mood of confidence among workers marked the Red Biennium before Fascism's rise. In general, European family ties became looser.

In England, men and women mixed more easily than they had before the war, a trend that resulted in a national debate on the place of women in society. Observers argued about whether women were the intellectual equals of men. Feminist organizations demanded political rights.

Society condemned abortion and punished it severely, as was seen in France, which enforced its abortion laws more strictly than before 1914. Birth control laws forced abstinence on couples who wanted to limit their families—wives frequently opting for separate rooms and barred doors. Despite the obstacles to birth control, however, fertility rates declined.

Women in Western Europe improved their political and legal status and attained greater social freedom. In Germany and Scandinavia, they received the right to vote. In Britain, the first woman entered Parliament in 1919, and women were admitted to full membership in the professions and academic life—despite professorial protests. Throughout the 1920s, Western countries progressively repealed many legal disabilities that hampered women's progress, and women's growing freedom encouraged discussions of formerly taboo topics, such as homosexuality.

Fashion

Women's fashions reflected their emancipation, and commentators complained that women dressed too scantily: short skirts, sleeves above the elbows, floppy hats, skimpy lingerie. High heels, long associated with the theater and immorality, became common. Only rich women could afford silk stockings to go with them, and middle-class women contented themselves with wool or cotton stockings. The 1920s "flapper" made her entrance with bobbed hair and dancing to jazz rhythms. American music and African American singers, such as Josephine Baker in France, became models for a new life criticized by traditionalists. The upper and middle classes set the dance styles at first but later preferred restaurants and supper clubs and left the dance halls to their lower-middle-class brethren. In Britain new dance palaces dotted the postwar landscape, and skill in ballroom dancing seemed inversely proportional to social status. The emphasis on life, enjoyment, and youth was a reaction to the deaths caused by the recent conflict. Age lost its social status to youth and trim physiques, as reflected in the less formal fashions for both sexes. Men's beards disappeared, and English children earned points with their playmates by shouting "Beaver" when they spotted a man with a beard.

Perhaps African-American Josephine Baker best epitomizes the changes in women's roles during the Interwar period. She lived in France where she became the best-known entertainer there and was a friend of the most important artists and writers of the period. During World War II, she worked in the French Resistance and later supported the American Civil Rights movement in the 1950s and 1960s. She died in France on April 12, 1975, and was buried with French military honors.

Tourism and Sports

The desire to live life more fully brought a greater appetite for tourism and sports. Both had grown before World War I, and the expansion continued after the conflict. In 1930, a million Britons vacationed on the continent, producing a boom in the number of travel agencies and hotels. Unlike the pre-1914 period, tourists required passports to travel even to other European countries. In England the number of people taking vacations increased even during the depression; by the late 1930s, one in three Britons, 15 million, spent at least a week away from home. Workers came to regard paid vacations as necessary to confront the stresses of modern life, and contracts awarding them proliferated in the 1920s and 1930s.

The vogue for tourism and vacations stimulated the growth of the automotive industry, and in England, the number of motor vehicles increased from 500,000 in 1920 to 1.5 million in 1930 and to 3 million in 1939. Congestion resulted, and traffic regulations proliferated. Paris adopted parking rules in 1930, pedestrian crossings in 1931, and hand-operated electric traffic lights in 1932. The Italians invented the limited-access highway, but the French considered toll roads Fascist. In France victims of traffic accidents increased from 2,042 in 1930 to 5,000 in 1934, and car insurance was introduced to compensate them. City roads improved, but rural ones still presented considerable challenges. In 1929, the hearse carrying the

Europeans began taking vacations on a large scale before World War I. This trend continued and grew after the conflict. Despite economic setbacks, by the Interwar period vacations were a staple of European life. Here is a poster from the period touting a vacation on the Italian seaside.

body of French statesman Georges Clemenceau to Paris bogged down in the mud and had to be pulled out by teams of oxen.

Besides vacations, Europeans emphasized physical fitness, especially outdoor recreational activities such as walking and hiking. In Germany, "Pathfinder" groups—including Nobel-winning physicist Werner Heisenberg's—trekked on difficult excursions through the wild, something the more casual British called rambling; in Italy another Nobel Prize winner, nuclear physicist Enrico Fermi, missed no opportunity to ski, swim, and play tennis.

Along with this trend, participatory sports grew enormously among the lower-middle and working classes—particularly women. Camping, cycling, and rambling boomed. Dealers sold more than 500,000 bicycles annually in England in the mid-1930s, while the 3,500 cycling clubs attracted 60,000 members. The radio, associations, and party organizations encouraged physical fitness through sports. Dog and motorcycle racing especially appealed to the working class. Women demonstrated their newfound independence through sports, and the number of women's sports association exploded. During the 1920s and 1930s, sports clothing revealed more of their bodies because physical activity demanded shorter skirts, shorts, pants—and briefer bathing suits. In 1922 the Women's Amateur Athletic

Association was founded, and in 1928 women participated in the Olympic games for the first time.

ENTERTAINMENT AND HIGH CULTURE

Major changes in entertainment and culture, especially the cinema, took place during the 1920s and 1930s and established the basis for the extraordinary world-wide cultural impact that European filmmakers achieved following World War II. The nature of the changes depended on technological changes and the war's terrible legacy.

Motion Pictures

Cinema matured during the war and exploded in popularity during the 1920s and 1930s. Besides their entertainment value, movies had an important social function as a leveling experience. To be sure, the rich watched movies in more luxurious theaters than did ordinary people, but they enjoyed the same films, cheered the same movie stars, and cried with them when Rudolph Valentino, an actor who captured the imagination of all classes, died prematurely. Movies encouraged families to go out together instead of the men leaving their wives and children at home to go drinking. Families went to the movies to laugh at Charlie Chaplin, one of the first movie superstars, who spoofed politicians and social customs during the 1920s and 1930s. American films became popular, and more films were directed at women.

Besides attracting families, movie theaters were attractive places to meet people and, for couples in love, to enjoy the privacy conferred by the dark. Statistics confirm the cinema's growing popularity. By 1937, 20 million Britons watched a movie once a week, showing that the depression did not reduce the size of audiences as theater owners successfully introduced double features, cartoons, and newsreels for the price of admission. In 1935, France counted 4,000 theaters, with 3,300 of them wired for "talkies."

The Flowering and Decline of German Cinema

Trends in high culture affecting literature and the arts influenced the movies through film reviews, theoretical journals, and film associations. Although American films tended to dominate the market, Europeans established film as a contemporary art form and as a serious field of study.

Weimar Germany unexpectedly flourished as the major center of cinema after the war and for a time challenged American commercial superiority. Germany had lagged behind other western countries, but World War I sowed the seeds for the startling development of German film. Seeking to combat Allied film propaganda and to jump-start the depressed film industry, the German government created a large subsidized film company, called the UFA, in 1917. After the war, the government sold its shares to private concerns, but by then Germany possessed the largest film studios in Europe. The pessimistic postwar atmosphere and the end of censorship encouraged experimentation and increased the quality of German films. The cinematic style that prevailed in early postwar Germany was *expressionism,* a term already familiar in prewar painting and postwar literature. Filmmakers belonging to this school explored not objective reality but the subjective feelings of artists responding to existence. Their film technique included abstraction, perceptive distortion, and symbolism. In 1919 the film that became the symbol of German filmmaking appeared: *The Cabinet of Dr. Caligari,* which launched the great decade of German cinema. This film, loosely based on a sex slaying of the period, was an attack on authority. The incongruously juxtaposed and strangely proportioned structures conveyed an unnatural feeling of doom; the film's atmosphere reflected the dismal postwar situation and inspired the American horror movies of the 1930s.

After 1925, expressionism's gloomy outlook fit in poorly with the renewed German economic prosperity, and German film turned toward other cinematic styles, such as the *Kammerspielfilm* (intimate theater) that essentially rejected expressionism and street realism, which accepted the world as it existed. By the late 1920s, however, economics and politics contributed to the demise of the German film as international agreements stabilizing the country's finances damaged the film industry, particularly an abortive agreement between the UFA and American film companies. Nationalist media magnate Alfred Hugenberg took over the UFA, and German studios turned to producing more nationalistic films and documentaries.

Despite the Great Depression, motion pictures, which existed even before World War I, became a mass industry during the Interwar period because movie theaters were cheap and provided a getaway for the family and privacy for young lovers. Here is a still from Fritz Lang's classic 1927 film, *Metropolis.*

Hugenberg's ownership of the UFA facilitated domination of the film industry by Nazi Propaganda Minister Joseph Goebbels after 1933. The Nazis specialized in the use of newsreels and documentaries for propaganda, as demonstrated by Leni Riefenstahl's famous *The Triumph of the Will,* presenting the 1934 Nuremberg party congress as a mystical-religious experience. The Nazis left the movie industry in private hands but would not allow films to criticize society, killing the German cinema's spirit.

Experimentation and Repression: Soviet Film

Film-as-documentary followed a similar trajectory in the USSR and flourished in the 1920s. In 1919 the government nationalized the film industry and put it under a committee headed by Nadezhda Krupskaya, Lenin's wife, who founded a film school in Moscow. Because of the shortage of equipment and film in the early days of the revolution, the committee concentrated on newsreels and documentaries. In the 1920s, Dziga Vertov, an early practitioner and theoretician of the documentary, developed imaginative means of organizing film to suit his propaganda purposes and produced a series of documentaries that were collectively known as film truth; in the process, he made a major contribution to the art of the montage that accounted for much of the style of Soviet films.

A great film director who ranks with American D. W. Griffith as "one of the two pioneering geniuses of the modern cinema," Sergei Eisenstein, emerged from the Soviet school. Eisenstein's 1925 masterpiece, *Battleship Potemkin,* tells the story of the 1905 revolution against the tsar and ranks as one of the most influential films in history. Eisenstein created modern editing techniques that emotionally involved the viewer in the events that were depicted. *Potemkin* gave Russian cinema an international influence it has lacked since.

Eisenstein and the Russian cinema eventually ran afoul of political interference. Eisenstein increasingly fell into disfavor with Stalin, who disparaged *October,* another masterpiece. Stalin recognized the cinema's power to move the masses and in 1928 and 1929 imposed greater party control on film as on all the arts, discouraging experimentation and proclaiming Socialist realism the official Soviet style.

New Cinematic Forms

Of the other major European countries, France was the most consistent center of experimentation. Cubism, surrealism, Dadaism, impressionism (unrelated to the school of painting), and other avant-garde movements flourished. Films analyzed Freudian-type sexual repression, the psychological basis of provincial middle-class marriages, and the lives of ordinary people and workers. The French film industry introduced several important technical innovations, such as portable cameras. The "Second" avant-garde cinema, inspired by Dadaism and surrealism, produced films without subjects based on a series of "subconscious" images, such as Luis Buñuel's *Un chien andalou.* The French confronted the challenge of sound in the 1930s more successfully than did either the Germans or the Russians. The most famous filmmaker during this period was Jean Renoir, whose film *Grand Illusion* described the crumbling of dominant cultures caused by the war.

The golden age of the Italian cinema had ended with the outbreak of World War I and did not recover during the 1920s. By 1930, Italian studios made only thirty films yearly, a situation that preoccupied Benito Mussolini. Well aware of the cinema's power—Il Duce enjoyed editing newsreels—he acted. In 1935, he established the only film school outside the USSR and ordered the building of studios that rivaled the UFA—*Cinecittà*. A theoretical journal also appeared, and the government placed strict quotas on the importation of foreign films. The Italians continued to produce films of a propaganda-documentary nature, but, paradoxically, out of them would emerge the influential postwar style known as neorealism that used similar techniques, such as nonprofessional actors, shooting on location, and the newsreel style. The film school also produced some of the most famous Italian post-1945 directors, including Pietro Germi, Roberto Rossellini, and Michelangelo Antonioni. Innovations and new ideas came into Italy and, ironically, served as vehicles of intellectual opposition to Fascism. Once considered a dead interlude in Italy's film history, the interwar period marked a crucial time for the Italian cinema.

The British film industry was in crisis until 1927, when it recovered thanks to legislation establishing quotas for foreign films that reduced American competition and stimulated domestic production, so that by the 1930s, British-produced films trailed only American productions. The British specialized in biographical costume dramas, but also produced the mysteries of Alfred Hitchcock and excellent documentaries.

Literature

Literature and painting during the interwar years worked through the implications of ideas that had been announced at the century's dawn. Affected by developments in science, the old certainties, unity, and continuity of Western culture broke up. Literature in particular took on modern characteristics similar to those in science, with doubt and subjectivity permeating modern novels, poetry, and plays. Literature and art, like physics, became difficult for educated nonspecialists to understand, a development that had disturbing consequences.

Ambiguity in the arts produced exasperation among ordinary people. Laypeople considered pure science an esoteric activity, did not comprehend it, and left it to the scientists—but not the arts. Modernism, with its advocacy of constant change and shock tactics, alienated a public opinion traumatized by the devastation of World War I and its turbulent aftereffects. Utilizing the principles of modern science in a famous manifesto, Russian novelist Yevgeny Zamyatin condemned anyone who remained static, arguing that revolution is everywhere and will never end. The confiscation of modern paintings by the police and riots in France that greeted exhibitions of modern art symbolized the chasm between artists and the public. In Weimar Germany, the center of the new culture, the majority considered modernism decadent and an assault on German history, while artists objected that they were attempting to get at the social reality behind appearances. The adverse reaction to the worldview of modern artists and their attack on German society contributed to the rise of Nazism. When the Nazi regime imposed

The revolutionary developments in art before World War I and during the 1920s caused consternation among the public and resulted in a backlash. In the USSR, the government put an end to experimental artistic forms and instituted "Socialist Realism," and in Nazi Germany the regime's opposition to modernism translated into conformist art. This watercolor from the Nazi period is an example of this trend.

its own hackneyed art preferences or when it burned books, public opinion did not come to the intellectuals' defense. In the USSR during the Bolshevik revolution's early years, an explosion of modernistic movements and experimentation with new forms in all artistic fields occurred, but Bolshevism imposed conformity on intellectuals when their works criticized the regime; few people protested when the Communists shot, jailed, silenced, or drove the best writers to suicide. In 1932, the Communists formally imposed the Socialist realism that forced artists to idealize Soviet life in trite ways.

In the West, the earliest revolutionary reactions to World War I in the artistic world, Dadaism and surrealism (already discussed) had antecedents in Futurism and in the psychological theories of Sigmund Freud. This influence petered out after Marinetti founded an ineffectual Futurist political party in 1918 and then allied himself with Mussolini. The Russian Futurists made a similar error by supporting the new Soviet state; Lenin put up with the antics of its leader, poet Vladimir Mayakovsky, despite his hatred for his poetry, because of the movement's propaganda value to the regime, but Stalin showed less deference to Mayakovsky, which contributed to Mayakovsky's suicide in 1930.

In the West, Freud's psychoanalysis influenced the best interwar literature. French novelist Marcel Proust had begun his massive work, *Remembrance of Things Past* in 1908 and completed it after 1918. Proust sought to understand how reality emerges from unconscious memory, a clear connection with Freud's concerns. Along with the scientists describing the natural world, Freud had demonstrated that reality was not what it seemed. Artists asked, in effect, "What is reality?" Playwright Luigi Pirandello, a Nobel Prize winner, answered in his masterpieces: *Right You Are If You Think You Are, Henry IV,* and *Six Characters in Search of an Author.*

Freud's work had also demonstrated that persons acted not by reason alone but through the spur of the subconscious world. The surrealists emphasized this view as well by arguing that artists did not rely primarily on reason to create their work, but that emotion, feeling, or even accident played decisive roles. These ideas led to the stream-of-consciousness method of writing. The most famous practitioner of this technique, Irish writer James Joyce, produced his masterpiece *Ulysses* in this manner, but was hardly alone. Joyce, a teacher of English in Trieste, encouraged Italo Svevo to continue his work on the psychological novel that he had begun during the late nineteenth century. In 1923 Svevo published his masterpiece, *The Conscience of Zeno.* British feminist Virginia Woolf wrote *To the Lighthouse,* a novel analyzing the difficulties of human relationships and the breakdown of social values in the British upper middle class.

Painting and the Bauhaus Style

Painting witnessed similar attempts to evoke the subconscious. Giorgio De Chirico in Italy best represented the metaphysical school that shocked spectators. These painters juxtaposed real objects in an unreal manner—like ancient statuary and machinery—hoping to create magical effects to stimulate the unconscious mind. This school predated surrealist artists, such as Salvador Dalí, who aimed at liberating the subconscious from the rationalist straitjacket. Along with surrealist writers, these painters advocated an automatic technique that supposedly freed artists from rationalist interference.

This method affected the approach of Paul Klee, perhaps the interwar period's most famous painter. Klee began his paintings with no clearly defined idea but with a splash of color or lines drawn according to his feelings at the moment. He took these first feelings as indications of the subconscious mind at work that would determine the shape of the finished product. In a final act of creation, Klee entitled his works only after he had completed them. For Klee, an excellent violinist, this technique resembled musical creation—contemplation winning out over pictorial composition. In 1920, a celebrated exhibition of Klee's work opened in Munich. Shortly thereafter, he joined his friend Wassily Kandinsky at the Bauhaus, the most celebrated German cultural school of the period.

Architect Walter Gropius founded the Bauhaus in 1919. He aimed to fuse an art academy with the applied arts, believing that buildings could bring together the crafts and the arts in a new unity. Gropius applied this synthesis to all areas of artistic life, including the design of everyday objects used by ordinary people.

The Bauhaus style founded by architect Walter Gropius in 1919 aimed to fuse modern art with practical life. He founded a school that trained students to accomplish this aim and became the most famous institution of its kind in Interwar Germany but had to close because of economic conditions and political turmoil. Here is the Bauhaus building of 1925.

Bauhaus designers created new shapes for lamps, furniture, pottery, rugs, type fonts, and utensils. Production ranging from Marcel Breuer's chair to Gropius's 1925 Bauhaus building, the most famous structure of this period, to the paintings of Klee and Kandinsky consolidated the Bauhaus's reputation. Experimentation, freedom, inventiveness, and community marked the school's atmosphere—principles that infuriated artistic and political conservatives alike. Gropius attempted to keep the school out of politics, but the Bauhaus lost popularity at home as quickly as it gained fame abroad. In 1925, it left Weimar for Dessau, but in 1932, the victim of economic conditions and rightist political turmoil, the school moved to Berlin where it later closed.

Political Philosophy

As fascism and Nazism spread during the 1920s and 1930s, important political philosophers defended parliamentary democracy and rebutted the notion that the one-party state was the wave of the future. In the classic work *The Revolt of the Masses,* Spanish republican José Ortega y Gasset labeled fascism and communism new but regressive and made a compelling case for the reform and updating of parliaments that would bring the masses peace and social justice without subjecting them to the violence of totalitarian governments. A German thinker, Hans Kelsen, also pronounced parliamentary institutions fundamentally sound because they permitted groups to organize, scrutinize the management of public affairs, and implement democracy by resolving the social problems of modern times.

Flanking these political defenses of democracy were Catholic thinkers, such as Jacques Maritain, and liberal socialists who tried to update democratic socialism. Despite the prevailing political atmosphere favoring dictatorship, the ideas of these political scientists defending parliamentary democracy and democratic socialism assured the success of these models after World War II.

TECHNOLOGY AND SOCIETY

The 1920s and 1930s were decades of important technological changes that directly affected daily life as few in history have. For example, airplanes crossed the Atlantic and achieved unheard-of speeds of 400 miles per hour, anticipating the time when airplanes would carry millions of passengers across the oceans at a reasonable cost.

Diffusion of Technology

European governments invested funds to bring technology to the greatest number of their people by subsidizing rural electrification, despite the opposition of traditionalists who objected because it encouraged people to stay up too late at night partying. Despite concerns that governments were moving too quickly, extensive electrification during the interwar years gave people access to many important devices.

Telephones, familiar since the 1880s, became widespread, and when the telephone dial became widely available in the 1930s, people could finally call without operators. Most telephones were black, with only the rich being able to afford white ones that were the symbols of affluence.

The decline in the labor supply because of the large number of deaths during the war affected the diffusion of technology because the increased cost of labor and servants favored the introduction of labor-saving appliances, such as the washing machine. However, since the first washing machines were hand cranked, most people preferred using the washtub or the local stream to wash their clothes until the electric washing machine was introduced and became widely available. Along with washing machines, primitive refrigerators appeared.

The Radio and Its Impact

In the 1920s, the radio revolutionized political and social life by making it possible for leaders to influence millions of people instead of thousands. Mussolini and Hitler encouraged the diffusion of radio sets that brought their speeches into homes and to the masses gathered in the remotest town squares, but radios also spread rapidly in the democracies.

The explosive growth of the radio raised the question of how to administer programs, which led to novel forms of public involvement in society. In 1926, the British established a public corporation, the British Broadcasting Corporation (BBC), as an independently run public company financed by a yearly fee paid by radio owners, a model that spread to other countries and was frequently applied to television after World War II. The BBC established trends and transformed performers overnight into stars, as well as disseminating the latest news and

This is the BBC Broadcasting House in London, built in London in 1932 as the first dedicated broadcasting studio. Music and dance were popular areas for radio programming during the Interwar years, and the Broadcasting House's first transmission featured the BBC Dance Orchestra on March 15, 1932.

influencing everyday life. Daily French radio newscasts began in 1925, and by 1934 the Paris police had radio cars to help them control crime. The radio also transmitted American popular culture to Europe.

By the 1920s and 1930s, as the price dropped, the radio's economic impact increased. Between 1927 and 1939, the number of British set owners grew from 2 million to more than 9 million; the BBC counted 773 employees in 1927 and 5,000 in 1939. The radio favored rapid growth in advertising, sports, and gambling, making it possible to create football and other pools, both legal and illegal, because it quickly reported scores to a vast audience. These activities related to the radio resulted in more work for thousands of people. Millions tuned in to sports events, and sports commentaries became a regular part of broadcasting. The radio had a fundamental role in knitting together society and in increasing employment.

The Depression

The technological innovations of the interwar period, however, could not reverse the economic slump, which forced pullbacks in many areas of social life. French critics attributed the decline of dinner parties to increased poverty, not only to the growing use of cigarettes that caused burns on furniture. Less frivolously, public health problems increased, and, with growing unemployment and increased prostitution, venereal diseases became more widespread. The alcoholism rate shot up: the average French adult drank a record of 250 liters of wine annually between 1930 and 1940. With increased drinking came a greater likelihood of contracting tuberculosis, which killed one-third of French men aged 35 to 50, and poverty intensified the virulence of more traditional diseases, such as typhoid and diphtheria. Fear of competition from immigrants prompted attacks against foreigners and Jews, and from 1932 to 1937, 500,000 foreigners left France.

PURE SCIENCE: REVOLUTION AND TRAVAIL

In pure science, the interwar years were the golden age of physics. Studying in cities, such as Copenhagen, Gottingen, Leipzig, Berlin, Cambridge, Rome, and Paris, physicists worked out the implications of the quantum theory that Max Planck had elaborated in 1900 and made fundamental progress in understanding the atomic nucleus. This knowledge eventually led to new weapons and energy sources that critically affected the modern world.

A New Revolution

Defeat in World War I did not end the primacy of German scientists, who continued to claim the lion's share of Nobel prizes. The Kaiser Wilhelm Institutes, founded by the former emperor to encourage science, were threatened by the loss of funding and by the hyperinflation. In response, German scholars employed modern methods of financing scientific research during the 1920s by giving research grants on the advice of committees and peer reviews of projects and seeking help from the Rockefeller Foundation. Crucially, the European tradition of collaboration among scientists of different countries survived the war, and the brightest physicists flocked to study with the best scientists, such as the Dane Niels Bohr in Copenhagen and Werner Heisenberg in Leipzig.

Research in the interwar period completed the revolutionary quantum theory, called quantum mechanics, by Heisenberg, Bohr, and other physicists. Between 1925 and 1927, the work of these physicists culminated in the uncertainty or indeterminacy principle enunciated by Heisenberg. Uncertainty meant that the velocity *or* the position of a subatomic particle could be determined at any one time, but not both; it demonstrated that the act of observation influenced the results of an experiment, a principle with enormous implications for other fields besides nuclear physics. At the subatomic level, statistical probabilities (separately worked out by Enrico Fermi and British scientist P. A. M. Dirac), not absolute values, best explained reality. In the visible world, the idea elevated uncertainty to a principle of nature for the real world. This concept coincided with the breakdown of European society and values brought about by World War I and corresponded to the chaos of life during the interwar period that affected the ordinary person. The certainties of the Newtonian worldview that had comforted Europeans since the eighteenth century and that had begun to crumble at the beginning of the twentieth ended during the 1920s and 1930s. Quantum mechanics and relativity set the state for the later development of the atomic bomb.

Important developments in the investigation of radioactivity that took place at the same time confirmed the hidden nature of reality theorized at the beginning of the century. In 1934, Madame Curie's daughter Iréne and her husband Frédéric Joliot discovered how to induce artificial radiation. In Rome, Enrico Fermi and his team systematically bombarded the different elements with neutrons, discovered by British scientist James Chadwick in 1932, as the best way to induce changes in the atomic nucleus. In the course of these experiments, the Rome team developed "slow neutrons" and probably split the atom. The Rome group failed to recognize this result, which was not given a theoretical explanation until 1939 by Austrian physicist Lise Meitner and her nephew Otto Frisch in a paper interpreting similar experimental results achieved by her old partner in Germany, Otto Hahn.

As a result of these developments, Fermi guided a project that produced the world's first controlled chain reaction on December 2, 1942, at the University of Chicago, a crucial event in the development of the atomic bomb and nuclear power plants.

BIOGRAPHICAL SKETCHES

Ettore Majorana
The Enduring Mystery

Ettore Majorana was perhaps the most brilliant of the brilliant physicists of the 1930s—certainly the most mysterious.

Born into a prominent Sicilian family, Majorana studied engineering at the University of Rome. In 1928, his friends encouraged him to switch to physics and study with Enrico Fermi. Majorana went to see Fermi, who had been working for some time on a new statistical method later named after him. Fermi showed Majorana a table of values that justified his method. Majorana returned the next day with a piece of paper and asked to see Fermi's table. He compared it to his results, pronounced Fermi's numbers correct, and consented to work with him.

Majorana revealed himself not only brilliant but eccentric. He kept to himself, published reluctantly, and refused to make his results known to the wider scientific community. A chain smoker, he neatly worked out complicated principles and formulas on his packs of Macedonia brand cigarettes, explained his ideas to his Rome colleagues, rejected their pleas to publish them, and casually flung the empty packs into the wastepaper basket. He published only nine articles, but anticipated many fundamental developments and principles that were elaborated as many as thirty years later. Fermi commented to a colleague: "You see, there are different categories of scientists in the world; there are second- and third-rate people who try hard but do not accomplish very much. There are first-rate people who make important, fundamental, discoveries for the development of science [Fermi considered himself one of them]. But then there are the geniuses, like Galileo and Newton. Ettore Majorana was one of those."

In order to bring Majorana out of his shell, Fermi secured a seven-month scholarship for him at Leipzig, where he impressed Werner Heisenberg. When he returned from Germany, Majorana became even stranger, refusing to leave his

continued

continued

apartment or even to shave, despite the urging of his friends. He spent his time thinking about physics, philosophy, and naval tactics. One of his favorite authors was fellow-Sicilian Luigi Pirandello, the playwright and distinguished novelist who speculated on the nature of reality. In November 1937, a committee named Majorana full professor at the University of Naples, based on his extraordinary merit, and he began teaching there.

On March 26, 1938, the head of his department received a puzzling telegram from Majorana from Palermo, telling him to disregard his previous letters and saying that a new letter would follow. A search of his hotel room revealed two suicide notes, but the later telegram and letter from Majorana said that he had changed his mind. That was the last time anyone heard from him.

An investigation produced sightings on the boat from Palermo to Naples, a witness who saw him in Naples, and a monk who identified him as asking if he could experiment with the monastic life. Benito Mussolini ordered the police to conduct a nationwide manhunt, and the Vatican scoured its monasteries. When he disappeared, Majorana had his passport and the equivalent of $10,000. Observers noted how the circumstances of his disappearance recalled a famous Pirandello novel. Almost thirty years later, stories surfaced about a person in Buenos Aires, Argentina, who called himself Ettore Majorana and wrote complicated formulas in neat handwriting on hotel napkins. Other sightings also occurred.

Writers and scientists have debated the Majorana case ever since. Suicide is probable, but why would Majorana recant his suicide letters and vanish with his passport and a large sum of money? Did he foresee the development of nuclear weapons and then disappear because he could no longer bear to work in the field, as some authors have speculated? Whatever the answer, one mild spring day in 1938, the world lost a person who might have been another Galileo or Newton.

BIOGRAPHICAL SKETCHES

Lise Meitner
The Role of Insight

As a shy young girl in Vienna, Lise Meitner, the first person to provide a theoretical explanation of the fission process that made the development of nuclear weapons possible, had an aptitude for mathematics and for physics. Her father, a Jewish lawyer with eight children, hired a private tutor to prepare his daughter to enter the University of Vienna, which rarely accepted females. In 1906, she received the first physics doctorate awarded to a woman by that institution.

In 1907, the young woman persuaded her parents to let her travel to Germany and attend Max Planck's lectures. There she met Otto Hahn, a chemist working at the Kaiser Wilhelm Institute, won a position as his assistant, and stayed for thirty years. The team achieved international recognition for its role in investigating the atomic nucleus, but could not end the irritating prejudices against Meitner because of her gender.

World War I fundamentally changed Meitner's world. During the conflict, she interrupted her work to serve as an X-ray technician at the front. Returning to her research after the war, she and Hahn discovered the ninety-first element of the periodic table (protactinium). Meitner became an assistant professor at the University of Berlin and headed a physics institute, but after 1933 Hitler's anti-Semitism threatened her career and her life, even though she had converted to Protestantism years before. In 1937, a courageous Max Planck objected to Hitler that famous scientists who were considered even one-quarter Jewish lost their positions. An enraged Fuehrer rejected Planck's appeal to let Jewish scientists keep their jobs; he thundered that they could not leave the Reich and would be detained pending charges. Meitner's Austrian citizenship protected her, but in 1938, Hitler annexed Austria, and she became subject to German anti-Jewish legislation. Denied an exit visa, she escaped Germany through the Netherlands into Sweden, where Niels Bohr had secured a position for her at the Nobel Institute of Theoretical Physics in Stockholm. In Sweden, Lise Meitner labored under poor conditions—but a flash of insight allowed her to make a great contribution to physics and history.

In 1934, Enrico Fermi had bombarded the uranium nucleus with neutrons, obtaining baffling results. According to the thinking at the time, the outcome should have been a new element heavier than uranium, an explanation that physicists continued to expound despite their uneasiness with it. On vacation at Christmastime in 1938, Meitner received a letter from Hahn in which he described chemical reactions resulting from bombardment of the uranium atom that he could not satisfactorily explain. The snow fell heavily as a radical idea suddenly struck Meitner. She paced in the snow and the cold as she considered it: the neutron bombardment had split the uranium atom, producing two different elements and releasing great amounts of energy according to Einstein's famous equation, $E = mc^2$! Unable to contain her excitement, Meitner summoned her nephew, physicist Otto Frisch, and worked out the details of the fission process that governs nuclear explosions.

Following World War II, the press hailed Meitner as the "mother of the atomic bomb," but she protested that she had always refused to work on the weapon. She spent the postwar years lecturing, teaching, continuing her research, and collecting a number of prestigious prizes and awards—except the big one. In 1946, the Nobel Committee awarded the Nobel Prize in physics to Otto Hahn and ignored Meitner. Meitner remained dignified until the end, and history does not record what she thought about this unfair denial, but she continued her friendship with Hahn even though he did not defend her. On October 27, 1968, a month before her ninetieth birthday, Lise Meitner died in a nursing home in Cambridge, England.

Science and Politics

The flash of insight that allowed Lise Meitner to explain nuclear fission came to her in Sweden, where she had fled from the Nazis. Meitner had worked in Germany for thirty years, but Hitler's persecution of the Jews and the dismissal of Jewish professors forced her and many German scientists of Jewish extraction to emigrate. The Nazis denounced Einstein and relativity as Jewish physics and non-Jewish Germans who accepted Einstein's conclusions as "white Jews." As one of these "white Jews," Werner Heisenberg stayed behind saying that he hoped to save German science as the Nazis replaced disgraced brilliant professors with third-rate hacks. Heisenberg emerged from suspicion to direct Germany's nuclear weapons program. In the meantime, anti-Semitic legislation drove Fermi—whose wife and several collaborators were Jewish—out of Italy. European émigré scientists joined American nuclear physicists in the Manhattan Project and built the atomic bomb.

The interwar period was a crucial turning point for scientists whose attempt to unlock the secrets of the subatomic world had appeared arcane. One reporter asked: "Professor Dirac solves all the problems of mathematical physics, but is unable to find a better way of figuring out Babe Ruth's batting average?" As searchers for basic truths, scientists had constituted a special kind of club that cut across national lines. The research they did during the 1920s and 1930s, however, would spell the difference between victory and defeat in the 1940s. From neglected ivory-tower intellectuals, physicists turned into warriors who were sworn to hold secrets instead of sharing information; the relationship that had linked them to a special mission vanished with the golden interwar years.

Bibliographical Essay

A. J. P. Taylor, *From Sarajevo to Potsdam* (London, 1965), is a brief, readable book that has interesting insights on culture and daily life during this period. James Walvin's excellent little book *Leisure and Society 1830–1950* (London and New York, 1978) has chapters on the interwar period. Robert Graves and Alan Hodge, *The Long Weekend: A Social History of Great Britain, 1918–1939* (New York, 1963), is a classic study of social developments in England between the wars. Charles Loch Mowat, *Britain Between the Wars: 1918–1940* (Chicago, 1963), while mainly concerned with economic and political history, also discusses social history, and A. J. P. Taylor, *English History 1914–1945* (New York, 1965), has important sections on social affairs. Matt Perry's *Bread and Work* (London, 2000) is about the experience of unemployment between 1918 and 1938. Eugen Weber, *The Hollow Years,* previously cited (New York, 1994), is an excellent social history of France during the 1930s that also discusses the war's effects and the 1920s. H. Stuart Hughes, *The Obstructed Path: French Social Thought in the Years of Desperation, 1930–1960* (New York, 1968), discusses social thought in France. Gary S. Cross devotes most of *Immigrant Workers in Industrial France: The Making of a New Laboring Class* (Philadelphia, 1983) to the period discussed in this chapter.

An interesting interpretation of cultural life during the Weimar Republic is Peter Gay, *Weimar Culture: The Outsider as Insider* (New York, 1968). For a detailed treatment of cultural affairs, see Walter Laqueur, *Weimar: A Cultural History* (New York, 1974). Connecting cultural refinement and society is Keith Bullivant, ed., *Culture and Society in the Weimar Republic* (Manchester, UK, 1977). On the plight of intellectuals, see the collected essays edited by Anthony Phelan, *The Weimar Dilemma: Intellectuals in the Weimar Republic* (Manchester, UK, 1985). John Willett, *The Weimar Years: A Culture Cut Short* (London, 1984), has good text and pictures. The Bauhaus from its beginnings to the cold war is discussed by Kathleen James, *Bauhaus Culture* (Minneapolis, Minn., 2006).

The mass media are treated by Ken Ward, *Mass Communications and the Modern Word* (Chicago, 1989), and Pierre Sorlin, *The Mass Media* (London, 1994). The best book on radio in England during this period is volume 2 of Asa Briggs's history of broadcasting in the United Kingdom, *The Golden Age of Wireless* (London, 1965). Aitor Anduaga published a book on the relationship among the British Empire, the radio, and atmospheric science between the wars: *Wireless and Empire* (Oxford, UK, 2009). There is not much in English on the radio outside of Britain, but see Philip Cannistraro, "The Radio in Fascist Italy," *Journal of European Studies* II, 2 (June 1972):127–54.

Sports and their influence are the subjects of three interesting books: Mike Huggins and Jack Williams, *Sport and the English* (London, 2006), and John Hargreaves,

Sport, Power and Culture: A Social and Historical Analysis of Popular Sports in Britain (New York, 1986), examine England, while France is the subject of Richard Holt's *Sport and Society in Modern France* (London, 1981).

A good general history of film is David A. Cook's *A History of Narrative Film,* 2d ed. (New York, 1990); the quotation on Eisenstein is on p. 142. The German film in its various aspects is discussed in Siegfried Kracauer, *From Caligari to Hitler: A Psychological History of the German Film* (Princeton, N.J., 1947), a fundamental work; David Welch, *Propaganda and the German Cinema 1933–1945* (Oxford, UK, 1983); and Erwin Leiser, *Nazi Cinema* (London, 1974). For French cinema, see Colin Crisp, *Classic French Cinema 1930–1960* (Bloomington, Ind., 1993). On Italian cinema, see the excellent general treatment by Pierre Leprohon, *The Italian Cinema* (New York, 1972), and the specialized works on the Fascist period: Marcia Landy, *Fascism in Film: The Italian Commercial Cinema, 1931–1943* (Princeton, N.J., 1986), and James Hay, *Popular Film Culture in Fascist Italy: The Passing of the Rex* (Bloomington, Ind., 1987). Roy Armes, *A Critical History of the British Cinema* (London, 1978), has several chapters on this period.

For a discussion of the political science aspects of the questions raised in this chapter, see the relevant chapters in Spencer M. Di Scala and Salvo Mastellone, *European Political Thought, 1815–1989* (Boulder, Colo., 1998).

A good introduction to the physics revolution of this period is Armin Hermann, *The New Physics: The Route into the Atomic Age* (Bonn, 1979), a collection of documents and photographs centered on Germany, and with a good chronology. Gino Segrè, *Faust in Copenhagen* (New York, 2007), is an examination of the "miracle year" 1932. An excellent book that stirred controversy when it appeared is Robert Jungk, *Brighter than a Thousand Suns: A Personal History of the Atomic Scientists* (New York, 1958). This work emphasizes the lives and research of the nuclear scientists and takes the story beyond the development of the atom bomb. On the most important physicists, see Abraham Pais, *Niels Bohr* (Oxford, UK, 1991), a biography by a physicist who knew him. David C. Cassidy, *Uncertainty: The Life and Science of Werner Heisenberg* (New York, 1992), is a massive but rewarding biography. Laura Fermi, *Atoms in the Family: My Life with Enrico Fermi* (Chicago, 1954), is a memoir by Enrico Fermi's wife. Emilio Segrè, *Enrico Fermi: Physicist* (Chicago, 1970), is a memoir by Fermi's Nobel Prize-winning student. Majorana has been the subject of increased interest; see, for example, Joao Magueijo, *A Brilliant Darkness* (New York, 2009). Deborah Crawford's short biography, *Lise Meitner, Atomic Pioneer* (New York, 1969), is a good portrait of the Austrian physicist who was the first woman to receive a doctorate in physics from the University of Vienna. Patricia Rife's *Lise Meitner and the Dawn of the Nuclear Age* (Boston, 2007) is a more complete biography. The quotation regarding Dirac is in Timothy Ferris, *The Whole Shebang: A State-of-the-Universe(s) Report* (New York, 1997), p. 209.

❧

CHAPTER 17

Diplomacy Between the Wars: The Collapse of Peace

CHAPTER OUTLINE

The Continent in the 1920s • Correcting Versailles • The Hitler Revolution • From Crisis to Crisis • A New War

BIOGRAPHICAL SKETCHES

Gustav Stresemann, Fulfillment • Aristide Briand, Man of Peace, "Father of Europe"

International relations during the 1920s and 1930s may be seen either as a lull in what was a "Thirty Years War" from 1914 to 1945, in which the victors of World War I imposed a harsh peace on Germany that led to World War II, or as a period in which diplomats made substantial progress reintegrating Germany into Europe by modifying the harsher features of the Versailles treaty.

THE CONTINENT IN THE 1920s

European diplomats confronted an unprecedented situation following World War I. The German, Russian, and Austro-Hungarian empires had vanished. In the East, new and/or greatly enlarged states with sizable ethnic minorities created special strategic dilemmas because the minorities destabilized the new nations. The instability would provide Germany and the USSR—temporarily weakened but desirous of recouping lost territory—with an opportunity to subvert the postwar settlement.

The French Military Dilemma

The temporary weakness of Germany and Russia made France dominant on the continent. The French constructed a network of alliances linking the small East European states that had benefited from the war. In February 1921, the French signed a Polish alliance and sponsored the Little Entente among Czechoslovakia, Romania, and Yugoslavia in order to defend the status quo and to help contain a possible resurgent Germany. The agreements also created a *cordon sanitaire* around Soviet Russia to isolate and prevent it from exporting the Bolshevik revolution to the West.

However, French preponderance in the East proved untenable after the revival of Germany and Russia in the 1930s. French resources could not match German or Russian resources, while the British considered French policy aggressive and risky. Because of the distance from its Eastern allies and shifting power relationships, France's Eastern policy became more dubious by the late 1920s. The only realistic hope for the small French allies in a German war was for an immediate French attack on Germany from the West. As long as the Rhineland remained demilitarized, France maintained a military advantage, but when Hitler remilitarized it in 1936, the French became more reluctant to take military initiatives and became more defensive minded because of its stagnating population and the unwillingness to risk another war and losses such as those it sustained during World War I. The supposedly impregnable Maginot line was a symbol of France's emphasis on defense.

Moreover, Germany and the USSR opposed the Paris peace settlement of 1919 and secretly collaborated to evade the disarmament clauses of the Versailles treaty. The Russians allowed the Germans to test weapons on their territory, and in April 1922 the two countries signed the Treaty of Rapallo that settled the outstanding issues between the former enemies. Rapallo was the first step in the emergence of both countries from isolation.

Mussolini's Revisionism

During the 1920s, it was Benito Mussolini whose revisionism was most serious because of his feelings that Italy had been cheated at the Paris Peace Conference. In 1923, he temporarily seized the Greek island of Corfu following the murder of Italian experts marking the Albanian-Greek border. Il Duce focused on the Balkans and Eastern Europe, traditional areas of Italian interest, and helped create the premises for a future alliance with Hitler. Yugoslavia's ethnic divisions encouraged Mussolini to finance separatist and terrorist organizations there and to plot Yugoslavia's disintegration. In November 1927 Yugoslavia signed a treaty with France, but Mussolini continued to stir up trouble by sheltering Croat separatists. In March 1932, he signed the Rome Protocols with Austria and Hungary, both revisionist states, and exploited Fascist influence in a failed attempt to bring Romania into his camp. In October 1934, Croat terrorists assassinated the king of Yugoslavia and the French foreign minister in Marseilles, and il Duce's support for the Croats was criticized.

Hitler's takeover in Germany exacerbated the revisionist debate. The French fretted about an eventual Italian-German rapprochement and attempted to placate Mussolini. Hitler's rise created a potential ally whom Mussolini believed he could exploit to subvert the Paris peace settlement.

CORRECTING VERSAILLES

With the exception of Mussolini's attempts to revise the peace settlement, Europe in the 1920s seemed to have returned to normal. Bolshevism seemed to have been

War Minister André Maginot gave his name to the spectacular—and very expensive—line of defensive fortifications between France and Germany, some of which are seen here. The line was built with the intention of stopping a German attack without the gigantic loss of life that France had suffered during World War I. A major weakness was that the Maginot Line could not be constructed on the Franco-Belgian border for political reasons: it would place Belgium on the "German" side of the fighting in case of war, "abandoning" Belgium to the Germans. When World War II broke out, the Germans outflanked the line.

contained by sealing off the USSR from the West, and the economic situation seemed to have calmed down. The efforts of Allied and German diplomats to correct the shortcomings of the Versailles treaty also seemed to be having success.

The "Spirit of Locarno"

In January and February 1925, German Foreign Minister Gustav Stresemann proposed to the British and French a series of agreements regarding Germany's western frontier that amounted to German recognition of the peace settlement of 1919. Stresemann aimed to calm both the French and domestic German unrest by accepting the verdict of Versailles.

BIOGRAPHICAL SKETCHES

Gustav Stresemann
Fulfillment

The man who, along with Aristide Briand, achieved the most success in attempting to reintegrate Germany into Europe following World War I came from an unlikely background. His father, a retailer of bottled beer, found prosperity as a small businessman. Gustav, born in Berlin on May 10, 1878, his mother's favorite, reportedly suffered from loneliness. The child had reddish hair, bright blue eyes, and an inclination toward literary romanticism. At the University of Berlin, his dissertation on the Berlin bottled beer industry demonstrated a flair for combining the theoretical with the practical that never left him.

In 1901, Stresemann took a position in Dresden as assistant manager of the German Chocolate Manufacturers' Association and championed small business against heavy industry. Because small businesspeople relied on cheap imported raw materials, they fought for low tariffs against large business interests and big landowners who wanted high duties. Following this job, Stresemann led the Union of Industrialists, a manufacturers' organization that affiliated with the Central Union of German Industrialists after 1914. The contacts he formed in the business world proved particularly useful to him during the postwar period when he needed support for his policy of reconciliation with the West.

Stresemann's parliamentary debut came in 1907 with his election as a Reichstag deputy as a member of the National Liberal Party, which he headed after July 1917. Before and during World War I, Stresemann favored a strong nationalist and expansionist policy. The Central Union of Industrialists, with Stresemann in its wake, became a powerful supporter of the Pan-German League, advocating peace only if Germany achieved substantial gains. Stresemann also joined the Wednesday Society, a nonpartisan group that sought to keep support for the war high. After the war ended, however, Stresemann shifted gears, realizing that Germany must accept defeat and follow a more conciliatory course that others had already advocated. His previous hawkishness allowed him to win over many resentful diehards to the policy. Albert Einstein wrote: "During the War [sic], Stresemann was warlike enough to be able, later on, to hold the confidence of those whom he wanted to win over to his own wise and noble purposes."

Following the war, Stresemann founded the People's Party, a small organization but one of the mainstays of the Weimar Republic. Between August 14 and November 23, 1923, he headed a coalition government that stabilized the country after Hitler's attempted *putsch,* confronted the hyperinflation crisis, and ended the passive resistance to the occupying French and Belgian forces in the Ruhr. When the cabinet resigned, Stresemann retained the office of foreign minister. He resisted a closer alliance with the USSR, which was desired by the army and elements in the foreign ministry, and attempted a rapprochement with the French. Through a dual policy of revision and fulfillment of the Versailles treaty, he initiated the moves that resulted in the Locarno treaties and in 1926 shared the Nobel Peace Prize with the French statesman Aristide Briand. Stresemann also negotiated the Dawes and Young Plans and brought Germany into the League of Nations with its status as a great power intact.

Stresemann married Kathe Kleefeld in 1906, his serene family life contributing greatly to his success. Stiff and formal in public life, his bald head shining, in private Stresemann displayed a lighter side. He loved food, a glass of beer or wine with dinner, and a good cigar. He greatly enjoyed spending time with his family and friends, and he entertained journalists at frequent teas. At Locarno, he frequented a small café. His health was poor, and he languished from a kidney ailment. In his last years, he refused to stop working despite the rapid deterioration in his health, and his death in Berlin from a stroke on October 3, 1929 surprised no one.

Negotiations with the Allies went forward in the Swiss resort of Locarno, and the agreements were signed in London on December 1, 1925. Germany, France, and Belgium accepted their common borders, and Britain and Italy acted as guarantors. In a crucial achievement, Germany freely accepted the demilitarization of the Rhineland that the Versailles treaty had once imposed. In addition, Germany, France, Belgium, Poland, and Czechoslovakia also signed treaties that bound them to submit disputes to outside arbitration. The lack of a German pledge to respect the borders of its eastern neighbors was a disappointment, but treaties of mutual assistance among France, Poland, and Czechoslovakia within the Locarno framework partially compensated for this deficiency. Continuing negotiations achieved other significant successes. The Allies agreed that Germany could join the League of Nations with a permanent seat on the Council and, by the end of 1926, that Allied inspection to enforce German disarmament would end.

Besides the formal agreements, the Locarno spirit buoyed European hopes. A special relationship seemed to link Stresemann and his French counterpart, Aristide Briand. Joy at achieving the Locarno agreements brought Briand and his British counterpart Austen Chamberlain to tears. An enthusiastic Mussolini kissed Mrs. Chamberlain's hands while bands played. *The New York Times* announced that Germany and France had barred war forever. In August 1928, twenty-three countries signed the Kellogg-Briand Pact, renouncing war. However, complications increasingly spoiled the spirit. The Reichstag received the Locarno agreements with little enthusiasm. An international controversy erupted when Germany applied for admission to the League of Nations and when President von Hindenburg publicly denied German responsibility for the outbreak of World War I. Diplomatic disputes continued over some areas in Germany that the French continued to occupy, and by mid-1927, the friendly feelings of Briand and Stresemann evaporated. Furthermore, it soon became obvious that the Kellogg-Briand Pact lacked teeth. The Locarno era failed to survive Stresemann's death and the Great Depression.

BIOGRAPHICAL SKETCHES

Aristide Briande
Man of Peace, "Father of Europe"

Aristide Briand's father, for love of his wife Magdeleine, settled down in Nantes, in Brittany, where he established an inn and prospered. Two years after their marriage, on March 26, 1862, Magdeleine gave birth to a son, Aristide.

An unruly student with no desire to study, the young Aristide met the famous novelist Jules Verne while attending the Nantes lycée (high school). Verne liked and befriended him, basing the character "Briant" on him in his novel *A Long Vacation*. Verne described "Briant" as a lively teenager unwilling to study but given to occasional bursts of energy during which he outperformed all his fellow students. Briand studied law but preferred journalism. He wrote for a number of influential newspapers, and after he joined the Socialist Party, he collaborated with its leader Jean Jaurès to found *L'Humanité*, the most famous French newspaper on the left. In 1902, Briand ran for election to the Chamber of Deputies and won.

Briand hit his stride as a politician. When the French decided to separate church and state in 1905, Briand headed the commission that was charged with drawing up the implementing legislation. He so impressed his colleagues that Premier Jean Sarrien invited him to join his cabinet in 1906 as minister of education and religion to ensure proper enforcement of the law. Briand accepted, but, because Socialist policy did not allow party members to join governments, the party expelled him. This exhilarating period also brought great personal satisfaction because Briand met the love of his life, actress Berthe Cerny. Briand never formed his own party, but his skill in Parliament, rhetorical ability, and intelligence made him one of the most successful French politicians of the era. In 1909, he became prime minister, heading the first of eleven cabinets he eventually formed. A man of peace, he found himself leading the French government during World War I from October 1915 to March 1917, during which he participated in military planning and strengthened the country's military institutions. His tenure as wartime premier ended amid criticism when he favored a negotiated peace with Germany.

Briand returned to the fore as Europe's most active diplomat in the 1920s, alternating in the offices of prime minister and foreign minister. In collaboration with German Foreign Minister Gustav Stresemann, he negotiated the Locarno Pact, a complex series of mutual guarantee and arbitration treaties that were designed to normalize German relations. This achievement won him the Nobel Peace Prize in 1926, which he shared with Stresemann.

A famous cartoon of the period summed up the French diplomat's association with peace in the popular mind. It depicted world leaders, except for Briand, smashing the statue of Mars. In the vignette, Briand tries to talk the ancient Roman god of war into committing suicide. An enthusiastic Briand greeted Germany's admittance to the League of Nations in September 1926 with the words: "Away with rifles and cannon; make place for arbitration and peace." The next year, Briand approached U.S. Secretary of State Frank B. Kellogg with the idea of renouncing war in favor of arbitration, which led to the Kellogg-Briand Pact. In May 1930, Briand proposed to twenty-six nations the creation of a European Union based on federative principles and linked to the League of Nations. For the first time, the French Foreign Office took concrete steps to implement the initiative, but the plan died when the cabinet of which Briand was part resigned. For the French, the effort was enough to baptize Briand "the father of Europe," and he deserves a high place along with other influential French proponents of European unity.

In May 1931, Briand attempted and failed to win election as French president. On March 7, 1932, he died suddenly. He lies buried at Cocherel, where he periodically took refuge from his intense political and diplomatic labors.

Economic Issues

Strengthening the good feelings during the Locarno period was the apparent resolution of the reparations issue, one of the major obstacles to a lasting peace. After the occupation of the Ruhr, the Allies created a committee to examine relevant issues. Headed by Charles G. Dawes, director of the American Budget Bureau, the committee made a series of recommendations in early 1924. It proposed stabilizing the German currency (ruined by hyperinflation) by pegging it to the British pound, a new schedule of reparations payments starting at 1,000 million gold marks and rising to 2,500 million after five years, and a foreign loan to back the new currency and help raise the amount needed for the first payment. A reparations agency including Allied representatives would oversee the details of payment and eventual variations.

The Dawes Plan achieved success. The French accepted it and withdrew from the Ruhr, while Germany made regular payments, demonstrating that reparations were not incompatible with Europe's economic recovery. In 1927 and 1928, the height of the Locarno era, a new committee, which was set up in 1929 and headed by American banker Owen D. Young, recommended reducing reparations by about a quarter and suggested a rising rate of annual payments that would definitively end reparations in 1988. The countries involved agreed, and Germany made the first payment under the new arrangement in May 1930.

German acceptance, however, did not come easily. Financial officials objected to the plan and wrestled with the German cabinet before finally agreeing to it, but a referendum on the plan aroused hostile feelings among the opponents of reparations and brought the Nazis greater recognition in the country as a result of their participation in the voting. Nevertheless, just before the Great Depression, Europe seemed to have achieved economic stability despite persistent problems. Germany had successfully replaced its currency, Britain had stabilized the pound sterling in 1925, and France, the franc in 1926. In 1924, French industrial production surpassed that of 1913, and in 1926, German production exceeded its prewar level. Moreover, trade increased substantially between France and Germany. Unclear at the time was the degree to which European economic progress depended on American loans. American capital flowing to Germany stimulated production and helped the Germans pay their reparations bill, which in turn allowed the Allies to pay their war debts to the Americans. When American money dried up because of the stock market crash in October 1929, the Americans called in their loans, and the system collapsed, but would it have done so without the shock of the ensuing depression?

Economic stabilization mirrored social stabilization. Following the war, revolution had shaken the continent, but, with the exception of Russia, the old social order had substantially survived. Europe's calm encouraged new efforts at cooperation as an antidote to conflict. In May 1930, Briand proposed restructuring Europe as a federal union. Its organization would be similar to the League of Nations, with an assembly representing all the states, a body representing the large countries, and a Secretariat. The proposal included a common market. The new European federal union would coordinate action with the League of Nations, which illustrated the high hopes that Europeans placed in the international organization.

THE HITLER REVOLUTION

Although the settlements of the 1920s had important defects, the flaws would not have necessarily been fatal without the political and economic destabilization caused by the depression, including Hitler's rise to power.

The Austrian Debacle

As was previously discussed, strong sectors of German and Austrian public opinion favored the union of Austria and Germany, known as the Anschluss.

The Allies, however, had forbidden any form of unity and in 1931 vetoed a customs union to combat the depression.

Austrian Chancellor Engelbert Dollfuss jealously guarded his country's independence. A rightist Catholic and Mussolini protégé, Dollfuss, in February 1934, destroyed his Social Democratic opposition, which left the Austrian Nazis as the main paramilitary force. On July 25, the Nazis attempted to overthrow the government. The *putsch* failed, but Dollfuss bled to death in the attempt. Hitler threatened to invade the country, but Mussolini dispatched several divisions to Italy's border with Austria and denounced the Fuehrer as "a horrible sexual degenerate, a dangerous fool." Hitler quickly backed down.

Il Duce recognized that German absorption of Austria would have put a dangerous power on its border. Furthermore, Italy had annexed the South Tyrol, an area populated by a restive Austrian minority that Mussolini sought to Italianize, and Germany's Austrian ambitions presented a clear enough danger that forced il Duce to act.

After Italian forces blocked the Anschluss, Britain, France, and Italy discussed ways of curbing future German aggression. Mussolini believed he deserved a reward for his action against Hitler. Over the next several months, however, he concluded that the British expected him to defend Austria without any compensation. Should he be relegated to the position of permanently defending Austria, it would spell the end of his ambitions in Eastern Europe and Africa. By 1935, he hoped to conquer Ethiopia in order to create an empire and to avenge a humiliating defeat that Italy had suffered in 1896 but could not do so while stationing forces on the Austrian border to stop Hitler. Despite Austria's importance for Italy, Mussolini informed the Germans that only Austria stood between them. This attitude signaled a basic reorientation of Italian foreign policy by loosening the ties that linked Italy to Britain and France and exploiting the threat posed by Hitler to induce them to agree to his demands.

Africa and Europe: Breakup of the Wartime Alliance

By January 1935, the French had become convinced that an agreement with the Duce was necessary to defend against Hitler. Prime Minister Pierre Laval met Mussolini in Rome and discussed a deal on the Ethiopian question, which had become critical because of a December 1934 military confrontation on the poorly demarcated border between Ethiopia and Italian Somaliland. The conflict produced an Ethiopian appeal to the League of Nations, and Mussolini accelerated his timetable to take over the country before the Ethiopians could modernize their army or gain world sympathy. He was prepared to make concessions to the French in return for their diplomatic backing and agreed to a greater role for the League of Nations in the Austrian question and to renouncing Italian rights in Tunisia. France made minor colonial adjustments in Africa, but the core of the agreement seems to have been a French promise of a free hand in Ethiopia. Exactly what this free hand meant has been disputed ever since. Both men preferred to keep things vague, but it seems likely that il Duce received French backing for his African plans. Mussolini also sought British acquiescence but failed to achieve it.

On March 16, 1935, Hitler denounced the disarmament clauses of the Versailles treaty. In discussing the Allied response, the British favored conciliating Hitler, but Mussolini argued that only a show of force would bring the Germans into line. At the Stresa Conference in April 1935, Mussolini demanded binding commitments and concerted action by the Western powers against aggressive German moves. The French agreed with him but went along with the British, who opposed strong action. Far from retaliating, the British negotiated a naval agreement with Hitler that sanctioned his building of a fleet up to 35 percent of theirs. In effect, this agreement endorsed Hitler's violation of the Versailles disarmament clauses.

The British attitude assured that no decisive step resulted from the Stresa consultations, an outcome that convinced Mussolini that the Western democracies were pusillanimous. Worse, the conference relegated Italian ambitions in Africa to talks among experts, where British opposition to Italy's African venture surfaced. In a contradictory move, however, the British agreed that the final communiqué would remain silent on the issue, suggesting to the Italians that Britain would not oppose Italy's African adventure.

The Stresa conference's failure and the Anglo-German naval agreement had major consequences. The Italians could not understand why the British opposed them in Africa while insisting that they protect Austria and concluding an agreement with Hitler that violated the Versailles treaty. The dispute between the British and Mussolini escalated during the Ethiopian affair and alienated Italy from the victorious World War I alliance.

The Ethiopian War and the Discredit of the League of Nations

As an Italian invasion of Ethiopia loomed in the fall of 1935, the British proposed that the League of Nations invoke collective security if the Italians attacked Ethiopia. On October 3, 1935, Italian troops entered the country. The league imposed sanctions on Italy but left petroleum off the list, the only commodity that could stop the Italian war effort. Sanctions caused the Italians hardship but transformed the Fascist adventure into a national crusade and boosted Mussolini's popularity. Sanctions were a test to determine if the League of Nations could be utilized against Germany in the future, but their failure destroyed the organization's reputation and irremediably weakened it. Consequently, the League of Nations would not be a significant factor in the crises that led to World War II.

For the big powers, the major focus of the dispute was Europe, not Africa. Italy's involvement in Ethiopia left Austria vulnerable to Germany and encouraged the British and French to halt the African conflict quickly. Discussions among Britain, France, and Italy culminated in the Hoare-Laval proposals, which offered the Italians major economic and territorial concessions in Ethiopia. The deal fell through because of leaks and the so-called Peace Poll that indicated popular support in Britain for the League of Nations and opposition to the dictators. Contemporaneously, Mussolini's archenemy Anthony Eden became British foreign minister, and the leftist Popular Front government came to power in France, producing further complications. At this crucial juncture, a new crisis diverted attention from the Ethiopian conflict.

Remilitarization of the Rhineland

The Treaty of Versailles had prohibited the Germans from keeping troops in or fortifying the Rhineland, but on March 7, 1936, Hitler remilitarized it, violating the treaty by sending troops into the area. This move clearly threatened France, but, led by a caretaker government, it did nothing. The British also did not react strongly. Many Europeans, convinced that the Germans had been treated too harshly after the war, accepted the fait accompli.

Astonished at the soft British reaction against Germany compared to the hard line taken against him over Ethiopia, Mussolini concluded that London plotted a general German agreement with a redistribution of colonies, leaving Italy out in the cold. On the other hand, Hitler's spectacular move helped Italy by taking the wind out of the drive for oil sanctions, which the British championed. These developments confirmed il Duce's alienation from the Western democracies, convinced him of their weakness, and demonstrated that the two dictators could benefit by cooperating.

In the meantime, the Italians rapidly conquered Ethiopia, although guerrilla activities continued until World War II. On May 9, 1936, they proclaimed the empire.

The Spanish Civil War and Its Impact

Following the Duce's victory in Ethiopia, the British and French sought to placate the Italians, hoping to gain Mussolini's support for the diplomatic containment of Germany. The British induced the League of Nations to remove the sanctions and reduced tensions in other ways. Despite serious differences with the democracies, il Duce had not irredeemably thrown in his lot with Hitler, but German revival had proved useful to him. However, the Spanish Civil War made a rapprochement less likely.

In July 1936, rightist forces, headed by General Francisco Franco, revolted against the Spanish Republican government. Despite initial hesitation, Mussolini dispatched forces to aid the rebels. Instead, the Spanish conflict escalated and ended only in 1939, becoming an ideological war that antifascists viewed as an opportunity to stop international fascism. Volunteers from all over the world fought on the Republican side and dealt the fascists an embarrassing defeat at the Battle of Guadalajara. With his prestige at stake, il Duce sent more troops and material to Spain. Mussolini had not coordinated his action with the Germans, but the Spanish war brought the dictators closer together as Hitler sent soldiers to Spain and the two collaborated. Hitler pledged to support Italian primacy in the Mediterranean, and on November 1, Mussolini baptized the new cooperative attitude between Germany and Italy the "Axis." In the same month, Germany and Japan signed the Anti-Comintern pact against the Soviet Union, with Italy joining later. In September 1937, Mussolini paid Hitler a friendly visit.

Besides producing a closer relationship between Hitler and Mussolini, the Spanish Civil War worsened relationships with the democracies. The British and the French advocated nonintervention by the big powers. The Germans and Italians agreed but violated their commitments. The Soviets sent military aid to the Spanish government, greatly increasing their influence over the Republican war effort. Moreover, Soviet predominance raised the specter of a Communist Spain, which weakened the British and French resolve and strengthened the Republican opponents. Furthermore, the German military performance had important repercussions. The Nazis tested new and fearful air power tactics—Pablo Picasso's *Guernica* captures the brutality of bombing helpless civilians in the city that gave the painting its name.

FROM CRISIS TO CRISIS

In 1938, the focus of diplomatic activity shifted from Spain to Eastern Europe as Hitler felt strong enough to escalate his challenge to the Allies.

The Austrian Crisis
Following the failed Nazi coup of 1934, Kurt Schuschnigg replaced Dollfuss as chancellor, but the increasingly close association between the Duce and the Fuehrer made Mussolini less inclined to oppose Hitler's Austrian policy. Already in July 1936, Schuschnigg had caved in to German pressure to accept several pro-Nazi Austrians into his cabinet, and the Duce had gone along with this arrangement.

On February 12, 1938, Hitler summoned Schuschnigg to his mountain headquarters in Berchtesgaden, berated him, and threatened to invade if he did not agree to Austria's Nazification. Schuschnigg consented, but once back in Vienna, he attempted to strengthen his hand against the Fuehrer by ordering a plebiscite on the Anschluss. A furious Hitler prepared to invade. Only a show of force by Italy could have stopped Germany from swallowing Austria, but the Duce refused to intervene. Schuschnigg called off the plebiscite, and Austrian Nazi leader and interior minister Arthur Seyss-Inquart invited German troops into the country.

The Austrians joyfully greeted the German soldiers, leading the Western powers to conclude that the Anschluss enjoyed majority support, but the absorption of Austria was a defeat for them and for Mussolini. The enlarged Reich increased German power, and Mussolini accepted the presence of a great power on his border that could threaten Italy's independence. This fact made it less likely that he would end his association with Hitler.

Czechoslovakia's Strategic Dilemma
Within a few months of the Anschluss, Hitler provoked a crisis over Czechoslovakia, exploiting the 3 million formerly Austrian Germans within its borders. A country of 10 million people with an efficient army and a strong armaments industry, Czechoslovakia could not defeat Germany in case of war, but could offer stiff resistance. President Beneš and Foreign Minister Thomas Masaryk had sought security by allying with France in 1924. There was no British pact, but the Czechs counted on British involvement in case of a conflict with Germany because of Britain's commitment to the French. Unfortunately for them, the British feared being drawn into a conflagration in Eastern Europe and, when a crisis broke out between Germany and Czechoslovakia in 1938, encouraged the French to accept the German demands.

The Czech Crisis

The Anschluss set the stage for the Czech crisis by absorbing Austria and creating a common German-Czech border. Hitler incited the Sudeten German minority, led by Nazi Konrad Heinlein, to make extreme demands on the Czech government. France and the USSR indicated they would aid Czechoslovakia, but the British, reluctant to be dragged into a conflict, pressured the Czechs to agree to concessions.

During the summer and fall of 1938, Hitler berated the Czechs for mistreating the Sudeten minority. In September, President Benes agreed to autonomy for the Germans, but the Nazis did not desist. British Prime Minister Neville Chamberlain cautioned Hitler that Britain and France would fight should his Czechoslovak policy lead to war, but his warning failed to dissuade the Fuehrer.

At Hitler's urging, the Sudeten Germans took to the streets, prompting Chamberlain to fly to Berchtesgaden for consultations on September 15. The two leaders agreed that Czechoslovakia should cede the Sudetenland to Germany. The loss of this mountainous, heavily fortified area rendered Czechoslovakia militarily helpless, but the British accepted this consequence because they believed it would produce peace. France, a possible obstacle because its treaty with Czechoslovakia committed it to war under such circumstances, backed off when the British intimated that they would not support the French in case of war. A stunned Benes could only acquiesce.

Just when the crisis seemed resolved, Hitler suddenly changed his mind. Alleging escalating Czech atrocities, he demanded more land, a plebiscite, and the immediate entrance of German troops into Czechoslovakia. A second meeting between Chamberlain and Hitler failed to settle the differences. The Fuehrer seemed determined to have a conflict, which prompted the Czechs to mobilize, the French to gear up for war, and the British to ready their fleet. As a last resort, however, the British appealed to Mussolini to intervene, and the powers agreed to a conference.

The Munich Conference

On September 29, 1938, Hitler, Mussolini, Chamberlain, and French Prime Minister Édouard Daladier, "The Bulldog," met at the infamous Munich conference without the Czechs or the Russians. At this meeting, the four statesmen agreed on the details of Czechoslovakia's dismemberment and saved the peace for a year. The Soviets offered to aid Czechoslovakia, but Poland and Romania objected to Soviet troops crossing their territory.

After the Munich Conference, the Poles seized the rich area of Teschen, Benes resigned, and Czechoslovakia reorganized itself into a feeble federation. The British and French guaranteed the new borders, but Hitler had no good reason to take them seriously. The Western democracies had in effect put the country into Germany's sphere of influence, and the Fuehrer soon dispensed with the formalities of Czech sovereignty. Slovakia broke off in March 1939 and became a German satellite. Hitler summoned the new Czech president, Emil Hácha, and subjected him to a violent tirade. German troops marched on Prague, and Hitler threatened to bomb the city if the president did not acknowledge a German protectorate. Hitler

Czechoslovakia's Strategic Predicament. The areas that Hitler claimed and eventually got were Czechoslovakia's strategic border, the Sudetenland, protected by mountains. By giving the Germans Czechoslovakia's strategic border, shaded in the map, the British and French rendered it militarily defenseless. The German minority living in this area had not been part of united Germany but of Austria-Hungary.

also allowed the Hungarians to take Ruthenia, a piece of the hapless state that they had long claimed. The British and French backed out of their pledge to preserve the borders of the rump state because it no longer existed.

A NEW WAR

After the Munich conference, Chamberlain announced: "Peace in our time." The conference had turned Europe away from the brink of war at the last minute, but a new crisis brewed.

Poland's Strategic Dilemma

The independent Poland that appeared after World War I faced the strategic dilemma of being located between an aggressive Germany and Russia and of lacking defensible frontiers. Even worse, the Polish Corridor contained a large German minority, and Poland had annexed large tracts of Soviet territory inhabited by former Russian subjects, primarily Ukrainians, that the USSR wanted to regain.

Polish political leaders based their foreign policy during the 1920s on a French alliance, but during the 1930s, France appeared weaker while German and

On September 29, 1938, the leaders of the big powers met at Munich at the behest of Mussolini to try to save the peace during the Czechoslovak crisis. They met without either the Czechs or the Russians being represented and agreed to resolve their differences by giving in to most of Hitler's demands. The Conference saved the peace, but at the cost of a French betrayal of its commitments to Czechoslovakia. In this photograph, from left to right, British Prime Minister Neville Chamberlain, French Prime Minister Édouard Deladier, Hitler, and Mussolini, pose for the camera. The man in uniform on the extreme right is Count Galeazzo Ciano, Mussolini's son-in-law and Italian Foreign Minister.

Russian power increased. With Hitler's takeover of Austria and Czechoslovakia, Poland's military situation deteriorated. The Poles had a longer border with German-controlled territory and, even if Hitler and Stalin clashed, the fighting would take place on Polish territory because Germany and the USSR lacked a common border. Furthermore, because of the distances involved, Western military support would not reach Poland in time to make a difference.

The Polish Crisis
After his successes in Austria and Czechoslovakia, Hitler raised the unresolved questions of the German minority and the Polish Corridor. In October 1938, he demanded the return of the former German port of Danzig, a road across the Polish Corridor connecting East Prussia with the rest of Germany, and Polish adherence to the Anti-Comintern Pact. After March 1939, Hitler made new demands, and on April 6, Chamberlain responded by guaranteeing Poland's borders; the French followed suit.

Probably the sudden British-French guarantee can be explained by Hitler's absorption of Prague in violation of the Munich agreements, after which they understood that the Fuehrer could not be appeased. Presenting Hitler with the

Poland's Quandary. Poland was caught between the claims of Germany and the USSR. Here the Polish Corridor and the territory desired and eventually annexed by the Soviet Union are shaded.

certainty of war to dissuade him from attacking Poland seems a likely explanation for the guarantee, although the British advised the Poles to negotiate with the Germans in a last-ditch effort to save the peace. The Poles refused, fearing that the British might withdraw their guarantee should they see an opening to maintain peace by yielding Polish territory.

The Nazi-Soviet Nonaggression Pact

The British-French guarantee thrust the USSR to the forefront of European diplomacy. Should war with Poland and the Allies break out, the Allies needed the Soviets in order to present Germany with a credible military threat on two fronts. Poland might be defeated, but the Germans would face a long war with the French and the Russians. If the Fuehrer ensured Russian neutrality, however, he could overrun Poland and then turn his attention to the Western front, or perhaps the West would not to go to war under circumstances in which it could not save Poland.

For the Allies as well, the USSR's attitude was crucial. To have any chance of saving Poland, they needed Soviet help. However, they were at a disadvantage in the negotiations during which the Soviets bargained with them and with the Germans. Stalin distrusted the Allies because of their anticommunism; moreover, the British and French had guaranteed Poland's borders and could not offer the Soviets what they wanted: the land Russia had lost to Poland after World War I. Even if their enmity made Nazis and Communists improbable friends, a deal

From the strategic viewpoint, modern Poland was doomed from the beginning, just as it was in the eighteenth century, because it was a large weak state with no defensible borders caught between hostile big powers. After World War I, the Poles alienated both Germany and Russia, and later it became impossible for the country to have friendly relations with either Nazi Germany or Soviet Russia without becoming the satellite of one or the other. In this photograph, a smiling Stalin seems satisfied with his pact with Hitler plotting the partition of Poland and the absorption of the Baltic States by the USSR. The Nazi-Soviet Non-Aggression Pact set the stage for World War II.

would give the USSR the territory it desired and, by pushing Soviet borders farther west, would create a buffer against an eventual German attack. For Stalin, there was the added prospect that Germany and the Western powers would wear each other down.

In order to get an agreement quickly, Hitler dispatched Foreign Minister Joachim von Ribbentrop to Moscow on August 23, 1939. Ribbentrop and the Soviets quickly agreed to a nonaggression treaty. The Soviets and Nazis pledged enduring friendship, promising not to attack each other or to join any third party that might attack their respective countries. Secret clauses split up Poland and left for later consideration whether a rump state would remain on the map. Germany recognized Latvia, Estonia, and Finland as belonging in the Soviet sphere of influence and declared its disinterest in Bessarabia, which Russia had lost to Romania after World War I. In return, Germany got Lithuania. By assuring that the USSR would remain neutral in a war with the Western democracies, the Nazi-Soviet Nonaggression Pact set the stage for war.

The Outbreak of War

Following up its pledge to guarantee Poland's borders, London signed a pact with Warsaw committing itself to war if the Germans attacked. In a last-ditch effort to save the peace, the British asked Mussolini to arrange a conference, but the Duce

Danzig, the German-inhabited free city in the "Polish Corridor" that had been a major bone of contention during the Polish crisis, heard the first shots of World War II, fired from a German warship, on September 1, 1939. This photograph shows a street in the historical city, now briefly German, decorated with swastikas. The city was mostly destroyed during the conflict.

refused, although he kept his country out of the imminent conflict by informing Germany that Italy was unprepared for war. The Japanese also refused to get involved. On September 1, 1939, German armies invaded Poland. Britain sent an ultimatum to Germany, and France also declared war.

World War II had begun only twenty years after the First World War ended, but on a different basis from the previous world conflict. The Germans had a tradition of expanding in the East, but Hitler based his *Lebensraum* on extreme racism that mandated the subservience and destruction of so-called inferior races, such as the Jews, Gypsies, and Slavs who lived in the area. While World War

Mussolini and Hitler dominated the international scene in the 1930s. They had similar foreign policy aims in that both opposed the post-World War I Versailles Settlement and wished to overthrow it. Hitler's goals, however, were much more ambitious than those of the Duce, who aimed primarily at a Mediterranean and colonial empire. Although this picture portrays Mussolini and Hitler as being solidly with each other, Mussolini distrusted Hitler and had doubts about joining him in World War II until mid-1940.

I had been a struggle against German domination, the new war was a fight for survival.

Bibliographical Essay

Two books that examine significant foreign policy issues during the 1920s are Piotr S. Wandycz, *France and Her Eastern Allies 1919–1925* (Westport, Conn., 1962), and Robert Machray, *The Little Entente* (New York, 1970). A good general account of the interwar years is Raymond J. Sontag, *A Broken World, 1919–1939* (New York, 1971). Patrick O. Cohrs, *The Unfinished Peace After World War I* (New York, 2006), is a thorough history of the attempt to stabilize Europe between 1919 and the rise of Hitler and includes the U.S. role.

Stephanie Salzmann emphasizes an important but neglected topic mentioned in this chapter in *Great Britain, Germany, and the Soviet Union: Rapallo and After, 1922–1934* (London, 2003). Jon Jacobson, *Locarno Diplomacy: Germany and the West 1925–1929* (Princeton, N.J., 1972), is a thorough examination of Locarno, while Anne Orde, *Great Britain and International Security 1920–1926* (London, 1978), describes the British perspective. Orde also published *British Policy and European Reconstruction After the*

First World War (Cambridge, UK, 2002). William J. Newman's *The Balance of Power in the Interwar Years, 1919–1939* (New York, 1968) is a clear discussion of the European balance during the years concerned through an examination of the Locarno agreement and its implications for wider policy. Stresemann's aims are examined by Henry L. Bretton, *Stresemann and the Revision of Versailles: A Fight for Reason* (Stanford, Conn., 1953). Hans W. Gatzke, ed., *European Diplomacy Between Two Wars, 1919–1939* (Chicago, 1972), contains a series of essays on major issues pertinent to the coming of war. Gordon A. Craig and Gilbert A. Felix, *The Diplomats 1919–1939,* 2 vols. (Princeton, N.J., 1953), is a classic treatment of interwar diplomacy. Winston Churchill's *The Gathering Storm* (Boston, 1948) is a protagonist's account that sets forward the case against appeasement while summarizing the dissolution of the postwar settlement.

The most comprehensive work on Mussolini's interwar diplomacy and goals is H. James Burgwyn, *Italian Foreign Policy in the Interwar Period 1918–1940* (Westport, 1997). MacGregor Knox, *Common Destiny: Dictatorship, Foreign Policy, and War in Fascist Italy and Nazi Germany* (Cambridge, UK, 2000), is an analysis of the Fascist and Nazi dictatorships and their foreign policies. Denis Mack Smith, *Mussolini's Roman Empire* (New York, 1976), covering the same period, is more impressionistic. John Gooch weighs in on an unusual topic: *Mussolini and His Generals: The Armed Forces and Fascist Foreign Policy* (New York, 2007); Gaetano Salvemini, an old enemy of Mussolini, sees the Duce as an important protagonist in the coming of World War II in *Prelude to World War II* (New York, 1954), a standard account. Older examinations of Mussolini's foreign policy that still have value include Elizabeth Wiskemann, *The Rome-Berlin Axis* (London, 1969); Mario Toscano, *The Origins of the Pact of Steel* (Baltimore, Md., 1967); and Maxwell H. H. Macartney and Paul Cremona, *Italy's Foreign and Colonial Policy, 1914–1937* (London, 1938). On the Ethiopian War, see George Baer, *The Coming of the Italian-Ethiopian War* (Cambridge, Mass., 1967). Franklin D. Laurens discusses the French position in *France and the Italo-Ethiopian Crisis, 1935–1936* (The Hague, 1968), while William I. Shorrock examines the general issue of Italian Fascism in French diplomacy in his *From Ally to Enemy* (Kent, Ohio, 1988). On the Spanish Civil War, John Coverdale, *Italian Intervention in the Spanish Civil War* (Princeton, N.J., 1975), debunks some of the myths about the ineffectiveness of Mussolini's participation in the conflict.

Felix John Vondracek's *The Foreign Policy of Czechoslovakia 1918–1935* (New York, 1968) is a thorough examination. Polish and Russian foreign policy up to the final crisis is analyzed by Bohdan B. Budurowycz, *Polish-Soviet Relations 1932–1932* (New York, 1963).

Hitler's foreign policy has been the subject of many works. See Christian Leitz, *Nazi Foreign Policy, 1933–1941: The Road to Global War* (New York, 2004). Consult Klaus Hildebrand, *The Foreign Policy of the Third Reich* (Berkeley, Calif., 1983). Gerhard Weinberg, *The Foreign Policy of Hitler's Germany: Starting World War II, 1937–1939,* 2 vols. (Chicago, 1994), argues that Hitler wanted war over Czechoslovakia, indeed, that he planned a series of conflicts. An earlier book by the same author describes how the coming of Hitler to power was a diplomatic revolution: *The Foreign Policy of Hitler* (Chicago, 1970). Williamson Murray rebuts commentators who argue that the allies profited by Munich, which allowed them to go to war a year later when they were supposedly better prepared. See *The Change in the Balance of Power, 1938–1939* (Princeton, N.J., 1984). E. M. Robertson discusses the relationship between Hitler's foreign policy and military planning in *Hitler's Pre-War Policy and Military Plans* (New York, 1963). Keith Eubank studies the problem of appeasement in *Munich* (Norman, Okla., 1963) and the coming of World War II in *The Origins of World War II,* 3rd ed. (Arlington Heights, Ill., 2004). On the question of appeasement, two works that examine the issue in detail are *Hitler, Chamberlain and Appeasement* (Cambridge, UK, 2002) by Frank McDonough, and *Public Opinion and the End of Appeasement in Britain and France* (Farnham, UK, 2010) by Daniel Hucker. Appeasement is inextricably involved with the question of whether or not the Western democracies were militarily prepared to fight successfully against Hitler. Discussions of this issue may be found in Gaines Post, *Dilemmas of Appeasement: British Deterrence and Defense* (Ithaca, NY, 1993), and Robert J. Young, *In Command of France: French Foreign Policy and Military Planning, 1933–1940* (Cambridge, Mass., 1978). Young also wrote *France and the Origins of the Second World War* (New York, 1996), a study of why France chose to enter a war for which it was so badly prepared. Donald Cameron Watt, *Too Serious a Business: European Armed Forces and the Approach to the Second World War* (New York, 1975), is a readable analysis of the European armed forces and the coming of World War II.

The role of the League of Nations is the subject of two books: Ruth B. Henig, *The League of Nations* (London, 2010), in the Makers of the Modern World series published by Haus, and Peter J. Yearwood's *Guarantee of Peace: The League of Nations in British Policy, 1914–1925* (New York, 2009).

Geoffrey Roberts examines the crucial relationship between the USSR and Nazi Germany from 1933 in *The Soviet Union and the Origins of the Second World War: Russo-German Relations and the Road to War, 1933–1941* (New York, 1995). Simon Newman dedicated a study to the all-important guarantee to Poland, *March 1939: The British Guarantee to Poland* (Oxford, UK, 1976). Poland's predicament during the interwar period is examined in Richard M. Wate, *Bitter Glory: Poland and its Fate, 1918* to 1939 (New York, 1998).

The book that reopened the question of the origins of the war is A. J. P. Taylor, *The Origins of the Second World War* (New York, 1961). E. M. Robertson, *The Origins of the Second World War: Historical Interpretations* (London, 1971), is a collection of articles that includes attention to Taylor. The debate itself may be followed in a series of works, including Wm. Roger Louis, ed., *The Origins of the Second World War: A. J. P. Taylor and His Critics* (New York, 1972), and Gordon Martel, *The Origins of the Second World War Reconsidered*, 2d ed. (London, 1999). Over the years, Taylor's book has led to extensive examinations by other authors of Hitler's motives and tactics. Andreas Hillgruber's *Germany and Two World Wars* (Cambridge, Mass., 1981) concludes that Hitler aimed at world power. Norman Rich, *Hitler's War Aims* (New York, 1974), argues that Hitler's racist ideology spurred him toward great territorial expansion. A detailed history of how the war actually broke out is Donald Cameron Watt's *How War Came: The Immediate Origins of the Second World War, 1938–1939* (New York, 1989). P. M. H. Bell, *The Origins of the Second World War in Europe*, 2d ed. (New York, 1997), does a good job of putting everything into perspective.

CHAPTER 18

✍

The German Tide Over Europe

CHAPTER OUTLINE

Confrontation • German Successes • The Home Fronts

BIOGRAPHICAL SKETCHES

Heinz Wilhelm Guderian, Panzer General • Maurice Gustave Gamelin,
Historical Footnote

With the beginning of World War II on September 1, 1939, the great struggle between Germany and Russia for supremacy in Eastern Europe, and perhaps the world, began anew, although ostensibly on a different basis: ideology.

After World War I, a class ideology dominated Russia, and a racist one, Germany. The accidents of history help explain Russia's choice, while historical continuity is more appropriate for Germany—but below the surface, history and national ambition guided their policies. Confronted with a German invasion in 1941, Stalin appealed to his people to defend "Mother Russia," and the Nazis invoked European civilization against the Asiatic hordes. After World War II, the Soviets exploited Communist ideology as a façade for their control of Eastern Europe, but the events of 1989, when communism collapsed, illustrated the fragility of ideology compared to national realities.

CONFRONTATION

Even though the major European powers expected a conflict when World War II broke out, they were less prepared for a war than in 1914.

The Allies

After World War I, British planners assumed that the country would not have to fight a major war for ten years, an assumption they abandoned in 1932, but only in theory. In February 1936, the British decided on a five-year rearmament program, but financial considerations and the government's reluctance to interfere with civilian production limited rearmament.

The need to protect its empire also limited Britain's ability to confront a European conflict. The doctrine of limited liability placed the major burden of fighting the Germans on the French. In 1938, 74 out of 138 British battalions served abroad. The lack of conscription limited the growth of the British army, making it much smaller than those of the other major powers. In early 1939, the government decided to raise thirty-two divisions within a year of the outbreak of war, and in April it announced conscription, but when the war began, only four British divisions departed for the continent.

Similar considerations affected the British navy and air force. The British had the strongest navy in Europe, but Britain's worldwide role made it less able to confront the combined German, Italian, and Japanese fleets. A building program, adopted in 1936, that would have doubled British cruisers and aircraft carriers and significantly increased the number of other ships, came too late to make a difference in 1939. In the air, the British hoped that a strong force would deter a German attack; between 1934 and 1938, they concentrated on building bombers, but in 1938 changed their emphasis to building fighters that were better able to protect British civilians. The quality of the planes increased dramatically with the introduction of the Hurricanes and Spitfires. Luckily, the secret British work on radar made it possible to intercept enemy bombers some distance away.

Unlike the British army, regular soldiers made up only the core of the French army, which was based on conscription. The French had periodically reduced the term of service but increased it to two years in 1935 to compensate for the low birthrate. After their active duty, these solders went into the reserves, which allowed the French to field eighty-four divisions when the war broke out. This force was better armed than its rapid defeat in May–June 1940 suggested. In the autumn of 1936, the French began an ambitious rearmament program to increase their tank forces and antitank capabilities. Much of the rearmament plan was completed, but the defense-mindedness of its generals hampered the army. Wanting to avoid the huge World War I-style offensives, they built the Maginot Line, a series of impregnable fortifications that, they hoped, would save their manpower and wait for reinforcements while the Allied fleets strangled Germany, as they had in World War I. The French generals expected a replay of the previous conflict in which the defense would be supreme.

The other French armed services were mixed. High quality and modern construction characterized the French navy, except for several old battleships. In combination with the British navy, the French fleet was a powerful force, in stark contrast to the air force, which consisted mainly of old planes. In 1933, the French instituted a new program to refit their air force, but planning and industrial difficulties hampered modernization. When war began, the French had just three hundred modern warplanes of a poorer quality than their German counterparts.

The Axis
Germany's rapid rearmament from the disarmed state imposed by the Versailles treaty stands out as an amazing achievement, but its stunning military achievements between 1939 and 1942 gave a false impression. After Hitler

announced conscription and rearmament in March 1935, the German army rapidly expanded from 7 to 21 divisions and by 1939 could field 103 divisions.

This quick expansion caused serious problems in recruiting, in training an adequate officer corps, and in producing the tanks that were needed to outfit the new armored (Panzer) divisions. In 1939 German equipment did not fulfill officers' expectations, deficiencies that help explain the caution of the German generals, who feared that Hitler's reckless foreign policy would embroil them in a war. Hitler's success in the Rhineland and the Czechoslovak crises, however, allowed him to brush the generals aside and take control of the command structure of the armed forces by establishing the High Command of the Armed Forces (*Oberkommando der Wehrmacht, OKW*).

The excellent performance of the German armed forces under these conditions says as much about the weakness of their opponents as it does about German military skill. Despite the strong influence of the traditional tactics of using tanks for infantry support, the Germans emphasized concentrated employment of tank divisions, along with close, dive-bomber support (*Blitzkrieg*), pioneered by General Heinz Guderian.

The Germans concentrated on their air force, the flower in the Nazi military lapel. In 1932, the air force possessed only a small number of military planes, and the aircraft industry had dwindled to just over 3,000 workers. Under Hitler crony Hermann Goering, the German air force began a spectacular expansion in 1933. Between 1936 and 1938, the number of workers in the German aircraft

Although the Germans were famous for their tank operations during World War II, their early tanks performed poorly. The Germans had a greater edge in the quality and design of their airplanes, and during the war developed models that were much more advanced than those of the Allies. However, by concentrating on ever more advanced weapons that could not be developed and put into production quickly enough they did not make a difference in the fighting. Here is a picture of a German "Komet," a rocket-propelled fighter that appeared in combat in May 1944, outperforming all other planes but with a very short powered flying time. It was credited with fewer than ten kills.

industry rose to more than 125,000, and production reached an annual average of over 5,000 planes. Even though the Germans had problems obtaining enough raw materials, deciding on which models to produce, and agreeing on the proportion of bombers and fighters, and never reached their ambitious targets, in 1939 the German air force was the strongest in Europe.

The Germans also embarked on an enormous naval building program, but the navy received low priority compared with the other services. By September 1939, the German navy boasted only two battle cruisers, three pocket battleships, and six cruisers among its capital ships, although the powerful battleships *Bismarck* and *Tirpitz* neared completion. The navy had only fifty-six submarines, of which twenty-six were capable of operating in the Atlantic Ocean. In 1939, Admiral Erich Raeder and Hitler agreed on "Plan Z," which would have given Germany a world-class fleet over the next several years, but war's outbreak in 1939 scuttled the ambitious naval plan.

Despite rearmament, Germany was not ready for a long conflict in 1939. Hitler consistently stated that a war would not break out before 1943 or 1944, and its early arrival caught the armed forces at a disadvantage. The country was militarily and economically prepared for short wars but had to import strategic raw materials in a long one, making it vulnerable to a blockade.

The Italian armed forces were the least prepared to fight a major war. The successes that they had achieved in Ethiopia and Spain during the 1930s drained their limited resources and made it less likely that they could sustain a full-blown European conflict. Furthermore, Fascist direction of war preparations was incompetent and bumbling. In theory, Fascism provided for central direction, with Mussolini holding the three cabinet military posts—the army, navy, and air force—in addition to being prime minister. Il Duce could not keep up with the work and did not coordinate his actions with the general staff. The different services did not have coherent military doctrines and did not work out consistent strategic plans for the likely war scenarios.

This confused situation had disastrous effects. The Italian army had a structure similar to the French army, but in order to increase the army's maneuverability in 1937, the Chief of Staff reduced the size of a division from three to two regiments. The reorganization began in late 1938, creating confusion, but that was not the only problem. Armaments were poor. Italian commanders had proposed forming a number of armored divisions, but by 1940 had not proceeded very far. Only a few medium tanks reached the armed forces, the main armed vehicle remaining a lightly armored tankette. The production of heavy artillery in 1939 stalled at about seventy pieces a month. Most of the army's artillery and its rifle, the Model 91, were of World War I vintage. Even Fascism's prize service, the air force, under Fascist hierarch Italo Balbo, was woefully unprepared for war, despite its prestige during the interwar period and the excellent models on the drawing boards. Mussolini claimed 8,500 planes, but the air force began the war with only 1,000 obsolete planes and did not coordinate its action with the army. The most efficient service was the navy, whose strength compared well with the British and the French fleets in the Mediterranean and could have dominated the central part of that sea. Unfortunately, the navy lacked fuel and did not have radar.

Compounding these issues, il Duce had never been able to gain control over the armed forces, which remained loyal to the king, the soldiers disliked their German allies, and there was a culture of disobedience to Fascist orders.

THE USSR

Given its military and geographic situation, the USSR's best course was neutrality in a European conflict, despite possessing Europe's largest armed force with a peacetime strength of almost a million soldiers in 1939. Estimates of its tanks range from 3,000 to 10,000, but several models proved unsatisfactory until production of the T-34 medium tank in 1940. From their military operations during the Spanish Civil War, the Soviets favored the organization of their tanks to support the infantry. When the German defeat of France proved the superiority of concentrating tank divisions in highly mobile attacks, the Soviets began reorganizing their tank forces on the German model and were in the process of this reorganization when the Germans attacked them with devastating results. Military doctrine was another problem. Because the Soviets assumed that any new conflict would be a class war and uprisings would take place behind enemy lines, they also believed that the Red Army would take the offensive; instead the German attack forced the Soviets to go on the defensive.

The Soviet air force was large but had a large number of obsolete planes, and serious problems afflicted the main bomber. As war approached, the Soviets began

Unlike the Germans, the Russians concentrated on producing reliable weapons rather than focusing on exotic ones. Here is the Soviet T-34 medium tank, the most effective and most common tank of World War II. It continued to be produced until 1958 and widely exported throughout the world. The picture shows a World War II era T-34 during a victory parade in October 2004. The flag is the one the Russians hoisted above the German Reichstag in 1945.

to deploy modern aircraft and, during the conflict, followed an intelligent policy of producing few but serviceable models in great quantity—a strategy that eventually overwhelmed German air superiority.

Two other major problems that affected Soviet military performance were poor training for recruits and damage done to the officer corps by the purges. The resulting weakness emerged dramatically in armed clashes with the Japanese in 1938 and 1939 and in a war against the Finns that began on November 30, 1939. The Russian difficulty in defeating the Finns encouraged Hitler to believe that he would win an easy victory over the USSR.

GERMAN SUCCESSES

Hitler's rapid victories in 1939 and 1940 allowed Germany to capture and utilize the resources of the defeated countries. Military observers expected Germany to defeat Poland in short order, and Hitler's pact with Stalin made the task easier. Two days after Warsaw's fall on September 27, 1939, the Nazis and Soviets formally divided the country between them. During the assault on Poland, the Germans fought a holding action against the French and British in the West, with the Allies missing the opportunity to help the Poles by launching a major offensive during what they called the "phony" war.

In April 1940, the Germans invaded Denmark and Norway. On May 10, they launched an offensive against France through Belgium, the Netherlands, and Luxembourg and defeated France in a month. Hitler then attempted to knock Britain out of the war through a massive air campaign that continued until June 1941. He failed to accomplish his goal, but the British remained isolated in their island fortress and could not take offensive action on the continent. Hitler then turned his attention against the USSR, which had been his prime target to achieve *Lebansraum* (living space) in the East. On June 22, 1941, German troops invaded Russia in the expectation of a quick victory

The Nazi-Soviet Assault on Poland and the Baltic

With the defeat of Poland, the Soviets and Nazis renegotiated their non-aggression pact. Germany gained a larger amount of Polish territory in return for letting the Russians take Lithuania. One quarter of a million Polish Jews escaped into Soviet territory, although many died on the way or were turned back by Soviet soldiers.

As the Nazis wreaked havoc in Poland, the Soviets deported hundreds of thousands of civilians to labor camps in the USSR and systematically murdered the Polish officers and specialists they captured. The most spectacular atrocity, known as the Katyn forest massacre, was part of Stalin's long-term objective to Sovietize Poland. Although the Germans later discovered mass graves, the Soviets denied responsibility until Premier Mikhail Gorbachev admitted it on April 13, 1990. Once they had achieved their immediate aims in Eastern Europe, the Nazis and Communists signed a treaty on February 11, 1940. In return for German manufactured goods, the Russians assured Germany the steady stream of strategic raw materials it needed for its military machine.

Expansion of Nazi Germany 1933–39.

The Germans had great success at the beginning of World War II thanks to their greater military preparation and tactics based on speed of action, concentration of their forces on vulnerable points of the enemy's defenses, and a skillful combination of land and air attacks—the "blitzkrieg." The most clamorous example of the effectiveness of these tactics was the rapid defeat of France. Here is General Erwin Rommel, one of the most brilliant practitioners of the new military method, and his staff planning their advance through France in May 1940.

Hitler Turns West

Before he could attack Russia, Hitler had to secure his western front. Following Poland's defeat, Hitler aimed to destroy the British and French armies by going through neutral Belgium and Holland, a plan the military establishment did not favor. Hitler endorsed a blueprint for the French campaign, prepared by Generals Erich von Manstein and Gerd von Runstedt, by which the Germans would draw the Franco-British forces north to save Holland and Belgium while they attacked in force through the Ardennes forest, cutting their enemies off and defeating them.

At the same time, driven by Admiral Raeder's desire for naval bases in Norway to confront the British, Hitler authorized an intrepid scheme to take over that country. In April 1940, utilizing the element of surprise, the Germans seized control of Norway and Denmark. A bumbling British effort to dislodge them failed miserably. Unfortunately for the Germans, the surface fleet sustained heavy losses in the conquest of Norway, ending any hope of defeating the British navy in an invasion of Britain itself. The Norwegian campaign was a warning to Sweden if it had any ideas about cutting off the vast quantities of high-grade iron ore it supplied to Germany. In the future, Sweden adjusted its neutrality to the demands of its aggressive neighbor and to the fortunes of war.

In Britain, the Norwegian debacle increased popular dissatisfaction with the government, which lost support in Parliament. Chamberlain lost control of his own Conservative Party and resigned. Led by its female deputies, the Labour Party favored a national coalition government headed by Winston Churchill, who had been tainted by the Norwegian disaster but had made his reputation in opposing appeasement and in pressing for resistance to Hitler. The new prime minister electrified Britain on May 13, 1940, offering his people nothing "but blood, toil, tears, and sweat" and by defining British policy as "Victory—victory at all costs."

France Falls

In the meantime, the Germans implemented their invasion of France using Heinz Guderian's *Blitzkrieg* tactics, perfected in Poland, of concentrating their armor to create an irresistible mobile mass supported by dive-bombers and in constant touch by radio. The French and British had a large number of tanks, and the French machines were superior to the German, but they failed to exploit the tank's speed or ability to roll over the most stubborn resistance.

The Germans unleashed their offensive on May 10, 1940, by attacking Holland and bombing Rotterdam, killing hundreds of civilians to terrorize the Dutch people. The Dutch army surrendered on May 15, and Queen Wilhelmina fled to London to set up a government in exile. On May 18, Belgium capitulated. When the British and French moved their best mobile forces far to the north to confront the German invasion of the Low Countries, the Germans attacked France through the Ardennes forest, splitting the Allied forces into northern and southern chunks. French commander Maurice Gamelin committed his reserves to the northern theater, leaving none to confront the deteriorating military situation. The Allies lacked an effective command structure, making it difficult to coordinate their actions as the Germans split the Allied armies. The Allies tried to stop the German advance by bombing the bridges, but their air forces proved unequal to the task. By May 20 and 21, the Germans had reached the channel coast.

BIOGRAPHICAL SKETCHES

Heinz Wilhelm Guderian
Panzer General

Heinz Guderian exemplifies the strength and weakness of German society during the Hitler era. Most Germans were not evil or committed Nazis but, frequently, talented people who lent their expertise to the regime without bothering about the consequences.

Born on June 17, 1888, in Culm (now in Poland), the son of an army officer, Guderian was educated in military schools. In 1908, he joined a ranger battalion commanded by his father, who in 1911 sent him to study wireless communications, an important component of his future military strategy. Guderian, who was a very serious student, exhibited an acerbic sense of humor that made him enemies. As a young lieutenant during World War I, he wrote a scathing report about his commander, displaying another character trait that would get him into trouble.

Guderian made a brilliant career in Germany's postwar *Reichswehr*, serving as the youngest staff officer on the general staff. An expert in tanks and motorized warfare, he took command of motorized (mostly supply) units. Because the Versailles treaty prohibited the German army from possessing tanks, the Germans secretly developed them in Russia with Soviet cooperation. Guderian participated in this activity and in 1937 published a seminal tract on tank warfare: *Achtung Panzer!* He called for the reorganization of the army around armored divisions, a proposal that upset traditional army commanders who favored the infantry, but one that Hitler supported by ordering the creation of three tank divisions. There followed the rapid promotion to general, full control of the army's armored units, and prestigious assignments leading German troops into Austria and Czechoslovakia.

During World War II, Guderian led an army corps in Poland, but his most famous victory came in France. Guderian fully implemented his *Blitzkrieg* tactics by disobeying the orders of his superiors, who, afraid of outflanking movements by the enemy, constantly ordered him to stop and wait for the infantry when his tanks outran it. Guderian remarked that it was more difficult to fight his superiors than the French. Aided not by better machines but by radio communication among his tanks and perfectly trained crews—his innovations—Guderian pushed his tank forces as far as they could go, broke through French lines, and delivered a spectacular victory. During the Russian invasion, Guderian commanded a Panzer army, but constant fighting with his commanding officer led to his removal and reassignment in February 1943. Put in charge of reorganizing German tank units and increasing the production of armored vehicles, he achieved great success. After the failure of a conspiracy by army officers to kill Hitler on July 20, 1944, he accepted the Fuehrer's nomination as the army chief of staff. Guderian loyally served until March 1945, when Hitler dismissed him because of military disagreements.

At the war's end, the Americans found no evidence of war crimes, but questions surfaced about Guderian's failure to support the July 20 conspiracy, acceptance of the post of army chief of staff, indifference to slave laborers in German arms factories, and fidelity to Hitler. Even after the conflict, he did not criticize Hitler or take a strong position on the persecution of the Jews.

After the war, Guderian participated in an American historical project on the German general staff, wrote several cold war tracts, and published *Panzer Leader*, a best-seller translated into ten languages. He died on May 17, 1954, and was lowered into his grave to the sound of West German frontier police firing a salute. His name remains identified with armored warfare, but he left an emblematic legacy symbolized by a 1960s proposal, rejected, to name a German army barracks after him.

The question for the Allies became what to do with the two chunks of their armies; for the Germans, how to destroy them. The British decided to evacuate the British Expeditionary Force (BEF) and as many French soldiers as possible from the northern theater so the army could be re-formed in Britain. On May 25, the Dunkirk evacuation began utilizing governmental vessels and private craft of all kinds. They saved about 340,000 men, including 120,000 French soldiers.

The German success in France almost destroyed the British Expeditionary Force operating in that country. In order to save their troops and surviving French soldiers the British mounted a massive evacuation effort from Dunkirk on May 25, 1940, using large ships but also small craft of all types. Most of the soldiers were saved so they could fight later. Here is a picture of Allied troops boarding a ship during the evacuation.

The overconfident Germans rested their victorious forces and prepared to move against French troops in the south, leaving the job of finishing off the soldiers trapped at Dunkirk to Goering's Luftwaffe. Weather and the British air force thwarted the Germans, and by the time they realized that a large number of troops were escaping, it was too late. On June 14, with the French army in an advanced state of disintegration, the Germans entered Paris.

The internal malaise that contributed to France's fall can be traced back to the beginning of the twentieth century: the profound social divisions among the classes; the political divisions that led some groups to support the USSR and others, Nazi Germany; the lack of significant reforms to address the complaints of different social strata; and the defense-mindedness.

In the military sphere, Hitler became overconfident. His spectacular success in France despite opposition from the generals had major repercussions in the conduct of the war by increasing his suspicion of the army and convincing him of his own military genius. He took greater direction of the conflict's military side and implemented his frequently mistaken decisions against the advice of his generals.

BIOGRAPHICAL SKETCHES

Maurice Gustave Gamelin
Historical Footnote

General Maurice Gamelin, commander in chief of Anglo-French forces at the beginning of World War II, served as a fitting foil to Heinz Guderian. From comparable backgrounds, both men had roughly similar careers, but a fatal timidity transformed Gamelin from a prominent general into a historical footnote.

Born in Paris on September 20, 1872, the son of a high army official, Gamelin attended the prestigious French military academy of Saint Cyr and served in North Africa from 1883 to 1897. Cultivated and brilliant, he impressed his superior officers and in 1906 published *Étude philosophique sur l'art de la guerre* (*Philosophical Studies on the Art of War*), a tract that revealed a good military mind. Two future commanders of the western front during World War I, Generals Ferdinand Foch and, especially, Joseph Joffre, strongly supported him and advanced his career.

During World War I, Gamelin participated in the most famous battles of the conflict and demonstrated talent as an administrator and tactician. Skilled in politics in addition to war, Gamelin achieved promotion to brigadier general on December 8, 1916. After the war, Gamelin headed the French military mission to Brazil and, in September 1924, took command of French troops in Syria, successfully restoring his country's shaky military position there. In February 1929, he assumed command of an army corps and the next year became the second highest officer on the French general staff. Within two years, he had replaced General Maxime Weygand as its chief. Through his political acumen and subsequent promotions, Gamelin became virtual head of the French army by 1935.

As an influential adviser to French governments and known to be admired by the British, Gamelin exercised more sway on French foreign policy than did other generals in the great democracies. Consequently, he bears a substantially greater responsibility for French indecisiveness toward Hitler in the 1930s. Especially critical was his abandonment of Czechoslovakia, despite that country's long alliance with France, and his personal promise of aid in case of a German threat.

Most seriously, his ineptitude helped set the stage for France's spectacular defeat by Germany despite the rough military equality between the two countries in armaments, training, and military tradition. Before the war, Gamelin did not seriously consider or implement modern doctrines that his military attachés reported were under discussion by foreign armies, particularly the use of tanks. As the commander of Allied forces from September 1939 to May 1940, he proved incompetent. He failed to deliver on a promise to the Poles to launch a powerful attack against the Germans while their army was engaged in Poland, a strategy with a good probability of success. Fearful of retaliation, Gamelin kept his forces on the defensive behind the Maginot Line. He established his headquarters far from the front, isolating himself and hindering good communication with his troops. He proved incapable of controlling the rivalries among his subordinates and issued commands in a hesitating manner, suggesting, rather than ordering, action. His most famous directive begins: "Having no wish to intervene in the battle currently underway. . . ." Gamelin also made a major error during the German offensive by committing most of his reserves in the wrong place. On May 19, 1940, the government dismissed him—too late to repair the damage and spare France its greatest defeat in modern times.

In February 1942, the Vichy government tried Gamelin and important politicians as responsible for the French disaster but recessed the trial. The Germans arrested him in April, but he went free in May 1945. From then on, Gamelin defended his role in the war but died in Paris on April 18, 1958, unsuccessful to the end.

Italian Intervention

With France defeated and Britain beleaguered, isolated, and on the brink of defeat, many Europeans believed that the war was almost over. This attitude encouraged Mussolini to enter the conflict.

Il Duce had kept Italy out of the war despite the "Pact of Steel" signed with the Germans on May 22, 1939. He had made it clear that Italy would be unprepared to fight a major war until 1943 and was unhappy when Germany touched off the conflict. Mussolini's son-in-law, Foreign Minister Galeazzo Ciano, took the lead in this effort by sending the Germans a long list of supplies that the Italians needed in order to join the Germans. Ciano and his friends fretted about the Italian position in a German-dominated Europe, although Mussolini himself seemed untroubled at the prospect. The Duce could not conceive of the war continuing for long after the French defeat and, after his initial doubts, worried that he could not get into the fray fast enough to claim French territory and build an empire in the Mediterranean. To his generals, who timidly pointed out the country's lack of preparation, he remarked that he required only a few thousand dead in order to sit at the peace table. On June 10, 1940, he declared war, not only militarily unprepared but without having made definite military plans.

The quick German defeat of France in May-June 1940 was one of the great shocks of World War II. The French had a great military tradition and, despite their defeat during the Franco-Prussian war of 1870, had a long history of defeating Germans in war. Hitler danced with joy at the news of his army's great success. After the Germans occupied the proud French capital, they staged a victory parade at the Arc de Triomphe, one of the most famous Parisian landmarks.

Britain Resists

Mussolini had made a monumental miscalculation. The British vowed to resist a anticipated German invasion by all possible means. They planned to use poison gas against the invaders; prepared to destroy bridges and other essential structures; and, if occupied, to continue the struggle from Canada. They attacked and destroyed most of the French fleet off North Africa on July 3, 1940, when it refused to surrender because of the fear that it would fall into German hands. They sought arms from the neutral Americans, who in June sent rifles, machine guns, artillery pieces, and ammunition. On September 2, 1940, the two countries concluded an agreement by which the Americans transferred fifty destroyers to the British in return for ninety-nine-year leases on a series of British bases close to their shores. This deal represented a step toward future American intervention.

Because of the overwhelming British superiority at sea, the air war took center stage. The Battle of Britain began in earnest in July and August 1940. The British and Germans lost a large number of airplanes, but Hitler made a fundamental error by ordering the Luftwaffe to change its targeting from fighter bases to London.

On September 17, Hitler postponed his invasion plans, cancelling them in October. The blitz followed as the Germans intensified their bombing of London and industrial centers in an attempt to break British morale. In May 1941, with Britain undefeated and German plans to attack Russia well advanced, the blitz ended, but the targeting of civilian areas had become a normal part of warfare and culminated in the carpet bombing of German cities and in the atomic bombing of Japan.

Italian Failures

While the Germans were preparing to attack the USSR, Italian intervention widened the war to the Mediterranean and Africa and diverted the Germans into areas where they did not want to be involved. Mussolini was jealous of Hitler's successes and dreamed of invading Yugoslavia and Greece. When German troops appeared in Romania in preparation for the Russian attack, Mussolini believed that Hitler was moving forward in southeastern Europe without regard for Italian interests. The Duce resolved that the next time he acted, he would not inform the Fuehrer, and in late October 1940, badly prepared, ill equipped, and badly led, the Italians invaded Greece while Mussolini informed Hitler only at the last moment. The Greeks threw them back and moved into Albania, and the Germans had to rescue the Italians by invading Greece and Yugoslavia.

The Italians did poorly not only in the Balkans, but in Africa. They initially advanced in North Africa, but the British defeated them in early 1941. This disaster forced the Germans to send an army under General Erwin Rommel to bolster their allies. In East Africa, which the Italians could not supply, they lost their newly acquired Ethiopian Empire and their old colonies.

The Assault on the USSR

In the East, Hitler hoped that early spectacular victories against Soviet forces would cause the Soviet state to collapse and give him the control of the East of which he dreamed. On June 22, 1941, three German army groups, known as north, center, and south, attacked the USSR. The Germans seized large stretches of Soviet territory, including the Polish lands they had taken, and inflicted a large number of casualties. By mid-July the Germans had taken 600,000 prisoners in the central portion of the front alone, had seized the Baltic states, moved into the Ukraine, and besieged Leningrad (now St. Petersburg). The German generals talked about the war in terms of mopping-up operations, and Hitler began claiming Germany's new borders and defining his plans for the territories to be incorporated.

Soviet Resistance

This optimistic scenario turned out to be unrealistic. The defeated Red Army retreated but did not collapse, nor did the Soviet state. Brutal German tactics helped attain these results. The Germans murdered captured Soviet political officers, slaughtered or starved prisoners of war, and liquidated tens of thousands of civilians and Jews. Aware of the fate that awaited them should they lose the struggle, the Russians fought harder than ever. Partisan activities tied down thousands of German troops. The Soviet government mobilized the economic and human resources of the country to fight the enemy.

The Germans had planned a brief war and consequently lacked reserves of men and equipment to win. By late July the German army stopped to rest its men, overhaul equipment, and fix damaged transportation facilities. Its long supply lines proved a major handicap, as they had for previous invading armies. As the Soviet government drew up plans to leave Moscow, the Germans failed to attain their objectives—to reach Murmansk and the Caucasus or to take Leningrad or Moscow—and failed to knock Russia out of the war before winter. The German invasion would soon take on the proportions of a military disaster.

Hitler had believed that the Germans would quickly annihilate the USSR and had earmarked Russian raw materials for the buildup of the navy and air force for the invasion of Britain. In September 1941, he reversed those orders and told German industry to concentrate on the production of weapons for the army so it could keep fighting the Soviets. The sacrifices of the Russian people made a major contribution to the ultimate Allied victory.

THE HOME FRONTS

The enormous amount of war materiel that was needed to fight World War II necessitated a more efficient mobilization of the home fronts than had been the case from 1914 to 1918. In theory the centralized administrations of the dictatorships should have made them more efficient than the democracies, but while the USSR mobilized its economy and citizens in an astonishingly successful but brutal manner, Britain rallied its population more effectively than did Nazi Germany.

Home Front: Britain

Total mobilization for war brought major changes to British society, helped, ironically, by the intense German aerial bombardment. British authorities issued gas masks that people carried around in cardboard boxes, ordered blackouts, and prevented motorists from turning on their headlights. They evacuated young children from endangered cities, along with their mothers and teachers. This step should have meant moving 4 million people, along with 2 million who left voluntarily, but only half the mandated evacuees left. The evacuation went smoothly only to encounter significant problems at the destination points. In the countryside, the evacuees found abominable weather and social conditions, since many children of the urban poor wound up staying with poor rural families who could not supply their needs, while the children of the richer classes were placed with wealthy families. This fact exposed the perversities of the British class system and would have an impact on British social policy after the war. Another problem was that the localities from which the evacuees came had the financial responsibility for paying expenses to the receiving areas, but the funds either arrived late or never; this put a tremendous burden on rural towns. In the cities, the children who remained found that their schools were frequently closed until November or later and that there was no governmental supply of free milk or food. In addition, the authorities reserved city hospitals for casualties that the "phony" war never produced and cut off access to them by the poor, including pregnant women. The evacuation during the "phony" war and a second one while the bombs fell during the Battle of Britain and the blitz revealed the conditions of the urban poor and spurred the government to take action to improve the living standards of distressed people both during and after the war. One observer wrote: "The Luftwaffe was a powerful missionary for the welfare state."

Besides the social impact of the evacuations, the "war socialism" resulting from the organization of the country for combat had major repercussions on the nation's future social and economic development. The British people supported the war against Nazism and did not allow the social discord of the 1914–1918 conflict to resurface. Governmental agencies elaborated an equitable and practical rationing system that was generally accepted as fair. The Labour Party sent the authoritative Ernest Bevin to participate in the cabinet as labor minister. Thanks to him, workers, including a large number of women, united to achieve the government's production goals.

The government's innovative financial policy kept social antagonism to a minimum. It did not attempt to contain inflation by using its wartime powers to depress wages but allowed them to rise with the aim of keeping the gap between national income and expenditures as narrow as possible. This policy allowed for some inflation but kept it at a minimum and had the important social consequence of evening out the imbalance in the sources of wealth. In fact, income from wages grew by 18 percent while earnings from property fell 15 percent and those from salaries fell 21 percent. The workers judged tax increases to be fair, and the taxes from labor paid for a greater percentage of expenditures than in World War I. The equitable economic regime helped the British government mobilize English society for war more effectively than did Nazi Germany.

Home Front: Germany

Because of its army's early successes, which allowed Germany to loot its victims and employ a large number of slave laborers, German citizens lived a relatively comfortable life, and the state faced less severe economic hardships than did Britain. Hitler deliberately followed this policy because of his conviction that during World War I, the hardships suffered by the German people because of the Allied blockade and the demands of war had led to disaffection and to the uprising that had defeated Germany.

The Germans instituted more generous rationing than did the other belligerents; allowed the production of consumer goods to remain high until 1942, when they ordered industry to concentrate on war-related items; and exempted an exceptionally high proportion of men from military service. Unlike the British or the Russians, the government did not mobilize women to work in the factories on a large scale until 1944, on the grounds that women should stay at home to tend their children and because of the large number of slave laborers who took the place of the men serving in the armed forces. Indeed, the government's generous subsidies to servicemen's families encouraged women to leave their jobs.

The Nazis were also less efficient than the British and Americans in mobilizing science for war. Nazi planners concentrated on developing weapons, such as the V-1 and V-2 and the jet fighter, but the use of slave laborers exposed the V-2 rocket project to frequent sabotage. They failed to recognize the importance of developing a nuclear weapon or to devote the necessary resources to it (perhaps because of Werner Heisenberg's influence), and the jet fighter arrived too late to affect the war's course.

Slave labor probably ended up damaging the war effort. Slave laborers were in poor physical condition, required guards, lacked motivation, and sabotaged the war effort when they could. Probably their greatest contribution to Germany's war effort was to free a greater proportion of men for service in the armed forces than was the case in other countries. Because they received no salaries or pensions, were overworked, underfed, and easily replaced upon death, slave laborers supplemented the profits of German companies, an issue that returned to haunt German industry during the 1990s. Slave laborers permitted Germans to live relatively well at the upper reaches of a racial hierarchy and, divided into racial categories that determined the severity of their maltreatment, provided a foretaste of Hitler's hopes and plans for Europe. However, they presented one overwhelming social hazard: possible sexual activity. The Nazis banned sexual relations, even touching, between the slave laborers and German women, and meted out ruthless punishment for infractions. Some Germans felt uncomfortable with the pervasive presence of slave laborers, but the majority profited or turned their eyes away.

The Germans tasted not only the future that Hitler held out for Europe, but the one he held for them. After the war began, Hitler ordered an intensification of the euthanasia program—the killing of selected categories of Germans whom the government considered useless. An October 1939 decree mandated the systematic removal and murder of patients with incurable physical and mental infirmities, of ailing elderly people in institutions, and of babies born with severe handicaps. Pervasive rumors placed severely wounded veterans of the current conflict on the list, although the government backtracked. Relatives and some institutions resisted the elimination of sick Germans, and scattered rioting occurred. In August 1941 the bishop of Munster, Clemens August von Galen, publicly protested, and the government temporarily backed off the most extreme aspects of its program. By then, the program had disposed of between 100,000 and 200,000 Germans and had important results with respect to the Jewish question. The euthanasia program required the collaboration of doctors, other medical personnel, and experts of all kinds, which favored the development of a core of workers specializing in methods of mass murder in the concentration camps.

The casualties of war created a novel problem. Because the Nazis feared that German women would marry men from stock they considered racially inferior, they planned ways of increasing the Aryan population during the postwar period without this inconvenience. The Nazis recognized the illegitimate children of SS members and of German soldiers with Germanic women of the occupied countries, extending subsidies to the mothers. They seized children from occupied Eastern Europe if they had the proper racial characteristics and raised them as Germans. For the future, SS head Himmler and other Nazi leaders advocated multiple wives for men, so they could breed more progeny, and proposed the procurement of wives from the United States and other areas of significant past German emigration. In the conquered East, Himmler planned for a large number of Germans to return to the soil as farmers and to have large families. These Germans would lord it over the local population that was to be kept poor.

The war witnessed an exponential growth of SS power in German society. Favored by Albert Speer, industrial tsar and Hitler's favorite architect, SS enterprises expanded rapidly at the expense of private industry, and its armed units, the Waffen SS, at the army's cost. Had the Nazis won the war, the SS would have become the major industrial power in a German-dominated postwar Europe. The Nazis also planned to continue the strict wartime regulation of private industry.

Flanking the SS, the Nazi Party intensified its presence in German society during the war. Hitler's secretary Martin Bormann expanded the party's power despite the decline of popular support owing to increasing realization that Germany would lose. Intensification of the Allied bombing campaign forced more people to depend for clothing and other necessities on social relief agencies, especially the party welfare organization. Welfare activities and the country's desperate efforts to raise more soldiers kept the party viable in the war's final years.

Hammered by the most devastating conventional bombing in history in the latter part of the conflict, German civilian morale dropped but induced passivity rather than rebellion. No matter how bad the bombing, the German people feared even more a Russian invasion and the fate of their country once the nature of its war crimes became general knowledge. The Germans grumbled but remained faithful to their Fuehrer, and his soldiers fought bravely for him until the end.

Home Front: Italy

Unlike Hitler, Benito Mussolini, could not count on the loyalty of his people, who had grown continually disaffected from the regime that brought them into the war unprepared. Opposition to Italian entrance into the conflict ranged from the highest levels of government to the ordinary citizen. The formerly pro-German Foreign Minister Ciano exclaimed in his diary for June 10, 1940: "May God help Italy!" Forced to fight, ordinary Italians would have preferred the Germans as enemies.

The National Fascist Party, long utilized to mobilize the masses, could not convince Italians to put their hearts into the conflict. Italian opinion became even more hostile to the Duce when he sent soldiers to fight in Russia, where they suffered high casualties for no vital interests. This campaign and the military defeats the Italian armed forces suffered sapped what little support il Duce had.

The Fascists made a greater attempt than the Nazis to mobilize women in an effort to support troops on the front. The regime removed its quotas on working women in June 1940, just before the country declared war, hoping that they could fill in for the men who were conscripted into the army. By 1943, when Mussolini was overthrown, women figured prominently in both private and public enterprises. By then, hunger stalked the country, and mass protests began. March 1943 witnessed widespread strikes in the important industrial center of Turin—the first in Axis Europe—with workers shouting "peace and bread." The largest target, Fiat, quickly agreed to pay overtime and to grant cost-of-living increases. Politically, the failure of the police and party authorities to intervene demonstrated that il Duce's authority had evaporated. Many of the strikers were women, a sign that the regime had lost their support. A strong Italian resistance movement took root, and women were prominent among the opponents of the Fascists and their Nazi allies even though the regime retained some support among women. In the last days of the war, 6,000 women answered the call to join a women's armed force in a last, desperate attempt to fight the Allies and anti-Fascist partisans.

These developments demonstrated the folly of Mussolini's participation in the war. Although it had made good progress during the Fascist era, Italian industry could not compete with the other combatants in the production of war materiel, a weakness compounded by the country's lack of raw materials. For example, the Italians manufactured 667 tanks in 1942, compared to the USSR's 25,000, and only 350 in 1943.

The war arrived at the Italian homeland with severe bombardments of the northern industrial cities of Milan and Turin in March 1943. Strikes, the loss of North Africa, and the invasion of Sicily by the Allies followed. Faced by the certainty of defeat, Fascist leaders rebelled against the Duce, and on July 25, the Fascist Grand Council voted a motion of no confidence in Mussolini and asked King Victor Emmanuel III to take charge of the country. The monarch had Mussolini arrested, prompting popular demonstrations that eliminated the vestiges of the Fascist regime. Hitler rescued his partner and placed him at the head of a satellite state in northern Italy. The story of Mussolini's last few months as titular head of the Italian Social Republic makes a degrading final chapter to a high-stakes gambler's amazing career.

Home Front: The USSR

At first it seemed that the Ukrainians and Russians would welcome the Germans, but they quickly discovered that Nazi racism and brutality outdid the horrors of Bolshevism and made them support their leaders despite the loss of over 20 million lives and the terrible misery caused by the war. Communist modernization during the 1930s had gotten the Soviet people used to working under abominable conditions and allowed Stalin to mobilize the country. Visitors' reports described shabbily dressed and severely overworked workers enjoying no privileges or breaks in their routine, toiling between twelve and sixteen hours a day. The state canceled all leaves and holidays for the war's duration, added three hours of compulsory overtime to the workday, put much of the Soviet workforce under military law, and sent habitual latecomers and slackers to labor camps.

Of all the combatants, the Soviet government succeeded best in militarizing society. It called up all men aged 18 to 50 and kept industrial and agricultural production high through the mass mobilization of women, who accounted for 40 percent of the industrial workforce in 1940 and over 50 percent in 1943; on the farms, women topped 85 percent. In 1944, over 80 percent of tractor drivers were women. After 1941, the Soviets called up women without children who were not working in critical industries to serve as fighter and bomber pilots, communication and transportation specialists, machine gunners, snipers, infantry, tank commanders, and anti-aircraft gunners, so that about 8 percent of the Soviet armed forces consisted of women. Women received 4 percent of the military medals and 1 percent of the highest decoration, the Hero of the Soviet Union, which indicate that their efforts were underrewarded. Besides appealing to nationalism, the government made workers who excelled at their jobs into national heroes and rewarded productive workers with extra food and fuel. Conversely, if workers failed to meet expectations, the government withheld food.

During the conflict, ideology faded as an incentive for hard work, despite the omnipresent propaganda and secret police. Nationalism and hatred of the Germans took the place of ideology. When the Germans invaded, they seized the Soviet industrial, mineral, and agricultural heartland. As a result, the Soviet supply of coal, iron, and steel fell by 75 percent, strategic raw materials by 66 percent, electricity by 40 percent, and meat and grain production by 50 percent. Nevertheless, between 1941 and the time the United States could gear up its vast industrial potential, the USSR carried the major burden of the war against the Nazis.

The Soviets accomplished this feat by evacuating entire industries to the Urals, Central Asia, and Siberia in the last five months of 1941. These industries included over 1,500 iron, steel, engineering, and other war-related industrial concerns, and the 16 million people and technicians who were needed to run them. What they

When the Germans invaded the USSR in June 1940 it seemed that the Russian people would welcome them. Once they experienced the Nazi occupation, however, they strongly supported their Fatherland despite great hardship, spurred by Stalin's appeals to nationalism. This photograph shows Russian women digging anti-tank traps outside Moscow.

could not relocate, they destroyed. The Soviets also built new industries, concentrating on giant plants that were needed to supply their forces with weapons. By 1942 the eastern regions produced 75 percent of Soviet arms and practically all the country's coal and steel. In an effort to get as much materiel as possible to their soldiers rapidly, the Soviets constructed tanks, airplanes, and artillery in only a few basic models of good quality, outproducing the Germans, despite more limited resources. In 1943, for example, 8 million tons of Soviet steel and 90 million tons of coal were transformed into 48,000 pieces of heavy artillery and 24,000 tanks. The Germans used 30 million tons of steel and 340 million tons of coal to make 24,000 guns and 17,000 tanks. After 1943 the production gap widened in favor of the Soviets.

Bibliographical Essay

The reader will find a flood of material on World War II, and no attempt to be exhaustive has been made here. P. M. H. Bell's *The Origins of the Second World War in Europe*, 3rd ed. (New York, 2007), is excellent on the situation of the different powers just before the outbreak of the conflict. Readers who are interested in the origins of the conflict now have a good choice, with books that include R. J. Overy, *The Origins of the Second World War* (New York, 2008), who looks at the issue of the short war; Jonathan Wright, *Germany and the Origins of the Second World War* (New York, 2007); and Victor Rothwell, *Origins of the Second World War* (New York, 2001). For considerations on the controversial book by A. J. P. Taylor on the problem, already cited, see Gordon Martel, *The Origins of the Second World War Reconsidered: A.J.P. Taylor and the Historians* (New York, 2002).

The best one-volume work on the fighting in Europe is Gerhard L. Weinberg, *A World at Arms: A Global History of World War II* (New York, 2005). This detailed, perceptive, and comprehensive work discusses all military aspects of the war in different parts of the world. Peter Calvocoressi and Guy Wint, *Total War: Causes and Courses of the Second World War* (New York, 1974), is excellent, also goes into detail on Europe, and has a large section on the Pacific. Both books are indispensable for an understanding of how the war developed. James L. Stokesbury, *A Short History of World War II* (New York, 1980), is a good representative of a numerous and growing class of books. *Europe at War: 1939–1945* (London, 2006) concentrates on the Nazi and Soviet regimes at war, reminding readers of the brutality of the Soviets as well as the Nazis. S. P. MacKenzie, *The Second World War in Europe* (New York, 2009), is a brief treatment. Lee Baker, *The Second World War on the Eastern Front* (New York, 2009), concentrates on the engagement between the USSR and Germany. Readers should be reminded of a classic— Gordon Wright, *The Ordeal of Total War 1939–1945* (New York, 1968), which analyzes the conflict from all aspects and includes information in one handy source.

Adrian Ball, *The Last Day of the Old World* (Westport, Conn., 1978), follows developments hour by hour on the last day of peace. John Lukacs, *The Last European War: September 1939/December 1945* (New York, 1976), contrasts people's everyday lives with the movement of armies and high politics during the conflict. Alan S. Milward, *War, Economy and Society* (Harmondsworth, UK, 1987), discusses the conflict's economic and social aspects. Richard J. Overy, in *War and Economy in the Third Reich* (Oxford, UK, 1995), does not believe that Hitler planned a brief war.

Anyone who is serious about understanding World War II should include a reading of Winston Churchill's classic account, *The Second World War*, 6 vols. (Boston, 1948–54). There are many good biographies of Churchill, including, among the best, Martin Gilbert, *Churchill: A Life* (New York, 1991); William Manchester, *The Last Lion: Winston Spencer Churchill* (New York, 1988); and John Lukas, *Churchill: Visionary, Statesman,*

Historian (New Haven, Conn., 2002). The appearance of revisionist accounts of Churchill's policies demonstrates that the subject is still lively. See John Charmley, *Churchill and the End of Glory* (New York, 1993), which argues that Churchill should have considered a compromise with Germany, and Robert Rhodes James, *Churchill: A Study in Failure* (New York, 1970), which faults Churchill's style. Roger Parkinson, *Blood, Toil, Tears and Sweat: The War History from Dunkirk to Alemein, Based on the War Cabinet Papers of 1940 to 1942* (New York, 1973), details the war from 1940 to 1942 from the British govern-ment's perspective. E. S. Turner's *The Phony War* (New York, 1961) is a social history of Britain during the period.

Specific books on the Battle of Britain include Francis K. Mason, *Battle Over Britain: A History of the German Air Assaults on Great Britain* (London, 1969), and Peter Townsend, *Duel of Eagles* (London, 1971). R. J. Overy's *The Battle of Britain: The Myth and the Reality* (New York, 2001) is a thorough scholarly coverage of the event. See Michael Korda's book on the same subject, *With Wings Like Eagles* (New York, 2009). The battle is well covered in more general histories of air operations during World War II. Philip Ziegler, *London at War* (New York, 1995), looks at the city up to the war's end.

Robert Mallett produced a closely argued book on *Mussolini and the Origins of the Second World War, 1933–1940* (New York, 2003). MacGregor Knox's *Mussolini Unleashed, 1938–1941* (Cambridge, UK, 1982) is a controversial book that discusses Italy's entrance into the war and the Duce's plans. The poor performance of the Italian armed forces should be considered in context. See James Sadkovich, "Understanding Defeat," *Journal of Contemporary History* 24 (1989): 27–61, and his *The Italian Navy in World War II* (Westport, Conn., 1994). See also Knox's *Hitler's Italian Allies: Royal Armed Forces, Fascist Regime, and the War of 1940–43* (New York, 2000). On the Russian women combatants, see the essay in Nancy Loring Goldman, ed., *Female Soldiers—Combatants or Noncombatants?* (Westport, Conn., 1982).

For the defeat of France, see Guy Chapman, *Why France Fell: The Defeat of the French Army in 1940* (New York, 1968), which gives a thorough account of why the French army was not successfully reconstituted before the war and of the fighting. Alistair Horne, *To Lose a Battle: France 1940* (Boston, 1969), is well written and complete. Other good works on the French collapse and its causes are A. Gunsberg, *Divided and Conquered: The French High Command and the Defeat of the West* (Westport, Conn., 1979); Brian Bond, *France and Belgium 1939–1940* (London, 1975); and William L. Shirer, *The Collapse of the Third Republic* (New York, 1969). Robert Jackson, *The Fall of France; May–June 1940* (London, 1975), describes the French defense-mindedness and its contribution to the country's defeat. Ernest R. May, *Strange Victory: Hitler's Conquest of France* (New York, 2000), rejects the standard view and considers France's military collapse to be the result of intelligence failures. Julian Jackson's *The Fall of France: The Nazi Invasion of 1940* (New York, 2003) incorporates the latest research on the subject. Gregory Blaxland, *Destination Dunkirk* (London, 1973), recounts the events leading up to the famous withdrawal from France, while *Dunkirk: Fight to the Last Man* (Cambridge, Mass., 2006), by Hugh Sebag-Montefiore, is a more recent account. Kenneth Macksey wrote a good biography of the German general who was most famous for his use of armor during this period: *Guderian: Panzer General* (London, 1975).

Richard J. Evans, *The Third Reich at War* (New York, 2009), is the most comprehen-sive account of Germany during the war years. Walter Ansel, *Hitler Confronts England* (Durham, N.C., 1960), reconstructs the project to assault England. Peter Fleming, *Opera-tion Sea Lion: The Projected Invasion of England in 1940* (New York, 1957), is a thorough account of the German preparations for invasion and British countermeasures. *Hitler's War Aims* (New York, 1973–74), by Norman Rich, includes views of works on German-occupied Europe. The campaign in northern Europe is chronicled by Earl F. Ziemke,

The German Northern Theater of Operations 1940–1945 (Washington, D.C., 1960). There is a good chapter on Finland in World War II in John H. Wuorinen, *A History of Finland* (New York, 1965). The Polish campaign is covered by Nicholas Bethell, *The War Hitler Won* (New York, 1972); the paucity of books in English on this subject has been partially alleviated by books on the Nazi-Soviet collaboration to destroy the country: *Poland Betrayed* (Barnsley, UK, 2009), by D. G. Williamson, and by a book on the German military campaign, Alexander B. Rossino, *Hitler Strikes Poland* (Lawrence, Kans., 2003). Allen Paul wrote a good account of the Katyn massacre: *Katyn: The Untold Story of Stalin's Polish Massacre* (New York, 1991). Allen Paul's *Katyn: Stalin's Massacre and the Triumph of Truth* (De Kalb, Ill., 2010) looks at the Soviet attempt to hide the facts. Michael Hope focuses on *Polish Deportees in the Soviet Union* (London, 2000). The Russian role in the East during this period is examined by Jan T. Gross, *Revolution from Abroad: The Soviet Conquest of Poland's Western Ukraine and Western Belorussia* (Princeton, N.J., 1988), and there are several interesting essays on various subjects dealing with the Baltic states, which fell into the Soviet sphere, in V. Stanley Vardis and Romuald J. Misiunas, eds., *The Baltic States in Peace and War 1917–1945* (University Park, Pa., 1978). For the East in general, see Robert Cecil, *Hitler's Decision to Invade Russia 1941* (London, 1975), and Gerhard L. Weinberg, *Germany and the Soviet Union, 1939–1941* (Leyden, 1972).

For discussions of the home fronts during the war, particularly Britain, consult Harold L. Smith, ed., *War and Social Change: British Society in the Second World War* (Manchester, UK, 1986). Leonard Moseley, *Backs to the Wall: London Under Fire, 1939–1945* (New York, 1971), emphasizes the social history of London. A. J. P. Taylor's *British History 1914–1945* (New York, 1965) has important sections on the same issue; the quotation about the Luftwaffe helping bring about the welfare state is on p. 455. Alan Milward discusses Germany at war in *The German Economy at War* (London, 1965). Goetz Aly focuses on the plunder of Europe for the benefit of Germans in *Hitler's Beneficiaries: Plunder, Racial War, and the Nazi Welfare State* (New York, 2007). An important aspect of the home front in Germany is treated in detail by Edward L. Homze, *Foreign Labor in Nazi Germany* (Princeton, N.J., 1967). For information about the Soviets, see John Barber and Mark Harrison, *The Soviet Home Front 1941–1945* (New York, 1991), and Mark Harrison, *Soviet Planning in Peace and War 1938–1945* (New York, 1985).

An interesting perspective on the influence of the smaller states during the conflict is offered by Annette Baker Fox, *The Power of Small States: Diplomacy in World War II* (Chicago, 1959), which covers Finland, Norway, Sweden, Spain, and Turkey. Several important books have been published on the European neutrals during World War II. They include Neville Wylie, *European Neutrals and Non-Belligerents During the Second World War* (New York, 2002), and, by the same author, *Switzerland: A Neutral of Distinction?* (n.p., 2002); Jerrold M. Packard, *Neither Friend nor Foe: The European Neutrals in World War II* (New York, 1992); and Christian Leitz, *Sympathy for the Devil: Neutral Europe and Nazi Germany in World War II* (New York, 2001).

CHAPTER 19

✍

Inside Hitler's Europe: Military Occupation and Genocide

CHAPTER OUTLINE

Short- and Long-Term Aims • Military Occupation in the East • Military Occupation in the West • The Holocaust • Genocide

BIBLIOGRAPHICAL SKETCHES

Heinrich Himmler, "Architect of Genocide" • Primo Levi, 174517

By early 1942, the Axis occupied most of Europe, and the process of reorganizing the continent according to Hitler's "New Order" had begun: a territorial and economic reordering for Germany's benefit and an alteration of Europe's racial composition.

SHORT- AND LONG-TERM AIMS

In line with Hitler's "living space" concept, the Nazi blueprint for reorganization of the conquered lands included unimagined brutality.

Territorial Designs

The Nazis slated substantial parts of the occupied regions for incorporation into the Reich, including most of Poland and occupied Soviet territory. In the West, the Nazis planned to incorporate Nordic areas, along with strategic sectors, including Norway, Denmark, Holland, Luxembourg, most of Belgium, and parts of France, and integrate the Nordic population into the Reich while killing off the Jews and other so-called inferior races.

The Nazis reserved their most brutal treatment for the inhabitants of Eastern Europe, exterminating or using them as slave labor. The Germans either immediately killed the Jews in the conquered regions or sent them to labor or death camps. The Nazis planned to reduce the non-Jewish population substantially through systematic murder—Himmler suggested a figure of 30 million for the Slavs—leaving the survivors to work in menial jobs for the Germans.

1942: German Europe. In 1942, German-occupied Europe briefly exceeded even the size of Napoleon's empire. German plans for the occupied areas varied depending on racial criteria, being particularly brutal in the East. The Germans encountered growing resistance everywhere as time passed.

They aimed to keep the number of subject peoples low by separating men and women and utilizing mass sterilization techniques and by ensuring their permanent subjugation through the mass murder of intellectuals and denying them all schooling. Hitler believed that the subject populations should "know just enough to understand road signs, so as not to get themselves run over by our vehicles. For them the word 'liberty' must mean the right to wash on holidays." Once the German inhabitants had increased sufficiently and no longer required extra labor, the Nazis would exterminate or expel the native populations from the areas of German colonization.

Economic Goals

The Nazis planned to restructure Europe economically by dividing the continent into an industrialized zone, consisting of a greatly enlarged Germany, and an agricultural one. One would produce arms and heavy machinery, the other would dedicate itself to farming and supplying raw materials for the Reich. In this way, the Nazis grotesquely claimed, Germany would provide Europe with centralized economic planning, a guaranteed export market, and a regulated labor supply that would eliminate waste and unemployment and establish a rational international planning mechanism.

In 1942, SS leader Himmler worked out a long-range Eastern plan for the next twenty-five years that described the details of Europe's Nazi future. He envisioned the construction of centrally located fortified areas garrisoned by peasant-soldiers, with the mission of defending the conquered regions and of colonizing the areas through increased birth rates. At the frontiers of the new German conquests, military settlements, modeled on the marches of the Middle Ages, would stand guard. These soldier peasant-colonists would rule over an impoverished, landless local population.

MILITARY OCCUPATION IN THE EAST

The areas of German military occupation suffered diverse fates. In the East, the Germans implemented harsh measures that resulted in millions of civilian deaths. In the West, the occupation was less harsh because the Germans wanted to gain the support of the Nordic populations, there was a smaller Jewish population, and the conquered countries could supply crucial industrial products. Moreover, the Germans worked through existing civil administrations and puppet governments that resulted in more moderate occupation administrations than in the East.

The brutal Nazi occupation of Czechoslovakia brought retaliation. In May of 1942, SS chief Reinhard Heydrich was assassinated. The assassination occasioned a vicious crackdown in the country. The town of Lidice was razed to the ground with its population either killed or sent to concentration camps, 10,000 arrests, and 1,500 deaths. These tactics were typical of the German occupation.

Northeastern Europe

The occupied areas of the Soviet Union and Poland suffered the most. Both had large Jewish populations, the Nazis considered the Slavs an inferior race to be killed or used for slave labor, and the USSR was Bolshevik. In both countries, the Germans immediately murdered millions of people, hoping to kill Jews and to decapitate the despised Communist ruling elite.

In the USSR on July 18, 1941, the Central Committee of the Communist Party gave the order for partisan warfare against the German invaders. On May 30, 1942, the Soviets formed the Central Partisan Staff, which centralized partisan activities during 1943. The Soviets armed hundreds of thousands of partisans in the occupied parts of the USSR and in eastern Poland and coordinated their actions with those of the regular armed forces. Jewish fighters had a significant part in these activities.

The Germans annexed large sections of Poland, killing, starving, or deporting the inhabitants to concentration camps or to Germany as slave laborers. They killed the Jews, expropriated Polish property, and sent to the Reich any children they believed possessed Aryan racial characteristics. The SS employed special police units to murder Jews and intellectuals—the *Einsatzgruppen* later used in the USSR. They sent millions of Poles to the Government General, an area of prewar Poland under their direct control but not incorporated into Germany and used as a dumping ground for deportees. The Nazis also introduced their program of murdering sick people. The Poles resisted this brutal occupation through military and passive means, attacking the occupying forces and performing important intelligence services for the Allies and the Polish government in exile.

The German army initially administered the eastern conquests, but in Poland, Hitler transferred authority to civilian administrators because he wanted the occupied territories to supply large quantities of raw materials, food, and industrial products. The Germans milked the considerable industrial potential of the protectorate of Bohemia and Moravia, the nucleus of the defunct Czechoslovakia. They ruled indirectly through Czech collaborators, some of whom hoped that cooperation would spare the population the more brutal aspects of German occupation, but in May 1942, Czech and Slovak resisters assassinated Reinhard Heydrich, SS chief of German administration. The Germans immediately killed 1,500 Czechs, then murdered or sent to concentration camps the entire population of the village of Lidice and then razed the village to the ground, and then made 10,000 arrests that practically wiped out the resistance.

Southeastern Europe

Southeastern Europe presented a more complex picture than did Poland and Czechoslovakia, including as it did such diverse countries as Greece and Yugoslavia, victims of Axis aggression, and Germany's allies Hungary, Romania, and Bulgaria.

After the defeat of Greece, the Germans and Italians divided the country into separate occupation zones. The Germans ruled through a Greek collaborationist government. Greek fighters, split between Communist partisans and anti-Communists, resisted the occupiers with varying effectiveness as the German army plundered the country, reneged on promises to supply food, stripped the country of its assets, and demanded exorbitant occupation costs. The result: wild inflation and a famine that killed 250,000 Greeks and that had social and political repercussions after World War II. The Germans destroyed the Jewish community of Salonika, one of the oldest in Europe, and killed more than 85 percent of the Jewish population of Greece. These developments shocked the Italians, who protested German plundering of the country and protected Jews in their zone of occupation.

Yugoslavia presented an even more confusing situation. The Germans invaded the country after a military revolt established a regime that was unfriendly to the Nazis. The Axis then occupied and dismembered the country, giving free rein to intense ethnic divisions. Germany and Italy annexed parts of the country, while Hungary and Bulgaria seized other areas. In the zones incorporated into the Reich, the Germans instituted measures favoring the inhabitants of German ancestry and then expelled and tried to murder the rest. The German army administered Serbia with a brutality second only to their administration of the East. In the remaining part of Yugoslavia, the Axis established an independent Croatia under Ante Pavelic, head of the Fascist *Ustasha*, who closely allied himself to the Germans. At Jasenovac, the "Auschwitz of the Balkans," the Croatians exterminated Jews, Serbs, Gypsies, and Muslims. A fierce guerilla war broke out in which Serb bands attacked the Croatians and the Germans. At the same time, Communist partisans under Tito fought against the occupiers and engaged in a civil war with the anti-Communist Serb nationalist fighters of Draza Mihailovic.

In the rest of southeastern Europe, there was an uneasy relationship between Germany and its allies.

The Hungarians were primarily interested in regaining territory lost to Romania after World War I, but resented Nazi support for the German minority in Hungary and attempts to take over Hungarian economic assets. The Germans viewed Hungary as useful in fighting the Russians, but Hungarian recalcitrance in handing over the Jews for liquidation angered them. In 1943, Hungarian losses in the USSR produced an anti-German government. The regent, Admiral Horthy, considered a separate peace with the Allies and resisted Hitler's demands for greater cooperation, and in 1944 the Germans occupied the country and installed a subservient government. The SS seized control of the Hungarian economy and slaughtered the Hungarian Jews. Horthy attempted to surrender to the Allies, but his efforts exacerbated the atrocities perpetrated by Hungarian collaborators.

The Germans valued Hungary's rival, Romania, for its oil reserves and for the large contingent of troops it sent to fight against the USSR. In 1940, Germany had forced Romania to surrender territory to Hungary, but Romanian policy makers calculated that if they sided with the Germans against the Soviets, they could retrieve these lands and retake territory lost to the Russians under the Nazi-Soviet Nonaggression Pact. Romania curried favor with Germany by sending troops to the Soviet front and by collaborating in the so-called Final Solution against the despised Jews. These hopes vanished with the destruction of their forces by the Russians. In August 1944, with the Soviets invading, Romania formally ended the German alliance, switched sides, and joined the Soviets in fighting the Germans. This timely action allowed the country to retain its prewar borders after the postwar settlement, but postwar Romania was dominated by the Soviets.

In August 1944 the German position in Bulgaria also deteriorated. Because of its sensitive geographic location close to Russia and the danger that a Bulgarian collapse would represent, the Germans exerted minimal pressure on Bulgaria to conform to its policies, such as handing over the Jews. The Bulgarians did not surrender Bulgarian Jews but did hand over Jews in their occupied areas. The Bulgarians profited from their military cooperation with the Germans by making gains in Greece, Yugoslavia, and Romania, but the Red Army overran the country after Romania's collapse and brought it into the Soviet orbit.

MILITARY OCCUPATION IN THE WEST

Even after France's stunning defeat, the possibilities that the French could revolt, continue the war from their colonies, or direct their fleet to assist the British gave the Germans reasons to avoid treating France too harshly. In addition, there were tendencies in France that were willing to accept a new, subordinate, position in a German-dominated Europe.

Defeated France and Its Divisions

After their victory, the Germans annexed Alsace and Lorraine, expelled the non-Aryan population, and occupied about 75 percent of France, including the entire coastline and the capital. They left the southeastern quarter of the country unoccupied but ruled by a collaborationist government headquartered at Vichy, a town famed for its mineral water. Prewar Premier Pierre Laval ran the government, and World War I hero Marshal Philippe Pétain served as the head of state. Laval cooperated with the Germans while seeking to gain advantage from the vestiges of French power and hoping to exploit the situation if the war worsened for the Germans. Hitler, a fanatic Francophobe, aimed to keep France quiet during the conflict so he could exploit its resources and industrial potential. Some semblance of independence for Vichy allowed the Germans to rule a large population at a minimal cost through the preexisting administrative structure.

The French defeat exacerbated the deep domestic divergences that had characterized the country during the twentieth century. Some leaders like General Charles de Gaulle favored continued resistance, while Pétain and Laval hoped that cooperation would spare the country the worst horrors of the Nazi occupation. Pétain rallied the country through his belief that after a temporary period of hardship, there would be a peace treaty and revival. Convinced that Britain could not hold out for long, Pétain's supporters favored a place for France in what would be the new Nazi, European order. They attributed the fall of France to the liberal principles of the Third Republic and wanted to restructure the country along conservative lines.

Vichy France brought to the fore the splits in French society of the previous hundred years. Prewar Prime Minister Pierre Laval, shown here sitting behind his desk, incarnated these divisions. Laval and other Vichy leaders thought that France still had an important role to play in what they believed would be a German-dominated future Europe. This idea gave rise to a strange policy of collaboration with the Nazis and an attempt to assert French rights within the new order. Laval was executed after the war.

The National Revolution

Many of Pétain's supporters were military leaders who considered the army the highest expression of fundamental French values. With German permission, they formed an armistice army of 100,000 soldiers, from which liberal officers were excluded, a force that could not threaten German control but was adequate to buttress conservative social values. They attributed the French defeat in 1940 to the Third Republic's liberal political and secular values and to the principles of the French Revolution of 1789: "Liberty, Equality, Fraternity," against which they presented their "National Revolution" and "Work, Family, Fatherland."

The Vichy rulers considered a radical change in social values as the key to French revival: the National Revolution guided by a stern, benevolent father chastising his children for their own good in return for obedience and loyalty. This theory implied that social groups had a specific place and function in French society and that agitators who disturbed this hierarchy must be weeded out. The Vichy government consequently proscribed intellectuals, foreign elements, and Jews; Vichy prefects complied with the German demands to hand over foreign Jews for deportation and vigorously applied their own government's anti-Jewish measures. The Vichy regime thus adopted the core of the fascist notion of the nation as an organic entity whose social groups worked in unison for the Fatherland's greatness.

Women and the Family

Because of Vichy's emphasis on France as a large family, the regime took particular care to spell out the role of men and women by defining their roles. Fathers had a duty to be the breadwinners and decision makers, and mothers must dedicate themselves to motherhood, children, and home. Vichy legislation reinforced the family's cohesion even while taking into account the large number of separations caused by soldiers who were still prisoners of war. A September 1942 law reaffirmed the authority of the man as the head of the family but accepted previous legislation that allowed mothers to make decisions in case of the fathers' absence. The concept of the man as head remained in French legislation until 1970, and as late as 1965, the husband had a legal veto on his wife taking a job. Since rejecting motherhood was evil, in February 1942, Vichy adopted stronger measures against abortion than those that passed in the 1920s (legal restrictions on abortion remained in France until 1975). A December 1942 law made a woman who left the home criminally liable, and adultery with the wife of a prisoner of war could be prosecuted as a crime against society. In 1943 the government abrogated a tacit understanding against the death penalty for women by executing a midwife for providing abortions. Vichy law also targeted fathers who did not provide for their families, convicting 4,000 transgressors a year between 1942 and 1944. In April 1941, Vichy reversed legislation passed in the 1930s easing restrictions on divorce.

Consistent with its view of women, Vichy discouraged women from working outside the home, an attitude reinforced after the 1940 defeat, demobilization, and increased unemployment. The government adopted harsh measures to prevent married women from working, but the French people received them with hostility. The officials responded that they had to implement temporary expedients to share the work, but the issue soon became moot. The Germans needed the products of French industry to support the war effort, which increased the demand and encouraged the growth of new industries, such as aluminum, the output of which surpassed prewar production. These relatively well-paying new jobs went to men, rather than women, who took poorly paying public jobs that men avoided.

Friction increased when the Germans demanded that women workers go to Germany, and the church and other organizations protested against the German insistence that single women work in the Reich. Despite these objections, Frenchwomen accounted for 2 percent of foreign females working in Germany in 1944.

Growth of Resistance

The forced incorporation of French women into the Reich's labor force contributed to a growing resistance movement. Initial French toleration for Vichy evaporated with increasing German reprisals for acts of resistance, the roundup of Jews, the expulsion of French citizens from parts of their own country, the deportations to labor camps, and the refusal to release French prisoners of war. Both passive and

As the Nazi occupation of different European countries lengthened it became more unbearable and generated more resistance. Here is a 1944 poster from Vichy France that shows both this growing resistance and the attempts to stop it. The poster shows pictures of condemned resisters and says: "Liberators? Liberation for an army of crime!"

active resistance increased after November 1942 when the Germans occupied the entire country. The French responded with silence when a German came into the room, mimicked German habits, hid resisters, allowed their houses to be used for intelligence activities, issued false documents, and refused to spend coins containing metals needed by the Germans. From these activities, many persons passed to sabotage and military action, tying down thousands of German troops and slowing the transfer of others to the front.

This pattern of opposition was repeated in the other occupied Western countries. Despite Hitler's invitation to the Nordic populations of Norway, Denmark, Luxembourg, Holland, and most of Belgium to join the "master race" after the cleansing of impure elements, they opposed him. In Norway, Vidkun Quisling ran the country for the benefit of the Germans, but his name became synonymous with *traitor*. The Norwegian resistance blew up the Vermork High Concentration Plant for the production of heavy water, depriving the Germans of a crucial resource for nuclear research and obliged them to station thirteen divisions and a large number of SS and naval personnel to police the country. In Denmark the Germans allowed the government to remain in power and initially ruled through it. The country provided food and important bases for the Nazi war effort until 1943, when Hitler ordered a change in the moderate German policy, provoking active resistance, the rescue of the country's Jewish population, and the dramatic flight of nuclear scientist Niels Bohr to England and later to the United States to work on the atomic bomb. The Danes then sabotaged German efforts to use Danish resources and later could field a significant number of resistance fighters.

The Dutch queen and government fled with her government to continue the fight against the German military administration in Holland, soon replaced by civilian authorities who attempted to assimilate the Germanic Dutch population into the Reich. The German policy of exploiting Dutch resources and liquidating the Jews provoked major strikes in February 1941, but the Nazis succeeded in wiping out most of the Dutch Jewish community. Few Jews lived in Luxembourg, but the Germans deported the foreign population in anticipation of annexation, policies that stimulated opposition. In Belgium the Germans succeeded in exploiting industry for their own purposes, but less than 30 percent of the Belgian Jews perished, thanks to the efforts of German commander Alexander von Falkenhausen's attenuation of measures to kill the Jews and starve the population; he was arrested for his effort. The Belgian king remained in the country but provided no leadership. Nevertheless, the majority of Belgians passively opposed the occupation, and by the end of the war, it is estimated that 120,000 of them were fighting in regular units against the Germans.

By 1943, opposition to the brutal German occupation had developed into armed resistance that tied up thousands of German troops and hampered their movements against the Allies. The Resistance compensated Western Europeans in some measure for the quick victory of the Germans and restored national pride. In the West many Resistance leaders became convinced that Europeans should never again fight against themselves and revived ideas of unity that were based on reciprocal respect for the different nationalities that would be important after the war.

THE HOLOCAUST

The Holocaust has come to mean the Nazi attempt to exterminate the Jewish people, but it was much wider. *Shoah*, or catastrophe, is a more appropriate term when referring to the destruction of European Jews, and it is important to remember that the slaughter in and out of the concentration camps included a large number of different victims: Jews, Gypsies (Roma or Sinti), Slavs, Russian prisoners of war, and other unfortunates from all the countries of occupied Europe.

The Holocaust Debate

In interpreting the Holocaust, historians have argued about when the Nazis decided to kill all members of the Jewish people. Because Hitler proclaimed his rage against the Jews most famously in the first volume of *Mein Kampf,* published in 1925, the attempt to eradicate all Jews during the World War II can be seen as a fulfillment of Hitler's intentions all along. Adding to the strength of this argument is a prophesy that Hitler made before the conflict that should another world war break out, the Jews would be annihilated. During the Holocaust, Hitler constantly stated that this prophecy was coming true. To most observers, it seemed obvi-ous that the Nazis always intended to eliminate the Jews and that they attempted to put this policy into effect when they had the power to do so. These are the "intentionalists."

Opposed to them, the "functionalists" (or "structuralists") argue that Hitler did not seek to eliminate the German Jews (about 570,000) when he came to power, only to pauperize and expel them. This policy of expulsion, they maintain, contin-ued well into 1941. The Nazis planned to resettle Eastern Europe according to their living space ideas, which meant expelling the inhabitants of Poland and the Jews farther to the East into the cold wastes of the Soviet Union. They planned to expel the Jews first, but when the Russian campaign bogged down, they could not fulfill their plans and turned to exterminating them. Contradicting this argument is the reality that the Germans began exterminating Jews immediately upon invading Russia, but the functionalist rebuttal points to the entire Nazi structure as evolv-ing the final solution through "the system's automatic mechanisms for 'cumulative radicalization.'" The Nazis supposedly did so through various unplanned stages that represented Nazi thinking on how to resolve the so-called Jewish question at the time of their implementation.

The important difference between the intentionalists and the functionalists thus appears to be that the first school attributes the Holocaust to premeditation while the second emphasizes the evolution of Nazi practice. Neither side in this

Jewish Population Killed During the Holocaust. This map provides estimates of the percentages of European Jews exterminated by the Germans during World War II.

There has been a historical debate about whether the Nazis planned to eliminate the Jews from the beginning of the movement or whether they decided on the "Final Solution of the Jewish Problem" after World War II began and they found themselves controlling a vast Jewish population. Whatever the answer, final agreement is supposed to have come at a conference of Hitler and Nazi officials at the Wannsee Conference on January 20, 1942. Here is the villa in which the meeting took place.

historical debate absolves the Germans for implementing the Final Solution to the Jewish question.

The Final Solution

The inhabitants of occupied Eastern Europe, slated for permanent German colonization, suffered most during World War II. Hitler talked about eliminating large segments of the Czechoslovak population, and, even before war broke out, SS and army heads discussed how the Polish intelligentsia would be killed along with the Jews. Hitler set up a research agency under ideologist Alfred Rosenberg to study the Jewish (and Communist) question in Poland and in the occupied Russian areas, and Rosenberg drew up plans for the disposition of the eastern territories and Russia that served as a cloak for SS mass murder operations.

SS chief Himmler took the lead in exterminating the Jews. He first supported expulsion of the Jews to Madagascar, an island off the East African coast, which proved impossible, then expulsion to the East, which proved impossible because of the lack of transportation facilities. In May 1940, Himmler proposed dumping 8 million "racially inferior" people into the General Government in the former Poland, an area that had not been annexed, which would serve as a source of labor. This policy brought complaints from German officials there who pushed for their extermination. Nazi thinking rapidly evolved away from eventually annihilating the Jews through expulsion and forced labor to eradicating them before the war ended. On January 20, 1942, Nazi officials held a conference at a villa on the Wannsee, a beautiful lake west of Berlin. Apparently Hitler had decided on the Final Solution several weeks before: immediate and complete eradication of the Jewish race by means of industrialized murder in death camps. The participants represented the SS, the Nazi Party, and the civil service. Heinrich Himmler and Reinhard Heydrich wanted to make certain that the entire apparatus of the German state understood that Hitler's plan to destroy the Jews worked smoothly and participated in the operation.

BIOGRAPHICAL SKETCHES

Heinrich Himmler
"Architect of Genocide"

When the Gestapo investigated Werner Heisenberg, the famous German nuclear scientist, on suspicion of anti-Nazi activities, his mother appealed for help to the mother of Heinrich Himmler, the leader of the SS and the German police. Himmler listened to his mother, and the SS cleared Heisenberg.

The irony of supposed soft-heartedness coexisting with fiendish brutality in the polite figure of the Final Solution's chief of operations emerges in other reported incidents. Shaken after witnessing the execution of a hundred people by the *Einsatzgruppen,* Himmler expressed concern about the emotional effects on the executioners, mostly married men, of shooting women and children. In order to help them, he favored more "humane" killing methods to achieve Hitler's aim of destroying the Jews and other groups, such as employing poison gas.

Himmler had not had a particularly brilliant career. Born into a Catholic family on October 7, 1900, in Munich, Himmler set his sights on becoming a farmer and studied agronomy. He seems to have believed in the application of animal breeding to human society. He served in the army at the end of World War I, and after the conflict, right-wing causes attracted him. By 1923, he had entered Adolf Hitler's orbit and participated in the *Putsch* of that year. Recognizing his loyalty and his outstanding organizational qualities, Hitler appointed Himmler head of the SS in 1929. From a small body of 300 men, Himmler expanded his organization to 50,000 by 1933. The SA's destruction after June 30, 1934, opened greater horizons for Himmler and the SS. Himmler controlled the Gestapo (the secret police), the SD (the SS's security service), and the concentration camps, and on June 17, 1936, became chief of the German police.

When World War II erupted, Himmler ran the camps that served as the main tools for Hitler's extermination policy. He saw the task of killing Jews as a duty and a glorious page in German history. He considered it a moral crusade and guarded against corruption. In October 1943, he admonished SS leaders not to enrich

continued

continued

themselves "even just with a fur or a watch or a Mark or a cigarette!" This principle, however, did not apply to the SS Empire, which he greatly expanded. Himmler established a huge industrial base and an enormous armed force, the *Waffen SS* (armed SS units), that rivaled the army. Within the Third Reich, his power also increased immensely during the conflict. In 1943, he became minister of the interior and, following the failed attempt to assassinate Hitler on July 20, 1944, took charge of the investigation and arrests of the conspirators. During the same year, he became the second most powerful figure in the Reich by achieving power over the Reserve Army and the People's militia.

"Loyal Heinrich" remained true to Hitler, but not quite until the end. Anticipating that Germany would lose the war, in October 1944 he tried to save his skin and position by secretly offering twenty-five German divisions to the Allies to fight communism, a ridiculous proposition. During the war's last days, he put out peace feelers through a Swedish intermediary, demonstrating a strong unwillingness to die with his Fuehrer. In the course of these talks, he released a small number of concentration camp inmates but regarded the others as hostages. When Hitler discovered his activities, as one of the last acts of his life in the bunker, he expelled Himmler from the party and removed him from all his offices.

Himmler had his files destroyed, disguised himself, and tried to flee the Reich using the papers of a victim of Nazism. Captured by the British on May 23, 1945, he bit down on a hidden cyanide capsule when a doctor attempted to examine his mouth; fifteen minutes later, he died. British doctors made casts of his face, removed part of his brain for study, and buried him in a secret grave. "The bastard's beat us!" exclaimed a British officer.

The *Einsatzgruppen*

In anticipation of the Russian invasion, the SS established four *Einsatzgruppen* consisting of 500 to 700 people each—special mobile police units trained for the task of killing German enemies in the occupied territories. Composed of Waffen SS, Gestapo, SD, police, and other personnel, these units took their orders directly from Himmler and, before his death, Reinhard Heydrich. These two leaders, who received their orders from Hitler, personally briefed the leaders of the special units on several occasions in June 1941. Their main task: to eliminate Jews, Gypsies, and political commissars in the occupied areas. They conducted massive roundups or forced Jewish leaders to assemble members of their communities, after which they shot and buried them in ditches that the victims had previously been forced to dig. Although most of their victims were Jews, the *Einsatzgruppen* also killed Russian prisoners of war and anyone they considered partisans or German opponents.

For the *Einsatzgruppen*, anyone who was a Jew was a partisan or a Bolshevik, and vice versa. Hitler had specified that pacifying the occupied areas meant shooting anyone who looked askance at the Germans. Consequently, the *Einsatzgruppen* butchered men, women, children, and elderly people. The murderers also confiscated the victims' property, not stopping at their clothing. At one famous operation, Babi Yar, on September 29 and 30, 1941, they killed 33,770 Jews. The killings took place primarily in the Ukraine and in the Baltic states, frequently with the assistance of Lithuanian and Ukrainian nationalists, and especially the *Wehrmacht*.

From a bureaucratic viewpoint, the *Einsatzgruppen* operated independently from the army, as the high command took pains to emphasize. However, the *Wehrmacht* and the SS collaborated closely to aid the *Einsatzgruppen's* work and even participated in it. Army commanders entreated their soldiers to act without pity in the struggle to liberate the Germans from the clutches of Jews and Bolsheviks, to avenge them, and to carry Volkish ideology eastward. Without the army's active cooperation, it would have been more difficult for the *Einsatzgruppen* to destroy the estimated 600,000 to 1.5 million human beings they are believed to have killed.

Despite the massive *Einsatzgruppen* operations, eliminating entire races and groups required the industrialization of murder, as exemplified by the concentration camps where most Nazi victims died.

The Concentration Camps

Originally established at Dachau in March 1933 to intern political enemies and intimidate the German population, the camps soon brimmed with prisoners of all kinds. There were two categories of camps. In the labor camps, inmates toiled for the German war effort and for giant German industrial concerns, such as I. G. Farben. Inmates worked until they died or until they could no longer toil for the Reich and were murdered. The normal survival rate in the labor camps was a few months.

The German victory over Poland, with its 3 million Jews, altered the scale and purpose of the camps. Poland became the major killing ground and home to six large death camps, including Auschwitz, and numerous satellite camps where Jews from all over Europe were exterminated. The death camps employed modern industrial methods to eliminate anyone who was judged incapable of working for Germany, regardless of age or gender. Camp officials deprived inmates of all their possessions upon arrival and selected those who were to die immediately, depending on their age and general health conditions. In order to get them to follow instructions, they lied to the new arrivals, sending them to showers that were really gas chambers. Children were gassed immediately, along with their mothers, if they objected to being separated. After their deaths, the camp officials had the victims' hair and gold teeth collected. The punctilious Germans carefully divided the booty among different agencies, with the SS profiting economically from the camps. The economic objective helps explain why the SS chose campsites close to cities, although not in easily accessible areas, and built good transportation facilities.

The camps had three major divisions: headquarters, an SS residential area, and the prisoners' compound. Luxury generally marked the headquarters and residential areas. At Buchenwald, the SS stocked a game preserve and fed the animals a richer diet than the inmates. In 1943 the SS also established a brothel there. Concentration camp prisoners lived in crowded, unhealthful, wooden or masonry barracks surrounded by barbed wire, electrified fences, and watch towers. The barracks might be several stories high and consist of two or four wings, including a day room and sleeping quarters. The small beds, divided into tiers, consisted of straw mattresses. The prisoners stored their canteens and spoons in wooden boxes. A typical barracks included a washroom and open toilets that the prisoners had to clean under humiliating circumstances. The camps also included a hospital, which sick prisoners usually did not leave alive and where SS doctors conducted outrageous medical experiments. Finally, in a large open space surrounded by a high wall stood the furnaces, with their enormous smokestacks, that consumed the inmates' bodies.

The camps were tightly organized. At the top of the hierarchy, the camp commandant and his staff had complete authority. The administrative officer handled day-to-day administration, working with the officer in charge and the roll-call officer, who had direct command over the prisoners through the block leaders. The block leaders, famed for their brutality, commanded individual barracks. A labor service officer determined inmate tasks and work organization, frequently holding in his hands the life and death of individual prisoners. SS Death Head units provided the guards, who were armed with weapons and with special dogs that were trained to attack the inmates. The camps included a political department run by the Gestapo. This hierarchical organization was reflected in the lives of the prisoners. Each barracks had a senior block inmate, approved by the camp administration, responsible to the block leader for everything that went on in the barracks and who had responsibility for keeping order and for disbursing rations. Prisoners, known as capos, ran the labor details. In most cases, egged on by their SS guards, prisoners who had some authority over their fellow inmates were known for their brutality.

BIOGRAPHICAL SKETCHES

Primo Levi, 174517

Primo Levi seemed destined for an ordinary though good career, but World War II intervened. Born on July 31, 1919, as a Jew living in Turin, he represented a minority of a minority because most Italian Jews lived in Rome or Milan. Levi, who traced his ancestry to Jews expelled from Spain in 1492, proved an outstanding student and attended the University of Turin despite the 1938 racial laws. In 1941, he received a chemistry degree. Some of his chemical texts were in German; his knowledge of the language and his chemical expertise would save his life.

The overthrow of Fascism and creation of a German puppet state in northern Italy prompted Levi and some friends to take to the mountains and join the resistance in 1943. Captured in December, he was sent to Auschwitz in February 1944, where he was assigned to a labor detail building a synthetic rubber factory. It is unlikely that Levi would have lived had it not become known that he was a skilled chemist who knew German. His reassignment to a camp laboratory with better rations and easier working conditions enabled him to survive.

Released at the war's end, Levi returned to Italy, a voyage described in *The Reawakening* (*La tregua*, or "The Truce," 1958, later made into a film). Back home, he resumed his career as an industrial chemist, working at a paint factory in his native Turin. Despite his profession, he felt the need to write. As he told an interviewer:

"After Auschwitz, I had an absolute need to write. Not only as a moral duty, but as a psychological need." In 1947, he published his famous *Se questo è un uomo* (published in English as *Survival in Auschwitz*). This book has become the classic account of life in the Nazi concentration camps.

Levi's masterpiece describes the creation of a full-blown society among the death camp prisoners and the relationship of that culture to the camp authorities in a detached, almost scientific, manner. Far from being a cold work, however, *Survival in Auschwitz* demonstrates in a graphic but matter-of-fact tone the total failure of the Nazis to achieve their objective—to dehumanize even more than to kill the inmates. Despite their suffering under intolerable conditions, the inmates expressed their full humanity, their strengths and their foibles, virtues and defects. In his work Levi fused the scientist-observer, philosopher, and poet. After writing *Survival in Auschwitz*, he published other important works on the camps and in 1974 retired to write full time.

At 10:00 A.M. on April 11, 1987, the concierge of the late nineteenth-century building in which Levi and his family had lived for three generations delivered the mail. Levi thanked her and closed the door of his third-floor apartment. Outside the apartment was a spiral staircase, an elevator enclosed by a cage, and an open space down to the ground floor. Moments after the mail delivery, Levi's body tumbled to the ground, crushing his head when he landed. The police ruled his death a suicide.

Despite the official ruling, a debate raged about whether Levi killed himself or fell accidentally. Levi constantly fought depression, and his son pointed to his conviction that the best people had died in Auschwitz and that only the worst survived. A friend stated that his death should be backdated to 1945 and that he killed himself when his writing was done. In 1962, Levi wrote about a recurrent dream: "I am in the Lager once more, and nothing is true outside the Lager." The chief rabbi of Rome disclosed that Levi had called him minutes before he died and said his terminally ill mother reminded him of the bodies at Auschwitz: He could not go on with life. Those who believed in an accidental death pointed to the lack of a note and to the difficulty of committing suicide in the physical circumstances of the building.

Whatever the answer, Levi's experiences in Auschwitz never left him. He lies buried in a Jewish cemetery near Turin under a headstone engraved: Primo Levi— 174517—1919–1987. That was the number that the Nazis tattooed on his arm.

Resistance in the Camps

Under these circumstances, resistance in the camps was very difficult, but it existed. Prisoners attempted to organize themselves in the best way possible in an attempt to survive physical destruction and lift their spirits. The SS tried to plant informers among the inmates but rarely succeeded. The inmates' resistance focused on two areas: they constructed a pervasive intelligence network, so they knew almost immediately what the SS planned, and they became skilled at sabotage.

Contrary to the conception that inmates went meekly to their fates, concentration camp inmates not only resisted their tormenters, but attempted to escape and revolted against them. Successful escapes were difficult because the surrounding population was generally hostile and feared ending up in the camps if they helped escaping prisoners. In the last years of the war, revolts occurred at Treblinka, Sobibor, and Auschwitz.

As much as possible, the prisoners also wrote descriptions of their ordeal. In 1947, Eugen Kogon published a detailed description of the camps, *The Theory and Practice of Hell*, and an Italian Jew, Primo Levi, published *Survival at Auschwitz* and several other classic works on the universe of the concentration camp, describing the psychology of the prisoners and the administrators and the daily operations of the camp.

Ghettoization

Besides the camps, the Germans employed ghettos to eliminate Jews. They obliged Jews to live in certain parts of the most important cities, then walled off the ghettos, systematically subjected the inhabitants to atrocities, and carefully restricted essential supplies. Overcrowding and maltreatment resulted in epidemics that killed hundreds of thousands. When the Nazis decided on the Final Solution, they methodically moved the ghetto inhabitants to extermination

During World War II, the Allies probably did not realize the full extent of the Holocaust, despite the many signs that pointed to mass killings, and did very little to stop it. Only in the later stages of the conflict did they see the consequences, and only later still did its full impact sink in. This May 1945 photograph shows American soldiers observing the consequences of the Nazi murders of Jews, Slavs, Gypsies, and political prisoners in a concentration camp around the city of Ohrdruf in Germany.

camps, lying to the ghetto populations that they would enjoy better conditions in the East.

Many ghettos existed in Eastern Europe, but the most infamous was the Warsaw Ghetto, created on October 2, 1940, in the slums of the Polish capital and holding a population of 500,000 at its height. The average person subsisted on only 184 calories per day, and hunger and epidemics decimated the population. The Germans used a supposedly self-governing Jewish organization, the *Judenrat*, the ghetto police, and collaborators to rule the area. In late 1941 and early 1942, reliable reports arrived at the ghetto about the Nazi gassing of Jews. This news and continual German atrocities prompted Jewish leaders to establish relations with the Polish resistance outside the ghetto and to plan a revolt.

The uprising began on April 19, 1943, when German troops entered the ghetto, and lasted a month as the resisters employed Molotov cocktails, handmade grenades, and weapons taken from fallen German soldiers against the attackers. The Warsaw Ghetto rebellion represented the zenith of Jewish resistance to the Nazis and was remarkable for military reasons and because the entire population of the Ghetto participated.

The West

Jews in a large Western country like France had a better chance of survival than did those in smaller countries, like Holland, even though France had a long and inglorious tradition of anti-Semitism; decades later, shameful cases of anti-Semitism during the conflict continued to emerge, and trials took place into the 1980s. Ironically, France's nationalistic pride mitigated the Jewish condition to some extent as Vichy handed over foreign Jews but balked at surrendering French and denaturalized Jews, stubbornly seeking to implement its own anti-Semitic measures. Many Jews survived by joining the Resistance or fleeing to the safety of the Italian zone.

The Phenomenon of Rescue

Despite intense pressure from the Germans, the Italians protected the Jews in their occupation zones in France, Yugoslavia, and Greece and were unique in protecting foreign Jews, not only the few Italian Jews present there.

In southern France, the Vichy government demanded that the Italians hand over Jews and sent its police into their zone to round them up, but the Italians asserted their complete legal authority as the occupying power and ordered the Vichy police to halt their activities. Laval complained to the Germans, who appealed to Mussolini to order his generals to arrest Jews on the grounds that they constituted a security risk. Il Duce then appointed a special police official to resolve the problem, but he appointed an Italian Jew as an adviser and avoided the German officials. The Italians then moved Jews to the interior, putting up the poorest in requisitioned hotels. In France about 50,000 Jews fled to the Italian zone. In the Italian occupation zones of the Balkans, Italian soldiers and diplomats followed similar policies and instituted bureaucratic obstacles, preventing the handing over of Jews to Germans and Croats that caused Jews all over the Balkans to flood into Italian-occupied areas.

While the Italian effort was unique because soldiers and diplomats obstructed the Final Solution, other rescue efforts should not be underestimated. The controversial Pope Pius XII has been harshly criticized for refusing publicly to denounce the Holocaust, but he ordered priests and nuns to open church buildings and monasteries to shelter Jews. In Hungary, diplomats from the neutral nations bonded together to rescue the Jews of Budapest. Swedish representative Raoul Wallenberg and his collaborators from other countries saved thousands. While most ordinary Europeans may have remained passive to the plight of Hitler's victims or to have behaved badly, many ordinary people risked their lives to hide and protect them. Despite the gloomy picture presented in occupied Europe in this respect, rescue was a significant humanitarian phenomenon whose importance has increasingly been recognized.

GENOCIDE

Of the 40 million to 55 million victims of World War II, about half were civilians. This figure resulted from the Nazis' attempts at not only physical destruction, but also cultural and social destruction,.The Polish lawyer Raphael Lemkin, who invented the term in 1943, wrote in his preface to *Axis Rule in Occupied Europe*:

> Genocide is effected through a synchronized attack on different aspects of life of the captive peoples: in the political field (by destroying institutions of self-government and imposing a German pattern of administration, and through colonization by Germans); in the social field (by disrupting the social cohesion of the nation involved and killing or removing elements such as the intelligentsia, which provide spiritual leadership . . .); in the cultural field (by prohibiting or destroying cultural institutions and cultural activities . . .); in the economic field (by shifting the wealth to Germans and by prohibiting the exercise of trades and occupation by people who do not promote germanism "without reservation"); in the biological field (by a policy of depopulation and promoting procreation by Germans in the occupied countries); in the field of physical existence (by introducing a starvation rationing system for non-Germans and by mass killing, mainly of Jews, Poles, Slovenes, and Russians); in the religious field (by interfering with the activities of the Church, which in many countries provides not only spiritual but also national leadership); in the field of morality (by attempts to create an atmosphere of moral debasement . . .).

The Techniques of Genocide
During World War II, the Germans implemented genocide on a wider scale than ever before. They attempted to eliminate races and national and cultural groups, trying at the same time to impose their own national patterns.

Depopulation
In accomplishing their aims, the Germans followed an organic program that was not limited to the elimination of undesirable groups by means of concentration camps and ghettos, but pursued vigorous depopulation policies to reduce

populations who were not related to the Germans by blood. This policy was intended to make room for future German generations and for Germans living in different parts of Europe where political agreements or other factors called for their transfer.

The German government instituted measures to decrease births among the defeated populace, combining them with steps favoring an increased German birthrate. Nazi doctors conducted sterilization experiments on concentration camp inmates. In the parts of Poland incorporated into the Reich, German officials required Polish couples to request special permission to marry—and then refused authorization. They physically separated men and women by deporting them for forced labor to different areas and by other means. They lowered rations for Poles because undernourishment reduces the birthrate and the chances that offspring will survive. At the same time, German families in Poland having at least three children received special subsidies. In Norway and Holland, populated by Germanic peoples, the Reich commissioners provided aid for the illegitimate children of German soldiers who were born to Norwegian and Dutch women.

Debilitation

The occupiers employed physical means to debilitate the races they earmarked for immediate or eventual eradication, providing them with little food of poor quality. The German rationing system allocated 93 percent of their prewar caloric intake to Germans and only 20 percent to Jews. With reference to quality, the percentages of meat rations that were earmarked to different national groups was as follows: Germans, 100; Czechs, 86; Dutch, 71; Poles (incorporated Poland), 78; Lithuanians, 57; French, 51; Belgians, 40; Poles (unincorporated Poland), 36; Serbs, 36; Slovenes, 29; Jews, 0. Similar proportions prevailed concerning other foods that are essential for good health, with Germans on top and Jews on the bottom. This policy greatly increased the death and illness rates for the subject populations. In Warsaw, anemia jumped 113 percent for Poles and 435 percent for Jews. The occupiers complemented their food rationing policy by withholding or requisitioning essential materials, such as medicine and, during the coldest parts of the winter, fuel and blankets.

The Germans sought to ensure the permanent impoverishment of the subservient populations and the economic superiority of Germanic elements by seeking to destroy the livelihood of the conquered peoples. In the parts of Poland that they incorporated, the Germans confiscated the property and bank accounts of Poles, allowing access only to German depositors of Polish banks who submitted a certificate of their national origin. They required licenses to exercise trades and issued them only to Germans. They closed cooperatives and associations that had been principal vehicles for improving the standards of living of Poles.

Denationalization

The Germans sought to obliterate the national identities of the people living in the areas they conquered by destroying their cultural and political heritage. They destroyed Jewish libraries and synagogues and burned Talmudic scrolls and other sacred items. In Poland, the Germans wrecked national monuments and demolished or confiscated the contents of libraries and museums. They dev-astated churches and attacked the clergy in order to destroy the Polish national religion and gave top priority to murdering the nation's intellectuals who might serve as future leaders.

In the eastern incorporated territories, German policy was to remove the inhabitants and replace them with *Volksdeutsche*, Germans who had lived else-where in Europe. These settlers received the property of the deported inhabitants and other economic inducements. Members of the subservient population could not access higher education.

In areas of Germanic populations that were destined for incorporation into the Reich, the Germans killed the Jews, expelled the foreign population, and gave special privileges to persons of German origin who cooperated with them. The authorities imposed German culture, instituted special agencies to control high culture through special agencies, and required licenses for artists and writers. They ordered changes in names of people, communities, enterprises, and signs to German forms. They forbade the teaching of the primary language of a conquered area, replacing it with German; inculcated National Socialist principles starting at age 6; and enticed children into Nazi organizations. German became the official language of the courts, and German law codes either replaced or modified local laws. Finally, the Germans banned local political organizations and supplanted them with local Nazi parties enjoying special legal privileges.

Had the Nazis won the war, the brutal application of this comprehensive program would have completely altered the face of Europe.

Bibliographical Essay

On the conduct of the war by German soldiers, see Omer Bartov, *The Eastern Front 1941–1945: German Troops and the Barbarization of Warfare* (New York, 1985). Richard Rhodes's *Masters of Death: The Einsatzgruppen and the Invention of the Holocaust* (New York, 2002), which shows Hitler's wider intentions. See as well, Wendy Lower, *Nazi Empire-Building and the Holocaust in Ukraine* (Chapel Hill, N.C., 2005). Heather Anne Pringle, *The Master Plan: Himmler's Scholars and the Holocaust* (New York, 2006), is the story of the SS chief's plan to create a new racially pure Europe.

For information on the organization of the German army and how it fought, see Tim Ripley, *The Wehrmacht* (London, 2003), and David Stone, *Hitler's Army* (London, 2009). For an analysis of the Nazi occupation, see Mark Mazower's *Hitler's Empire: How the Nazis Ruled Europe* (New York, 2008). The mistreatment of occupied Eastern Europe is treated by Alexander Dallin, *German Rule in Russia 1941–1945* (London, 1957). Hitler's remark on keeping the subject populations ignorant is quoted by Peter Cavalcoressi and Guy Wint, *Total War* (New York, 1974), previously cited, p. 212. Theo Schulte discusses the army in *The German Army and Nazi Politics in Occupied Russia* (Oxford, UK, 1989). Poland is discussed by Richard C. Lukas, *The Forgotten Holocaust: The Poles Under German Occupation, 1939–1944* (Lexington, Ky., 1986), and Stefan Korbonski and F. B. Czarnomski, *Fighting Warsaw: The Story of the Polish Underground State, 1939–1945* (New York, 2004). There are five essays on Czechoslovakia during the World War II period in Victor S. Mamatey and Radomir Luza, eds., *A History of the Czechoslovak Republic, 1918–1948* (Princeton, N.J., 1973); C. A. MacDonald and Jan Kaplan published a study on *Prague in the Shadow of the Swastika: A History of the German Occupation* (n.p., 2001). On Vichy France, see Robert Paxton, *Parades and Politics at Vichy: The French Officer Corps*

Under Marshal Pétain (Princeton, N.J., 1966), an examination of the French officer corps, and *Vichy France: Old Guard and New Order* (New York, 2001). Julian Jackson, *France: The Dark Years, 1940–1944* (New York, 2001), is a thorough analysis of France under the German occupation and its effects on the country; see also *Marianne in Chains: Everyday Life in the French Heartland Under the German Occupation* (New York, 2003), by Robert Gildea. With regard to "undesirables" in Vichy, Shannon L. Fogg published *The Politics of Everyday Life in Vichy France* (Cambridge, UK, 2008). The debate on the Vichy experience continued long after the war. See Éric Conan and Henry Rousso, *Vichy: An Ever-Present Past* (Hanover, N.H., 1998); Richard Golsan, *Vichy's Afterlife: History and Counterhistory in Postwar France* (Lincoln, Nebr., 2000); and Michael Curtis, *Verdict on Vichy* (London, 2004). On Vichy's foreign affairs, see Adrienne Doris Hytier, *Two Years of French Foreign Policy: Vichy 1940–1942* (Westport, Conn., 1974). On the relationship with Britain, see R. T. Thomas, *Britain and Vichy: The Dilemma of Anglo-French Relations, 1940–42* (New York, 1979). P. M. H. Bell, *A Certain Eventuality: Britain and the Fall of France* (n.p., 1974), analyzes relations between Britain and France before and after the defeat. Eleanor M. Gates, *End of the Affair: The Collapse of the Anglo-French Alliance, 1939–1940* (London, 1981), is an account of the breakdown of the Anglo-French alliance. On the question of collaboration, there is Philippe Burrin, *France Under the Germans: Collaboration and Compromise* (New York, 1996). Bertram M. Gordon also examines France in *Collaborationism in France During the Second World War* (Ithaca, N.Y., 1980). On the resistance to the German occupation, see the results of an international conference held in 2007: Jun Glasgow et al., *Partisan and Anti-Partisan Warfare in German-Occupied Europe 1939–1945* (Basingstoke, UK, 2010). On the behavior of business under the German occupation, there is Joachim Lund, *Working for the New Order* (Copenhagen, 2006).

Mark Mazower wrote an excellent and readable work on the Axis occupation of Greece, *Inside Hitler's Greece* (New Haven, Conn., 1993). The Italian occupation is examined, controversially, by Davide Rodogno, *Fascism's European Empire* (Cambridge, UK, 2006), and by H. James Burgwyn, *Empire on the Adriatic: Mussolini's Conquest of Yugoslavia 1941–1943* (New York, 2005). Dietrich Orlow's *The Nazis in the Balkans: A Case Study in Totalitarian Politics* (Pittsburgh, 1968) examines the role of an important agency operating in the area. Ilija Jukic, *The Fall of Yugoslavia* (New York, 1974), gives good, firsthand information. Walter R. Roberts, *Tito, Mihailovic and the Allies* (New Brunswick, N.J., 1973), examines the resistance and its divisions in Yugoslavia.

The reader will find many good books on the Holocaust; a good introduction is Doris L. Bergen, *War and Genocide: A Concise History of the Holocaust* (Lanham, Md., 2003). The most thorough and complete work is the excellent Raul Hilberg, *The Destruction of the European Jews*, 3 vols., rev. and definitive edition (New York, 1985). This book goes into all the details about the roundup of the Jews, the organization of the concentration camps and ghettos, the disposition of the victims and their property, and the number and modalities of Jewish deportation from all the European countries. Shorter general histories include Neil Tonge, *The Holocaust* (New York, 2009). *A Mosaic of Victims* (New York, 1990), edited by Michael Berenbaum, discusses the non-Jewish victims of the Nazis. Raphael Lemkin, *Axis Rule in Occupied Europe: Laws of Occupation, Analysis of Government, Proposals for Redress* (New York, 1973), observes the administrative and legal position of occupied Europe, attempts to put it within the context of accepted international law, and suggests legal remedies; the book, originally published in 1944, also has a wealth of difficult-to-find documents. Gotz Aly's *"Final Solution": Nazi Population Policy and the Murder of the European Jews* (New York, 1999) analyzes developments leading to the Nazi genocide. David A. Hackett, ed., *The Buchenwald Report* (Boulder, Colo., 1995), provides brief accounts by victims about their treatment and the organization of one of the most infamous concentration camps. Eugen Kogon, *The Theory and Practice of Hell: The German Concentration Camps and the System Behind Them* (New York, 1975), is an early but accurate account (original publication date in English, 1950) describing the setup of the concentration camp system. Auschwitz is described by Yisrael Gutman and Michael Berenbaum, *Anatomy of the Auschwitz Death Camp* (Indianapolis, Ind., 1994). *The Business of Genocide: The SS, Slave Labor, and the Concentration Camps* (Chapel Hill, N.C., 2002), by Michael Thad Allen, examines the modern management aspects of the concentration camps. James Caplan and Nikolaus Wachsmann produced a book of essays providing new scholarship on the concentration camp system: *Concentration Camps in Nazi Germany: The New Histories* (New York, 2010). Lucy S. Dawidowicz, *The War Against the Jews 1933–1945* (New York, 1975), attempts to answer the questions of how a modern state could bring itself to institute the Holocaust and how its people could have followed it. George M. Kren and Leon Rappaport examine *The Holocaust and the Crisis of Human Behavior* (New York, 1994). Richard Breitman, *The Architect of Genocide: Himmler and the Final Solution* (New York, 1991), examines Himmler's role in the Holocaust.

Women are treated by Vera Laska, *Women in the Resistance and in the Holocaust* (Westport, Conn., 1983), which describes sterilization and other experiments; Lenore J. Weitzman and Dalia Ofer, *Women in the Holocaust* (New Haven, Conn., 1998), which discusses the conditions for women in the camps; Carol Ann Rittner and John R. Roth, eds., *Different Voices: Women and the Holocaust* (New York, 1993), which contains essays by survivors and observers; and Roger A. Ritvo and Diane M. Plotkin, *Sisters of Sorrow: Voices of Care in the Holocaust* (Austin, Tex., 1998).

Two interesting books on how and why the Holocaust was actually begun are Philippe Burrin, *Hitler and the Jews: The Genesis of the Holocaust* (London, 1994), dating the decision to late 1941, and, especially, Christopher Browning, *The Path to Genocide: Essays on the Launching of the Final Solution* (New York, 1995), which does a good job of discussing the intentionalist and functionalist theories and the debate's evolution; the quotation on cumulative radicalization of the Nazi system is on p. 87. *Ordinary Men* (New York, 1992) is an attempt by Browning to analyze the composition of some of the killing groups and their mentality. Browning also published *Nazi Policy, Jewish Labor, German Killers* (New York, 2000), on the evolution of Nazi methods from 1939 to 1941. The question of the willingness of Germans to kill Jews is discussed in the controversial Daniel Goldhagen, *Hitler's Willing Executioners: Ordinary Germans and the Holocaust* (New York, 1997); see Chapter 15 for books discussing the debate on Goldhagen's work. Henry Friedlaender, *The Origins of Nazi Genocide: Ordinary Germans and the Holocaust* (Chapel Hill, N.C., 1995), traces events from euthanasia to the final solution. Saul Friedlaender wrote *Nazi Germany and the Jews* (New York, 1998).

Controversy surrounds the question of whether the pope at the time, Pius XII, should have spoken out forcefully against the Holocaust. This issue has brought up the question of anti-Semitism in the Catholic Church. The most outspoken and controversial books are John Cornwell, *Hitler's Pope: The Secret History of Pius XII* (New York, 1999), and Daniel Jonah Goldhagen, *Moral Reckoning: The Role of the Catholic Church in the Holocaust and Its Unfulfilled Duty of Repair* (New York, 2002). More balanced treatments may be found in Susan Zuccotti, *Under His Very Windows: The Vatican and the Holocaust in Italy* (New Haven, Conn., 2000) and Michael Phayer, *The Catholic Church and the Holocaust, 1930–1963* (Bloomington, Ind., 2000). Ronald J. Rychlak, *Hitler, the War, and the Pope* (Columbus, Mo., 2000) maintains that Pius acted wisely in being circumspect but signaling to the faithful that they should help people in need.

On Jewish resistance, Reuben Ainztein's, *Jewish Resistance in Nazi-Occupied Eastern Europe: With a Historical Survey of the Jew as Fighter and Soldier in the Diaspora*

(London, 1974) is a comprehensive work. On the wider topic, see Yuri Suhl, *They Fought Back: The Story of Jewish Resistance in Europe* (New York, 1978). There are a number of good books on the Warsaw Ghetto. Israel Gutman's *The Warsaw Ghetto Uprising* (Boston, 1994) is a good account.

On rescue, Martin Gilbert's *The Righteous: the Unsung Heroes of the Holocaust* (New York, 2003) is a general history. For the little-known story of how Italian soldiers and diplomats protected Jews in Greece, Yugoslavia, and France, see Jonathan Steinberg's *All or Nothing: The Axis and the Holocaust 1941–1943* (London, 1990). Documents related to these events, with commentaries, are published in Léon Poliakov and Jacques Sabille, *Jews Under the Italian Occupation* (Paris, 1954); see also Susan Zuccotti's *The Italians and the Holocaust* (New York, 1987) and Charles T. O'Reilly, *The Jews of Italy, 1938–1945* (Jefferson, Mo., 2007). Tela Zasloff, *A Rescurer's Story* (Madison, Wis., 2003), is an example of a rescue in Vichy France. Karen Gray Ruelle and Deborah Durland De Saix, *The Grand Mosque of Paris* (New York, 2008), tells how Muslims saved Jews during the Holocaust. Suzanne Vromen, *Hidden Children of the Holocaust* (New York, 2008), describes how Belgian nuns rescued young Jews. The Bulgarian case is examined by Frederick B. Chary, *The Bulgarian Jews and the Final Solution 1940–1944* (Pittsburgh, 1972). The case of Wallenberg is the most famous also because he disappeared when the Russians took over Hungary. See John Bierman, *Righteous Gentile: The Story of Raoul Wallenberg, Missing Hero of the Holocaust* (New York, 1981); Andrew Handler, *A Man for all Generations—Raoul Wallenberg and the Hungarian Apparatus, 1944–1945* (Westport, Conn., 1996); and Alan Gersten, *A Conspiracy of Indifference: The Raoul Wallenbeg Story* (Philadelphia, 2001).

CHAPTER 20

✍

How the War Was Won

CHAPTER OUTLINE

Weapons • Wartime Production • Battles • Resistance • The Future •
Ideology: Nationalism's Handmaiden?

BIOGRAPHICAL SKETCHES

Erwin Rommel, The Desert Fox • Bernard Law Montgomery, Hero of
El Alamein

Their early victories allowed the Germans to exploit Europe's resources and
productive capacities, and between 1940 and 1942, the Nazis enjoyed an aura
of invincibility and important bases from which they would be difficult to dislodge,
while their opponents had no convenient staging areas for war operations. However,
the fortunes of the war slowly shifted against the Germans because the Americans
joined the British and the Soviets. On December 7, 1941, the Japanese bombed
Pearl Harbor, and the Germans and Italians declared war on the United States.

WEAPONS

During World War II, the Allies emphasized the large-scale production of
reliable weapons rather than seeking to perfect ever more advanced ones, as did
the Germans.

Armies and Armor

For land armies, the rifle remained the fundamental weapon. The major
innovations were ammunition clips and rapid-fire submachine guns. Machine
guns became lighter but remained fundamentally the same. With reference to
another basic weapon, the belligerents (except Germany) entered the war with
artillery manufactured during World War I, but innovations that combined
heavy artillery with rapid-fire ability made it necessary to shift to more modern
guns. Heavier artillery forced armies to mount them on vehicles, giving rise to

self-propelled artillery. The Russians adapted rockets to artillery uses, employing a bank of them, the *katyusha*. The design of shells accounted for the most important change in the evolution of the artillery because changes allowed them to penetrate thicker armor and to explode in the proximity of targets without direct hits.

Tanks developed into reliable vehicles and conferred great mobility to the battles of World War II. Ironically, the Germans did not enjoy qualitative superiority at first; the Mark III and IV were disappointments, and they utilized Czech-built T-38 medium tanks that they had taken after the Munich crisis to great effect during the early days of the war. The French had better tanks than the Germans but used them poorly. The Russian T-34 was clearly superior to the German Mark III and IV and equal to the later Mark V and VI. The Americans intervened with the heavily armored and reliable Shermans that also replaced earlier British armor, but they were inferior to later German models. The tank initially gave the offensive the edge over the defense through its ability to roll over machine guns, but the Germans in North Africa discovered that they could stop them with the use of anti-aircraft weapons. Handheld tank-killing rockets could also destroy tanks, but subsequent changes in the tank meant that neither offense nor defense had a clear superiority.

Another weapon that was commonly employed in World War I, poison gas, was not used in World War II despite ominous developments in its effectiveness. Both sides possessed it, and the Allies threatened massive retaliation against the Germans should they employ it, especially on the eastern front where its use appeared most probable. Given the scarcity of gas masks and the subjection of Germany to mammoth air raids, German leaders heeded the warning—luckily, because the Germans had invented nerve gas, against which no defense existed, and Hitler mistakenly assumed that the Allies also had it. There was some attempt to develop biological weapons, especially anthrax, but they were not a significant factor in the war.

War in the Air

Greater changes occurred in the air than on land, even with regard to personnel. With the exception of the USSR, where women saw significant action in the army in addition to the air force, female service in the air corps captured the public's imagination in the Allied countries. By 1939, single-winged warplanes had substantially replaced biplanes, and American development of long-range fighters revolutionized the air war by permitting these fighters to escort bombers to strike enemy territory. Twin-engine bombers continued to be used for combat support, but the four-engine airplane set the standard for the long-range bomber carrying large loads.

Allied strategic bombing of Germany spurred the development of famous four-engine bombers, such as the American B-17 Flying Fortress and the B-29 that dropped the first atomic weapons on Japan. The Germans had begun the tradition of heavily bombing cities and civilian populations during the Spanish Civil War, but the British and Americans mastered the technique. They implemented the ideas of prewar theorists who had argued that air power alone could break the will of populations to continue fighting and spur them to revolt. Allied carpet bombing claimed many victims; the bombing of Dresden, for example, created ferocious firestorms and is estimated to have killed 70,000 people. The bombing of Germany did not induce the Germans to revolt and force their government to surrender, but it severely damaged the production of war materiel and the ability to keep armed forces in the field. The Germans ultimately proved less efficient than the Allies in the air war because, impressed by the achievements of their dive-bombers in the opening months of the war, they concentrated on perfecting them, which proved to be a dead end, instead of developing more potent four-engine bombers.

On the other hand, the Germans excelled in advanced air weapons that did not affect the course of the war but were important for the future. The V-1 "flying bomb," utilizing a jet engine and capable of being dropped from airplanes, foreshadowed the cruise missile. Because its low speed made it vulnerable to being shot down by fighters, the Germans developed the V-2, a true rocket and ancestor of the ballistic missile against which no defense existed. Despite its late employment, its early stage of perfection, and Allied bombing against research and assembly bases, it killed 15,000 persons. The Germans' use of slave labor on this project, however, subjected the weapon to sabotage. The Germans had in the works the V-4, a rocket capable of reaching the United States. Luckily for the Allies, the Germans had previously interrupted earlier research on missiles because they believed the war would be a brief one.

The Germans made progress in the development of jet fighters, but too late to affect the course of the conflict. In 1943, they flew a jet fighter and a jet bomber that was more advanced than any similar weapon the Allies had. Because Allied bombing had become so efficient, the Germans had to scatter their aircraft production facilities, which delayed the deployment of the jet aircraft. Disputes over how the aircraft should be used, the inability to train pilots, and the capture of a manufacturing plant prevented the Germans from exploiting their technical advantage.

Naval Warfare

On the sea, there were fewer changes in weaponry, and battleships and submarines remained essentially the same as those of the World War I. The Germans built powerful battleships, such as the *Bismarck,* that raided the Atlantic and gained great notoriety, but had a minimal effect on the war. For the Germans, the real challenge in World War II was to destroy the shipping that carried American supplies and troops to Europe, and as in World War I, their most potent weapon was the submarine. With the exception of Admiral Karl Doentiz, German leaders failed to give submarines high priority, building fewer of them than was required to fulfill their mission and employing mistaken tactics. Even so, it is doubtful that the submarine could have been successful because it still traveled too slowly under water and had to surface and move significant distances to find targets, making it vulnerable. The convoy system proved as effective as it had been in World War I, even against improved German "wolf pack" tactics that pitted groups of submarines against convoys. The slow American response to the German strategy resulted in

As the war began turning against the Germans, they developed more advanced weapons, such as the V-2 rocket. Although the new weapons came too late to affect the war's outcome, they were important for the future. As the war came to a close, the Americans scrambled to bring German scientists as to the United States in order to keep them out of Soviet hands and to take advantage of their expertise. Werner von Braun, developer of the V-2, helped develop the Intermediate Range Ballistic Missile (IRBM) during the Cold War and the Saturn booster that was essential in the successful effort to land Americans on the moon in July 1969.

the loss of a significant number of American ships to submarines, but eventually the Allies responded with improved convoy schemes and high-frequency direction finders that defeated the submarine menace.

The most important innovation in naval warfare was the development of radar, which gave the Allies great advantages over the Germans and Italians. In another electronic area, radio communication among the fighting forces became commonplace, making the interception of messages and the breaking of secret codes an essential element of warfare on land, air, and sea. A war within the war took place in which the belligerents tried to break each other's codes and then struggled to keep the development secret so they could continue to learn of the other's plans and operations. In a field related to naval warfare, the need to land in occupied Europe spurred the development of amphibious craft capable of landing troops and tanks from naval transports. These craft played a crucial part in Asia as well.

Atomic Weapons

The most radical development for the future of the world, however, was the successful production of nuclear weapons—the culmination the progress made in understanding the nucleus made in the 1930s. The idea that splitting the atom would yield enormous amounts of energy was implicit in Einstein's 1905 relativity theory, but whether the theory could be used to develop a bomb was a question. Einstein doubted it until he was confronted with the work of Enrico Fermi and Hungarian physicist Leo Szilard. Einstein then wrote to President Franklin D. Roosevelt, and the Americans, spurred by the fear that the Nazis would develop the bomb first, began an expensive but successful crash project to develop nuclear weapons. Also aware of the possibilities, the Germans sponsored nuclear research as well, but they underestimated the possibility of producing such weapons in time to make a difference in the war. The American bomb came too late to use against Germany but was used against Japan.

Wartime Propaganda

Finally, propaganda—print, film, and radio—was utilized during the conflict, but, at least until the later stages, it probably had more effect on the home front than against the enemy. Radio broadcasts inducing enemy soldiers to give up usually produced a good laugh, as did propaganda leaflets. Toward the end of the war, the Americans dropped leaflets with passes promising safety to German troops if they surrendered. Although the soldiers used them, it is doubtful that they persuaded anybody. Probably the most effective propaganda weapon in the war was the truth about the war's course. BBC broadcasts gave hope to people in occupied areas and encouraged them to resist. The United States was particularly successful in getting Americans to buy war bonds to support the war effort.

WARTIME PRODUCTION

Napoleon Bonaparte stated that armies marched on their bellies. Modern armies, however, march thanks to economics because in the twentieth century, machines achieved domination over the battlefield, and soldiers depended on the weapons and supplies produced by their workers at home.

Axis Inferiority

In the field of production, the Axis was decidedly inferior to the allies, especially in the long run. Hitler's successful dismantling of Czechoslovakia in 1938 brought him control of that country's considerable reserve of armaments and its industrial plant. The time that elapsed between the Munich Pact and the outbreak of war did not permit the British and the French to fill the gap in armaments opened by the German rearmament program, but the inability of the Germans to win the war quickly and the entrance of the United States into the conflict meant that the Axis lost the arms race.

The manufacture of weapons that the armies needed to fight World War II required about twenty essential materials and a host of other natural products ranging from petroleum and coal for fuel; to lead for ammunition; to cotton, mercury, and glycerin for explosives; to antimony, nickel, and manganese for steel; to copper for electric wire. With the exception of coal, Germany produced none of them in substantial amounts. The Germans did succeed in obtaining indispensable primary materials, either from their conquests or from their allies, and in producing some substitutes, but not enough. Germany's major ally, Italy, had to import almost everything it needed and was a drain on Axis resources. In contrast, the USSR had large reserves of raw materials despite its vast territorial losses in the west, Britain could import key materials from its empire and the United States, and the Americans constituted an "arsenal of democracy." The United States produced about 66 percent of the world's petroleum and 50 percent of its cotton and copper and, with the exception of a handful, had a sufficient supply of the other necessary minerals.

In addition, the Germans turned out to be much less efficient in producing war materiel than the Allies. The Soviets ploughed ahead, used to their command economy, while the Americans relied on informality to spur industrialists—but both undertook the greatest war effort yet known—while Germany produced military equipment well below its capacity to do so. Hitler issued orders, but a vast bureaucratic and corrupt party network overwhelmed them. Moreover, unlike the United States, the German armed forces determined the kind of weapons to be produced. The Germans prided themselves on a tradition of skilled craftsmanship and looked down on American mass production techniques. They produced high-quality weapons and numerous models that had to be constantly modified and slowed production.

The Germans failed to exploit the economies of scale until Hitler appointed his favorite architect Albert Speer as the armaments minister. Speer introduced the mass production methods that proved so effective for the Allies, reducing the number of models and concentrating on bigger manufacturing plants. German efficiency finally approximated that of the Allies, but too late. The fierce Allied bombing campaign made it impossible to continue production of war materiel undisturbed, and the Germans had to move and camouflage their factories. The Germans' reliance on poorly paid and unmotivated foreign workers and slave laborers also hampered their war effort. Furthermore, the continuous bombing sapped the will of German workers and prompted the Gestapo and the SS to intervene against them. The security services harassed industrialists, whom they could send to concentration camps. Threats and coercion proved poor motivators. Thus, the Americans outclassed the highly skilled German industrial workforce and entrepreneurs who looked down upon them as producers of shoddy goods.

BIOGRAPHICAL SKETCHES

Erwin Rommel
The Desert Fox

Adolf Hitler named Erwin Rommel a field marshal, at the young age of 50, because of Rommel's exploits against the British in North Africa. Sent to bolster the faltering Italians, Rommel soon had the British on the run despite his inferiority in armaments. His style contrasted vividly with that of his desert enemy, the meticulous Eighth Army commander General Bernard Montgomery. By contrast, Rommel was daring, impulsive, and imaginative. In 1941 and 1942, he developed such a great reputation among his enemies that the British launched an extraordinary propaganda campaign to convince their soldiers that he was not a magician but an ordinary German general.

Rommel served as an infantry officer on the western front during World War I, winning medals for bravery and receiving his country's highest decoration on the Italian front in 1917. His tactics foreshadowed the Blitzkrieg employed during World War II and his development into the perfect fighting animal.

Ironically, Rommel in war contrasted with his tranquil, middle-class— even dull—existence during peacetime. He was born on November 15, 1891, in Heidenheim, near Ulm, in southwestern Germany. His mother, the daughter of an important local official, and his father, a mathematics teacher, ensured practicality in his life. After planning to study engineering, Rommel joined the army in July 1910. In 1911, while studying to be an officer, he met Lucie Maria Mollin, the daughter of a Prussian landowner and his future wife. They married in 1916 and had their only child Manfred in 1928. Aside from her, he was uninterested in women.

After World War I, Rommel settled down to the normal life of a German career officer. He wrote *Infantry Attacks*, which became a training manual for the army and brought him to Hitler's attention. By 1938, he commanded the Fuehrer's bodyguard, but, despite his closeness to Hitler, he kept out of politics throughout his life.

During the German Blitzkrieg against France in May 1940, Rommel headed a Panzer army, demonstrating the dash and intuition that made him and his Afrika Korps legendary in the North African desert fighting between February 1941 and March 1943. He fought at the head of his troops, often risking his life; he ate the same rations and slept in the open with them. After he left North Africa, Rommel undertook a series of important assignments in the last phases of the war. He designed Axis—the successful operation to take over Italy after it surrendered. By November 1943, he was engaged in the building of the Atlantic Wall, consisting of concrete blockhouses and other obstacles, 4 million mines, and the so-called Rommel Asparagus—anti-aircraft barriers—to prevent an Allied landing. The Allied success prompted him to tell Hitler that Germany should ask for peace.

Given Hitler's refusal, Rommel looked favorably on the possibility of the Fuehrer's overthrow. Not involved with the July 20 plot to kill Hitler, he nonetheless was the conspirators' choice for temporary president of Germany after Hitler's planned assassination. When the plot failed, Hitler also took his revenge on Rommel. On October 14, 1944, while recovering from wounds inflicted when a British plane strafed his car, two generals brought Hitler's ultimatum: commit suicide (a hero's funeral and safety for his family) or go on trial (execution and retaliation against his family). Rommel left with them in a green car, took poison, and died.

Four days later, a day of national mourning, Rommel's body lay in state, with his coffin covered by an enormous Swastika flag, a general at each corner of his bier, his many decorations prominently displayed on a velvet cushion, and his family forced to take part in the charade. The funeral oration written by Hitler ended the sham with a lie: "His heart belonged to the Fuehrer."

American Production Techniques

The United States performed an economic miracle; despite a weak tradition of military production, workers initially opposed to war, and industrialists unhappy about taking orders from the government, the Americans produced more than all the Axis powers combined by the end of 1942; in four years they doubled their industrial capacity. The United States produced two-thirds of the equipment used by the Allies during World War II—297,000 airplanes, 86,000 tanks, 193,000 artillery pieces, 8,800 ships, 87,000 amphibious assault vessels, and 2 million trucks.

American industry, government, and labor worked together in an imaginative way. The government listened to the suggestions of entrepreneurs and gave them practically free rein to institute unusual ideas instead of giving them orders. Unconventional contracts left production details and methods up to the industrialists. The Americans regulated the economy as little as possible, implementing only absolutely necessary wartime controls. The industrialists responded with flexibility and commitment. They swiftly converted peacetime industries to wartime uses, built gigantic factories bigger than those in the Soviet Union, and perfected mass production methods and applied them in such unorthodox fields as shipbuilding and the manufacture of complex modern aircraft. In the process, American manufacturers made a fortune, but a workforce just emerging from high unemployment also shared the wealth through higher wages that outpaced the high inflation rate. High wages drew the workers from the impoverished South to the booming North and attracted women to take jobs in the armaments factories. "Rosie the Riveter" became an American staple and a symbol of American production. Social disruption, juvenile delinquency, shortages, and racial tension accompanied this progress, but a productive workforce was effectively mobilized to make the equipment that won the battles.

BATTLES

The European war encompassed three broad fronts: southern, eastern, and western.

The South

The Allies focused on the South first, where Italy was the weak link. The Italians' inability to supply their isolated East African colonies led to their rapid loss, but in North Africa, their lack of modern tanks made the Italians succumb to the

Besides the size of its armed forces, the greatest American contribution of World War II was the country's military production capacity. It is estimated, for example, that the Americans provided the USSR with about 10 billion dollars worth of war materiel. If it had not been for American production techniques and workers, the course of the war would have been very different. Here Douglas Aircraft Corporation workers in Long Beach, California, greet the 3,000th C-47 "Skytrain" transport airplane to come off the assembly line of their factory just before it heads off to the war zone.

British despite their superior numbers. The brilliant general Erwin Rommel and his Afrika Korps arrived in Libya to rescue them and in April 1941 pushed the British back into Egypt despite his inferiority in men and equipment.

The rest of the year witnessed back-and-forth battles between the British and Axis forces. Operation Battleaxe, designed to wipe out Rommel, failed when Rommel drew the British Matilda tanks into traps, destroying them with anti-aircraft guns and proving that it was possible to resist armored vehicles. After Battleaxe, Operation Crusader also failed in November, despite British numerical superiority on the ground and in the air. In 1942, both the Allied and Axis forces received reinforcements, but the Axis inferiority in tanks did not prevent Rommel from unleashing an offensive that nearly won him Egypt. By October 23 and 24, however, Montgomery's Eighth Army had recovered and unleashed an offensive at El Alamein. On November 4, the Germans fled before an irresistible British advance. On November 8, when American and British troops landed in northwestern Africa, the battle heated up.

BIOGRAPHICAL SKETCHES

Bernard Law Montgomery
Hero of El Alamein

Erwin Rommel's antagonist, Bernard Montgomery, presented a different picture than "the Desert Fox." In his personal life, Montgomery was flamboyant; in public relations, skilled; in his public pronouncements, arrogant. As a general, however, he moved deliberately and only when he had superior means.

Montgomery had a miserable childhood because of his mother, with whom he was always in a state of war that he always lost. The fourth of nine children, Montgomery had a cool relationship with his siblings, with the partial exception of his younger sister Una. Relations with his saintly father Henry, who came from a long line of clergymen, were good. Henry became Episcopal bishop of Tasmania (Australia) when Bernard, born in London on November 17, 1887, was not yet 2. Bernard grew up in Tasmania with a well-earned reputation for bad behavior.

The family returned to England in late 1901, and in 1907, Montgomery entered the Royal military college at Sandhurst. He was an indifferent student, and an officer told him he was useless. He fought on the western front during World War I, learning, as Rommel did, from his early combat experience. Montgomery concluded that a successful general had to have a plan and to implement it with certainty. He lived and breathed the army and paid attention to nothing else. This focus gave him a reputation as an eccentric, but one who steadily moved up through the ranks.

After the war, Montgomery served in a series of positions and in different overseas posts. In 1926, he decided to marry and began looking for a wife as if he was conducting a campaign. He met a war widow with two children and—surprisingly for a person so much in control of everything—fell in love. Unusual for a husband, he took command of the household, arranging for its orderly functioning down to the grocery shopping. His wife Betty Carver allowed him to do so, but while he reigned, she got her way on the major issues. After ten years of a happy marriage, however, tragedy struck when an insect bit his wife on the leg. Infection spread, and on October 19, 1937, she died. He never married again and could still write emotionally about the incident in 1961.

Montgomery commanded a division in France at the outbreak of World War II. After Dunkirk, he received important commissions in Britain and helped plan important aspects of a 1942 raid on Dieppe, a French port that could have served as a landing area when the British returned to the continent. With the operation's failure, a debate began on his military qualities, despite his disavowal of the raid and his transfer to Africa.

Montgomery rebuilt the demoralized Eighth Army, fighting a losing war against a legend. He became a legend himself by beating Rommel. He had a different style of fighting than did Rommel, but he also was a master at establishing rapport with the troops. Montgomery had the gift of communicating with individual soldiers, who willingly died for him. Long before, Montgomery had become convinced that a successful general had to learn where the enemy was weak and then hurl overwhelmingly superior forces against that point. Using this strategy, he waited until he had accumulated greater resources than his enemy did and won the breakthrough victory at El Alamein.

continued

continued

Following his service in North Africa, Montgomery fought in Italy, participated in the planning for D-Day, and held crucial commands in Western Europe.
The polemical field marshal criticized his American allies and received blame for
faulty planning in a number of operations, especially Arnhem. After the war, he
became the military commander of Germany, commander of the Imperial General
Staff (CIGS), and the deputy supreme commander of NATO. Montgomery retired in
1958, controversial as always, and wrote his memoirs. On March 24, 1976, "Monty"
died, in the world's imagination still the hero of El Alamein.

The Fight for North Africa

With the North African landing (Operation Torch), the Germans and Italians
decided to make a stand in Tunisia and sent reinforcements to the country. The
Axis forces that were employed in the Tunisian campaign were unavailable for
combat elsewhere and weakened the Germans in the Soviet Union at a crucial
time. The Americans did poorly, taking 2,000 casualties at the Battle of Kassarine
Pass, but their losses helped them make adjustments in their training that transformed them into an effective fighting force. The Allies had hoped for a quick
victory, but it was April before the Axis had been defeated in North Africa;
however, in the final battles, 275,000 Axis troops surrendered to the Allies.

At the Casablanca Conference between Churchill and Roosevelt from January
14 to 23, 1943, the two leaders recognized that Axis resistance in North Africa had
made an Allied invasion of France impossible in 1943 and postponed it until 1944.
In a major step toward that objective, U.S. general George Marshall successfully
insisted on the creation of a staff to begin preparations for the French invasion.
The Allies also agreed on the invasion of Sicily by July.

The Italian Surrender

The successful Sicilian invasion, Husky, began on July 10, 1943. The Italian situation had been unstable because the population blamed Mussolini for the string of
Italian defeats. The disaffection had spread to the highest levels of the government
and the Fascist Party. After the fall of Sicily, Fascists who believed the war had been
lost scheduled a meeting of the Fascist Grand Council. The council turned against
Mussolini at a long meeting held on July 24 and 25, voting to return power to the
king. When Mussolini went to discuss the situation with Victor Emanuel, the king
removed him from office, named a military government under Marshal Pietro
Badoglio, and had il Duce arrested.

Badoglio announced that "the war continues," but he opened negotiations
with the Allies. The ruse did not fool Hitler who, in anticipation of Mussolini's
overthrow and an Italian attempt to switch sides, had sent a number of crack divisions into the country. The Badoglio government botched the armistice talks with
the Allies and bungled the military preparations for turning against the Germans.
As a result, plans for the participation of American troops in the operation were
canceled, and, worse, the government left the armed forces without orders and
fled with the king to the Allied-occupied part of Italy. The Germans disarmed the

Italian units and took Rome after a brief battle. The Germans also moved into the Italian-occupied zones in the Balkans and in France. In a daring operation, they liberated Mussolini and brought him to the north, where he led a puppet regime called the Italian Social Republic (or the Salò Republic).

Operations on the Italian mainland went poorly for the Allies. The German troops they had allowed to escape from Sicily continued the battle, taking advantage of the rugged Italian terrain. An Allied amphibious operation in September 1943 at Salerno, near Naples, stalled despite its establishment of a beachhead. Montgomery's Eighth Army crossed the Straits of Messina onto the Italian boot but made slow headway, as did the Americans. Nevertheless, the Allies had returned to the European heartland and diverted a great number of German troops from the crucial eastern front.

The East

In Eastern Europe, the tide of war turned against Germany in 1942. As the winter ended, Hitler planned a new offensive despite the Germans' weakened state caused by the transfer of forces and supplies to Tunisia.

The Germans planned to undertake their major efforts on the southern flank, where they had the best chance of a breakthrough in areas rich in minerals that they required for the war. At the same time, however, they projected taking Leningrad in the north, assuming that they would win and then could move a large number of troops to Leningrad. In June, the Germans launched attacks aimed at taking the Caucasus oil fields, but the offensive failed as Stalin relied more than he previously had on the professionals in his military and Hitler took exactly the reverse action by interfering more than before. By late summer, activities on the southern flank of the eastern front soon concentrated on the strategic city of Stalingrad, whose importance the Germans had initially failed to consider.

Stalingrad, January 26, 1943. In addition to the strategic value of this city, it had great symbolic worth for being named after the Soviet dictator and because Hitler vowed to capture it. The battle was a disaster for the Germans as Hitler forbade even a tactical retreat and the Axis armies suffered tens of thousands dead or taken prisoner. In the photograph, Red Army soldiers advance among the city's ruins.

Stalingrad

The loss of Stalingrad, a major industrial center, would have been a blow to the Soviet war effort, and in German hands could block all trade on the Volga. Besides its strategic value, Stalingrad had the great symbolic significance of being named for the Soviet dictator. As the battle unfolded, Hitler continually swore that he would take the city, while the Russians resolved to hold it at any cost. By September 3, the battle for Stalingrad was in full swing, and fighting devastated the city. The Germans made slow headway, entering the city that the Soviets defended block by block and house by house (the film *Enemy at the Gates* gives a good idea of the ferocity involved in the fighting). Hitler promised that he would take it, but the Germans failed to see the larger picture and their own potential weaknesses, which Georgi Zhukov, V. I. Chuikov, and A. I. Eremenko—the Soviet generals defending Stalingrad— exploited. Between September and November, the Soviets quietly assembled massive forces for a surprise counterattack against the Germans' Romanian allies and on November 19 unleashed a huge infantry and tank offensive that broke through and surrounded the German army besieging Stalingrad. The Germans could have either elected to break out of the pocket, as the generals wanted, or to resist until reinforcements arrived, as Hitler ordered. The Germans could not send enough soldiers and supplies to relieve the encircled troops, and the operation failed. In lifting the siege of Stalingrad, the Russians took over 90,000 German prisoners, while 150,000 others died either from combat or the cold. The Romanian, Italian, and Hungarian losses weakened the German hold over those countries. The German loss at Stalingrad dealt a devastating moral blow to Germany and gave the Allies a tremendous lift.

Progress of the Russian Fighting

In the north, the Germans also failed to take Leningrad, and in January 1943, the Soviets broke the siege. In the central part of the front, the German drive to take Moscow failed as well. Fighting on the Soviet fronts progressed with victories and defeats on both sides, but while the Soviets could replace men and materiel, the Germans found it increasingly difficult to do so. In July and August 1943, the Russians won the battle of Kursk, breaking the German ability to mount offensives in the east. In June and July 1944, at the same time that the Americans and British came ashore at Normandy, successful Russian offensives began sowing panic in the German ranks, and many soldiers surrendered. The central portion of the German lines collapsed, and the Russians began their march toward Warsaw. By the fall, the Finns withdrew from the war, and the Soviets extended their military and political influence westward.

The German army commanders implemented defensive tactics that slowed the Soviet advance but were hampered by Hitler's opposition to retreat, forcing the army to take greater losses of men and equipment than would otherwise have been the case.

The West

Faced with an improving but still difficult situation, Stalin continued to insist that the Anglo-Americans immediately establish a second front to take the pressure off the Soviets. He suspected that the western Allies delayed this move in order

On D-Day, June 6, 1944, American troops landed on the Normandy coast of France and began their assault of the German-dominated European continent. Historians debate whether the Normandy invasion or the Battle of Kursk in which the Russians defeated the Germans in July/August 1943 was the turning point of World War II, but either way the tide had turned against Hitler. This photograph shows American marines landing on one of the four Normandy beachheads on June 7, 1944.

to weaken him, but the military situation precluded the possibility of a second front until 1944. The western Allies had to assemble a great invasion force on the British Isles that was capable of dislodging the Germans from their heavily fortified positions on the European coastline by bringing men and equipment from the faraway United States.

D-Day

Led by U.S. General Dwight D. Eisenhower and Montgomery, the Allies launched the invasion of France on D-Day, June 6, 1944. The invasion force successfully established bridgeheads in Normandy and landed a huge army in the following weeks.

Several factors explain the Allied success in this arduous breach of the German Atlantic Wall. They included the crushing Allied air superiority and, on the German side, a dispute about exactly where the Allies planned a landing and how to confront it. Thus, the Germans had only one Panzer division near the zone where the Allies landed. The German commander Erwin Rommel had pleaded in vain with his colleagues to station strong mobile forces closer to where the invasion actually occurred, and the debate about how they would meet the invaders ended in a compromise that worked poorly. In this case as well, Hitler constantly interfered with the generals and hampered German military operations. Rounding out the picture and ultimately accounting for the German defeat was the inability of the Germans to match Allied resources in tanks and aircraft.

The Battle of the Bulge

Given the advance of the Allied armies in the West, Hitler decided to risk everything on a last throw of the dice. He planned an offensive against the Americans with thirty reformed divisions and six hundred tanks. He counted on a heavy American defeat to break the will of Americans at home to continue the war. While he envisioned a break in the Allied coalition, even if it did not come, a victory in the West would allow him to shift his troops again to the East to defeat the advancing Soviets.

On December 16, 1944, with bad weather grounding the Allied air forces, the Germans threw 200,000 men against a sector of the front held by 80,000 Americans—the Battle of the Bulge. This attack achieved surprise and caused the American defenders to waver. The Germans achieved a temporary success, but the American lines held, and they soon passed to the counterattack. Hitler's last, desperate plans to recoup his position failed and worsened the German situation because the Germans had exhausted their last reserves and their best equipment.

The Strategic Bombing Campaign

As a major part of their strategy to defeat the Germans, the Anglo-Americans conducted increasingly heavy strategic bombing of Germany. The effectiveness of this campaign has been debated because in 1942 and 1943, strategic bombing did not have great effects either on German civilian morale or on production, which actually increased because of Speer's reorganization of German industry.

In 1944, the Americans introduced long-range fighters that were capable of escorting bombers to distant targets. This development, along with refined navigational aids, radar-evading devices, and improved night capabilities, allowed the Allies to area and carpet-bomb more cities and disrupt production to a greater degree than had been possible before. Raids included hundreds of bombers, thousands of tons of ordnance, and tens of thousands of civilian casualties. Whether bombing civilians was the best use of air power or whether it might have shortened the war by concentrating on military targets is still disputed.

RESISTANCE

The German occupation stimulated both collaboration and resistance. Collaborators were motivated by self-interest or by a belief that given the new European order, cooperation was better for their countries. As German exploitation and atrocities increased, resistance movements appeared that saved the honor of the conquered countries and gave them the self-confidence to rebuild after the liberation even though the number of those who actively resisted is still in dispute. The European Resistance can be considered a combination of patriotic, class, and civil warfare.

Divisions

Despite the common goal of fighting the occupiers, divisions regarding the future organization of their countries and the desire for revenge against collaborators remained strong, and the Resistance movements in Western and Eastern Europe took on the aspects of a civil war. In Italy, the fight between the Fascists and the partisans is graphically illustrated in the film *The Night of the Shooting Stars*. In Yugoslavia, a civil war openly raged during the German occupation, and in Greece, following the occupation. In Poland, the underground movement barely tolerated Jewish resisters and hardly cooperated with them. After the conflict, the Communists in Eastern Europe eliminated the non-Communist resisters.

In the Balkans, Yugoslav Communist leader Josip Broz, called Tito, conducted an all-out war against the Germans and Cetniks, Serb partisans, skillfully cooperating with the different nationalities and gaining Allied support. When the Germans withdrew, he took control of Yugoslavia without the help of the Red Army and achieved a measure of independence from the USSR.

In Greece, the Communist-controlled ELAS and the monarchist EDES Resistance organizations competed against each other. After the war, the British supported the monarchists against the Communists in a brutal civil war that led the Americans to declare that they would contain communism (the Truman Doctrine). With Greece solidly in the Western zone of influence, the Communists lost, but in neighboring Albania, Communist resistance leader Enver Hoxha took control and ruled the country until his death in 1986.

Different Phases

The course of resistance may be divided into stages, although not all of them occurred at the same time in different countries. Humor frequently marked the beginnings of the process. In Paris, the following story circulated: Hitler had discovered an old rabbi whose family had handed down the secret of parting the seas so that people could cross them in safety. Hoping to send his army across the channel to attack Britain, the Fuehrer promised the rabbi that thousands of Jews could go free if he revealed the secret. The rabbi quickly agreed. A special little wand waved over the seas caused them to part. Hitler asked where the wand was. The answer: "In the British museum."

Other modest actions, such as scraps of information passed to opponents of the occupying power, solidarity toward its victims, telling others of brutal behavior, or helping someone escape a roundup, preceded the organizational phase that was usually provoked by brutal acts of repression. Finally came the entrance into battle—hiding Allied airmen, stealing secret information, assassinating Nazi officials, fomenting strikes, sabotaging and attacking military installations, and joining partisan bands. The British conducted operations in concert with the Resistance movements through their Special Operations Executive (SOE), the Americans through the Office of Strategic Services (OSS). Many Resistance leaders hoped that their opposition would culminate in uprisings against the occupier and in political and social revolutions, although the western Allies rejected them.

Toward the end of the war in the West, the Resistance movements in France and Italy, organized by secret committees, constructed important military formations. In France, armed resistance took on a new dimension in early 1944 when the different Resistance forces joined in the *Forces Français de l' Intérieur* (French Forces of the Interior, FFI). Guerrilla bands usually numbered about fifty, but toward the end of the conflict fielded thousands of fighters. They engaged in pitched battles with the Germans and obstructed the movement of troops to important battles. Eisenhower believed that they were worth fifteen divisions.

The Italian Communists played a crucial role in the Resistance, aided by their underground experience in fighting Fascism. The Italian Resistance opposed the Nazis and Fascists in occupied northern Italy following creation of the Salò Republic. The political organization of the Italian Resistance took the form of committees of national liberation consisting of six-party coalitions that included the mass parties—Communists, Socialists, and Christian Democrats. This coalition formed governments recognized by the Allies after the war.

The Italian Communists and Socialists aimed at a revolution, but, ironically, the Communists were most apt to compromise the revolutionary ideal. Because Stalin knew that Italy would be in the Western sphere of influence following the war, he insisted that the Communists come to power by legal means, through elections. Upon his return from the Soviet Union, Communist leader Palmiro Togliatti announced at Salerno on March 24, 1944, that the Communists would cooperate with the conservatives and monarchists to rid the country of the Germans. At the same time, guerrilla bands carried out daring raids, some of them described in Elio Vittorini's masterpiece *Men and Non-Men* and in the works of Beppe Fenoglio. The most famous was an action that killed thirty-three German soldiers in Rome that provoked the brutal execution of 335 civilians. The guerilla bands helped clear northern cities and forced a retreating German column to hand over Mussolini, after which they executed him and his mistress Claretta Petacci. They also executed major Fascist hierarchs and minor officials and continued their actions after the war in the hopes of eliminating potential political enemies; estimates of persons who were murdered after the war because of revenge or politics, primarily by Communists, range up to 100,000. The Italian Resistance, however, claimed to have created the ideological basis for a new republic set up after the war.

In Poland a large underground army had the support of the population and collected arms for a planned rural insurrection. It gathered intelligence on German military movements, tactics, and secret weapons and forwarded the information to London. The underground army perished during the last days of the war when it was called upon by the Red Army to rise in Warsaw. The Soviets then halted their advance while the Germans eliminated the rebels and destroyed the city. The Soviet goal: to facilitate the establishment of a pliable Communist regime in postwar Poland.

Different Groups

The Resistance movements included diverse groups. Jews figured prominently in the national Resistance movements and developed their own tradition of opposition. In addition to the spectacular Warsaw Ghetto uprising of April 1943, Jewish partisans operated independently of other groups in the forests of Poland,

During the latter part of World War II, resistance to the German occupation became widespread even though the number of people involved in the Resistance has been debated. Throughout Europe the probability of a Nazi defeat emboldened people to fight Nazism and contributed to its overthrow. Women made a notable contribution to the Resistance movements all over Europe as indicated in this picture of a woman Resistance fighter in France.

Lithuania, and the Ukraine even though they frequently faced anti-Semitism among the Christian partisans.

Women participated in Resistance movements in both the East and the West. They took part in operations, as novels such as *L'Agnese va a morire* [Agnese Goes to Her Death] illustrate. In the West, women excelled in operating printing presses and distributing clandestine material. Different French accounts emphasize their capacity as liaison officers, fomenters of demonstrations and strikes, and agitators against the forced deportation of laborers—dangerous activities in occupied Europe. Many women resisters belonged to the middle- and lower-middle classes, the strongest repositories of national feeling and resistance.

Workers did not distinguish themselves early as resisters because of their need for employment, but became strong opponents when confronted with increases in the draft and in forced labor. They tended to support Communist groups, but in France the so-called Worker Priest movement strengthened the church's presence among them.

Opposition in Germany

In Germany, passive rather than active resistance had existed since Hitler had come to power, but was confined to restricted circles because any kind of opposition led to execution. A desire to save persecuted Jews and to get the Catholic Church to intervene forcefully against the Nazis motivated some people, such as Margerete Sommer. Other opponents formed discussion groups. The most significant of these groups was Helmut von Moltke's Kreisau Circle, which discussed Germany's future should Hitler be overthrown. As German losses mounted in Russia, opposition increased. In Munich, university students established the White Rose organization, which distributed leaflets calling for opposition to the Nazis. In 1943, the Nazis executed the leaders of this group, including sister and brother Sophie and Hans Scholl.

The German Catholics had been among the political groups that supported Hitler the least, but after Hitler's accession, the Vatican preferred to leave opposition to the German bishops on the grounds that they knew more about local conditions. During the war, Pope Pius XII did not openly condemn the Germans, believing that he risked Nazi military action against the church and that conditions would worsen if he did so. Although church authorities, priests, and nuns helped persecuted Jews with the pope's knowledge, Pius's failure publicly to denounce German genocide produced furious debate after the war.

The German military hierarchy was uneasy with Hitler for different reasons, but the Fuehrer constantly outmaneuvered the generals. As the situation became increasingly desperate during World War II, some of his opponents, such as Colonel Claus von Stauffenberg, chief of staff of the reserve army, came together in a conspiracy to assassinate him and overthrow the regime. On July 20, 1944, Stauffenberg successfully planted a bomb close to Hitler in a conference room. The Fuehrer miraculously survived the blast, retained the army's loyalty, and struck back savagely. He ordered the traitors brutally tortured and murdered and eliminated what opposition remained in the armed forces and in the country.

Despite their variety and complexity, the significance of the European Resistance movements may be summarized in a few points. The movements demonstrated the depth of a prostrate continent's opposition to German conquest and suggested that the Germans would have had a difficult time implementing their ultimate aims even if they had won. They brought right and left together to fight a common enemy, but also highlighted civil strife. They positioned the Communists politically for a major role in the politics and society of postwar Western Europe and provided a fig leaf for Soviet expansion in the East. The Resistance contributed to the Allied victory, restored the hope and self-assurance of European nations who were crushed by defeat and dictatorship, and rekindled confidence in a united Europe that would prevent future wars.

THE FUTURE

As the defeat of Nazi Germany loomed, the Allied leaders met to plan their military strategy and Europe's future.

Conferences

The British and Americans met to discuss their military options at conferences in Quebec, Moscow, Cairo, and Teheran in 1943.

The British insisted on military priority for operations in Italy and the Eastern Mediterranean; the Americans demanded precedence for a cross-channel invasion by May 1944, proposing that battle-hardened divisions be withdrawn from the Mediterranean to support the invasion. Churchill feared that the invasion would fail, leading to another Dunkirk or a stalemate similar to the one that had occurred in World War I. The Americans disagreed and had the resources to try again in case of failure. They worried that the Russians would defeat Germany quickly and establish their hegemony in areas overrun by the Red Army, possibly including regions of Western Europe. In late 1943, Stalin settled the question at the Teheran Conference by insisting on the invasion of northwest Europe while stiff German military resistance preventing Stalin's implementation of any plans he may have had for rapid westward expansion calmed immediate American fears. Planning for Overlord, the Normandy invasion of June 1944, went into high gear under General Dwight D. Eisenhower.

The political issues among the Allies proved knottier to resolve. At the Moscow Conference in October 1943, the Allies agreed on trying German war criminals and on the disarmament and denazification of Germany itself. But the participants reached no agreement on Germany's future borders or whether the country should be dismembered. The Americans focused on Allied agreement on the unconditional surrender of Germany, the establishment of a postwar international organization to safeguard the peace, and recognition of China as a major power. The Soviets raised the problem of future borders, but the Americans were reluctant to make commitments while the war raged. The British went along with Soviets' insistence that their partners agree that their western border include territory annexed as a result of their 1939 pact with the Nazis, on the grounds that that the Red Army would conquer the East anyway and would make concessions in the West in return and that the proposed boundary coincided roughly with one drawn up in 1919 by British Foreign Secretary Lord Curzon. The British were also willing to allow the Soviets wide latitude in setting postwar boundaries in the entire East. The Western Allies were anxious to secure the USSR's commitment to military strategy in the Pacific, and Stalin agreed to attack Japan following Germany's defeat.

The Teheran Conference (November 28, 1943–January 12, 1944) ratified the border decisions taken at earlier meetings. The Russians would get large areas of prewar Poland, compensating Poland with German territory. In practice, the Western Allies also acquiesced to the expulsion of the German population of Eastern Europe, which would make Poland and the states that emerged from the conflict ethnically homogeneous.

Yalta and Potsdam—and the Cold War

The consensus on Eastern Europe that was ratified at Teheran went a long way toward implementation at the Yalta Conference, held February 4 through 11, 1945. The Russians promised to allow free elections, but this pledge conflicted with their

Of the World War II conferences, Yalta, held February 4–11, 1945 remains the most controversial. Although the "Big Three" settled the fate of postwar Germany and compromised on setting up the United Nations, they essentially divided Europe into a Western and a Soviet sphere of influence. This picture shows the British, American, and Russian leaders in a convivial moment. From left to right, Winston Churchill, a visibly ill Franklin D. Roosevelt, and Joseph Stalin. Roosevelt died on April 12, 1945.

desire to retain control of the region for security purposes. Because the Communists did not win power legally after the war, the Soviets imposed regimes that were favorable to them, alienated Western opinion, contributed to the beginning of the cold war, and gave them a bad reputation among the American public. At the same conference, the participants compromised on the structure of the United Nations, which had been causing difficulties. From the Soviet geopolitical viewpoint, the arrangement in the East counterbalanced Allied supremacy in Western Europe and Greece. The Yalta Conference also divided Germany into occupation zones, including one for the French carved out of the American and British occupation areas.

At the end of February 1945, Western public opinion hardened against the USSR following a Soviet-sponsored coup in Romania, the arrest of non-Communist Polish underground leaders, and the refusal to hold free elections. The Potsdam Conference, held in July 1945, hammered out the last details with regard to reparations and the new Polish borders and set the first international trials of war criminals. Harry S. Truman, who had succeeded to the presidency following Roosevelt's death, secured a definitive agreement from the Russians to enter the war against Japan on August 15, which was projected to last until 1947 until the atomic bomb was used. Most ominously, an Allied control council set up at Yalta proved unworkable. The Soviets moved toward the establishment of a de facto govern-

On May 8, 1945, World War II came to an end in Europe with the German surrender. The continent was devastated. This picture shows a street scene in Berlin. German officials forced Nazi Party members to clear the once-impassible street of rubble.

ment in their zone, eventually precipitating the creation of two German states that would reunite only after the end of the cold war.

End of the War in Europe

On April 29, 1945, with Soviet soldiers entering Berlin, Hitler married his mistress Eva Braun in the depths of his Reich Chancellery. The couple, Hitler's staff, and his loyal followers drank champagne, ate sandwiches, and reminisced about the past. Later Hitler retired with his secretary to dictate his last will and political testament, including naming a government to succeed him. On the same day, he had had his dog poisoned. After lunch on April 30 and chats with his staff, Hitler and Eva Braun retired to his study. Ten minutes later, they were both dead—Braun from poison and Hitler from a gunshot wound. Their associates took the bodies to be burned with some gas set aside for the purpose. It was not enough, and Soviet soldiers had no difficulty identifying the remains.

On May 8, the Germans surrendered unconditionally. The war in Europe had left 55 million to 60 million dead.

IDEOLOGY: NATIONALISM'S HANDMAIDEN?

The civilian deaths caused by World War II outnumbered those of any previous war or revolution. Competing ideologies help account for the brutality demonstrated by the combatants during the conflict, but this is not the full explanation.

Nazism and Nationalism

Nazism aimed at the racial restructuring of Europe and to make Germany supreme in Europe. The wholesale destruction of the Jews, the attempt to exploit Slavic slave laborers for the benefit of future German generations while eliminating them from history, and the efforts to murder the cultures of other nationalities were revolutionary goals. Although Imperial Germany shared the characteristic of nationalism and considered Germans superior to other European "races," it did not plan their destruction.

Italian Fascism, the regime that initially served as a model for Hitler, was openly nationalistic but not racist until 1938. It was a reaction to a parliamentary regime that was considered weak domestically and neither warlike nor success-ful in the scramble for colonies. The Fascists pledged to reverse this situation; to construct a strong state where a fragile one had existed; to make the country's voice heard in Europe where it had been ignored; to win colonies that had been denied to it; and, finally, to transform Italians into warriors where they had been too peaceful. That the Fascists failed miserably in all their goals only highlights their nationalistic objectives.

Communism and Russian Nationalism

Communist ideology posited class domination instead of racial control. In practice, however, nationalism triumphed in Russia, and the foreign policy of the USSR came to resemble that of the old tsarist Russian Empire. The Russians were supreme over the other republics of the USSR, and the Communist state expanded toward the west in order to create a buffer zone around itself, as had the Russian Empire. Both sought aggrandizement in Asia. Like the tsars, the Communists participated in the partition of Poland and incorporated the Baltic States. Communists alleged that capitalism wanted to destroy them and that they had to take measures to defend themselves; the tsars did their utmost to kept Western influence from contaminating the country, as did the Soviets, and pursued a similar expansionist policy. Making due allowance for the difference in technology, both regimes used similar means to maintain internal control, although the Communists were harsher and more destructive.

Like the Nazis, the Communist leaders justified themselves as people with a mission to fulfill. At the same time, the Russian motherland drew ben-efits from this mission. The Communists absorbed vast amounts of territory and derived economic advantages from their satellite states. They supported, morally and financially, vast flanking organizations in the Western states and manipulated them for the benefit of the USSR's foreign or domestic policies. They slaughtered the elites of other nationalities and suppressed their culture, as did the Nazis; to call those cultures bourgeois mattered little. After the war, the Communist countries exploited Marxist ideology to expel and subjugate German and other ethnic minorities and confiscate their property. Ironically, while the Nazis exploited other nationalities and passed some of the material benefits to their people, Soviet Communism transmitted fewer advantages to its citizens.

Nationalism and Democracy

Finally, what of democratic ideologies? Nationalism is not an overt part of democracy, but it was present nonetheless. After World War I, the two greatest imperial powers, Britain and France, took the lion's share of German and Turkish colonies on the grounds that they had to teach the natives about democracy. It took them decades to give up their mandates, in effect, colonies taken from the losers in World War I, and they did not do so willingly. Both countries exploited the natural resources of their empires even though economic forces spurred the British to move toward a commonwealth. Both democracies suppressed revolts in colonies against the conquerors. Winston Churchill fought against his countrymen to hold on to India, made deals with Stalin over spheres of influence, championed continued British supremacy in the Mediterranean, and wanted to retain discredited monarchies in Italy and Greece because he thought they suited British interests. The United States is not immune from similar charges and interfered in the political workings of foreign countries after World War II.

In Western Europe, recognition of the destructive role that extreme nationalism played in the twentieth century produced a strong movement favoring unification. This idea had been discussed before, was lost in the war, but reemerged powerfully during the darkest days of the conflict. A common political structure that allowed full expression of national differences, the proponents of a united Europe argued, was the only way to exorcise the scourge of nationalistic wars from the continent. What better time to begin the process than after the most destructive conflict in history had taught all the European nations a lesson they resolved not to forget?

Bibliographical Essay

Readers should refer to the previous chapter for other books on World War II.

Richard Overy, *Why the Allies Won* (New York, 1995), is an excellent work stressing the production of war materiel and other reasons accounting for the Allied victory. Besides the works cited in previous chapters, the famous military analyst B. H. Liddell Hart published the very readable and clear *History of the Second World War* (New York, 1970). The same author also published *The Other Side of the Hill: Germany's Generals, Their Rise and Fall, with Their Own Account of Military Events* (London, 1951), an enlarged edition of *The German Generals Talk*, originally published in 1948. Gerhard L. Weinberg, *A World at Arms* (New York, 1994), previously cited, is the best one-volume work on the fighting of World War II. Norman Davies also wrote a general history: *No Simple Victory: World War II in Europe, 1939–1945* (New York, 2008). Ralf Blank et al. published a book on German wartime society during the war: *Germany and the Second World War* (New York, 2008).

In contrast to the long works already cited, there is an excellent very brief book that considers all aspects of the war, including intelligence and weapons, and that can be used for further research into the different issues: Anthony Wood, *War in Europe 1939–1945* (London, 1987). A good account of the war's overall course is Chester Wilmot, *The Struggle for Europe* (Westport, Conn., 1972).

For the North African campaigns, see Robin Neillands, *Eighth Army: From the Western Desert to the Alps* (London, 2004). On the commanders, see Ronald Lewin, *Rommel as Military Commander* (Princeton, N.J., 1968), and Charles Douglas-Home,

Rommel (London, 1973). On Montgomery as a soldier, consult Alun Chalfont, *Montgomery of Alamein* (London, 1976); Nigel Hamilton's massive biography *Montgomery of Alamein, 1887–1942* (London, 2001); and Hamilton's *Monty: Final Years of the Field Marshal, 1944–1976* (New York, 1987). On Italy's surrender and the consequences, see Elena Aga Rossi, *A Nation Collapses* (Cambridge, UK, 2000). The relationship between Mussolini and Hitler during this period is examined by F. W. Deakin, *The Brutal Friendship: Mussolini, Hitler, and the Fall of Italian Fascism* (London, 1962).

For specific books on the fighting in the East, see Alan Clark, *Barbarossa: The Russo-German Conflict* (Harmondsworth, UK, 1985); Rold Dieter Muller and Gerd R. Uebershar, *Hitler's War in the East* (Providence, R.I., 1997); Paul Schmidt, *Hitler's War on Russia* (London, 1964); Earl Frederick Ziemke, *Moscow to Stalingrad: Decision in the East* (Washington, D.C., 1987); and John Ericson, *The Road to Stalingrad* (London, 1993). On the most important fighting in the European theater, see Stephen E. Ambrose's excellent account of *D-Day, June 6, 1944: The Climactic Battle of World War II* (New York, 1994). The Battle of the Bulge is analyzed in two books: Trevor N. Dupuy, David L. Bongard, and Richard C. Anderson, Jr., *Hitler's Last Gamble* (New York, 1994), and Jacques Nobecourt, *Hitler's Last Gamble: The Battle of the Bulge, December 1944–January 1945* (New York, 1967). The best book on the atomic bomb is Richard Rhodes, *The Making of the Atomic Bomb* (New York, 1986), a comprehensive work that traces the story back to the earliest developments.

Many books have been written on the air war, but among the best comprehensive overall treatments is Richard Overy's *The Air War 1939–1945* (New York, 1980). An official history in four volumes, *Strategic Air Offensive Against Germany 1939–1945* (East Sussex, UK, 2006), by Charles Webster and Noble Frankland, also gives a good account. Good works on more specialized aspects of the air war include Mark K. Wells, *Courage and Air Warfare: The Allied Aircrew Experience in the Second World War* (London, 1995), an account of the selection and experiences of Allied air crews; David MacIssac, *Strategic Bombing in World War II* (New York, 1976), which discusses the doctrine and organization of strategic bombing; and Anthony Verrier, *The Bomber Offensive* (New York, 1968), the story of bombing from the beginning until the end of the war. An idea of what it was like to be on the receiving end of the bombs may be gleaned from Earl R. Beck's *Under the Bombs: The German Home Front 1942–1945* (Lexington, Ky., 1986). For the German side, see Werner Baumback, *The Life and Death of the Luftwaffe* (New York, 1960). Many treatments also exist about the war at sea, but a good overall picture can still be obtained from Samuel E. Morison, *History of the United States Naval Operations in World War II. Volume One: The Battle of the Atlantic* (Boston, 1947); and for the British side, Stephen W. Roskill, *The War at Sea, 1939–1945* (Ukfield, UK, 2004). See also Jurgen Rohmer, *War At Sea, 1939–1945* (Annapolis, Md., 1996). On the submarine struggle, see Clay Blair, *Hitler's U-Boat War* (New York, 1996), and Peter Padfield, *War Beneath the Sea, 1939–1945* (London, 1997).

Many books on the Resistance movements in different countries and the attitude and operations of the Allies have been written, but Henri Michel's *The Shadow War: European Resistance 1939–1945* (New York, 1972) is outstanding on the general structure, purposes, and organization of the movements. Other general treatments are Jorgen Haestrup, *European Resistance Movements (1939–1945)* (Westport, Conn., 1981), and, by the same author, *Europe Ablaze: An Analysis of the History of the European Resistance Movements* (Odense, 1978). Also, see Stephen Hawes and Ralph White, eds., *Resistance in Europe 1939–1945: A Complete History* (Harmondsworth, UK, 1976). *The Intellectual Resistance in Europe* (Cambridge, Mass., 1981), by James D. Wilkinson, discusses French, Italian, and German intellectuals. For the resistance in France, see Matthew Cobb, *The*

Resistance: The French Fight against the Nazis (London, 2009); *In Search of the Maquis* (Oxford, UK, 1994) and *Resistance in Vichy France: A Study of Ideas and Motivation in the Southern Zone, 1940–1942* (New York, 1983) both by H. Roderick Kedward; and H. R. Kedward and Roger Austin, eds., *Vichy France and the Resistance: Culture and Ideology* (London, 1985). Everyday life is examined by Denis Peschanski et al., *Collaboration and Resistance: Images of Life in Vichy France, 1940–1944* (New York, 2000) and *Between Resistance and Collaboration* (New York, 2000), which describes the impact of occupation. For Eastern Europe, there is *War in a Twilight World* (New York, 2010), essays edited by Juiliette Pattinson and Ben Shepherd. On Yugoslavia, see Marcia Christoff Kuropovna's *Shadows on the Mountain* (New York, 2009); *Tito's Partisans 1941–45* (Oxford, UK, 2003) by V. Vuksic; and Walter R. Roberts's *Tito, Mihailovic and the Allies 1941–1945* (Durham, N.C., 1987). For Italy, there is a classic by Charles Delzell, *Mussolini's Enemies: The Italian Anti-Fascist Resistance* (Princeton, N.J., 1961), and books by Tom Behan, *The Italian Resistance* (New York, 2009), and Philip E. Cooke, *The Legacy of the Italian Resistance* (New York, 2011), which takes important cultural factors into consideration. For the complicated situation following the Italian surrender, see David W. Ellwood, *Italy 1943–1945* (Leicester, UK, 1985). On the Jewish Resistance, see *Caged* (Sydney, 2000), by David Landau. On the other side, there is Colin D. Heaton, *German Anti-Partisan Warfare in Europe, 1939–1945* (Atglen, Pa., 2001). On Germany, there is the standard work by Peter Hoffman, *The History of the German Resistance 1933–1945* (Cambridge, Mass., 1977), and books by Ruth Bernadette Melon, *Journey to the White Rose in Germany* (Indianapolis, Ind., 2007), and John J. Michalczyk, *Confront* (New York, 2004), a book of essays; but more than resistance, the literature shows that the opposition consisted of limited circles. The lack of effective resistance to Hitler is a point made by Joachim Fest in his history of the plot to assassinate Hitler: *Plotting Hitler's Death: The Story of the German Resistance* (New York, 1996). On this subject, see also Roger Moorhouse's *Killing Hitler* (London, 2006). Klemens von Klemperer's *The German Resistance Against Hitler* (Oxford, UK, 1994) looks at the failure to find support abroad. Michael Geyer and John Boyer, *Resistance Against the Third Reich* (Chicago, 1994), includes wide-ranging essays.

Religious opposition to the Nazis is an interesting subject in the context of the German Resistance. The role of women resisters is discussed by Theodore N. Thomas, *Women Against Hitler: Christian Resistance in the Third Reich* (Westport, Conn., 1994), and Michael Phayer, *Cries in the Night: Women Who Challenged the Holocaust* (Kansas City, Mo., 1990). John E. Morley analyzes Vatican policy in *Vatican Diplomacy and the Jews During the Holocaust* (New York, 1980). Gordon Zahn wrote a perceptive study on *German Catholics and Hitler's Wars* (Notre Dame, Ind., 1989).

A complete understanding of the role of women in the Resistance awaits further research. Two good works on the subject are Margaret Collins Weitz, *Sisters in the Resistance: How Women Fought to Free France, 1940–1945* (New York, 1995), which discusses the French Resistance, and Jane Slaughter's *Women in the Italian Resistance* (Denver, 1997). Chris Corrin published *Women in a Violent World: Feminist Analyses and Resistance Across Europe* (Edinburgh, 1996). The Polish Resistance is analyzed by Stefan Korbonski, *Fighting Warsaw: The Story of the Polish Underground State* (New York, 1956); an organizer of the Polish Resistance and later its commander, T. Bor-Komorowski, wrote his memoirs, *The Secret Army* (New York, 1951). On the Greek Resistance, see Stefanos Sarafis, *ELAS: Greek Resistance Army* (Atlantic Highlands, N.J., 1980). For more information on Greece and Yugoslavia from the Allied side, consult *British Policy Towards Wartime Resistance in Yugoslavia and Greece* (London, 1975), a collection of important papers and interesting discussions.

On the diplomacy among the Allies and the conferences discussed in this chapter, see Martin Kitchen, *British Policy Towards the Soviet Union During the Second World War* (New York, 1986). Mark A. Stoler gives a detailed account of American military policy in the coalition between 1941 and 1943 and American differences with the British in *The Politics of the Second Front: American Military Planning and Diplomacy in Coalition Warfare, 1941–1943* (Westport, Conn., 1977). On the difficult relationship between the British and DeGaulle, see François Kersandy, *Churchill and DeGaulle* (New York, 1982). Herbert Feis's *Churchill, Roosevelt, Stalin* (Princeton, N.J., 1957) analyzes the relationships among the three leaders, as well as the conferences. Keith Sainsbury, *The Turning Point: Roosevelt, Stalin, Churchill and Chiang-Kai-Shek, 1943* (Oxford, UK, 1985), is the best account of the Moscow, Cairo, and Teheran conferences and the discussions among Roosevelt, Churchill, and Stalin. On the 1943 Teheran summit, see also Paul D. Mayle, *Eureka Summit: Agreement in Principle and the Big Three at Tehran, 1943* (Newark, N.J., 1987). On the pivotal Yalta Conference, see Fraser J. Harbutt, *Yalta 1945* (New York, 2010), and Russell D. Buhite, *Decisions at Yalta: An Appraisal of Summit Diplomacy* (Wilmington, Del., 1986); Diane

Shaver Clemens, *Yalta* (New York, 1970); and the essays by prominent scholars in John L. Snell et al. *The Meaning of Yalta* (Baton Rouge, La., 1956). Herbert Feis published a standard account of the Potsdam Conference, *Between War and Peace: The Potsdam Conference* (Princeton, N.J., 1960).

IMAGE SOURCES AND CREDITS

Introduction: © Burstein Collection / CORBIS.

Chapter 1: pg. 8 © Bettmann / CORBIS; pg. 11 Courtesy of the Library of Congress; pg. 23 © Alinari Archives / CORBIS.

Chapter 2: pg. 36 Hulton Archive / Getty Images.

Chapter 3: pg. 55 Courtesy of the Library of Congress; pg. 71 Courtesy of the Library of Congress; pg. 72 © Bettmann / CORBIS.

Chapter 4: pg. 83 Courtesy of the Library of Congress; pg. 86 © Bettmann / CORBIS; pg. 91 akg-images / Jean-Pierre Verney; pg. 95 (top) © Hulton-Deutsch Collection / CORBIS; pg. 95 (bottom) Courtesy of the Library of Congress.

Chapter 5: pg. 107 © Christophe Boisvieux / Corbis; pg. 111 © Kirn Vintage Stock / Corbis; pg. 114 © Bettmann / CORBIS; pg. 118 © Bettmann / CORBIS; pg. 121 © No Credit Given / National Geographic Society / Corbis; pg. 125 © Bettmann / CORBIS.

Chapter 6: pg. 136 © Bettmann / CORBIS; pg. 138 © Hulton-Deutsch Collection / CORBIS; pg. 140 © Hulton-Deutsch Collection / CORBIS; pg. 142 © Bettmann / CORBIS; pg. 143 © Bettmann / CORBIS; pg. 147 © CORBIS; pg. 150 Courtesy of the Library of Congress; pg. 156 © Lebrecht / Lebrecht Music & Arts / Corbis; pg. 160 The Granger Collection.

Chapter 7: pg. 166 © CORBIS; pg. 168 © CORBIS; pg. 170 © Hulton-Deutsch Collection / CORBIS; pg. 179 Courtesy of the Library of Congress; pg. 181 © Hulton-Deutsch Collection / CORBIS; pg. 186 © Stefano Bianchetti / CORBIS.

Chapter 8: pg. 200 Courtesy of the Library of Congress; pg. 205 © E.O. Hoppé / CORBIS; pg. 206 © Bettmann / CORBIS.

Chapter 9: pg. 215 © BBC / Corbis; pg. 217 © Bettmann / CORBIS; pg. 223 © Stefano Bianchetti / Corbis; pg. 227 © Hulton-Deutsch Collection / CORBIS.

Chapter 10: pg. 241 © Hulton-Deutsch Collection / CORBIS; pg. 242 Courtesy of the Library of Congress; pg. 247 © Bettmann / CORBIS; pg. 251 © G. Jackson / Arcaid / Corbis.

Chapter 11: pg. 265 © Hulton-Deutsch Collection / CORBIS; pg. 267 © CORBIS; pg. 268 © Hulton-Deutsch Collection / CORBIS; pg. 271 © Hulton-Deutsch Collection / CORBIS; pg. 275 © Bettmann / CORBIS; pg. 278 © Bettmann / CORBIS.

Chapter 12: pg. 284 © Hulton-Deutsch Collection / CORBIS; pg. 288 © Hulton-Deutsch Collection / CORBIS; pg. 293 (top) akg-images / Interfoto; pg. 293 (bottom) © Bettmann / Corbis; pg. 296 © Hulton-Deutsch Collection / CORBIS.

Chapter 13: pg. 304 © Bettmann / CORBIS; pg. 307 © Bettmann / CORBIS; pg. 309 © Bettmann / CORBIS; pg. 311 Courtesy of the Library of Congress; pg. 316 © Bettmann / CORBIS.

Chapter 14: pg. 326 © Austrian Archives / CORBIS; pg. 328 © Lebrecht Authors / Lebrecht Music & Arts / Corbis; pg. 332 © Hulton-Deutsch Collection / CORBIS; pg. 333 © Hulton-Deutsch Collection / CORBIS.

Chapter 15: pg. 338 © Bettmann / CORBIS; pg. 340 Courtesy of the Library of Congress; pg. 343 © MAURIZIO GAMBARINI / epa / Corbis; pg. 344 © Bettmann / CORBIS; pg. 349 © Hulton-Deutsch Collection / CORBIS; pg. 351 Courtesy of the Library of Congress.

Chapter 16: pg. 362 akg-images; pg. 365 © Stapleton Collection / Corbis; pg. 367 © Dave G. Houser / Corbis; pg. 369 © Richard Bryant / Arcaid / Corbis.

Chapter 17: pg. 378 © Charles & Josette Lenars / CORBIS; pg. 389 © CORBIS; pg. 391 © CORBIS; pg. 392 © Bettmann / CORBIS; pg. 393 © Bettmann / CORBIS.

Chapter 18: pg. 400 © GLEB GARANICH / Reuters / Corbis; pg. 402 © CORBIS; pg. 405 © Hulton-Deutsch Collection / CORBIS; pg. 408 © Bettmann / Corbis; pg. 415 © Dmitri Baltermants / The Dmitri Baltermants Collection / Corbis.

Chapter 19: pg. 421 © CORBIS; pg. 425 © Bettmann / CORBIS; pg. 427 © Leonard de Selva / CORBIS; pg. 430 © Bettmann / CORBIS; pg. 436 © Bettmann / Corbis.

Chapter 20: pg. 447 © CORBIS; pg. 455 © Bettmann / CORBIS; pg. 461 © Hulton-Deutsch Collection / CORBIS; pg. 464 Courtesy of the Library of Congress.

Chapter 21: pg. 476 © Lebrecht Authors / Lebrecht Music & Arts / Corbis; pg. 478 Courtesy of the Library of Congress; pg. 487 Courtesy of the Library of Congress; pg. 489 Courtesy of the Library of Congress; pg. 490 Getty Images; pg. 493 © CORBIS.

Chapter 22: pg. 503 Courtesy of the Library of Congress; pg. 505 © Bettmann / CORBIS; pg. 506 Courtesy of the Library of Congress; pg. 515 © Bettmann / CORBIS; pg. 518 © Ted Spiegel / CORBIS.

Chapter 23: pg. 530 © SALVATORE DI NOLFI / epa / Corbis; pg. 534 © Ingrid Rossi / Sygma / Corbis; pg. 535 Courtesy of the Library of Congress; pg. 539 © Bettmann / CORBIS.

Chapter 24: pg. 552 © - / BELGA / epa / Corbi; pg. 553 © Bettmann / CORBIS; pg. 557 © Swim Ink 2, LLC / CORBIS.

Chapter 25: pg. 570 © Hulton-Deutsch Collection / CORBIS; pg. 571 © CORBIS; pg. 572 © Bettmann / CORBIS; pg. 576 © Bettmann / CORBIS.

Chapter 26: pg. 582 © Hulton-Deutsch Collection / CORBIS; pg. 583 Courtesy of the Library of Congress; pg. 586 © Bettmann / CORBIS; pg. 588 © Hulton-Deutsch Collection / CORBIS; pg. 590 © Tibor Hollos / epa / Corbis; pg. 594 © Bettmann / CORBIS; pg. 600 © Bettmann / CORBIS.

Chapter 27: pg. 606 © Hulton-Deutsch Collection / CORBIS; pg. 611 © Annie Griffiths Belt / Corbis; pg. 618 © Fabian Cevallos / Sygma /Corbis; pg. 624 akg-images.

Chapter 28: pg. 630 © Jack Burlot / Apis / Sygma / Corbis; pg. 633 © Regis Bossu / Sygma / Corbis; pg. 638 © Regis Bossu / Sygma / Corbis.

Chapter 29: pg. 643 © James Leynse / Corbis; pg. 648 © Hulton-Deutsch Collection / CORBIS; pg. 651 © Raymond Reuter / Sygma / Corbis; pg. 653 © John Garrett / CORBIS; pg. 655 © Julia Waterlow / Eye Ubiquitous / Corbis.

Chapter 30: pg. 661 © Bettmann / CORBIS; pg. 662 © Mike Kemp / In Pictures / Corbis; pg. 666 © Bettmann / CORBIS; pg. 668 © David Lees / CORBIS; pg. 673 © Gideon Mendel / Corbis.

Chapter 31: pg. 681 © Frederic Pitchal / Sygma / Corbis; pg. 686 © Bettmann / CORBIS; pg. 690 © Bob Krist / CORBIS.

Chapter 32: pg. 698 © Wally McNamee / CORBIS; pg. 699 © Reuters / CORBIS; pg. 705 © Jacques Langevin / Sygma / Corbis; pg. 709 © Peter Turnley / CORBIS; pg. 715 Hulton Archive / Getty Images; pg. 718 © Robert Maass / CORBIS.

Chapter 33: pg. 724 © Karlheinz Schindler / dpa / Corbis; pg. 725 © Andrew Holbrooke / Corbis; pg. 728 © Robert Wallis / Corbis; pg. 730 © David Turnley / CORBIS; pg. 734 © Reuters / CORBIS; pg. 743 © Gary Trotter / Eye Ubiquitous / Corbis.

Chapter 34: pg. 757 © Gary Knight / VII / Corbis; pg. 761 © Alberto Pizzoli / Sygma / Corbis; pg. 768 © Brooks Kraft / CORBIS; pg. 774 © Thierry Tronnel / Corbis; pg. 777 © Jean-Michel Turpin / Corbis.

---

*All images, unless otherwise noted, are within the public domain.

INDEX

Communist Party control centralized by, 576–77
cultural revolution under, 312–14
Eastern Europe controlled by, 474–75
Eastern Europe purges of, 569
Eastern Europe show trials and, 572–73
German strategy of, 490–91
Great Purge of, 317–18
Kirov burial and, 316, 317
lying in state, 582
prison camp inmate labor used by, 578
science advances and, 315–16
social category purges in, 573
strange death of, 581
Tito defying, 480
Titoism and, 569
totalitarian regime established by, 318
USSR denouncing crimes of, 575, 587
USSR Five-Year Plan from, 491
war with capitalism possibility from, 577
wife's death of, 316
women's liberation stifled under, 312
Stalingrad, 455, 456
Stalinism, 302–3, 565
Stamboliisky, Alexander, 272
Stambolov, Stefan, 123
standard of living, 612
Stanislaw, Joseph, 607
Starhemberg, E. R. von, 270
state industries, 611–12
state institutions, 283–84
state power, 157–58
Stauffenberg, Claus von, 462
Stavisky, Serge, 246
Stavisky scandal, 246
steel production, 82
Steinche, Karl Kristian, 252
sterilization techniques, 420, 671
Sternhell, Zeev, 27, 42
Stimson, Henry, 473
stock market, 652
stock market crash, 239
Stolypin, Peter, 71, 73, 74–75
Storm Troopers (SA), 325, 326
Strachey, John, 245
Strasser, Gregor, 332
Strategic Arms Limitation Talks (SALT), 713
Strategic Defense Initiative (Star Wars), 717, 722
strategic material production, 82t–83t
Strauss, Franz-Josef, 511, 623

Strength Through Joy movement, 348
Stresa Conference, 384
Stresemann, Gustav, xxxii, 228
biography of, 378–79
Einstein's comments on, 379
fulfillment policy of, 229
Nobel Peace Prize won by, 381
Strindberg, August, 101
structural continuity, 225–26
structuralism, 684
Struve, Peter B., 72
Stürmer, Boris, 167
Sturzo, Don Luigi, 220
subatomic world, 187
submachine guns, 444
submarines, 151, 446
subnuclear particles, 681
Sudetenland, 387, 388
Suez Crisis, 504, 558
suffragists, 8
Superconducting Supercollider, 681
superior race, 337–38
surrealism, 186, 186–87, 365
Survival in Auschwitz (Levi), 435–36
Svevo, Italo, 366
Sweden
democratic constitution of, 102–3
economic challenges in, 642
economic progress in, 103–4
electoral reforms in, 250–51
as EU member, 642
Keynes theories applied in, 252
modern furniture designs from, 251
neutralist policies of, 533
Norway's union ending with, 104–5
universal male suffrage in, 103
women's voting rights in, 103
Swept Away (film), 688
Swing Youth, 350
Swiss Social Democratic Party, 254
Switzerland
citizens military training in, 115
direct democracy in, 115–16
economic development in, 116–17
fascist groups appearing in, 255
Holocaust victims assets exploited by, 536–37, 647
interwar economic difficulties of, 254–55
League of Nations joined by, 255
official languages of, 116

Truman Doctrine, 491–92
Tukhachevsky, Mikhail, 318
Turati, Filippo, 9, 43, 46
Turkey
    Italy's declaration of war on, 96–98
    NATO joined by, 522
    World War I with, 145–46
twentieth century
    citizen's expectations rising in, 4–5
    cultural and political revolutions in, 22
    European society in, 27
    factors characterizing, 3–4
    rationalism declining in, 24
    scientific revolution in, 18–22
typhoid fever, 158
Tzara, Tristan, 186

UDF. *See* Union of Democratic Forces
Ukraine, 576
Ukrainian Communist Party, 582
Ulbricht, Walter, 585–86, 707
Ulmanis, Karlis, 259
Ulyanov, Vladimir Ilych. *See* Lenin, Vladimir Ilych
Ulysses (Joyce), 366
U.N. *See* United Nations
uncertainty principle, 22
underground army, 460
unemployed workers, 322
unicameral (single-body) legislatures, 641
Union of Democratic Forces (UDF), 733
Union of Kalmar, 101
Union of Soviet Socialist Republics
    (USSR). *See also* Russia
    air force of, 400–401
    Bolsheviks creating, 176
    bourgeois nationalism in, 669
    Brezhnev and decline of, 712–13
    collective leadership in, 581–82
    collectives forced on families in, 308
    colonialism opposed by, 547
    communism model of, 562–63
    Confederation of Independent States
        replacing, 742
    consumer goods in, 669
    coup d'état plot in, 744
    Czechoslovakia and intervention of, 600
    dissent in, 697–700
    Eastern Europe power struggle in, 584
    East Germany riot intervention of,
        585–86, 586

East Germany tensions with, 707
fall of, xxxiv
film industry in, 363
Finland's treaty with, 540
five-year plan for industrialization of,
    309–10
Five-Year Plan of, 491
foreign policy difficulties of, 593–94
German occupied areas of, 422
Gorbachev's failed reforms ending,
    718–19
green movement damaging reputation
    of, 725
Hitler attacking, 409
human rights violations in, 698
Hungary invaded by, 591, 706
ideology and decline of, 713
independent states after end of, 756
industry evacuation by, 415–16
Khrushchev's decentralization in, 697
metal plant in, 311
nationalism weakened in, 741
Nazi treaty signed with, 401
NEP debate in, 230
new flag signaling end of, 743
peasants challenge in, 230–31
perestroika rupturing structure of, 738
Poland caught between Germany and,
    390
political and ideological transition in,
    713–14
postwar reconstruction costs of, 578–79
power struggle in, 740–43
Rákosi' resignation forced by, 590
resistance against Germany of, 409–10
Romania dominated by, 479
satellite country exploitation by, 495
satellite states independence from, 723–24
socialism in, 305
Socialist Realism artform in, 365
society militarized by, 414–15
space race with, 681–82
Stalin's crimes denounced, 575, 587
tank disassembled by, 724
U.S. nuclear weapons and, 492
Warsaw Pact established by, 592
women's status in, 577–78
unions
    Clemenceau's government opposing, 44
    House of Lords ruling on, 35–36
    labor militancy and, 36–37